EP Seventh Reader

Days 91-180

EP Reader Series

Volume 7

Updated Edition

ISBN-13: 978-1506005331
ISBN-10: 1506005330

CONTENTS

The Spy (continued) 1
Treasure Island 78
The Talisman 204
The King Will Make a Way 436
Answers 540
About 551

ACKNOWLEDGEMENTS

Thank you to Abigail Baia for her beautiful cover art.

Welcome to Easy Peasy All-in-One Homeschool's Seventh Reader Lessons 91-180

We hope you enjoy curling up with this book of books.

This is Easy Peasy's offline version of its assignments for the second half of Reading 7. The novels and poetry included are found in the public domain and have been gathered here along with each lesson's directions. Care was taken to ensure the children don't miss out on any important lessons or activities. Online lessons from Easy Peasy's website have been replaced with offline lessons found in this book.

This book covers the second half of the course only, lessons 91-180. The rest of the course is in the first book, EP Seventh Reader Days 1-90.

Lesson 91

1. Read chapter 25.
2. As Frances talked with Katy on the way up the mountain, what did she learn about Birch's former housekeeper's opinion about where his loyalties lay? (Answers)

Vocabulary

1. Choose the word that is best described by the definition. Write the numbers and letters of the answers on a separate piece of paper.

1. an unprincipled person
A) reprobate B) conveyance C) prudence D) destitute

2. give up
A) waft B) destitute C) relinquish D) reprobate

3. without the basic necessities of life
A) prudence B) reprobate C) defraud D) destitute

4. with a boastful showiness, conspicuously
A) conveyance B) prudence C) ostentatiously D) relinquish

5. illegally obtain money through deception
A) defraud B) destitute C) relinquish D) reprobate

6. to carry lightly through air or over water
A) waft B) impel C) relinquish D) reprobate

7. caution with regard to practical matters
A) reprobate B) conveyance C) prudence D) destitute

8. to force or urge to do something
A) waft B) impel C) conveyance D) defraud

9. a means of transportation
A) waft B) conveyance C) prudence D) destitute

CHAPTER XXV

No vernal blooms their torpid rocks array,
But winter, lingering, chills the lap of May;
No zephyr fondly sues the mountain's breast,
But meteors glare, and stormy glooms invest.
—GOLDSMITH.

The roads of Westchester are, at this hour, below the improvements of the country. Their condition at the time of the tale has already been alluded to in these pages; and the reader will, therefore, easily imagine the task assumed by Caesar, when he undertook to guide the translated chariot of the English prelate through their windings, into one of the less frequented passes of the Highlands of the Hudson.

While Caesar and his steeds were contending with these difficulties, the inmates of the carriage were too much engrossed with their own cares to attend to those who served them. The mind of Sarah had ceased to wander so wildly as at first; but at every advance that she made towards reason, she seemed to retire a step from animation; from being excited and flighty, she was gradually becoming moody and melancholy. There were moments, indeed, when her anxious companions thought that they could discern marks of recollection; but the expression of exquisite woe that accompanied these transient gleams of reason, forced them to the dreadful alternative of wishing that she might forever be spared the agony of thought. The day's march was performed chiefly in silence, and the party found shelter for the night in different farmhouses.

The following morning the cavalcade dispersed. The wounded diverged towards the river, with the intention of taking water at Peekskill, in order to be transported to the hospitals of the American army above. The litter of Singleton was conveyed to a part of the Highlands where his father held his quarters, and where it was intended that the youth should complete his cure; the carriage of Mr. Wharton, accompanied by a wagon conveying the housekeeper and what baggage had been saved, and could be transported, resumed its route towards the place where Henry Wharton was held in duress, and where he only waited their arrival to be put on trial for his life.

The country which lies between the waters of the Hudson and Long Island Sound, is, for the first forty miles from their junction, a succession of hills and dales. The land bordering on the latter then becomes less abrupt, and gradually assumes a milder appearance, until it finally melts into the lovely plains and meadows of the Connecticut. But as you approach the Hudson, the rugged aspect increases, until you at length meet with the formidable barrier of the Highlands. Here the neutral ground ceased. The royal army held the two points of land that commanded the southern entrance of the river into the mountains; but all the remaining passes were guarded by the Americans.

We have already stated that the pickets of the continental army were sometimes pushed low into the country, and that the hamlet of the White Plains was occasionally maintained by parties of its troops. At other times, the advanced guards were withdrawn to the northern extremity of the country, and, as has been shown, the intermediate country was abandoned to the ravages of the miscreants who plundered between both armies, serving neither.

The road taken by our party was not the one that communicates between the two principal cities of the states, but was a retired and unfrequented pass, that to this hour is but little known, and which, entering the hills near the eastern boundary, emerges into the plain above, many miles from the Hudson.

It would have been impossible for the tired steeds of Mr. Wharton to drag the heavy chariot up the lengthened and steep ascents which now lay before them; and a pair of country horses were procured, with but little regard to their owner's wishes, by the two dragoons who still continued to accompany the party. With their assistance, Caesar was enabled to advance, by slow and toilsome steps, into the bosom of the hills. Willing to relieve her own melancholy by breathing a fresher air, and also to lessen the weight, Frances alighted as they reached the foot of the mountain. She found that Katy had made similar preparations, with the like intention of walking to the summit. It was near the setting of the sun, and, from the top of the mountain, their guard had declared that the end of their journey might be discerned. Frances moved forward with the elastic step of youth; and, followed by the housekeeper at a little distance, she soon lost sight of the sluggish carriage, that was slowly toiling up the hill, occasionally halting to allow the cattle to breathe.

"Oh, Miss Fanny, what dreadful times these be!" said Katy, when they paused for breath themselves. "I know'd that calamity was about to befall, ever sin' the streak of blood was seen in the clouds."

"There has been blood upon earth, Katy, though but little is ever seen in the clouds."

"Not blood in the clouds!" echoed the housekeeper. "Yes, that there has, often, and comets with fiery, smoking tails. Didn't people see armed men in the heavens, the year the war began? And, the night before the battle of the Plains, wasn't there thunder, like the cannon themselves? Ah! Miss Fanny, I'm fearful that no good can follow rebellion against the Lord's anointed!"

"These events are certainly dreadful," returned Frances, "and enough to sicken the stoutest heart. But what can be done, Katy? Gallant and independent men are unwilling to submit to oppression; and I am fearful that such scenes are but too common in war."

"If I could but see anything to fight about," said Katy, renewing her walk as the young lady proceeded, "I shouldn't mind it so much. 'Twas said the king wanted all the tea for his own family, at one time; and then again, that he meant the colonies should pay over to him all their earnings. Now this is matter enough to fight about—for I'm sure that no one, however he may be lord or king, has a right to the hard earnings of another. Then it was all contradicted, and some said Washington wanted to be king himself; so that, between the two, one doesn't know which to believe."

"Believe neither—for neither is true. I do not pretend to understand, myself, all the merits of this war, Katy; but to me it seems unnatural, that a country like this should be ruled by another so distant as England."

"So I have heard Harvey say to his father, that is dead and in his grave," returned Katy, approaching nearer to the young lady, and lowering her voice. "Many is the good time that I've listened to them talking, when all the neighborhood was asleep; and such conversations, Miss

Fanny, that you can have no idea on! Well, to say the truth, Harvey was a mystified body, and he was like the winds in the good book; no one could tell whence he came, or whither he went."

Frances glanced her eye at her companion with an apparent desire to hear more.

"There are rumors abroad relative to the character of Harvey," she said, "that I should be sorry were true."

"'Tis a disparagement, every word on't," cried Katy, vehemently. "Harvey had no more dealings with Beelzebub than you or I had. I'm sure if Harvey had sold himself, he would take care to be better paid; though, to speak the truth, he was always a wasteful and disregardful man."

"Nay, nay," returned the smiling Frances, "I have no such injurious suspicion of him; but has he not sold himself to an earthly prince—one too much attached to the interests of his native island to be always just to this country?"

"To the king's majesty!" replied Katy. "Why, Miss Fanny, your own brother that's in jail serves King George."

"True," said Frances, "but not in secret—openly, manfully, and bravely."

"'Tis said he is a spy, and why ain't one spy as bad as another?"

"'Tis untrue; no act of deception is worthy of my brother; nor of any would he be guilty, for so base a purpose as gain or promotion."

"Well, I'm sure," said Katy, a little appalled at the manner of the young lady, "if a body does the work, he should be paid for it. Harvey is by no means partic'lar about getting his lawful dues; and I dar'st to say, if the truth was forthcoming, King George owes him money this very minute."

"Then you acknowledge his connection with the British army," said Frances. "I confess there have been moments when I have thought differently."

"Lord, Miss Fanny, Harvey is a man that no calculation can be made on. Though I lived in his house for a long concourse of years, I have never known whether he belonged above or below [Footnote: The American party was called the party belonging 'above,' and the British that of 'below.' The terms had reference to the course of the Hudson.]. The time that Burg'yne was taken he came home, and there was great doings between him and the old gentleman, but for my life I couldn't tell if 'twas joy or grief. Then, here, the other day, when the great British general—I'm sure I have been so flurried with losses and troubles, that I forget his name—"

"Andre," said Frances.

"Yes, Ondree; when he was hanged, acrost the Tappan, the old gentleman was near hand to going crazy about it, and didn't sleep for night nor day, till Harvey got back; and then his money was mostly golden guineas; but the Skinners took it all, and now he is a beggar, or, what's the same thing, despisable for poverty and want."

To this speech Frances made no reply, but continued her walk up the hill, deeply engaged in her own reflections. The allusion to Andre had recalled her thoughts to the situation of her own brother.

They soon reached the highest point in their toilsome progress to the summit, and Frances seated herself on a rock to rest and to admire. Immediately at her feet lay a deep dell, but little altered by cultivation, and dark with the gloom of a November sunset. Another hill rose opposite to the place where she sat, at no great distance, along whose rugged sides nothing was to be seen but shapeless rocks, and oaks whose stunted growth showed a meager soil.

To be seen in their perfection, the Highlands must be passed immediately after the fall of the leaf. The scene is then the finest, for neither the scanty foliage which the summer lends the trees, nor the snows of winter, are present to conceal the minutest objects from the eye. Chilling solitude is the characteristic of the scenery; nor is the mind at liberty, as in March, to look forward to a renewed vegetation that is soon to check, without improving, the view.

The day had been cloudy and cool, and thin fleecy clouds hung around the horizon, often promising to disperse, but as frequently disappointing Frances in the hope of catching a parting beam from the setting sun. At length a solitary gleam struck on the base of the mountain on which she was gazing, and moved gracefully up its side, until reaching the summit, it stood for a minute, forming a crown of glory to the somber pile. So strong were the rays, that what was before indistinct now clearly opened to the view. With a feeling of awe at being thus unexpectedly admitted, as it were, into the secrets of that desert place, Frances gazed intently, until, among the scattered trees and fantastic rocks, something like a rude structure was seen. It was low, and so obscured by the color of its materials, that but for its roof, and the glittering of a window, it must have escaped her notice. While yet lost in the astonishment created by discovering a habitation in such a spot, on moving her eyes she perceived another object that increased her wonder. It apparently was a human figure, but of singular mold and unusual deformity. It stood on the edge of a rock, a little above the hut, and it was no difficult task for our heroine to fancy it was gazing at the vehicles that were ascending the side of the mountain beneath her. The distance, however, was too great to distinguish with precision. After looking at it a moment in breathless wonder, Frances had just come to the conclusion that it was ideal, and that what she saw was a part of the rock itself, when the object moved swiftly from its position, and glided into the hut, at once removing every doubt as to the nature of either. Whether it was owing to the recent conversation that she had been holding with Katy, or to some fancied resemblance that she discerned, Frances thought, as the figure vanished from her view, that it bore a marked likeness to Birch, moving under the weight of his pack. She continued to gaze towards the mysterious residence, when the gleam of light passed away, and at the same instant the tones of a bugle rang through the glens and hollows, and were reechoed in every direction. Springing on her feet, the alarmed girl heard the trampling of horses, and directly a party in the well-known uniform of the Virginians came sweeping round the point of a rock near her, and drew up at a short distance. Again the bugle sounded a lively strain, and before the agitated Frances had time to rally her thoughts, Dunwoodie dashed by the party of dragoons, threw himself from his charger, and advanced to her side.

His manner was earnest and interested, but in a slight degree constrained. In a few words he explained that he had been ordered up, with a party of Lawton's men, in the absence of the captain himself, to attend the trial of Henry, which was fixed for the morrow; and that, anxious for their safety in the rude passes of the mountain, he had ridden a mile or two in quest of the travelers. Frances explained, with trembling voice, the reason of her being in advance, and taught him momentarily to expect the arrival of her father. The constraint of his manner had, however, unwillingly on her part, communicated itself to her own deportment, and the approach of the chariot was a relief to both. The major handed her in, spoke a few words of encouragement to Mr. Wharton and Miss Peyton, and, again mounting, led the way towards the plains of Fishkill, which broke on their sight, on turning the rock, with the effect of enchantment. A short half hour brought them to the door of the farmhouse which the care of Dunwoodie had already prepared for their reception, and where Captain Wharton was anxiously expecting their arrival.

Lesson 92

1. Read chapter 26.
2. What was the turning point in Captain Wharton's trial? (Answers)

CHAPTER XXVI

These limbs are strengthened with a soldier's toil,
Nor has this cheek been ever blanched with fear—
But this sad tale of thine enervates all
Within me that I once could boast as man;
Chill trembling agues seize upon my frame,
And tears of childish sorrow pour, apace,
Through scarred channels that were marked by wounds.

—*Duo.*

The friends of Henry Wharton had placed so much reliance on his innocence, that they were unable to see the full danger of his situation. As the moment of trial, however, approached, the uneasiness of the youth himself increased; and after spending most of the night with his afflicted family, he awoke, on the following morning, from a short and disturbed slumber, to a clearer sense of his condition, and a survey of the means that were to extricate him from it with life. The rank of Andre, and the importance of the measures he was plotting, together with the powerful intercessions that had been made in his behalf, occasioned his execution to be stamped with greater notoriety than the ordinary events of the war. But spies were frequently arrested; and the instances that occurred of summary punishment for this crime were numerous. These were facts that were well known to both Dunwoodie and the prisoner; and to their experienced judgments the preparations for the trial were indeed alarming. Notwithstanding their apprehensions, they succeeded so far in concealing them, that neither Miss Peyton nor Frances was aware of their extent. A strong guard was stationed in the outbuilding of the farmhouse where the prisoner was quartered, and several sentinels watched the avenues that approached the dwelling. Another was constantly near the room of the British officer. A court was already detailed to examine into the circumstances; and upon their decision the fate of Henry rested.

The moment at length arrived, and the different actors in the approaching investigation assembled. Frances experienced a feeling like suffocation, as, after taking her seat in the midst of her family, her eyes wandered over the group who were thus collected. The judges, three in number, sat by themselves, clad in the vestments of their profession, and maintained a gravity worthy of the occasion, and becoming in their rank. In the center was a man of advanced years, and whose whole exterior bore the stamp of early and long-tried military habits. This was the president of the court; and Frances, after taking a hasty and unsatisfactory view of his associates, turned to his benevolent countenance as to the harbinger of mercy to her brother. There was a melting and subdued expression in the features of the veteran, that, contrasted with the rigid decency and composure of the others, could not fail to attract her notice. His attire was strictly in conformity to the prescribed rules of the service to which he belonged; but while his air was erect and military, his fingers trifled with a kind of convulsive and unconscious motion, with a bit of crape that entwined the hilt of the sword on which his body partly reclined, and which, like himself, seemed a relic of older times. There were the workings of an unquiet soul within; but his military front blended awe with the pity that its exhibition excited. His associates were officers selected from the eastern troops, who held the fortresses of West Point and the adjacent passes; they were men who had attained the meridian of life, and the eye sought in vain the expression of any passion or emotion on which it might seize as an indication of human infirmity. In their demeanor there was a mild, but a grave, intellectual reserve. If there was no ferocity nor harshness to chill, neither was there compassion nor interest to attract. They were men who had long acted under the dominion of a prudent reason, and whose feelings seemed trained to a perfect submission to their judgments.

Before these arbiters of his fate Henry Wharton was ushered under the custody of armed men. A profound and awful silence succeeded his entrance, and the blood of Frances chilled as she noted the grave character of the whole proceedings. There was but little of pomp in the preparations, to impress her imagination; but the reserved, businesslike air of the whole scene made it seem, indeed, as if the destinies of life awaited the result. Two of the judges sat in grave reserve, fixing their inquiring eyes on the object of their investigation; but the president continued gazing around with uneasy, convulsive motions of the muscles of the face, that indicated a restlessness foreign to his years and duty. It was Colonel Singleton, who, but the day before, had learned the fate of Isabella, but who stood forth in the discharge of a duty that his country required at his hands. The silence, and the expectation in every eye, at length struck him, and making an effort to collect himself, he spoke, in the tones of one used to authority.

"Bring forth the prisoner," he said, with a wave of the hand.

The sentinels dropped the points of their bayonets towards the judges, and Henry Wharton advanced, with a firm step, into the center of the apartment. All was now anxiety and eager curiosity. Frances turned for a moment in grateful emotion, as the deep and perturbed breathing of Dunwoodie reached her ears; but her brother again concentrated all her interest in one feeling of intense care. In the background were arranged the inmates of the family who owned the dwelling, and behind them, again, was a row of shining faces of ebony, glistening with pleased wonder. Amongst these was the faded luster of Caesar Thompson's countenance.

"You are said," continued the president, "to be Henry Wharton, a captain in his Britannic Majesty's 60th regiment of foot."

"I am."

"I like your candor, sir; it partakes of the honorable feelings of a soldier, and cannot fail to impress your judges favorably."

"It would be prudent," said one of his companions, "to advise the prisoner that he is bound to answer no more than he deems necessary; although we are a court of martial law, yet, in this respect, we own the principles of all free governments."

A nod of approbation from the silent member was bestowed on this remark, and the president proceeded with caution, referring to the minutes he held in his hand.

"It is an accusation against you, that, being an officer of the enemy, you passed the pickets of the American army at the White Plains, in disguise, on the 29th of October last, whereby you are suspected of views hostile to the interests of America, and have subjected yourself to the punishment of a spy."

The mild but steady tones of the speaker, as he slowly repeated the substance of this charge, were full of authority. The accusation was so plain, the facts so limited, the proof so obvious, and the penalty so well established, that escape seemed impossible. But Henry replied, with earnest grace,—

"That I passed your pickets in disguise, is true; but—"

"Peace!" interrupted the president. "The usages of war are stern enough in themselves; you need not aid them to your own condemnation."

"The prisoner can retract that declaration, if he please," remarked another judge. "His confession, if taken, goes fully to prove the charge."

"I retract nothing that is true," said Henry proudly.

The two nameless judges heard him in silent composure, yet there was no exultation mingled with their gravity. The president now appeared, however, to take new interest in the scene.

"Your sentiment is noble, sir," he said. "I only regret that a youthful soldier should so far be misled by loyalty as to lend himself to the purposes of deceit."

"Deceit!" echoed Wharton. "I thought it prudent to guard against capture from my enemies."

"A soldier, Captain Wharton, should never meet his enemy but openly, and with arms in his hands. I have served two kings of England, as I now serve my native land; but never did I approach a foe, unless under the light of the sun, and with honest notice that an enemy was nigh."

"You are at liberty to explain what your motives were in entering the ground held by our army in disguise," said the other judge, with a slight movement of the muscles of his mouth.

"I am the son of this aged man before you," continued Henry. "It was to visit him that I encountered the danger. Besides, the country below is seldom held by your troops, and its very name implies a right to either party to move at pleasure over its territory."

"Its name, as a neutral ground, is unauthorized by law; it is an appellation that originates with the condition of the country. But wherever an army goes, it carries its rights along, and the first is the ability to protect itself."

"I am no casuist, sir," returned the youth; "but I feel that my father is entitled to my affection, and I would encounter greater risks to prove it to him in his old age."

"A very commendable spirit," cried the veteran. "Come, gentlemen, this business brightens. I confess, at first, it was very bad, but no man can censure him for desiring to see his parents."

"And have you proof that such only was your intention?"

"Yes—here," said Henry, admitting a ray of hope. "Here is proof—my father, my sister, Major Dunwoodie, all know it."

"Then, indeed," returned his immovable judge, "we may be able to save you. It would be well, sir, to examine further into this business."

"Certainly," said the president, with alacrity. "Let the elder Mr. Wharton approach and take the oath."

The father made an effort at composure, and, advancing with a feeble step, he complied with the necessary forms of the court.

"You are the father of the prisoner?" said Colonel Singleton, in a subdued voice, after pausing a moment in respect for the agitation of the witness.

"He is my only son."

"And what do you know of his visit to your house, on the 29th day of October last?"

"He came, as he told you, to see me and his sisters."

"Was he in disguise?" asked the other judge.

"He did not wear the uniform of the 60th."

"To see his sisters, too!" said the president with great emotion. "Have you daughters, sir?"

"I have two—both are in this house."

"Had he a wig?" interrupted the officer.

"There was some such thing I do believe, upon his head."

"And how long had you been separated?" asked the president.

"One year and two months."

"Did he wear a loose greatcoat of coarse materials?" inquired the officer, referring to the paper that contained the charges.

"There was an overcoat."

"And you think that it was to see you, only, that he came out?"

"Me, and my daughters."

"A boy of spirit," whispered the president to his silent comrade. "I see but little harm in such a freak; 'twas imprudent, but then it was kind."

"Do you know that your son was intrusted with no commission from Sir Henry Clinton, and that the visit to you was not merely a cloak to other designs?"

"How can I know it?" said Mr. Wharton, in alarm. "Would Sir Henry intrust me with such a business?"

"Know you anything of this pass?" exhibiting the paper that Dunwoodie had retained when Wharton was taken.

"Nothing—upon my honor, nothing," cried the father, shrinking from the paper as from contagion.

"On your oath?"

"Nothing."

"Have you other testimony? This does not avail you, Captain Wharton. You have been taken in a situation where your life is forfeited; the labor of proving your innocence rests with yourself. Take time to reflect, and be cool."

There was a frightful calmness in the manner of this judge that appalled the prisoner. In the sympathy of Colonel Singleton, he could easily lose sight of his danger; but the obdurate and collected air of the others was ominous of his fate. He continued silent, casting imploring glances towards his friend. Dunwoodie understood the appeal, and offered himself as a witness. He was sworn, and desired to relate what he knew. His statement did not materially alter the case, and Dunwoodie felt that it could not. To him personally but little was known, and that little rather militated against the safety of Henry than otherwise. His account was listened to in silence, and the significant shake of the head that was made by the silent member spoke too plainly what effect it had produced.

"Still you think that the prisoner had no other object than what he has avowed?" said the president, when he had ended.

"None other, I will pledge my life," cried the major, with fervor.

"Will you swear it?" asked the immovable judge.

"How can I? God alone can tell the heart; but I have known this gentleman from a boy; deceit never formed part of his character. He is above it."

"You say that he escaped, and was retaken in open arms?" said the president.

"He was; nay, he received a wound in the combat. You see he yet moves his arm with difficulty. Would he, think you, sir, have trusted himself where he could fall again into our hands, unless conscious of innocence?"

"Would Andre have deserted a field of battle, Major Dunwoodie, had he encountered such an event, near Tarrytown?" asked his deliberate examiner. "Is it not natural to youth to seek glory?"

"Do you call this glory?" exclaimed the major: "an ignominious death and a tarnished name."

"Major Dunwoodie," returned the other, still with inveterate gravity, "you have acted nobly; your duty has been arduous and severe, but it has been faithfully and honorably discharged; ours must not be less so."

During the examination, the most intense interest prevailed among the hearers. With that kind of feeling which could not separate the principle from the cause, most of the auditors thought that if Dunwoodie failed to move the hearts of Henry's judges, no other possessed the power. Caesar thrust his misshapen form forward and his features, so expressive of the concern he felt, and so different from the vacant curiosity pictured in the countenance of the other blacks, caught the attention of the silent judge. For the first time he spoke:—

"Let that black be brought forward."

It was too late to retreat, and Caesar found himself confronted with a row of rebel officers, before he knew what was uppermost in his thoughts. The others yielded the examination to the one who suggested it, and using all due deliberation, he proceeded accordingly.

"You know the prisoner?"

"I t'ink he ought," returned the black, in a manner as sententious as that of his examiner.

"Did he give you the wig when he threw it aside?"

"I don't want 'em," grumbled Caesar; "got a berry good hair heself."

"Were you employed in carrying any letters or messages of any kind while Captain Wharton was in your master's house?"

"I do what a tell me," returned the black.

"But what did they tell you to do?"

"Sometime a one ting—sometime anoder."

"Enough," said Colonel Singleton, with dignity. "You have the noble acknowledgment of a gentleman, what more can you obtain from this slave?—Captain Wharton, you perceive the unfortunate impression against you. Have you other testimony to adduce?"

To Henry there now remained but little hope; his confidence in his security was fast ebbing, but with an indefinite expectation of assistance from the loveliness of his sister, he fixed an earnest gaze on the pallid features of Frances. She arose, and with a tottering step moved towards the judges; the paleness of her cheek continued but for a moment, and gave place to a flush of fire, and with a light but firm tread, she stood before them. Raising her hand to her polished forehead, Frances threw aside her exuberant locks, and displayed a picture of beauty and innocence to their view that might have moved even sterner natures. The president shrouded his eyes for a moment, as if the wild eye and speaking countenance recalled the image of another. The movement was transient, and recovering himself, with an earnestness that betrayed his secret wishes,—

"To you, then, your brother previously communicated his intention of paying your family a secret visit?"

"No!—no!" said Frances, pressing her hand on her brain, as if to collect her thoughts; "he told me nothing—we knew not of the visit until he arrived; but can it be necessary to explain to gallant men, that a child would incur hazard to meet his only parent, and that in times like these, and in a situation like ours?"

"But was this the first time? Did he never even talk of doing so before?" inquired the colonel, leaning towards her with paternal interest.

"Certainly—certainly," cried Frances, catching the expression of his own benevolent countenance. "This is but the fourth of his visits."

"I knew it!" exclaimed the veteran, rubbing his hands with delight. "An adventurous, warm-hearted son—I warrant me, gentlemen, a fiery soldier in the field! In what disguises did he come?"

"In none, for none were then necessary; the royal troops covered the country, and gave him safe passage."

"And was this the first of his visits out of the uniform of his regiment?" asked the colonel, in a suppressed voice, avoiding the penetrating looks of his companions.

"Oh! the very first," exclaimed the eager girl. "His first offense, I do assure you, if offense it be."

"But you wrote him—you urged the visit; surely, young lady, you wished to see your brother?" added the impatient colonel.

"That we wished it, and prayed for it,—oh, how fervently we prayed for it!—is true; but to have held communion with the royal army would have endangered our father, and we dared not."

"Did he leave the house until taken, or had he intercourse with any out of your own dwelling?"

"With none—no one, excepting our neighbor, the peddler Birch."

"With whom!" exclaimed the colonel, turning pale, and shrinking as from the sting of an adder.

Dunwoodie groaned aloud, and striking his head with his hand, cried in piercing tones, "He is lost!" and rushed from the apartment.

"But Harvey Birch," repeated Frances, gazing wildly at the door through which her lover had disappeared.

"Harvey Birch!" echoed all the judges. The two immovable members of the court exchanged looks, and threw an inquisitive glance at the prisoner.

"To you, gentlemen, it can be no new intelligence to hear that Harvey Birch is suspected of favoring the royal cause," said Henry, again advancing before the judges; "for he has already been condemned by your tribunals to the fate that I now see awaits myself. I will therefore explain, that it was by his assistance I procured the disguise, and passed your pickets; but to my dying moments, and with my dying breath, I will avow, that my intentions were as pure as the innocent being before you."

"Captain Wharton," said the president, solemnly, "the enemies of American liberty have made mighty and subtle efforts to overthrow our power. A more dangerous man, for his means and education, is not ranked among our foes than this peddler of Westchester. He is a spy—artful, delusive, and penetrating, beyond the abilities of any of his class. Sir Henry could not do better than to associate him with the officer in his next attempt. He would have saved Andre. Indeed, young man, this is a connection that may prove fatal to you!"

The honest indignation that beamed on the countenance of the aged warrior was met by a look of perfect conviction on the part of his comrades.

"I have ruined him!" cried Frances, clasping her hands in terror. "Do you desert us? then he is lost, indeed!"

"Forbear! lovely innocent, forbear!" said the colonel, with strong emotion; "you injure none, but distress us all."

"Is it then such a crime to possess natural affection?" said Frances wildly. "Would Washington—the noble, upright, impartial Washington, judge so harshly? Delay, till Washington can hear his tale."

"It is impossible," said the president, covering his eyes, as if to hide her beauty from his view.

"Impossible! oh! but for a week suspend your judgment. On my knees I entreat you, as you will expect mercy yourself, when no human power can avail you, give him but a day."

"It is impossible," repeated the colonel, in a voice that was nearly choked. "Our orders are peremptory, and too long delay has been given already."

He turned from the kneeling suppliant, but could not, or would not, extricate that hand that she grasped with frenzied fervor.

"Remand your prisoner," said one of the judges to the officer who had the charge of Henry. "Colonel Singleton, shall we withdraw?"

"Singleton! Singleton!" echoed Frances. "Then you are a father, and know how to pity a father's woes; you cannot, will not, wound a heart that is now nearly crushed. Hear me, Colonel Singleton; as God will listen to your dying prayers, hear me, and spare my brother!"

"Remove her," said the colonel, gently endeavoring to extricate his hand; but none appeared disposed to obey. Frances eagerly strove to read the expression of his averted face, and resisted all his efforts to retire.

"Colonel Singleton! how lately was your own son in suffering and in danger! Under the roof of my father he was cherished-under my father's roof he found shelter and protection. Oh! suppose that son the pride of your age, the solace and protection of your infant children, and then pronounce my brother guilty, if you dare!"

"What right has Heath to make an executioner of me!" exclaimed the veteran fiercely, rising with a face flushed like fire, and every vein and artery swollen with suppressed emotion. "But I forget myself; come, gentlemen, let us mount, our painful duty must be done."

"Mount not! go not!" shrieked Frances. "Can you tear a son from his parent—a brother from his sister, so coldly? Is this the cause I have so ardently loved? Are these the men that I have been taught to reverence? But you relent, you do hear me, you will pity and forgive."

"Lead on, gentlemen," said the colonel, motioning towards the door, and erecting himself into an air of military grandeur, in the vain hope of quieting his feelings.

"Lead not on, but hear me," cried Frances, grasping his hand convulsively. "Colonel Singleton, you are a father!—pity—mercy—mercy for the son! mercy for the daughter! Yes—you had a daughter. On this bosom she poured out her last breath; these hands closed her eyes; these very hands, that are now clasped in prayer, did those offices for her that you condemn my poor, poor brother, to require."

One mighty emotion the veteran struggled with, and quelled; but with a groan that shook his whole frame. He even looked around in conscious pride at his victory; but a second burst of feeling conquered. His head, white with the frost of seventy winters, sank upon the shoulder of the frantic suppliant. The sword that had been his companion in so many fields of blood dropped from his nerveless hand, and as he cried, "May God bless you for the deed!" he wept aloud.

Long and violent was the indulgence that Colonel Singleton yielded to his feelings. On recovering, he gave the senseless Frances into the arms of her aunt, and, turning with an air of fortitude to his comrades, he said,—

"Still, gentlemen, we have our duty as officers to discharge; our feelings as men may be indulged hereafter. What is your pleasure with the prisoner?"

One of the judges placed in his hand a written sentence, that he had prepared while the colonel was engaged with Frances, and declared it to be the opinion of himself and his companion.

It briefly stated that Henry Wharton had been detected in passing the lines of the American army as a spy, and in disguise. That thereby, according to the laws of war, he was liable to suffer death, and that this court adjudged him to the penalty; recommending him to be executed by hanging, before nine o'clock on the following morning.

It was not usual to inflict capital punishments, even on the enemy, without referring the case to the commander in chief, for his approbation; or, in his absence, to the officer commanding for the time being. But, as Washington held his headquarters at New Windsor, on the western bank of the Hudson, there was sufficient time to receive his answer.

"This is short notice," said the veteran, holding the pen in his hand, in a suspense that had no object; "not a day to fit one so young for heaven?"

"The royal officers gave Hale [Footnote: An American officer of this name was detected within the British lines, in disguise, in search of military information. He was tried and executed, as stated in the text, as soon as the preparations could be made. It is said that he was reproached under the gallows with dishonoring the rank he held by his fate. 'What a death for an officer to die!' said one of his captors. 'Gentlemen, any death is honorable when a man dies in a cause like that of America,' was his answer. Andre was executed amid the tears of his enemies; Hale died unpitied and with reproaches in his ears; and yet one was the victim of ambition, and the other of devotion to his country. Posterity will do justice between them.] but an hour," returned his comrade; "we have granted the usual time. But Washington has the power to extend it, or to pardon."

"Then to Washington will I go," cried the colonel, returning the paper with his signature; "and if the services of an old man like me, or that brave boy of mine, entitle me to his ear, I will yet save the youth."

So saying, he departed, full of his generous intentions in favor of Henry Wharton.

The sentence of the court was communicated, with proper tenderness, to the prisoner; and after giving a few necessary instructions to the officer in command, and dispatching a courier to headquarters with their report, the remaining judges mounted, and rode to their own quarters, with the same unmoved exterior, but with the consciousness of the same dispassionate integrity, that they had maintained throughout the trial.

Lesson 93

1. Read chapter 27.
2. Recount briefly the emotional ups and downs experienced by the family in this chapter as they waited to see what Capt. Wharton's fate would be. (Answers)

CHAPTER XXVII

Have you no countermand for Claudio yet,
But he must die to-morrow?
—*Measure for Measure.*

A few hours were passed by the prisoner, after his sentence was received, in the bosom of his family. Mr. Wharton wept in hopeless despondency over the untimely fate of his son; and Frances, after recovering from her insensibility, experienced an anguish of feeling to which the bitterness of death itself would have been comparatively light. Miss Peyton alone retained a vestige of hope, or presence of mind to suggest what might be proper to be done under their circumstances. The comparative composure of the good aunt arose in no degree from any want of interest in the welfare of her nephew, but it was founded in a kind of instinctive dependence on the character of Washington. He was a native of the same colony with herself; and although his early military services, and her frequent visits to the family of her sister, and subsequent establishment at its head, had prevented their ever meeting, still she was familiar with his domestic virtues, and well knew that the rigid inflexibility for which his public acts were distinguished formed no part of his reputation in private life. He was known in Virginia as a consistent but just and lenient master; and she felt a kind of pride in associating in her mind her countryman with the man who led the armies, and in a great measure controlled the destinies, of America. She knew that Henry was innocent of the crime for which he was condemned to suffer, and, with that kind of simple faith that is ever to be found in the most ingenuous characters, could not conceive of those constructions and interpretations of law that inflicted punishment without the actual existence of crime. But even her confiding hopes were doomed to meet with a speedy termination. Towards noon, a regiment of militia, that were quartered on the banks of the river, moved to the ground in front of the house that held our heroine and her family, and deliberately pitched their tents, with the avowed intention of remaining until the following morning, to give solemnity and effect to the execution of a British spy.

Dunwoodie had performed all that was required of him by his orders, and was at liberty to retrace his steps to his expectant squadron, which was impatiently waiting his return to be led against a detachment of the enemy that was known to be slowly moving up the banks of the river, in order to cover a party of foragers in its rear. He was accompanied by a small party of Lawton's troop, under the expectation that their testimony might be required to convict the prisoner; and Mason, the lieutenant, was in command. But the confession of Captain Wharton had removed the necessity of examining any witnesses on behalf of the people. [Footnote: In America justice is administered in the name of "the good people," etc., etc., the sovereignty residing with them.] The major, from an unwillingness to encounter the distress of Henry's friends, and a dread of trusting himself within its influence, had spent the time we have mentioned in walking by himself, in keen anxiety, at a short distance from the dwelling. Like Miss Peyton, he had some reliance on the mercy of Washington, although moments of terrific doubt and despondency were continually crossing his mind. To him the rules of service were familiar, and he was more accustomed to consider his general in the capacity of a ruler, than as exhibiting the characteristics of the individual. A dreadful instance had too recently occurred, which fully proved that Washington was above the weakness of sparing another in mercy to himself. While pacing, with hurried steps, through the orchard, laboring under these constantly recurring doubts, enlivened by transient rays of hope, Mason approached, accoutered completely for the saddle.

"Thinking you might have forgotten the news brought this morning from below, sir, I have taken the liberty to order the detachment under arms," said the lieutenant, very coolly, cutting down with his sheathed saber the mullein tops that grew within his reach.

"What news?" cried the major, starting.

"Only that John Bull is out in Westchester, with a train of wagons, which, if he fills, will compel us to retire through these cursed hills, in search of provender. These greedy Englishmen are so shut up on York Island, that when they do venture out, they seldom leave straw enough to furnish the bed of a Yankee heiress."

"Where did the express leave them, did you say? The intelligence has entirely escaped my memory."

"On the heights above Sing Sing," returned the lieutenant, with no little amazement. "The road below looks like a hay market, and all the swine are sighing forth their lamentations, as the corn passes them towards King's Bridge. George Singleton's orderly, who brought up the tidings, says that our horses were holding consultation if they should not go down without their riders, and eat another meal, for it is questionable with them whether they can get a full stomach again. If they are suffered to get back with their plunder, we shall not be able to find a piece of pork at Christmas fat enough to fry itself."

"Peace, with all this nonsense of Singleton's orderly, Mr. Mason," cried Dunwoodie, impatiently; "let him learn to wait the orders of his superiors."

"I beg pardon in his name, Major Dunwoodie," said the subaltern; "but, like myself, he was in error. We both thought it was the order of General Heath, to attack and molest the enemy whenever he ventured out of his nest."

"Recollect yourself, Lieutenant Mason," said the major, "or I may have to teach you that your orders pass through me."

"I know it, Major Dunwoodie—I know it; and I am sorry that your memory is so bad as to forget that I never have yet hesitated to obey them."

"Forgive me, Mason," cried Dunwoodie, taking both his hands. "I do know you for a brave and obedient soldier; forget my humor. But this business—had you ever a friend?"

"Nay, nay," interrupted the lieutenant, "forgive me and my honest zeal. I knew of the orders, and was fearful that censure might fall on my officer. But remain, and let a man breathe a syllable against the corps, and every sword will start from the scabbard of itself; besides, they are still moving up, and it is a long road from Croton to King's Bridge. Happen what may, I see plainly that we shall be on their heels before they are housed again."

"Oh! that the courier was returned from headquarters!" exclaimed Dunwoodie. "This suspense is insupportable."

"You have your wish," cried Mason. "Here he is at the moment, and riding like the bearer of good news. God send it may be so; for I can't say that I particularly like myself to see a brave young fellow dancing upon nothing."

Dunwoodie heard but very little of this feeling declaration; for, ere half of it was uttered, he had leaped the fence and stood before the messenger.

"What news?" cried the major, the moment that the soldier stopped his horse.

"Good!" exclaimed the man; and feeling no hesitation to intrust an officer so well known as Major Dunwoodie, he placed the paper in his hands, as he added, "but you can read it, sir, for yourself."

Dunwoodie paused not to read; but flew, with the elastic spring of joy, to the chamber of the prisoner. The sentinel knew him, and he was suffered to pass without question.

"Oh! Peyton," cried Frances, as he entered the apartment, "you look like a messenger from heaven! Bring you tidings of mercy?"

"Here, Frances—here, Henry—here, dear cousin Jeanette," cried the youth, as with trembling hands he broke the seal; "here is the letter itself, directed to the captain of the guard. But listen-"

All did listen with intense anxiety; and the pang of blasted hope was added to their misery, as they saw the glow of delight which had beamed on the countenance of the major give place to a look of horror. The paper contained the sentence of the court, and underneath was written these simple words,—

"Approved—GEO. WASHINGTON."

"He's lost, he's lost!" cried Frances, sinking into the arms of her aunt.

"My son! my son!" sobbed the father, "there is mercy in heaven, if there is none on earth. May Washington never want that mercy he thus denies to my innocent child!"

"Washington!" echoed Dunwoodie, gazing around him in vacant horror. "Yes, 'tis the act of Washington himself; these are his characters; his very name is here, to sanction the dreadful deed."

"Cruel, cruel Washington!" cried Miss Peyton. "How has familiarity with blood changed his nature!"

"Blame him not," said Dunwoodie; "it is the general, and not the man; my life on it, he feels the blow he is compelled to inflict."

"I have been deceived in him," cried Frances. "He is not the savior of his country; but a cold and merciless tyrant. Oh! Peyton, Peyton! how have you misled me in his character!"

"Peace, dear Frances; peace, for God's sake; use not such language. He is but the guardian of the law."

"You speak the truth, Major Dunwoodie," said Henry, recovering from the shock of having his last ray of hope extinguished, and advancing from his seat by the side of his father. "I, who am to suffer, blame him not. Every indulgence has been granted me that I can ask. On the verge of the grave I cannot continue unjust. At such a moment, with so recent an instance of danger to your cause from treason, I wonder not at Washington's unbending justice. Nothing now remains but to prepare for that fate which so speedily awaits me. To you, Major Dunwoodie, I make my first request."

"Name it," said the major, giving utterance with difficulty.

Henry turned, and pointing to the group of weeping mourners near him, he continued,—

"Be a son to this aged man; help his weakness, and defend him from any usage to which the stigma thrown upon me may subject him. He has not many friends amongst the rulers of this country; let your powerful name be found among them."

"It shall."

"And this helpless innocent," continued Henry, pointing to where Sarah sat, unconscious of what was passing, "I had hoped for an opportunity to revenge her wrongs;" a flush of excitement passed over his features; "but such thoughts are evil—I feel them to be wrong. Under your care, Peyton, she will find sympathy and refuge."

"She shall," whispered Dunwoodie.

"This good aunt has claims upon you already; of her I will not speak; but here," taking the hand of Frances, and dwelling upon her countenance with an expression of fraternal affection, "here is the choicest gift of all. Take her to your bosom, and cherish her as you would cultivate innocence and virtue."

The major could not repress the eagerness with which he extended his hand to receive the precious boon; but Frances, shrinking from his touch, hid her face in the bosom of her aunt.

"No, no, no!" she murmured. "None can ever be anything to me who aid in my brother's destruction."

Henry continued gazing at her in tender pity for several moments, before he again resumed a discourse that all felt was most peculiarly his own.

"I have been mistaken, then. I did think, Peyton, that your worth, your noble devotion to a cause that you have been taught to revere, that your kindness to our father when in imprisonment, your friendship for me,—in short, that your character was understood and valued by my sister."

"It is—it is," whispered Frances, burying her face still deeper in the bosom of her aunt.

"I believe, dear Henry," said Dunwoodie, "this is a subject that had better not be dwelt upon now."

"You forget," returned the prisoner, with a faint smile, "how much I have to do, and how little time is left to do it in."

"I apprehend," continued the major, with a face of fire, "that Miss Wharton has imbibed some opinions of me that would make a compliance with your request irksome to her—opinions that it is now too late to alter."

"No, no, no," cried Frances, quickly, "you are exonerated, Peyton—with her dying breath she removed my doubts."

"Generous Isabella!" murmured Dunwoodie; "but, still, Henry, spare your sister now; nay, spare even me."

"I speak in pity to myself," returned the brother, gently removing Frances from the arms of her aunt. "What a time is this to leave two such lovely females without a protector! Their abode is destroyed, and misery will speedily deprive them of their last male friend," looking at his father; "can I die in peace with the knowledge of the danger to which they will be exposed?"

"You forget me," said Miss Peyton, shrinking at the idea of celebrating nuptials at such a moment.

"No, my dear aunt, I forget you not, nor shall I, until I cease to remember; but you forget the times and the danger. The good woman who lives in this house has already dispatched a messenger for a man of God, to smooth my passage to another world. Frances, if you would wish me to die in peace, to feel a security that will allow me to turn my whole thoughts to heaven, you will let this clergyman unite you to Dunwoodie."

Frances shook her head, but remained silent.

"I ask for no joy—no demonstration of a felicity that you will not, cannot feel, for months to come; but obtain a right to his powerful name—give him an undisputed title to protect you—"

Again the maid made an impressive gesture of denial.

"For the sake of that unconscious sufferer"—pointing to Sarah, "for your sake—for my sake—my sister—"

"Peace, Henry, or you will break my heart," cried the agitated girl. "Not for worlds would I at such a moment engage in the solemn vows that you wish. It would render me miserable for life."

"You love him not," said Henry, reproachfully. "I cease to importune you to do what is against your inclinations."

Frances raised one hand to conceal her countenance, as she extended the other towards Dunwoodie, and said earnestly,—

"Now you are unjust to me—before, you were unjust to yourself."

"Promise me, then," said Wharton, musing awhile in silence, "that as soon as the recollection of my fate is softened, you will give my friend that hand for life, and I am satisfied."

"I do promise," said Frances, withdrawing the hand that Dunwoodie delicately relinquished, without even presuming to press it to his lips.

"Well, then, my good aunt," continued Henry, "will you leave me for a short time alone with my friend? I have a few melancholy commissions with which to intrust him, and would spare you and my sister the pain of hearing them."

"There is yet time to see Washington again," said Miss Peyton, moving towards the door; and then, speaking with extreme dignity, she continued, "I will go myself; surely he must listen to a woman from his own colony!—and we are in some degree connected with his family."

"Why not apply to Mr. Harper?" said Frances, recollecting the parting words of their guest for the first time.

"Harper!" echoed Dunwoodie, turning towards her with the swiftness of lightning; "what of him? Do you know him?"

"It is in vain," said Henry, drawing him aside; "Frances clings to hope with the fondness of a sister. Retire, my love, and leave me with my friend."

But Frances read an expression in the eye of Dunwoodie that chained her to the spot. After struggling to command her feelings, she continued,—

"He stayed with us for two days—he was with us when Henry was arrested."

"And—and—did you know him?"

"Nay," continued Frances, catching her breath as she witnessed the intense interest of her lover, "we knew him not; he came to us in the night, a stranger, and remained with us during the severe storm; but he seemed to take an interest in Henry, and promised him his friendship,"

"What!" exclaimed the youth in astonishment. "Did he know your brother?"

"Certainly; it was at his request that Henry threw aside his disguise."

"But," said Dunwoodie, turning pale with suspense, "he knew him not as an officer of the royal army?"

"Indeed he did," cried Miss Peyton; "and he cautioned us against this very danger."

Dunwoodie caught up the fatal paper, that still lay where it had fallen from his own hands, and studied its characters intently. Something seemed to bewilder his brain. He passed his hand over his forehead, while each eye was fixed on him in dreadful suspense—all feeling afraid to admit those hopes anew that had been so sadly destroyed.

"What said he? What promised he?" at length Dunwoodie asked, with feverish impatience.

"He bid Henry apply to him when in danger, and promised to requite the son for the hospitality of the father."

"Said he this, knowing him to be a British officer?"

"Most certainly; and with a view to this very danger."

"Then," cried the youth aloud, and yielding to his rapture, "then you are safe—then will I save him; yes, Harper will never forget his word."

"But has he the power to?" said Frances. "Can he move the stubborn purpose of Washington?"

"Can he? If he cannot," shouted the youth, "if he cannot, who can? Greene, and Heath, and young Hamilton are nothing compared to this Harper. But," rushing to his mistress, and pressing her hands convulsively, "repeat to me—you say you have his promise?"

"Surely, surely, Peyton; his solemn, deliberate promise, knowing all the circumstances."

"Rest easy," cried Dunwoodie, holding her to his bosom for a moment, "rest easy, for Henry is safe."

He waited not to explain, but darting from the room, he left the family in amazement. They continued in silent wonder until they heard the feet of his charger, as he dashed from the door with the speed of an arrow.

A long time was spent after this abrupt departure of the youth, by the anxious friends he had left, in discussing the probability of his success. The confidence of his manner had, however, communicated to his auditors something of his own spirit. Each felt that the prospects of Henry were again brightening, and with their reviving hopes they experienced a renewal of spirits, which in all but Henry himself amounted to pleasure; with him, indeed, his state was too awful to admit of trifling, and for a few hours he was condemned to feel how much more intolerable was suspense than even the certainty of calamity. Not so with Frances. She, with all the reliance of affection, reposed in security on the assurance of Dunwoodie, without harassing herself with doubts that she possessed not the means of satisfying; but believing her lover able to accomplish everything that man could do, and retaining a vivid recollection of the manner and benevolent appearance of Harper, she abandoned herself to all the felicity of renovated hope.

The joy of Miss Peyton was more sobered, and she took frequent occasions to reprove her niece for the exuberance of her spirits, before there was a certainty that their expectations were to be realized. But the slight smile that hovered around the lips of the virgin contradicted the very sobriety of feeling that she inculcated.

"Why, dearest aunt," said Frances, playfully, in reply to one of her frequent reprimands, "would you have me repress the pleasure that I feel at Henry's deliverance, when you yourself have so often declared it to be impossible that such men as ruled in our country could sacrifice an innocent man?"

"Nay, I did believe it impossible, my child, and yet think so; but still there is a discretion to be shown in joy as well as in sorrow."

Frances recollected the declaration of Isabella, and turned an eye filled with tears of gratitude on her excellent aunt, as she replied,—

"True; but there are feelings that will not yield to reason. Ah! here are those monsters, who have come to witness the death of a fellow creature, moving around yon field, as if life was, to them, nothing but a military show."

"It is but little more to the hireling soldier," said Henry, endeavoring to forget his uneasiness.

"You gaze, my love, as if you thought a military show of some importance," said Miss Peyton, observing her niece to be looking from the window with a fixed and abstracted attention. But Frances answered not.

From the window where she stood, the pass that they had traveled through the Highlands was easily to be seen; and the mountain which held on its summit the mysterious hut was directly before her. Its side was rugged and barren; huge and apparently impassable barriers of rocks presenting themselves through the stunted oaks, which, stripped of their foliage, were scattered over its surface. The base of the hill was not half a mile from the house, and the object which attracted the notice of Frances was the figure of a man emerging from behind a rock of remarkable formation, and as suddenly disappearing. The maneuver was several times repeated, as if it were the intention of the fugitive (for such by his air he seemed to be) to reconnoiter the proceedings of the soldiery, and assure himself of the position of things on the plain. Notwithstanding the distance, Frances instantly imbibed the opinion that it was Birch. Perhaps this impression was partly owing to the air and figure of the man, but in a great measure to the idea that presented itself on formerly beholding the object at the summit of the mountain. That they were the same figure she was confident, although this wanted the appearance which, in the other, she had taken for the pack of the peddler. Harvey had so connected himself with the mysterious deportment of Harper, within her imagination, that under circumstances of less agitation than those in which she had labored since her arrival, she would have kept her suspicions to herself. Frances, therefore, sat ruminating on this second appearance in silence, and endeavoring to trace what possible connection this extraordinary man could have with the fortunes of her own family. He had certainly saved Sarah in some degree, from the blow that had partially alighted on her, and in no instance had he proved himself to be hostile to their interests.

After gazing for a long time at the point where she had last seen the figure, in the vain expectation of its reappearance, she turned to her friends in the apartment. Miss Peyton was sitting by Sarah, who gave some slight additional signs of observing what passed, but who still continued insensible either to joy or grief.

"I suppose, by this time, my love, that you are well acquainted with the maneuvers of a regiment," said Miss Peyton. "It is no bad quality in a soldier's wife, at all events."

"I am not a wife yet," said Frances, coloring to the eyes; "and we have little reason to wish for another wedding in our family."

"Frances!" exclaimed her brother, starting from his seat, and pacing the floor in violent agitation. "Touch not the chord again, I entreat you. While my fate is uncertain, I would wish to be at peace with all men."

"Then let the uncertainty cease," cried Frances, springing to the door, "for here comes Peyton with the joyful intelligence of your release."

The words were hardly uttered, before the door opened, and the major entered. In his air there was the appearance of neither success nor defeat, but there was a marked display of vexation. He took the hand that Frances, in the fullness of her heart, extended towards him, but instantly relinquishing it, threw himself into a chair, in evident fatigue.

"You have failed," said Wharton, with a bound of his heart, but an appearance of composure.

"Have you seen Harper?" cried Frances, turning pale.

"I have not. I crossed the river in one boat as he must have been coming to this side, in another. I returned without delay, and traced him for several miles into the Highlands, by the western pass, but there I unaccountably lost him. I have returned here to relieve your uneasiness, but see him I will this night, and bring a respite for Henry."

"But saw you Washington?" asked Miss Peyton.

Dunwoodie gazed at her a moment in abstracted musing, and the question was repeated. He answered gravely, and with some reserve,—

"The commander in chief had left his quarters."

"But, Peyton," cried Frances, in returning terror, "if they should not see each other, it will be too late. Harper alone will not be sufficient."

Her lover turned his eyes slowly on her anxious countenance, and dwelling a moment on her features, said, still musing,—

"You say that he promised to assist Henry."

"Certainly, of his own accord and in requital for the hospitality he had received."

Dunwoodie shook his head, and began to look grave.

"I like not that word hospitality—it has an empty sound; there must be something more reasonable to tie Harper. I dread some mistake; repeat to me all that passed."

Frances, in a hurried and earnest voice, complied with his request. She related particularly the manner of his arrival at the Locusts, the reception that he received, and the events that passed as minutely as her memory could supply her with the means. As she alluded to the conversation that occurred between her father and his guest, the major smiled but remained silent. She then gave a detail of Henry's arrival, and the events of the following day. She dwelt upon the part where Harper had desired her brother to throw aside his disguise, and recounted, with wonderful accuracy, his remarks upon the hazard of the step that the youth had taken. She even remembered a remarkable expression of his to her brother, "that he was safer from Harper's knowledge of his person, than he would be without it." Frances mentioned, with the warmth of youthful admiration, the benevolent character of his deportment to herself, and gave a minute relation of his adieus to the whole family.

Dunwoodie at first listened with grave attention; evident satisfaction followed as she proceeded. When she spoke of herself in connection with their guest, he smiled with pleasure, and as she concluded, he exclaimed, with delight,—

"We are safe!—we are safe!"

But he was interrupted, as will be seen in the following chapter.

Lesson 94

1. Read chapter 28.
2. In the midst of the escape attempt, Birch again mentions a mysterious person to whom he has promised to save Capt. Wharton. Recall he mentioned this same person previously, but when questioned about who it is, says "No one." Any guesses as to who this may be?

CHAPTER XXVIII

The owlet loves the gloom of night,
  The lark salutes the day,
The timid dove will coo at hand—
  But falcons soar away.
          —*Song in Duo.*

In a country settled, like these states, by a people who fled their native land and much-loved firesides, victims of consciences and religious zeal, none of the decencies and solemnities of a Christian death are dispensed with, when circumstances will admit of their exercise. The good woman of the house was a strict adherent to the forms of the church to which she belonged; and having herself been awakened to a sense of her depravity, by the ministry of the divine who harangued the people of the adjoining parish, she thought it was from his exhortations only that salvation could be meted out to the short-lived hopes of Henry Wharton. Not that the kind-hearted matron was so ignorant of the doctrines of the religion which she professed, as to depend, theoretically, on mortal aid for protection; but she had, to use her own phrase, "sat so long under the preaching of good Mr.——," that she had unconsciously imbibed a practical reliance on his assistance, for that which her faith should have taught her could come from the Deity alone. With her, the consideration of death was at all times awful, and the instant that the sentence of the prisoner was promulgated, she dispatched Caesar, mounted on one of her husband's best horses, in quest of her clerical monitor. This step had been taken without consulting either Henry or his friends; and it was only when the services of Caesar were required on some domestic emergency, that she explained the nature of his absence. The youth heard her, at first, with an unconquerable reluctance to admit of such a spiritual guide; but as our view of the things of this life becomes less vivid, our prejudices and habits cease to retain their influence; and a civil bow of thanks was finally given, in requital for the considerate care of the well-meaning woman.

The black returned early from his expedition, and, as well as could be gathered from his somewhat incoherent narrative, a minister of God might be expected to arrive in the course of the day. The interruption that we mentioned in our preceding chapter was occasioned by the entrance of the landlady. At the intercession of Dunwoodie, orders had been given to the sentinel who guarded the door of Henry's room, that the members of the prisoner's family should, at all times, have free access to his apartment. Caesar was included in this arrangement, as a matter of convenience, by the officer in command; but strict inquiry and examination was made into the errand of every other applicant for admission. The major had, however, included himself among the relatives of the British officer; and one pledge, that no rescue should be attempted, was given in his name, for them all. A short conversation was passing between the woman of the house and the corporal of the guard, before the door that the sentinel had already opened in anticipation of the decision of his noncommissioned commandant.

"Would you refuse the consolations of religion to a fellow creature about to suffer death?" said the matron, with earnest zeal. "Would you plunge a soul into the fiery furnace, and a minister at hand to point out the straight and narrow path?"

"I'll tell you what, good woman," returned the corporal, gently pushing her away; "I've no notion of my back being a highway for any man to walk to heaven upon. A pretty figure I should make at the pickets, for disobeying orders. Just step down and ask Lieutenant Mason, and you may bring in a whole congregation. We have not taken the guard from the foot soldiers, but an hour, and I shouldn't like to have it said that we know less than the militia."

"Admit the woman," said Dunwoodie, sternly, observing, for the first time, that one of his own corps was on post.

The corporal raised his hand to his cap, and fell back in silence; the soldier stood to his arms, and the matron entered.

"Here is a reverend gentleman below, come to soothe the parting soul, in the place of our own divine, who is engaged with an appointment that could not be put aside; 'tis to bury old Mr.—-"

"Show him in at once," said Henry, with feverish impatience.

"But will the sentinel let him pass? I would not wish a friend of Mr.—to be rudely stopped on the threshold, and he a stranger."

All eyes were now turned on Dunwoodie, who, looking at his watch, spoke a few words with Henry, in an undertone, and hastened from the apartment, followed by Frances. The subject of their conversation was a wish expressed by the prisoner for a clergyman of his own persuasion, and a promise from the major, that one should be sent from Fishkill town, through which he was about to pass, on his way to the ferry to intercept the expected return of Harper. Mason soon made his bow at the door, and willingly complied with the wishes of the landlady; and the divine was invited to make his appearance accordingly.

The person who was ushered into the apartment, preceded by Caesar, and followed by the matron, was a man beyond the middle age, or who might rather be said to approach the downhill of life. In stature he was above the size of ordinary men, though his excessive leanness might contribute in deceiving as to his height; his countenance was sharp and unbending, and every muscle seemed set in rigid compression. No joy or relaxation appeared ever to have dwelt on features that frowned habitually, as if in detestation of the vices of mankind. The brows were beetling, dark, and forbidding, giving the promise of eyes of no less repelling expression; but the organs were concealed beneath a pair of enormous green goggles, through which they glared around with a fierceness that denounced the coming day of wrath. All was fanaticism, uncharitableness, and denunciation. Long, lank hair, a mixture of gray and black, fell down his neck, and in some degree obscured the sides of his face, and, parting on his forehead, fell in either direction in straight and formal screens. On the top of this ungraceful exhibition was laid impending forward, so as to overhang in some measure the whole fabric, a large hat of three equal cocks. His coat was of a rusty black, and his breeches and stockings were of the same color; his shoes without luster, and half-concealed beneath huge plated buckles. He stalked into the room, and giving a stiff nod with his head, took the chair offered him by the black, in dignified silence. For several minutes no one broke this ominous pause in the conversation; Henry feeling a repugnance to his guest, that he was vainly endeavoring to conquer, and the stranger himself drawing forth occasional sighs and groans, that threatened a dissolution of the unequal connection between his sublimated soul and its ungainly tenement. During this, deathlike preparation, Mr. Wharton, with a feeling nearly allied to that of his son, led Sarah from the apartment. His retreat was noticed by the divine, in a kind of scornful disdain, who began to hum the air of a popular psalm tune, giving it the full richness of the twang that distinguishes the Eastern [Footnote: By "Eastern" is meant the states of New England, which, being originally settled by Puritans, still retain many distinct shades of character.] psalmody.

"Caesar," said Miss Peyton, "hand the gentleman some refreshment; he must need it after his ride."

"My strength is not in the things of this life," said the divine, speaking in a hollow, sepulchral voice. "Thrice have I this day held forth in my Master's service, and fainted not; still it is prudent to help this frail tenement of clay, for, surely, 'the laborer is worthy of his hire.'"

Opening a pair of enormous jaws, he took a good measure of the proffered brandy, and suffered it to glide downwards, with that sort of facility with which man is prone to sin.

"I apprehend, then, sir, that fatigue will disable you from performing the duties which kindness has induced you to attempt."

"Woman!" exclaimed the stranger, with energy, "when was I ever known to shrink from a duty? But 'judge not lest ye be judged,' and fancy not that it is given to mortal eyes to fathom the intentions of the Deity."

"Nay," returned the maiden, meekly, and slightly disgusted with his jargon, "I pretend not to judge of either events, or the intentions of my fellow creatures, much less of those of Omnipotence."

"'Tis well, woman,—'tis well," cried the minister, moving his head with supercilious disdain; "humility becometh thy sex and lost condition; thy weakness driveth thee on headlong like 'unto the bosom of destruction.'"

Surprised at this extraordinary deportment, but yielding to that habit which urges us to speak reverently on sacred subjects, even when perhaps we had better continue silent, Miss Peyton replied,—

"There is a Power above, that can and will sustain us all in well-doing, if we seek its support in humility and truth."

The stranger turned a lowering look at the speaker, and then composing himself into an air of self-abasement, he continued in the same repelling tones,—

"It is not everyone that crieth out for mercy, that will be heard. The ways of Providence are not to be judged by men—'Many are called, but few chosen.' It is easier to talk of humility than to feel it. Are you so humble, vile worm, as to wish to glorify God by your own damnation? If not, away with you for a publican and a Pharisee!"

Such gross fanaticism was uncommon in America, and Miss Peyton began to imbibe the impression that her guest was deranged; but remembering that he had been sent by a well-known divine, and one of reputation, she discarded the idea, and, with some forbearance, observed,—

"I may deceive myself, in believing that mercy is proffered to all, but it is so soothing a doctrine, that I would not willingly be undeceived."

"Mercy is only for the elect," cried the stranger, with an unaccountable energy; "and you are in the 'valley of the shadow of death.' Are you not a follower of idle ceremonies, which belong to the vain church that our tyrants would gladly establish here, along with their stamp acts and tea laws? Answer me that, woman; and remember, that Heaven hears your answer; are you not of that idolatrous communion?"

"I worship at the altars of my fathers," said Miss Peyton, motioning to Henry for silence; "but bow to no other idol than my own infirmities."

"Yes, yes, I know ye, self-righteous and papal as ye are—followers of forms, and listeners to bookish preaching; think you, woman, that holy Paul had notes in his hand to propound the Word to the believers?"

"My presence disturbs you," said Miss Peyton, rising. "I will leave you with my nephew, and offer those prayers in private that I did wish to mingle with his."

So saying, she withdrew, followed by the landlady, who was not a little shocked, and somewhat surprised, by the intemperate zeal of her new acquaintance; for, although the good woman believed that Miss Peyton and her whole church were on the highroad to destruction, she was by no means accustomed to hear such offensive and open avowals of their fate.

Henry had with difficulty repressed the indignation excited by this unprovoked attack on his meek and unresisting aunt; but as the door closed on her retiring figure, he gave way to his feelings.

"I must confess, sir," he exclaimed with heat, "that in receiving a minister of God, I thought I was admitting a Christian; and one who, by feeling his own weaknesses, knew how to pity the frailties of others. You have wounded the meek spirit of an excellent woman, and I acknowledge but little inclination to mingle in prayer with so intolerant a spirit."

The minister stood erect, with grave composure, following with his eyes, in a kind of scornful pity, the retiring females, and suffered the expostulation of the youth to be given, as if unworthy of his notice. A third voice, however, spoke,—

"Such a denunciation would have driven many women into fits; but it has answered the purpose well enough, as it is."

"Who's that?" cried the prisoner, in amazement, gazing around the room in quest of the speaker.

"It is I, Captain Wharton," said Harvey Birch, removing the spectacles, and exhibiting his piercing eyes, shining under a pair of false eyebrows.

"Good heavens—Harvey!"

"Silence!" said the peddler, solemnly. "'Tis a name not to be mentioned, and least of all here, within the heart of the American army." Birch paused and gazed around him for a moment, with an emotion exceeding the base passion of fear, and then continued in a gloomy tone, "There are a thousand halters in that very name, and little hope would there be left me of another escape, should I be again taken. This is a fearful venture that I am making; but I could not sleep in quiet, and know that an innocent man was about to die the death of a dog, when I might save him."

"No," said Henry, with a glow of generous feeling on his cheek, "if the risk to yourself be so heavy, retire as you came, and leave me to my fate. Dunwoodie is making, even now, powerful exertions in my behalf; and if he meets with Mr. Harper in the course of the night, my liberation is certain."

"Harper!" echoed the peddler, remaining with his hands raised, in the act of replacing the spectacles. "What do you know of Harper? And why do you think he will do you service?"

"I have his promise; you remember our recent meeting in my father's dwelling, and he then gave an unasked promise to assist me."

"Yes—but do you know him? That is—why do you think he has the power? Or what reason have you for believing he will remember his word?"

"If there ever was the stamp of truth, or simple, honest benevolence, in the countenance of man, it shone in his," said Henry. "Besides, Dunwoodie has powerful friends in the rebel army, and it would be better that I take the chance where I am, than thus to expose you to certain death, if detected."

"Captain Wharton," said Birch, looking guardedly around and speaking with impressive seriousness of manner, "if I fail you, all fail you. No Harper nor Dunwoodie can save your life; unless you get out with me, and that within the hour, you die to-morrow on the gallows of a murderer. Yes, such are their laws; the man who fights, and kills, and plunders, is honored; but he who serves his country as a spy, no matter how faithfully, no matter how honestly, lives to be reviled, or dies like the vilest criminal!"

"You forget, Mr. Birch," said the youth, a little indignantly, "that I am not a treacherous, lurking spy, who deceives to betray; but innocent of the charge imputed to me."

The blood rushed over the pale, meager features of the peddler, until his face was one glow of fire; but it passed quickly away, as he replied,—

"I have told you truth. Caesar met me, as he was going on his errand this morning, and with him I have laid the plan which, if executed as I wish, will save you—otherwise you are lost; and I again tell you, that no other power on earth, not even Washington, can save you."

"I submit," said the prisoner, yielding to his earnest manner, and goaded by the fears that were thus awakened anew.

The peddler beckoned him to be silent, and walking to the door, opened it, with the stiff, formal air with which he had entered the apartment.

"Friend, let no one enter," he said to the sentinel. "We are about to go to prayer, and would wish to be alone."

"I don't know that any will wish to interrupt you," returned the soldier, with a waggish leer of his eye; "but, should they be so disposed, I have no power to stop them, if they be of the prisoner's friends. I have my orders, and must mind them, whether the Englishman goes to heaven, or not."

"Audacious sinner!" said the pretended priest, "have you not the fear of God before your eyes? I tell you, as you will dread punishment at the last day, to let none of the idolatrous communion enter, to mingle in the prayers of the righteous."

"Whew-ew-ew—what a noble commander you'd make for Sergeant Hollister! You'd preach him dumb in a roll call. Harkee, I'll thank you not to make such a noise when you hold forth, as to drown our bugles, or you may get a poor fellow a short horn at his grog, for not turning out to the evening parade. If you want to be alone, have you no knife to stick over the door latch, that you must have a troop of horse to guard your meetinghouse?"

The peddler took the hint, and closed the door immediately, using the precaution suggested by the dragoon.

"You overact your part," said young Wharton, in constant apprehension of discovery; "your zeal is too intemperate."

"For a foot soldier and them Eastern militia, it might be," said Harvey, turning a bag upside down, that Caesar now handed him; "but these dragoons are fellows that you must brag down. A faint heart, Captain Wharton, would do but little here; but come, here is a black shroud for your good-looking countenance," taking, at the same time, a parchment mask, and fitting it to the face of Henry. "The master and the man must change places for a season."

"I don't t'ink he look a bit like me," said Caesar, with disgust, as he surveyed his young master with his new complexion.

"Stop a minute, Caesar," said the peddler, with the lurking drollery that at times formed part of his manner, "till we get on the wool."

"He worse than ebber now," cried the discontented African. "A t'ink colored man like a sheep! I nebber see sich a lip, Harvey; he most as big as a sausage!"

Great pains had been taken in forming the different articles used in the disguise of Captain Wharton, and when arranged, under the skillful superintendence of the peddler, they formed together a transformation that would easily escape detection, from any but an extraordinary observer.

The mask was stuffed and shaped in such a manner as to preserve the peculiarities, as well as the color, of the African visage; and the wig was so artfully formed of black and white wool, as to imitate the pepper-and-salt color of Caesar's own head, and to exact plaudits from the black himself, who thought it an excellent counterfeit in everything but quality.

"There is but one man in the American army who could detect you, Captain Wharton," said the peddler, surveying his work with satisfaction, "and he is just now out of our way."

"And who is he?"

"The man who made you prisoner. He would see your white skin through a plank. But strip, both of you; your clothes must be exchanged from head to foot."

Caesar, who had received minute instructions from the peddler in their morning interview, immediately commenced throwing aside his coarse garments, which the youth took up and prepared to invest himself with; unable, however, to repress a few signs of loathing.

In the manner of the peddler there was an odd mixture of care and humor; the former was the result of a perfect knowledge of their danger, and the means necessary to be used in avoiding it; and the latter proceeded from the unavoidably ludicrous circumstances before him, acting on an indifference which sprang from habit, and long familiarity with such scenes as the present.

"Here, captain," he said, taking up some loose wool, and beginning to stuff the stockings of Caesar, which were already on the leg of the prisoner; "some judgment is necessary in shaping this limb. You will have to display it on horseback; and the Southern dragoons are so used to the brittle-shins, that should they notice your well-turned calf, they'd know at once it never belonged to a black."

"Golly!" said Caesar, with a chuckle, that exhibited a mouth open from ear to ear, "Massa Harry breeches fit."

"Anything but your leg," said the peddler, coolly pursuing the toilet of Henry. "Slip on the coat, captain, over all. Upon my word, you'd pass well at a pinkster frolic; and here, Caesar, place this powdered wig over your curls, and be careful and look out of the window, whenever the door is open, and on no account speak, or you will betray all."

"I s'pose Harvey t'ink a colored man ain't got a tongue like oder folk," grumbled the black, as he took the station assigned to him.

Everything now was arranged for action, and the peddler very deliberately went over the whole of his injunctions to the two actors in the scene. The captain he conjured to dispense with his erect military carriage, and for a season to adopt the humble paces of his father's slave; and Caesar he enjoined to silence and disguise, so long as he could possibly maintain them. Thus prepared, he opened the door, and called aloud to the sentinel, who had retired to the farthest end of the passage, in order to avoid receiving any of that spiritual comfort, which he felt was the sole property of another.

"Let the woman of the house be called," said Harvey, in the solemn key of his assumed character; "and let her come alone. The prisoner is in a happy train of meditation, and must not be led from his devotions."

Caesar sank his face between his hands; and when the soldier looked into the apartment, he thought he saw his charge in deep abstraction. Casting a glance of huge contempt at the divine, he called aloud for the good woman of the house. She hastened at the summons, with earnest zeal, entertaining a secret hope that she was to be admitted to the gossip of a death-bed repentance.

"Sister," said the minister, in the authoritative tones of a master, "have you in the house `The Christian Criminal's last Moments, or Thoughts on Eternity, for them who die a violent Death'?"

"I never heard of the book!" said the matron in astonishment.

"'Tis not unlikely; there are many books you have never heard of: it is impossible for this poor penitent to pass in peace, without the consolations of that volume. One hour's reading in it is worth an age of man's preaching."

"Bless me, what a treasure to possess! When was it put out?"

"It was first put out at Geneva in the Greek language, and then translated at Boston. It is a book, woman, that should be in the hands of every Christian, especially such as die upon the gallows. Have a horse prepared instantly for this black, who shall accompany me to my brother—, and I will send down the volume yet in season. Brother, compose thy mind; you are now in the narrow path to glory."

Caesar wriggled a little in his chair, but he had sufficient recollection to conceal his face with hands that were, in their turn, concealed by gloves. The landlady departed, to comply with this very reasonable request, and the group of conspirators were again left to themselves.

"This is well," said the peddler; "but the difficult task is to deceive the officer who commands the guard—he is lieutenant to Lawton, and has learned some of the captain's own cunning in these things. Remember, Captain Wharton," continued he with an air of pride, "that now is the moment when everything depends on our coolness."

"My fate can be made but little worse than it is at present, my worthy fellow," said Henry; "but for your sake I will do all that in me lies."

"And wherein can I be more forlorn and persecuted than I now am?" asked the peddler, with that wild incoherence which often crossed his manner. "But I have promised *one* to save you, and to him I have never yet broken my word."

"And who is he?" said Henry, with awakened interest.

"No one."

The man soon returned, and announced that the horses were at the door. Harvey gave the captain a glance, and led the way down the stairs, first desiring the woman to leave the prisoner to himself, in order that he might digest the wholesome mental food that he had so lately received.

A rumor of the odd character of the priest had spread from the sentinel at the door to his comrades; so that when Harvey and Wharton reached the open space before the building, they found a dozen idle dragoons loitering about with the waggish intention of quizzing the fanatic, and employed in affected admiration of the steeds.

"A fine horse!" said the leader in this plan of mischief; "but a little low in flesh. I suppose from hard labor in your calling."

"My calling may be laborsome to both myself and this faithful beast, but then a day of settling is at hand, that will reward me for all my outgoings and incomings," said Birch, putting his foot in the stirrup, and preparing to mount.

"You work for pay, then, as we fight for't?" cried another of the party.

"Even so—is not the laborer worthy of his hire?"

"Come, suppose you give us a little preaching; we have a leisure moment just now, and there's no telling how much good you might do a set of reprobates like us, in a few words. Here, mount this horseblock, and take your text where you please."

The men now gathered in eager delight around the peddler, who, glancing his eye expressively towards the captain, who had been suffered to mount, replied,—

"Doubtless, for such is my duty. But, Caesar, you can ride up the road and deliver the note—the unhappy prisoner will be wanting the book, for his hours are numbered."

"Aye, aye, go along, Caesar, and get the book," shouted half a dozen voices, all crowding eagerly around the ideal priest, in anticipation of a frolic.

The peddler inwardly dreaded, that, in their unceremonious handling of himself and garments, his hat and wig might be displaced, when detection would be certain; he was therefore fain to comply with their request. Ascending the horseblock, after hemming once or twice, and casting several glances at the captain, who continued immovable, he commenced as follows:—

"I shall call your attention, my brethren, to that portion of Scripture which you will find in the second book of Samuel, and which is written in the following words:—'*And the king lamented over Abner, and said. Died Abner as a fool dieth? Thy hands were not bound, nor thy feet put into fetters: as a man falleth before wicked men, so fellest thou. And all the people wept again over him.*' Caesar, ride forward, I say, and obtain the book as directed; thy master is groaning in spirit even now for the want of it."

"An excellent text!" cried the dragoons. "Go on—go on—let the snowball stay; he wants to be edified as well as another."

"What are you at there, scoundrels?" cried Lieutenant Mason, as he came in sight from a walk he had taken to sneer at the evening parade of the regiment of militia. "Away with every man of you to your quarters, and let me find that each horse is cleaned and littered, when I come round." The sound of the officer's voice operated like a charm, and no priest could desire a more silent congregation, although he might possibly have wished for one that was more numerous. Mason had not done speaking, when it was reduced to the image of Caesar only. The peddler took that opportunity to mount, but he had to preserve the gravity of his movements, for the remark of the troopers upon the condition of their beasts was but too just, and a dozen dragoon horses stood saddled and bridled at hand, ready to receive their riders at a moment's warning.

"Well, have you bitted the poor fellow within," said Mason, "that he can take his last ride under the curb of divinity, old gentleman?"

"There is evil in thy conversation, profane man," cried the priest, raising his hands and casting his eyes upwards in holy horror; "so I will depart from thee unhurt, as Daniel was liberated from the lions' den."

"Off with you, for a hypocritical, psalm-singing, canting rogue in disguise," said Mason scornfully. "By the life of Washington! it worries an honest fellow to see such voracious beasts of prey ravaging a country for which he sheds his blood. If I had you on a Virginia plantation for a quarter of an hour, I'd teach you to worm the tobacco with the turkeys."

"I leave you, and shake the dust off my shoes, that no remnant of this wicked hole may tarnish the vestments of the godly."

"Start, or I will shake the dust from your jacket, designing knave! A fellow to be preaching to my men! There's Hollister put the devil in them by his exhorting; the rascals were getting too conscientious to strike a blow that would raze the skin. But hold! Whither do you travel, Master Blackey, in such godly company?"

"He goes," said the minister, hastily speaking for his companion, "to return with a book of much condolence and virtue to the sinful youth above, whose soul will speedily become white, even as his outwards are black and unseemly. Would you deprive a dying man of the consolation of religion?"

"No, no, poor fellow, his fate is bad enough; a famous good breakfast his prim body of an aunt gave us. But harkee, Mr. Revelation, if the youth must die *secundum arlem*, let it be under a gentleman's directions, and my advice is, that you never trust that skeleton of yours among us again, or I will take the skin off and leave you naked."

"Out upon thee for a reviler and scoffer of goodness!" said Birch, moving slowly, and with a due observance of clerical dignity, down the road, followed by the imaginary Caesar. "But I leave thee, and that behind me that will prove thy condemnation, and take from thee a hearty and joyful deliverance."

"Damn him," muttered the trooper. "The fellow rides like a stake, and his legs stick out like the cocks of his hat. I wish I had him below these hills, where the law is not over-particular, I'd—-"

"Corporal of the guard!—corporal of the guard!" shouted the sentinel in the passage to the chambers, "corporal of the guard!—corporal of the guard!"

The subaltern flew up the narrow stairway that led to the room of the prisoner, and demanded the meaning of the outcry.

The soldier was standing at the open door of the apartment, looking in with a suspicious eye on the supposed British officer. On observing his lieutenant, he fell back with habitual respect, and replied, with an air of puzzled thought,—

"I don't know, sir; but just now the prisoner looked queer. Ever since the preacher has left him, he don't look as he used to do—but," gazing intently over the shoulder of his officer, "it must be him, too! There is the same powdered head, and the darn in the coat, where he was hit the day we had the last brush with the enemy."

"And then all this noise is occasioned by your doubting whether that poor gentleman is your prisoner, or not, is it, sirrah? Who the devil do you think it can be, else?"

"I don't know who else it can be," returned the fellow, sullenly; "but he has grown thicker and shorter, if it is he; and see for yourself, sir, he shakes all over, like a man in an ague."

This was but too true. Caesar was an alarmed auditor of this short conversation, and, from congratulating himself upon the dexterous escape of his young master, his thoughts were very naturally beginning to dwell upon the probable consequences to his own person. The pause that succeeded the last remark of the sentinel, in no degree contributed to the restoration of his faculties. Lieutenant Mason was busied in examining with his own eyes the suspected person of the black, and Caesar was aware of the fact, by stealing a look through a passage under one of his arms, that he had left expressly for the purpose of reconnoitering. Captain Lawton would have discovered the fraud immediately, but Mason was by no means so quick-sighted as his commander. He therefore turned rather contemptuously to the soldier, and, speaking in an undertone, observed,

"That anabaptist, methodistical, quaker, psalm-singing rascal has frightened the boy, with his farrago about flames and brimstone. I'll step in and cheer him with a little rational conversation."

"I have heard of fear making a man white," said the soldier, drawing back, and staring as if his eyes would start from their sockets, "but it has changed the royal captain to a black!"

The truth was, that Caesar, unable to hear what Mason uttered in a low voice, and having every fear aroused in him by what had already passed, incautiously removed the wig a little from one of his ears, in order to hear the better, without in the least remembering that its color might prove fatal to his disguise. The sentinel had kept his eyes fastened on his prisoner, and noticed the action. The attention of Mason was instantly drawn to the same object; and, forgetting all delicacy for a brother officer in distress, or, in short, forgetting everything but the censure that might alight on his corps, the lieutenant sprang forward and seized the terrified African by the throat; for no sooner had Caesar heard his color named, than he knew his discovery was certain; and at the first sound of Mason's heavy boot on the floor, he arose from his seat, and retreated precipitately to a corner of the room.

"Who are you?" cried Mason, dashing the head of the old man against the angle of the wall at each interrogatory. "Who the devil are you, and where is the Englishman? Speak, thou thundercloud! Answer me, you jackdaw, or I'll hang you on the gallows of the spy!"

Caesar continued firm. Neither the threats nor the blows could extract any reply, until the lieutenant, by a very natural transition in the attack, sent his heavy boot forward in a direction that brought it in direct contact with the most sensitive part of the man—his shin. The most obdurate heart could not have exacted further patience, and Caesar instantly gave in. The first words he spoke were—

"Golly! massa, you t'ink I got no feelin'?"

"By heavens!" shouted the lieutenant, "it is him! Scoundrel! where is your master, and who was the priest?" While speaking, he made a movement as if about to renew the attack; but Caesar cried aloud for mercy, promising to tell all that he knew.

"Who was the priest?" repeated the dragoon, drawing back his formidable leg, and holding it in threatening suspense. "Harvey, Harvey!" cried Caesar, dancing from one leg to the other, as he thought each member in turn might be assailed.

"Harvey who, you black villain?" cried the impatient lieutenant, as he executed a full measure of vengeance by letting his leg fly.

"Birch!" shrieked Caesar, falling on his knees, the tears rolling in large drops over his shining face.

"Harvey Birch!" echoed the trooper, hurling the black from him, and rushing from the room. "To arms! to arms! Fifty guineas for the life of the peddler spy—give no quarter to either. Mount, mount! to arms! to horse!"

During the uproar occasioned by the assembling of the dragoons, who all rushed tumultuously to their horses, Caesar rose from the floor, where he had been thrown by Mason, and began to examine into his injuries. Happily for himself, he had alighted on his head, and consequently sustained no material damage.

Lesson 95

1. Read chapter 29.
2. Imagine how Capt. Wharton felt as he saw the gallows. What might your feelings have been had you been in the same situation?

CHAPTER XXIX

Away went Gilpin, neck or nought,
Away went hat and wig;
He little dreamt, when he set out,
Of running such a rig.
—COWPER.

The road which it was necessary for the peddler and the English captain to travel, in order to reach the shelter of the hills, lay, for a half mile, in full view from the door of the building that had so recently been the prison of the latter; running for the whole distance over the rich plain, that spreads to the very foot of the mountains, which here rise in a nearly perpendicular ascent from their bases; it then turned short to the right, and was obliged to follow the windings of nature, as it won its way into the bosom of the Highlands.

To preserve the supposed difference in their stations, Harvey rode a short distance ahead of his companion, and maintained the sober, dignified pace, that was suited to his assumed character. On their right, the regiment of foot, that we have already mentioned, lay, in tents; and the sentinels who guarded their encampment were to be seen moving with measured tread under the hills themselves.

The first impulse of Henry was, certainly, to urge the beast he rode to his greatest speed at once, and by a coup de main not only accomplish his escape, but relieve himself from the torturing suspense of his situation. But the forward movement that the youth made for this purpose was instantly checked by the peddler.

"Hold up!" he cried, dexterously reining his own horse across the path of the other. "Would you ruin us both? Fall into the place of a black, following his master. Did you not see their blooded chargers, all saddled and bridled, standing in the sun before the house? How long do you think that miserable Dutch horse you are on would hold his speed, if pursued by the Virginians? Every foot that we can gain, without giving the alarm, counts a day in our lives. Ride steadily after me, and on no account look back. They are as subtle as foxes, aye, and as ravenous for blood as wolves!"

Henry reluctantly restrained his impatience, and followed the direction of the peddler. His imagination, however, continually alarmed him with the fancied sounds of pursuit, though Birch, who occasionally looked back under the pretense of addressing his companion, assured him that all continued quiet and peaceful.

"But," said Henry, "it will not be possible for Caesar to remain long undiscovered. Had we not better put our horses to the gallop, and by the time they can reflect on the cause of our flight, we can reach the corner of the woods?"

"Ah! you little know them, Captain Wharton," returned the peddler. "There is a sergeant at this moment looking after us, as if he thought all was not right; the keen-eyed fellow watches me like a tiger lying in wait for his leap. When I stood on the horseblock, he half suspected that something was wrong. Nay, check your beast—we must let the animals walk a little, for he is laying his hand on the pommel of his saddle. If he mounts, we are gone. The foot-soldiers could reach us with their muskets."

"What does he now?" asked Henry, reining his horse to a walk, but at the same time pressing his heels into the animal's sides, to be in readiness for a spring.

"He turns from his charger, and looks the other way, now trot on gently—not so fast—not so fast. Observe the sentinel in the field, a little ahead of us—he eyes us keenly."

"Never mind the footman," said Henry, impatiently, "he can do nothing but shoot us—whereas these dragoons may make me a captive again. Surely, Harvey, there are horse moving down the road behind us. Do you see nothing particular?"

"Humph!" ejaculated the peddler. "There is something particular, indeed, to be seen behind the thicket on our left. Turn your head a little, and you may see and profit by it too."

Henry eagerly seized this permission to look aside, and the blood curdled to his heart as he observed that they were passing a gallows, which unquestionably had been erected for his own execution. He turned his face from the sight, in undisguised horror.

"There is a warning to be prudent," said the peddler, in the sententious manner that he often adopted.

"It is a terrific sight, indeed!" cried Henry, for a moment veiling his eyes with his hand, as if to drive a vision from before him.

The peddler moved his body partly around, and spoke with energetic but gloomy bitterness, "And yet, Captain Wharton, you see it where the setting sun shines full upon you; the air you breathe is clear, and fresh from the hills before you. Every step that you take leaves that hated gallows behind; and every dark hollow, and every shapeless rock in the mountains, offers you a hiding place from the vengeance of your enemies. But I have seen the gibbet raised, when no place of refuge offered. Twice have I been buried in dungeons, where, fettered and in chains, I have passed nights in torture, looking forward to the morning's dawn that was to light me to a death of infamy. The sweat has started from limbs that seemed already drained of their moisture; and if I ventured to the hole that admitted air through grates of iron to look out upon the smiles of nature, which God has bestowed for the meanest of His creatures, the gibbet has glared before my eyes, like an evil conscience harrowing the soul of a dying man. Four times have I been in their power, besides this last; but—twice—did I think my hour had come. It is hard to die at the best, Captain Wharton; but to spend your last moments alone and unpitied, to know that none near you so much as think of the fate that is to you the closing of all that is earthly; to think that, in a few hours, you are to be led from the gloom, which, as you dwell on what follows, becomes dear to you, to the face of day, and there to meet all eyes fixed upon you, as if you were a wild beast; and to lose sight of everything amidst the jeers and scoffs of your fellow creatures—that, Captain Wharton, that indeed is to die!"

Henry listened in amazement, as his companion uttered this speech with a vehemence altogether new to him; both seemed to have forgotten their danger and their disguises.

"What! were you ever so near death as that?"

"Have I not been the hunted beast of these hills for three years past?" resumed Harvey; "and once they even led me to the foot of the gallows itself, and I escaped only by an alarm from the royal troops. Had they been a quarter of an hour later, I must have died. There was I placed in the midst of unfeeling men, and gaping women and children, as a monster to be cursed. When I would pray to God, my ears were insulted with the history of my crimes; and when, in all that multitude, I looked around for a single face that showed me any pity, I could find none—no, not even one; all cursed me as a wretch who would sell his country for gold. The sun was brighter to my eyes than common—but it was the last time I should see it. The fields were gay and pleasant, and everything seemed as if this world was a kind of heaven. Oh, how sweet life was to me at that moment! 'Twas a dreadful hour, Captain Wharton, and such as you have never known. You have friends to feel for you, but I had none but a father to mourn my loss, when he might hear of it; but there was no pity, no consolation near, to soothe my anguish. Everything seemed to have deserted me. I even thought that HE had forgotten that I lived."

"What! did you feel that God Himself had forgotten you, Harvey?"

"God never forsakes His servants," returned Birch, with reverence, and exhibiting naturally a devotion that hitherto he had only assumed.

"And whom did you mean by HE?"

The peddler raised himself in his saddle to the stiff and upright posture that was suited to his outward appearance. The look of fire, that for a short time glowed on his countenance, disappeared in the solemn lines of unbending self-abasement, and, speaking as if addressing a slave, he replied,—

"In heaven there is no distinction of color, my brother, therefore you have a precious charge within you, that you must hereafter render an account of;" dropping his voice—"this is the last sentinel near the road; look not back, as you value your life."

Henry remembered his situation, and instantly assumed the humble demeanor of his adopted character. The unaccountable energy of the peddler's manner was soon forgotten in the sense of his own immediate danger; and with the recollection of his critical situation, returned all the uneasiness that he had momentarily forgotten.

"What see you, Harvey?" he cried, observing the peddler to gaze towards the building they had left, with ominous interest. "What see you at the house?"

"That which bodes no good to us," returned the pretended priest. "Throw aside the mask and wig; you will need all your senses without much delay; throw them in the road. There are none before us that I dread, but there are those behind who will give us a fearful race!"

"Nay, then," cried the captain, casting the implements of his disguise into the highway, "let us improve our time to the utmost. We want a full quarter to the turn; why not push for it, at once?"

"Be cool; they are in alarm, but they will not mount without an officer, unless they see us fly—now he comes, he moves to the stables; trots briskly; a dozen are in their saddles, but the officer stops to tighten his girths; they hope to steal a march upon us; he is mounted; now ride, Captain Wharton, for your life, and keep at my heels. If you quit me, you will be lost!"

A second request was unnecessary. The instant that Harvey put his horse to his speed Captain Wharton was at his heels, urging the miserable animal he rode to the utmost. Birch had selected his own beast; and although vastly inferior to the high-fed and blooded chargers of the dragoons, still it was much superior to the little pony that had been thought good enough to carry Caesar Thompson on an errand. A very few jumps convinced the captain that his companion was fast leaving him, and a fearful glance thrown behind informed the fugitive that his enemies were as speedily approaching. With that abandonment that makes misery doubly grievous, when it is to be supported alone, Henry cried aloud to the peddler not to desert him. Harvey instantly drew up, and suffered his companion to run alongside of his own horse. The cocked hat and wig of the peddler fell from his head the moment that his steed began to move briskly, and this development of their disguise, as it might be termed, was witnessed by the dragoons, who announced their observation by a boisterous shout, that seemed to be uttered in the very ears of the fugitives; so loud was the cry, and so short the distance between them.

"Had we not better leave our horses," said Henry, "and make for the hills across the fields, on our left? The fence will stop our pursuers."

"That way lies the gallows," returned the peddler. "These fellows go three feet to our two, and would mind the fences no more than we do these ruts; but it is a short quarter to the turn, and there are two roads behind the wood. They may stand to choose until they can take the track, and we shall gain a little upon them there."

"But this miserable horse is blown already," cried Henry, urging his beast with the end of his bridle, at the same time that Harvey aided his efforts by applying the lash of a heavy riding whip he carried. "He will never stand it for half a mile farther."

"A quarter will do; a quarter will do," said the peddler, "a single quarter will save us, if you follow my directions."

Somewhat cheered by the cool and confident manner of his companion, Henry continued silently urging his horse forward. A few moments brought them to the desired turn, and as they doubled round a point of low underbrush, the fugitives caught a glimpse of their pursuers scattered along the highway. Mason and the sergeant, being better mounted than the rest of the party, were much nearer to their heels than even the peddler thought could be possible.

At the foot of the hills, and for some distance up the dark valley that wound among the mountains, a thick underwood of saplings had been suffered to shoot up, where the heavier growth was felled for the sake of the fuel. At the sight of this cover, Henry again urged the peddler to dismount, and to plunge into the woods; but his request was promptly refused. The two roads, before mentioned, met at very sharp angles at a short distance from the turn, and both were circuitous, so that but little of either could be seen at a time. The peddler took the one which led to the left, but held it only a moment, for, on reaching a partial opening in the thicket, he darted across into the right-hand path and led the way up a steep ascent, which lay directly before them. This maneuver saved them. On reaching the fork, the dragoons followed the track and passed the spot where the fugitives had crossed to the other road, before they missed the marks of the footsteps. Their loud cries were heard by Henry and the peddler, as their wearied and breathless animals toiled up the hill, ordering their comrades in the rear to ride in the right direction. The captain again proposed to leave their horses and dash into the thicket.

"Not yet, not yet," said Birch, in a low voice. "The road falls from the top of this hill as steep as it rises; first let us gain the top." While speaking, they reached the desired summit, and both threw themselves from their horses, Henry plunging into the thick underwood, which covered the side of the mountain for some distance above them. Harvey stopped to give each of their beasts a few severe blows of his whip, that drove them headlong down the path on the other side of the eminence, and then followed his example.

The peddler entered the thicket with a little caution, and avoided, as much as possible, rustling or breaking the branches in his way. There was but time only to shelter his person from view when a dragoon led up the ascent, and on reaching the height, he cried aloud,—

"I saw one of their horses turning the hill this minute."

"Drive on, spur forward, my lads," shouted Mason; "give the Englishman quarter, but cut down the peddler, and make an end of him."

Henry felt his companion grip his arm hard, as he listened in a great tremor to this cry, which was followed by the passage of a dozen horsemen, with a vigor and speed that showed too plainly how little security their overtired steeds could have afforded them.

"Now," said the peddler, rising from the cover to reconnoiter, and standing for a moment in suspense, "all that we gain is clear gain; for, as we go up, they go down. Let us be stirring."

"But will they not follow us, and surround this mountain?" said Henry, rising, and imitating the labored but rapid progress of his companion. "Remember, they have foot as well as horse, and, at any rate, we shall starve in the hills."

"Fear nothing, Captain Wharton," returned the peddler, with confidence; "this is not the mountain that I would be on, but necessity has made me a dexterous pilot among these hills. I will lead you where no man will dare to follow. See, the sun is already setting behind the tops of the western mountains, and it will be two hours to the rising of the moon. Who, think you, will follow us far, on a November night, among these rocks and precipices?"

"Listen!" exclaimed Henry; "the dragoons are shouting to each other; they miss us already."

"Come to the point of this rock, and you may see them," said Harvey, composedly setting himself down to rest. "Nay, they can see us—observe, they are pointing up with their fingers. There! one has fired his pistol, but the distance is too great even for a musket."

"They will pursue us," cried the impatient Henry, "let us be moving."

"They will not think of such a thing," returned the peddler, picking the checkerberries that grew on the thin soil where he sat, and very deliberately chewing them, leaves and all, to refresh his mouth. "What progress could they make here, in their heavy boots and spurs, and long swords? No, no—they may go back and turn out the foot, but the horse pass through these defiles, when they can keep the saddle, with fear and trembling. Come, follow me, Captain Wharton; we have a troublesome march before us, but I will bring you where none will think of venturing this night."

So saying, they both arose, and were soon hid from view amongst the rocks and caverns of the mountain.

The conjecture of the peddler was true. Mason and his men dashed down the hill, in pursuit, as they supposed, of their victims, but, on reaching the bottom lands, they found only the deserted horses of the fugitives. Some little time was spent in examining the woods near them, and in endeavoring to take the trail on such ground as might enable the horse to pursue, when one of the party descried the peddler and Henry seated on the rock already mentioned.

"He's off," muttered Mason, eying Harvey, with fury; "he's off, and we are disgraced. By heavens, Washington will not trust us with the keeping of a suspected Tory, if we let the rascal trifle in this manner with the corps; and there sits the Englishman, too, looking down upon us with a smile of benevolence! I fancy that I can see it. Well, well, my lad, you are comfortably seated, I will confess, and that is something better than dancing upon nothing; but you are not to the west of the Harlem River yet, and I'll try your wind before you tell Sir Henry what you have seen."

"Shall I fire and frighten the peddler?" asked one of the men, drawing his pistol from the holster.

"Aye, startle the birds from their perch—let us see how they can use the wing." The man fired the pistol, and Mason continued—"'Fore George, I believe the scoundrels laugh at us. But homeward, or we shall have them rolling stones upon our heads, and the royal gazettes teeming with an account of a rebel regiment routed by two loyalists. They have told bigger lies than that, before now."

The dragoons moved sullenly after their officer, who rode towards their quarters, musing on the course it behooved him to pursue in the present dilemma. It was twilight when Mason's party reached the dwelling, before the door of which were collected a great number of the officers and men, busily employed in giving and listening to the most exaggerated accounts of the escape of the spy. The mortified dragoons gave their ungrateful tidings with the sullen air of disappointed men; and most of the officers gathered round Mason, to consult of the steps that ought to be taken. Miss Peyton and Frances were breathless and unobserved listeners to all that passed between them, from the window of the chamber immediately above their heads.

"Something must be done, and that speedily," observed the commanding officer of the regiment, which lay encamped before the house. "This English officer is doubtless an instrument in the great blow aimed at us by the enemy lately; besides, our honor is involved in his escape."

"Let us beat the woods!" cried several at once. "By morning we shall have them both again."

"Softly, softly, gentlemen," returned the colonel. "No man can travel these hills after dark, unless used to the passes. Nothing but horse can do service in this business, and I presume Lieutenant Mason hesitates to move without the orders of his major."

"I certainly dare not," replied the subaltern, gravely shaking his head, "unless you will take the responsibility of an order; but Major Dunwoodie will be back again in two hours, and we can carry the tidings through the hills before daylight; so that by spreading patrols across, from one river to the other, and offering a reward to the country people, their escape will yet be impossible, unless they can join the party that is said to be out on the Hudson."

"A very plausible plan," cried the colonel, "and one that must succeed; but let a messenger be dispatched to Dunwoodie, or he may continue at the ferry until it proves too late; though doubtless the runaways will lie in the mountains to-night."

To this suggestion Mason acquiesced, and a courier was sent to the major with the important intelligence of the escape of Henry, and an intimation of the necessity of his presence to conduct the pursuit. After this arrangement, the officers separated.

When Miss Peyton and her niece first learned the escape of Captain Wharton, it was with difficulty they could credit their senses. They both relied so implicitly on the success of Dunwoodie's exertions, that they thought the act, on the part of their relative, extremely imprudent; but it was now too late to mend it. While listening to the conversation of the officers, both were struck with the increased danger of Henry's situation, if recaptured, and they trembled to think of the great exertions that would be made to accomplish this object. Miss Peyton consoled herself, and endeavored to cheer her niece, with the probability that the fugitives would pursue their course with unremitting diligence, so that they might reach the neutral ground before the horse would carry down the tidings of their flight. The absence of Dunwoodie seemed to her all-important, and the artless lady was anxiously devising some project that might detain her kinsman, and thus give her nephew the longest possible time. But very different were the reflections of Frances. She could no longer doubt that the figure she had seen on the hill was Birch, and she felt certain that, instead of flying to the friendly forces below, her brother would be taken to the mysterious hut to pass the night.

Frances and her aunt held a long and animated discussion by themselves, when the good spinster reluctantly yielded to the representation of her niece, and folding her in her arms, she kissed her cold cheek, and, fervently blessing her, allowed her to depart on an errand of fraternal love.

Lesson 96

1. Read chapter 30.
2. Why might Harper have been so insistent that Capt. Wharton not see him together with Birch? (Answers)

Vocabulary

1. Review your vocabulary words from Lesson 91.

CHAPTER XXX

And here, forlorn and lost, I tread,
With fainting steps, and slow;
Where wilds, immeasurably spread,
Seem length'ning as I go.
—GOLDSMITH.

The night had set in dark and chilling, as Frances Wharton, with a beating heart but light step, moved through the little garden that lay behind the farmhouse which had been her brother's prison, and took her way to the foot of the mountain, where she had seen the figure of him she supposed to be the peddler. It was still early, but the darkness and the dreary nature of a November evening would, at any other moment, or with less inducement to exertion, have driven her back in terror to the circle she had left. Without pausing to reflect, however, she flew over the ground with a rapidity that seemed to bid defiance to all impediments, nor stopped even to breathe, until she had gone half the distance to the rock that she had marked as the spot where Birch made his appearance on that very morning.

The good treatment of their women is the surest evidence that a people can give of their civilization; and there is no nation which has more to boast of, in this respect, than the Americans. Frances felt but little apprehension from the orderly and quiet troops who were taking their evening's repast on the side of the highway, opposite to the field through which she was flying. They were her countrymen, and she knew that her sex would be respected by the Eastern militia, who composed this body; but in the volatile and reckless character of the Southern horse she had less confidence. Outrages of any description were seldom committed by the really American soldiery; but she recoiled, with exquisite delicacy, from even the appearance of humiliation. When, therefore, she heard the footsteps of a horse moving slowly up the road, she shrank, timidly, into a little thicket of wood which grew around the spring that bubbled from the side of a hillock near her. The vidette, for such it proved to be, passed her without noticing her form, which was so enveloped as to be as little conspicuous as possible, humming a low air to himself, and probably thinking of some other fair that he had left on the banks of the Potomac.

Frances listened anxiously to the retreating footsteps of his horse, and, as they died upon her ear, she ventured from her place of secrecy, and advanced a short distance into the field, where, startled at the gloom, and appalled with the dreariness of the prospect, she paused to reflect on what she had undertaken. Throwing back the hood of her cardinal, she sought the support of a tree, and gazed towards the summit of the mountain that was to be the goal of her enterprise. It rose from the plain like a huge pyramid, giving nothing to the eye but its outlines. The pinnacle could be faintly discerned in front of a lighter background of clouds, between which a few glimmering stars occasionally twinkled in momentary brightness, and then gradually became obscured by the passing vapor that was moving before the wind, at a vast distance below the clouds themselves. Should she return, Henry and the peddler would most probably pass the night in fancied security upon that very hill towards which she was straining her eyes, in the vain hope of observing some light that might encourage her to proceed. The deliberate, and what to her seemed cold-blooded, project of the officer for the recapture of the fugitives, still rang in her ears, and stimulated her to go on; but the solitude into which she must venture, the time, the actual danger of the ascent, and the uncertainty of her finding the hut, or what was still more disheartening, the chance that it might be occupied by unknown tenants, and those of the worst description—urged her to retreat.

The increasing darkness was each moment rendering objects less and less distinct, and the clouds were gathering more gloomily in the rear of the hill, until its form could no longer be discerned. Frances threw back her rich curls with both hands on her temples, in order to possess her senses in their utmost keenness; but the towering hill was entirely lost to the eye. At length she discovered a faint and twinkling blaze in the direction in which she thought the building stood, that, by its reviving and receding luster, might be taken for the glimmering of a fire. But the delusion vanished, as the horizon again cleared, and the star of evening shone forth from a cloud, after struggling hard, as if for existence. She now saw the mountain to the left of the place where the planet was shining, and suddenly a streak of mellow light burst upon the fantastic oaks that were thinly scattered over its summit, and gradually moved down its side, until the whole pile became distinct under the rays of the rising moon. Although it would have been physically impossible for our heroine to advance without the aid of the friendly light, which now gleamed on the long line of level land before her, yet she was not encouraged to proceed. If she could see the goal of her wishes, she could also perceive the difficulties that must attend her reaching it.

While deliberating in distressing incertitude, now shrinking with the timidity of her sex and years from the enterprise, and now resolving to rescue her brother at every hazard, Frances turned her looks towards the east, in earnest gaze at the clouds which constantly threatened to involve her again in comparative darkness. Had an adder stung her, she could not have sprung with greater celerity than she recoiled from the object against which she was leaning, and which she for the first time noticed. The two upright posts, with a crossbeam on their tops, and a rude platform beneath, told but too plainly the nature of the structure; even the cord was suspended from an iron staple, and was swinging to and fro, in the night air. Frances hesitated no longer, but rather flew than ran across the meadow, and was soon at the base of the rock, where she hoped to find something like a path to the summit of the mountain. Here she was compelled to pause for breath, and she improved the leisure by surveying the ground about her. The ascent was quite abrupt, but she soon found a sheep path that wound among the shelving rocks and through the trees, so as to render her labor much less tiresome than it otherwise would have been. Throwing a fearful glance behind, the determined girl commenced her journey upwards. Young, active, and impelled by her generous motive, she moved up the hill with elastic steps, and very soon emerged from the cover of the woods, into an open space of more level ground, that had evidently been cleared of its timber, for the purpose of cultivation. But either the war or the sterility of the soil had compelled the adventurer to abandon the advantages that he had obtained over the wilderness, and already the bushes and briers were springing up afresh, as if the plow had never traced furrows through the mold which nourished them. Frances felt her spirits invigorated by these faint vestiges of the labor of man, and she walked up the gentle acclivity with renewed hopes of success. The path now diverged in so many different directions, that she soon saw it would be useless to follow their windings, and abandoning it, at the first turn, she labored forward towards what she thought was the nearest point of the summit. The cleared ground was soon past, and woods and rocks, clinging to the precipitous sides of the mountain, again opposed themselves to her progress. Occasionally, the path was to be seen running along the verge of the clearing, and then striking off into the scattering patches of grass and herbage, but in no instance could she trace it upward. Tufts of wool, hanging to the briers, sufficiently denoted the origin of these tracks, and Frances rightly conjectured that whoever descended the mountain, would avail himself of their existence, to lighten the labor. Seating herself on a stone, the wearied girl again paused to rest and to reflect; the clouds were rising before the moon, and the whole scene at her feet lay pictured in softest colors.

The white tents of the militia were stretched in regular lines immediately beneath her. The light was shining in the window of her aunt, who, Frances easily fancied, was watching the mountain, racked with all the anxiety she might be supposed to feel for her niece. Lanterns were playing about in the stable yard, where she knew the horses of the dragoons were kept, and believing them to be preparing for their night march, she again sprang upon her feet, and renewed her toil.

Our heroine had to ascend more than a quarter of a mile farther, although she had already conquered two thirds of the height of the mountain. But she was now without a path or any guide to direct her in her course. Fortunately, the hill was conical, like most of the mountains in that range, and, by advancing upwards, she was certain of at length reaching the desired hut, which hung, as it were, on the very pinnacle. Nearly an hour did she struggle with the numerous difficulties that she was obliged to overcome, when, having been repeatedly exhausted with her efforts, and, in several instances, in great danger from falls, she succeeded in gaining the small piece of tableland on the summit.

Faint with her exertions, which had been unusually severe for so slight a frame, she sank on a rock, to recover her strength and fortitude for the approaching interview. A few moments sufficed for this purpose, when she proceeded in quest of the hut. All of the neighboring hills were distinctly visible by the aid of the moon, and Frances was able, where she stood, to trace the route of the highway, from the plains into the mountains. By following this line with her eyes, she soon discovered the point whence she had seen the mysterious dwelling, and directly opposite to that point she well knew the hut must stand.

The chilling air sighed through the leafless branches of the gnarled and crooked oaks, as with a step so light as hardly to rustle the dry leaves on which she trod, Frances moved forward to that part of the hill where she expected to find this secluded habitation; but nothing could she discern that in the least resembled a dwelling of any sort. In vain she examined every recess of the rocks, or inquisitively explored every part of the summit that she thought could hold the tenement of the peddler. No hut, nor any vestige of a human being could she trace. The idea of her solitude struck on the terrified mind of the affrighted girl, and approaching to the edge of a shelving rock, she bent forward to gaze on the signs of life in the vale, when a ray of keen light dazzled her eyes, and a warm ray diffused itself over her whole frame. Recovering from her surprise, Frances looked on the ledge beneath her, and at once perceived that she stood directly over the object of her search. A hole through its roof afforded a passage to the smoke, which, as it blew aside, showed her a clear and cheerful fire crackling and snapping on a rude hearth of stone. The approach to the front of the hut was by a winding path around the point of the rock on which she stood, and by this, she advanced to its door.

Three sides of this singular edifice, if such it could be called, were composed of logs laid alternately on each other, to a little more than the height of a man; and the fourth was formed by the rock against which it leaned. The roof was made of the bark of trees, laid in long strips from the rock to its eaves; the fissures between the logs had been stuffed with clay, which in many places had fallen out, and dried leaves were made use of as a substitute, to keep out the wind. A single window of four panes of glass was in front, but a board carefully closed it, in such a manner as to emit no light from the fire within. After pausing some time to view this singularly constructed hiding place, for such Frances well knew it to be, she applied her eye to a crevice to examine the inside. There was no lamp or candle, but the blazing fire of dry wood made the interior of the hut light enough to read by. In one corner lay a bed of straw, with a pair of blankets thrown carelessly over it, as if left where they had last been used. Against the walls and rock were suspended, from pegs forced into the crevices, various garments, and such as were apparently fitted for all ages and conditions, and for either sex. British and American uniforms hung peaceably by the side of each other; and on the peg that supported a gown of striped calico, such as was the usual country wear, was also depending a well-powdered wig: in short, the attire was numerous and as various as if a whole parish were to be equipped from this one wardrobe.

In the angle against the rock, and opposite to the fire which was burning in the other corner, was an open cupboard, that held a plate or two, a mug, and the remains of some broken meat. Before the fire was a table, with one of its legs fractured, and made of rough boards; these, with a single stool, composed the furniture, if we except a few articles of cooking. A book, that by its size and shape, appeared to be a Bible, was lying on the table, unopened. But it was the occupant of the hut in whom Frances was chiefly interested. This was a man, sitting on the stool, with his head leaning on his hand, in such a manner as to conceal his features, and deeply occupied in examining some open papers. On the table lay a pair of curiously and richly mounted horseman's pistols, and the handle of a sheathed rapier, of exquisite workmanship, protruded from between the legs of the gentleman, one of whose hands carelessly rested on its guard. The tall stature of this unexpected tenant of the hut, and his form, much more athletic than that of either Harvey or her brother, told Frances, without the aid of his dress, that it was neither of those she sought. A close surtout was buttoned high in the throat of the stranger, and parting at his knees, showed breeches of buff, with military boots and spurs. His hair was dressed so as to expose the whole face; and, after the fashion of that day, it was profusely powdered. A round hat was laid on the stones that formed a paved floor to the hut, as if to make room for a large map, which, among the other papers, occupied the table.

This was an unexpected event to our adventurer. She had been so confident that the figure twice seen was the peddler, that on learning his agency in her brother's escape, she did not in the least doubt of finding them both in the place, which, she now discovered, was occupied by another and a stranger. She stood, earnestly looking through the crevice, hesitating whether to retire, or to wait with the expectation of yet meeting Henry, as the stranger moved his hand from before his eyes, and raised his face, apparently in deep musing, when Frances instantly recognized the benevolent and strongly marked, but composed features of Harper.

All that Dunwoodie had said of his power and disposition, all that he had himself promised her brother, and all the confidence that had been created by his dignified and paternal manner, rushed across the mind of Frances, who threw open the door of the hut, and falling at his feet, clasped his knees with her arms, as she cried,—

"Save him—save him—save my brother; remember your promise, and save him!"

Harper had risen as the door opened, and there was a slight movement of one hand towards his pistols; but it was cool and instantly checked. He raised the hood of the cardinal, which had fallen over her features, and exclaimed, with some uneasiness,—

"Miss Wharton! But you cannot be alone?"

"There is none here but my God and you; and by His sacred name, I conjure you to remember your promise, and save my brother!"

Harper gently raised her from her knees, and placed her on the stool, begging her at the same time to be composed, and to acquaint him with the nature of her errand. This Frances instantly did, ingenuously admitting him to a knowledge of all her views in visiting that lone spot at such an hour, and by herself.

It was at all times difficult to probe the thoughts of one who held his passions in such disciplined subjection as Harper, but still there was a lighting of his thoughtful eye, and a slight unbending of his muscles, as the hurried and anxious girl proceeded in her narrative. His interest, as she dwelt upon the manner of Henry's escape, and the flight to the woods, was deep and manifest, and he listened to the remainder of her tale with a marked expression of benevolent indulgence. Her apprehensions, that her brother might still be too late through the mountains, seemed to have much weight with him, for, as she concluded, he walked a turn or two across the hut, in silent musing.

Frances hesitated, and unconsciously played with the handle of one of the pistols, and the paleness that her fears had spread over her fine features began to give place to a rich tint, as, after a short pause, she added,—

"We can depend much on the friendship of Major Dunwoodie, but his sense of honor is so pure, that—that—notwithstanding his—his—feelings—his desire to serve us—he will conceive it to be his duty to apprehend my brother again. Besides, he thinks there will be no danger in so doing, as he relies greatly on your interference."

"On mine," said Harper, raising his eyes in surprise.

"Yes, on yours. When we told him of your kind language, he at once assured us all that you had the power, and, if you had promised, would have the inclination, to procure Henry's pardon."

"Said he more?" asked Harper, who appeared slightly uneasy.

"Nothing but reiterated assurances of Henry's safety; even now he is in quest of you."

"Miss Wharton, that I bear no mean part, in the unhappy struggle between England and America, it might now be useless to deny. You owe your brother's escape, this night, to my knowledge of his innocence, and the remembrance of my word. Major Dunwoodie is mistaken when he says that I might openly have procured his pardon. I now, indeed, can control his fate, and I pledge to you a word which has some influence with Washington, that means shall be taken to prevent his recapture. But from you, also, I exact a promise, that this interview, and all that has passed between us, remain confined to your own bosom, until you have my permission to speak upon the subject."

Frances gave the desired assurance, and he continued,—

"The peddler and your brother will soon be here, but I must not be seen by the royal officer, or the life of Birch might be the forfeiture."

"Never!" cried Frances, ardently. "Henry could never be so base as to betray the man who saved him."

"It is no childish game that we are now playing, Miss Wharton. Men's lives and fortunes hang upon slender threads, and nothing must be left to accident that can be guarded against. Did Sir Henry Clinton know that the peddler had communion with me, and under such circumstances, the life of the miserable man would be taken instantly; therefore, as you value human blood, or remember the rescue of your brother, be prudent, and be silent. Communicate what you know to them both, and urge them to instant departure. If they can reach the last pickets of our army before morning, it shall be my care that there are none to intercept them. There is better work for Major Dunwoodie than to be exposing the life of his friend."

While Harper was speaking, he carefully rolled up the map he had been studying, and placed it, together with sundry papers that were also open, into his pocket. He was still occupied in this manner, when the voice of the peddler, talking in unusually loud tones, was heard directly over their heads.

"Stand farther this way, Captain Wharton, and you can see the tents in the moonshine. But let them mount and ride; I have a nest here, that will hold us both, and we will go in at our leisure."

"And where is this nest? I confess that I have eaten but little the last two days, and I crave some of the cheer you mention."

"Hem!" said the peddler, exerting his voice still more. "Hem—this fog has given me a cold; but move slow—and be careful not to slip, or you may land on the bayonet of the sentinel on the flats; 'tis a steep hill to rise, but one can go down it with ease."

Harper pressed his finger on his lip, to remind Frances of her promise, and, taking his pistols and hat, so that no vestige of his visit remained, he retired deliberately to a far corner of the hut, where, lifting several articles of dress, he entered a recess in the rock, and, letting them fall again, was hid from view. Frances noticed, by the strong firelight, as he entered, that it was a natural cavity, and contained nothing but a few more articles of domestic use.

The surprise of Henry and the peddler, on entering and finding Frances in possession of the hut, may be easily imagined. Without waiting for explanations or questions, the warm-hearted girl flew into the arms of her brother, and gave a vent to her emotions in tears. But the peddler seemed struck with very different feelings. His first look was at the fire, which had been recently supplied with fuel; he then drew open a small drawer of the table, and looked a little alarmed at finding it empty.

"Are you alone, Miss Fanny?" he asked, in a quick voice. "You did not come here alone?"

"As you see me, Mr. Birch," said Frances, raising herself from her brother's arms, and turning an expressive glance towards the secret cavern, that the quick eye of the peddler instantly understood.

"But why and wherefore are you here?" exclaimed her astonished brother; "and how knew you of this place at all?"

Frances entered at once into a brief detail of what had occurred at the house since their departure, and the motives which induced her to seek them.

"But," said Birch, "why follow us here, when we were left on the opposite hill?"

Frances related the glimpse that she had caught of the hut and peddler, in her passage through the Highlands, as well as her view of him on that day, and her immediate conjecture that the fugitives would seek the shelter of this habitation for the night. Birch examined her features as, with open ingenuousness, she related the simple incidents that had made her mistress of his secret; and, as she ended, he sprang upon his feet, and, striking the window with the stick in his hand, demolished it at a blow.

"'Tis but little luxury or comfort that I know," he said, "but even that little cannot be enjoyed in safety! Miss Wharton," he added, advancing before Frances, and speaking with the bitter melancholy that was common to him, "I am hunted through these hills like a beast of the forest; but whenever, tired with my toils, I can reach this spot, poor and dreary as it is, I can spend my solitary nights in safety. Will you aid to make the life of a wretch still more miserable?"

"Never!" cried Frances, with fervor; "your secret is safe with me."

"Major Dunwoodie"—said the peddler, slowly, turning an eye upon her that read her soul.

Frances lowered her head upon her bosom, for a moment, in shame; then, elevating her fine and glowing face, she added, with enthusiasm,—

"Never, never, Harvey, as God may hear my prayers!"

The peddler seemed satisfied; for he drew back, and, watching his opportunity, unseen by Henry, slipped behind the screen, and entered the cavern.

Frances and her brother, who thought his companion had passed through the door, continued conversing on the latter's situation for several minutes, when the former urged the necessity of expedition on his part, in order to precede Dunwoodie, from whose sense of duty they knew they had no escape. The captain took out his pocketbook, and wrote a few lines with his pencil; then folding the paper, he handed it to his sister.

"Frances," he said, "you have this night proved yourself to be an incomparable woman. As you love me, give that unopened to Dunwoodie, and remember that two hours may save my life."

"I will—I will; but why delay? Why not fly, and improve these precious moments?"

"Your sister says well, Captain Wharton," exclaimed Harvey, who had reentered unseen; "we must go at once. Here is food to eat, as we travel."

"But who is to see this fair creature in safety?" cried the captain. "I can never desert my sister in such a place as this."

"Leave me! leave me!" said Frances. "I can descend as I came up. Do not doubt me; you know not my courage nor my strength."

"I have not known you, dear girl, it is true; but now, as I learn your value, can I quit you here? Never, never!"

"Captain Wharton," said Birch, throwing open the door, "you can trifle with your own lives, if you have many to spare; I have but one, and must nurse it. Do I go alone, or not?"

"Go, go, dear Henry," said Frances, embracing him; "go; remember our father; remember Sarah." She waited not for his answer, but gently forced him through the door, and closed it with her own hands.

For a short time there was a warm debate between Henry and the peddler; but the latter finally prevailed, and the breathless girl heard the successive plunges, as they went down the sides of the mountain at a rapid rate.

Immediately after the noise of their departure had ceased, Harper reappeared. He took the arm of Frances in silence, and led her from the hut. The way seemed familiar to him; for, ascending to the ledge above them, he led his companion across the tableland tenderly, pointing out the little difficulties in their route, and cautioning her against injury.

Frances felt, as she walked by the side of this extraordinary man, that she was supported by one of no common stamp. The firmness of his step, and the composure of his manner, seemed to indicate a mind settled and resolved. By taking a route over the back of the hill, they descended with great expedition, and but little danger. The distance it had taken Frances an hour to conquer, was passed by Harper and his companion in ten minutes, and they entered the open space already mentioned. He struck into one of the sheep paths, and, crossing the clearing with rapid steps, they came suddenly upon a horse, caparisoned for a rider of no mean rank. The noble beast snorted and pawed the earth, as his master approached and replaced the pistols in the holsters.

Harper then turned, and, taking the hand of Frances, spoke as follows:—

"You have this night saved your brother, Miss Wharton. It would not be proper for me to explain why there are limits to my ability to serve him; but if you can detain the horse for two hours, he is assuredly safe. After what you have already done, I can believe you equal to any duty. God has denied to me children, young lady; but if it had been His blessed will that my marriage should not have been childless, such a treasure as yourself would I have asked from His mercy. But you are my child: all who dwell in this broad land are my children, and my care; and take the blessing of one who hopes yet to meet you in happier days."

As he spoke, with a solemnity that touched Frances to the heart, he laid his hand impressively upon her head. The guileless girl turned her face towards him, and the hood again falling back, exposed her lovely features to the moonbeams. A tear was glistening on either cheek, and her mild blue eyes were gazing upon him in reverence. Harper bent and pressed a paternal kiss upon her forehead, and continued: "Any of these sheep paths will take you to the plain; but here we must part—I have much to do and far to ride; forget me in all but your prayers."

He then mounted his horse, and lifting his hat, rode towards the back of the mountain, descending at the same time, and was soon hid by the trees. Frances sprang forward with a lightened heart, and taking the first path that led downwards, in a few minutes she reached the plain in safety. While busied in stealing through the meadows towards the house, the noise of horse approaching startled her, and she felt how much more was to be apprehended from man, in some situations, than from solitude. Hiding her form in the angle of a fence near the road, she remained quiet for a moment, and watched their passage. A small party of dragoons, whose dress was different from the Virginians, passed at a brisk trot. They were followed by a gentleman, enveloped in a large cloak, whom she at once knew to be Harper. Behind him rode a black in livery, and two youths in uniform brought up the rear. Instead of taking the road that led by the encampment, they turned short to the left and entered the hills.

Wondering who this unknown but powerful friend of her brother could be, Frances glided across the fields, and using due precautions in approaching the dwelling, regained her residence undiscovered and in safety.

Lesson 97

1. Read chapter 31.
2. What are two reasons why Frances agreed to marry Dunwoodie so quickly, right on the spot? (Answers)

CHAPTER XXXI

Hence, bashful cunning!
And prompt me, plain and holy innocence;
I am your wife, if you will marry me.

—*Tempest.*

On joining Miss Peyton, Frances learned that Dunwoodie was not yet returned; although, with a view to relieve Henry from the importunities of the supposed fanatic, he had desired a very respectable divine of their own church to ride up from the river and offer his services. This gentleman was already arrived, and had been passing the half hour he had been there, in a sensible and well-bred conversation with the spinster, that in no degree touched upon their domestic affairs.

To the eager inquiries of Miss Peyton, relative to her success in her romantic excursion, Frances could say no more than that she was bound to be silent, and to recommend the same precaution to the good maiden also. There was a smile playing around the beautiful mouth of Frances, while she uttered this injunction, which satisfied her aunt that all was as it should be. She was urging her niece to take some refreshment after her fatiguing expedition, when the noise of a horseman riding to the door, announced the return of the major. He had been found by the courier who was dispatched by Mason, impatiently waiting the return of Harper to the ferry, and immediately flew to the place where his friend had been confined, tormented by a thousand conflicting fears. The heart of Frances bounded as she listened to his approaching footsteps. It wanted yet an hour to the termination of the shortest period that the peddler had fixed as the time necessary to effect his escape. Even Harper, powerful and well-disposed as he acknowledged himself to be, had laid great stress upon the importance of detaining the Virginians during that hour. She, however, had not time to rally her thoughts, before Dunwoodie entered one door, as Miss Peyton, with the readiness of female instinct, retired through another.

The countenance of Peyton was flushed, and an air of vexation and disappointment pervaded his manner.

"'Twas imprudent, Frances; nay, it was unkind," he cried, throwing himself in a chair, "to fly at the very moment that I had assured him of safety! I can almost persuade myself that you delight in creating points of difference in our feelings and duties."

"In our duties there may very possibly be a difference," returned his mistress, approaching, and leaning her slender form against the wall; "but not in our feelings, Peyton. You must certainly rejoice in the escape of Henry!"

"There was no danger impending. He had the promise of Harper; and it is a word never to be doubted. O Frances! Frances! had you known the man, you would never have distrusted his assurance; nor would you have again reduced me to this distressing alternative."

"What alternative?" asked Frances, pitying his emotions deeply, but eagerly seizing upon every circumstance to prolong the interview.

"What alternative! Am I not compelled to spend this night in the saddle to recapture your brother, when I had thought to lay my head on its pillow, with the happy consciousness of having contributed to his release? You make me seem your enemy; I, who would cheerfully shed the last drop of blood in your service. I repeat, Frances, it was rash; it was unkind; it was a sad, sad mistake."

She bent towards him and timidly took one of his hands, while with the other she gently removed the curls from his burning brow.

"Why go at all, dear Peyton?" she asked. "You have done much for your country, and she cannot exact such a sacrifice as this at your hand."

"Frances! Miss Wharton!" exclaimed the youth, springing on his feet, and pacing the floor with a cheek that burned through its brown covering, and an eye that sparkled with wounded integrity. "It is not my country, but my honor, that requires the sacrifice. Has he not fled from a guard of my own corps? But for this, I might have been spared the blow! But if the eyes of the Virginians are blinded to deception and artifice, their horses are swift of foot, and their sabers keen. We shall see, before to-morrow's sun, who will presume to hint that the beauty of the sister furnished a mask to conceal the brother! Yes, yes, I should like, even now," he continued, laughing bitterly, "to hear the villain who would dare to surmise that such treachery existed!"

"Peyton, dear Peyton," said Frances, recoiling from his angry eye, "you curdle my blood—would you kill my brother?"

"Would I not die for him!" exclaimed Dunwoodie, as he turned to her more mildly. "You know I would; but I am distracted with the cruel surmise to which this step of Henry's subjects me. What will Washington think of me, should he learn that I ever became your husband?"

"If that alone impels you to act so harshly towards my brother," returned Frances, with a slight tremor in her voice, "let it never happen for him to learn."

"And this is consolation, Frances!"

"Nay, dear Dunwoodie, I meant nothing harsh or unkind; but are you not making us both of more consequence with Washington than the truth will justify?"

"I trust that my name is not entirely unknown to the commander in chief," said the major, a little proudly; "nor are you as obscure as your modesty would make you. I believe you, Frances, when you say that you pity me, and it must be my task to continue worthy of such feelings. But I waste the precious moments; we must go through the hills to-night, that we may be refreshed in time for the duty of to-morrow. Mason is already waiting my orders to mount. Frances, I leave you with a heavy heart; pity me, but feel no concern for your brother; he must again become a prisoner, but every hair of his head is sacred."

"Stop! Dunwoodie, I conjure you," cried Frances, gasping for breath, as she noticed that the hand of the clock still wanted many minutes to the desired hour. "Before you go on your errand of fastidious duty, read this note that Henry has left for you, and which, doubtless, he thought he was writing to the friend of his youth."

"Frances, I excuse your feelings; but the time will come when you will do me justice."

"That time is now," she answered, extending her hand, unable any longer to feign a displeasure that she did not feel.

"Where got you this note?" exclaimed the youth, glancing his eyes over its contents. "Poor Henry, you are indeed my friend! If anyone wishes me happiness, it is you!"

"He does, he does," cried Frances, eagerly; "he wishes you every happiness; believe what he tells you; every word is true."

"I do believe him, lovely girl, and he refers me to you for its confirmation. Would that I could trust equally to your affections!"

"You may, Peyton," said Frances, looking up with innocent confidence towards her lover.

"Then read for yourself, and verify your words," interrupted Dunwoodie, holding the note towards her.

Frances received it in astonishment, and read the following:

"Life is too precious to be trusted to uncertainties. I leave you, Peyton, unknown to all but Caesar, and I recommend him to your mercy. But there is a care that weighs me to the earth. Look at my aged and infirm parent. He will be reproached for the supposed crime of his son. Look at those helpless sisters that I leave behind me without a protector. Prove to me that you love us all. Let the clergyman whom you will bring with you, unite you this night to Frances, and become at once, brother, son, and husband."

The paper fell from the hands of Frances, and she endeavored to raise her eyes to the face of Dunwoodie, but they sank abashed to the floor.

"Am I worthy of this confidence? Will you send me out this night, to meet my own brother? or will it be the officer of Congress in quest of the officer of Britain?"

"And would you do less of your duty because I am your wife, Major Dunwoodie? In what degree would it better the condition of Henry?"

"Henry, I repeat, is safe. The word of Harper is his guarantee; but I will show the world a bridegroom," continued the youth, perhaps deceiving himself a little, "who is equal to the duty of arresting the brother of his bride."

"And will the world comprehend this refinement?" said Frances, with a musing air, that lighted a thousand hopes in the bosom of her lover. In fact, the temptation was mighty. Indeed, there seemed no other way to detain Dunwoodie until the fatal hour had elapsed. The words of Harper himself, who had so lately told her that openly he could do but little for Henry, and that everything depended upon gaining time, were deeply engraved upon her memory. Perhaps there was also a fleeting thought of the possibility of an eternal separation from her lover, should he proceed and bring back her brother to punishment. It is difficult at all times to analyze human emotions, and they pass through the sensitive heart of a woman with the rapidity and nearly with the vividness of lightning.

"Why do you hesitate, dear Frances?" cried Dunwoodie, who was studying her varying countenance. "A few minutes might give me a husband's claim to protect you."

Frances grew giddy. She turned an anxious eye to the clock, and the hand seemed to linger over its face, as if with intent to torture her.

"Speak, Frances," murmured Dunwoodie; "may I summon my good kinswoman? Determine, for time presses."

She endeavored to reply, but could only whisper something that was inaudible, but which her lover, with the privilege of immemorial custom, construed into assent. He turned and flew to the door, when his mistress recovered her voice:—

"Stop, Peyton! I cannot enter into such a solemn engagement with a fraud upon my conscience. I have seen Henry since his escape, and time is all-important to him. Here is my hand; if, with this knowledge of the consequences of delay, you will not reject it, it is freely yours."

"Reject it!" cried the delighted youth. "I take it as the richest gift of heaven. There is time enough for us all. Two hours will take me through the hills; and by noon to-morrow I will return with Washington's pardon for your brother, and Henry will help to enliven our nuptials."

"Then meet me here, in ten minutes," said Frances, greatly relieved by unburdening her mind, and filled with the hope of securing Henry's safety, "and I will return and take those vows which will bind me to you forever."

Dunwoodie paused only to press her once to his bosom, and flew to communicate his wishes to the priest.

Miss Peyton received the avowal of her niece with infinite astonishment, and a little displeasure. It was violating all the order and decorum of a wedding to get it up so hastily, and with so little ceremony. But Frances, with modest firmness, declared that her resolution was taken; she had long possessed the consent of her friends, and their nuptials, for months, had only waited her pleasure. She had now promised Dunwoodie; and it was her wish to comply; more she dare not say without committing herself, by entering into explanations that might endanger Birch, or Harper, or both. Unused to contention, and really much attached to her kinsman, the feeble objections of Miss Peyton gave way to the firmness of her niece. Mr. Wharton was too completely a convert to the doctrine of passive obedience and nonresistance, to withstand any solicitation from an officer of Dunwoodie's influence in the rebel armies; and the maid returned to the apartment, accompanied by her father and aunt, at the expiration of the time that she had fixed. Dunwoodie and the clergyman were already there. Frances, silently, and without the affectation of reserve, placed in his hand the wedding ring of her own mother, and after some little time spent in arranging Mr. Wharton and herself, Miss Peyton suffered the ceremony to proceed.

The clock stood directly before the eyes of Frances, and she turned many an anxious glance at the dial; but the solemn language of the priest soon caught her attention, and her mind became intent upon the vows she was uttering. The ceremony was quickly over, and as the clergyman closed the words of benediction, the clock told the hour of nine. This was the time that Harper had deemed so important, and Frances felt as if a mighty load was at once removed from her heart.

Dunwoodie folded her in his arms, saluted the mild aunt again and again, and shook Mr. Wharton and the divine repeatedly by the hands. In the midst of the felicitation, a tap was heard at the door. It was opened, and Mason appeared.

"We are in the saddle," said the lieutenant, "and, with your permission, I will lead on; as you are so well mounted, you can overtake us at your leisure."

"Yes, yes, my good fellow; march," cried Dunwoodie, gladly seizing an excuse to linger. "I will reach you at the first halt."

The subaltern retired to execute these orders; he was followed by Mr. Wharton and the divine.

"Now, Peyton," said Frances, "it is indeed a brother that you seek; I am sure I need not caution you in his behalf, should you unfortunately find him."

"Say fortunately," cried the youth, "for I am determined he shall yet dance at my wedding. Would that I could win him to our cause. It is the cause of his country; and I could fight with more pleasure, Frances, with your brother by my side."

"Oh! mention it not! You awaken terrible reflections."

"I will not mention it," returned her husband; "but I must now leave you. But the sooner I go, Frances, the sooner I shall return."

The noise of a horseman was heard approaching the house, and Dunwoodie was yet taking leave of his bride and her aunt, when an officer was shown into the room by his own man.

The gentleman wore the dress of an aid-de-camp, and the major at once knew him to be one of the military family of Washington.

"Major Dunwoodie," he said, after bowing to the ladies, "the commander in chief has directed me to give you these orders."

He executed his mission, and, pleading duty, took his leave immediately.

"Here, indeed!" cried the major, "is an unexpected turn in the whole affair; but I understand it: Harper has got my letter, and already we feel his influence."

"Have you news affecting Henry?" cried Frances, springing to his side.

"Listen, and you shall judge."

> SIR,—Upon the receipt of this, you will concentrate your squadron, so as to be in front of a covering party which the enemy has sent up in front of his foragers, by ten o'clock to-morrow, on the heights of Croton, where you will find a body of foot to support you. The escape of the English spy has been reported to me, but his arrest is unimportant, compared with the duty I now assign you. You will, therefore, recall your men, if any are in pursuit, and endeavor to defeat the enemy forthwith."
>
> Your obedient servant,
> GEO. WASHINGTON.

"Thank God!" cried Dunwoodie, "my hands are washed of Henry's recapture; I can now move to my duty with honor."

"And with prudence, too, dear Peyton," said Frances, with a face as pale as death. "Remember, Dunwoodie, you leave behind you new claims on your life."

The youth dwelt on her lovely but pallid features with rapture; and, as he folded her to his heart, exclaimed,—

"For your sake, I will, lovely innocent!" Frances sobbed a moment on his bosom, and he tore himself from her presence.

Miss Peyton retired with her niece, to whom she conceived it necessary, before they separated for the night, to give an admonitory lecture on the subject of matrimonial duty. Her instruction was modestly received, if not properly digested. We regret that history has not handed down to us this precious dissertation; but the result of all our investigation has been to learn that it partook largely of those peculiarities which are said to tincture the rules prescribed to govern bachelors' children. We shall now leave the ladies of the Wharton family, and return to Captain Wharton and Harvey Birch.

Lesson 98

1. Read chapter 32. I actually skipped the last part of the chapter. You don't need to read it. British soldiers hang a Skinner who was deserting from the American army. Would you have trusted him?
2. What became of Captain Wharton? (Answers)

CHAPTER XXXII

Allow him not a parting word;
Short be the shrift, and sure the cord!
—*Rokeby*.

The peddler and his companion soon reached the valley, and after pausing to listen, and hearing no sounds which announced that pursuers were abroad, they entered the highway. Acquainted with every step that led through the mountains, and possessed of sinews inured to toil, Birch led the way, with the lengthened strides that were peculiar to the man and his profession; his pack alone was wanting to finish the appearance of his ordinary business air. At times, when they approached one of those little posts held by the American troops, with which the Highlands abounded, he would take a circuit to avoid the sentinels, and plunge fearlessly into a thicket, or ascend a rugged hill, that to the eye seemed impassable. But the peddler was familiar with every turn in their difficult route, knew where the ravines might be penetrated, or where the streams were fordable. In one or two instances, Henry thought that their further progress was absolutely at an end, but the ingenuity, or knowledge, of his guide, conquered every difficulty. After walking at a great rate for three hours, they suddenly diverged from the road, which inclined to the east, and held their course directly across the hills, in a due south direction. This movement was made, the peddler informed his companion, in order to avoid the parties who constantly patrolled in the southern entrance of the Highlands, as well as to shorten the distance, by traveling in a straight line. After reaching the summit of a hill, Harvey seated himself by the side of a little run, and opening a wallet, that he had slung where his pack was commonly suspended, he invited his comrade to partake of the coarse fare it contained. Henry had kept pace with the peddler, more by the excitement natural to his situation, than by the equality of his physical powers. The idea of a halt was unpleasant, so long as there existed a possibility of the horse getting below him in time to intercept their retreat through the neutral ground. He therefore stated his apprehensions to his companion, and urged a wish to proceed.

"Follow my example, Captain Wharton," said the peddler, commencing his frugal meal. "If the horse have started, it will be more than man can do to head them; and if they have not, work is cut out for them, that will drive all thoughts of you and me from their brains."

"You said yourself, that two hours' detention was all-important to us, and if we loiter here, of what use will be the advantage that we may have already obtained?"

"The time is past, and Major Dunwoodie thinks little of following two men, when hundreds are waiting for him on the banks of the river."

"Listen!" interrupted Henry, "there are horse at this moment passing the foot of the hill. I hear them even laughing and talking to each other. Hist! there is the voice of Dunwoodie himself; he calls to his comrade in a manner that shows but little uneasiness. One would think that the situation of his friend would lower his spirits; surely Frances could not have given him the letter."

On hearing the first exclamation of the captain, Birch arose from his seat, and approached cautiously to the brow of the hill, taking care to keep his body in the shadow of the rocks, so as to be unseen at any distance, and earnestly reconnoitered the group of passing horsemen. He continued listening, until their quick footsteps were no longer audible, and then quietly returned to his seat, and with incomparable coolness resumed his meal.

"You have a long walk, and a tiresome one, before you, Captain Wharton; you had better do as I do—you were eager for food at the hut above Fishkill, but traveling seems to have worn down your appetite."

"I thought myself safe, then, but the information of my sister fills me with uneasiness, and I cannot eat."

"You have less reason to be troubled now than at any time since the night before you were taken, when you refused my advice, and an offer to see you in safety," returned the peddler. "Major Dunwoodie is not a man to laugh and be gay when his friend is in difficulty. Come, then, and eat, for no horse will be in our way, if we can hold our legs for four hours longer, and the sun keeps behind the hills as long as common."

There was a composure in the peddler's manner that encouraged his companion; and having once determined to submit to Harvey's government, he suffered himself to be persuaded into a tolerable supper, if quantity be considered without any reference to the quality. After completing their repast, the peddler resumed his journey.

Henry followed in blind submission to his will. For two hours more they struggled with the difficult and dangerous passes of the Highlands, without road, or any other guide than the moon, which was traveling the heavens, now wading through flying clouds, and now shining brightly. At length they arrived at a point where the mountains sank into rough and unequal hillocks, and passed at once from the barren sterility of the precipices, to the imperfect culture of the neutral ground.

The peddler now became more guarded in the manner in which they proceeded, and took divers precautions to prevent meeting any moving parts of the Americans. With the stationary posts he was too familiar to render it probable he might fall upon any of them unawares. He wound among the hills and vales, now keeping the highways and now avoiding them, with a precision that seemed instinctive. There was nothing elastic in his tread, but he glided over the ground with enormous strides, and a body bent forward, without appearing to use exertion, or know weariness.

The moon had set, and a faint streak of light was beginning to show itself in the east. Captain Wharton ventured to express a sense of fatigue, and to inquire if they were not yet arrived at a part of the country where it might be safe to apply at some of the farmhouses for admission.

"See here," said the peddler, pointing to a hill, at a short distance in the rear, "do you not see a man walking on the point of that rock? Turn, so as to bring the daylight in the range—now, see, he moves, and seems to be looking earnestly at something to the eastward. That is a royal sentinel; two hundred of the rig'lar troops lay on that hill, no doubt sleeping on their arms."

"Then," cried Henry, "let us join them, and our danger is ended."

"Softly, softly, Captain Wharton," said the peddler, dryly, "you've once been in the midst of three hundred of them, but there was a man who could take you out; see you not yon dark body, on the side of the opposite hill, just above the cornstalks? There are the—the rebels (since that is the word for us loyal subjects), waiting only for day, to see who will be master of the ground."

"Nay, then," exclaimed the fiery youth, "I will join the troops of my prince, and share their fortune, be it good or be it bad."

"You forget that you fight with a halter round your neck; no, no—I have promised one whom I must not disappoint, to carry you safe in; and unless you forget what I have already done, and what I have risked for you, Captain Wharton, you will turn and follow me to Harlem."

To this appeal the youth felt unwillingly obliged to submit; and they continued their course towards the city. It was not long before they gained the banks of the Hudson. After searching for a short time under the shore, the peddler discovered a skiff, that appeared to be an old acquaintance; and entering it with his companion he landed him on the south side of the Croton. Here Birch declared they were in safety; for the royal troops held the continentals at bay, and the former were out in too great strength for the light parties of the latter to trust themselves below that river, on the immediate banks of the Hudson.

Throughout the whole of this arduous flight, the peddler had manifested a coolness and presence of mind that nothing appeared to disturb. All his faculties seemed to be of more than usual perfection, and the infirmities of nature to have no dominion over him. Henry had followed him like a child in leading strings, and he now reaped his reward, as he felt a bound of pleasure at his heart, on hearing that he was relieved from apprehension, and permitted to banish every doubt of security.

A steep and laborious ascent brought them from the level of the tidewaters to the high lands that form, in this part of the river, the eastern banks of the Hudson. Retiring a little from the highway, under the shelter of a thicket of cedars, the peddler threw his form on a flat rock, and announced to his companion that the hour for rest and refreshment was at length arrived. The day was now opened, and objects could be seen in the distance, with distinctness. Beneath them lay the Hudson, stretching to the south in a straight line, as far as the eye could reach. To the north, the broken fragments of the Highlands threw upwards their lofty heads, above masses of fog that hung over the water, and by which the course of the river could be traced into the bosom of hills whose conical summits were grouping togather, one behind another, in that disorder which might be supposed to have succeeded their gigantic, but fruitless, efforts to stop the progress of the flood. Emerging from these confused piles, the river, as if rejoicing at its release from the struggle, expanded into a wide bay, which was ornamented by a few fertile and low points that jutted humbly into its broad basin. On the opposite, or western shore, the rocks of Jersey were gathered into an array that has obtained for them the name of the "Palisades," elevating themselves for many hundred feet, as if to protect the rich country in their rear from the inroads of the conqueror; but, disdaining such an enemy, the river swept proudly by their feet, and held its undeviating way to the ocean. A ray of the rising sun darted upon the slight cloud that hung over the placid river, and at once the whole scene was in motion, changing and assuming new forms, and exhibiting fresh objects in each successive moment. At the daily rising of this great curtain of nature, at the present time, scores of white sails and sluggish vessels are seen thickening on the water, with that air of life which denotes the neighborhood to the metropolis of a great and flourishing empire; but to Henry and the peddler it displayed only the square yards and lofty masts of a vessel of war, riding a few miles below them. Before the fog had begun to move, the tall spars were seen above it, and from one of them a long pennant was feebly borne abroad in the current of night air, that still quivered along the river; but as the smoke arose, the black hull, the crowded and complicated mass of rigging, and the heavy yards and booms, spreading their arms afar, were successively brought into view.

"There, Captain Wharton," said the peddler, "there is a safe resting place for you; America has no arm that can reach you, if you gain the deck of that ship. She is sent up to cover the foragers, and support the troops; the rig'lar officers are fond of the sound of cannon from their shipping."

Without condescending to reply to the sarcasm conveyed in this speech, or perhaps not noticing it, Henry joyfully acquiesced in the proposal, and it was accordingly arranged between them, that, as soon as they were refreshed, he should endeavor to get on board the vessel.

While busily occupied in the very indispensable operation of breaking their fast, our adventurers were startled with the sound of distant firearms. At first a few scattering shots were fired, which were succeeded by a long and animated roll of musketry, and then quick and heavy volleys followed each other.

"Your prophecy is made good," cried the English officer, springing upon his feet. "Our troops and the rebels are at it! I would give six months' pay to see the charge."

"Umph!" returned his companion, without ceasing his meal, "they do very well to look at from a distance; I can't say but the company of this bacon, cold as it is, is more to my taste, just now, than a hot fire from the continentals."

"The discharges are heavy for so small a force; but the fire seems irregular."

"The scattering guns are from the Connecticut militia," said Harvey, raising his head to listen; "they rattle it off finely, and are no fools at a mark. The volleys are the rig'lars, who, you know, fire by word—as long as they can."

"I like not the warmth of what you call a scattering fire," exclaimed the captain, moving about with uneasiness; "it is more like the roll of a drum than skirmishers' shooting."

"No, no; I said not skrimmagers," returned the other, raising himself upon a knee, and ceasing to eat; "so long as they stand, they are too good for the best troops in the royal army. Each man does his work as if fighting by the job; and then, they think while they fight, and don't send bullets to the clouds, that were meant to kill men on earth."

"You talk and look, sir, as if you wished them success," said Henry, sternly.

"I wish success to the good cause only, Captain Wharton. I thought you knew me too well, to be uncertain which party I favored."

"Oh! you are reputed loyal, Mr. Birch. But the volleys have ceased!"

Both now listened intently for a little while, during which the irregular reports became less brisk, and suddenly heavy and repeated volleys followed.

"They've been at the bayonet," said the peddler; "the rig'lars have tried the bayonet, and the rebels are driven."

"Aye, Mr. Birch, the bayonet is the thing for the British soldier, after all. They delight in the bayonet!"

"Well, to my notion," said the peddler, "there's but little delight to be taken in any such fearful weapon. I dare say the militia are of my mind, for half of them don't carry the ugly things. Lord! Lord! captain, I wish you'd go with me once into the rebel camp, and hear what lies the men will tell about Bunker Hill and Burg'yne; you'd think they loved the bayonet as much as they do their dinners."

There was a chuckle, and an air of affected innocency about his companion, that rather annoyed Henry, and he did not deign to reply.

The firing now became desultory, occasionally intermingled with heavy volleys. Both of the fugitives were standing, listening with much anxiety, when a man, armed with a musket, was seen stealing towards them, under the shelter of the cedar bushes, that partially covered the hill. Henry first observed this suspicious-looking stranger, and instantly pointed him out to his companion. Birch started, and certainly made an indication of sudden flight; but recollecting himself, he stood, in sullen silence, until the stranger was within a few yards of them.

"'Tis friends," said the fellow, clubbing his gun, but apparently afraid to venture nearer.

"You had better retire," said Birch; "here are rig'lars at hand. We are not near Dunwoodie's horse now, and you will not find me an easy prize to-day."

"Damn Major Dunwoodie and his horse!" cried the leader of the Skinners (for it was he); "God bless King George! and a speedy end to the rebellion, say I. If you would show me the safe way in to the refugees, Mr. Birch, I'll pay you well, and ever after stand your friend, in the bargain."

"The road is as open to you as to me," said Birch, turning from him in ill-concealed disgust. "If you want to find the refugees, you know well where they lay."

"Aye, but I'm a little doubtful of going in upon them by myself; now, you are well known to them all, and it will be no detriment to you just to let me go in with you."

Henry here interfered, and after holding a short dialogue with the fellow, he entered into a compact with him, that, on condition of surrendering his arms, he might join the party. The man complied instantly, and Birch received his gun with eagerness; nor did he lay it upon his shoulder to renew their march, before he had carefully examined the priming, and ascertained, to his satisfaction, that it contained a good, dry, ball cartridge.

As soon as this engagement was completed, they commenced their journey anew. By following the bank of the river, Birch led the way free from observation, until they reached the point opposite to the frigate, when, by making a signal, a boat was induced to approach. Some time was spent, and much precaution used, before the seamen would trust themselves ashore; but Henry having finally succeeded in making the officer who commanded the party credit his assertions, he was able to rejoin his companions in arms in safety. Before taking leave of Birch, the captain handed him his purse, which was tolerably well supplied for the times; the peddler received it, and, watching an opportunity, he conveyed it, unnoticed by the Skinner, to a part of his dress that was ingeniously contrived to hold such treasures.

The boat pulled from the shore, and Birch turned on his heel, drawing his breath, like one relieved, and shot up the hills with the strides for which he was famous. The Skinner followed, and each party pursued the common course, casting frequent and suspicious glances at the other, and both maintaining a most impenetrable silence.

Wagons were moving along the river road, and occasional parties of horse were seen escorting the fruits of the inroad towards the city. As the peddler had views of his own, he rather avoided falling in with any of these patrols, than sought their protection. But, after traveling a few miles on the immediate banks of the river, during which, notwithstanding the repeated efforts of the Skinner to establish something like sociability, he maintained a most determined silence, keeping a firm hold of the gun, and always maintaining a jealous watchfulness of his associate, the peddler suddenly struck into the highway, with an intention of crossing the hills towards Harlem. At the moment he gained the path, a body of horse came over a little eminence, and was upon him before he perceived them. It was too late to retreat, and after taking a view of the materials that composed this party, Birch rejoiced in the rencounter, as a probable means of relieving him from his unwelcome companion. There were some eighteen or twenty men, mounted and equipped as dragoons, though neither their appearance nor manners denoted much discipline. At their head rode a heavy, middle-aged man, whose features expressed as much of animal courage, and as little of reason, as could be desired for such an occupation. He wore the dress of an officer, but there was none of that neatness in his attire, nor grace in his movements, that was usually found about the gentlemen who bore the royal commission. His limbs were firm, and not pliable, and he sat his horse with strength and confidence, but his bridle hand would have been ridiculed by the meanest rider amongst the Virginians. As he expected, this leader instantly hailed the peddler, in a voice by no means more conciliating than his appearance.

"Hey! my gentlemen, which way so fast?" he cried, "Has Washington sent you down as spies?"

"I am an innocent peddler," returned Harvey meekly, "and am going below, to lay in a fresh stock of goods."

"And how do you expect to get below, my innocent peddler? Do you think we hold the forts at King's Bridge to cover such peddling rascals as you, in your goings in and comings out?"

"I believe I hold a pass that will carry me through," said the peddler, handing him a paper, with an air of indifference.

The officer, for such he was, read it, and cast a look of surprise and curiosity at Harvey, when he had done.

Then turning to one or two of his men, who had officiously stopped the way, he cried,—

"Why do you detain the man? Give way, and let him pass in peace. But whom have we here? Your name is not mentioned in the pass!"

"No, sir," said the Skinner, lifting his hat with humility. "I have been a poor, deluded man, who has been serving in the rebel army; but, thank God, I've lived to see the error of my ways, and am now come to make reparation, by enlisting under the Lord's anointed."

Lesson 99

1. Read chapter 33.
2. Why did Major Dunwoodie's being wounded turn out for his and Frances' good? (Answers)

CHAPTER XXXIII

Green be the turf above thee,
Friend of my better days;
None knew thee but to love thee,
None named thee but to praise.
—HALLECK.

While the scenes and events that we have recorded were occurring, Captain Lawton led his small party, by slow and wary marches, from the Four Corners to the front of a body of the enemy; where he so successfully maneuvered, for a short time, as completely to elude all their efforts to entrap him, and yet so disguised his own force as to excite the constant apprehension of an attack from the Americans. This forbearing policy, on the side of the partisan, was owing to positive orders received from his commander. When Dunwoodie left his detachment, the enemy were known to be slowly advancing, and he directed Lawton to hover around them, until his own return, and the arrival of a body of foot, might enable him to intercept their retreat.

The trooper discharged his duty to the letter but with no little of the impatience that made part of his character when restrained from the attack.

During these movements, Betty Flanagan guided her little cart with indefatigable zeal among the rocks of Westchester, now discussing with the sergeant the nature of evil spirits, and now combating with the surgeon sundry points of practice that were hourly arising between them. But the moment arrived that was to decide the temporary mastery of the field. A detachment of the eastern militia moved out from their fastnesses, and approached the enemy.

The junction between Lawton and his auxiliaries was made at midnight, and an immediate consultation was held between him and the leader of the foot soldiers. After listening to the statements of the partisan, who rather despised the prowess of his enemy, the commandant of the party determined to attack the British, the moment daylight enabled him to reconnoiter their position, without waiting for the aid of Dunwoodie and his horse. So soon as this decision was made, Lawton retired from the building where the consultation was held, and rejoined his own small command.

The few troopers who were with the captain had fastened their horses in a spot adjacent to a haystack, and laid their own frames under its shelter, to catch a few hours' sleep. But Dr. Sitgreaves, Sergeant Hollister, and Betty Flanagan were congregated at a short distance by themselves, having spread a few blankets upon the dry surface of a rock. Lawton threw his huge frame by the side of the surgeon, and folding his cloak about him, leaned his head upon one hand, and appeared deeply engaged in contemplating the moon as it waded through the heavens. The sergeant was sitting upright, in respectful deference to the surgeon, and the washerwoman was now raising her head, in order to vindicate some of her favorite maxims, and now composing it to sleep.

"So, sergeant," continued Sitgreaves, following up a previous position, "if you cut upwards, the blow, by losing the additional momentum of your weight, will be less destructive, and at the same time effect the true purpose of war, that of disabling your enemy."

"Pooh! pooh! sergeant dear," said the washerwoman, raising her head from the blanket, "where's the harm of taking a life, jist in the way of battle? Is it the rig'lars who'll show favor, and they fighting? Ask Captain Jack there, if the country could get free, and the boys no strike their might. I wouldn't have them disparage the whisky so much."

"It is not to be expected that an ignorant female like yourself, Mrs. Flanagan," returned the surgeon, with a calmness that only rendered his contempt more stinging to Betty, "can comprehend the distinctions of surgical science; neither are you accomplished in the sword exercise; so that dissertations upon the judicious use of that weapon could avail you nothing either in theory or in practice."

"It's hut little I care, anyway, for such botherment; but fighting is no play, and a body shouldn't be particular how they strike, or who they hit, so it's the inimy."

"Are we likely to have a warm day, Captain Lawton?"

"'Tis more than probable," replied the trooper; "these militia seldom fail of making a bloody field, either by their cowardice or their ignorance, and the real soldier is made to suffer for their bad conduct."

"Are you ill, John?" said the surgeon, passing his hand along the arm of the captain, until it instinctively settled on his pulse; but the steady, even beat announced neither bodily nor mental malady.

"Sick at heart, Archibald, at the folly of our rulers, in believing that battles are to be fought and victories won, by fellows who handle a musket as they would a flail; lads who wink when they pull a trigger, and form a line like a hoop pole. The dependence we place on these men spills the best blood of the country."

The surgeon listened with amazement. It was not the matter, but the manner that surprised him. The trooper had uniformly exhibited, on the eve of battle, an animation, and an eagerness to engage, that was directly at variance with the admirable coolness of his manner at other times. But now there was a despondency in the tones of his voice, and a listlessness in his air, that was entirely different. The operator hesitated a moment, to reflect in what manner he could render this change of service in furthering his favorite system, and then continued,—

"It would be wise, John, to advise the colonel to keep at long shot; a spent ball will disable—"

"No!" exclaimed the trooper, impatiently, "let the rascals singe their whiskers at the muzzles of the British muskets, if they can be driven there. But, enough of them. Archibald, do you deem that moon to be a world like this, containing creatures like ourselves?"

"Nothing more probable, dear John; we know its size and, reasoning from analogy, may easily conjecture its use. Whether or not its inhabitants have attained to that perfection in the sciences which we have acquired, must depend greatly on the state of its society, and in some measure upon its physical influences."

"I care nothing about their learning, Archibald; but 'tis a wonderful power that can create such worlds, and control them in their wanderings. I know not why, but there is a feeling of melancholy excited within me as I gaze on that body of light, shaded as it is by your fancied sea and land. It seems to be the resting place of departed spirits!"

"Take a drop, darling," said Betty, raising her head once more, and proffering her own bottle. "'Tis the night damp that chills the blood—and then the talk with the cursed militia is no good for a fiery temper. Take a drop, darling, and ye'll sleep till the morning. I fed Roanoke myself, for I thought ye might need hard riding the morrow."

"'Tis a glorious heaven to look upon," continued the trooper, in the same tone, disregarding the offer of Betty, "and 'tis a thousand pities that such worms as men should let their vile passions deface such goodly work."

"You speak the truth, dear John; there is room for all to live and enjoy themselves in peace, if each could be satisfied with his own. Still, war has its advantages; it particularly promotes the knowledge of surgery; and—"

"There is a star," continued Lawton, still bent on his own ideas, "struggling to glitter through a few driving clouds; perhaps that too is a world, and contains its creatures endowed with reason like ourselves. Think you that they know of war and bloodshed?"

"If I might be so bold," said Sergeant Hollister, mechanically raising his hand to his cap, "'tis mentioned in the good book, that the Lord made the sun to stand still while Joshua was charging the enemy, in order, sir, as I suppose, that they might have daylight to turn their flank, or perhaps make a feint in the rear, or some such maneuver. Now, if the Lord would lend them a hand, fighting cannot be sinful. I have often been nonplused, though, to find that they used them chariots instead of heavy dragoons, who are, in all comparison, better to break a line of infantry, and who, for the matter of that, could turn such wheel carriages, and getting into the rear, play the very devil with them, horse and all."

"It is because you do not understand the construction of those ancient vehicles, Sergeant Hollister, that you judge of them so erroneously," said the surgeon. "They were armed with sharp weapons that protruded from their wheels, and which broke up the columns of foot, like dismembered particles of matter. I doubt not, if similar instruments were affixed to the cart of Mrs. Flanagan, that great confusion might be carried into the ranks of the enemy thereby, this very day."

"It's but little that the mare would go, and the rig'lars firing at her," grumbled Betty, from under her blanket. "When we got the plunder, the time we drove them through the Jarseys it was, I had to back the baste up to the dead; for the divil the foot would she move, fornent the firing, wid her eyes open. Roanoke and Captain Jack are good enough for the redcoats, letting alone myself and the mare."

A long roll of the drums, from the hill occupied by the British, announced that they were on the alert; and a corresponding signal was immediately heard from the Americans. The bugle of the Virginians struck up its martial tones; and in a few moments both the hills, the one held by the royal troops and the other by their enemies, were alive with armed men. Day had begun to dawn, and preparations were making by both parties, to give and to receive the attack. In numbers the Americans had greatly the advantage; but in discipline and equipment the superiority was entirely with their enemies. The arrangements for the battle were brief, and by the time the sun rose the militia moved forward.

The ground did not admit of the movements of horse; and the only duty that could be assigned to the dragoons was to watch the moment of victory, and endeavor to improve the success to the utmost. Lawton soon got his warriors into the saddle; and leaving them to the charge of Hollister, he rode himself along the line of foot, who, in varied dresses, and imperfectly armed, were formed in a shape that in some degree resembled a martial array. A scornful smile lowered about the lip of the trooper as he guided Roanoke with a skillful hand through the windings of their ranks; and when the word was given to march, he turned the flank of the regiment, and followed close in the rear. The Americans had to descend into a little hollow, and rise a hill on its opposite side, to approach the enemy.

The descent was made with tolerable steadiness, until near the foot of the hill, when the royal troops advanced in a beautiful line, with their flanks protected by the formation of the ground. The appearance of the British drew a fire from the militia, which was given with good effect, and for a moment staggered the regulars. But they were rallied by their officers, and threw in volley after volley with great steadiness. For a short time the fire was warm and destructive, until the English advanced with the bayonet. This assault the militia had not sufficient discipline to withstand. Their line wavered, then paused, and finally broke into companies and fragments of companies, keeping up at the same time a scattering and desultory fire.

Lawton witnessed these operations in silence, nor did he open his mouth until the field was covered with parties of the flying Americans. Then, indeed, he seemed stung with the disgrace thus heaped upon the arms of his country. Spurring Roanoke along the side of the hill, he called to the fugitives in all the strength of his powerful voice. He pointed to the enemy, and assured his countrymen that they had mistaken the way. There was such a mixture of indifference and irony in his exhortations that a few paused in surprise—more joined them, until, roused by the example of the trooper, and stimulated by their own spirit, they demanded to be led against their foe once more.

"Come on, then, my brave friends!" shouted the trooper, turning his horse's head towards the British line, one flank of which was very near him; "come on, and hold your fire until it will scorch their eyebrows."

The men sprang forward, and followed his example, neither giving nor receiving a fire until they had come within a very short distance of the enemy. An English sergeant, who had been concealed by a rock, enraged with the audacity of the officer who thus dared their arms, stepped from behind his cover, and leveled his musket.

"Fire and you die!" cried Lawton, spurring his charger, which leaped forward at the instant. The action and the tone of his voice shook the nerves of the Englishman, who drew his trigger with an uncertain aim. Roanoke sprang with all his feet from the earth, and, plunging, fell headlong and lifeless at the feet of his destroyer. Lawton kept his feet, standing face to face with his enemy. The latter presented his bayonet, and made a desperate thrust at the trooper's heart. The steel of their weapons emitted sparks of fire, and the bayonet flew fifty feet in the air. At the next moment its owner lay a quivering corpse.

"Come on!" shouted the trooper, as a body of English appeared on the rock, and threw in a close fire. "Come on!" he repeated, and brandished his saber fiercely. Then his gigantic form fell backward, like a majestic pine yielding to the ax; but still, as he slowly fell, he continued to wield his saber, and once more the deep tones of his voice were heard uttering, "Come on!"

The advancing Americans paused aghast, and, turning, they abandoned the field to the royal troops.

It was neither the intention nor the policy of the English commander to pursue his success, for he well knew that strong parties of the Americans would soon arrive; accordingly he only tarried to collect his wounded, and forming in a square, he commenced his retreat towards the shipping. Within twenty minutes of the fall of Lawton, the ground was deserted by both English and Americans. When the inhabitants of the country were called upon to enter the field, they were necessarily attended by such surgical advisers as were furnished by the low state of the profession in the interior at that day. Dr. Sitgreaves entertained quite as profound a contempt for the medical attendants of the militia as the captain did of the troops themselves. He wandered, therefore, around the field, casting many a glance of disapprobation at the slight operations that came under his eye; but when, among the flying troops, he found that his comrade and friend was nowhere to be seen, he hastened back to the spot at which Hollister was posted, to inquire if the trooper had returned. Of course, the answer was in the negative. Filled with a thousand uneasy conjectures, the surgeon, without regarding, or indeed without at all reflecting upon any dangers that might lie in his way, strode over the ground at an enormous rate, to the point where he knew the final struggle had been. Once before, the surgeon had rescued his friend from death in a similar situation; and he felt a secret joy in his own conscious skill, as he perceived Betty Flanagan seated on the ground, holding in her lap the head of a man whose size and dress he knew could belong only to the trooper. As he approached the spot, the surgeon became alarmed at the aspect of the washerwoman. Her little black bonnet was thrown aside, and her hair, which was already streaked with gray, hung around her face in disorder.

"John! dear John!" said the doctor, tenderly, as he bent and laid his hand upon the senseless wrist of the trooper, from which it recoiled with an intuitive knowledge of his fate. "John! where are you hurt?—can I help you?"

"Ye talk to the senseless clay," said Betty, rocking her body, and unconsciously playing with the raven ringlets of the trooper's hair; "it's no more will he hear, and it's but little will he mind yeer probes and yeer med'cines. Och hone, och hone!—and where will be the liberty now? or who will there be to fight the battle, or gain the day?"

"John!" repeated the surgeon, still unwilling to believe the evidence of his unerring senses. "Dear John, speak to me; say what you will, that you do but speak. Oh, God! he is dead; would that I had died with him!"

"There is but little use in living and fighting now," said Betty. "Both him and the baste! see, there is the poor cratur, and here is the master! I fed the horse with my own hands, the day; and the last male that *he* ate was of my own cooking. Och hone! och hone!—that Captain Jack should live to be killed by the rig'lars!"

"John! my dear John!" said the surgeon, with convulsive sobs, "thy hour has come, and many a more prudent man survives thee; but none better, nor braver. O John, thou wert to me a kind friend, and very dear; it is unphilosophical to grieve; but for thee I must weep, in bitterness of heart."

The doctor buried his face in his hands, and for several minutes sat yielding to an ungovernable burst of sorrow; while the washerwoman gave vent to her grief in words, moving her body in a kind of writhing, and playing with different parts of her favorite's dress with her fingers.

"And who'll there be to encourage the boys now?" she said. "O Captain Jack! ye was the sowl of the troop, and it was but little we knowed of the danger, and ye fighting. Och! he was no maly-mouthed, that quarreled wid a widowed woman for the matter of a burn in the mate, or the want of a breakfast. Taste a drop, darling, and it may be, 'twill revive ye. Och! and he'll niver taste ag'in; here's the doctor, honey, him ye used to blarney wid, waping as if the poor sowl would die for ye. Och! he's gone, he's gone; and the liberty is gone with him."

A thundering sound of horses' feet came rolling along the road which led near the place where Lawton lay, and directly the whole body of Virginians appeared, with Dunwoodie at their head. The news of the captain's fate had reached him, for the instant that he saw the body he halted the squadron, and, dismounting, approached the spot. The countenance of Lawton was not in the least distorted, but the angry frown which had lowered over his brow during the battle was fixed even in death. His frame was composed, and stretched as in sleep. Dunwoodie took hold of his hand, and gazed a moment in silence; his own dark eye kindled, and the paleness which had overspread his features was succeeded by a spot of deep red in either cheek.

"With his own sword will I avenge him!" he cried, endeavoring to take the weapon from the hand of Lawton; but the grasp resisted his utmost strength. "It shall be buried with him. Sitgreaves, take care of our friend, while I revenge his death."

The major hastened back to his charger, and led the way in pursuit of the enemy.

While Dunwoodie had been thus engaged, the body of Lawton lay in open view of the whole squadron. He was a universal favorite, and the sight inflamed the men to the utmost: neither officers nor soldiers possessed that coolness which is necessary to insure success in military operations; they spurred after their enemies, burning for vengeance.

The English were formed in a hollow square, which contained their wounded, who were far from numerous, and were marching steadily across a very uneven country as the dragoons approached. The horse charged in column, and were led by Dunwoodie, who, burning with revenge, thought to ride through their ranks, and scatter them at a blow. But the enemy knew their own strength too well, and, standing firm, they received the charge on the points of their bayonets. The horses of the Virginians recoiled, and the rear rank of the foot throwing in a close fire, the major, with a few men, fell. The English continued their retreat the moment they were extricated from their assailants; and Dunwoodie, who was severely, but not dangerously wounded, recalled his men from further attempts, which must be fruitless.

A sad duty remained to be fulfilled. The dragoons retired slowly through the hills, conveying their wounded commander, and the body of Lawton. The latter they interred under the ramparts of one of the Highland forts, and the former they consigned to the tender care of his afflicted bride.

Many weeks were gone before the major was restored to sufficient strength to be removed. During those weeks, how often did he bless the moment that gave him a right to the services of his beautiful nurse! She hung around his couch with fond attention, administered with her own hands every prescription of the indefatigable Sitgreaves, and grew each hour in the affections and esteem of her husband. An order from Washington soon sent the troops into winter quarters, and permission was given to Dunwoodie to repair to his own plantation, with the rank of lieutenant colonel, in order to complete the restoration of his health. Captain Singleton made one of the party; and the whole family retired from the active scenes of the war, to the ease and plenty of the major's own estate. Before leaving Fishkill, however, letters were conveyed to them, through an unknown hand, acquainting them with Henry's safety and good health; and also that Colonel Wellmere had left the continent for his native island, lowered in the estimation of every honest man in the royal army.

It was a happy winter for Dunwoodie, and smiles once more began to play around the lovely mouth of Frances.

Lesson 100

1. Read chapter 34.
2. What is revealed in this chapter about Birch's loyalties and whom he has been serving? (Answers)
3. How would you feel about serving a cause you believed in, but getting no recognition for it or even being maligned by the very ones who are serving the same cause and should be on your side?

CHAPTER XXXIV

'Midst furs, and silks, and jewels' sheen,
He stood, in simple Lincoln green,
The center of the glittering ring;
And Snowdon's knight is Scotland's king!
—*Lady of the Lake*.

The commencement of the following year was passed, on the part of the Americans, in making great preparations, in conjunction with their allies, to bring the war to a close. In the South, Greene and Rawdon made a bloody campaign, that was highly honorable to the troops of the latter, but which, by terminating entirely to the advantage of the former, proved him to be the better general of the two.

New York was the point that was threatened by the allied armies; and Washington, by exciting a constant apprehension for the safety of that city, prevented such reinforcements from being sent to Cornwallis as would have enabled him to improve his success.

At length, as autumn approached, every indication was given that the final moment had arrived.

The French forces drew near to the royal lines, passing through the neutral ground, and threatened an attack in the direction of King's Bridge, while large bodies of Americans were acting in concert. By hovering around the British posts, and drawing nigh in the Jerseys, they seemed to threaten the royal forces from that quarter also. The preparations partook of the nature of both a siege and a storm. But Sir Henry Clinton, in the possession of intercepted letters from Washington, rested within his lines, and cautiously disregarded the solicitations of Cornwallis for succor.

It was at the close of a stormy day in the month of September, that a large assemblage of officers was collected near the door of a building that was situated in the heart of the Americans troops, who held the Jerseys. The age, the dress, and the dignity of deportment of most of these warriors, indicated them to be of high rank; but to one in particular was paid a deference and obedience that announced him to be of the highest. His dress was plain, but it bore the usual military distinctions of command. He was mounted on a noble animal, of a deep bay; and a group of young men, in gayer attire, evidently awaited his pleasure and did his bidding. Many a hat was lifted as its owner addressed this officer; and when he spoke, a profound attention, exceeding the respect of mere professional etiquette, was exhibited on every countenance. At length the general raised his own hat, and bowed gravely to all around him. The salute was returned, and the party dispersed, leaving the officer without a single attendant, except his body servants and one aid-de-camp. Dismounting, he stepped back a few paces, and for a moment viewed the condition of his horse with the eye of one who well understood the animal, and then, casting a brief but expressive glance at his aid, he retired into the building, followed by that gentleman.

On entering an apartment that was apparently fitted for his reception, he took a seat, and continued for a long time in a thoughtful attitude, like one in the habit of communing much with himself. During this silence, the aid-de-camp stood in expectation of his orders. At length the general raised his eyes, and spoke in those low, placid tones that seemed natural to him.

"Has the man whom I wished to see arrived, sir?"

"He waits the pleasure of your excellency."

"I will receive him here, and alone, if you please."

The aid bowed and withdrew. In a few minutes the door again opened, and a figure, gliding into the apartment, stood modestly at a distance from the general, without speaking. His entrance was unheard by the officer, who sat gazing at the fire, still absorbed in his own meditations. Several minutes passed, when he spoke to himself in an undertone,—

"To-morrow we must raise the curtain, and expose our plans. May Heaven prosper them!"

A slight movement made by the stranger caught his ear, and he turned his head, and saw that he was not alone. He pointed silently to the fire, toward which the figure advanced, although the multitude of his garments, which seemed more calculated for disguise than comfort, rendered its warmth unnecessary. A second mild and courteous gesture motioned to a vacant chair, but the stranger refused it with a modest acknowledgment. Another pause followed, and continued for some time. At length the officer arose, and opening a desk that was laid upon the table near which he sat, took from it a small, but apparently heavy bag.

"Harvey Birch," he said, turning to the stranger, "the time has arrived when our connection must cease; henceforth and forever we must be strangers."

The peddler dropped the folds of the greatcoat that concealed his features, and gazed for a moment earnestly at the face of the speaker; then dropping his head upon his bosom, he said, meekly,—

"If it be your excellency's pleasure."

"It is necessary. Since I have filled the station which I now hold, it has become my duty to know many men, who, like yourself, have been my instruments in procuring intelligence. You have I trusted more than all; I early saw in you a regard to truth and principle, that, I am pleased to say, has never deceived me—you alone know my secret agents in the city, and on your fidelity depend, not only their fortunes, but their lives."

He paused, as if to reflect in order that full justice might be done to the peddler, and then continued,—

"I believe you are one of the very few that I have employed who have acted faithfully to our cause; and, while you have passed as a spy of the enemy, have never given intelligence that you were not permitted to divulge. To me, and to me only of all the world, you seem to have acted with a strong attachment to the liberties of America."

During this address, Harvey gradually raised his head from his bosom, until it reached the highest point of elevation; a faint tinge gathered in his cheeks, and, as the officer concluded, it was diffused over his whole countenance in a deep glow, while he stood proudly swelling with his emotions, but with eyes that sought the feet of the speaker.

"It is now my duty to pay you for these services; hitherto you have postponed receiving your reward, and the debt has become a heavy one—I wish not to undervalue your dangers; here are a hundred doubloons; remember the poverty of our country, and attribute to it the smallness of your pay."

The peddler raised his eyes to the countenance of the speaker; but, as the other held forth the money, he moved back, as if refusing the bag.

"It is not much for your services and risks, I acknowledge," continued the general, "but it is all that I have to offer; hereafter, it may be in my power to increase it."

"Does your excellency think that I have exposed my life, and blasted my character, for money?"

"If not for money, what then?"

"What has brought your excellency into the field? For what do you daily and hourly expose your precious life to battle and the halter? What is there about me to mourn, when such men as you risk their all for our country? No, no, no—not a dollar of your gold will I touch; poor America has need of it all!"

The bag dropped from the hand of the officer, and fell at the feet of the peddler, where it lay neglected during the remainder of the interview. The officer looked steadily at the face of his companion, and continued,—

"There are many motives which might govern me, that to you are unknown. Our situations are different; I am known as the leader of armies—but you must descend into the grave with the reputation of a foe to your native land. Remember that the veil which conceals your true character cannot be raised in years—perhaps never."

Birch again lowered his face, but there was no yielding of the soul in the movement.

"You will soon be old; the prime of your days is already past; what have you to subsist on?"

"These!" said the peddler, stretching forth his hands, that were already embrowned with toil.

"But those may fail you; take enough to secure a support to your age. Remember your risks and cares. I have told you that the characters of men who are much esteemed in life depend on your secrecy; what pledge can I give them of your fidelity?"

"Tell them," said Birch, advancing and unconsciously resting one foot on the bag, "tell them that I would not take the gold!"

The composed features of the officer relaxed into a smile of benevolence, and he grasped the hand of the peddler firmly.

"Now, indeed, I know you; and although the same reasons which have hitherto compelled me to expose your valuable life will still exist, and prevent my openly asserting your character, in private I can always be your friend; fail not to apply to me when in want or suffering, and so long as God giveth to me, so long will I freely share with a man who feels so nobly and acts so well. If sickness or want should ever assail you and peace once more smile upon our efforts, seek the gate of him whom you have so often met as Harper, and he will not blush to acknowledge you."

"It is little that I need in this life," said Harvey; "so long as God gives me health and honest industry, I can never want in this country; but to know that your excellency is my friend is a blessing that I prize more than all the gold of England's treasury."

The officer stood for a few moments in the attitude of intense thought. He then drew to him the desk, and wrote a few lines on a piece of paper, and gave it to the peddler.

"That Providence destines this country to some great and glorious fate I must believe, while I witness the patriotism that pervades the bosoms of her lowest citizens," he said. "It must be dreadful to a mind like yours to descend into the grave, branded as a foe to liberty; but you already know the lives that would be sacrificed, should your real character be revealed. It is impossible to do you justice now, but I fearlessly entrust you with this certificate; should we never meet again, it may be serviceable to your children."

"Children!" exclaimed the peddler, "can I give to a family the infamy of my name?"

The officer gazed at the strong emotion he exhibited with pain, and he made a slight movement towards the gold; but it was arrested by the expression of his companion's face. Harvey saw the intention, and shook his head, as he continued more mildly,—

"It is, indeed, a treasure that your excellency gives me: it is safe, too. There are men living who could say that my life was nothing to me, compared to your secrets. The paper that I told you was lost I swallowed when taken last by the Virginians. It was the only time I ever deceived your excellency, and it shall be the last; yes, this is, indeed, a treasure to me; perhaps," he continued, with a melancholy smile, "it may be known after my death who was my friend; but if it should not, there are none to grieve for me."

"Remember," said the officer, with strong emotion, "that in me you will always have a secret friend; but openly I cannot know you."

"I know it, I know it," said Birch; "I knew it when I took the service. 'Tis probably the last time that I shall ever see your excellency. May God pour down His choicest blessings on your head!" He paused, and moved towards the door. The officer followed him with eyes that expressed deep interest. Once more the peddler turned, and seemed to gaze on the placid, but commanding features of the general with regret and reverence, and, bowing low, he withdrew.

The armies of America and France were led by their illustrious commander against the enemy under Cornwallis, and terminated a campaign in triumph that had commenced in difficulties.

Great Britain soon after became disgusted with the war; and the States' independence was acknowledged.

As years rolled by, it became a subject of pride among the different actors in the war, and their descendants, to boast of their efforts in the cause which had confessedly heaped so many blessings upon their country; but the name of Harvey Birch died away among the multitude of agents who were thought to have labored in secret against the rights of their countrymen. His image, however, was often present to the mind of the powerful chief, who alone knew his true character; and several times did he cause secret inquiries to be made into the other's fate, one of which only resulted in any success. By this he learned that a peddler of a different name, but similar appearance, was toiling through the new settlements that were springing up in every direction, and that he was struggling with the advance of years and apparent poverty. Death prevented further inquiries on the part of the officer, and a long period passed before he was again heard of.

Lesson 101

1. Read chapter 35.
2. Describe the final end of Harvey Birch. (Answers)

CHAPTER XXXV

Some village Hampden, that with dauntless breast
The village tyrant of his fields withstood—
Some mute, inglorious Milton here may rest;
Some Cromwell, guiltless of his country's blood.
—GRAY.

It was thirty-three years after the interview which we have just related that an American army was once more arrayed against the troops of England; but the scene was transferred from Hudson's banks to those of the Niagara.

The body of Washington had long lain moldering in the tomb; but as time was fast obliterating the slight impressions of political enmity or personal envy, his name was hourly receiving new luster, and his worth and integrity each moment became more visible, not only to his countrymen, but to the world. He was already the acknowledged hero of an age of reason and truth; and many a young heart, amongst those who formed the pride of our army in 1814, was glowing with the recollection of the one great name of America, and inwardly beating with the sanguine expectation of emulating, in some degree, its renown. In no one were these virtuous hopes more vivid than in the bosom of a young officer who stood on the table rock, contemplating the great cataract, on the evening of the 25th of July of that bloody year. The person of this youth was tall and finely molded, indicating a just proportion between strength and activity; his deep black eyes were of a searching and dazzling brightness. At times, as they gazed upon the flood of waters that rushed tumultuously at his feet, there was a stern and daring look that flashed from them, which denoted the ardor of an enthusiast. But this proud expression was softened by the lines of a mouth around which there played a suppressed archness, that partook of feminine beauty. His hair shone in the setting sun like ringlets of gold, as the air from the falls gently moved the rich curls from a forehead whose whiteness showed that exposure and heat alone had given their darker hue to a face glowing with health. There was another officer standing by the side of this favored youth; and both seemed, by the interest they betrayed, to be gazing, for the first time, at the wonder of the western world. A profound silence was observed by each, until the companion of the officer that we have described suddenly started, and pointing eagerly with his sword into the abyss beneath, exclaimed,—

"See! Wharton, there is a man crossing in the very eddies of the cataract, and in a skiff no bigger than an eggshell."

"He has a knapsack—it is probably a soldier," returned the other. "Let us meet him at the ladder, Mason, and learn his tidings."

Some time was expended in reaching the spot where the adventurer was intercepted. Contrary to the expectations of the young soldiers, he proved to be a man far advanced in life, and evidently no follower of the camp. His years might be seventy, and they were indicated more by the thin hairs of silver that lay scattered over his wrinkled brow, than by any apparent failure of his system. His frame was meager and bent; but it was the attitude of habit, for his sinews were strung with the toil of half a century. His dress was mean, and manifested the economy of its owner, by the number and nature of its repairs. On his back was a scantily furnished pack, that had led to the mistake in his profession. A few words of salutation, and, on the part of the young men, of surprise, that one so aged should venture so near the whirlpools of the cataract, were exchanged; when the old man inquired, with a voice that began to manifest the tremor of age, the news from the contending armies.

"We whipped the redcoats here the other day, among the grass on the Chippewa plains," said the one who was called Mason; "since when, we have been playing hide and go seek with the ships: but we are now marching back from where we started, shaking our heads, and as surly as the devil."

"Perhaps you have a son among the soldiers," said his companion, with a milder demeanor, and an air of kindness; "if so, tell me his name and regiment, and I will take you to him."

The old man shook his head, and, passing his hand over his silver locks, with an air of meek resignation, he answered,—

"No; I am alone in the world!"

"You should have added, Captain Dunwoodie," cried his careless comrade, "if you could find either; for nearly half our army has marched down the road, and may be, by this time, under the walls of Fort George, for anything that we know to the contrary."

The old man stopped suddenly, and looked earnestly from one of his companions to the other; the action being observed by the soldiers, they paused also.

"Did I hear right?" the stranger uttered, raising his hand to screen his eyes from the rays of the setting sun. "What did he call you?" "My name is Wharton Dunwoodie," replied the youth, smiling. The stranger motioned silently for him to remove his hat, which the youth did accordingly, and his fair hair blew aside like curls of silk, and opened the whole of his ingenuous countenance to the inspection of the other. "'Tis like our native land!" exclaimed the old man with vehemence, "improving with time; God has blessed both." "Why do you stare thus, Lieutenant Mason?" cried Captain Dunwoodie, laughing a little. "You show more astonishment than when you saw the falls." "Oh, the falls!—they are a thing to be looked at on a moonshiny night, by your Aunt Sarah and that gay old bachelor, Colonel Singleton; but a fellow like myself never shows surprise, unless it may be at such a touch as this." The extraordinary vehemence of the stranger's manner had passed away as suddenly as it was exhibited, but he listened to this speech with deep interest, while Dunwoodie replied, a little gravely,—"Come, come, Tom, no jokes about my good aunt, I beg; she is kindness itself, and I have heard it whispered that her youth was not altogether happy." "Why, as to rumor," said Mason, "there goes one in Accomac, that Colonel Singleton offers himself to her regularly every Valentine's day; and there are some who add that your old great-aunt helps his suit." "Aunt Jeanette!" said Dunwoodie, laughing. "Dear, good soul, she thinks but little of marriage in any shape, I believe, since the death of Dr. Sitgreaves. There were some whispers of a courtship between them formerly, but it ended in nothing but civilities, and I suspect that the whole story arises from the intimacy of Colonel Singleton and my father. You know they were comrades in the horse, as indeed was your own father."

"I know all that, of course; but you must not tell me that the particular, prim bachelor goes so often to General Dunwoodie's plantation merely for the sake of talking old soldier with your father. The last time I was there, that yellow, sharp-nosed housekeeper of your mother's took me into the pantry, and said that the colonel was no despisable match, as she called it, and how the sale of his plantation in Georgia had brought him—oh, Lord! I don't know how much."

"Quite likely," returned the captain, "Katy Haynes is no bad calculator."

They had stopped during this conversation, in uncertainty whether their new companion was to be left or not.

The old man listened to each word as it was uttered, with the most intense interest; but, towards the conclusion of the dialogue, the earnest attention of his countenance changed to a kind of inward smile. He shook his head, and, passing his hands over his forehead, seemed to be thinking of other times. Mason paid but little attention to the expression of his features, and continued,—

"To me, she is selfishness embodied!"

"Her selfishness does but little harm," returned Dunwoodie. "One of her greatest difficulties is her aversion to the blacks. She says that she never saw but one she liked."

"And who was he?"

"His name was Caesar; he was a house servant of my late grandfather Wharton. You don't remember him, I believe; he died the same year with his master, while we were children. Katy yearly sings his requiem, and, upon my word, I believe he deserved it. I have heard something of his helping my English uncle, as we call General Wharton, in some difficulty that occurred in the old war. My mother always speaks of him with great affection. Both Caesar and Katy came to Virginia with my mother when she married. My mother was—"

"An angel!" interrupted the old man, in a voice that startled the young soldiers by its abruptness and energy.

"Did you know her?" cried the son, with a glow of pleasure on his cheek.

The reply of the stranger was interrupted by sudden and heavy explosions of artillery, which were immediately followed by continued volleys of small arms, and in a few minutes the air was filled with the tumult of a warm and well-contested battle.

The two soldiers hastened with precipitation towards the camp, accompanied by their new acquaintance. The excitement and anxiety created by the approaching fight prevented a continuance of the conversation, and the three held their way to the army, making occasional conjectures on the cause of the fire, and the probability of a general engagement. During their short and hurried walk, Captain Dunwoodie, however, threw several friendly glances at the old man, who moved over the ground with astonishing energy for his years, for the heart of the youth was warmed by an eulogium on a mother that he adored. In a short time they joined the regiment to which the officers belonged, when the captain, squeezing the stranger's hand, earnestly begged that he would make inquiries after him on the following morning, and that he might see him in his own tent. Here they separated.

Everything in the American camp announced an approaching struggle. At a distance of a few miles, the sound of cannon and musketry was heard above the roar of the cataract. The troops were soon in motion, and a movement made to support the division of the army which was already engaged. Night had set in before the reserve and irregulars reached the foot of Lundy's Lane, a road that diverged from the river and crossed a conical eminence, at no great distance from the Niagara highway. The summit of this hill was crowned with the cannon of the British, and in the flat beneath was the remnant of Scott's gallant brigade, which for a long time had held an unequal contest with distinguished bravery. A new line was interposed, and one column of the Americans directed to charge up the hill, parallel to the road. This column took the English in flank, and, bayoneting their artillerists, gained possession of the cannon. They were immediately joined by their comrades, and the enemy was swept from the hill. But large reinforcements were joining the English general momentarily, and their troops were too brave to rest easy under the defeat. Repeated and bloody charges were made to recover the guns, but in all they were repulsed with slaughter. During the last of these struggles, the ardor of the youthful captain whom we have mentioned urged him to lead his men some distance in advance, to scatter a daring party of the enemy. He succeeded, but in returning to the line missed his lieutenant from the station that he ought to have occupied. Soon after this repulse, which was the last, orders were given to the shattered troops to return to the camp. The British were nowhere to be seen, and preparations were made to take in such of the wounded as could be moved. At this moment Wharton Dunwoodie, impelled by affection for his friend, seized a lighted fuse, and taking two of his men went himself in quest of his body, where he was supposed to have fallen. Mason was found on the side of the hill, seated with great composure, but unable to walk from a fractured leg. Dunwoodie saw and flew to the side of his comrade, saying,—

"Ah! dear Tom, I knew I should find you the nearest man to the enemy."

"Softly, softly; handle me tenderly," replied the lieutenant. "No, there is a brave fellow still nearer than myself, and who he can be I know not. He rushed out of our smoke, near my platoon, to make a prisoner or some such thing, but, poor fellow, he never came back; there he lies just over the hillock. I have spoken to him several times, but I fancy he is past answering."

Dunwoodie went to the spot, and to his astonishment beheld the aged stranger.

"It is the old man who knew my mother!" cried the youth. "For her sake he shall have honorable burial; lift him, and let him be carried in; his bones shall rest on native soil."

The men approached to obey. He was lying on his back, with his face exposed to the glaring light of the fusee; his eyes were closed, as if in slumber; his lips, sunken with years, were slightly moved from their natural position, but it seemed more like a smile than a convulsion which had caused the change. A soldier's musket lay near him; his hands were pressed upon his breast, and one of them contained a substance that glittered like silver. Dunwoodie stooped, and removing the limbs, perceived the place where the bullet had found a passage to his heart. The subject of his last care was a tin box, through which the fatal lead had gone; and the dying moments of the old man must have passed in drawing it from his bosom. Dunwoodie opened it, and found a paper in which, to his astonishment, he read the following:

> Circumstances of political importance, which involve the lives and fortunes of many, have hitherto kept secret what this paper now reveals. Harvey Birch has for years been a faithful and unrequited servant of his country. Though man does not, may God reward him for his conduct!
>
> GEO. WASHINGTON.

It was the SPY OF THE NEUTRAL GROUND, who died as he had lived, devoted to his country, and a martyr to her liberties.

Lesson 102

1. Read a biography of the new author you will be reading, Robert Louis Stevenson. The book is *Treasure Island.*
2. When did he write the book and who did he write it for?
3. Read the introduction to *Treasure Island.*

Biography: Stevenson was born in 1850 in Scotland. His father was an engineer who built lighthouses. He wanted Robert to follow in his footsteps and study engineering, but Stevenson took up writing, publishing his first book at twenty-eight. He married a woman with two children and wrote the book you're going to read for his step-son. It was his first popular novel, but it was first published in 1881 as a series in a children's magazine, meaning the story was published bit by bit in the issues of the magazine. Most of his books were not for children.

Introduction:

(The picture and intro are from the book online at https://archive.org/details/treasureisland00stev2.)

"ONE MORE CHEER FOR CAP'N SMOLLETT," CRIED LONG JOHN

IT was in 1880 and 1881 that Stevenson wrote *Treasure Island*, which was begun at Braemar, Scotland, where his father aided him with suggestions from his own seafaring experiences. It was finished in the course of his second visit to Davos in the winter of 1881-82. In 1878 he had published his first book, *The Island Voyage*, which was followed by *Travels with a Donkey*. He had also written the tales known as "The New Arabian Nights," the essays collected under the title of *Virginibus Puerisque*, and other stories and essays, but *Treasure Island*, which appeared when the author was thirty-one, was his first long romance, and it brought to him his first taste of popular success, when the story was published in book form.

It was in October, 1881, that this story began to appear as a serial in an English magazine called *Young Folks*. The title then was "The Sea Cook, or Treasure Island," but when published in book form in May, 1883, the name was simply *Treasure Island*, a name which has taken its place among the titles of far older classics. I remember well that as a boy in England I was obliged to satisfy my craving for sea-stories with books like *Captain Cook's Voyages* and *The Mutiny of the "Bounty."* The latter dreadful tale must have been read by Stevenson and perhaps afforded some suggestions. It has seemed to me that before *Treasure Island* there was no really great sea-tale for younger readers. The immortal *Swiss Family Robinson* and *Robinson Crusoe* belonged to a different category, and Dana's *Two Years before the Mast* was little known to English youth. It seems to me fair to say that *Treasure Island* is the only great modern classic written especially for younger readers.

I find that girls enjoy *Treasure Island* just as well as boys. The book stands alone in its wonderfully vivid and dramatic story-telling, which is characterized throughout by an entirely sane and wholesome tone and purpose. When I imagine myself again a boyish reader comparing this story with the old favorites like *Robinson Crusoe, Gulliver s Travels, The Pilgrim s Progress, The Swiss Family Robinson*, and *Tom Brown at Rugby*—the first three not written originally for children—I find myself impelled to rank *Treasure Island* as an equal and in some points as a superior. This may seem heresy, but it is the result of a peculiarly close and sympathetic study of these and other famous books for boys and girls.

Although this was Stevenson's first long romantic story, he showed the born story-teller's instinct for a beginning which seizes upon the reader at once. We are absorbed in the first few lines and the interest deepens as we go on. How it moves and holds us—the advent of that precious trio, Billy Bones, Old Pew, and Black Dog, and their performances at the "Admiral Benbow." It is so apt an introduction to the strange tale of after happenings. And from a boy's viewpoint the end is perfect.

Lesson 103

1. Read the first two chapters of *Treasure Island.*
2. Write a description of the characters, setting and plot you've encountered so far.

Vocabulary

1. Start an illustrated dictionary. You'll write the word and a definition and draw a picture.
2. Bucaneer is your first word.

The Old Sea-dog at the "Admiral Benbow"

SQUIRE TRELAWNEY, Dr. Livesey, and the rest of these gentlemen having asked me to write down the whole particulars about Treasure Island, from the beginning to the end, keeping nothing back but the bearings of the island, and that only because there is still treasure not yet lifted, I take up my pen in the year of grace 17__ and go back to the time when my father kept the Admiral Benbow inn and the brown old seaman with the sabre cut first took up his lodging under our roof.

I remember him as if it were yesterday, as he came plodding to the inn door, his sea-chest following behind him in a hand-barrow—a tall, strong, heavy, nut-brown man, his tarry pigtail falling over the shoulder of his soiled blue coat, his hands ragged and scarred, with black, broken nails, and the sabre cut across one cheek, a dirty, livid white. I remember him looking round the cover and whistling to himself as he did so, and then breaking out in that old sea-song that he sang so often afterwards:

"Fifteen men on the dead man's chest—

Yo-ho-ho, and a bottle of rum!"

in the high, old tottering voice that seemed to have been tuned and broken at the capstan bars. Then he rapped on the door with a bit of stick like a handspike that he carried, and when my father appeared, called roughly for a glass of rum. This, when it was brought to him, he drank slowly, like a connoisseur, lingering on the taste and still looking about him at the cliffs and up at our signboard.

"This is a handy cove," says he at length; "and a pleasant sittyated grog-shop. Much company, mate?"

My father told him no, very little company, the more was the pity.

"Well, then," said he, "this is the berth for me. Here you, matey," he cried to the man who trundled the barrow; "bring up alongside and help up my chest. I'll stay here a bit," he continued. "I'm a plain man; rum and bacon and eggs is what I want, and that head up there for to watch ships off. What you mought call me? You mought call me captain. Oh, I see what you're at—there"; and he threw down three or four gold pieces on the threshold. "You can tell me when I've worked through that," says he, looking as fierce as a commander.

And indeed bad as his clothes were and coarsely as he spoke, he had none of the appearance of a man who sailed before the mast, but seemed like a mate or skipper accustomed to be obeyed or to strike. The man who came with the barrow told us the mail had set him down the morning before at the Royal George, that he had inquired what inns there were along the coast, and hearing ours well spoken of, I suppose, and described as lonely, had chosen it from the others for his place of residence. And that was all we could learn of our guest.

He was a very silent man by custom. All day he hung round the cove or upon the cliffs with a brass telescope; all evening he sat in a corner of the parlour next the fire and drank rum and water very strong. Mostly he would not speak when spoken to, only look up sudden and fierce and blow through his nose like a fog-horn; and we and the people who came about our house soon learned to let him be. Every day when he came back from his stroll he would ask if any seafaring men had gone by along the road. At first we thought it was the want of company of his own kind that made him ask this question, but at last we began to see he was desirous to avoid them. When a seaman did put up at the Admiral Benbow (as now and then some did, making by the coast road for Bristol) he would look in at him through the curtained door before he entered the parlour; and he was always sure to be as silent as a mouse when any such was present. For me, at least, there was no secret about the matter, for I was, in a way, a sharer in his alarms. He had taken me aside one day and promised me a silver fourpenny on the first of every month if I would only keep my "weather-eye open for a seafaring man with one leg" and let him know the moment he appeared. Often enough when the first of the month came round and I applied to him for my wage, he would only blow through his nose at me and stare me down, but before the week was out he was sure to think better of it, bring me my four-penny piece, and repeat his orders to look out for "the seafaring man with one leg."

How that personage haunted my dreams, I need scarcely tell you. On stormy nights, when the wind shook the four corners of the house and the surf roared along the cove and up the cliffs, I would see him in a thousand forms, and with a thousand diabolical expressions. Now the leg would be cut off at the knee, now at the hip; now he was a monstrous kind of a creature who had never had but the one leg, and that in the middle of his body. To see him leap and run and pursue me over hedge and ditch was the worst of nightmares. And altogether I paid pretty dear for my monthly fourpenny piece, in the shape of these abominable fancies.

But though I was so terrified by the idea of the seafaring man with one leg, I was far less afraid of the captain himself than anybody else who knew him. There were nights when he took a deal more rum and water than his head would carry; and then he would sometimes sit and sing his wicked, old, wild sea-songs, minding nobody; but sometimes he would call for glasses round and force all the trembling company to listen to his stories or bear a chorus to his singing. Often I have heard the house shaking with "Yo-ho-ho, and a bottle of rum," all the neighbours joining in for dear life, with the fear of death upon them, and each singing louder than the other to avoid remark. For in these fits he was the most overriding companion ever known; he would slap his hand on the table for silence all round; he would fly up in a passion of anger at a question, or sometimes because none was put, and so he judged the company was not following his story. Nor would he allow anyone to leave the inn till he had drunk himself sleepy and reeled off to bed.

His stories were what frightened people worst of all. Dreadful stories they were—about hanging, and walking the plank, and storms at sea, and the Dry Tortugas, and wild deeds and places on the Spanish Main. By his own account he must have lived his life among some of the wickedest men that God ever allowed upon the sea, and the language in which he told these stories shocked our plain country people almost as much as the crimes that he described. My father was always saying the inn would be ruined, for people would soon cease coming there to be tyrannized over and put down, and sent shivering to their beds; but I really believe his presence did us good. People were frightened at the time, but on looking back they rather liked it; it was a fine excitement in a quiet country life, and there was even a party of the younger men who pretended to admire him, calling him a "true sea-dog" and a "real old salt" and such like names, and saying there was the sort of man that made England terrible at sea.

In one way, indeed, he bade fair to ruin us, for he kept on staying week after week, and at last month after month, so that all the money had been long exhausted, and still my father never plucked up the heart to insist on having more. If ever he mentioned it, the captain blew through his nose so loudly that you might say he roared, and stared my poor father out of the room. I have seen him wringing his hands after such a rebuff, and I am sure the annoyance and the terror he lived in must have greatly hastened his early and unhappy death.

All the time he lived with us the captain made no change whatever in his dress but to buy some stockings from a hawker. One of the cocks of his hat having fallen down, he let it hang from that day forth, though it was a great annoyance when it blew. I remember the appearance of his coat, which he patched himself upstairs in his room, and which, before the end, was nothing but patches. He never wrote or received a letter, and he never spoke with any but the neighbours, and with these, for the most part, only when drunk on rum. The great sea-chest none of us had ever seen open.

He was only once crossed, and that was towards the end, when my poor father was far gone in a decline that took him off. Dr. Livesey came late one afternoon to see the patient, took a bit of dinner from my mother, and went into the parlour to smoke a pipe until his horse should come down from the hamlet, for we had no stabling at the old Benbow. I followed him in, and I remember observing the contrast the neat, bright doctor, with his powder as white as snow and his bright, black eyes and pleasant manners, made with the coltish country folk, and above all, with that filthy, heavy, bleared scarecrow of a pirate of ours, sitting, far gone in rum, with his arms on the table. Suddenly he—the captain, that is—began to pipe up his eternal song:

"Fifteen men on the dead man's chest—

Yo-ho-ho, and a bottle of rum!

Drink and the devil had done for the rest—

Yo-ho-ho, and a bottle of rum!"

At first I had supposed "the dead man's chest" to be that identical big box of his upstairs in the front room, and the thought had been mingled in my nightmares with that of the one-legged seafaring man. But by this time we had all long ceased to pay any particular notice to the song; it was new, that night, to nobody but Dr. Livesey, and on him I observed it did not produce an agreeable effect, for he looked up for a moment quite angrily before he went on with his talk to old Taylor, the gardener, on a new cure for the rheumatics. In the meantime, the captain gradually brightened up at his own music, and at last flapped his hand upon the table before him in a way we all knew to mean silence. The voices stopped at once, all but Dr. Livesey's; he went on as before speaking clear and kind and drawing briskly at his pipe between every word or two. The captain glared at him for a while, flapped his hand again, glared still harder, and at last broke out with a villainous, low oath, "Silence, there, between decks!"

"Were you addressing me, sir?" says the doctor; and when the ruffian had told him, with another oath, that this was so, "I have only one thing to say to you, sir," replies the doctor, "that if you keep on drinking rum, the world will soon be quit of a very dirty scoundrel!"

The old fellow's fury was awful. He sprang to his feet, drew and opened a sailor's clasp-knife, and balancing it open on the palm of his hand, threatened to pin the doctor to the wall.

The doctor never so much as moved. He spoke to him as before, over his shoulder and in the same tone of voice, rather high, so that all the room might hear, but perfectly calm and steady: "If you do not put that knife this instant in your pocket, I promise, upon my honour, you shall hang at the next assizes."

Black Dog Appears and Disappears

It was not very long after this that there occurred the first of the mysterious events that rid us at last of the captain, though not, as you will see, of his affairs. It was a bitter cold winter, with long, hard frosts and heavy gales; and it was plain from the first that my poor father was little likely to see the spring. He sank daily, and my mother and I had all the inn upon our hands, and were kept busy enough without paying much regard to our unpleasant guest.

It was one January morning, very early—a pinching, frosty morning—the cove all grey with hoar-frost, the ripple lapping softly on the stones, the sun still low and only touching the hilltops and shining far to seaward. The captain had risen earlier than usual and set out down the beach, his cutlass swinging under the broad skirts of the old blue coat, his brass telescope under his arm, his hat tilted back upon his head. I remember his breath hanging like smoke in his wake as he strode off, and the last sound I heard of him as he turned the big rock was a loud snort of indignation, as though his mind was still running upon Dr. Livesey.

Well, mother was upstairs with father and I was laying the breakfast-table against the captain's return when the parlour door opened and a man stepped in on whom I had never set my eyes before. He was a pale, tallowy creature, wanting two fingers of the left hand, and though he wore a cutlass, he did not look much like a fighter. I had always my eye open for seafaring men, with one leg or two, and I remember this one puzzled me. He was not sailorly, and yet he had a smack of the sea about him too.

I asked him what was for his service, and he said he would take rum; but as I was going out of the room to fetch it, he sat down upon a table and motioned me to draw near. I paused where I was, with my napkin in my hand.

"Come here, sonny," says he. "Come nearer here."

I took a step nearer.

"Is this here table for my mate Bill?" he asked with a kind of leer.

I told him I did not know his mate Bill, and this was for a person who stayed in our house whom we called the captain.

"Well," said he, "my mate Bill would be called the captain, as like as not. He has a cut on one cheek and a mighty pleasant way with him, particularly in drink, has my mate Bill. We'll put it, for argument like, that your captain has a cut on one cheek—and we'll put it, if you like, that that cheek's the right one. Ah, well! I told you. Now, is my mate Bill in this here house?"

I told him he was out walking.

"Which way, sonny? Which way is he gone?"

And when I had pointed out the rock and told him how the captain was likely to return, and how soon, and answered a few other questions, "Ah," said he, "this'll be as good as drink to my mate Bill."

The expression of his face as he said these words was not at all pleasant, and I had my own reasons for thinking that the stranger was mistaken, even supposing he meant what he said. But it was no affair of mine, I thought; and besides, it was difficult to know what to do. The stranger kept hanging about just inside the inn door, peering round the corner like a cat waiting for a mouse. Once I stepped out myself into the road, but he immediately called me back, and as I did not obey quick enough for his fancy, a most horrible change came over his tallowy face, and he ordered me in with an oath that made me jump. As soon as I was back again he returned to his former manner, half fawning, half sneering, patted me on the shoulder, told me I was a good boy and he had taken quite a fancy to me. "I have a son of my own," said he, "as like you as two blocks, and he's all the pride of my 'art. But the great thing for boys is discipline, sonny—discipline. Now, if you had sailed along of Bill, you wouldn't have stood there to be spoke to twice—not you. That was never Bill's way, nor the way of sich as sailed with him. And here, sure enough, is my mate Bill, with a spy-glass under his arm, bless his old 'art, to be sure. You and me'll just go back into the parlour, sonny, and get behind the door, and we'll give Bill a little surprise—bless his 'art, I say again."

So saying, the stranger backed along with me into the parlour and put me behind him in the corner so that we were both hidden by the open door. I was very uneasy and alarmed, as you may fancy, and it rather added to my fears to observe that the stranger was certainly frightened himself. He cleared the hilt of his cutlass and loosened the blade in the sheath; and all the time we were waiting there he kept swallowing as if he felt what we used to call a lump in the throat.

At last in strode the captain, slammed the door behind him, without looking to the right or left, and marched straight across the room to where his breakfast awaited him.

"Bill," said the stranger in a voice that I thought he had tried to make bold and big.

The captain spun round on his heel and fronted us; all the brown had gone out of his face, and even his nose was blue; he had the look of a man who sees a ghost, or the evil one, or something worse, if anything can be; and upon my word, I felt sorry to see him all in a moment turn so old and sick.

"Come, Bill, you know me; you know an old shipmate, Bill, surely," said the stranger.

The captain made a sort of gasp.

"Black Dog!" said he.

"And who else?" returned the other, getting more at his ease. "Black Dog as ever was, come for to see his old shipmate Billy, at the Admiral Benbow inn. Ah, Bill, Bill, we have seen a sight of times, us two, since I lost them two talons," holding up his mutilated hand.

"Now, look here," said the captain; "you've run me down; here I am; well, then, speak up; what is it?"

"That's you, Bill," returned Black Dog, "you're in the right of it, Billy. I'll have a glass of rum from this dear child here, as I've took such a liking to; and we'll sit down, if you please, and talk square, like old shipmates."

When I returned with the rum, they were already seated on either side of the captain's breakfast-table—Black Dog next to the door and sitting sideways so as to have one eye on his old shipmate and one, as I thought, on his retreat.

He bade me go and leave the door wide open. "None of your keyholes for me, sonny," he said; and I left them together and retired into the bar.

For a long time, though I certainly did my best to listen, I could hear nothing but a low gattling; but at last the voices began to grow higher, and I could pick up a word or two, mostly oaths, from the captain.

"No, no, no, no; and an end of it!" he cried once. And again, "If it comes to swinging, swing all, say I."

Then all of a sudden there was a tremendous explosion of oaths and other noises—the chair and table went over in a lump, a clash of steel followed, and then a cry of pain, and the next instant I saw Black Dog in full flight, and the captain hotly pursuing, both with drawn cutlasses, and the former streaming blood from the left shoulder. Just at the door the captain aimed at the fugitive one last tremendous cut, which would certainly have split him to the chine had it not been intercepted by our big signboard of Admiral Benbow. You may see the notch on the lower side of the frame to this day.

That blow was the last of the battle. Once out upon the road, Black Dog, in spite of his wound, showed a wonderful clean pair of heels and disappeared over the edge of the hill in half a minute. The captain, for his part, stood staring at the signboard like a bewildered man. Then he passed his hand over his eyes several times and at last turned back into the house.

"Jim," says he, "rum"; and as he spoke, he reeled a little, and caught himself with one hand against the wall.

"Are you hurt?" cried I.

"Rum," he repeated. "I must get away from here. Rum! Rum!"

I ran to fetch it, but I was quite unsteadied by all that had fallen out, and I broke one glass and fouled the tap, and while I was still getting in my own way, I heard a loud fall in the parlour, and running in, beheld the captain lying full length upon the floor. At the same instant my mother, alarmed by the cries and fighting, came running downstairs to help me. Between us we raised his head. He was breathing very loud and hard, but his eyes were closed and his face a horrible colour.

"Dear, deary me," cried my mother, "what a disgrace upon the house! And your poor father sick!"

In the meantime, we had no idea what to do to help the captain, nor any other thought but that he had got his death-hurt in the scuffle with the stranger. I got the rum, to be sure, and tried to put it down his throat, but his teeth were tightly shut and his jaws as strong as iron. It was a happy relief for us when the door opened and Doctor Livesey came in, on his visit to my father.

"Oh, doctor," we cried, "what shall we do? Where is he wounded?"

"Wounded? A fiddle-stick's end!" said the doctor. "No more wounded than you or I. The man has had a stroke, as I warned him. Now, Mrs. Hawkins, just you run upstairs to your husband and tell him, if possible, nothing about it. For my part, I must do my best to save this fellow's trebly worthless life; Jim, you get me a basin."

When I got back with the basin, the doctor had already ripped up the captain's sleeve and exposed his great sinewy arm. It was tattooed in several places. "Here's luck," "A fair wind," and "Billy Bones his fancy," were very neatly and clearly executed on the forearm; and up near the shoulder there was a sketch of a gallows and a man hanging from it—done, as I thought, with great spirit.

"Prophetic," said the doctor, touching this picture with his finger. "And now, Master Billy Bones, if that be your name, we'll have a look at the colour of your blood. Jim," he said, "are you afraid of blood?"

"No, sir," said I.

"Well, then," said he, "you hold the basin"; and with that he took his lancet and opened a vein.

A great deal of blood was taken before the captain opened his eyes and looked mistily about him. First he recognized the doctor with an unmistakable frown; then his glance fell upon me, and he looked relieved. But suddenly his colour changed, and he tried to raise himself, crying, "Where's Black Dog?"

"There is no Black Dog here," said the doctor, "except what you have on your own back. You have been drinking rum; you have had a stroke, precisely as I told you; and I have just, very much against my own will, dragged you headforemost out of the grave. Now, Mr. Bones—"

"That's not my name," he interrupted.

"Much I care," returned the doctor. "It's the name of a buccaneer of my acquaintance; and I call you by it for the sake of shortness, and what I have to say to you is this; one glass of rum won't kill you, but if you take one you'll take another and another, and I stake my wig if you don't break off short, you'll die—do you understand that?—die, and go to your own place, like the man in the Bible. Come, now, make an effort. I'll help you to your bed for once."

Between us, with much trouble, we managed to hoist him upstairs, and laid him on his bed, where his head fell back on the pillow as if he were almost fainting.

"Now, mind you," said the doctor, "I clear my conscience—the name of rum for you is death."

And with that he went off to see my father, taking me with him by the arm.

"This is nothing," he said as soon as he had closed the door. "I have drawn blood enough to keep him quiet awhile; he should lie for a week where he is—that is the best thing for him and you; but another stroke would settle him."

Lesson 104

1. Read chapters three and four of *Treasure Island.*
2. Write a summary of the chapter "The Black Spot." How is the plot advanced?

Vocabulary

1. Add a spy-glass. The words don't have to be in alphabetical order. But if you are doing it on the computer, then they *should* be in alphabetical order.

The Black Spot

About noon I stopped at the captain's door with some cooling drinks and medicines. He was lying very much as we had left him, only a little higher, and he seemed both weak and excited.

"Jim," he said, "you're the only one here that's worth anything, and you know I've been always good to you. Never a month but I've given you a silver fourpenny for yourself. And now you see, mate, I'm pretty low, and deserted by all; and Jim, you'll bring me one noggin of rum, now, won't you, matey?"

"The doctor—" I began.

But he broke in cursing the doctor, in a feeble voice but heartily. "Doctors is all swabs," he said; "and that doctor there, why, what do he know about seafaring men? I been in places hot as pitch, and mates dropping round with Yellow Jack, and the blessed land a-heaving like the sea with earthquakes—what to the doctor know of lands like that?—and I lived on rum, I tell you. It's been meat and drink, and man and wife, to me; and if I'm not to have my rum now I'm a poor old hulk on a lee shore, my blood'll be on you, Jim, and that doctor swab"; and he ran on again for a while with curses. "Look, Jim, how my fingers fidges," he continued in the pleading tone. "I can't keep 'em still, not I. I haven't had a drop this blessed day. That doctor's a fool, I tell you. If I don't have a drain o' rum, Jim, I'll have the horrors; I seen some on 'em already. I seen old Flint in the corner there, behind you; as plain as print, I seen him; and if I get the horrors, I'm a man that has lived rough, and I'll raise Cain. Your doctor hisself said one glass wouldn't hurt me. I'll give you a golden guinea for a noggin, Jim."

He was growing more and more excited, and this alarmed me for my father, who was very low that day and needed quiet; besides, I was reassured by the doctor's words, now quoted to me, and rather offended by the offer of a bribe.

"I want none of your money," said I, "but what you owe my father. I'll get you one glass, and no more."

When I brought it to him, he seized it greedily and drank it out.

"Aye, aye," said he, "that's some better, sure enough. And now, matey, did that doctor say how long I was to lie here in this old berth?"

"A week at least," said I.

"Thunder!" he cried. "A week! I can't do that; they'd have the black spot on me by then. The lubbers is going about to get the wind of me this blessed moment; lubbers as couldn't keep what they got, and want to nail what is another's. Is that seamanly behaviour, now, I want to know? But I'm a saving soul. I never wasted good money of mine, nor lost it neither; and I'll trick 'em again. I'm not afraid on 'em. I'll shake out another reef, matey, and daddle 'em again."

As he was thus speaking, he had risen from bed with great difficulty, holding to my shoulder with a grip that almost made me cry out, and moving his legs like so much dead weight. His words, spirited as they were in meaning, contrasted sadly with the weakness of the voice in which they were uttered. He paused when he had got into a sitting position on the edge.

"That doctor's done me," he murmured. "My ears is singing. Lay me back."

Before I could do much to help him he had fallen back again to his former place, where he lay for a while silent.

"Jim," he said at length, "you saw that seafaring man today?"

"Black Dog?" I asked.

"Ah! Black Dog," says he. "*He's* a bad un; but there's worse that put him on. Now, if I can't get away nohow, and they tip me the black spot, mind you, it's my old sea-chest they're after; you get on a horse—you can, can't you? Well, then, you get on a horse, and go to—well, yes, I will!—to that eternal doctor swab, and tell him to pipe all hands—magistrates and sich—and he'll lay 'em aboard at the Admiral Benbow—all old Flint's crew, man and boy, all on 'em that's left. I was first mate, I was, old Flint's first mate, and I'm the on'y one as knows the place. He gave it me at Savannah, when he lay a-dying, like as if I was to now, you see. But you won't peach unless they get the black spot on me, or unless you see that Black Dog again or a seafaring man with one leg, Jim—him above all."

"But what is the black spot, captain?" I asked.

"That's a summons, mate. I'll tell you if they get that. But you keep your weather-eye open, Jim, and I'll share with you equals, upon my honour."

He wandered a little longer, his voice growing weaker; but soon after I had given him his medicine, which he took like a child, with the remark, "If ever a seaman wanted drugs, it's me," he fell at last into a heavy, swoon-like sleep, in which I left him. What I should have done had all gone well I do not know. Probably I should have told the whole story to the doctor, for I was in mortal fear lest the captain should repent of his confessions and make an end of me. But as things fell out, my poor father died quite suddenly that evening, which put all other matters on one side. Our natural distress, the visits of the neighbours, the arranging of the funeral, and all the work of the inn to be carried on in the meanwhile kept me so busy that I had scarcely time to think of the captain, far less to be afraid of him.

He got downstairs next morning, to be sure, and had his meals as usual, though he ate little and had more, I am afraid, than his usual supply of rum, for he helped himself out of the bar, scowling and blowing through his nose, and no one dared to cross him. On the night before the funeral he was as drunk as ever; and it was shocking, in that house of mourning, to hear him singing away at his ugly old sea-song; but weak as he was, we were all in the fear of death for him, and the doctor was suddenly taken up with a case many miles away and was never near the house after my father's death. I have said the captain was weak, and indeed he seemed rather to grow weaker than regain his strength. He clambered up and down stairs, and went from the parlour to the bar and back again, and sometimes put his nose out of doors to smell the sea, holding on to the walls as he went for support and breathing hard and fast like a man on a steep mountain. He never particularly addressed me, and it is my belief he had as good as forgotten his confidences; but his temper was more flighty, and allowing for his bodily weakness, more violent than ever. He had an alarming way now when he was drunk of drawing his cutlass and laying it bare before him on the table. But with all that, he minded people less and seemed shut up in his own thoughts and rather wandering. Once, for instance, to our extreme wonder, he piped up to a different air, a kind of country love-song that he must have learned in his youth before he had begun to follow the sea.

So things passed until, the day after the funeral, and about three o'clock of a bitter, foggy, frosty afternoon, I was standing at the door for a moment, full of sad thoughts about my father, when I saw someone drawing slowly near along the road. He was plainly blind, for he tapped before him with a stick and wore a great green shade over his eyes and nose; and he was hunched, as if with age or weakness, and wore a huge old tattered sea-cloak with a hood that made him appear positively deformed. I never saw in my life a more dreadful-looking figure. He stopped a little from the inn, and raising his voice in an odd sing-song, addressed the air in front of him, "Will any kind friend inform a poor blind man, who has lost the precious sight of his eyes in the gracious defence of his native country, England—and God bless King George!—where or in what part of this country he may now be?"

"You are at the Admiral Benbow, Black Hill Cove, my good man," said I.

"I hear a voice," said he, "a young voice. Will you give me your hand, my kind young friend, and lead me in?"

I held out my hand, and the horrible, soft-spoken, eyeless creature gripped it in a moment like a vise. I was so much startled that I struggled to withdraw, but the blind man pulled me close up to him with a single action of his arm.

"Now, boy," he said, "take me in to the captain."

"Sir," said I, "upon my word I dare not."

"Oh," he sneered, "that's it! Take me in straight or I'll break your arm."

And he gave it, as he spoke, a wrench that made me cry out.

"Sir," said I, "it is for yourself I mean. The captain is not what he used to be. He sits with a drawn cutlass. Another gentleman—"

"Come, now, march," interrupted he; and I never heard a voice so cruel, and cold, and ugly as that blind man's. It cowed me more than the pain, and I began to obey him at once, walking straight in at the door and towards the parlour, where our sick old buccaneer was sitting, dazed with rum. The blind man clung close to me, holding me in one iron fist and leaning almost more of his weight on me than I could carry. "Lead me straight up to him, and when I'm in view, cry out, 'Here's a friend for you, Bill.' If you don't, I'll do this," and with that he gave me a twitch that I thought would have made me faint. Between this and that, I was so utterly terrified of the blind beggar that I forgot my terror of the captain, and as I opened the parlour door, cried out the words he had ordered in a trembling voice.

The poor captain raised his eyes, and at one look the rum went out of him and left him staring sober. The expression of his face was not so much of terror as of mortal sickness. He made a movement to rise, but I do not believe he had enough force left in his body.

"Now, Bill, sit where you are," said the beggar. "If I can't see, I can hear a finger stirring. Business is business. Hold out your left hand. Boy, take his left hand by the wrist and bring it near to my right."

We both obeyed him to the letter, and I saw him pass something from the hollow of the hand that held his stick into the palm of the captain's, which closed upon it instantly.

"And now that's done," said the blind man; and at the words he suddenly left hold of me, and with incredible accuracy and nimbleness, skipped out of the parlour and into the road, where, as I still stood motionless, I could hear his stick go tap-tap-tapping into the distance.

It was some time before either I or the captain seemed to gather our senses, but at length, and about at the same moment, I released his wrist, which I was still holding, and he drew in his hand and looked sharply into the palm.

"Ten o'clock!" he cried. "Six hours. We'll do them yet," and he sprang to his feet.

Even as he did so, he reeled, put his hand to his throat, stood swaying for a moment, and then, with a peculiar sound, fell from his whole height face foremost to the floor.

I ran to him at once, calling to my mother. But haste was all in vain. The captain had been struck dead by thundering apoplexy. It is a curious thing to understand, for I had certainly never liked the man, though of late I had begun to pity him, but as soon as I saw that he was dead, I burst into a flood of tears. It was the second death I had known, and the sorrow of the first was still fresh in my heart.

The Sea-chest

I lost no time, of course, in telling my mother all that I knew, and perhaps should have told her long before, and we saw ourselves at once in a difficult and dangerous position. Some of the man's money—if he had any—was certainly due to us, but it was not likely that our captain's shipmates, above all the two specimens seen by me, Black Dog and the blind beggar, would be inclined to give up their booty in payment of the dead man's debts. The captain's order to mount at once and ride for Doctor Livesey would have left my mother alone and unprotected, which was not to be thought of. Indeed, it seemed impossible for either of us to remain much longer in the house; the fall of coals in the kitchen grate, the very ticking of the clock, filled us with alarms. The neighbourhood, to our ears, seemed haunted by approaching footsteps; and what between the dead body of the captain on the parlour floor and the thought of that detestable blind beggar hovering near at hand and ready to return, there were moments when, as the saying goes, I jumped in my skin for terror. Something must speedily be resolved upon, and it occurred to us at last to go forth together and seek help in the neighbouring hamlet. No sooner said than done. Bare-headed as we were, we ran out at once in the gathering evening and the frosty fog.

The hamlet lay not many hundred yards away, though out of view, on the other side of the next cove; and what greatly encouraged me, it was in an opposite direction from that whence the blind man had made his appearance and whither he had presumably returned. We were not many minutes on the road, though we sometimes stopped to lay hold of each other and hearken. But there was no unusual sound—nothing but the low wash of the ripple and the croaking of the inmates of the wood.

It was already candle-light when we reached the hamlet, and I shall never forget how much I was cheered to see the yellow shine in doors and windows; but that, as it proved, was the best of the help we were likely to get in that quarter. For—you would have thought men would have been ashamed of themselves—no soul would consent to return with us to the Admiral Benbow. The more we told of our troubles, the more—man, woman, and child—they clung to the shelter of their houses. The name of Captain Flint, though it was strange to me, was well enough known to some there and carried a great weight of terror. Some of the men who had been to field-work on the far side of the Admiral Benbow remembered, besides, to have seen several strangers on the road, and taking them to be smugglers, to have bolted away; and one at least had seen a little lugger in what we called Kitt's Hole. For that matter, anyone who was a comrade of the captain's was enough to frighten them to death. And the short and the long of the matter was, that while we could get several who were willing enough to ride to Dr. Livesey's, which lay in another direction, not one would help us to defend the inn.

They say cowardice is infectious; but then argument is, on the other hand, a great emboldener; and so when each had said his say, my mother made them a speech. She would not, she declared, lose money that belonged to her fatherless boy; "If none of the rest of you dare," she said, "Jim and I dare. Back we will go, the way we came, and small thanks to you big, hulking, chicken-hearted men. We'll have that chest open, if we die for it. And I'll thank you for that bag, Mrs. Crossley, to bring back our lawful money in."

Of course I said I would go with my mother, and of course they all cried out at our foolhardiness, but even then not a man would go along with us. All they would do was to give me a loaded pistol lest we were attacked, and to promise to have horses ready saddled in case we were pursued on our return, while one lad was to ride forward to the doctor's in search of armed assistance.

My heart was beating finely when we two set forth in the cold night upon this dangerous venture. A full moon was beginning to rise and peered redly through the upper edges of the fog, and this increased our haste, for it was plain, before we came forth again, that all would be as bright as day, and our departure exposed to the eyes of any watchers. We slipped along the hedges, noiseless and swift, nor did we see or hear anything to increase our terrors, till, to our relief, the door of the Admiral Benbow had closed behind us.

I slipped the bolt at once, and we stood and panted for a moment in the dark, alone in the house with the dead captain's body. Then my mother got a candle in the bar, and holding each other's hands, we advanced into the parlour. He lay as we had left him, on his back, with his eyes open and one arm stretched out.

"Draw down the blind, Jim," whispered my mother; "they might come and watch outside. And now," said she when I had done so, "we have to get the key off *that*; and who's to touch it, I should like to know!" and she gave a kind of sob as she said the words.

I went down on my knees at once. On the floor close to his hand there was a little round of paper, blackened on the one side. I could not doubt that this was the *black spot*; and taking it up, I found written on the other side, in a very good, clear hand, this short message: "You have till ten tonight."

"He had till ten, Mother," said I; and just as I said it, our old clock began striking. This sudden noise startled us shockingly; but the news was good, for it was only six.

"Now, Jim," she said, "that key."

I felt in his pockets, one after another. A few small coins, a thimble, and some thread and big needles, a piece of pigtail tobacco bitten away at the end, his gully with the crooked handle, a pocket compass, and a tinder box were all that they contained, and I began to despair.

"Perhaps it's round his neck," suggested my mother.

Overcoming a strong repugnance, I tore open his shirt at the neck, and there, sure enough, hanging to a bit of tarry string, which I cut with his own gully, we found the key. At this triumph we were filled with hope and hurried upstairs without delay to the little room where he had slept so long and where his box had stood since the day of his arrival.

It was like any other seaman's chest on the outside, the initial "B" burned on the top of it with a hot iron, and the corners somewhat smashed and broken as by long, rough usage.

"Give me the key," said my mother; and though the lock was very stiff, she had turned it and thrown back the lid in a twinkling.

A strong smell of tobacco and tar rose from the interior, but nothing was to be seen on the top except a suit of very good clothes, carefully brushed and folded. They had never been worn, my mother said. Under that, the miscellany began—a quadrant, a tin canikin, several sticks of tobacco, two brace of very handsome pistols, a piece of bar silver, an old Spanish watch and some other trinkets of little value and mostly of foreign make, a pair of compasses mounted with brass, and five or six curious West Indian shells. I have often wondered since why he should have carried about these shells with him in his wandering, guilty, and hunted life.

In the meantime, we had found nothing of any value but the silver and the trinkets, and neither of these were in our way. Underneath there was an old boat-cloak, whitened with sea-salt on many a harbour-bar. My mother pulled it up with impatience, and there lay before us, the last things in the chest, a bundle tied up in oilcloth, and looking like papers, and a canvas bag that gave forth, at a touch, the jingle of gold.

"I'll show these rogues that I'm an honest woman," said my mother. "I'll have my dues, and not a farthing over. Hold Mrs. Crossley's bag." And she began to count over the amount of the captain's score from the sailor's bag into the one that I was holding.

It was a long, difficult business, for the coins were of all countries and sizes—doubloons, and louis d'ors, and guineas, and pieces of eight, and I know not what besides, all shaken together at random. The guineas, too, were about the scarcest, and it was with these only that my mother knew how to make her count.

When we were about half-way through, I suddenly put my hand upon her arm, for I had heard in the silent frosty air a sound that brought my heart into my mouth—the tap-tapping of the blind man's stick upon the frozen road. It drew nearer and nearer, while we sat holding our breath. Then it struck sharp on the inn door, and then we could hear the handle being turned and the bolt rattling as the wretched being tried to enter; and then there was a long time of silence both within and without. At last the tapping recommenced, and, to our indescribable joy and gratitude, died slowly away again until it ceased to be heard.

"Mother," said I, "take the whole and let's be going," for I was sure the bolted door must have seemed suspicious and would bring the whole hornet's nest about our ears, though how thankful I was that I had bolted it, none could tell who had never met that terrible blind man.

But my mother, frightened as she was, would not consent to take a fraction more than was due to her and was obstinately unwilling to be content with less. It was not yet seven, she said, by a long way; she knew her rights and she would have them; and she was still arguing with me when a little low whistle sounded a good way off upon the hill. That was enough, and more than enough, for both of us.

"I'll take what I have," she said, jumping to her feet.

"And I'll take this to square the count," said I, picking up the oilskin packet.

Next moment we were both groping downstairs, leaving the candle by the empty chest; and the next we had opened the door and were in full retreat. We had not started a moment too soon. The fog was rapidly dispersing; already the moon shone quite clear on the high ground on either side; and it was only in the exact bottom of the dell and round the tavern door that a thin veil still hung unbroken to conceal the first steps of our escape. Far less than half-way to the hamlet, very little beyond the bottom of the hill, we must come forth into the moonlight. Nor was this all, for the sound of several footsteps running came already to our ears, and as we looked back in their direction, a light tossing to and fro and still rapidly advancing showed that one of the newcomers carried a lantern.

"My dear," said my mother suddenly, "take the money and run on. I am going to faint."

This was certainly the end for both of us, I thought. How I cursed the cowardice of the neighbours; how I blamed my poor mother for her honesty and her greed, for her past foolhardiness and present weakness! We were just at the little bridge, by good fortune; and I helped her, tottering as she was, to the edge of the bank, where, sure enough, she gave a sigh and fell on my shoulder. I do not know how I found the strength to do it at all, and I am afraid it was roughly done, but I managed to drag her down the bank and a little way under the arch. Farther I could not move her, for the bridge was too low to let me do more than crawl below it. So there we had to stay—my mother almost entirely exposed and both of us within earshot of the inn.

Lesson 105

1. Read chapters five and six of *Treasure Island.*
2. The sea-chest is an object that the author chose to include in the novel. Write: Why did the author include it? How does it help the story? What part does it play?

Vocabulary

1. Add a sea-chest.
2. Add a character from the book.

The Last of the Blind Man

My curiosity, in a sense, was stronger than my fear, for I could not remain where I was, but crept back to the bank again, whence, sheltering my head behind a bush of broom, I might command the road before our door. I was scarcely in position ere my enemies began to arrive, seven or eight of them, running hard, their feet beating out of time along the road and the man with the lantern some paces in front. Three men ran together, hand in hand; and I made out, even through the mist, that the middle man of this trio was the blind beggar. The next moment his voice showed me that I was right.

"Down with the door!" he cried.

"Aye, aye, sir!" answered two or three; and a rush was made upon the Admiral Benbow, the lantern-bearer following; and then I could see them pause, and hear speeches passed in a lower key, as if they were surprised to find the door open. But the pause was brief, for the blind man again issued his commands. His voice sounded louder and higher, as if he were afire with eagerness and rage.

"In, in, in!" he shouted, and cursed them for their delay.

Four or five of them obeyed at once, two remaining on the road with the formidable beggar. There was a pause, then a cry of surprise, and then a voice shouting from the house, "Bill's dead."

But the blind man swore at them again for their delay.

"Search him, some of you shirking lubbers, and the rest of you aloft and get the chest," he cried.

I could hear their feet rattling up our old stairs, so that the house must have shook with it. Promptly afterwards, fresh sounds of astonishment arose; the window of the captain's room was thrown open with a slam and a jingle of broken glass, and a man leaned out into the moonlight, head and shoulders, and addressed the blind beggar on the road below him.

"Pew," he cried, "they've been before us. Someone's turned the chest out alow and aloft."

"Is it there?" roared Pew.

"The money's there."

The blind man cursed the money.

"Flint's fist, I mean," he cried.

"We don't see it here nohow," returned the man.

"Here, you below there, is it on Bill?" cried the blind man again.

At that another fellow, probably him who had remained below to search the captain's body, came to the door of the inn. "Bill's been overhauled a'ready," said he; "nothin' left."

"It's these people of the inn—it's that boy. I wish I had put his eyes out!" cried the blind man, Pew. "There were no time ago—they had the door bolted when I tried it. Scatter, lads, and find 'em."

"Sure enough, they left their glim here," said the fellow from the window.

"Scatter and find 'em! Rout the house out!" reiterated Pew, striking with his stick upon the road.

Then there followed a great to-do through all our old inn, heavy feet pounding to and fro, furniture thrown over, doors kicked in, until the very rocks re-echoed and the men came out again, one after another, on the road and declared that we were nowhere to be found. And just the same whistle that had alarmed my mother and myself over the dead captain's money was once more clearly audible through the night, but this time twice repeated. I had thought it to be the blind man's trumpet, so to speak, summoning his crew to the assault, but I now found that it was a signal from the hillside towards the hamlet, and from its effect upon the buccaneers, a signal to warn them of approaching danger.

"There's Dirk again," said one. "Twice! We'll have to budge, mates."

"Budge, you skulk!" cried Pew. "Dirk was a fool and a coward from the first—you wouldn't mind him. They must be close by; they can't be far; you have your hands on it. Scatter and look for them, dogs! Oh, shiver my soul," he cried, "if I had eyes!"

This appeal seemed to produce some effect, for two of the fellows began to look here and there among the lumber, but half-heartedly, I thought, and with half an eye to their own danger all the time, while the rest stood irresolute on the road.

"You have your hands on thousands, you fools, and you hang a leg! You'd be as rich as kings if you could find it, and you know it's here, and you stand there skulking. There wasn't one of you dared face Bill, and I did it—a blind man! And I'm to lose my chance for you! I'm to be a poor, crawling beggar, sponging for rum, when I might be rolling in a coach! If you had the pluck of a weevil in a biscuit you would catch them still."

"Hang it, Pew, we've got the doubloons!" grumbled one.

"They might have hid the blessed thing," said another. "Take the Georges, Pew, and don't stand here squalling."

Squalling was the word for it; Pew's anger rose so high at these objections till at last, his passion completely taking the upper hand, he struck at them right and left in his blindness and his stick sounded heavily on more than one.

These, in their turn, cursed back at the blind miscreant, threatened him in horrid terms, and tried in vain to catch the stick and wrest it from his grasp.

This quarrel was the saving of us, for while it was still raging, another sound came from the top of the hill on the side of the hamlet—the tramp of horses galloping. Almost at the same time a pistol-shot, flash and report, came from the hedge side. And that was plainly the last signal of danger, for the buccaneers turned at once and ran, separating in every direction, one seaward along the cove, one slant across the hill, and so on, so that in half a minute not a sign of them remained but Pew. Him they had deserted, whether in sheer panic or out of revenge for his ill words and blows I know not; but there he remained behind, tapping up and down the road in a frenzy, and groping and calling for his comrades. Finally he took a wrong turn and ran a few steps past me, towards the hamlet, crying, "Johnny, Black Dog, Dirk," and other names, "you won't leave old Pew, mates—not old Pew!"

Just then the noise of horses topped the rise, and four or five riders came in sight in the moonlight and swept at full gallop down the slope.

At this Pew saw his error, turned with a scream, and ran straight for the ditch, into which he rolled. But he was on his feet again in a second and made another dash, now utterly bewildered, right under the nearest of the coming horses.

The rider tried to save him, but in vain. Down went Pew with a cry that rang high into the night; and the four hoofs trampled and spurned him and passed by. He fell on his side, then gently collapsed upon his face and moved no more.

I leaped to my feet and hailed the riders. They were pulling up, at any rate, horrified at the accident; and I soon saw what they were. One, tailing out behind the rest, was a lad that had gone from the hamlet to Dr. Livesey's; the rest were revenue officers, whom he had met by the way, and with whom he had had the intelligence to return at once. Some news of the lugger in Kitt's Hole had found its way to Supervisor Dance and set him forth that night in our direction, and to that circumstance my mother and I owed our preservation from death.

Pew was dead, stone dead. As for my mother, when we had carried her up to the hamlet, a little cold water and salts and that soon brought her back again, and she was none the worse for her terror, though she still continued to deplore the balance of the money. In the meantime the supervisor rode on, as fast as he could, to Kitt's Hole; but his men had to dismount and grope down the dingle, leading, and sometimes supporting, their horses, and in continual fear of ambushes; so it was no great matter for surprise that when they got down to the Hole the lugger was already under way, though still close in. He hailed her. A voice replied, telling him to keep out of the moonlight or he would get some lead in him, and at the same time a bullet whistled close by his arm. Soon after, the lugger doubled the point and disappeared. Mr. Dance stood there, as he said, "like a fish out of water," and all he could do was to dispatch a man to B—— to warn the cutter. "And that," said he, "is just about as good as nothing. They've got off clean, and there's an end. Only," he added, "I'm glad I trod on Master Pew's corns," for by this time he had heard my story.

I went back with him to the Admiral Benbow, and you cannot imagine a house in such a state of smash; the very clock had been thrown down by these fellows in their furious hunt after my mother and myself; and though nothing had actually been taken away except the captain's money-bag and a little silver from the till, I could see at once that we were ruined. Mr. Dance could make nothing of the scene.

"They got the money, you say? Well, then, Hawkins, what in fortune were they after? More money, I suppose?"

"No, sir; not money, I think," replied I. "In fact, sir, I believe I have the thing in my breast pocket; and to tell you the truth, I should like to get it put in safety."

"To be sure, boy; quite right," said he. "I'll take it, if you like."

"I thought perhaps Dr. Livesey—" I began.

"Perfectly right," he interrupted very cheerily, "perfectly right—a gentleman and a magistrate. And, now I come to think of it, I might as well ride round there myself and report to him or squire. Master Pew's dead, when all's done; not that I regret it, but he's dead, you see, and people will make it out against an officer of his Majesty's revenue, if make it out they can. Now, I'll tell you, Hawkins, if you like, I'll take you along."

I thanked him heartily for the offer, and we walked back to the hamlet where the horses were. By the time I had told mother of my purpose they were all in the saddle.

"Dogger," said Mr. Dance, "you have a good horse; take up this lad behind you."

As soon as I was mounted, holding on to Dogger's belt, the supervisor gave the word, and the party struck out at a bouncing trot on the road to Dr. Livesey's house.

The Captain's Papers

He rode hard all the way till we drew up before Dr. Livesey's door. The house was all dark to the front.

Mr. Dance told me to jump down and knock, and Dogger gave me a stirrup to descend by. The door was opened almost at once by the maid.

"Is Dr. Livesey in?" I asked.

No, she said, he had come home in the afternoon but had gone up to the hall to dine and pass the evening with the squire.

"So there we go, boys," said Mr. Dance.

This time, as the distance was short, I did not mount, but ran with Dogger's stirrup-leather to the lodge gates and up the long, leafless, moonlit avenue to where the white line of the hall buildings looked on either hand on great old gardens. Here Mr. Dance dismounted, and taking me along with him, was admitted at a word into the house.

The servant led us down a matted passage and showed us at the end into a great library, all lined with bookcases and busts upon the top of them, where the squire and Dr. Livesey sat, pipe in hand, on either side of a bright fire.

I had never seen the squire so near at hand. He was a tall man, over six feet high, and broad in proportion, and he had a bluff, rough-and-ready face, all roughened and reddened and lined in his long travels. His eyebrows were very black, and moved readily, and this gave him a look of some temper, not bad, you would say, but quick and high.

"Come in, Mr. Dance," says he, very stately and condescending.

"Good evening, Dance," says the doctor with a nod. "And good evening to you, friend Jim. What good wind brings you here?"

The supervisor stood up straight and stiff and told his story like a lesson; and you should have seen how the two gentlemen leaned forward and looked at each other, and forgot to smoke in their surprise and interest. When they heard how my mother went back to the inn, Dr. Livesey fairly slapped his thigh, and the squire cried "Bravo!" and broke his long pipe against the grate. Long before it was done, Mr. Trelawney (that, you will remember, was the squire's name) had got up from his seat and was striding about the room, and the doctor, as if to hear the better, had taken off his powdered wig and sat there looking very strange indeed with his own close-cropped black poll.

At last Mr. Dance finished the story.

"Mr. Dance," said the squire, "you are a very noble fellow. And as for riding down that black, atrocious miscreant, I regard it as an act of virtue, sir, like stamping on a cockroach. This lad Hawkins is a trump, I perceive. Hawkins, will you ring that bell? Mr. Dance must have some ale."

"And so, Jim," said the doctor, "you have the thing that they were after, have you?"

"Here it is, sir," said I, and gave him the oilskin packet.

The doctor looked it all over, as if his fingers were itching to open it; but instead of doing that, he put it quietly in the pocket of his coat.

"Squire," said he, "when Dance has had his ale he must, of course, be off on his Majesty's service; but I mean to keep Jim Hawkins here to sleep at my house, and with your permission, I propose we should have up the cold pie and let him sup."

"As you will, Livesey," said the squire; "Hawkins has earned better than cold pie."

So a big pigeon pie was brought in and put on a sidetable, and I made a hearty supper, for I was as hungry as a hawk, while Mr. Dance was further complimented and at last dismissed.

"And now, squire," said the doctor.

"And now, Livesey," said the squire in the same breath.

"One at a time, one at a time," laughed Dr. Livesey. "You have heard of this Flint, I suppose?"

"Heard of him!" cried the squire. "Heard of him, you say! He was the bloodthirstiest buccaneer that sailed. Blackbeard was a child to Flint. The Spaniards were so prodigiously afraid of him that, I tell you, sir, I was sometimes proud he was an Englishman. I've seen his top-sails with these eyes, off Trinidad, and the cowardly son of a rum-puncheon that I sailed with put back—put back, sir, into Port of Spain."

"Well, I've heard of him myself, in England," said the doctor. "But the point is, had he money?"

"Money!" cried the squire. "Have you heard the story? What were these villains after but money? What do they care for but money? For what would they risk their rascal carcasses but money?"

"That we shall soon know," replied the doctor. "But you are so confoundedly hot-headed and exclamatory that I cannot get a word in. What I want to know is this: Supposing that I have here in my pocket some clue to where Flint buried his treasure, will that treasure amount to much?"

"Amount, sir!" cried the squire. "It will amount to this: If we have the clue you talk about, I fit out a ship in Bristol dock, and take you and Hawkins here along, and I'll have that treasure if I search a year."

"Very well," said the doctor. "Now, then, if Jim is agreeable, we'll open the packet"; and he laid it before him on the table.

The bundle was sewn together, and the doctor had to get out his instrument case and cut the stitches with his medical scissors. It contained two things—a book and a sealed paper.

"First of all we'll try the book," observed the doctor.

The squire and I were both peering over his shoulder as he opened it, for Dr. Livesey had kindly motioned me to come round from the side-table, where I had been eating, to enjoy the sport of the search. On the first page there were only some scraps of writing, such as a man with a pen in his hand might make for idleness or practice. One was the same as the tattoo mark, "Billy Bones his fancy"; then there was "Mr. W. Bones, mate," "No more rum," "Off Palm Key he got itt," and some other snatches, mostly single words and unintelligible. I could not help wondering who it was that had "got itt," and what "itt" was that he got. A knife in his back as like as not.

"Not much instruction there," said Dr. Livesey as he passed on.

The next ten or twelve pages were filled with a curious series of entries. There was a date at one end of the line and at the other a sum of money, as in common account-books, but instead of explanatory writing, only a varying number of crosses between the two. On the 12th of June, 1745, for instance, a sum of seventy pounds had plainly become due to someone, and there was nothing but six crosses to explain the cause. In a few cases, to be sure, the name of a place would be added, as "Offe Caraccas," or a mere entry of latitude and longitude, 62o 17' 20", 19o 2' 40".

The record lasted over nearly twenty years, the amount of the separate entries growing larger as time went on, and at the end a grand total had been made out after five or six wrong additions, and these words appended, "Bones, his pile."

"I can't make head or tail of this," said Dr. Livesey.

"The thing is as clear as noonday," cried the squire. "This is the black-hearted hound's account-book. These crosses stand for the names of ships or towns that they sank or plundered. The sums are the scoundrel's share, and where he feared an ambiguity, you see he added something clearer. 'Offe Caraccas,' now; you see, here was some unhappy vessel boarded off that coast. God help the poor souls that manned her—coral long ago."

"Right!" said the doctor. "See what it is to be a traveller. Right! And the amounts increase, you see, as he rose in rank."

There was little else in the volume but a few bearings of places noted in the blank leaves towards the end and a table for reducing French, English, and Spanish moneys to a common value.

"Thrifty man!" cried the doctor. "He wasn't the one to be cheated."

"And now," said the squire, "for the other."

The paper had been sealed in several places with a thimble by way of seal; the very thimble, perhaps, that I had found in the captain's pocket. The doctor opened the seals with great care, and there fell out the map of an island, with latitude and longitude, soundings, names of hills and bays and inlets, and every particular that would be needed to bring a ship to a safe anchorage upon its shores. It was about nine miles long and five across, shaped, you might say, like a fat dragon standing up, and had two fine land-locked harbours, and a hill in the centre part marked "The Spy-glass." There were several additions of a later date, but above all, three crosses of red ink—two on the north part of the island, one in the southwest—and beside this last, in the same red ink, and in a small, neat hand, very different from the captain's tottery characters, these words: "Bulk of treasure here."

Over on the back the same hand had written this further information:

Tall tree, Spy-glass shoulder, bearing a point to the N. of N.N.E.

Skeleton Island E.S.E. and by E.

Ten feet.

The bar silver is in the north cache; you can find it by the trend of the east hummock, ten fathoms south of the black crag with the face on it.

The arms are easy found, in the sand-hill, N. point of north inlet cape, bearing E. and a quarter N.

J.F.

That was all; but brief as it was, and to me incomprehensible, it filled the squire and Dr. Livesey with delight.

"Livesey," said the squire, "you will give up this wretched practice at once. Tomorrow I start for Bristol. In three weeks' time—three weeks!—two weeks—ten days—we'll have the best ship, sir, and the choicest crew in England. Hawkins shall come as cabin-boy. You'll make a famous cabin-boy, Hawkins. You, Livesey, are ship's doctor; I am admiral. We'll take Redruth, Joyce, and Hunter. We'll have favourable winds, a quick passage, and not the least difficulty in finding the spot, and money to eat, to roll in, to play duck and drake with ever after."

"Trelawney," said the doctor, "I'll go with you; and I'll go bail for it, so will Jim, and be a credit to the undertaking. There's only one man I'm afraid of."

"And who's that?" cried the squire. "Name the dog, sir!"

"You," replied the doctor; "for you cannot hold your tongue. We are not the only men who know of this paper. These fellows who attacked the inn tonight—bold, desperate blades, for sure—and the rest who stayed aboard that lugger, and more, I dare say, not far off, are, one and all, through thick and thin, bound that they'll get that money. We must none of us go alone till we get to sea. Jim and I shall stick together in the meanwhile; you'll take Joyce and Hunter when you ride to Bristol, and from first to last, not one of us must breathe a word of what we've found."

"Livesey," returned the squire, "you are always in the right of it. I'll be as silent as the grave."

Lesson 106

1. Read chapters 7 and 8. A “Black Dog” is counterfeit money.
2. Add Long John Silver to your pictionary.

Speech

1. Read aloud the letter from chapter 7 in front of an audience.

PART TWO—The Sea-cook

I Go to Bristol

It was longer than the squire imagined ere we were ready for the sea, and none of our first plans—not even Dr. Livesey's, of keeping me beside him—could be carried out as we intended. The doctor had to go to London for a physician to take charge of his practice; the squire was hard at work at Bristol; and I lived on at the hall under the charge of old Redruth, the gamekeeper, almost a prisoner, but full of sea-dreams and the most charming anticipations of strange islands and adventures. I brooded by the hour together over the map, all the details of which I well remembered. Sitting by the fire in the housekeeper's room, I approached that island in my fancy from every possible direction; I explored every acre of its surface; I climbed a thousand times to that tall hill they call the Spy-glass, and from the top enjoyed the most wonderful and changing prospects. Sometimes the isle was thick with savages, with whom we fought, sometimes full of dangerous animals that hunted us, but in all my fancies nothing occurred to me so strange and tragic as our actual adventures.

So the weeks passed on, till one fine day there came a letter addressed to Dr. Livesey, with this addition, "To be opened, in the case of his absence, by Tom Redruth or young Hawkins." Obeying this order, we found, or rather I found—for the gamekeeper was a poor hand at reading anything but print—the following important news:

Old Anchor Inn, Bristol, March 1, 17—

Dear Livesey—As I do not know whether you are at the hall or still in London, I send this in double to both places.

The ship is bought and fitted. She lies at anchor, ready for sea. You never imagined a sweeter schooner—a child might sail her—two hundred tons; name, Hispaniola.

I got her through my old friend, Blandly, who has proved himself throughout the most surprising trump. The admirable fellow literally slaved in my interest, and so, I may say, did everyone in Bristol, as soon as they got wind of the port we sailed for—treasure, I mean.

"Redruth," said I, interrupting the letter, "Dr. Livesey will not like that. The squire has been talking, after all."

"Well, who's a better right?" growled the gamekeeper. "A pretty rum go if squire ain't to talk for Dr. Livesey, I should think."

At that I gave up all attempts at commentary and read straight on:

Blandly himself found the Hispaniola, and by the most admirable management got her for the merest trifle. There is a class of men in Bristol monstrously prejudiced against Blandly. They go the length of declaring that this honest creature would do anything for money, that the Hispaniolabelonged to him, and that he sold it me absurdly high—the most transparent calumnies. None of them dare, however, to deny the merits of the ship.

So far there was not a hitch. The workpeople, to be sure—riggers and what not—were most annoyingly slow; but time cured that. It was the crew that troubled me.

> *I wished a round score of men—in case of natives, buccaneers, or the odious French—and I had the worry of the deuce itself to find so much as half a dozen, till the most remarkable stroke of fortune brought me the very man that I required.*
>
> *I was standing on the dock, when, by the merest accident, I fell in talk with him. I found he was an old sailor, kept a public-house, knew all the seafaring men in Bristol, had lost his health ashore, and wanted a good berth as cook to get to sea again. He had hobbled down there that morning, he said, to get a smell of the salt.*
>
> *I was monstrously touched—so would you have been—and, out of pure pity, I engaged him on the spot to be ship's cook. Long John Silver, he is called, and has lost a leg; but that I regarded as a recommendation, since he lost it in his country's service, under the immortal Hawke. He has no pension, Livesey. Imagine the abominable age we live in!*

Well, sir, I thought I had only found a cook, but it was a crew I had discovered. Between Silver and myself we got together in a few days a company of the toughest old salts imaginable—not pretty to look at, but fellows, by their faces, of the most indomitable spirit. I declare we could fight a frigate.

Long John even got rid of two out of the six or seven I had already engaged. He showed me in a moment that they were just the sort of fresh-water swabs we had to fear in an adventure of importance.

I am in the most magnificent health and spirits, eating like a bull, sleeping like a tree, yet I shall not enjoy a moment till I hear my old tarpaulins tramping round the capstan. Seaward, ho! Hang the treasure! It's the glory of the sea that has turned my head. So now, Livesey, come post; do not lose an hour, if you respect me.

Let young Hawkins go at once to see his mother, with Redruth for a guard; and then both come full speed to Bristol.

John Trelawney

Postscript—I did not tell you that Blandly, who, by the way, is to send a consort after us if we don't turn up by the end of August, had found an admirable fellow for sailing master—a stiff man, which I regret, but in all other respects a treasure. Long John Silver unearthed a very competent man for a mate, a man named Arrow. I have a boatswain who pipes, Livesey; so things shall go man-o'-war fashion on board the good ship Hispaniola.

I forgot to tell you that Silver is a man of substance; I know of my own knowledge that he has a banker's account, which has never been overdrawn. He leaves his wife to manage the inn; and as she is a woman of colour, a pair of old bachelors like you and I may be excused for guessing that it is the wife, quite as much as the health, that sends him back to roving.

J. T.

P.P.S.—Hawkins may stay one night with his mother.

J. T.

You can fancy the excitement into which that letter put me. I was half beside myself with glee; and if ever I despised a man, it was old Tom Redruth, who could do nothing but grumble and lament. Any of the under-gamekeepers would gladly have changed places with him; but such was not the squire's pleasure, and the squire's pleasure was like law among them all. Nobody but old Redruth would have dared so much as even to grumble.

The next morning he and I set out on foot for the Admiral Benbow, and there I found my mother in good health and spirits. The captain, who had so long been a cause of so much discomfort, was gone where the wicked cease from troubling. The squire had had everything repaired, and the public rooms and the sign repainted, and had added some furniture—above all a beautiful armchair for mother in the bar. He had found her a boy as an apprentice also so that she should not want help while I was gone.

It was on seeing that boy that I understood, for the first time, my situation. I had thought up to that moment of the adventures before me, not at all of the home that I was leaving; and now, at sight of this clumsy stranger, who was to stay here in my place beside my mother, I had my first attack of tears. I am afraid I led that boy a dog's life, for as he was new to the work, I had a hundred opportunities of setting him right and putting him down, and I was not slow to profit by them.

The night passed, and the next day, after dinner, Redruth and I were afoot again and on the road. I said good-bye to Mother and the cove where I had lived since I was born, and the dear old Admiral Benbow—since he was repainted, no longer quite so dear. One of my last thoughts was of the captain, who had so often strode along the beach with his cocked hat, his sabre-cut cheek, and his old brass telescope. Next moment we had turned the corner and my home was out of sight.

The mail picked us up about dusk at the Royal George on the heath. I was wedged in between Redruth and a stout old gentleman, and in spite of the swift motion and the cold night air, I must have dozed a great deal from the very first, and then slept like a log up hill and down dale through stage after stage, for when I was awakened at last it was by a punch in the ribs, and I opened my eyes to find that we were standing still before a large building in a city street and that the day had already broken a long time.

"Where are we?" I asked.

"Bristol," said Tom. "Get down."

Mr. Trelawney had taken up his residence at an inn far down the docks to superintend the work upon the schooner. Thither we had now to walk, and our way, to my great delight, lay along the quays and beside the great multitude of ships of all sizes and rigs and nations. In one, sailors were singing at their work, in another there were men aloft, high over my head, hanging to threads that seemed no thicker than a spider's. Though I had lived by the shore all my life, I seemed never to have been near the sea till then. The smell of tar and salt was something new. I saw the most wonderful figureheads, that had all been far over the ocean. I saw, besides, many old sailors, with rings in their ears, and whiskers curled in ringlets, and tarry pigtails, and their swaggering, clumsy sea-walk; and if I had seen as many kings or archbishops I could not have been more delighted.

And I was going to sea myself, to sea in a schooner, with a piping boatswain and pig-tailed singing seamen, to sea, bound for an unknown island, and to seek for buried treasure!

While I was still in this delightful dream, we came suddenly in front of a large inn and met Squire Trelawney, all dressed out like a sea-officer, in stout blue cloth, coming out of the door with a smile on his face and a capital imitation of a sailor's walk.

"Here you are," he cried, "and the doctor came last night from London. Bravo! The ship's company complete!"

"Oh, sir," cried I, "when do we sail?"

"Sail!" says he. "We sail tomorrow!"

At the Sign of the Spy-glass

When I had done breakfasting the squire gave me a note addressed to John Silver, at the sign of the Spy-glass, and told me I should easily find the place by following the line of the docks and keeping a bright lookout for a little tavern with a large brass telescope for sign. I set off, overjoyed at this opportunity to see some more of the ships and seamen, and picked my way among a great crowd of people and carts and bales, for the dock was now at its busiest, until I found the tavern in question.

It was a bright enough little place of entertainment. The sign was newly painted; the windows had neat red curtains; the floor was cleanly sanded. There was a street on each side and an open door on both, which made the large, low room pretty clear to see in, in spite of clouds of tobacco smoke.

The customers were mostly seafaring men, and they talked so loudly that I hung at the door, almost afraid to enter.

As I was waiting, a man came out of a side room, and at a glance I was sure he must be Long John. His left leg was cut off close by the hip, and under the left shoulder he carried a crutch, which he managed with wonderful dexterity, hopping about upon it like a bird. He was very tall and strong, with a face as big as a ham—plain and pale, but intelligent and smiling. Indeed, he seemed in the most cheerful spirits, whistling as he moved about among the tables, with a merry word or a slap on the shoulder for the more favoured of his guests.

Now, to tell you the truth, from the very first mention of Long John in Squire Trelawney's letter I had taken a fear in my mind that he might prove to be the very one-legged sailor whom I had watched for so long at the old Benbow. But one look at the man before me was enough. I had seen the captain, and Black Dog, and the blind man, Pew, and I thought I knew what a buccaneer was like—a very different creature, according to me, from this clean and pleasant-tempered landlord.

I plucked up courage at once, crossed the threshold, and walked right up to the man where he stood, propped on his crutch, talking to a customer.

"Mr. Silver, sir?" I asked, holding out the note.

"Yes, my lad," said he; "such is my name, to be sure. And who may you be?" And then as he saw the squire's letter, he seemed to me to give something almost like a start.

"Oh!" said he, quite loud, and offering his hand. "I see. You are our new cabin-boy; pleased I am to see you."

And he took my hand in his large firm grasp.

Just then one of the customers at the far side rose suddenly and made for the door. It was close by him, and he was out in the street in a moment. But his hurry had attracted my notice, and I recognized him at glance. It was the tallow-faced man, wanting two fingers, who had come first to the Admiral Benbow.

"Oh," I cried, "stop him! It's Black Dog!"

"I don't care two coppers who he is," cried Silver. "But he hasn't paid his score. Harry, run and catch him."

One of the others who was nearest the door leaped up and started in pursuit.

"If he were Admiral Hawke he shall pay his score," cried Silver; and then, relinquishing my hand, "Who did you say he was?" he asked. "Black what?"

"Dog, sir," said I. "Has Mr. Trelawney not told you of the buccaneers? He was one of them."

"So?" cried Silver. "In my house! Ben, run and help Harry. One of those swabs, was he? Was that you drinking with him, Morgan? Step up here."

The man whom he called Morgan—an old, grey-haired, mahogany-faced sailor—came forward pretty sheepishly, rolling his quid.

"Now, Morgan," said Long John very sternly, "you never clapped your eyes on that Black—Black Dog before, did you, now?"

"Not I, sir," said Morgan with a salute.

"You didn't know his name, did you?"

"No, sir."

"By the powers, Tom Morgan, it's as good for you!" exclaimed the landlord. "If you had been mixed up with the like of that, you would never have put another foot in my house, you may lay to that. And what was he saying to you?"

"I don't rightly know, sir," answered Morgan.

"Do you call that a head on your shoulders, or a blessed dead-eye?" cried Long John. "Don't rightly know, don't you! Perhaps you don't happen to rightly know who you was speaking to, perhaps? Come, now, what was he jawing—v'yages, cap'ns, ships? Pipe up! What was it?"

"We was a-talkin' of keel-hauling," answered Morgan.

"Keel-hauling, was you? And a mighty suitable thing, too, and you may lay to that. Get back to your place for a lubber, Tom."

And then, as Morgan rolled back to his seat, Silver added to me in a confidential whisper that was very flattering, as I thought, "He's quite an honest man, Tom Morgan, on'y stupid. And now," he ran on again, aloud, "let's see—Black Dog? No, I don't know the name, not I. Yet I kind of think I've—yes, I've seen the swab. He used to come here with a blind beggar, he used."

"That he did, you may be sure," said I. "I knew that blind man too. His name was Pew."

"It was!" cried Silver, now quite excited. "Pew! That were his name for certain. Ah, he looked a shark, he did! If we run down this Black Dog, now, there'll be news for Cap'n Trelawney! Ben's a good runner; few seamen run better than Ben. He should run him down, hand over hand, by the powers! He talked o' keel-hauling, did he? *I'll* keel-haul him!"

All the time he was jerking out these phrases he was stumping up and down the tavern on his crutch, slapping tables with his hand, and giving such a show of excitement as would have convinced an Old Bailey judge or a Bow Street runner. My suspicions had been thoroughly reawakened on finding Black Dog at the Spy-glass, and I watched the cook narrowly. But he was too deep, and too ready, and too clever for me, and by the time the two men had come back out of breath and confessed that they had lost the track in a crowd, and been scolded like thieves, I would have gone bail for the innocence of Long John Silver.

"See here, now, Hawkins," said he, "here's a blessed hard thing on a man like me, now, ain't it? There's Cap'n Trelawney—what's he to think? Here I have this confounded son of a Dutchman sitting in my own house drinking of my own rum! Here you comes and tells me of it plain; and here I let him give us all the slip before my blessed deadlights! Now, Hawkins, you do me justice with the cap'n. You're a lad, you are, but you're as smart as paint. I see that when you first come in. Now, here it is: What could I do, with this old timber I hobble on? When I was an A B master mariner I'd have come up alongside of him, hand over hand, and broached him to in a brace of old shakes, I would; but now—"

And then, all of a sudden, he stopped, and his jaw dropped as though he had remembered something.

"The score!" he burst out. "Three goes o' rum! Why, shiver my timbers, if I hadn't forgotten my score!"

And falling on a bench, he laughed until the tears ran down his cheeks. I could not help joining, and we laughed together, peal after peal, until the tavern rang again.

"Why, what a precious old sea-calf I am!" he said at last, wiping his cheeks. "You and me should get on well, Hawkins, for I'll take my davy I should be rated ship's boy. But come now, stand by to go about. This won't do. Dooty is dooty, messmates. I'll put on my old cockerel hat, and step along of you to Cap'n Trelawney, and report this here affair. For mind you, it's serious, young Hawkins; and neither you nor me's come out of it with what I should make so bold as to call credit. Nor you neither, says you; not smart—none of the pair of us smart. But dash my buttons! That was a good un about my score."

And he began to laugh again, and that so heartily, that though I did not see the joke as he did, I was again obliged to join him in his mirth.

On our little walk along the quays, he made himself the most interesting companion, telling me about the different ships that we passed by, their rig, tonnage, and nationality, explaining the work that was going forward—how one was discharging, another taking in cargo, and a third making ready for sea—and every now and then telling me some little anecdote of ships or seamen or repeating a nautical phrase till I had learned it perfectly. I began to see that here was one of the best of possible shipmates.

When we got to the inn, the squire and Dr. Livesey were seated together, finishing a quart of ale with a toast in it, before they should go aboard the schooner on a visit of inspection.

Long John told the story from first to last, with a great deal of spirit and the most perfect truth. "That was how it were, now, weren't it, Hawkins?" he would say, now and again, and I could always bear him entirely out.

The two gentlemen regretted that Black Dog had got away, but we all agreed there was nothing to be done, and after he had been complimented, Long John took up his crutch and departed.

"All hands aboard by four this afternoon," shouted the squire after him.

"Aye, aye, sir," cried the cook, in the passage.

"Well, squire," said Dr. Livesey, "I don't put much faith in your discoveries, as a general thing; but I will say this, John Silver suits me."

"The man's a perfect trump," declared the squire.

"And now," added the doctor, "Jim may come on board with us, may he not?"

"To be sure he may," says squire. "Take your hat, Hawkins, and we'll see the ship."

Lesson 107

1. Read chapters 9 and 10.
2. Tell someone what happened in these chapters.

Powder and Arms

The *Hispaniola* lay some way out, and we went under the figureheads and round the sterns of many other ships, and their cables sometimes grated underneath our keel, and sometimes swung above us. At last, however, we got alongside, and were met and saluted as we stepped aboard by the mate, Mr. Arrow, a brown old sailor with earrings in his ears and a squint. He and the squire were very thick and friendly, but I soon observed that things were not the same between Mr. Trelawney and the captain.

This last was a sharp-looking man who seemed angry with everything on board and was soon to tell us why, for we had hardly got down into the cabin when a sailor followed us.

"Captain Smollett, sir, axing to speak with you," said he.

"I am always at the captain's orders. Show him in," said the squire.

The captain, who was close behind his messenger, entered at once and shut the door behind him.

"Well, Captain Smollett, what have you to say? All well, I hope; all shipshape and seaworthy?"

"Well, sir," said the captain, "better speak plain, I believe, even at the risk of offence. I don't like this cruise; I don't like the men; and I don't like my officer. That's short and sweet."

"Perhaps, sir, you don't like the ship?" inquired the squire, very angry, as I could see.

"I can't speak as to that, sir, not having seen her tried," said the captain. "She seems a clever craft; more I can't say."

"Possibly, sir, you may not like your employer, either?" says the squire.

But here Dr. Livesey cut in.

"Stay a bit," said he, "stay a bit. No use of such questions as that but to produce ill feeling. The captain has said too much or he has said too little, and I'm bound to say that I require an explanation of his words. You don't, you say, like this cruise. Now, why?"

"I was engaged, sir, on what we call sealed orders, to sail this ship for that gentleman where he should bid me," said the captain. "So far so good. But now I find that every man before the mast knows more than I do. I don't call that fair, now, do you?"

"No," said Dr. Livesey, "I don't."

"Next," said the captain, "I learn we are going after treasure—hear it from my own hands, mind you. Now, treasure is ticklish work; I don't like treasure voyages on any account, and I don't like them, above all, when they are secret and when (begging your pardon, Mr. Trelawney) the secret has been told to the parrot."

"Silver's parrot?" asked the squire.

"It's a way of speaking," said the captain. "Blabbed, I mean. It's my belief neither of you gentlemen know what you are about, but I'll tell you my way of it—life or death, and a close run."

"That is all clear, and, I dare say, true enough," replied Dr. Livesey. "We take the risk, but we are not so ignorant as you believe us. Next, you say you don't like the crew. Are they not good seamen?"

"I don't like them, sir," returned Captain Smollett. "And I think I should have had the choosing of my own hands, if you go to that."

"Perhaps you should," replied the doctor. "My friend should, perhaps, have taken you along with him; but the slight, if there be one, was unintentional. And you don't like Mr. Arrow?"

"I don't, sir. I believe he's a good seaman, but he's too free with the crew to be a good officer. A mate should keep himself to himself—shouldn't drink with the men before the mast!"

"Do you mean he drinks?" cried the squire.

"No, sir," replied the captain, "only that he's too familiar."

"Well, now, and the short and long of it, captain?" asked the doctor. "Tell us what you want."

"Well, gentlemen, are you determined to go on this cruise?"

"Like iron," answered the squire.

"Very good," said the captain. "Then, as you've heard me very patiently, saying things that I could not prove, hear me a few words more. They are putting the powder and the arms in the fore hold. Now, you have a good place under the cabin; why not put them there?—first point. Then, you are bringing four of your own people with you, and they tell me some of them are to be berthed forward. Why not give them the berths here beside the cabin?—second point."

"Any more?" asked Mr. Trelawney.

"One more," said the captain. "There's been too much blabbing already."

"Far too much," agreed the doctor.

"I'll tell you what I've heard myself," continued Captain Smollett: "that you have a map of an island, that there's crosses on the map to show where treasure is, and that the island lies—" And then he named the latitude and longitude exactly.

"I never told that," cried the squire, "to a soul!"

"The hands know it, sir," returned the captain.

"Livesey, that must have been you or Hawkins," cried the squire.

"It doesn't much matter who it was," replied the doctor. And I could see that neither he nor the captain paid much regard to Mr. Trelawney's protestations. Neither did I, to be sure, he was so loose a talker; yet in this case I believe he was really right and that nobody had told the situation of the island.

"Well, gentlemen," continued the captain, "I don't know who has this map; but I make it a point, it shall be kept secret even from me and Mr. Arrow. Otherwise I would ask you to let me resign."

"I see," said the doctor. "You wish us to keep this matter dark and to make a garrison of the stern part of the ship, manned with my friend's own people, and provided with all the arms and powder on board. In other words, you fear a mutiny."

"Sir," said Captain Smollett, "with no intention to take offence, I deny your right to put words into my mouth. No captain, sir, would be justified in going to sea at all if he had ground enough to say that. As for Mr. Arrow, I believe him thoroughly honest; some of the men are the same; all may be for what I know. But I am responsible for the ship's safety and the life of every man Jack aboard of her. I see things going, as I think, not quite right. And I ask you to take certain precautions or let me resign my berth. And that's all."

"Captain Smollett," began the doctor with a smile, "did ever you hear the fable of the mountain and the mouse? You'll excuse me, I dare say, but you remind me of that fable. When you came in here, I'll stake my wig, you meant more than this."

"Doctor," said the captain, "you are smart. When I came in here I meant to get discharged. I had no thought that Mr. Trelawney would hear a word."

"No more I would," cried the squire. "Had Livesey not been here I should have seen you to the deuce. As it is, I have heard you. I will do as you desire, but I think the worse of you."

"That's as you please, sir," said the captain. "You'll find I do my duty."

And with that he took his leave.

"Trelawney," said the doctor, "contrary to all my notions, I believed you have managed to get two honest men on board with you—that man and John Silver."

"Silver, if you like," cried the squire; "but as for that intolerable humbug, I declare I think his conduct unmanly, unsailorly, and downright un-English."

"Well," says the doctor, "we shall see."

When we came on deck, the men had begun already to take out the arms and powder, yo-ho-ing at their work, while the captain and Mr. Arrow stood by superintending.

The new arrangement was quite to my liking. The whole schooner had been overhauled; six berths had been made astern out of what had been the after-part of the main hold; and this set of cabins was only joined to the galley and forecastle by a sparred passage on the port side. It had been originally meant that the captain, Mr. Arrow, Hunter, Joyce, the doctor, and the squire were to occupy these six berths. Now Redruth and I were to get two of them and Mr. Arrow and the captain were to sleep on deck in the companion, which had been enlarged on each side till you might almost have called it a round-house. Very low it was still, of course; but there was room to swing two hammocks, and even the mate seemed pleased with the arrangement. Even he, perhaps, had been doubtful as to the crew, but that is only guess, for as you shall hear, we had not long the benefit of his opinion.

We were all hard at work, changing the powder and the berths, when the last man or two, and Long John along with them, came off in a shore-boat.

The cook came up the side like a monkey for cleverness, and as soon as he saw what was doing, "So ho, mates!" says he. "What's this?"

"We're a-changing of the powder, Jack," answers one.

"Why, by the powers," cried Long John, "if we do, we'll miss the morning tide!"

"My orders!" said the captain shortly. "You may go below, my man. Hands will want supper."

"Aye, aye, sir," answered the cook, and touching his forelock, he disappeared at once in the direction of his galley.

"That's a good man, captain," said the doctor.

"Very likely, sir," replied Captain Smollett. "Easy with that, men—easy," he ran on, to the fellows who were shifting the powder; and then suddenly observing me examining the swivel we carried amidships, a long brass nine, "Here you, ship's boy," he cried, "out o' that! Off with you to the cook and get some work."

And then as I was hurrying off I heard him say, quite loudly, to the doctor, "I'll have no favourites on my ship."

I assure you I was quite of the squire's way of thinking, and hated the captain deeply.

The Voyage

All that night we were in a great bustle getting things stowed in their place, and boatfuls of the squire's friends, Mr. Blandly and the like, coming off to wish him a good voyage and a safe return. We never had a night at the Admiral Benbow when I had half the work; and I was dog-tired when, a little before dawn, the boatswain sounded his pipe and the crew began to man the capstan-bars. I might have been twice as weary, yet I would not have left the deck, all was so new and interesting to me—the brief commands, the shrill note of the whistle, the men bustling to their places in the glimmer of the ship's lanterns.

"Now, Barbecue, tip us a stave," cried one voice.

"The old one," cried another.

"Aye, aye, mates," said Long John, who was standing by, with his crutch under his arm, and at once broke out in the air and words I knew so well:

"Fifteen men on the dead man's chest—"

And then the whole crew bore chorus:—

"Yo-ho-ho, and a bottle of rum!"

And at the third "Ho!" drove the bars before them with a will.

Even at that exciting moment it carried me back to the old Admiral Benbow in a second, and I seemed to hear the voice of the captain piping in the chorus. But soon the anchor was short up; soon it was hanging dripping at the bows; soon the sails began to draw, and the land and shipping to flit by on either side; and before I could lie down to snatch an hour of slumber the *Hispaniola* had begun her voyage to the Isle of Treasure.

I am not going to relate that voyage in detail. It was fairly prosperous. The ship proved to be a good ship, the crew were capable seamen, and the captain thoroughly understood his business. But before we came the length of Treasure Island, two or three things had happened which require to be known.

Mr. Arrow, first of all, turned out even worse than the captain had feared. He had no command among the men, and people did what they pleased with him. But that was by no means the worst of it, for after a day or two at sea he began to appear on deck with hazy eye, red cheeks, stuttering tongue, and other marks of drunkenness. Time after time he was ordered below in disgrace. Sometimes he fell and cut himself; sometimes he lay all day long in his little bunk at one side of the companion; sometimes for a day or two he would be almost sober and attend to his work at least passably.

In the meantime, we could never make out where he got the drink. That was the ship's mystery. Watch him as we pleased, we could do nothing to solve it; and when we asked him to his face, he would only laugh if he were drunk, and if he were sober deny solemnly that he ever tasted anything but water.

He was not only useless as an officer and a bad influence amongst the men, but it was plain that at this rate he must soon kill himself outright, so nobody was much surprised, nor very sorry, when one dark night, with a head sea, he disappeared entirely and was seen no more.

"Overboard!" said the captain. "Well, gentlemen, that saves the trouble of putting him in irons."

But there we were, without a mate; and it was necessary, of course, to advance one of the men. The boatswain, Job Anderson, was the likeliest man aboard, and though he kept his old title, he served in a way as mate. Mr. Trelawney had followed the sea, and his knowledge made him very useful, for he often took a watch himself in easy weather. And the coxswain, Israel Hands, was a careful, wily, old, experienced seaman who could be trusted at a pinch with almost anything.

He was a great confidant of Long John Silver, and so the mention of his name leads me on to speak of our ship's cook, Barbecue, as the men called him.

Aboard ship he carried his crutch by a lanyard round his neck, to have both hands as free as possible. It was something to see him wedge the foot of the crutch against a bulkhead, and propped against it, yielding to every movement of the ship, get on with his cooking like someone safe ashore. Still more strange was it to see him in the heaviest of weather cross the deck. He had a line or two rigged up to help him across the widest spaces—Long John's earrings, they were called; and he would hand himself from one place to another, now using the crutch, now trailing it alongside by the lanyard, as quickly as another man could walk. Yet some of the men who had sailed with him before expressed their pity to see him so reduced.

"He's no common man, Barbecue," said the coxswain to me. "He had good schooling in his young days and can speak like a book when so minded; and brave—a lion's nothing alongside of Long John! I seen him grapple four and knock their heads together—him unarmed."

All the crew respected and even obeyed him. He had a way of talking to each and doing everybody some particular service. To me he was unweariedly kind, and always glad to see me in the galley, which he kept as clean as a new pin, the dishes hanging up burnished and his parrot in a cage in one corner.

"Come away, Hawkins," he would say; "come and have a yarn with John. Nobody more welcome than yourself, my son. Sit you down and hear the news. Here's Cap'n Flint—I calls my parrot Cap'n Flint, after the famous buccaneer—here's Cap'n Flint predicting success to our v'yage. Wasn't you, cap'n?"

And the parrot would say, with great rapidity, "Pieces of eight! Pieces of eight! Pieces of eight!" till you wondered that it was not out of breath, or till John threw his handkerchief over the cage.

"Now, that bird," he would say, "is, maybe, two hundred years old, Hawkins—they live forever mostly; and if anybody's seen more wickedness, it must be the devil himself. She's sailed with England, the great Cap'n England, the pirate. She's been at Madagascar, and at Malabar, and Surinam, and Providence, and Portobello. She was at the fishing up of the wrecked plate ships. It's there she learned 'Pieces of eight,' and little wonder; three hundred and fifty thousand of 'em,

Hawkins! She was at the boarding of the viceroy of the Indies out of Goa, she was; and to look at her you would think she was a babby. But you smelt powder—didn't you, cap'n?"

"Stand by to go about," the parrot would scream.

"Ah, she's a handsome craft, she is," the cook would say, and give her sugar from his pocket, and then the bird would peck at the bars and swear straight on, passing belief for wickedness. "There," John would add, "you can't touch pitch and not be mucked, lad. Here's this poor old innocent bird o' mine swearing blue fire, and none the wiser, you may lay to that. She would swear the same, in a manner of speaking, before chaplain." And John would touch his forelock with a solemn way he had that made me think he was the best of men.

In the meantime, the squire and Captain Smollett were still on pretty distant terms with one another. The squire made no bones about the matter; he despised the captain. The captain, on his part, never spoke but when he was spoken to, and then sharp and short and dry, and not a word wasted. He owned, when driven into a corner, that he seemed to have been wrong about the crew, that some of them were as brisk as he wanted to see and all had behaved fairly well. As for the ship, he had taken a downright fancy to her. "She'll lie a point nearer the wind than a man has a right to expect of his own married wife, sir. But," he would add, "all I say is, we're not home again, and I don't like the cruise."

The squire, at this, would turn away and march up and down the deck, chin in air.

"A trifle more of that man," he would say, "and I shall explode."

We had some heavy weather, which only proved the qualities of the *Hispaniola*. Every man on board seemed well content, and they must have been hard to please if they had been otherwise, for it is my belief there was never a ship's company so spoiled since Noah put to sea. Double grog was going on the least excuse; there was duff on odd days, as, for instance, if the squire heard it was any man's birthday, and always a barrel of apples standing broached in the waist for anyone to help himself that had a fancy.

"Never knew good come of it yet," the captain said to Dr. Livesey. "Spoil forecastle hands, make devils. That's my belief."

But good did come of the apple barrel, as you shall hear, for if it had not been for that, we should have had no note of warning and might all have perished by the hand of treachery.

This was how it came about.

We had run up the trades to get the wind of the island we were after—I am not allowed to be more plain—and now we were running down for it with a bright lookout day and night. It was about the last day of our outward voyage by the largest computation; some time that night, or at latest before noon of the morrow, we should sight the Treasure Island. We were heading S.S.W. and had a steady breeze abeam and a quiet sea. The *Hispaniola* rolled steadily, dipping her bowsprit now and then with a whiff of spray. All was drawing alow and aloft; everyone was in the bravest spirits because we were now so near an end of the first part of our adventure.

Now, just after sundown, when all my work was over and I was on my way to my berth, it occurred to me that I should like an apple. I ran on deck. The watch was all forward looking out for the island. The man at the helm was watching the luff of the sail and whistling away gently to himself, and that was the only sound excepting the swish of the sea against the bows and around the sides of the ship.

In I got bodily into the apple barrel, and found there was scarce an apple left; but sitting down there in the dark, what with the sound of the waters and the rocking movement of the ship, I had either fallen asleep or was on the point of doing so when a heavy man sat down with rather a clash close by. The barrel shook as he leaned his shoulders against it, and I was just about to jump up when the man began to speak. It was Silver's voice, and before I had heard a dozen words, I would not have shown myself for all the world, but lay there, trembling and listening, in the extreme of fear and curiosity, for from these dozen words I understood that the lives of all the honest men aboard depended upon me alone.

Lesson 108

1. Read chapters 11 and 12.
2. Tell someone about the chapters.

What I Heard in the Apple Barrel

“No, not I," said Silver. "Flint was cap'n; I was quartermaster, along of my timber leg. The same broadside I lost my leg, old Pew lost his deadlights. It was a master surgeon, him that ampytated me—out of college and all—Latin by the bucket, and what not; but he was hanged like a dog, and sun-dried like the rest, at Corso Castle. That was Roberts' men, that was, and comed of changing names to their ships—*Royal Fortune* and so on. Now, what a ship was christened, so let her stay, I says. So it was with the *Cassandra*, as brought us all safe home from Malabar, after England took the viceroy of the Indies; so it was with the old *Walrus*, Flint's old ship, as I've seen amuck with the red blood and fit to sink with gold."

"Ah!" cried another voice, that of the youngest hand on board, and evidently full of admiration. "He was the flower of the flock, was Flint!"

"Davis was a man too, by all accounts," said Silver. "I never sailed along of him; first with England, then with Flint, that's my story; and now here on my own account, in a manner of speaking. I laid by nine hundred safe, from England, and two thousand after Flint. That ain't bad for a man before the mast—all safe in bank. 'Tain't earning now, it's saving does it, you may lay to that. Where's all England's men now? I dunno. Where's Flint's? Why, most on 'em aboard here, and glad to get the duff—been begging before that, some on 'em. Old Pew, as had lost his sight, and might have thought shame, spends twelve hundred pound in a year, like a lord in Parliament. Where is he now? Well, he's dead now and under hatches; but for two year before that, shiver my timbers, the man was starving! He begged, and he stole, and he cut throats, and starved at that, by the powers!"

"Well, it ain't much use, after all," said the young seaman.

"'Tain't much use for fools, you may lay to it—that, nor nothing," cried Silver. "But now, you look here: you're young, you are, but you're as smart as paint. I see that when I set my eyes on you, and I'll talk to you like a man."

You may imagine how I felt when I heard this abominable old rogue addressing another in the very same words of flattery as he had used to myself. I think, if I had been able, that I would have killed him through the barrel. Meantime, he ran on, little supposing he was overheard.

"Here it is about gentlemen of fortune. They lives rough, and they risk swinging, but they eat and drink like fighting-cocks, and when a cruise is done, why, it's hundreds of pounds instead of hundreds of farthings in their pockets. Now, the most goes for rum and a good fling, and to sea again in their shirts. But that's not the course I lay. I puts it all away, some here, some there, and none too much anywheres, by reason of suspicion. I'm fifty, mark you; once back from this cruise, I set up gentleman in earnest. Time enough too, says you. Ah, but I've lived easy in the meantime, never denied myself o' nothing heart desires, and slep' soft and ate dainty all my days but when at sea. And how did I begin? Before the mast, like you!"

"Well," said the other, "but all the other money's gone now, ain't it? You daren't show face in Bristol after this."

"Why, where might you suppose it was?" asked Silver derisively.

"At Bristol, in banks and places," answered his companion.

"It were," said the cook; "it were when we weighed anchor. But my old missis has it all by now. And the Spy-glass is sold, lease and goodwill and rigging; and the old girl's off to meet me. I would tell you where, for I trust you, but it'd make jealousy among the mates."

"And can you trust your missis?" asked the other.

"Gentlemen of fortune," returned the cook, "usually trusts little among themselves, and right they are, you may lay to it. But I have a way with me, I have. When a mate brings a slip on his cable—one as knows me, I mean—it won't be in the same world with old John. There was some that was feared of Pew, and some that was feared of Flint; but Flint his own self was feared of me. Feared he was, and proud. They was the roughest crew afloat, was Flint's; the devil himself would have been feared to go to sea with them. Well now, I tell you, I'm not a boasting man, and you seen yourself how easy I keep company, but when I was quartermaster, *lambs* wasn't the word for Flint's old buccaneers. Ah, you may be sure of yourself in old John's ship."

"Well, I tell you now," replied the lad, "I didn't half a quarter like the job till I had this talk with you, John; but there's my hand on it now."

"And a brave lad you were, and smart too," answered Silver, shaking hands so heartily that all the barrel shook, "and a finer figurehead for a gentleman of fortune I never clapped my eyes on."

By this time I had begun to understand the meaning of their terms. By a "gentleman of fortune" they plainly meant neither more nor less than a common pirate, and the little scene that I had overheard was the last act in the corruption of one of the honest hands—perhaps of the last one left aboard. But on this point I was soon to be relieved, for Silver giving a little whistle, a third man strolled up and sat down by the party.

"Dick's square," said Silver.

"Oh, I know'd Dick was square," returned the voice of the coxswain, Israel Hands. "He's no fool, is Dick." And he turned his quid and spat. "But look here," he went on, "here's what I want to know, Barbecue: how long are we a-going to stand off and on like a blessed bumboat? I've had a'most enough o' Cap'n Smollett; he's hazed me long enough, by thunder! I want to go into that cabin, I do. I want their pickles and wines, and that."

"Israel," said Silver, "your head ain't much account, nor ever was. But you're able to hear, I reckon; leastways, your ears is big enough. Now, here's what I say: you'll berth forward, and you'll live hard, and you'll speak soft, and you'll keep sober till I give the word; and you may lay to that, my son."

"Well, I don't say no, do I?" growled the coxswain. "What I say is, when? That's what I say."

"When! By the powers!" cried Silver. "Well now, if you want to know, I'll tell you when. The last moment I can manage, and that's when. Here's a first-rate seaman, Cap'n Smollett, sails the blessed ship for us. Here's this squire and doctor with a map and such—I don't know where it is, do I? No more do you, says you. Well then, I mean this squire and doctor shall find the stuff, and help us to get it aboard, by the powers. Then we'll see. If I was sure of you all, sons of double Dutchmen, I'd have Cap'n Smollett navigate us half-way back again before I struck."

"Why, we're all seamen aboard here, I should think," said the lad Dick.

"We're all forecastle hands, you mean," snapped Silver. "We can steer a course, but who's to set one? That's what all you gentlemen split on, first and last. If I had my way, I'd have Cap'n Smollett work us back into the trades at least; then we'd have no blessed miscalculations and a spoonful of water a day. But I know the sort you are. I'll finish with 'em at the island, as soon's the blunt's on board, and a pity it is. But you're never happy till you're drunk. Split my sides, I've a sick heart to sail with the likes of you!"

"Easy all, Long John," cried Israel. "Who's a-crossin' of you?"

"Why, how many tall ships, think ye, now, have I seen laid aboard? And how many brisk lads drying in the sun at Execution Dock?" cried Silver. "And all for this same hurry and hurry and hurry. You hear me? I seen a thing or two at sea, I have. If you would on'y lay your course, and a p'int to windward, you would ride in carriages, you would. But not you! I know you. You'll have your mouthful of rum tomorrow, and go hang."

"Everybody knowed you was a kind of a chapling, John; but there's others as could hand and steer as well as you," said Israel. "They liked a bit o' fun, they did. They wasn't so high and dry, nohow, but took their fling, like jolly companions every one."

"So?" says Silver. "Well, and where are they now? Pew was that sort, and he died a beggar-man. Flint was, and he died of rum at Savannah. Ah, they was a sweet crew, they was! On'y, where are they?"

"But," asked Dick, "when we do lay 'em athwart, what are we to do with 'em, anyhow?"

"There's the man for me!" cried the cook admiringly. "That's what I call business. Well, what would you think? Put 'em ashore like maroons? That would have been England's way. Or cut 'em down like that much pork? That would have been Flint's, or Billy Bones's."

"Billy was the man for that," said Israel. "'Dead men don't bite,' says he. Well, he's dead now hisself; he knows the long and short on it now; and if ever a rough hand come to port, it was Billy."

"Right you are," said Silver; "rough and ready. But mark you here, I'm an easy man—I'm quite the gentleman, says you; but this time it's serious. Dooty is dooty, mates. I give my vote—death. When I'm in Parlyment and riding in my coach, I don't want none of these sea-lawyers in the cabin a-coming home, unlooked for, like the devil at prayers. Wait is what I say; but when the time comes, why, let her rip!"

"John," cries the coxswain, "you're a man!"

"You'll say so, Israel when you see," said Silver. "Only one thing I claim—I claim Trelawney. I'll wring his calf's head off his body with these hands, Dick!" he added, breaking off. "You just jump up, like a sweet lad, and get me an apple, to wet my pipe like."

You may fancy the terror I was in! I should have leaped out and run for it if I had found the strength, but my limbs and heart alike misgave me. I heard Dick begin to rise, and then someone seemingly stopped him, and the voice of Hands exclaimed, "Oh, stow that! Don't you get sucking of that bilge, John. Let's have a go of the rum."

"Dick," said Silver, "I trust you. I've a gauge on the keg, mind. There's the key; you fill a pannikin and bring it up."

Terrified as I was, I could not help thinking to myself that this must have been how Mr. Arrow got the strong waters that destroyed him.

Dick was gone but a little while, and during his absence Israel spoke straight on in the cook's ear. It was but a word or two that I could catch, and yet I gathered some important news, for besides other scraps that tended to the same purpose, this whole clause was audible: "Not another man of them'll jine." Hence there were still faithful men on board.

When Dick returned, one after another of the trio took the pannikin and drank—one "To luck," another with a "Here's to old Flint," and Silver himself saying, in a kind of song, "Here's to ourselves, and hold your luff, plenty of prizes and plenty of duff."

Just then a sort of brightness fell upon me in the barrel, and looking up, I found the moon had risen and was silvering the mizzen-top and shining white on the luff of the fore-sail; and almost at the same time the voice of the lookout shouted, "Land ho!"

Council of War

There was a great rush of feet across the deck. I could hear people tumbling up from the cabin and the forecastle, and slipping in an instant outside my barrel, I dived behind the fore-sail, made a double towards the stern, and came out upon the open deck in time to join Hunter and Dr. Livesey in the rush for the weather bow.

There all hands were already congregated. A belt of fog had lifted almost simultaneously with the appearance of the moon. Away to the south-west of us we saw two low hills, about a couple of miles apart, and rising behind one of them a third and higher hill, whose peak was still buried in the fog. All three seemed sharp and conical in figure.

So much I saw, almost in a dream, for I had not yet recovered from my horrid fear of a minute or two before. And then I heard the voice of Captain Smollett issuing orders. The *Hispaniola* was laid a couple of points nearer the wind and now sailed a course that would just clear the island on the east.

"And now, men," said the captain, when all was sheeted home, "has any one of you ever seen that land ahead?"

"I have, sir," said Silver. "I've watered there with a trader I was cook in."

"The anchorage is on the south, behind an islet, I fancy?" asked the captain.

"Yes, sir; Skeleton Island they calls it. It were a main place for pirates once, and a hand we had on board knowed all their names for it. That hill to the nor'ard they calls the Fore-mast Hill; there are three hills in a row running south'ard—fore, main, and mizzen, sir. But the main—that's the big un, with the cloud on it—they usually calls the Spy-glass, by reason of a lookout they kept when they was in the anchorage cleaning, for it's there they cleaned their ships, sir, asking your pardon."

"I have a chart here," says Captain Smollett. "See if that's the place."

Long John's eyes burned in his head as he took the chart, but by the fresh look of the paper I knew he was doomed to disappointment. This was not the map we found in Billy Bones's chest, but an accurate copy, complete in all things—names and heights and soundings—with the single exception of the red crosses and the written notes. Sharp as must have been his annoyance, Silver had the strength of mind to hide it.

"Yes, sir," said he, "this is the spot, to be sure, and very prettily drawed out. Who might have done that, I wonder? The pirates were too ignorant, I reckon. Aye, here it is: 'Capt. Kidd's Anchorage'—just the name my shipmate called it. There's a strong current runs along the south, and then away nor'ard up the west coast. Right you was, sir," says he, "to haul your wind and keep the weather of the island. Leastways, if such was your intention as to enter and careen, and there ain't no better place for that in these waters."

"Thank you, my man," says Captain Smollett. "I'll ask you later on to give us a help. You may go."

I was surprised at the coolness with which John avowed his knowledge of the island, and I own I was half-frightened when I saw him drawing nearer to myself. He did not know, to be sure, that I had overheard his council from the apple barrel, and yet I had by this time taken such a horror of his cruelty, duplicity, and power that I could scarce conceal a shudder when he laid his hand upon my arm.

"Ah," says he, "this here is a sweet spot, this island—a sweet spot for a lad to get ashore on. You'll bathe, and you'll climb trees, and you'll hunt goats, you will; and you'll get aloft on them hills like a goat yourself. Why, it makes me young again. I was going to forget my timber leg, I was. It's a pleasant thing to be young and have ten toes, and you may lay to that. When you want to go a bit of exploring, you just ask old John, and he'll put up a snack for you to take along."

And clapping me in the friendliest way upon the shoulder, he hobbled off forward and went below.

Captain Smollett, the squire, and Dr. Livesey were talking together on the quarter-deck, and anxious as I was to tell them my story, I durst not interrupt them openly. While I was still casting about in my thoughts to find some probable excuse, Dr. Livesey called me to his side. He had left his pipe below, and being a slave to tobacco, had meant that I should fetch it; but as soon as I was near enough to speak and not to be overheard, I broke immediately, "Doctor, let me speak. Get the captain and squire down to the cabin, and then make some pretence to send for me. I have terrible news."

The doctor changed countenance a little, but next moment he was master of himself.

"Thank you, Jim," said he quite loudly, "that was all I wanted to know," as if he had asked me a question.

And with that he turned on his heel and rejoined the other two. They spoke together for a little, and though none of them started, or raised his voice, or so much as whistled, it was plain enough that Dr. Livesey had communicated my request, for the next thing that I heard was the captain giving an order to Job Anderson, and all hands were piped on deck.

"My lads," said Captain Smollett, "I've a word to say to you. This land that we have sighted is the place we have been sailing for. Mr. Trelawney, being a very open-handed gentleman, as we all know, has just asked me a word or two, and as I was able to tell him that every man on board had done his duty, alow and aloft, as I never ask to see it done better, why, he and I and the doctor are going below to the cabin to drink *your* health and luck, and you'll have grog served out for you to drink *our* health and luck. I'll tell you what I think of this: I think it handsome. And if you think as I do, you'll give a good sea-cheer for the gentleman that does it."

The cheer followed—that was a matter of course; but it rang out so full and hearty that I confess I could hardly believe these same men were plotting for our blood.

"One more cheer for Cap'n Smollett," cried Long John when the first had subsided.

And this also was given with a will.

On the top of that the three gentlemen went below, and not long after, word was sent forward that Jim Hawkins was wanted in the cabin.

I found them all three seated round the table, a bottle of Spanish wine and some raisins before them, and the doctor smoking away, with his wig on his lap, and that, I knew, was a sign that he was agitated. The stern window was open, for it was a warm night, and you could see the moon shining behind on the ship's wake.

"Now, Hawkins," said the squire, "you have something to say. Speak up."

I did as I was bid, and as short as I could make it, told the whole details of Silver's conversation. Nobody interrupted me till I was done, nor did any one of the three of them make so much as a movement, but they kept their eyes upon my face from first to last.

"Jim," said Dr. Livesey, "take a seat."

And they made me sit down at table beside them, poured me out a glass of wine, filled my hands with raisins, and all three, one after the other, and each with a bow, drank my good health, and their service to me, for my luck and courage.

"Now, captain," said the squire, "you were right, and I was wrong. I own myself an ass, and I await your orders."

"No more an ass than I, sir," returned the captain. "I never heard of a crew that meant to mutiny but what showed signs before, for any man that had an eye in his head to see the mischief and take steps according. But this crew," he added, "beats me."

"Captain," said the doctor, "with your permission, that's Silver. A very remarkable man."

"He'd look remarkably well from a yard-arm, sir," returned the captain. "But this is talk; this don't lead to anything. I see three or four points, and with Mr. Trelawney's permission, I'll name them."

"You, sir, are the captain. It is for you to speak," says Mr. Trelawney grandly.

"First point," began Mr. Smollett. "We must go on, because we can't turn back. If I gave the word to go about, they would rise at once. Second point, we have time before us—at least until this treasure's found. Third point, there are faithful hands. Now, sir, it's got to come to blows sooner or later, and what I propose is to take time by the forelock, as the saying is, and come to blows some fine day when they least expect it. We can count, I take it, on your own home servants, Mr. Trelawney?"

"As upon myself," declared the squire.

"Three," reckoned the captain; "ourselves make seven, counting Hawkins here. Now, about the honest hands?"

"Most likely Trelawney's own men," said the doctor; "those he had picked up for himself before he lit on Silver."

"Nay," replied the squire. "Hands was one of mine."

"I did think I could have trusted Hands," added the captain.

"And to think that they're all Englishmen!" broke out the squire. "Sir, I could find it in my heart to blow the ship up."

"Well, gentlemen," said the captain, "the best that I can say is not much. We must lay to, if you please, and keep a bright lookout. It's trying on a man, I know. It would be pleasanter to come to blows. But there's no help for it till we know our men. Lay to, and whistle for a wind, that's my view."

"Jim here," said the doctor, "can help us more than anyone. The men are not shy with him, and Jim is a noticing lad."

"Hawkins, I put prodigious faith in you," added the squire.

I began to feel pretty desperate at this, for I felt altogether helpless; and yet, by an odd train of circumstances, it was indeed through me that safety came. In the meantime, talk as we pleased, there were only seven out of the twenty-six on whom we knew we could rely; and out of these seven one was a boy, so that the grown men on our side were six to their nineteen.

Lesson 109

1. Read chapters 13 and 14.
2. What is Jim's problem? (Answers)

PART THREE—My Shore Adventure

How My Shore Adventure Began

The appearance of the island when I came on deck next morning was altogether changed. Although the breeze had now utterly ceased, we had made a great deal of way during the night and were now lying becalmed about half a mile to the south-east of the low eastern coast. Grey-coloured woods covered a large part of the surface. This even tint was indeed broken up by streaks of yellow sand-break in the lower lands, and by many tall trees of the pine family, out-topping the others—some singly, some in clumps; but the general colouring was uniform and sad. The hills ran up clear above the vegetation in spires of naked rock. All were strangely shaped, and the Spy-glass, which was by three or four hundred feet the tallest on the island, was likewise the strangest in configuration, running up sheer from almost every side and then suddenly cut off at the top like a pedestal to put a statue on.

The *Hispaniola* was rolling scuppers under in the ocean swell. The booms were tearing at the blocks, the rudder was banging to and fro, and the whole ship creaking, groaning, and jumping like a manufactory. I had to cling tight to the backstay, and the world turned giddily before my eyes, for though I was a good enough sailor when there was way on, this standing still and being rolled about like a bottle was a thing I never learned to stand without a qualm or so, above all in the morning, on an empty stomach.

Perhaps it was this—perhaps it was the look of the island, with its grey, melancholy woods, and wild stone spires, and the surf that we could both see and hear foaming and thundering on the steep beach—at least, although the sun shone bright and hot, and the shore birds were fishing and crying all around us, and you would have thought anyone would have been glad to get to land after being so long at sea, my heart sank, as the saying is, into my boots; and from the first look onward, I hated the very thought of Treasure Island.

We had a dreary morning's work before us, for there was no sign of any wind, and the boats had to be got out and manned, and the ship warped three or four miles round the corner of the island and up the narrow passage to the haven behind Skeleton Island. I volunteered for one of the boats, where I had, of course, no business. The heat was sweltering, and the men grumbled fiercely over their work. Anderson was in command of my boat, and instead of keeping the crew in order, he grumbled as loud as the worst.

"Well," he said with an oath, "it's not forever."

I thought this was a very bad sign, for up to that day the men had gone briskly and willingly about their business; but the very sight of the island had relaxed the cords of discipline.

All the way in, Long John stood by the steersman and conned the ship. He knew the passage like the palm of his hand, and though the man in the chains got everywhere more water than was down in the chart, John never hesitated once.

"There's a strong scour with the ebb," he said, "and this here passage has been dug out, in a manner of speaking, with a spade."

We brought up just where the anchor was in the chart, about a third of a mile from each shore, the mainland on one side and Skeleton Island on the other. The bottom was clean sand. The plunge of our anchor sent up clouds of birds wheeling and crying over the woods, but in less than a minute they were down again and all was once more silent.

The place was entirely land-locked, buried in woods, the trees coming right down to high-water mark, the shores mostly flat, and the hilltops standing round at a distance in a sort of amphitheatre, one here, one there. Two little rivers, or rather two swamps, emptied out into this pond, as you might call it; and the foliage round that part of the shore had a kind of poisonous brightness. From the ship we could see nothing of the house or stockade, for they were quite buried among trees; and if it had not been for the chart on the companion, we might have been the first that had ever anchored there since the island arose out of the seas.

There was not a breath of air moving, nor a sound but that of the surf booming half a mile away along the beaches and against the rocks outside. A peculiar stagnant smell hung over the anchorage—a smell of sodden leaves and rotting tree trunks. I observed the doctor sniffing and sniffing, like someone tasting a bad egg.

"I don't know about treasure," he said, "but I'll stake my wig there's fever here."

If the conduct of the men had been alarming in the boat, it became truly threatening when they had come aboard. They lay about the deck growling together in talk. The slightest order was received with a black look and grudgingly and carelessly obeyed. Even the honest hands must have caught the infection, for there was not one man aboard to mend another. Mutiny, it was plain, hung over us like a thunder-cloud.

And it was not only we of the cabin party who perceived the danger. Long John was hard at work going from group to group, spending himself in good advice, and as for example no man could have shown a better. He fairly outstripped himself in willingness and civility; he was all smiles to everyone. If an order were given, John would be on his crutch in an instant, with the cheeriest "Aye, aye, sir!" in the world; and when there was nothing else to do, he kept up one song after another, as if to conceal the discontent of the rest.

Of all the gloomy features of that gloomy afternoon, this obvious anxiety on the part of Long John appeared the worst.

We held a council in the cabin.

"Sir," said the captain, "if I risk another order, the whole ship'll come about our ears by the run. You see, sir, here it is. I get a rough answer, do I not? Well, if I speak back, pikes will be going in two shakes; if I don't, Silver will see there's something under that, and the game's up. Now, we've only one man to rely on."

"And who is that?" asked the squire.

"Silver, sir," returned the captain; "he's as anxious as you and I to smother things up. This is a tiff; he'd soon talk 'em out of it if he had the chance, and what I propose to do is to give him the chance. Let's allow the men an afternoon ashore. If they all go, why we'll fight the ship. If they none of them go, well then, we hold the cabin, and God defend the right. If some go, you mark my words, sir, Silver'll bring 'em aboard again as mild as lambs."

It was so decided; loaded pistols were served out to all the sure men; Hunter, Joyce, and Redruth were taken into our confidence and received the news with less surprise and a better spirit than we had looked for, and then the captain went on deck and addressed the crew.

"My lads," said he, "we've had a hot day and are all tired and out of sorts. A turn ashore'll hurt nobody—the boats are still in the water; you can take the gigs, and as many as please may go ashore for the afternoon. I'll fire a gun half an hour before sundown."

I believe the silly fellows must have thought they would break their shins over treasure as soon as they were landed, for they all came out of their sulks in a moment and gave a cheer that started the echo in a faraway hill and sent the birds once more flying and squalling round the anchorage.

The captain was too bright to be in the way. He whipped out of sight in a moment, leaving Silver to arrange the party, and I fancy it was as well he did so. Had he been on deck, he could no longer so much as have pretended not to understand the situation. It was as plain as day. Silver was the captain, and a mighty rebellious crew he had of it. The honest hands—and I was soon to see it proved that there were such on board—must have been very stupid fellows. Or rather, I suppose the truth was this, that all hands were disaffected by the example of the ringleaders—only some more, some less; and a few, being good fellows in the main, could neither be led nor driven any further. It is one thing to be idle and skulk and quite another to take a ship and murder a number of innocent men.

At last, however, the party was made up. Six fellows were to stay on board, and the remaining thirteen, including Silver, began to embark.

Then it was that there came into my head the first of the mad notions that contributed so much to save our lives. If six men were left by Silver, it was plain our party could not take and fight the ship; and since only six were left, it was equally plain that the cabin party had no present need of my assistance. It occurred to me at once to go ashore. In a jiffy I had slipped over the side and curled up in the fore-sheets of the nearest boat, and almost at the same moment she shoved off.

No one took notice of me, only the bow oar saying, "Is that you, Jim? Keep your head down." But Silver, from the other boat, looked sharply over and called out to know if that were me; and from that moment I began to regret what I had done.

The crews raced for the beach, but the boat I was in, having some start and being at once the lighter and the better manned, shot far ahead of her consort, and the bow had struck among the shore-side trees and I had caught a branch and swung myself out and plunged into the nearest thicket while Silver and the rest were still a hundred yards behind.

"Jim, Jim!" I heard him shouting.

But you may suppose I paid no heed; jumping, ducking, and breaking through, I ran straight before my nose till I could run no longer.

The First Blow

I was so pleased at having given the slip to Long John that I began to enjoy myself and look around me with some interest on the strange land that I was in.

I had crossed a marshy tract full of willows, bulrushes, and odd, outlandish, swampy trees; and I had now come out upon the skirts of an open piece of undulating, sandy country, about a mile long, dotted with a few pines and a great number of contorted trees, not unlike the oak in growth, but pale in the foliage, like willows. On the far side of the open stood one of the hills, with two quaint, craggy peaks shining vividly in the sun.

I now felt for the first time the joy of exploration. The isle was uninhabited; my shipmates I had left behind, and nothing lived in front of me but dumb brutes and fowls. I turned hither and thither among the trees. Here and there were flowering plants, unknown to me; here and there I saw snakes, and one raised his head from a ledge of rock and hissed at me with a noise not unlike the spinning of a top. Little did I suppose that he was a deadly enemy and that the noise was the famous rattle.

Then I came to a long thicket of these oaklike trees—live, or evergreen, oaks, I heard afterwards they should be called—which grew low along the sand like brambles, the boughs curiously twisted, the foliage compact, like thatch. The thicket stretched down from the top of one of the sandy knolls, spreading and growing taller as it went, until it reached the margin of the broad, reedy fen, through which the nearest of the little rivers soaked its way into the anchorage.

The marsh was steaming in the strong sun, and the outline of the Spy-glass trembled through the haze.

All at once there began to go a sort of bustle among the bulrushes; a wild duck flew up with a quack, another followed, and soon over the whole surface of the marsh a great cloud of birds hung screaming and circling in the air. I judged at once that some of my shipmates must be drawing near along the borders of the fen. Nor was I deceived, for soon I heard the very distant and low tones of a human voice, which, as I continued to give ear, grew steadily louder and nearer.

This put me in a great fear, and I crawled under cover of the nearest live-oak and squatted there, hearkening, as silent as a mouse.

Another voice answered, and then the first voice, which I now recognized to be Silver's, once more took up the story and ran on for a long while in a stream, only now and again interrupted by the other. By the sound they must have been talking earnestly, and almost fiercely; but no distinct word came to my hearing.

At last the speakers seemed to have paused and perhaps to have sat down, for not only did they cease to draw any nearer, but the birds themselves began to grow more quiet and to settle again to their places in the swamp.

And now I began to feel that I was neglecting my business, that since I had been so foolhardy as to come ashore with these desperadoes, the least I could do was to overhear them at their councils, and that my plain and obvious duty was to draw as close as I could manage, under the favourable ambush of the crouching trees.

I could tell the direction of the speakers pretty exactly, not only by the sound of their voices but by the behaviour of the few birds that still hung in alarm above the heads of the intruders.

Crawling on all fours, I made steadily but slowly towards them, till at last, raising my head to an aperture among the leaves, I could see clear down into a little green dell beside the marsh, and closely set about with trees, where Long John Silver and another of the crew stood face to face in conversation.

The sun beat full upon them. Silver had thrown his hat beside him on the ground, and his great, smooth, blond face, all shining with heat, was lifted to the other man's in a kind of appeal.

"Mate," he was saying, "it's because I thinks gold dust of you—gold dust, and you may lay to that! If I hadn't took to you like pitch, do you think I'd have been here a-warning of you? All's up—you can't make nor mend; it's to save your neck that I'm a-speaking, and if one of the wild uns knew it, where'd I be, Tom—now, tell me, where'd I be?"

"Silver," said the other man—and I observed he was not only red in the face, but spoke as hoarse as a crow, and his voice shook too, like a taut rope—"Silver," says he, "you're old, and you're honest, or has the name for it; and you've money too, which lots of poor sailors hasn't; and you're brave, or I'm mistook. And will you tell me you'll let yourself be led away with that kind of a mess of swabs? Not you! As sure as God sees me, I'd sooner lose my hand. If I turn agin my dooty—"

And then all of a sudden he was interrupted by a noise. I had found one of the honest hands—well, here, at that same moment, came news of another. Far away out in the marsh there arose, all of a sudden, a sound like the cry of anger, then another on the back of it; and then one horrid, long-drawn scream. The rocks of the Spy-glass re-echoed it a score of times; the whole troop of marsh-birds rose again, darkening heaven, with a simultaneous whirr; and long after that death yell was still ringing in my brain, silence had re-established its empire, and only the rustle of the redescending birds and the boom of the distant surges disturbed the languor of the afternoon.

Tom had leaped at the sound, like a horse at the spur, but Silver had not winked an eye. He stood where he was, resting lightly on his crutch, watching his companion like a snake about to spring.

"John!" said the sailor, stretching out his hand.

"Hands off!" cried Silver, leaping back a yard, as it seemed to me, with the speed and security of a trained gymnast.

"Hands off, if you like, John Silver," said the other. "It's a black conscience that can make you feared of me. But in heaven's name, tell me, what was that?"

"That?" returned Silver, smiling away, but warier than ever, his eye a mere pin-point in his big face, but gleaming like a crumb of glass. "That? Oh, I reckon that'll be Alan."

And at this point Tom flashed out like a hero.

"Alan!" he cried. "Then rest his soul for a true seaman! And as for you, John Silver, long you've been a mate of mine, but you're mate of mine no more. If I die like a dog, I'll die in my dooty. You've killed Alan, have you? Kill me too, if you can. But I defies you."

And with that, this brave fellow turned his back directly on the cook and set off walking for the beach. But he was not destined to go far. With a cry John seized the branch of a tree, whipped the crutch out of his armpit, and sent that uncouth missile hurtling through the air. It struck poor Tom, point foremost, and with stunning violence, right between the shoulders in the middle of his back. His hands flew up, he gave a sort of gasp, and fell.

Whether he were injured much or little, none could ever tell. Like enough, to judge from the sound, his back was broken on the spot. But he had no time given him to recover. Silver, agile as a monkey even without leg or crutch, was on the top of him next moment and buried his knife in that defenceless body.

I do not know what it rightly is to faint, but I do know that for the next little while the whole world swam away from before me in a whirling mist; Silver and the birds, and the tall Spy-glass hilltop, going round and round and topsy-turvy before my eyes, and all manner of bells ringing and distant voices shouting in my ear.

When I came again to myself the monster had pulled himself together, his crutch under his arm, his hat upon his head. Just before him Tom lay motionless upon the sward; but the murderer minded him not a whit, cleansing his blood-stained knife the while upon a wisp of grass. Everything else was unchanged, the sun still shining mercilessly on the steaming marsh and the tall pinnacle of the mountain, and I could scarce persuade myself that murder had been actually done and a human life cruelly cut short a moment since before my eyes.

But now John put his hand into his pocket, brought out a whistle, and blew upon it several modulated blasts that rang far across the heated air. I could not tell, of course, the meaning of the signal, but it instantly awoke my fears. More men would be coming. I might be discovered. They had already slain two of the honest people; after Tom and Alan, might not I come next?

Instantly I began to extricate myself and crawl back again, with what speed and silence I could manage, to the more open portion of the wood. As I did so, I could hear hails coming and going between the old buccaneer and his comrades, and this sound of danger lent me wings. As soon as I was clear of the thicket, I ran as I never ran before, scarce minding the direction of my flight, so long as it led me from the murderers; and as I ran, fear grew and grew upon me until it turned into a kind of frenzy.

Indeed, could anyone be more entirely lost than I? When the gun fired, how should I dare to go down to the boats among those fiends, still smoking from their crime? Would not the first of them who saw me wring my neck like a snipe's? Would not my absence itself be an evidence to them of my alarm, and therefore of my fatal knowledge? It was all over, I thought. Good-bye to the *Hispaniola*; good-bye to the squire, the doctor, and the captain! There was nothing left for me but death by starvation or death by the hands of the mutineers.

All this while, as I say, I was still running, and without taking any notice, I had drawn near to the foot of the little hill with the two peaks and had got into a part of the island where the live-oaks grew more widely apart and seemed more like forest trees in their bearing and dimensions. Mingled with these were a few scattered pines, some fifty, some nearer seventy, feet high. The air too smelt more freshly than down beside the marsh.

And here a fresh alarm brought me to a standstill with a thumping heart.

Lesson 110

1. Read chapters 15 and 16.
2. Who narrates chapter 16? (Answers)
3. A new narrator means a new perspective, a new **point of view**. He sees things Jim couldn't have seen.

The Man of the Island

From the side of the hill, which was here steep and stony, a spout of gravel was dislodged and fell rattling and bounding through the trees. My eyes turned instinctively in that direction, and I saw a figure leap with great rapidity behind the trunk of a pine. What it was, whether bear or man or monkey, I could in no wise tell. It seemed dark and shaggy; more I knew not. But the terror of this new apparition brought me to a stand.

I was now, it seemed, cut off upon both sides; behind me the murderers, before me this lurking nondescript. And immediately I began to prefer the dangers that I knew to those I knew not. Silver himself appeared less terrible in contrast with this creature of the woods, and I turned on my heel, and looking sharply behind me over my shoulder, began to retrace my steps in the direction of the boats.

Instantly the figure reappeared, and making a wide circuit, began to head me off. I was tired, at any rate; but had I been as fresh as when I rose, I could see it was in vain for me to contend in speed with such an adversary. From trunk to trunk the creature flitted like a deer, running manlike on two legs, but unlike any man that I had ever seen, stooping almost double as it ran. Yet a man it was, I could no longer be in doubt about that.

I began to recall what I had heard of cannibals. I was within an ace of calling for help. But the mere fact that he was a man, however wild, had somewhat reassured me, and my fear of Silver began to revive in proportion. I stood still, therefore, and cast about for some method of escape; and as I was so thinking, the recollection of my pistol flashed into my mind. As soon as I remembered I was not defenceless, courage glowed again in my heart and I set my face resolutely for this man of the island and walked briskly towards him.

He was concealed by this time behind another tree trunk; but he must have been watching me closely, for as soon as I began to move in his direction he reappeared and took a step to meet me. Then he hesitated, drew back, came forward again, and at last, to my wonder and confusion, threw himself on his knees and held out his clasped hands in supplication.

At that I once more stopped.

"Who are you?" I asked.

"Ben Gunn," he answered, and his voice sounded hoarse and awkward, like a rusty lock. "I'm poor Ben Gunn, I am; and I haven't spoke with a Christian these three years."

I could now see that he was a white man like myself and that his features were even pleasing. His skin, wherever it was exposed, was burnt by the sun; even his lips were black, and his fair eyes looked quite startling in so dark a face. Of all the beggar-men that I had seen or fancied, he was the chief for raggedness. He was clothed with tatters of old ship's canvas and old sea-cloth, and this extraordinary patchwork was all held together by a system of the most various and incongruous fastenings, brass buttons, bits of stick, and loops of tarry gaskin. About his waist he wore an old brass-buckled leather belt, which was the one thing solid in his whole accoutrement.

"Three years!" I cried. "Were you shipwrecked?"

"Nay, mate," said he; "marooned."

I had heard the word, and I knew it stood for a horrible kind of punishment common enough among the buccaneers, in which the offender is put ashore with a little powder and shot and left behind on some desolate and distant island.

"Marooned three years agone," he continued, "and lived on goats since then, and berries, and oysters. Wherever a man is, says I, a man can do for himself. But, mate, my heart is sore for Christian diet. You mightn't happen to have a piece of cheese about you, now? No? Well, many's the long night I've dreamed of cheese—toasted, mostly—and woke up again, and here I were."

"If ever I can get aboard again," said I, "you shall have cheese by the stone."

All this time he had been feeling the stuff of my jacket, smoothing my hands, looking at my boots, and generally, in the intervals of his speech, showing a childish pleasure in the presence of a fellow creature. But at my last words he perked up into a kind of startled slyness.

"If ever you can get aboard again, says you?" he repeated. "Why, now, who's to hinder you?"

"Not you, I know," was my reply.

"And right you was," he cried. "Now you—what do you call yourself, mate?"

"Jim," I told him.

"Jim, Jim," says he, quite pleased apparently. "Well, now, Jim, I've lived that rough as you'd be ashamed to hear of. Now, for instance, you wouldn't think I had had a pious mother—to look at me?" he asked.

"Why, no, not in particular," I answered.

"Ah, well," said he, "but I had—remarkable pious. And I was a civil, pious boy, and could rattle off my catechism that fast, as you couldn't tell one word from another. And here's what it come to, Jim, and it begun with chuck-farthen on the blessed grave-stones! That's what it begun with, but it went further'n that; and so my mother told me, and predicked the whole, she did, the pious woman! But it were Providence that put me here. I've thought it all out in this here lonely island, and I'm back on piety. You don't catch me tasting rum so much, but just a thimbleful for luck, of course, the first chance I have. I'm bound I'll be good, and I see the way to. And, Jim"—looking all round him and lowering his voice to a whisper—"I'm rich."

I now felt sure that the poor fellow had gone crazy in his solitude, and I suppose I must have shown the feeling in my face, for he repeated the statement hotly: "Rich! Rich! I says. And I'll tell you what: I'll make a man of you, Jim. Ah, Jim, you'll bless your stars, you will, you was the first that found me!"

And at this there came suddenly a lowering shadow over his face, and he tightened his grasp upon my hand and raised a forefinger threateningly before my eyes.

"Now, Jim, you tell me true: that ain't Flint's ship?" he asked.

At this I had a happy inspiration. I began to believe that I had found an ally, and I answered him at once.

"It's not Flint's ship, and Flint is dead; but I'll tell you true, as you ask me—there are some of Flint's hands aboard; worse luck for the rest of us."

"Not a man—with one—leg?" he gasped.

"Silver?" I asked.

"Ah, Silver!" says he. "That were his name."

"He's the cook, and the ringleader too."

He was still holding me by the wrist, and at that he give it quite a wring.

"If you was sent by Long John," he said, "I'm as good as pork, and I know it. But where was you, do you suppose?"

I had made my mind up in a moment, and by way of answer told him the whole story of our voyage and the predicament in which we found ourselves. He heard me with the keenest interest, and when I had done he patted me on the head.

"You're a good lad, Jim," he said; "and you're all in a clove hitch, ain't you? Well, you just put your trust in Ben Gunn—Ben Gunn's the man to do it. Would you think it likely, now, that your squire would prove a liberal-minded one in case of help—him being in a clove hitch, as you remark?"

I told him the squire was the most liberal of men.

"Aye, but you see," returned Ben Gunn, "I didn't mean giving me a gate to keep, and a suit of livery clothes, and such; that's not my mark, Jim. What I mean is, would he be likely to come down to the toon of, say one thousand pounds out of money that's as good as a man's own already?"

"I am sure he would," said I. "As it was, all hands were to share."

"*And* a passage home?" he added with a look of great shrewdness.

"Why," I cried, "the squire's a gentleman. And besides, if we got rid of the others, we should want you to help work the vessel home."

"Ah," said he, "so you would." And he seemed very much relieved.

"Now, I'll tell you what," he went on. "So much I'll tell you, and no more. I were in Flint's ship when he buried the treasure; he and six along—six strong seamen. They was ashore nigh on a week, and us standing off and on in the old *Walrus*. One fine day up went the signal, and here come Flint by himself in a little boat, and his head done up in a blue scarf. The sun was getting up, and mortal white he looked about the cutwater. But, there he was, you mind, and the six all dead—dead and buried. How he done it, not a man aboard us could make out. It was battle, murder, and sudden death, leastways—him against six. Billy Bones was the mate; Long John, he was quartermaster; and they asked him where the treasure was. 'Ah,' says he, 'you can go ashore, if you like, and stay,' he says; 'but as for the ship, she'll beat up for more, by thunder!' That's what he said.

"Well, I was in another ship three years back, and we sighted this island. 'Boys,' said I, 'here's Flint's treasure; let's land and find it.' The cap'n was displeased at that, but my messmates were all of a mind and landed. Twelve days they looked for it, and every day they had the worse word for me, until one fine morning all hands went aboard. 'As for you, Benjamin Gunn,' says they, 'here's a musket,' they says, 'and a spade, and pick-axe. You can stay here and find Flint's money for yourself,' they says.

"Well, Jim, three years have I been here, and not a bite of Christian diet from that day to this. But now, you look here; look at me. Do I look like a man before the mast? No, says you. Nor I weren't, neither, I says."

And with that he winked and pinched me hard.

"Just you mention them words to your squire, Jim," he went on. "Nor he weren't, neither—that's the words. Three years he were the man of this island, light and dark, fair and rain; and sometimes he would maybe think upon a prayer (says you), and sometimes he would maybe think of his old mother, so be as she's alive (you'll say); but the most part of Gunn's time (this is what you'll say)—the most part of his time was took up with another matter. And then you'll give him a nip, like I do."

And he pinched me again in the most confidential manner.

"Then," he continued, "then you'll up, and you'll say this: Gunn is a good man (you'll say), and he puts a precious sight more confidence—a precious sight, mind that—in a gen'leman born than in these gen'leman of fortune, having been one hisself."

"Well," I said, "I don't understand one word that you've been saying. But that's neither here nor there; for how am I to get on board?"

"Ah," said he, "that's the hitch, for sure. Well, there's my boat, that I made with my two hands. I keep her under the white rock. If the worst come to the worst, we might try that after dark. Hi!" he broke out. "What's that?"

For just then, although the sun had still an hour or two to run, all the echoes of the island awoke and bellowed to the thunder of a cannon.

"They have begun to fight!" I cried. "Follow me."

And I began to run towards the anchorage, my terrors all forgotten, while close at my side the marooned man in his goatskins trotted easily and lightly.

"Left, left," says he; "keep to your left hand, mate Jim! Under the trees with you! Theer's where I killed my first goat. They don't come down here now; they're all mastheaded on them mountings for the fear of Benjamin Gunn. Ah! And there's the cetemery"—cemetery, he must have meant. "You see the mounds? I come here and prayed, nows and thens, when I thought maybe a Sunday would be about doo. It weren't quite a chapel, but it seemed more solemn like; and then, says you, Ben Gunn was short-handed—no chapling, nor so much as a Bible and a flag, you says."

So he kept talking as I ran, neither expecting nor receiving any answer.

The cannon-shot was followed after a considerable interval by a volley of small arms.

Another pause, and then, not a quarter of a mile in front of me, I beheld the Union Jack flutter in the air above a wood.

PART FOUR—The Stockade

Narrative Continued by the Doctor: How the Ship Was Abandoned

It was about half past one—three bells in the sea phrase—that the two boats went ashore from the *Hispaniola*. The captain, the squire, and I were talking matters over in the cabin. Had there been a breath of wind, we should have fallen on the six mutineers who were left aboard with us, slipped our cable, and away to sea. But the wind was wanting; and to complete our helplessness, down came Hunter with the news that Jim Hawkins had slipped into a boat and was gone ashore with the rest.

It never occurred to us to doubt Jim Hawkins, but we were alarmed for his safety. With the men in the temper they were in, it seemed an even chance if we should see the lad again. We ran on deck. The pitch was bubbling in the seams; the nasty stench of the place turned me sick; if ever a man smelt fever and dysentery, it was in that abominable anchorage. The six scoundrels were sitting grumbling under a sail in the forecastle; ashore we could see the gigs made fast and a man sitting in each, hard by where the river runs in. One of them was whistling "Lillibullero."

Waiting was a strain, and it was decided that Hunter and I should go ashore with the jolly-boat in quest of information.

The gigs had leaned to their right, but Hunter and I pulled straight in, in the direction of the stockade upon the chart. The two who were left guarding their boats seemed in a bustle at our appearance; "Lillibullero" stopped off, and I could see the pair discussing what they ought to do. Had they gone and told Silver, all might have turned out differently; but they had their orders, I suppose, and decided to sit quietly where they were and hark back again to "Lillibullero."

There was a slight bend in the coast, and I steered so as to put it between us; even before we landed we had thus lost sight of the gigs. I jumped out and came as near running as I durst, with a big silk handkerchief under my hat for coolness' sake and a brace of pistols ready primed for safety.

I had not gone a hundred yards when I reached the stockade.

This was how it was: a spring of clear water rose almost at the top of a knoll. Well, on the knoll, and enclosing the spring, they had clapped a stout loghouse fit to hold two score of people on a pinch and loopholed for musketry on either side. All round this they had cleared a wide space, and then the thing was completed by a paling six feet high, without door or opening, too strong to pull down without time and labour and too open to shelter the besiegers. The people in the log-house had them in every way; they stood quiet in shelter and shot the others like partridges. All they wanted was a good watch and food; for, short of a complete surprise, they might have held the place against a regiment.

What particularly took my fancy was the spring. For though we had a good enough place of it in the cabin of the *Hispaniola*, with plenty of arms and ammunition, and things to eat, and excellent wines, there had been one thing overlooked—we had no water. I was thinking this over when there came ringing over the island the cry of a man at the point of death. I was not new to violent death—I have served his Royal Highness the Duke of Cumberland, and got a wound myself at Fontenoy—but I know my pulse went dot and carry one. "Jim Hawkins is gone," was my first thought.

It is something to have been an old soldier, but more still to have been a doctor. There is no time to dilly-dally in our work. And so now I made up my mind instantly, and with no time lost returned to the shore and jumped on board the jolly-boat.

By good fortune Hunter pulled a good oar. We made the water fly, and the boat was soon alongside and I aboard the schooner.

I found them all shaken, as was natural. The squire was sitting down, as white as a sheet, thinking of the harm he had led us to, the good soul! And one of the six forecastle hands was little better.

"There's a man," says Captain Smollett, nodding towards him, "new to this work. He came nigh-hand fainting, doctor, when he heard the cry. Another touch of the rudder and that man would join us."

I told my plan to the captain, and between us we settled on the details of its accomplishment.

We put old Redruth in the gallery between the cabin and the forecastle, with three or four loaded muskets and a mattress for protection. Hunter brought the boat round under the stern-port, and Joyce and I set to work loading her with powder tins, muskets, bags of biscuits, kegs of pork, a cask of cognac, and my invaluable medicine chest.

In the meantime, the squire and the captain stayed on deck, and the latter hailed the coxswain, who was the principal man aboard.

"Mr. Hands," he said, "here are two of us with a brace of pistols each. If any one of you six make a signal of any description, that man's dead."

They were a good deal taken aback, and after a little consultation one and all tumbled down the fore companion, thinking no doubt to take us on the rear. But when they saw Redruth waiting for them in the sparred galley, they went about ship at once, and a head popped out again on deck.

"Down, dog!" cries the captain.

And the head popped back again; and we heard no more, for the time, of these six very faint-hearted seamen.

By this time, tumbling things in as they came, we had the jolly-boat loaded as much as we dared. Joyce and I got out through the stern-port, and we made for shore again as fast as oars could take us.

This second trip fairly aroused the watchers along shore. "Lillibullero" was dropped again; and just before we lost sight of them behind the little point, one of them whipped ashore and disappeared. I had half a mind to change my plan and destroy their boats, but I feared that Silver and the others might be close at hand, and all might very well be lost by trying for too much.

We had soon touched land in the same place as before and set to provision the block house. All three made the first journey, heavily laden, and tossed our stores over the palisade. Then, leaving Joyce to guard them—one man, to be sure, but with half a dozen muskets—Hunter and I returned to the jolly-boat and loaded ourselves once more. So we proceeded without pausing to take breath, till the whole cargo was bestowed, when the two servants took up their position in the block house, and I, with all my power, sculled back to the *Hispaniola*.

That we should have risked a second boat load seems more daring than it really was. They had the advantage of numbers, of course, but we had the advantage of arms. Not one of the men ashore had a musket, and before they could get within range for pistol shooting, we flattered ourselves we should be able to give a good account of a half-dozen at least.

The squire was waiting for me at the stern window, all his faintness gone from him. He caught the painter and made it fast, and we fell to loading the boat for our very lives. Pork, powder, and biscuit was the cargo, with only a musket and a cutlass apiece for the squire and me and Redruth and the captain. The rest of the arms and powder we dropped overboard in two fathoms and a half of water, so that we could see the bright steel shining far below us in the sun, on the clean, sandy bottom.

By this time the tide was beginning to ebb, and the ship was swinging round to her anchor. Voices were heard faintly halloaing in the direction of the two gigs; and though this reassured us for Joyce and Hunter, who were well to the eastward, it warned our party to be off.

Redruth retreated from his place in the gallery and dropped into the boat, which we then brought round to the ship's counter, to be handier for Captain Smollett.

"Now, men," said he, "do you hear me?"

There was no answer from the forecastle.

"It's to you, Abraham Gray—it's to you I am speaking."

Still no reply.

"Gray," resumed Mr. Smollett, a little louder, "I am leaving this ship, and I order you to follow your captain. I know you are a good man at bottom, and I dare say not one of the lot of you's as bad as he makes out. I have my watch here in my hand; I give you thirty seconds to join me in."

There was a pause.

"Come, my fine fellow," continued the captain; "don't hang so long in stays. I'm risking my life and the lives of these good gentlemen every second."

There was a sudden scuffle, a sound of blows, and out burst Abraham Gray with a knife cut on the side of the cheek, and came running to the captain like a dog to the whistle.

"I'm with you, sir," said he.

And the next moment he and the captain had dropped aboard of us, and we had shoved off and given way.

We were clear out of the ship, but not yet ashore in our stockade.

Lesson 111

1. Read chapters 17 and 18.
2. Did you find the change in narrators confusing or interesting? Why?

Vocabulary

1. Analogies are word comparisons. Here is an analogy: a sock is to a foot as a glove is to a hand — sock and glove correspond and foot and hand correspond. Can you see that? Another way to write an analogy is like this — sock:foot :: glove:hand.
2. Fill in the blanks to complete the analogies. Write your answers on a separate piece of paper.

   1. four is to square as six is to _____________
   2. sky is to blue as grass is to _____________
   3. period is to sentence as question mark is to _______________
   4. classroom is to teacher as car repair shop is to _______________
   5. boy is to girl as man is to ______________

Narrative Continued by the Doctor: The Jolly-boat's Last Trip

This fifth trip was quite different from any of the others. In the first place, the little gallipot of a boat that we were in was gravely overloaded. Five grown men, and three of them—Trelawney, Redruth, and the captain—over six feet high, was already more than she was meant to carry. Add to that the powder, pork, and bread-bags. The gunwale was lipping astern. Several times we shipped a little water, and my breeches and the tails of my coat were all soaking wet before we had gone a hundred yards.

The captain made us trim the boat, and we got her to lie a little more evenly. All the same, we were afraid to breathe.

In the second place, the ebb was now making—a strong rippling current running westward through the basin, and then south'ard and seaward down the straits by which we had entered in the morning. Even the ripples were a danger to our overloaded craft, but the worst of it was that we were swept out of our true course and away from our proper landing-place behind the point. If we let the current have its way we should come ashore beside the gigs, where the pirates might appear at any moment.

"I cannot keep her head for the stockade, sir," said I to the captain. I was steering, while he and Redruth, two fresh men, were at the oars. "The tide keeps washing her down. Could you pull a little stronger?"

"Not without swamping the boat," said he. "You must bear up, sir, if you please—bear up until you see you're gaining."

I tried and found by experiment that the tide kept sweeping us westward until I had laid her head due east, or just about right angles to the way we ought to go.

"We'll never get ashore at this rate," said I.

"If it's the only course that we can lie, sir, we must even lie it," returned the captain. "We must keep upstream. You see, sir," he went on, "if once we dropped to leeward of the landing-place, it's hard to say where we should get ashore, besides the chance of being boarded by the gigs; whereas, the way we go the current must slacken, and then we can dodge back along the shore."

"The current's less a'ready, sir," said the man Gray, who was sitting in the fore-sheets; "you can ease her off a bit."

"Thank you, my man," said I, quite as if nothing had happened, for we had all quietly made up our minds to treat him like one of ourselves.

Suddenly the captain spoke up again, and I thought his voice was a little changed.

"The gun!" said he.

"I have thought of that," said I, for I made sure he was thinking of a bombardment of the fort. "They could never get the gun ashore, and if they did, they could never haul it through the woods."

"Look astern, doctor," replied the captain.

We had entirely forgotten the long nine; and there, to our horror, were the five rogues busy about her, getting off her jacket, as they called the stout tarpaulin cover under which she sailed. Not only that, but it flashed into my mind at the same moment that the round-shot and the powder for the gun had been left behind, and a stroke with an axe would put it all into the possession of the evil ones abroad.

"Israel was Flint's gunner," said Gray hoarsely.

At any risk, we put the boat's head direct for the landing-place. By this time we had got so far out of the run of the current that we kept steerage way even at our necessarily gentle rate of rowing, and I could keep her steady for the goal. But the worst of it was that with the course I now held we turned our broadside instead of our stern to the *Hispaniola* and offered a target like a barn door.

I could hear as well as see that brandy-faced rascal Israel Hands plumping down a round-shot on the deck.

"Who's the best shot?" asked the captain.

"Mr. Trelawney, out and away," said I.

"Mr. Trelawney, will you please pick me off one of these men, sir? Hands, if possible," said the captain.

Trelawney was as cool as steel. He looked to the priming of his gun.

"Now," cried the captain, "easy with that gun, sir, or you'll swamp the boat. All hands stand by to trim her when he aims."

The squire raised his gun, the rowing ceased, and we leaned over to the other side to keep the balance, and all was so nicely contrived that we did not ship a drop.

They had the gun, by this time, slewed round upon the swivel, and Hands, who was at the muzzle with the rammer, was in consequence the most exposed. However, we had no luck, for just as Trelawney fired, down he stooped, the ball whistled over him, and it was one of the other four who fell.

The cry he gave was echoed not only by his companions on board but by a great number of voices from the shore, and looking in that direction I saw the other pirates trooping out from among the trees and tumbling into their places in the boats.

"Here come the gigs, sir," said I.

"Give way, then," cried the captain. "We mustn't mind if we swamp her now. If we can't get ashore, all's up."

"Only one of the gigs is being manned, sir," I added; "the crew of the other most likely going round by shore to cut us off."

"They'll have a hot run, sir," returned the captain. "Jack ashore, you know. It's not them I mind; it's the round-shot. Carpet bowls! My lady's maid couldn't miss. Tell us, squire, when you see the match, and we'll hold water."

In the meanwhile we had been making headway at a good pace for a boat so overloaded, and we had shipped but little water in the process. We were now close in; thirty or forty strokes and we should beach her, for the ebb had already disclosed a narrow belt of sand below the clustering trees. The gig was no longer to be feared; the little point had already concealed it from our eyes. The ebb-tide, which had so cruelly delayed us, was now making reparation and delaying our assailants. The one source of danger was the gun.

"If I durst," said the captain, "I'd stop and pick off another man."

But it was plain that they meant nothing should delay their shot. They had never so much as looked at their fallen comrade, though he was not dead, and I could see him trying to crawl away.

"Ready!" cried the squire.

"Hold!" cried the captain, quick as an echo.

And he and Redruth backed with a great heave that sent her stern bodily under water. The report fell in at the same instant of time. This was the first that Jim heard, the sound of the squire's shot not having reached him. Where the ball passed, not one of us precisely knew, but I fancy it must have been over our heads and that the wind of it may have contributed to our disaster.

At any rate, the boat sank by the stern, quite gently, in three feet of water, leaving the captain and myself, facing each other, on our feet. The other three took complete headers, and came up again drenched and bubbling.

So far there was no great harm. No lives were lost, and we could wade ashore in safety. But there were all our stores at the bottom, and to make things worse, only two guns out of five remained in a state for service. Mine I had snatched from my knees and held over my head, by a sort of instinct. As for the captain, he had carried his over his shoulder by a bandoleer, and like a wise man, lock uppermost. The other three had gone down with the boat.

To add to our concern, we heard voices already drawing near us in the woods along shore, and we had not only the danger of being cut off from the stockade in our half-crippled state but the fear before us whether, if Hunter and Joyce were attacked by half a dozen, they would have the sense and conduct to stand firm. Hunter was steady, that we knew; Joyce was a doubtful case—a pleasant, polite man for a valet and to brush one's clothes, but not entirely fitted for a man of war.

With all this in our minds, we waded ashore as fast as we could, leaving behind us the poor jolly-boat and a good half of all our powder and provisions.

Narrative Continued by the Doctor: End of the First Day's Fighting

We made our best speed across the strip of wood that now divided us from the stockade, and at every step we took the voices of the buccaneers rang nearer. Soon we could hear their footfalls as they ran and the cracking of the branches as they breasted across a bit of thicket.

I began to see we should have a brush for it in earnest and looked to my priming.

"Captain," said I, "Trelawney is the dead shot. Give him your gun; his own is useless."

They exchanged guns, and Trelawney, silent and cool as he had been since the beginning of the bustle, hung a moment on his heel to see that all was fit for service. At the same time, observing Gray to be unarmed, I handed him my cutlass. It did all our hearts good to see him spit in his hand, knit his brows, and make the blade sing through the air. It was plain from every line of his body that our new hand was worth his salt.

Forty paces farther we came to the edge of the wood and saw the stockade in front of us. We struck the enclosure about the middle of the south side, and almost at the same time, seven mutineers—Job Anderson, the boatswain, at their head—appeared in full cry at the southwestern corner.

They paused as if taken aback, and before they recovered, not only the squire and I, but Hunter and Joyce from the block house, had time to fire. The four shots came in rather a scattering volley, but they did the business: one of the enemy actually fell, and the rest, without hesitation, turned and plunged into the trees.

After reloading, we walked down the outside of the palisade to see to the fallen enemy. He was stone dead—shot through the heart.

We began to rejoice over our good success when just at that moment a pistol cracked in the bush, a ball whistled close past my ear, and poor Tom Redruth stumbled and fell his length on the ground. Both the squire and I returned the shot, but as we had nothing to aim at, it is probable we only wasted powder. Then we reloaded and turned our attention to poor Tom.

The captain and Gray were already examining him, and I saw with half an eye that all was over.

I believe the readiness of our return volley had scattered the mutineers once more, for we were suffered without further molestation to get the poor old gamekeeper hoisted over the stockade and carried, groaning and bleeding, into the log-house.

Poor old fellow, he had not uttered one word of surprise, complaint, fear, or even acquiescence from the very beginning of our troubles till now, when we had laid him down in the log-house to die. He had lain like a Trojan behind his mattress in the gallery; he had followed every order silently, doggedly, and well; he was the oldest of our party by a score of years; and now, sullen, old, serviceable servant, it was he that was to die.

The squire dropped down beside him on his knees and kissed his hand, crying like a child.

"Be I going, doctor?" he asked.

"Tom, my man," said I, "you're going home."

"I wish I had had a lick at them with the gun first," he replied.

"Tom," said the squire, "say you forgive me, won't you?"

"Would that be respectful like, from me to you, squire?" was the answer. "Howsoever, so be it, amen!"

After a little while of silence, he said he thought somebody might read a prayer. "It's the custom, sir," he added apologetically. And not long after, without another word, he passed away.

In the meantime the captain, whom I had observed to be wonderfully swollen about the chest and pockets, had turned out a great many various stores—the British colours, a Bible, a coil of stoutish rope, pen, ink, the log-book, and pounds of tobacco. He had found a longish fir-tree lying felled and trimmed in the enclosure, and with the help of Hunter he had set it up at the corner of the log-house where the trunks crossed and made an angle. Then, climbing on the roof, he had with his own hand bent and run up the colours.

This seemed mightily to relieve him. He re-entered the log-house and set about counting up the stores as if nothing else existed. But he had an eye on Tom's passage for all that, and as soon as all was over, came forward with another flag and reverently spread it on the body.

"Don't you take on, sir," he said, shaking the squire's hand. "All's well with him; no fear for a hand that's been shot down in his duty to captain and owner. It mayn't be good divinity, but it's a fact."

Then he pulled me aside.

"Dr. Livesey," he said, "in how many weeks do you and squire expect the consort?"

I told him it was a question not of weeks but of months, that if we were not back by the end of August Blandly was to send to find us, but neither sooner nor later. "You can calculate for yourself," I said.

"Why, yes," returned the captain, scratching his head; "and making a large allowance, sir, for all the gifts of Providence, I should say we were pretty close hauled."

"How do you mean?" I asked.

"It's a pity, sir, we lost that second load. That's what I mean," replied the captain. "As for powder and shot, we'll do. But the rations are short, very short—so short, Dr. Livesey, that we're perhaps as well without that extra mouth."

And he pointed to the dead body under the flag.

Just then, with a roar and a whistle, a round-shot passed high above the roof of the log-house and plumped far beyond us in the wood.

"Oho!" said the captain. "Blaze away! You've little enough powder already, my lads."

At the second trial, the aim was better, and the ball descended inside the stockade, scattering a cloud of sand but doing no further damage.

"Captain," said the squire, "the house is quite invisible from the ship. It must be the flag they are aiming at. Would it not be wiser to take it in?"

"Strike my colours!" cried the captain. "No, sir, not I"; and as soon as he had said the words, I think we all agreed with him. For it was not only a piece of stout, seamanly, good feeling; it was good policy besides and showed our enemies that we despised their cannonade.

All through the evening they kept thundering away. Ball after ball flew over or fell short or kicked up the sand in the enclosure, but they had to fire so high that the shot fell dead and buried itself in the soft sand. We had no ricochet to fear, and though one popped in through the roof of the log-house and out again through the floor, we soon got used to that sort of horse-play and minded it no more than cricket.

"There is one good thing about all this," observed the captain; "the wood in front of us is likely clear. The ebb has made a good while; our stores should be uncovered. Volunteers to go and bring in pork."

Gray and Hunter were the first to come forward. Well armed, they stole out of the stockade, but it proved a useless mission. The mutineers were bolder than we fancied or they put more trust in Israel's gunnery. For four or five of them were busy carrying off our stores and wading out with them to one of the gigs that lay close by, pulling an oar or so to hold her steady against the current. Silver was in the stern-sheets in command; and every man of them was now provided with a musket from some secret magazine of their own.

The captain sat down to his log, and here is the beginning of the entry:

Alexander Smollett, master; David Livesey, ship's doctor; Abraham Gray, carpenter's mate; John Trelawney, owner; John Hunter and Richard Joyce, owner's servants, landsmen—being all that is left faithful of the ship's company—with stores for ten days at short rations, came ashore this day and flew British colours on the log-house in Treasure Island. Thomas Redruth, owner's servant, landsman, shot by the mutineers; James Hawkins, cabin-boy—

And at the same time, I was wondering over poor Jim Hawkins' fate.

A hail on the land side.

"Somebody hailing us," said Hunter, who was on guard.

"Doctor! Squire! Captain! Hullo, Hunter, is that you?" came the cries.

And I ran to the door in time to see Jim Hawkins, safe and sound, come climbing over the stockade.

Lesson 112

1. Read chapters 19 and 20.
2. Who is narrating chapter 19? (Answers)
3. Are there good guys and bad guys in this book? (Answers)
4. Write a summary of chapter 20.
5. Inferences are conclusions we draw from the clues we received. Authors don't always tell us everything. Often you do it without thinking about it, but it's a good practice to think! While you are reading, think about what's happening and what you think is going to happen.
6. What conclusions can you draw from the following scenarios? (Answers)
    - Todd looked down at the mess on the floor and wished he could just hide.
        - What do you think might have happened?
        - What do you think he's feeling?
    - Mary coughed, again, blew her nose and rolled over to reach for her phone. She called her boss to let her know she wouldn't be in to work.
        - Why isn't Mary going to work?
    - Thomas dropped his coat on the floor when he came in. He left dirty footprints across the floor as he headed to the kitchen. He knocked over three cups when he got one out of the cupboard. He spilled milk on the counter when he poured his cup.
        - What do you know about Thomas?

Narrative Resumed by Jim Hawkins: The Garrison in the Stockade

As soon as Ben Gunn saw the colours he came to a halt, stopped me by the arm, and sat down.

"Now," said he, "there's your friends, sure enough."

"Far more likely it's the mutineers," I answered.

"That!" he cried. "Why, in a place like this, where nobody puts in but gen'lemen of fortune, Silver would fly the Jolly Roger, you don't make no doubt of that. No, that's your friends. There's been blows too, and I reckon your friends has had the best of it; and here they are ashore in the old stockade, as was made years and years ago by Flint. Ah, he was the man to have a headpiece, was Flint! Barring rum, his match were never seen. He were afraid of none, not he; on'y Silver—Silver was that genteel."

"Well," said I, "that may be so, and so be it; all the more reason that I should hurry on and join my friends."

"Nay, mate," returned Ben, "not you. You're a good boy, or I'm mistook; but you're on'y a boy, all told. Now, Ben Gunn is fly. Rum wouldn't bring me there, where you're going—not rum wouldn't, till I see your born gen'leman and gets it on his word of honour. And you won't forget my words; 'A precious sight (that's what you'll say), a precious sight more confidence'—and then nips him."

And he pinched me the third time with the same air of cleverness.

"And when Ben Gunn is wanted, you know where to find him, Jim. Just wheer you found him today. And him that comes is to have a white thing in his hand, and he's to come alone. Oh! And you'll say this: 'Ben Gunn,' says you, 'has reasons of his own.'"

"Well," said I, "I believe I understand. You have something to propose, and you wish to see the squire or the doctor, and you're to be found where I found you. Is that all?"

"And when? says you," he added. "Why, from about noon observation to about six bells."

"Good," said I, "and now may I go?"

"You won't forget?" he inquired anxiously. "Precious sight, and reasons of his own, says you. Reasons of his own; that's the mainstay; as between man and man. Well, then"—still holding me—"I reckon you can go, Jim. And, Jim, if you was to see Silver, you wouldn't go for to sell Ben Gunn? Wild horses wouldn't draw it from you? No, says you. And if them pirates camp ashore, Jim, what would you say but there'd be widders in the morning?"

Here he was interrupted by a loud report, and a cannonball came tearing through the trees and pitched in the sand not a hundred yards from where we two were talking. The next moment each of us had taken to his heels in a different direction.

For a good hour to come frequent reports shook the island, and balls kept crashing through the woods. I moved from hiding-place to hiding-place, always pursued, or so it seemed to me, by these terrifying missiles. But towards the end of the bombardment, though still I durst not venture in the direction of the stockade, where the balls fell oftenest, I had begun, in a manner, to pluck up my heart again, and after a long detour to the east, crept down among the shore-side trees.

The sun had just set, the sea breeze was rustling and tumbling in the woods and ruffling the grey surface of the anchorage; the tide, too, was far out, and great tracts of sand lay uncovered; the air, after the heat of the day, chilled me through my jacket.

The *Hispaniola* still lay where she had anchored; but, sure enough, there was the Jolly Roger—the black flag of piracy—flying from her peak. Even as I looked, there came another red flash and another report that sent the echoes clattering, and one more round-shot whistled through the air. It was the last of the cannonade.

I lay for some time watching the bustle which succeeded the attack. Men were demolishing something with axes on the beach near the stockade—the poor jolly-boat, I afterwards discovered. Away, near the mouth of the river, a great fire was glowing among the trees, and between that point and the ship one of the gigs kept coming and going, the men, whom I had seen so gloomy, shouting at the oars like children. But there was a sound in their voices which suggested rum.

At length I thought I might return towards the stockade. I was pretty far down on the low, sandy spit that encloses the anchorage to the east, and is joined at half-water to Skeleton Island; and now, as I rose to my feet, I saw, some distance further down the spit and rising from among low bushes, an isolated rock, pretty high, and peculiarly white in colour. It occurred to me that this might be the white rock of which Ben Gunn had spoken and that some day or other a boat might be wanted and I should know where to look for one.

Then I skirted among the woods until I had regained the rear, or shoreward side, of the stockade, and was soon warmly welcomed by the faithful party.

I had soon told my story and began to look about me. The log-house was made of unsquared trunks of pine—roof, walls, and floor. The latter stood in several places as much as a foot or a foot and a half above the surface of the sand. There was a porch at the door, and under this porch the little spring welled up into an artificial basin of a rather odd kind—no other than a great ship's kettle of iron, with the bottom knocked out, and sunk "to her bearings," as the captain said, among the sand.

Little had been left besides the framework of the house, but in one corner there was a stone slab laid down by way of hearth and an old rusty iron basket to contain the fire.

The slopes of the knoll and all the inside of the stockade had been cleared of timber to build the house, and we could see by the stumps what a fine and lofty grove had been destroyed. Most of the soil had been washed away or buried in drift after the removal of the trees; only where the streamlet ran down from the kettle a thick bed of moss and some ferns and little creeping bushes were still green among the sand. Very close around the stockade—too close for defence, they said—the wood still flourished high and dense, all of fir on the land side, but towards the sea with a large admixture of live-oaks.

The cold evening breeze, of which I have spoken, whistled through every chink of the rude building and sprinkled the floor with a continual rain of fine sand. There was sand in our eyes, sand in our teeth, sand in our suppers, sand dancing in the spring at the bottom of the kettle, for all the world like porridge beginning to boil. Our chimney was a square hole in the roof; it was but a little part of the smoke that found its way out, and the rest eddied about the house and kept us coughing and piping the eye.

Add to this that Gray, the new man, had his face tied up in a bandage for a cut he had got in breaking away from the mutineers and that poor old Tom Redruth, still unburied, lay along the wall, stiff and stark, under the Union Jack.

If we had been allowed to sit idle, we should all have fallen in the blues, but Captain Smollett was never the man for that. All hands were called up before him, and he divided us into watches. The doctor and Gray and I for one; the squire, Hunter, and Joyce upon the other. Tired though we all were, two were sent out for firewood; two more were set to dig a grave for Redruth; the doctor was named cook; I was put sentry at the door; and the captain himself went from one to another, keeping up our spirits and lending a hand wherever it was wanted.

From time to time the doctor came to the door for a little air and to rest his eyes, which were almost smoked out of his head, and whenever he did so, he had a word for me.

"That man Smollett," he said once, "is a better man than I am. And when I say that it means a deal, Jim."

Another time he came and was silent for a while. Then he put his head on one side, and looked at me.

"Is this Ben Gunn a man?" he asked.

"I do not know, sir," said I. "I am not very sure whether he's sane."

"If there's any doubt about the matter, he is," returned the doctor. "A man who has been three years biting his nails on a desert island, Jim, can't expect to appear as sane as you or me. It doesn't lie in human nature. Was it cheese you said he had a fancy for?"

"Yes, sir, cheese," I answered.

"Well, Jim," says he, "just see the good that comes of being dainty in your food. You've seen my snuff-box, haven't you? And you never saw me take snuff, the reason being that in my snuff-box I carry a piece of Parmesan cheese—a cheese made in Italy, very nutritious. Well, that's for Ben Gunn!"

Before supper was eaten we buried old Tom in the sand and stood round him for a while bare-headed in the breeze. A good deal of firewood had been got in, but not enough for the captain's fancy, and he shook his head over it and told us we "must get back to this tomorrow rather livelier." Then, when we had eaten our pork and each had a good stiff glass of brandy grog, the three chiefs got together in a corner to discuss our prospects.

It appears they were at their wits' end what to do, the stores being so low that we must have been starved into surrender long before help came. But our best hope, it was decided, was to kill off the buccaneers until they either hauled down their flag or ran away with the *Hispaniola*. From nineteen they were already reduced to fifteen, two others were wounded, and one at least—the man shot beside the gun—severely wounded, if he were not dead. Every time we had a crack at them, we were to take it, saving our own lives, with the extremest care. And besides that, we had two able allies—rum and the climate.

As for the first, though we were about half a mile away, we could hear them roaring and singing late into the night; and as for the second, the doctor staked his wig that, camped where they were in the marsh and unprovided with remedies, the half of them would be on their backs before a week.

"So," he added, "if we are not all shot down first they'll be glad to be packing in the schooner. It's always a ship, and they can get to buccaneering again, I suppose."

"First ship that ever I lost," said Captain Smollett.

I was dead tired, as you may fancy; and when I got to sleep, which was not till after a great deal of tossing, I slept like a log of wood.

The rest had long been up and had already breakfasted and increased the pile of firewood by about half as much again when I was wakened by a bustle and the sound of voices.

"Flag of truce!" I heard someone say; and then, immediately after, with a cry of surprise, "Silver himself!"

And at that, up I jumped, and rubbing my eyes, ran to a loophole in the wall.

Silver's Embassy

Sure enough, there were two men just outside the stockade, one of them waving a white cloth, the other, no less a person than Silver himself, standing placidly by.

It was still quite early, and the coldest morning that I think I ever was abroad in—a chill that pierced into the marrow. The sky was bright and cloudless overhead, and the tops of the trees shone rosily in the sun. But where Silver stood with his lieutenant, all was still in shadow, and they waded knee-deep in a low white vapour that had crawled during the night out of the morass. The chill and the vapour taken together told a poor tale of the island. It was plainly a damp, feverish, unhealthy spot.

"Keep indoors, men," said the captain. "Ten to one this is a trick."

Then he hailed the buccaneer.

"Who goes? Stand, or we fire."

"Flag of truce," cried Silver.

The captain was in the porch, keeping himself carefully out of the way of a treacherous shot, should any be intended. He turned and spoke to us, "Doctor's watch on the lookout. Dr. Livesey take the north side, if you please; Jim, the east; Gray, west. The watch below, all hands to load muskets. Lively, men, and careful."

And then he turned again to the mutineers.

"And what do you want with your flag of truce?" he cried.

This time it was the other man who replied.

"Cap'n Silver, sir, to come on board and make terms," he shouted.

"Cap'n Silver! Don't know him. Who's he?" cried the captain. And we could hear him adding to himself, "Cap'n, is it? My heart, and here's promotion!"

Long John answered for himself. "Me, sir. These poor lads have chosen me cap'n, after your desertion, sir"—laying a particular emphasis upon the word "desertion." "We're willing to submit, if we can come to terms, and no bones about it. All I ask is your word, Cap'n Smollett, to let me safe and sound out of this here stockade, and one minute to get out o' shot before a gun is fired."

"My man," said Captain Smollett, "I have not the slightest desire to talk to you. If you wish to talk to me, you can come, that's all. If there's any treachery, it'll be on your side, and the Lord help you."

"That's enough, cap'n," shouted Long John cheerily. "A word from you's enough. I know a gentleman, and you may lay to that."

We could see the man who carried the flag of truce attempting to hold Silver back. Nor was that wonderful, seeing how cavalier had been the captain's answer. But Silver laughed at him aloud and slapped him on the back as if the idea of alarm had been absurd. Then he advanced to the stockade, threw over his crutch, got a leg up, and with great vigour and skill succeeded in surmounting the fence and dropping safely to the other side.

I will confess that I was far too much taken up with what was going on to be of the slightest use as sentry; indeed, I had already deserted my eastern loophole and crept up behind the captain, who had now seated himself on the threshold, with his elbows on his knees, his head in his hands, and his eyes fixed on the water as it bubbled out of the old iron kettle in the sand. He was whistling "Come, Lasses and Lads."

Silver had terrible hard work getting up the knoll. What with the steepness of the incline, the thick tree stumps, and the soft sand, he and his crutch were as helpless as a ship in stays. But he stuck to it like a man in silence, and at last arrived before the captain, whom he saluted in the handsomest style. He was tricked out in his best; an immense blue coat, thick with brass buttons, hung as low as to his knees, and a fine laced hat was set on the back of his head.

"Here you are, my man," said the captain, raising his head. "You had better sit down."

"You ain't a-going to let me inside, cap'n?" complained Long John. "It's a main cold morning, to be sure, sir, to sit outside upon the sand."

"Why, Silver," said the captain, "if you had pleased to be an honest man, you might have been sitting in your galley. It's your own doing. You're either my ship's cook—and then you were treated handsome—or Cap'n Silver, a common mutineer and pirate, and then you can go hang!"

"Well, well, cap'n," returned the sea-cook, sitting down as he was bidden on the sand, "you'll have to give me a hand up again, that's all. A sweet pretty place you have of it here. Ah, there's Jim! The top of the morning to you, Jim. Doctor, here's my service. Why, there you all are together like a happy family, in a manner of speaking."

"If you have anything to say, my man, better say it," said the captain.

"Right you were, Cap'n Smollett," replied Silver. "Dooty is dooty, to be sure. Well now, you look here, that was a good lay of yours last night. I don't deny it was a good lay. Some of you pretty handy with a handspike-end. And I'll not deny neither but what some of my people was shook—maybe all was shook; maybe I was shook myself; maybe that's why I'm here for terms. But you mark me, cap'n, it won't do twice, by thunder! We'll have to do sentry-go and ease off a point or so on the rum. Maybe you think we were all a sheet in the wind's eye. But I'll tell you I was sober; I was on'y dog tired; and if I'd awoke a second sooner, I'd 'a caught you at the act, I would. He wasn't dead when I got round to him, not he."

"Well?" says Captain Smollett as cool as can be.

All that Silver said was a riddle to him, but you would never have guessed it from his tone. As for me, I began to have an inkling. Ben Gunn's last words came back to my mind. I began to suppose that he had paid the buccaneers a visit while they all lay drunk together round their fire, and I reckoned up with glee that we had only fourteen enemies to deal with.

"Well, here it is," said Silver. "We want that treasure, and we'll have it—that's our point! You would just as soon save your lives, I reckon; and that's yours. You have a chart, haven't you?"

"That's as may be," replied the captain.

"Oh, well, you have, I know that," returned Long John. "You needn't be so husky with a man; there ain't a particle of service in that, and you may lay to it. What I mean is, we want your chart. Now, I never meant you no harm, myself."

"That won't do with me, my man," interrupted the captain. "We know exactly what you meant to do, and we don't care, for now, you see, you can't do it."

And the captain looked at him calmly and proceeded to fill a pipe.

"If Abe Gray—" Silver broke out.

"Avast there!" cried Mr. Smollett. "Gray told me nothing, and I asked him nothing; and what's more, I would see you and him and this whole island blown clean out of the water into blazes first. So there's my mind for you, my man, on that."

This little whiff of temper seemed to cool Silver down. He had been growing nettled before, but now he pulled himself together.

"Like enough," said he. "I would set no limits to what gentlemen might consider shipshape, or might not, as the case were. And seein' as how you are about to take a pipe, cap'n, I'll make so free as do likewise."

And he filled a pipe and lighted it; and the two men sat silently smoking for quite a while, now looking each other in the face, now stopping their tobacco, now leaning forward to spit. It was as good as the play to see them.

"Now," resumed Silver, "here it is. You give us the chart to get the treasure by, and drop shooting poor seamen and stoving of their heads in while asleep. You do that, and we'll offer you a choice. Either you come aboard along of us, once the treasure shipped, and then I'll give you my affy-davy, upon my word of honour, to clap you somewhere safe ashore. Or if that ain't to your fancy, some of my hands being rough and having old scores on account of hazing, then you can stay here, you can. We'll divide stores with you, man for man; and I'll give my affy-davy, as before to speak the first ship I sight, and send 'em here to pick you up. Now, you'll own that's talking. Handsomer you couldn't look to get, now you. And I hope"—raising his voice—"that all hands in this here block house will overhaul my words, for what is spoke to one is spoke to all."

Captain Smollett rose from his seat and knocked out the ashes of his pipe in the palm of his left hand.

"Is that all?" he asked.

"Every last word, by thunder!" answered John. "Refuse that, and you've seen the last of me but musket-balls."

"Very good," said the captain. "Now you'll hear me. If you'll come up one by one, unarmed, I'll engage to clap you all in irons and take you home to a fair trial in England. If you won't, my name is Alexander Smollett, I've flown my sovereign's colours, and I'll see you all to Davy Jones. You can't find the treasure. You can't sail the ship—there's not a man among you fit to sail the ship. You can't fight us—Gray, there, got away from five of you. Your ship's in irons, Master Silver; you're on a lee shore, and so you'll find. I stand here and tell you so; and they're the last good words you'll get from me, for in the name of heaven, I'll put a bullet in your back when next I meet you. Tramp, my lad. Bundle out of this, please, hand over hand, and double quick."

Silver's face was a picture; his eyes started in his head with wrath. He shook the fire out of his pipe.

"Give me a hand up!" he cried.

"Not I," returned the captain.

"Who'll give me a hand up?" he roared.

Not a man among us moved. Growling the foulest imprecations, he crawled along the sand till he got hold of the porch and could hoist himself again upon his crutch. Then he spat into the spring.

"There!" he cried. "That's what I think of ye. Before an hour's out, I'll stove in your old block house like a rum puncheon. Laugh, by thunder, laugh! Before an hour's out, ye'll laugh upon the other side. Them that die'll be the lucky ones."

And with a dreadful oath he stumbled off, ploughed down the sand, was helped across the stockade, after four or five failures, by the man with the flag of truce, and disappeared in an instant afterwards among the trees.

Lesson 113

1. Read chapters 21 and 22.
2. Write a one-sentence summary of each chapter.

Vocabulary

1. Try another analogy set. (Answers)

   1. minute:hour::second:_____________
   2. meter:centimeter::yard(measurement):_______________
   3. floor:down::ceiling:______________
   4. hammer:nail::screwdriver:_____________
   5. loud:quiet::big:_____________

The Attack

As soon as Silver disappeared, the captain, who had been closely watching him, turned towards the interior of the house and found not a man of us at his post but Gray. It was the first time we had ever seen him angry.

"Quarters!" he roared. And then, as we all slunk back to our places, "Gray," he said, "I'll put your name in the log; you've stood by your duty like a seaman. Mr. Trelawney, I'm surprised at you, sir. Doctor, I thought you had worn the king's coat! If that was how you served at Fontenoy, sir, you'd have been better in your berth."

The doctor's watch were all back at their loopholes, the rest were busy loading the spare muskets, and everyone with a red face, you may be certain, and a flea in his ear, as the saying is.

The captain looked on for a while in silence. Then he spoke.

"My lads," said he, "I've given Silver a broadside. I pitched it in red-hot on purpose; and before the hour's out, as he said, we shall be boarded. We're outnumbered, I needn't tell you that, but we fight in shelter; and a minute ago I should have said we fought with discipline. I've no manner of doubt that we can drub them, if you choose."

Then he went the rounds and saw, as he said, that all was clear.

On the two short sides of the house, east and west, there were only two loopholes; on the south side where the porch was, two again; and on the north side, five. There was a round score of muskets for the seven of us; the firewood had been built into four piles—tables, you might say—one about the middle of each side, and on each of these tables some ammunition and four loaded muskets were laid ready to the hand of the defenders. In the middle, the cutlasses lay ranged.

"Toss out the fire," said the captain; "the chill is past, and we mustn't have smoke in our eyes."

The iron fire-basket was carried bodily out by Mr. Trelawney, and the embers smothered among sand.

"Hawkins hasn't had his breakfast. Hawkins, help yourself, and back to your post to eat it," continued Captain Smollett. "Lively, now, my lad; you'll want it before you've done. Hunter, serve out a round of brandy to all hands."

And while this was going on, the captain completed, in his own mind, the plan of the defence.

"Doctor, you will take the door," he resumed. "See, and don't expose yourself; keep within, and fire through the porch. Hunter, take the east side, there. Joyce, you stand by the west, my man. Mr. Trelawney, you are the best shot—you and Gray will take this long north side, with the five loopholes; it's there the danger is. If they can get up to it and fire in upon us through our own ports, things would begin to look dirty. Hawkins, neither you nor I are much account at the shooting; we'll stand by to load and bear a hand."

As the captain had said, the chill was past. As soon as the sun had climbed above our girdle of trees, it fell with all its force upon the clearing and drank up the vapours at a draught. Soon the sand was baking and the resin melting in the logs of the block house. Jackets and coats were flung aside, shirts thrown open at the neck and rolled up to the shoulders; and we stood there, each at his post, in a fever of heat and anxiety.

An hour passed away.

"Hang them!" said the captain. "This is as dull as the doldrums. Gray, whistle for a wind."

And just at that moment came the first news of the attack.

"If you please, sir," said Joyce, "if I see anyone, am I to fire?"

"I told you so!" cried the captain.

"Thank you, sir," returned Joyce with the same quiet civility.

Nothing followed for a time, but the remark had set us all on the alert, straining ears and eyes—the musketeers with their pieces balanced in their hands, the captain out in the middle of the block house with his mouth very tight and a frown on his face.

So some seconds passed, till suddenly Joyce whipped up his musket and fired. The report had scarcely died away ere it was repeated and repeated from without in a scattering volley, shot behind shot, like a string of geese, from every side of the enclosure. Several bullets struck the log-house, but not one entered; and as the smoke cleared away and vanished, the stockade and the woods around it looked as quiet and empty as before. Not a bough waved, not the gleam of a musket-barrel betrayed the presence of our foes.

"Did you hit your man?" asked the captain.

"No, sir," replied Joyce. "I believe not, sir."

"Next best thing to tell the truth," muttered Captain Smollett. "Load his gun, Hawkins. How many should say there were on your side, doctor?"

"I know precisely," said Dr. Livesey. "Three shots were fired on this side. I saw the three flashes—two close together—one farther to the west."

"Three!" repeated the captain. "And how many on yours, Mr. Trelawney?"

But this was not so easily answered. There had come many from the north—seven by the squire's computation, eight or nine according to Gray. From the east and west only a single shot had been fired. It was plain, therefore, that the attack would be developed from the north and that on the other three sides we were only to be annoyed by a show of hostilities. But Captain Smollett made no change in his arrangements. If the mutineers succeeded in crossing the stockade, he argued, they would take possession of any unprotected loophole and shoot us down like rats in our own stronghold.

Nor had we much time left to us for thought. Suddenly, with a loud huzza, a little cloud of pirates leaped from the woods on the north side and ran straight on the stockade. At the same moment, the fire was once more opened from the woods, and a rifle ball sang through the doorway and knocked the doctor's musket into bits.

The boarders swarmed over the fence like monkeys. Squire and Gray fired again and yet again; three men fell, one forwards into the enclosure, two back on the outside. But of these, one was evidently more frightened than hurt, for he was on his feet again in a crack and instantly disappeared among the trees.

Two had bit the dust, one had fled, four had made good their footing inside our defences, while from the shelter of the woods seven or eight men, each evidently supplied with several muskets, kept up a hot though useless fire on the log-house.

The four who had boarded made straight before them for the building, shouting as they ran, and the men among the trees shouted back to encourage them. Several shots were fired, but such was the hurry of the marksmen that not one appears to have taken effect. In a moment, the four pirates had swarmed up the mound and were upon us.

The head of Job Anderson, the boatswain, appeared at the middle loophole.

"At 'em, all hands—all hands!" he roared in a voice of thunder.

At the same moment, another pirate grasped Hunter's musket by the muzzle, wrenched it from his hands, plucked it through the loophole, and with one stunning blow, laid the poor fellow senseless on the floor. Meanwhile a third, running unharmed all around the house, appeared suddenly in the doorway and fell with his cutlass on the doctor.

Our position was utterly reversed. A moment since we were firing, under cover, at an exposed enemy; now it was we who lay uncovered and could not return a blow.

The log-house was full of smoke, to which we owed our comparative safety. Cries and confusion, the flashes and reports of pistol-shots, and one loud groan rang in my ears.

"Out, lads, out, and fight 'em in the open! Cutlasses!" cried the captain.

I snatched a cutlass from the pile, and someone, at the same time snatching another, gave me a cut across the knuckles which I hardly felt. I dashed out of the door into the clear sunlight. Someone was close behind, I knew not whom. Right in front, the doctor was pursuing his assailant down the hill, and just as my eyes fell upon him, beat down his guard and sent him sprawling on his back with a great slash across the face.

"Round the house, lads! Round the house!" cried the captain; and even in the hurly-burly, I perceived a change in his voice.

Mechanically, I obeyed, turned eastwards, and with my cutlass raised, ran round the corner of the house. Next moment I was face to face with Anderson. He roared aloud, and his hanger went up above his head, flashing in the sunlight. I had not time to be afraid, but as the blow still hung impending, leaped in a trice upon one side, and missing my foot in the soft sand, rolled headlong down the slope.

When I had first sallied from the door, the other mutineers had been already swarming up the palisade to make an end of us. One man, in a red night-cap, with his cutlass in his mouth, had even got upon the top and thrown a leg across. Well, so short had been the interval that when I found my feet again all was in the same posture, the fellow with the red night-cap still half-way over, another still just showing his head above the top of the stockade. And yet, in this breath of time, the fight was over and the victory was ours.

Gray, following close behind me, had cut down the big boatswain ere he had time to recover from his last blow. Another had been shot at a loophole in the very act of firing into the house and now lay in agony, the pistol still smoking in his hand. A third, as I had seen, the doctor had disposed of at a blow. Of the four who had scaled the palisade, one only remained unaccounted for, and he, having left his cutlass on the field, was now clambering out again with the fear of death upon him.

"Fire—fire from the house!" cried the doctor. "And you, lads, back into cover."

But his words were unheeded, no shot was fired, and the last boarder made good his escape and disappeared with the rest into the wood. In three seconds nothing remained of the attacking party but the five who had fallen, four on the inside and one on the outside of the palisade.

The doctor and Gray and I ran full speed for shelter. The survivors would soon be back where they had left their muskets, and at any moment the fire might recommence.

The house was by this time somewhat cleared of smoke, and we saw at a glance the price we had paid for victory. Hunter lay beside his loophole, stunned; Joyce by his, shot through the head, never to move again; while right in the centre, the squire was supporting the captain, one as pale as the other.

"The captain's wounded," said Mr. Trelawney.

"Have they run?" asked Mr. Smollett.

"All that could, you may be bound," returned the doctor; "but there's five of them will never run again."

"Five!" cried the captain. "Come, that's better. Five against three leaves us four to nine. That's better odds than we had at starting. We were seven to nineteen then, or thought we were, and that's as bad to bear."*

*The mutineers were soon only eight in number, for the man shot by Mr. Trelawney on board the schooner died that same evening of his wound. But this was, of course, not known till after by the faithful party.

PART FIVE—My Sea Adventure

How My Sea Adventure Began

There was no return of the mutineers—not so much as another shot out of the woods. They had "got their rations for that day," as the captain put it, and we had the place to ourselves and a quiet time to overhaul the wounded and get dinner. Squire and I cooked outside in spite of the danger, and even outside we could hardly tell what we were at, for horror of the loud groans that reached us from the doctor's patients.

Out of the eight men who had fallen in the action, only three still breathed—that one of the pirates who had been shot at the loophole, Hunter, and Captain Smollett; and of these, the first two were as good as dead; the mutineer indeed died under the doctor's knife, and Hunter, do what we could, never recovered consciousness in this world. He lingered all day, breathing loudly like the old buccaneer at home in his apoplectic fit, but the bones of his chest had been crushed by the blow and his skull fractured in falling, and some time in the following night, without sign or sound, he went to his Maker.

As for the captain, his wounds were grievous indeed, but not dangerous. No organ was fatally injured. Anderson's ball—for it was Job that shot him first—had broken his shoulder-blade and touched the lung, not badly; the second had only torn and displaced some muscles in the calf. He was sure to recover, the doctor said, but in the meantime, and for weeks to come, he must not walk nor move his arm, nor so much as speak when he could help it.

My own accidental cut across the knuckles was a flea-bite. Doctor Livesey patched it up with plaster and pulled my ears for me into the bargain.

After dinner the squire and the doctor sat by the captain's side awhile in consultation; and when they had talked to their hearts' content, it being then a little past noon, the doctor took up his hat and pistols, girt on a cutlass, put the chart in his pocket, and with a musket over his shoulder crossed the palisade on the north side and set off briskly through the trees.

Gray and I were sitting together at the far end of the block house, to be out of earshot of our officers consulting; and Gray took his pipe out of his mouth and fairly forgot to put it back again, so thunder-struck he was at this occurrence.

"Why, in the name of Davy Jones," said he, "is Dr. Livesey mad?"

"Why no," says I. "He's about the last of this crew for that, I take it."

"Well, shipmate," said Gray, "mad he may not be; but if *he's* not, you mark my words, *I* am."

"I take it," replied I, "the doctor has his idea; and if I am right, he's going now to see Ben Gunn."

I was right, as appeared later; but in the meantime, the house being stifling hot and the little patch of sand inside the palisade ablaze with midday sun, I began to get another thought into my head, which was not by any means so right. What I began to do was to envy the doctor walking in the cool shadow of the woods with the birds about him and the pleasant smell of the pines, while I sat grilling, with my clothes stuck to the hot resin, and so much blood about me and so many poor dead bodies lying all around that I took a disgust of the place that was almost as strong as fear.

All the time I was washing out the block house, and then washing up the things from dinner, this disgust and envy kept growing stronger and stronger, till at last, being near a bread-bag, and no one then observing me, I took the first step towards my escapade and filled both pockets of my coat with biscuit.

I was a fool, if you like, and certainly I was going to do a foolish, over-bold act; but I was determined to do it with all the precautions in my power. These biscuits, should anything befall me, would keep me, at least, from starving till far on in the next day.

The next thing I laid hold of was a brace of pistols, and as I already had a powder-horn and bullets, I felt myself well supplied with arms.

As for the scheme I had in my head, it was not a bad one in itself. I was to go down the sandy spit that divides the anchorage on the east from the open sea, find the white rock I had observed last evening, and ascertain whether it was there or not that Ben Gunn had hidden his boat, a thing quite worth doing, as I still believe. But as I was certain I should not be allowed to leave the enclosure, my only plan was to take French leave and slip out when nobody was watching, and that was so bad a way of doing it as made the thing itself wrong. But I was only a boy, and I had made my mind up.

Well, as things at last fell out, I found an admirable opportunity. The squire and Gray were busy helping the captain with his bandages, the coast was clear, I made a bolt for it over the stockade and into the thickest of the trees, and before my absence was observed I was out of cry of my companions.

This was my second folly, far worse than the first, as I left but two sound men to guard the house; but like the first, it was a help towards saving all of us.

I took my way straight for the east coast of the island, for I was determined to go down the sea side of the spit to avoid all chance of observation from the anchorage. It was already late in the afternoon, although still warm and sunny. As I continued to thread the tall woods, I could hear from far before me not only the continuous thunder of the surf, but a certain tossing of foliage and grinding of boughs which showed me the sea breeze had set in higher than usual. Soon cool draughts of air began to reach me, and a few steps farther I came forth into the open borders of the grove, and saw the sea lying blue and sunny to the horizon and the surf tumbling and tossing its foam along the beach.

I have never seen the sea quiet round Treasure Island. The sun might blaze overhead, the air be without a breath, the surface smooth and blue, but still these great rollers would be running along all the external coast, thundering and thundering by day and night; and I scarce believe there is one spot in the island where a man would be out of earshot of their noise.

I walked along beside the surf with great enjoyment, till, thinking I was now got far enough to the south, I took the cover of some thick bushes and crept warily up to the ridge of the spit.

Behind me was the sea, in front the anchorage. The sea breeze, as though it had the sooner blown itself out by its unusual violence, was already at an end; it had been succeeded by light, variable airs from the south and south-east, carrying great banks of fog; and the anchorage, under lee of Skeleton Island, lay still and leaden as when first we entered it. The *Hispaniola*, in that unbroken mirror, was exactly portrayed from the truck to the waterline, the Jolly Roger hanging from her peak.

Alongside lay one of the gigs, Silver in the stern-sheets—him I could always recognize—while a couple of men were leaning over the stern bulwarks, one of them with a red cap—the very rogue that I had seen some hours before stride-legs upon the palisade. Apparently they were talking and laughing, though at that distance—upwards of a mile—I could, of course, hear no word of what was said. All at once there began the most horrid, unearthly screaming, which at first startled me badly, though I had soon remembered the voice of Captain Flint and even thought I could make out the bird by her bright plumage as she sat perched upon her master's wrist.

Soon after, the jolly-boat shoved off and pulled for shore, and the man with the red cap and his comrade went below by the cabin companion.

Just about the same time, the sun had gone down behind the Spy-glass, and as the fog was collecting rapidly, it began to grow dark in earnest. I saw I must lose no time if I were to find the boat that evening.

The white rock, visible enough above the brush, was still some eighth of a mile further down the spit, and it took me a goodish while to get up with it, crawling, often on all fours, among the scrub. Night had almost come when I laid my hand on its rough sides. Right below it there was an exceedingly small hollow of green turf, hidden by banks and a thick underwood about knee-deep, that grew there very plentifully; and in the centre of the dell, sure enough, a little tent of goat-skins, like what the gipsies carry about with them in England.

I dropped into the hollow, lifted the side of the tent, and there was Ben Gunn's boat—home-made if ever anything was home-made; a rude, lop-sided framework of tough wood, and stretched upon that a covering of goat-skin, with the hair inside. The thing was extremely small, even for me, and I can hardly imagine that it could have floated with a full-sized man. There was one thwart set as low as possible, a kind of stretcher in the bows, and a double paddle for propulsion.

I had not then seen a coracle, such as the ancient Britons made, but I have seen one since, and I can give you no fairer idea of Ben Gunn's boat than by saying it was like the first and the worst coracle ever made by man. But the great advantage of the coracle it certainly possessed, for it was exceedingly light and portable.

Well, now that I had found the boat, you would have thought I had had enough of truantry for once, but in the meantime I had taken another notion and become so obstinately fond of it that I would have carried it out, I believe, in the teeth of Captain Smollett himself. This was to slip out under cover of the night, cut the *Hispaniola* adrift, and let her go ashore where she fancied. I had quite made up my mind that the mutineers, after their repulse of the morning, had nothing nearer their hearts than to up anchor and away to sea; this, I thought, it would be a fine thing to prevent, and now that I had seen how they left their watchmen unprovided with a boat, I thought it might be done with little risk.

Down I sat to wait for darkness, and made a hearty meal of biscuit. It was a night out of ten thousand for my purpose. The fog had now buried all heaven. As the last rays of daylight dwindled and disappeared, absolute blackness settled down on Treasure Island. And when, at last, I shouldered the coracle and groped my way stumblingly out of the hollow where I had supped, there were but two points visible on the whole anchorage.

One was the great fire on shore, by which the defeated pirates lay carousing in the swamp. The other, a mere blur of light upon the darkness, indicated the position of the anchored ship. She had swung round to the ebb—her bow was now towards me—the only lights on board were in the cabin, and what I saw was merely a reflection on the fog of the strong rays that flowed from the stern window.

The ebb had already run some time, and I had to wade through a long belt of swampy sand, where I sank several times above the ankle, before I came to the edge of the retreating water, and wading a little way in, with some strength and dexterity, set my coracle, keel downwards, on the surface.

Lesson 114

1. Read chapters 23 and 24.
2. "I was just thinking how busy the drink and the devil were at that very moment in the cabin..." What does it mean that drink and the devil were busy? (Answers)
3. When you make inferences, you are reading between the lines. When you hear or see an ad, you need to read between the lines sometimes as well, and especially read the details. Read these ads. Do the headlines really tell the truth? What does the ad really say? (Answers)
    - Buy one get one free! *Second pair must be less than the first. Good through 8/31.

- Our brand is the best!
- Mr. Brown will fight for you. Vote Brown!

The Ebb-tide Runs

The coracle—as I had ample reason to know before I was done with her—was a very safe boat for a person of my height and weight, both buoyant and clever in a seaway; but she was the most cross-grained, lop-sided craft to manage. Do as you pleased, she always made more leeway than anything else, and turning round and round was the manoeuvre she was best at. Even Ben Gunn himself has admitted that she was "queer to handle till you knew her way."

Certainly I did not know her way. She turned in every direction but the one I was bound to go; the most part of the time we were broadside on, and I am very sure I never should have made the ship at all but for the tide. By good fortune, paddle as I pleased, the tide was still sweeping me down; and there lay the *Hispaniola* right in the fairway, hardly to be missed.

First she loomed before me like a blot of something yet blacker than darkness, then her spars and hull began to take shape, and the next moment, as it seemed (for, the farther I went, the brisker grew the current of the ebb), I was alongside of her hawser and had laid hold.

The hawser was as taut as a bowstring, and the current so strong she pulled upon her anchor. All round the hull, in the blackness, the rippling current bubbled and chattered like a little mountain stream. One cut with my sea-gully and the *Hispaniola* would go humming down the tide.

So far so good, but it next occurred to my recollection that a taut hawser, suddenly cut, is a thing as dangerous as a kicking horse. Ten to one, if I were so foolhardy as to cut the *Hispaniola* from her anchor, I and the coracle would be knocked clean out of the water.

This brought me to a full stop, and if fortune had not again particularly favoured me, I should have had to abandon my design. But the light airs which had begun blowing from the south-east and south had hauled round after nightfall into the south-west. Just while I was meditating, a puff came, caught the *Hispaniola*, and forced her up into the current; and to my great joy, I felt the hawser slacken in my grasp, and the hand by which I held it dip for a second under water.

With that I made my mind up, took out my gully, opened it with my teeth, and cut one strand after another, till the vessel swung only by two. Then I lay quiet, waiting to sever these last when the strain should be once more lightened by a breath of wind.

All this time I had heard the sound of loud voices from the cabin, but to say truth, my mind had been so entirely taken up with other thoughts that I had scarcely given ear. Now, however, when I had nothing else to do, I began to pay more heed.

One I recognized for the coxswain's, Israel Hands, that had been Flint's gunner in former days. The other was, of course, my friend of the red night-cap. Both men were plainly the worse of drink, and they were still drinking, for even while I was listening, one of them, with a drunken cry, opened the stern window and threw out something, which I divined to be an empty bottle. But they were not only tipsy; it was plain that they were furiously angry. Oaths flew like hailstones, and every now and then there came forth such an explosion as I thought was sure to end in blows. But each time the quarrel passed off and the voices grumbled lower for a while, until the next crisis came and in its turn passed away without result.

On shore, I could see the glow of the great camp-fire burning warmly through the shore-side trees. Someone was singing, a dull, old, droning sailor's song, with a droop and a quaver at the end of every verse, and seemingly no end to it at all but the patience of the singer. I had heard it on the voyage more than once and remembered these words:

"But one man of her crew alive,

What put to sea with seventy-five."

And I thought it was a ditty rather too dolefully appropriate for a company that had met such cruel losses in the morning. But, indeed, from what I saw, all these buccaneers were as callous as the sea they sailed on.

At last the breeze came; the schooner sidled and drew nearer in the dark; I felt the hawser slacken once more, and with a good, tough effort, cut the last fibres through.

The breeze had but little action on the coracle, and I was almost instantly swept against the bows of the *Hispaniola*. At the same time, the schooner began to turn upon her heel, spinning slowly, end for end, across the current.

I wrought like a fiend, for I expected every moment to be swamped; and since I found I could not push the coracle directly off, I now shoved straight astern. At length I was clear of my dangerous neighbour, and just as I gave the last impulsion, my hands came across a light cord that was trailing overboard across the stern bulwarks. Instantly I grasped it.

Why I should have done so I can hardly say. It was at first mere instinct, but once I had it in my hands and found it fast, curiosity began to get the upper hand, and I determined I should have one look through the cabin window.

I pulled in hand over hand on the cord, and when I judged myself near enough, rose at infinite risk to about half my height and thus commanded the roof and a slice of the interior of the cabin.

By this time the schooner and her little consort were gliding pretty swiftly through the water; indeed, we had already fetched up level with the camp-fire. The ship was talking, as sailors say, loudly, treading the innumerable ripples with an incessant weltering splash; and until I got my eye above the window-sill I could not comprehend why the watchmen had taken no alarm. One glance, however, was sufficient; and it was only one glance that I durst take from that unsteady skiff. It showed me Hands and his companion locked together in deadly wrestle, each with a hand upon the other's throat.

I dropped upon the thwart again, none too soon, for I was near overboard. I could see nothing for the moment but these two furious, encrimsoned faces swaying together under the smoky lamp, and I shut my eyes to let them grow once more familiar with the darkness.

The endless ballad had come to an end at last, and the whole diminished company about the camp-fire had broken into the chorus I had heard so often:

"Fifteen men on the dead man's chest—

Yo-ho-ho, and a bottle of rum!

Drink and the devil had done for the rest—

Yo-ho-ho, and a bottle of rum!"

I was just thinking how busy drink and the devil were at that very moment in the cabin of the *Hispaniola*, when I was surprised by a sudden lurch of the coracle. At the same moment, she yawed sharply and seemed to change her course. The speed in the meantime had strangely increased.

I opened my eyes at once. All round me were little ripples, combing over with a sharp, bristling sound and slightly phosphorescent. The *Hispaniola* herself, a few yards in whose wake I was still being whirled along, seemed to stagger in her course, and I saw her spars toss a little against the blackness of the night; nay, as I looked longer, I made sure she also was wheeling to the southward.

I glanced over my shoulder, and my heart jumped against my ribs. There, right behind me, was the glow of the camp-fire. The current had turned at right angles, sweeping round along with it the tall schooner and the little dancing coracle; ever quickening, ever bubbling higher, ever muttering louder, it went spinning through the narrows for the open sea.

Suddenly the schooner in front of me gave a violent yaw, turning, perhaps, through twenty degrees; and almost at the same moment one shout followed another from on board; I could hear feet pounding on the companion ladder and I knew that the two drunkards had at last been interrupted in their quarrel and awakened to a sense of their disaster.

I lay down flat in the bottom of that wretched skiff and devoutly recommended my spirit to its Maker. At the end of the straits, I made sure we must fall into some bar of raging breakers, where all my troubles would be ended speedily; and though I could, perhaps, bear to die, I could not bear to look upon my fate as it approached.

So I must have lain for hours, continually beaten to and fro upon the billows, now and again wetted with flying sprays, and never ceasing to expect death at the next plunge. Gradually weariness grew upon me; a numbness, an occasional stupor, fell upon my mind even in the midst of my terrors, until sleep at last supervened and in my sea-tossed coracle I lay and dreamed of home and the old Admiral Benbow.

The Cruise of the Coracle

It was broad day when I awoke and found myself tossing at the south-west end of Treasure Island. The sun was up but was still hid from me behind the great bulk of the Spy-glass, which on this side descended almost to the sea in formidable cliffs.

Haulbowline Head and Mizzen-mast Hill were at my elbow, the hill bare and dark, the head bound with cliffs forty or fifty feet high and fringed with great masses of fallen rock. I was scarce a quarter of a mile to seaward, and it was my first thought to paddle in and land.

That notion was soon given over. Among the fallen rocks the breakers spouted and bellowed; loud reverberations, heavy sprays flying and falling, succeeded one another from second to second; and I saw myself, if I ventured nearer, dashed to death upon the rough shore or spending my strength in vain to scale the beetling crags.

Nor was that all, for crawling together on flat tables of rock or letting themselves drop into the sea with loud reports I beheld huge slimy monsters—soft snails, as it were, of incredible bigness—two or three score of them together, making the rocks to echo with their barkings.

I have understood since that they were sea lions, and entirely harmless. But the look of them, added to the difficulty of the shore and the high running of the surf, was more than enough to disgust me of that landing-place. I felt willing rather to starve at sea than to confront such perils.

In the meantime I had a better chance, as I supposed, before me. North of Haulbowline Head, the land runs in a long way, leaving at low tide a long stretch of yellow sand. To the north of that, again, there comes another cape—Cape of the Woods, as it was marked upon the chart—buried in tall green pines, which descended to the margin of the sea.

I remembered what Silver had said about the current that sets northward along the whole west coast of Treasure Island, and seeing from my position that I was already under its influence, I preferred to leave Haulbowline Head behind me and reserve my strength for an attempt to land upon the kindlier-looking Cape of the Woods.

There was a great, smooth swell upon the sea. The wind blowing steady and gentle from the south, there was no contrariety between that and the current, and the billows rose and fell unbroken.

Had it been otherwise, I must long ago have perished; but as it was, it is surprising how easily and securely my little and light boat could ride. Often, as I still lay at the bottom and kept no more than an eye above the gunwale, I would see a big blue summit heaving close above me; yet the coracle would but bounce a little, dance as if on springs, and subside on the other side into the trough as lightly as a bird.

I began after a little to grow very bold and sat up to try my skill at paddling. But even a small change in the disposition of the weight will produce violent changes in the behaviour of a coracle. And I had hardly moved before the boat, giving up at once her gentle dancing movement, ran straight down a slope of water so steep that it made me giddy, and struck her nose, with a spout of spray, deep into the side of the next wave.

I was drenched and terrified, and fell instantly back into my old position, whereupon the coracle seemed to find her head again and led me as softly as before among the billows. It was plain she was not to be interfered with, and at that rate, since I could in no way influence her course, what hope had I left of reaching land?

I began to be horribly frightened, but I kept my head, for all that. First, moving with all care, I gradually baled out the coracle with my sea-cap; then, getting my eye once more above the gunwale, I set myself to study how it was she managed to slip so quietly through the rollers.

I found each wave, instead of the big, smooth glossy mountain it looks from shore or from a vessel's deck, was for all the world like any range of hills on dry land, full of peaks and smooth places and valleys. The coracle, left to herself, turning from side to side, threaded, so to speak, her way through these lower parts and avoided the steep slopes and higher, toppling summits of the wave.

"Well, now," thought I to myself, "it is plain I must lie where I am and not disturb the balance; but it is plain also that I can put the paddle over the side and from time to time, in smooth places, give her a shove or two towards land." No sooner thought upon than done. There I lay on my elbows in the most trying attitude, and every now and again gave a weak stroke or two to turn her head to shore.

It was very tiring and slow work, yet I did visibly gain ground; and as we drew near the Cape of the Woods, though I saw I must infallibly miss that point, I had still made some hundred yards of easting. I was, indeed, close in. I could see the cool green tree-tops swaying together in the breeze, and I felt sure I should make the next promontory without fail.

It was high time, for I now began to be tortured with thirst. The glow of the sun from above, its thousandfold reflection from the waves, the sea-water that fell and dried upon me, caking my very lips with salt, combined to make my throat burn and my brain ache. The sight of the trees so near at hand had almost made me sick with longing, but the current had soon carried me past the point, and as the next reach of sea opened out, I beheld a sight that changed the nature of my thoughts.

Right in front of me, not half a mile away, I beheld the *Hispaniola* under sail. I made sure, of course, that I should be taken; but I was so distressed for want of water that I scarce knew whether to be glad or sorry at the thought, and long before I had come to a conclusion, surprise had taken entire possession of my mind and I could do nothing but stare and wonder.

The *Hispaniola* was under her main-sail and two jibs, and the beautiful white canvas shone in the sun like snow or silver. When I first sighted her, all her sails were drawing; she was lying a course about north-west, and I presumed the men on board were going round the island on their way back to the anchorage. Presently she began to fetch more and more to the westward, so that I thought they had sighted me and were going about in chase. At last, however, she fell right into the wind's eye, was taken dead aback, and stood there awhile helpless, with her sails shivering.

"Clumsy fellows," said I; "they must still be drunk as owls." And I thought how Captain Smollett would have set them skipping.

Meanwhile the schooner gradually fell off and filled again upon another tack, sailed swiftly for a minute or so, and brought up once more dead in the wind's eye. Again and again was this repeated. To and fro, up and down, north, south, east, and west, the *Hispaniola* sailed by swoops and dashes, and at each repetition ended as she had begun, with idly flapping canvas. It became plain to me that nobody was steering. And if so, where were the men? Either they were dead drunk or had deserted her, I thought, and perhaps if I could get on board I might return the vessel to her captain.

The current was bearing coracle and schooner southward at an equal rate. As for the latter's sailing, it was so wild and intermittent, and she hung each time so long in irons, that she certainly gained nothing, if she did not even lose. If only I dared to sit up and paddle, I made sure that I could overhaul her. The scheme had an air of adventure that inspired me, and the thought of the water breaker beside the fore companion doubled my growing courage.

Up I got, was welcomed almost instantly by another cloud of spray, but this time stuck to my purpose and set myself, with all my strength and caution, to paddle after the unsteered*Hispaniola*. Once I shipped a sea so heavy that I had to stop and bail, with my heart fluttering like a bird, but gradually I got into the way of the thing and guided my coracle among the waves, with only now and then a blow upon her bows and a dash of foam in my face.

I was now gaining rapidly on the schooner; I could see the brass glisten on the tiller as it banged about, and still no soul appeared upon her decks. I could not choose but suppose she was deserted. If not, the men were lying drunk below, where I might batten them down, perhaps, and do what I chose with the ship.

For some time she had been doing the worse thing possible for me—standing still. She headed nearly due south, yawing, of course, all the time. Each time she fell off, her sails partly filled, and these brought her in a moment right to the wind again. I have said this was the worst thing possible for me, for helpless as she looked in this situation, with the canvas cracking like cannon and the blocks trundling and banging on the deck, she still continued to run away from me, not only with the speed of the current, but by the whole amount of her leeway, which was naturally great.

But now, at last, I had my chance. The breeze fell for some seconds, very low, and the current gradually turning her, the *Hispaniola* revolved slowly round her centre and at last presented me her stern, with the cabin window still gaping open and the lamp over the table still burning on into the day. The main-sail hung drooped like a banner. She was stock-still but for the current.

For the last little while I had even lost, but now redoubling my efforts, I began once more to overhaul the chase.

I was not a hundred yards from her when the wind came again in a clap; she filled on the port tack and was off again, stooping and skimming like a swallow.

My first impulse was one of despair, but my second was towards joy. Round she came, till she was broadside on to me—round still till she had covered a half and then two thirds and then three quarters of the distance that separated us. I could see the waves boiling white under her forefoot. Immensely tall she looked to me from my low station in the coracle.

And then, of a sudden, I began to comprehend. I had scarce time to think—scarce time to act and save myself. I was on the summit of one swell when the schooner came stooping over the next. The bowsprit was over my head. I sprang to my feet and leaped, stamping the coracle under water. With one hand I caught the jib-boom, while my foot was lodged between the stay and the brace; and as I still clung there panting, a dull blow told me that the schooner had charged down upon and struck the coracle and that I was left without retreat on the *Hispaniola*.

Lesson 115

1. Read chapters 25 and 26.
2. Tell someone what is happening in the book.

I Strike the Jolly Roger

I had scarce gained a position on the bowsprit when the flying jib flapped and filled upon the other tack, with a report like a gun. The schooner trembled to her keel under the reverse, but next moment, the other sails still drawing, the jib flapped back again and hung idle.

This had nearly tossed me off into the sea; and now I lost no time, crawled back along the bowsprit, and tumbled head foremost on the deck.

I was on the lee side of the forecastle, and the mainsail, which was still drawing, concealed from me a certain portion of the after-deck. Not a soul was to be seen. The planks, which had not been swabbed since the mutiny, bore the print of many feet, and an empty bottle, broken by the neck, tumbled to and fro like a live thing in the scuppers.

Suddenly the *Hispaniola* came right into the wind. The jibs behind me cracked aloud, the rudder slammed to, the whole ship gave a sickening heave and shudder, and at the same moment the main-boom swung inboard, the sheet groaning in the blocks, and showed me the lee after-deck.

There were the two watchmen, sure enough: red-cap on his back, as stiff as a handspike, with his arms stretched out like those of a crucifix and his teeth showing through his open lips; Israel Hands propped against the bulwarks, his chin on his chest, his hands lying open before him on the deck, his face as white, under its tan, as a tallow candle.

For a while the ship kept bucking and sidling like a vicious horse, the sails filling, now on one tack, now on another, and the boom swinging to and fro till the mast groaned aloud under the strain. Now and again too there would come a cloud of light sprays over the bulwark and a heavy blow of the ship's bows against the swell; so much heavier weather was made of it by this great rigged ship than by my home-made, lop-sided coracle, now gone to the bottom of the sea.

At every jump of the schooner, red-cap slipped to and fro, but—what was ghastly to behold—neither his attitude nor his fixed teeth-disclosing grin was anyway disturbed by this rough usage. At every jump too, Hands appeared still more to sink into himself and settle down upon the deck, his feet sliding ever the farther out, and the whole body canting towards the stern, so that his face became, little by little, hid from me; and at last I could see nothing beyond his ear and the frayed ringlet of one whisker.

At the same time, I observed, around both of them, splashes of dark blood upon the planks and began to feel sure that they had killed each other in their drunken wrath.

While I was thus looking and wondering, in a calm moment, when the ship was still, Israel Hands turned partly round and with a low moan writhed himself back to the position in which I had seen him first. The moan, which told of pain and deadly weakness, and the way in which his jaw hung open went right to my heart. But when I remembered the talk I had overheard from the apple barrel, all pity left me.

I walked aft until I reached the main-mast.

"Come aboard, Mr. Hands," I said ironically.

He rolled his eyes round heavily, but he was too far gone to express surprise. All he could do was to utter one word, "Brandy."

It occurred to me there was no time to lose, and dodging the boom as it once more lurched across the deck, I slipped aft and down the companion stairs into the cabin.

It was such a scene of confusion as you can hardly fancy. All the lockfast places had been broken open in quest of the chart. The floor was thick with mud where ruffians had sat down to drink or consult after wading in the marshes round their camp. The bulkheads, all painted in clear white and beaded round with gilt, bore a pattern of dirty hands. Dozens of empty bottles clinked together in corners to the rolling of the ship. One of the doctor's medical books lay open on the table, half of the leaves gutted out, I suppose, for pipelights. In the midst of all this the lamp still cast a smoky glow, obscure and brown as umber.

I went into the cellar; all the barrels were gone, and of the bottles a most surprising number had been drunk out and thrown away. Certainly, since the mutiny began, not a man of them could ever have been sober.

Foraging about, I found a bottle with some brandy left, for Hands; and for myself I routed out some biscuit, some pickled fruits, a great bunch of raisins, and a piece of cheese. With these I came on deck, put down my own stock behind the rudder head and well out of the coxswain's reach, went forward to the water-breaker, and had a good deep drink of water, and then, and not till then, gave Hands the brandy.

He must have drunk a gill before he took the bottle from his mouth.

"Aye," said he, "by thunder, but I wanted some o' that!"

I had sat down already in my own corner and begun to eat.

"Much hurt?" I asked him.

He grunted, or rather, I might say, he barked.

"If that doctor was aboard," he said, "I'd be right enough in a couple of turns, but I don't have no manner of luck, you see, and that's what's the matter with me. As for that swab, he's good and dead, he is," he added, indicating the man with the red cap. "He warn't no seaman anyhow. And where mought you have come from?"

"Well," said I, "I've come aboard to take possession of this ship, Mr. Hands; and you'll please regard me as your captain until further notice."

He looked at me sourly enough but said nothing. Some of the colour had come back into his cheeks, though he still looked very sick and still continued to slip out and settle down as the ship banged about.

"By the by," I continued, "I can't have these colours, Mr. Hands; and by your leave, I'll strike 'em. Better none than these."

And again dodging the boom, I ran to the colour lines, handed down their cursed black flag, and chucked it overboard.

"God save the king!" said I, waving my cap. "And there's an end to Captain Silver!"

He watched me keenly and slyly, his chin all the while on his breast.

"I reckon," he said at last, "I reckon, Cap'n Hawkins, you'll kind of want to get ashore now. S'pose we talks."

"Why, yes," says I, "with all my heart, Mr. Hands. Say on." And I went back to my meal with a good appetite.

"This man," he began, nodding feebly at the corpse "—O'Brien were his name, a rank Irelander—this man and me got the canvas on her, meaning for to sail her back. Well, *he's* dead now, he is—as dead as bilge; and who's to sail this ship, I don't see. Without I gives you a hint, you ain't that man, as far's I can tell. Now, look here, you gives me food and drink and a old scarf or ankecher to tie my wound up, you do, and I'll tell you how to sail her, and that's about square all round, I take it."

"I'll tell you one thing," says I: "I'm not going back to Captain Kidd's anchorage. I mean to get into North Inlet and beach her quietly there."

"To be sure you did," he cried. "Why, I ain't sich an infernal lubber after all. I can see, can't I? I've tried my fling, I have, and I've lost, and it's you has the wind of me. North Inlet? Why, I haven't no ch'ice, not I! I'd help you sail her up to Execution Dock, by thunder! So I would."

Well, as it seemed to me, there was some sense in this. We struck our bargain on the spot. In three minutes I had the *Hispaniola* sailing easily before the wind along the coast of Treasure Island, with good hopes of turning the northern point ere noon and beating down again as far as North Inlet before high water, when we might beach her safely and wait till the subsiding tide permitted us to land.

Then I lashed the tiller and went below to my own chest, where I got a soft silk handkerchief of my mother's. With this, and with my aid, Hands bound up the great bleeding stab he had received in the thigh, and after he had eaten a little and had a swallow or two more of the brandy, he began to pick up visibly, sat straighter up, spoke louder and clearer, and looked in every way another man.

The breeze served us admirably. We skimmed before it like a bird, the coast of the island flashing by and the view changing every minute. Soon we were past the high lands and bowling beside low, sandy country, sparsely dotted with dwarf pines, and soon we were beyond that again and had turned the corner of the rocky hill that ends the island on the north.

I was greatly elated with my new command, and pleased with the bright, sunshiny weather and these different prospects of the coast. I had now plenty of water and good things to eat, and my conscience, which had smitten me hard for my desertion, was quieted by the great conquest I had made. I should, I think, have had nothing left me to desire but for the eyes of the coxswain as they followed me derisively about the deck and the odd smile that appeared continually on his face. It was a smile that had in it something both of pain and weakness—a haggard old man's smile; but there was, besides that, a grain of derision, a shadow of treachery, in his expression as he craftily watched, and watched, and watched me at my work.

Israel Hands

The wind, serving us to a desire, now hauled into the west. We could run so much the easier from the north-east corner of the island to the mouth of the North Inlet. Only, as we had no power to anchor and dared not beach her till the tide had flowed a good deal farther, time hung on our hands. The coxswain told me how to lay the ship to; after a good many trials I succeeded, and we both sat in silence over another meal.

"Cap'n," said he at length with that same uncomfortable smile, "here's my old shipmate, O'Brien; s'pose you was to heave him overboard. I ain't partic'lar as a rule, and I don't take no blame for settling his hash, but I don't reckon him ornamental now, do you?"

"I'm not strong enough, and I don't like the job; and there he lies, for me," said I.

"This here's an unlucky ship, this *Hispaniola*, Jim," he went on, blinking. "There's a power of men been killed in this *Hispaniola*—a sight o' poor seamen dead and gone since you and me took ship to Bristol. I never seen sich dirty luck, not I. There was this here O'Brien now—he's dead, ain't he? Well now, I'm no scholar, and you're a lad as can read and figure, and to put it straight, do you take it as a dead man is dead for good, or do he come alive again?"

"You can kill the body, Mr. Hands, but not the spirit; you must know that already," I replied. "O'Brien there is in another world, and may be watching us."

"Ah!" says he. "Well, that's unfort'nate—appears as if killing parties was a waste of time. Howsomever, sperrits don't reckon for much, by what I've seen. I'll chance it with the sperrits, Jim. And now, you've spoke up free, and I'll take it kind if you'd step down into that there cabin and get me a—well, a—shiver my timbers! I can't hit the name on 't; well, you get me a bottle of wine, Jim—this here brandy's too strong for my head."

Now, the coxswain's hesitation seemed to be unnatural, and as for the notion of his preferring wine to brandy, I entirely disbelieved it. The whole story was a pretext. He wanted me to leave the deck—so much was plain; but with what purpose I could in no way imagine. His eyes never met mine; they kept wandering to and fro, up and down, now with a look to the sky, now with a flitting glance upon the dead O'Brien. All the time he kept smiling and putting his tongue out in the most guilty, embarrassed manner, so that a child could have told that he was bent on some deception. I was prompt with my answer, however, for I saw where my advantage lay and that with a fellow so densely stupid I could easily conceal my suspicions to the end.

"Some wine?" I said. "Far better. Will you have white or red?"

"Well, I reckon it's about the blessed same to me, shipmate," he replied; "so it's strong, and plenty of it, what's the odds?"

"All right," I answered. "I'll bring you port, Mr. Hands. But I'll have to dig for it."

With that I scuttled down the companion with all the noise I could, slipped off my shoes, ran quietly along the sparred gallery, mounted the forecastle ladder, and popped my head out of the fore companion. I knew he would not expect to see me there, yet I took every precaution possible, and certainly the worst of my suspicions proved too true.

He had risen from his position to his hands and knees, and though his leg obviously hurt him pretty sharply when he moved—for I could hear him stifle a groan—yet it was at a good, rattling rate that he trailed himself across the deck. In half a minute he had reached the port scuppers and picked, out of a coil of rope, a long knife, or rather a short dirk, discoloured to the hilt with blood. He looked upon it for a moment, thrusting forth his under jaw, tried the point upon his hand, and then, hastily concealing it in the bosom of his jacket, trundled back again into his old place against the bulwark.

This was all that I required to know. Israel could move about, he was now armed, and if he had been at so much trouble to get rid of me, it was plain that I was meant to be the victim. What he would do afterwards—whether he would try to crawl right across the island from North Inlet to the camp among the swamps or whether he would fire Long Tom, trusting that his own comrades might come first to help him—was, of course, more than I could say.

Yet I felt sure that I could trust him in one point, since in that our interests jumped together, and that was in the disposition of the schooner. We both desired to have her stranded safe enough, in a sheltered place, and so that, when the time came, she could be got off again with as little labour and danger as might be; and until that was done I considered that my life would certainly be spared.

While I was thus turning the business over in my mind, I had not been idle with my body. I had stolen back to the cabin, slipped once more into my shoes, and laid my hand at random on a bottle of wine, and now, with this for an excuse, I made my reappearance on the deck.

Hands lay as I had left him, all fallen together in a bundle and with his eyelids lowered as though he were too weak to bear the light. He looked up, however, at my coming, knocked the neck off the bottle like a man who had done the same thing often, and took a good swig, with his favourite toast of "Here's luck!" Then he lay quiet for a little, and then, pulling out a stick of tobacco, begged me to cut him a quid.

"Cut me a junk o' that," says he, "for I haven't no knife and hardly strength enough, so be as I had. Ah, Jim, Jim, I reckon I've missed stays! Cut me a quid, as'll likely be the last, lad, for I'm for my long home, and no mistake."

"Well," said I, "I'll cut you some tobacco, but if I was you and thought myself so badly, I would go to my prayers like a Christian man."

"Why?" said he. "Now, you tell me why."

"Why?" I cried. "You were asking me just now about the dead. You've broken your trust; you've lived in sin and lies and blood; there's a man you killed lying at your feet this moment, and you ask me why! For God's mercy, Mr. Hands, that's why."

I spoke with a little heat, thinking of the bloody dirk he had hidden in his pocket and designed, in his ill thoughts, to end me with. He, for his part, took a great draught of the wine and spoke with the most unusual solemnity.

"For thirty years," he said, "I've sailed the seas and seen good and bad, better and worse, fair weather and foul, provisions running out, knives going, and what not. Well, now I tell you, I never seen good come o' goodness yet. Him as strikes first is my fancy; dead men don't bite; them's my views—amen, so be it. And now, you look here," he added, suddenly changing his tone, "we've had about enough of this foolery. The tide's made good enough by now. You just take my orders, Cap'n Hawkins, and we'll sail slap in and be done with it."

All told, we had scarce two miles to run; but the navigation was delicate, the entrance to this northern anchorage was not only narrow and shoal, but lay east and west, so that the schooner must be nicely handled to be got in. I think I was a good, prompt subaltern, and I am very sure that Hands was an excellent pilot, for we went about and about and dodged in, shaving the banks, with a certainty and a neatness that were a pleasure to behold.

Scarcely had we passed the heads before the land closed around us. The shores of North Inlet were as thickly wooded as those of the southern anchorage, but the space was longer and narrower and more like, what in truth it was, the estuary of a river. Right before us, at the southern end, we saw the wreck of a ship in the last stages of dilapidation. It had been a great vessel of three masts but had lain so long exposed to the injuries of the weather that it was hung about with great webs of dripping seaweed, and on the deck of it shore bushes had taken root and now flourished thick with flowers. It was a sad sight, but it showed us that the anchorage was calm.

"Now," said Hands, "look there; there's a pet bit for to beach a ship in. Fine flat sand, never a cat's paw, trees all around of it, and flowers a-blowing like a garding on that old ship."

"And once beached," I inquired, "how shall we get her off again?"

"Why, so," he replied: "you take a line ashore there on the other side at low water, take a turn about one of them big pines; bring it back, take a turn around the capstan, and lie to for the tide. Come high water, all hands take a pull upon the line, and off she comes as sweet as natur'. And now, boy, you stand by. We're near the bit now, and she's too much way on her. Starboard a little—so—steady—starboard—larboard a little—steady—steady!"

So he issued his commands, which I breathlessly obeyed, till, all of a sudden, he cried, "Now, my hearty, luff!" And I put the helm hard up, and the *Hispaniola* swung round rapidly and ran stem on for the low, wooded shore.

The excitement of these last manoeuvres had somewhat interfered with the watch I had kept hitherto, sharply enough, upon the coxswain. Even then I was still so much interested, waiting for the ship to touch, that I had quite forgot the peril that hung over my head and stood craning over the starboard bulwarks and watching the ripples spreading wide before the bows. I might have fallen without a struggle for my life had not a sudden disquietude seized upon me and made me turn my head. Perhaps I had heard a creak or seen his shadow moving with the tail of my eye; perhaps it was an instinct like a cat's; but, sure enough, when I looked round, there was Hands, already half-way towards me, with the dirk in his right hand.

We must both have cried out aloud when our eyes met, but while mine was the shrill cry of terror, his was a roar of fury like a charging bully's. At the same instant, he threw himself forward and I leapt sideways towards the bows. As I did so, I let go of the tiller, which sprang sharp to leeward, and I think this saved my life, for it struck Hands across the chest and stopped him, for the moment, dead.

Before he could recover, I was safe out of the corner where he had me trapped, with all the deck to dodge about. Just forward of the main-mast I stopped, drew a pistol from my pocket, took a cool aim, though he had already turned and was once more coming directly after me, and drew the trigger. The hammer fell, but there followed neither flash nor sound; the priming was useless with sea-water. I cursed myself for my neglect. Why had not I, long before, reprimed and reloaded my only weapons? Then I should not have been as now, a mere fleeing sheep before this butcher.

Wounded as he was, it was wonderful how fast he could move, his grizzled hair tumbling over his face, and his face itself as red as a red ensign with his haste and fury. I had no time to try my other pistol, nor indeed much inclination, for I was sure it would be useless. One thing I saw plainly: I must not simply retreat before him, or he would speedily hold me boxed into the bows, as a moment since he had so nearly boxed me in the stern. Once so caught, and nine or ten inches of the blood-stained dirk would be my last experience on this side of eternity. I placed my palms against the main-mast, which was of a goodish bigness, and waited, every nerve upon the stretch.

Seeing that I meant to dodge, he also paused; and a moment or two passed in feints on his part and corresponding movements upon mine. It was such a game as I had often played at home about the rocks of Black Hill Cove, but never before, you may be sure, with such a wildly beating heart as now. Still, as I say, it was a boy's game, and I thought I could hold my own at it against an elderly seaman with a wounded thigh. Indeed my courage had begun to rise so high that I allowed myself a few darting thoughts on what would be the end of the affair, and while I saw certainly that I could spin it out for long, I saw no hope of any ultimate escape.

Well, while things stood thus, suddenly the *Hispaniola* struck, staggered, ground for an instant in the sand, and then, swift as a blow, canted over to the port side till the deck stood at an angle of forty-five degrees and about a puncheon of water splashed into the scupper holes and lay, in a pool, between the deck and bulwark.

We were both of us capsized in a second, and both of us rolled, almost together, into the scuppers, the dead red-cap, with his arms still spread out, tumbling stiffly after us. So near were we, indeed, that my head came against the coxswain's foot with a crack that made my teeth rattle. Blow and all, I was the first afoot again, for Hands had got involved with the dead body. The sudden canting of the ship had made the deck no place for running on; I had to find some new way of escape, and that upon the instant, for my foe was almost touching me. Quick as thought,

I sprang into the mizzen shrouds, rattled up hand over hand, and did not draw a breath till I was seated on the cross-trees.

I had been saved by being prompt; the dirk had struck not half a foot below me as I pursued my upward flight; and there stood Israel Hands with his mouth open and his face upturned to mine, a perfect statue of surprise and disappointment.

Now that I had a moment to myself, I lost no time in changing the priming of my pistol, and then, having one ready for service, and to make assurance doubly sure, I proceeded to draw the load of the other and recharge it afresh from the beginning.

My new employment struck Hands all of a heap; he began to see the dice going against him, and after an obvious hesitation, he also hauled himself heavily into the shrouds, and with the dirk in his teeth, began slowly and painfully to mount. It cost him no end of time and groans to haul his wounded leg behind him, and I had quietly finished my arrangements before he was much more than a third of the way up. Then, with a pistol in either hand, I addressed him.

"One more step, Mr. Hands," said I, "and I'll blow your brains out! Dead men don't bite, you know," I added with a chuckle.

He stopped instantly. I could see by the working of his face that he was trying to think, and the process was so slow and laborious that, in my new-found security, I laughed aloud. At last, with a swallow or two, he spoke, his face still wearing the same expression of extreme perplexity. In order to speak he had to take the dagger from his mouth, but in all else he remained unmoved.

"Jim," says he, "I reckon we're fouled, you and me, and we'll have to sign articles. I'd have had you but for that there lurch, but I don't have no luck, not I; and I reckon I'll have to strike, which comes hard, you see, for a master mariner to a ship's younker like you, Jim."

I was drinking in his words and smiling away, as conceited as a cock upon a wall, when, all in a breath, back went his right hand over his shoulder. Something sang like an arrow through the air; I felt a blow and then a sharp pang, and there I was pinned by the shoulder to the mast. In the horrid pain and surprise of the moment—I scarce can say it was by my own volition, and I am sure it was without a conscious aim—both my pistols went off, and both escaped out of my hands. They did not fall alone; with a choked cry, the coxswain loosed his grasp upon the shrouds and plunged head first into the water.

Lesson 116

1. Read chapters 27 and 28.
2. The chapter is called, "Pieces of Eight." Where does that come into the chapter? Do we know what it means? (Answers)
3. "Pieces of Eight" is a bit of **foreshadowing**. It's throwing us a clue about something to come to make us interested to find out.

4. Before, Stevenson changed narrators to give us another **point of view**. When Silver tells a story about meeting with the doctor, we hear the story from his perspective, from his **point of view**.
5. Tell someone what is happening the book.
6. Complete the analogies. Write your answers on a separate piece of paper. (Answers)
    - goose:geese::mouse:___________
    - student:class:(soccer)player:___________
    - thankful:thanks::thoughtful:___________
    - frigid:balmy::boiling:___________
    - beef:meat::carrot:___________

"Pieces of Eight"

Owing to the cant of the vessel, the masts hung far out over the water, and from my perch on the cross-trees I had nothing below me but the surface of the bay. Hands, who was not so far up, was in consequence nearer to the ship and fell between me and the bulwarks. He rose once to the surface in a lather of foam and blood and then sank again for good. As the water settled, I could see him lying huddled together on the clean, bright sand in the shadow of the vessel's sides. A fish or two whipped past his body. Sometimes, by the quivering of the water, he appeared to move a little, as if he were trying to rise. But he was dead enough, for all that, being both shot and drowned, and was food for fish in the very place where he had designed my slaughter.

I was no sooner certain of this than I began to feel sick, faint, and terrified. The hot blood was running over my back and chest. The dirk, where it had pinned my shoulder to the mast, seemed to burn like a hot iron; yet it was not so much these real sufferings that distressed me, for these, it seemed to me, I could bear without a murmur; it was the horror I had upon my mind of falling from the cross-trees into that still green water, beside the body of the coxswain.

I clung with both hands till my nails ached, and I shut my eyes as if to cover up the peril. Gradually my mind came back again, my pulses quieted down to a more natural time, and I was once more in possession of myself.

It was my first thought to pluck forth the dirk, but either it stuck too hard or my nerve failed me, and I desisted with a violent shudder. Oddly enough, that very shudder did the business. The knife, in fact, had come the nearest in the world to missing me altogether; it held me by a mere pinch of skin, and this the shudder tore away. The blood ran down the faster, to be sure, but I was my own master again and only tacked to the mast by my coat and shirt.

These last I broke through with a sudden jerk, and then regained the deck by the starboard shrouds. For nothing in the world would I have again ventured, shaken as I was, upon the overhanging port shrouds from which Israel had so lately fallen.

I went below and did what I could for my wound; it pained me a good deal and still bled freely, but it was neither deep nor dangerous, nor did it greatly gall me when I used my arm. Then I looked around me, and as the ship was now, in a sense, my own, I began to think of clearing it from its last passenger—the dead man, O'Brien.

He had pitched, as I have said, against the bulwarks, where he lay like some horrible, ungainly sort of puppet, life-size, indeed, but how different from life's colour or life's comeliness! In that position I could easily have my way with him, and as the habit of tragical adventures had worn off almost all my terror for the dead, I took him by the waist as if he had been a sack of bran and with one good heave, tumbled him overboard. He went in with a sounding plunge; the red cap came off and remained floating on the surface; and as soon as the splash subsided, I could see him and Israel lying side by side, both wavering with the tremulous movement of the water. O'Brien, though still quite a young man, was very bald. There he lay, with that bald head across the knees of the man who had killed him and the quick fishes steering to and fro over both.

I was now alone upon the ship; the tide had just turned. The sun was within so few degrees of setting that already the shadow of the pines upon the western shore began to reach right across the anchorage and fall in patterns on the deck. The evening breeze had sprung up, and though it was well warded off by the hill with the two peaks upon the east, the cordage had begun to sing a little softly to itself and the idle sails to rattle to and fro.

I began to see a danger to the ship. The jibs I speedily doused and brought tumbling to the deck, but the main-sail was a harder matter. Of course, when the schooner canted over, the boom had swung out-board, and the cap of it and a foot or two of sail hung even under water. I thought this made it still more dangerous; yet the strain was so heavy that I half feared to meddle. At last I got my knife and cut the halyards. The peak dropped instantly, a great belly of loose canvas floated broad upon the water, and since, pull as I liked, I could not budge the downhall, that was the extent of what I could accomplish. For the rest, the *Hispaniola* must trust to luck, like myself.

By this time the whole anchorage had fallen into shadow—the last rays, I remember, falling through a glade of the wood and shining bright as jewels on the flowery mantle of the wreck. It began to be chill; the tide was rapidly fleeting seaward, the schooner settling more and more on her beam-ends.

I scrambled forward and looked over. It seemed shallow enough, and holding the cut hawser in both hands for a last security, I let myself drop softly overboard. The water scarcely reached my waist; the sand was firm and covered with ripple marks, and I waded ashore in great spirits, leaving the *Hispaniola* on her side, with her main-sail trailing wide upon the surface of the bay. About the same time, the sun went fairly down and the breeze whistled low in the dusk among the tossing pines.

At least, and at last, I was off the sea, nor had I returned thence empty-handed. There lay the schooner, clear at last from buccaneers and ready for our own men to board and get to sea again. I had nothing nearer my fancy than to get home to the stockade and boast of my achievements. Possibly I might be blamed a bit for my truantry, but the recapture of the *Hispaniola*was a clenching answer, and I hoped that even Captain Smollett would confess I had not lost my time.

So thinking, and in famous spirits, I began to set my face homeward for the block house and my companions. I remembered that the most easterly of the rivers which drain into Captain Kidd's anchorage ran from the two-peaked hill upon my left, and I bent my course in that direction that I might pass the stream while it was small. The wood was pretty open, and keeping along the lower spurs, I had soon turned the corner of that hill, and not long after waded to the mid-calf across the watercourse.

This brought me near to where I had encountered Ben Gunn, the maroon; and I walked more circumspectly, keeping an eye on every side. The dusk had come nigh hand completely, and as I opened out the cleft between the two peaks, I became aware of a wavering glow against the sky, where, as I judged, the man of the island was cooking his supper before a roaring fire. And yet I wondered, in my heart, that he should show himself so careless. For if I could see this radiance, might it not reach the eyes of Silver himself where he camped upon the shore among the marshes?

Gradually the night fell blacker; it was all I could do to guide myself even roughly towards my destination; the double hill behind me and the Spy-glass on my right hand loomed faint and fainter; the stars were few and pale; and in the low ground where I wandered I kept tripping among bushes and rolling into sandy pits.

Suddenly a kind of brightness fell about me. I looked up; a pale glimmer of moonbeams had alighted on the summit of the Spy-glass, and soon after I saw something broad and silvery moving low down behind the trees, and knew the moon had risen.

With this to help me, I passed rapidly over what remained to me of my journey, and sometimes walking, sometimes running, impatiently drew near to the stockade. Yet, as I began to thread the grove that lies before it, I was not so thoughtless but that I slacked my pace and went a trifle warily. It would have been a poor end of my adventures to get shot down by my own party in mistake.

The moon was climbing higher and higher, its light began to fall here and there in masses through the more open districts of the wood, and right in front of me a glow of a different colour appeared among the trees. It was red and hot, and now and again it was a little darkened—as it were, the embers of a bonfire smouldering.

For the life of me I could not think what it might be.

At last I came right down upon the borders of the clearing. The western end was already steeped in moonshine; the rest, and the block house itself, still lay in a black shadow chequered with long silvery streaks of light. On the other side of the house an immense fire had burned itself into clear embers and shed a steady, red reverberation, contrasted strongly with the mellow paleness of the moon. There was not a soul stirring nor a sound beside the noises of the breeze.

I stopped, with much wonder in my heart, and perhaps a little terror also. It had not been our way to build great fires; we were, indeed, by the captain's orders, somewhat niggardly of firewood, and I began to fear that something had gone wrong while I was absent.

I stole round by the eastern end, keeping close in shadow, and at a convenient place, where the darkness was thickest, crossed the palisade.

To make assurance surer, I got upon my hands and knees and crawled, without a sound, towards the corner of the house. As I drew nearer, my heart was suddenly and greatly lightened. It is not a pleasant noise in itself, and I have often complained of it at other times, but just then it was like music to hear my friends snoring together so loud and peaceful in their sleep. The sea-cry of the watch, that beautiful "All's well," never fell more reassuringly on my ear.

In the meantime, there was no doubt of one thing; they kept an infamous bad watch. If it had been Silver and his lads that were now creeping in on them, not a soul would have seen daybreak. That was what it was, thought I, to have the captain wounded; and again I blamed myself sharply for leaving them in that danger with so few to mount guard.

By this time I had got to the door and stood up. All was dark within, so that I could distinguish nothing by the eye. As for sounds, there was the steady drone of the snorers and a small occasional noise, a flickering or pecking that I could in no way account for.

With my arms before me I walked steadily in. I should lie down in my own place (I thought with a silent chuckle) and enjoy their faces when they found me in the morning.

My foot struck something yielding—it was a sleeper's leg; and he turned and groaned, but without awaking.

And then, all of a sudden, a shrill voice broke forth out of the darkness:

"Pieces of eight! Pieces of eight! Pieces of eight! Pieces of eight! Pieces of eight!" and so forth, without pause or change, like the clacking of a tiny mill.

Silver's green parrot, Captain Flint! It was she whom I had heard pecking at a piece of bark; it was she, keeping better watch than any human being, who thus announced my arrival with her wearisome refrain.

I had no time left me to recover. At the sharp, clipping tone of the parrot, the sleepers awoke and sprang up; and with a mighty oath, the voice of Silver cried, "Who goes?"

I turned to run, struck violently against one person, recoiled, and ran full into the arms of a second, who for his part closed upon and held me tight.

"Bring a torch, Dick," said Silver when my capture was thus assured.

And one of the men left the log-house and presently returned with a lighted brand.

PART SIX—Captain Silver

In the Enemy's Camp

The red glare of the torch, lighting up the interior of the block house, showed me the worst of my apprehensions realized. The pirates were in possession of the house and stores: there was the cask of cognac, there were the pork and bread, as before, and what tenfold increased my horror, not a sign of any prisoner. I could only judge that all had perished, and my heart smote me sorely that I had not been there to perish with them.

There were six of the buccaneers, all told; not another man was left alive. Five of them were on their feet, flushed and swollen, suddenly called out of the first sleep of drunkenness. The sixth had only risen upon his elbow; he was deadly pale, and the blood-stained bandage round his head told that he had recently been wounded, and still more recently dressed. I remembered the man who had been shot and had run back among the woods in the great attack, and doubted not that this was he.

The parrot sat, preening her plumage, on Long John's shoulder. He himself, I thought, looked somewhat paler and more stern than I was used to. He still wore the fine broadcloth suit in which he had fulfilled his mission, but it was bitterly the worse for wear, daubed with clay and torn with the sharp briers of the wood.

"So," said he, "here's Jim Hawkins, shiver my timbers! Dropped in, like, eh? Well, come, I take that friendly."

And thereupon he sat down across the brandy cask and began to fill a pipe.

"Give me a loan of the link, Dick," said he; and then, when he had a good light, "That'll do, lad," he added; "stick the glim in the wood heap; and you, gentlemen, bring yourselves to! You needn't stand up for Mr. Hawkins; *he'll* excuse you, you may lay to that. And so, Jim"—stopping the tobacco—"here you were, and quite a pleasant surprise for poor old John. I see you were smart when first I set my eyes on you, but this here gets away from me clean, it do."

To all this, as may be well supposed, I made no answer. They had set me with my back against the wall, and I stood there, looking Silver in the face, pluckily enough, I hope, to all outward appearance, but with black despair in my heart.

Silver took a whiff or two of his pipe with great composure and then ran on again.

"Now, you see, Jim, so be as you *are* here," says he, "I'll give you a piece of my mind. I've always liked you, I have, for a lad of spirit, and the picter of my own self when I was young and handsome. I always wanted you to jine and take your share, and die a gentleman, and now, my cock, you've got to. Cap'n Smollett's a fine seaman, as I'll own up to any day, but stiff on discipline. 'Dooty is dooty,' says he, and right he is. Just you keep clear of the cap'n. The doctor himself is gone dead again you—'ungrateful scamp' was what he said; and the short and the long of the whole story is about here: you can't go back to your own lot, for they won't have you; and without you start a third ship's company all by yourself, which might be lonely, you'll have to jine with Cap'n Silver."

So far so good. My friends, then, were still alive, and though I partly believed the truth of Silver's statement, that the cabin party were incensed at me for my desertion, I was more relieved than distressed by what I heard.

"I don't say nothing as to your being in our hands," continued Silver, "though there you are, and you may lay to it. I'm all for argyment; I never seen good come out o' threatening. If you like the service, well, you'll jine; and if you don't, Jim, why, you're free to answer no—free and welcome, shipmate; and if fairer can be said by mortal seaman, shiver my sides!"

"Am I to answer, then?" I asked with a very tremulous voice. Through all this sneering talk, I was made to feel the threat of death that overhung me, and my cheeks burned and my heart beat painfully in my breast.

"Lad," said Silver, "no one's a-pressing of you. Take your bearings. None of us won't hurry you, mate; time goes so pleasant in your company, you see."

"Well," says I, growing a bit bolder, "if I'm to choose, I declare I have a right to know what's what, and why you're here, and where my friends are."

"Wot's wot?" repeated one of the buccaneers in a deep growl. "Ah, he'd be a lucky one as knowed that!"

"You'll perhaps batten down your hatches till you're spoke to, my friend," cried Silver truculently to this speaker. And then, in his first gracious tones, he replied to me, "Yesterday morning, Mr. Hawkins," said he, "in the dog-watch, down came Doctor Livesey with a flag of truce. Says he, 'Cap'n Silver, you're sold out. Ship's gone.' Well, maybe we'd been taking a glass, and a song to help it round. I won't say no. Leastways, none of us had looked out. We looked out, and by thunder, the old ship was gone! I never seen a pack o' fools look fishier; and you may lay to that, if I tells you that looked the fishiest. 'Well,' says the doctor, 'let's bargain.' We bargained, him and I, and here we are: stores, brandy, block house, the firewood you was thoughtful enough to cut, and in a manner of speaking, the whole blessed boat, from cross-trees to kelson. As for them, they've tramped; I don't know where's they are."

He drew again quietly at his pipe.

"And lest you should take it into that head of yours," he went on, "that you was included in the treaty, here's the last word that was said: 'How many are you,' says I, 'to leave?' 'Four,' says he; 'four, and one of us wounded. As for that boy, I don't know where he is, confound him,' says he, 'nor I don't much care. We're about sick of him.' These was his words.

"Is that all?" I asked.

"Well, it's all that you're to hear, my son," returned Silver.

"And now I am to choose?"

"And now you are to choose, and you may lay to that," said Silver.

"Well," said I, "I am not such a fool but I know pretty well what I have to look for. Let the worst come to the worst, it's little I care. I've seen too many die since I fell in with you. But there's a thing or two I have to tell you," I said, and by this time I was quite excited; "and the first is this: here you are, in a bad way—ship lost, treasure lost, men lost, your whole business gone to wreck; and if you want to know who did it—it was I! I was in the apple barrel the night we sighted land, and I heard you, John, and you, Dick Johnson, and Hands, who is now at the bottom of the sea, and told every word you said before the hour was out. And as for the schooner, it was I who cut her cable, and it was I that killed the men you had aboard of her, and it was I who brought her where you'll never see her more, not one of you. The laugh's on my side; I've had the top of this business from the first; I no more fear you than I fear a fly. Kill me, if you please, or spare me. But one thing I'll say, and no more; if you spare me, bygones are bygones, and when you fellows are in court for piracy, I'll save you all I can. It is for you to choose. Kill another and do yourselves no good, or spare me and keep a witness to save you from the gallows."

I stopped, for, I tell you, I was out of breath, and to my wonder, not a man of them moved, but all sat staring at me like as many sheep. And while they were still staring, I broke out again, "And now, Mr. Silver," I said, "I believe you're the best man here, and if things go to the worst, I'll take it kind of you to let the doctor know the way I took it."

"I'll bear it in mind," said Silver with an accent so curious that I could not, for the life of me, decide whether he were laughing at my request or had been favourably affected by my courage.

"I'll put one to that," cried the old mahogany-faced seaman—Morgan by name—whom I had seen in Long John's public-house upon the quays of Bristol. "It was him that knowed Black Dog."

"Well, and see here," added the sea-cook. "I'll put another again to that, by thunder! For it was this same boy that faked the chart from Billy Bones. First and last, we've split upon Jim Hawkins!"

"Then here goes!" said Morgan with an oath.

And he sprang up, drawing his knife as if he had been twenty.

"Avast, there!" cried Silver. "Who are you, Tom Morgan? Maybe you thought you was cap'n here, perhaps. By the powers, but I'll teach you better! Cross me, and you'll go where many a good man's gone before you, first and last, these thirty year back—some to the yard-arm, shiver my timbers, and some by the board, and all to feed the fishes. There's never a man looked me between the eyes and seen a good day a'terwards, Tom Morgan, you may lay to that."

Morgan paused, but a hoarse murmur rose from the others.

"Tom's right," said one.

"I stood hazing long enough from one," added another. "I'll be hanged if I'll be hazed by you, John Silver."

"Did any of you gentlemen want to have it out with *me*?" roared Silver, bending far forward from his position on the keg, with his pipe still glowing in his right hand. "Put a name on what you're at; you ain't dumb, I reckon. Him that wants shall get it. Have I lived this many years, and a son of a rum puncheon cock his hat athwart my hawse at the latter end of it? You know the way; you're all gentlemen o' fortune, by your account. Well, I'm ready. Take a cutlass, him that dares, and I'll see the colour of his inside, crutch and all, before that pipe's empty."

Not a man stirred; not a man answered.

"That's your sort, is it?" he added, returning his pipe to his mouth. "Well, you're a gay lot to look at, anyway. Not much worth to fight, you ain't. P'r'aps you can understand King George's English. I'm cap'n here by 'lection. I'm cap'n here because I'm the best man by a long sea-mile. You won't fight, as gentlemen o' fortune should; then, by thunder, you'll obey, and you may lay to it! I like that boy, now; I never seen a better boy than that. He's more a man than any pair of rats of you in this here house, and what I say is this: let me see him that'll lay a hand on him—that's what I say, and you may lay to it."

There was a long pause after this. I stood straight up against the wall, my heart still going like a sledge-hammer, but with a ray of hope now shining in my bosom. Silver leant back against the wall, his arms crossed, his pipe in the corner of his mouth, as calm as though he had been in church; yet his eye kept wandering furtively, and he kept the tail of it on his unruly followers. They, on their part, drew gradually together towards the far end of the block house, and the low hiss of their whispering sounded in my ear continuously, like a stream. One after another, they would look up, and the red light of the torch would fall for a second on their nervous faces; but it was not towards me, it was towards Silver that they turned their eyes.

"You seem to have a lot to say," remarked Silver, spitting far into the air. "Pipe up and let me hear it, or lay to."

"Ax your pardon, sir," returned one of the men; "you're pretty free with some of the rules; maybe you'll kindly keep an eye upon the rest. This crew's dissatisfied; this crew don't vally bullying a marlin-spike; this crew has its rights like other crews, I'll make so free as that; and by your own rules, I take it we can talk together. I ax your pardon, sir, acknowledging you for to be captaing at this present; but I claim my right, and steps outside for a council."

And with an elaborate sea-salute, this fellow, a long, ill-looking, yellow-eyed man of five and thirty, stepped coolly towards the door and disappeared out of the house. One after another the rest followed his example, each making a salute as he passed, each adding some apology. "According to rules," said one. "Forecastle council," said Morgan. And so with one remark or another all marched out and left Silver and me alone with the torch.

The sea-cook instantly removed his pipe.

"Now, look you here, Jim Hawkins," he said in a steady whisper that was no more than audible, "you're within half a plank of death, and what's a long sight worse, of torture. They're going to throw me off. But, you mark, I stand by you through thick and thin. I didn't mean to; no, not till you spoke up. I was about desperate to lose that much blunt, and be hanged into the bargain. But I see you was the right sort. I says to myself, you stand by Hawkins, John, and Hawkins'll stand by you. You're his last card, and by the living thunder, John, he's yours! Back to back, says I. You save your witness, and he'll save your neck!"

I began dimly to understand.

"You mean all's lost?" I asked.

"Aye, by gum, I do!" he answered. "Ship gone, neck gone—that's the size of it. Once I looked into that bay, Jim Hawkins, and seen no schooner—well, I'm tough, but I gave out. As for that lot and their council, mark me, they're outright fools and cowards. I'll save your life—if so be as I can—from them. But, see here, Jim—tit for tat—you save Long John from swinging."

I was bewildered; it seemed a thing so hopeless he was asking—he, the old buccaneer, the ringleader throughout.

"What I can do, that I'll do," I said.

"It's a bargain!" cried Long John. "You speak up plucky, and by thunder, I've a chance!"

He hobbled to the torch, where it stood propped among the firewood, and took a fresh light to his pipe.

"Understand me, Jim," he said, returning. "I've a head on my shoulders, I have. I'm on squire's side now. I know you've got that ship safe somewheres. How you done it, I don't know, but safe it is. I guess Hands and O'Brien turned soft. I never much believed in neither of *them*. Now you mark me. I ask no questions, nor I won't let others. I know when a game's up, I do; and I know a lad that's staunch. Ah, you that's young—you and me might have done a power of good together!"

He drew some cognac from the cask into a tin cannikin.

"Will you taste, messmate?" he asked; and when I had refused: "Well, I'll take a drain myself, Jim," said he. "I need a caulker, for there's trouble on hand. And talking o' trouble, why did that doctor give me the chart, Jim?"

My face expressed a wonder so unaffected that he saw the needlessness of further questions.

"Ah, well, he did, though," said he. "And there's something under that, no doubt—something, surely, under that, Jim—bad or good."

And he took another swallow of the brandy, shaking his great fair head like a man who looks forward to the worst.

Lesson 117

1. Read chapters 29 and 30.
2. What complaints do the pirates' have? (Answers)
3. Tell someone what is happening the book.

The Black Spot Again

The council of buccaneers had lasted some time, when one of them re-entered the house, and with a repetition of the same salute, which had in my eyes an ironical air, begged for a moment's loan of the torch. Silver briefly agreed, and this emissary retired again, leaving us together in the dark.

"There's a breeze coming, Jim," said Silver, who had by this time adopted quite a friendly and familiar tone.

I turned to the loophole nearest me and looked out. The embers of the great fire had so far burned themselves out and now glowed so low and duskily that I understood why these conspirators desired a torch. About half-way down the slope to the stockade, they were collected in a group; one held the light, another was on his knees in their midst, and I saw the blade of an open knife shine in his hand with varying colours in the moon and torchlight. The rest were all somewhat stooping, as though watching the manoeuvres of this last. I could just make out that he had a book as well as a knife in his hand, and was still wondering how anything so incongruous had come in their possession when the kneeling figure rose once more to his feet and the whole party began to move together towards the house.

"Here they come," said I; and I returned to my former position, for it seemed beneath my dignity that they should find me watching them.

"Well, let 'em come, lad—let 'em come," said Silver cheerily. "I've still a shot in my locker."

The door opened, and the five men, standing huddled together just inside, pushed one of their number forward. In any other circumstances it would have been comical to see his slow advance, hesitating as he set down each foot, but holding his closed right hand in front of him.

"Step up, lad," cried Silver. "I won't eat you. Hand it over, lubber. I know the rules, I do; I won't hurt a depytation."

Thus encouraged, the buccaneer stepped forth more briskly, and having passed something to Silver, from hand to hand, slipped yet more smartly back again to his companions.

The sea-cook looked at what had been given him.

"The black spot! I thought so," he observed. "Where might you have got the paper? Why, hillo! Look here, now; this ain't lucky! You've gone and cut this out of a Bible. What fool's cut a Bible?"

"Ah, there!" said Morgan. "There! Wot did I say? No good'll come o' that, I said."

"Well, you've about fixed it now, among you," continued Silver. "You'll all swing now, I reckon. What soft-headed lubber had a Bible?"

"It was Dick," said one.

"Dick, was it? Then Dick can get to prayers," said Silver. "He's seen his slice of luck, has Dick, and you may lay to that."

But here the long man with the yellow eyes struck in.

"Belay that talk, John Silver," he said. "This crew has tipped you the black spot in full council, as in dooty bound; just you turn it over, as in dooty bound, and see what's wrote there. Then you can talk."

"Thanky, George," replied the sea-cook. "You always was brisk for business, and has the rules by heart, George, as I'm pleased to see. Well, what is it, anyway? Ah! 'Deposed'—that's it, is it? Very pretty wrote, to be sure; like print, I swear. Your hand o' write, George? Why, you was gettin' quite a leadin' man in this here crew. You'll be cap'n next, I shouldn't wonder. Just oblige me with that torch again, will you? This pipe don't draw."

"Come, now," said George, "you don't fool this crew no more. You're a funny man, by your account; but you're over now, and you'll maybe step down off that barrel and help vote."

"I thought you said you knowed the rules," returned Silver contemptuously. "Leastways, if you don't, I do; and I wait here—and I'm still your cap'n, mind—till you outs with your grievances and I reply; in the meantime, your black spot ain't worth a biscuit. After that, we'll see."

"Oh," replied George, "you don't be under no kind of apprehension; *we're* all square, we are. First, you've made a hash of this cruise—you'll be a bold man to say no to that. Second, you let the enemy out o' this here trap for nothing. Why did they want out? I dunno, but it's pretty plain they wanted it. Third, you wouldn't let us go at them upon the march. Oh, we see through you, John Silver; you want to play booty, that's what's wrong with you. And then, fourth, there's this here boy."

"Is that all?" asked Silver quietly.

"Enough, too," retorted George. "We'll all swing and sun-dry for your bungling."

"Well now, look here, I'll answer these four p'ints; one after another I'll answer 'em. I made a hash o' this cruise, did I? Well now, you all know what I wanted, and you all know if that had been done that we'd 'a been aboard the *Hispaniola* this night as ever was, every man of us alive, and fit, and full of good plum-duff, and the treasure in the hold of her, by thunder! Well, who crossed me? Who forced my hand, as was the lawful cap'n? Who tipped me the black spot the day we landed and began this dance? Ah, it's a fine dance—I'm with you there—and looks mighty like a hornpipe in a rope's end at Execution Dock by London town, it does. But who done it? Why, it was Anderson, and Hands, and you, George Merry! And you're the last above board of that same meddling crew; and you have the Davy Jones's insolence to up and stand for cap'n over me—you, that sank the lot of us! By the powers! But this tops the stiffest yarn to nothing."

Silver paused, and I could see by the faces of George and his late comrades that these words had not been said in vain.

"That's for number one," cried the accused, wiping the sweat from his brow, for he had been talking with a vehemence that shook the house. "Why, I give you my word, I'm sick to speak to you. You've neither sense nor memory, and I leave it to fancy where your mothers was that let you come to sea. Sea! Gentlemen o' fortune! I reckon tailors is your trade."

"Go on, John," said Morgan. "Speak up to the others."

"Ah, the others!" returned John. "They're a nice lot, ain't they? You say this cruise is bungled. Ah! By gum, if you could understand how bad it's bungled, you would see! We're that near the gibbet that my neck's stiff with thinking on it. You've seen 'em, maybe, hanged in chains, birds about 'em, seamen p'inting 'em out as they go down with the tide. 'Who's that?' says one. 'That! Why, that's John Silver. I knowed him well,' says another. And you can hear the chains a-jangle as you go about and reach for the other buoy. Now, that's about where we are, every mother's son of us, thanks to him, and Hands, and Anderson, and other ruination fools of you. And if you want to know about number four, and that boy, why, shiver my timbers, isn't he a hostage? Are we a-going to waste a hostage? No, not us; he might be our last chance, and I shouldn't wonder. Kill that boy? Not me, mates! And number three? Ah, well, there's a deal to say to number three. Maybe you don't count it nothing to have a real college doctor to see you every day—you, John, with your head broke—or you, George Merry, that had the ague shakes upon you not six hours agone, and has your eyes the colour of lemon peel to this same moment on the clock? And maybe, perhaps, you didn't know there was a consort coming either? But there is, and not so long till then; and we'll see who'll be glad to have a hostage when it comes to that. And as for number two, and why I made a bargain—well, you came crawling on your knees to me to make it—on your knees you came, you was that downhearted—and you'd have starved too if I hadn't—but that's a trifle! You look there—that's why!"

And he cast down upon the floor a paper that I instantly recognized—none other than the chart on yellow paper, with the three red crosses, that I had found in the oilcloth at the bottom of the captain's chest. Why the doctor had given it to him was more than I could fancy.

But if it were inexplicable to me, the appearance of the chart was incredible to the surviving mutineers. They leaped upon it like cats upon a mouse. It went from hand to hand, one tearing it from another; and by the oaths and the cries and the childish laughter with which they accompanied their examination, you would have thought, not only they were fingering the very gold, but were at sea with it, besides, in safety.

"Yes," said one, "that's Flint, sure enough. J. F., and a score below, with a clove hitch to it; so he done ever."

"Mighty pretty," said George. "But how are we to get away with it, and us no ship."

Silver suddenly sprang up, and supporting himself with a hand against the wall: "Now I give you warning, George," he cried. "One more word of your sauce, and I'll call you down and fight you. How? Why, how do I know? You had ought to tell me that—you and the rest, that lost me my schooner, with your interference, burn you! But not you, you can't; you hain't got the invention of a cockroach. But civil you can speak, and shall, George Merry, you may lay to that."

"That's fair enow," said the old man Morgan.

"Fair! I reckon so," said the sea-cook. "You lost the ship; I found the treasure. Who's the better man at that? And now I resign, by thunder! Elect whom you please to be your cap'n now; I'm done with it."

"Silver!" they cried. "Barbecue forever! Barbecue for cap'n!"

"So that's the toon, is it?" cried the cook. "George, I reckon you'll have to wait another turn, friend; and lucky for you as I'm not a revengeful man. But that was never my way. And now, shipmates, this black spot? 'Tain't much good now, is it? Dick's crossed his luck and spoiled his Bible, and that's about all."

"It'll do to kiss the book on still, won't it?" growled Dick, who was evidently uneasy at the curse he had brought upon himself.

"A Bible with a bit cut out!" returned Silver derisively. "Not it. It don't bind no more'n a ballad-book."

"Don't it, though?" cried Dick with a sort of joy. "Well, I reckon that's worth having too."

"Here, Jim—here's a cur'osity for you," said Silver, and he tossed me the paper.

It was around about the size of a crown piece. One side was blank, for it had been the last leaf; the other contained a verse or two of Revelation—these words among the rest, which struck sharply home upon my mind: "Without are dogs and murderers." The printed side had been blackened with wood ash, which already began to come off and soil my fingers; on the blank side had been written with the same material the one word "Depposed." I have that curiosity beside me at this moment, but not a trace of writing now remains beyond a single scratch, such as a man might make with his thumb-nail.

That was the end of the night's business. Soon after, with a drink all round, we lay down to sleep, and the outside of Silver's vengeance was to put George Merry up for sentinel and threaten him with death if he should prove unfaithful.

It was long ere I could close an eye, and heaven knows I had matter enough for thought in the man whom I had slain that afternoon, in my own most perilous position, and above all, in the remarkable game that I saw Silver now engaged upon—keeping the mutineers together with one hand and grasping with the other after every means, possible and impossible, to make his peace and save his miserable life. He himself slept peacefully and snored aloud, yet my heart was sore for him, wicked as he was, to think on the dark perils that environed and the shameful gibbet that awaited him.

On Parole

I was wakened—indeed, we were all wakened, for I could see even the sentinel shake himself together from where he had fallen against the door-post—by a clear, hearty voice hailing us from the margin of the wood:

"Block house, ahoy!" it cried. "Here's the doctor."

And the doctor it was. Although I was glad to hear the sound, yet my gladness was not without admixture. I remembered with confusion my insubordinate and stealthy conduct, and when I saw where it had brought me—among what companions and surrounded by what dangers—I felt ashamed to look him in the face.

He must have risen in the dark, for the day had hardly come; and when I ran to a loophole and looked out, I saw him standing, like Silver once before, up to the mid-leg in creeping vapour.

"You, doctor! Top o' the morning to you, sir!" cried Silver, broad awake and beaming with good nature in a moment. "Bright and early, to be sure; and it's the early bird, as the saying goes, that gets the rations. George, shake up your timbers, son, and help Dr. Livesey over the ship's side. All a-doin' well, your patients was—all well and merry."

So he pattered on, standing on the hilltop with his crutch under his elbow and one hand upon the side of the log-house—quite the old John in voice, manner, and expression.

"We've quite a surprise for you too, sir," he continued. "We've a little stranger here—he! he! A noo boarder and lodger, sir, and looking fit and taut as a fiddle; slep' like a supercargo, he did, right alongside of John—stem to stem we was, all night."

Dr. Livesey was by this time across the stockade and pretty near the cook, and I could hear the alteration in his voice as he said, "Not Jim?"

"The very same Jim as ever was," says Silver.

The doctor stopped outright, although he did not speak, and it was some seconds before he seemed able to move on.

"Well, well," he said at last, "duty first and pleasure afterwards, as you might have said yourself, Silver. Let us overhaul these patients of yours."

A moment afterwards he had entered the block house and with one grim nod to me proceeded with his work among the sick. He seemed under no apprehension, though he must have known that his life, among these treacherous demons, depended on a hair; and he rattled on to his patients as if he were paying an ordinary professional visit in a quiet English family. His manner, I suppose, reacted on the men, for they behaved to him as if nothing had occurred, as if he were still ship's doctor and they still faithful hands before the mast.

"You're doing well, my friend," he said to the fellow with the bandaged head, "and if ever any person had a close shave, it was you; your head must be as hard as iron. Well, George, how goes it? You're a pretty colour, certainly; why, your liver, man, is upside down. Did you take that medicine? Did he take that medicine, men?"

"Aye, aye, sir, he took it, sure enough," returned Morgan.

"Because, you see, since I am mutineers' doctor, or prison doctor as I prefer to call it," says Doctor Livesey in his pleasantest way, "I make it a point of honour not to lose a man for King George (God bless him!) and the gallows."

The rogues looked at each other but swallowed the home-thrust in silence.

"Dick don't feel well, sir," said one.

"Don't he?" replied the doctor. "Well, step up here, Dick, and let me see your tongue. No, I should be surprised if he did! The man's tongue is fit to frighten the French. Another fever."

"Ah, there," said Morgan, "that comed of sp'iling Bibles."

"That comes—as you call it—of being arrant asses," retorted the doctor, "and not having sense enough to know honest air from poison, and the dry land from a vile, pestiferous slough. I think it most probable—though of course it's only an opinion—that you'll all have the deuce to pay before you get that malaria out of your systems. Camp in a bog, would you? Silver, I'm surprised at you. You're less of a fool than many, take you all round; but you don't appear to me to have the rudiments of a notion of the rules of health.

"Well," he added after he had dosed them round and they had taken his prescriptions, with really laughable humility, more like charity schoolchildren than blood-guilty mutineers and pirates—"well, that's done for today. And now I should wish to have a talk with that boy, please."

And he nodded his head in my direction carelessly.

George Merry was at the door, spitting and spluttering over some bad-tasted medicine; but at the first word of the doctor's proposal he swung round with a deep flush and cried "No!" and swore.

Silver struck the barrel with his open hand.

"Si-lence!" he roared and looked about him positively like a lion. "Doctor," he went on in his usual tones, "I was a-thinking of that, knowing as how you had a fancy for the boy. We're all humbly grateful for your kindness, and as you see, puts faith in you and takes the drugs down like that much grog. And I take it I've found a way as'll suit all. Hawkins, will you give me your word of honour as a young gentleman—for a young gentleman you are, although poor born—your word of honour not to slip your cable?"

I readily gave the pledge required.

"Then, doctor," said Silver, "you just step outside o' that stockade, and once you're there I'll bring the boy down on the inside, and I reckon you can yarn through the spars. Good day to you, sir, and all our dooties to the squire and Cap'n Smollett."

The explosion of disapproval, which nothing but Silver's black looks had restrained, broke out immediately the doctor had left the house. Silver was roundly accused of playing double—of trying to make a separate peace for himself, of sacrificing the interests of his accomplices and victims, and, in one word, of the identical, exact thing that he was doing. It seemed to me so obvious, in this case, that I could not imagine how he was to turn their anger. But he was twice the man the rest were, and his last night's victory had given him a huge preponderance on their minds. He called them all the fools and dolts you can imagine, said it was necessary I should talk to the doctor, fluttered the chart in their faces, asked them if they could afford to break the treaty the very day they were bound a-treasure-hunting.

"No, by thunder!" he cried. "It's us must break the treaty when the time comes; and till then I'll gammon that doctor, if I have to ile his boots with brandy."

And then he bade them get the fire lit, and stalked out upon his crutch, with his hand on my shoulder, leaving them in a disarray, and silenced by his volubility rather than convinced.

"Slow, lad, slow," he said. "They might round upon us in a twinkle of an eye if we was seen to hurry."

Very deliberately, then, did we advance across the sand to where the doctor awaited us on the other side of the stockade, and as soon as we were within easy speaking distance Silver stopped.

"You'll make a note of this here also, doctor," says he, "and the boy'll tell you how I saved his life, and were deposed for it too, and you may lay to that. Doctor, when a man's steering as near the wind as me—playing chuck-farthing with the last breath in his body, like—you wouldn't think it too much, mayhap, to give him one good word? You'll please bear in mind it's not my life only now—it's that boy's into the bargain; and you'll speak me fair, doctor, and give me a bit o' hope to go on, for the sake of mercy."

Silver was a changed man once he was out there and had his back to his friends and the block house; his cheeks seemed to have fallen in, his voice trembled; never was a soul more dead in earnest.

"Why, John, you're not afraid?" asked Dr. Livesey.

"Doctor, I'm no coward; no, not I—not *so* much!" and he snapped his fingers. "If I was I wouldn't say it. But I'll own up fairly, I've the shakes upon me for the gallows. You're a good man and a true; I never seen a better man! And you'll not forget what I done good, not any more than you'll forget the bad, I know. And I step aside—see here—and leave you and Jim alone. And you'll put that down for me too, for it's a long stretch, is that!"

So saying, he stepped back a little way, till he was out of earshot, and there sat down upon a tree-stump and began to whistle, spinning round now and again upon his seat so as to command a sight, sometimes of me and the doctor and sometimes of his unruly ruffians as they went to and fro in the sand between the fire—which they were busy rekindling—and the house, from which they brought forth pork and bread to make the breakfast.

"So, Jim," said the doctor sadly, "here you are. As you have brewed, so shall you drink, my boy. Heaven knows, I cannot find it in my heart to blame you, but this much I will say, be it kind or unkind: when Captain Smollett was well, you dared not have gone off; and when he was ill and couldn't help it, by George, it was downright cowardly!"

I will own that I here began to weep. "Doctor," I said, "you might spare me. I have blamed myself enough; my life's forfeit anyway, and I should have been dead by now if Silver hadn't stood for me; and doctor, believe this, I can die—and I dare say I deserve it—but what I fear is torture. If they come to torture me—"

"Jim," the doctor interrupted, and his voice was quite changed, "Jim, I can't have this. Whip over, and we'll run for it."

"Doctor," said I, "I passed my word."

"I know, I know," he cried. "We can't help that, Jim, now. I'll take it on my shoulders, holus bolus, blame and shame, my boy; but stay here, I cannot let you. Jump! One jump, and you're out, and we'll run for it like antelopes."

"No," I replied; "you know right well you wouldn't do the thing yourself—neither you nor squire nor captain; and no more will I. Silver trusted me; I passed my word, and back I go. But, doctor, you did not let me finish. If they come to torture me, I might let slip a word of where the ship is, for I got the ship, part by luck and part by risking, and she lies in North Inlet, on the southern beach, and just below high water. At half tide she must be high and dry."

"The ship!" exclaimed the doctor.

Rapidly I described to him my adventures, and he heard me out in silence.

"There is a kind of fate in this," he observed when I had done. "Every step, it's you that saves our lives; and do you suppose by any chance that we are going to let you lose yours? That would be a poor return, my boy. You found out the plot; you found Ben Gunn—the best deed that ever you did, or will do, though you live to ninety. Oh, by Jupiter, and talking of Ben Gunn! Why, this is the mischief in person. Silver!" he cried. "Silver! I'll give you a piece of advice," he continued as the cook drew near again; "don't you be in any great hurry after that treasure."

"Why, sir, I do my possible, which that ain't," said Silver. "I can only, asking your pardon, save my life and the boy's by seeking for that treasure; and you may lay to that."

"Well, Silver," replied the doctor, "if that is so, I'll go one step further: look out for squalls when you find it."

"Sir," said Silver, "as between man and man, that's too much and too little. What you're after, why you left the block house, why you given me that there chart, I don't know, now, do I? And yet I done your bidding with my eyes shut and never a word of hope! But no, this here's too much. If you won't tell me what you mean plain out, just say so and I'll leave the helm."

"No," said the doctor musingly; "I've no right to say more; it's not my secret, you see, Silver, or, I give you my word, I'd tell it you. But I'll go as far with you as I dare go, and a step beyond, for I'll have my wig sorted by the captain or I'm mistaken! And first, I'll give you a bit of hope; Silver, if we both get alive out of this wolf-trap, I'll do my best to save you, short of perjury."

Silver's face was radiant. "You couldn't say more, I'm sure, sir, not if you was my mother," he cried.

"Well, that's my first concession," added the doctor. "My second is a piece of advice: keep the boy close beside you, and when you need help, halloo. I'm off to seek it for you, and that itself will show you if I speak at random. Good-bye, Jim."

And Dr. Livesey shook hands with me through the stockade, nodded to Silver, and set off at a brisk pace into the wood.

Lesson 118

1. Read chapters 31 and 32.
2. Silver has at times acted like a caring father toward Jim, but when it comes to the treasure he changes. How does he act toward Jim in this chapter when the treasure (money) is at stake? What does that say about where his heart is? (Answers)
3. Tell someone what is happening in the book.

The Treasure-hunt—Flint's Pointer

"JIM," said Silver when we were alone, "if I saved your life, you saved mine; and I'll not forget it. I seen the doctor waving you to run for it—with the tail of my eye, I did; and I seen you say no, as plain as hearing. Jim, that's one to you. This is the first glint of hope I had since the attack failed, and I owe it you. And now, Jim, we're to go in for this here treasure-hunting, with sealed orders too, and I don't like it; and you and me must stick close, back to back like, and we'll save our necks in spite o' fate and fortune."

Just then a man hailed us from the fire that breakfast was ready, and we were soon seated here and there about the sand over biscuit and fried junk. They had lit a fire fit to roast an ox, and it was now grown so hot that they could only approach it from the windward, and even there not without precaution. In the same wasteful spirit, they had cooked, I suppose, three times more than we could eat; and one of them, with an empty laugh, threw what was left into the fire, which blazed and roared again over this unusual fuel. I never in my life saw men so careless of the morrow; hand to mouth is the only word that can describe their way of doing; and what with wasted food and sleeping sentries, though they were bold enough for a brush and be done with it, I could see their entire unfitness for anything like a prolonged campaign.

Even Silver, eating away, with Captain Flint upon his shoulder, had not a word of blame for their recklessness. And this the more surprised me, for I thought he had never shown himself so cunning as he did then.

"Aye, mates," said he, "it's lucky you have Barbecue to think for you with this here head. I got what I wanted, I did. Sure enough, they have the ship. Where they have it, I don't know yet; but once we hit the treasure, we'll have to jump about and find out. And then, mates, us that has the boats, I reckon, has the upper hand."

Thus he kept running on, with his mouth full of the hot bacon; thus he restored their hope and confidence, and, I more than suspect, repaired his own at the same time.

"As for hostage," he continued, "that's his last talk, I guess, with them he loves so dear. I've got my piece o' news, and thanky to him for that; but it's over and done. I'll take him in a line when we go treasure-hunting, for we'll keep him like so much gold, in case of accidents, you mark, and in the meantime. Once we got the ship and treasure both and off to sea like jolly companions, why then we'll talk Mr. Hawkins over, we will, and we'll give him his share, to be sure, for all his kindness."

It was no wonder the men were in a good humour now. For my part, I was horribly cast down. Should the scheme he had now sketched prove feasible, Silver, already doubly a traitor, would not hesitate to adopt it. He had still a foot in either camp, and there was no doubt he would prefer wealth and freedom with the pirates to a bare escape from hanging, which was the best he had to hope on our side.

Nay, and even if things so fell out that he was forced to keep his faith with Dr. Livesey, even then what danger lay before us! What a moment that would be when the suspicions of his followers turned to certainty and he and I should have to fight for dear life—he a cripple and I a boy—against five strong and active seamen!

Add to this double apprehension the mystery that still hung over the behaviour of my friends, their unexplained desertion of the stockade, their inexplicable cession of the chart, or harder still to understand, the doctor's last warning to Silver, "Look out for squalls when you find it," and you will readily believe how little taste I found in my breakfast and with how uneasy a heart I set forth behind my captors on the quest for treasure.

We made a curious figure, had anyone been there to see us—all in soiled sailor clothes and all but me armed to the teeth. Silver had two guns slung about him—one before and one behind—besides the great cutlass at his waist and a pistol in each pocket of his square-tailed coat. To complete his strange appearance, Captain Flint sat perched upon his shoulder and gabbling odds and ends of purposeless sea-talk. I had a line about my waist and followed obediently after the sea-cook, who held the loose end of the rope, now in his free hand, now between his powerful teeth. For all the world, I was led like a dancing bear.

The other men were variously burthened, some carrying picks and shovels—for that had been the very first necessary they brought ashore from the *Hispaniola*—others laden with pork, bread, and brandy for the midday meal. All the stores, I observed, came from our stock, and I could see the truth of Silver's words the night before. Had he not struck a bargain with the doctor, he and his mutineers, deserted by the ship, must have been driven to subsist on clear water and the proceeds of their hunting. Water would have been little to their taste; a sailor is not usually a good shot; and besides all that, when they were so short of eatables, it was not likely they would be very flush of powder.

Well, thus equipped, we all set out—even the fellow with the broken head, who should certainly have kept in shadow—and straggled, one after another, to the beach, where the two gigs awaited us. Even these bore trace of the drunken folly of the pirates, one in a broken thwart, and both in their muddy and unbailed condition. Both were to be carried along with us for the sake of safety; and so, with our numbers divided between them, we set forth upon the bosom of the anchorage.

As we pulled over, there was some discussion on the chart. The red cross was, of course, far too large to be a guide; and the terms of the note on the back, as you will hear, admitted of some ambiguity. They ran, the reader may remember, thus:

Tall tree, Spy-glass shoulder, bearing a point to the N. of N.N.E.

Skeleton Island E.S.E. and by E.

Ten feet.

A tall tree was thus the principal mark. Now, right before us the anchorage was bounded by a plateau from two to three hundred feet high, adjoining on the north the sloping southern shoulder of the Spy-glass and rising again towards the south into the rough, cliffy eminence called the Mizzen-mast Hill. The top of the plateau was dotted thickly with pine-trees of varying height. Every here and there, one of a different species rose forty or fifty feet clear above its neighbours, and which of these was the particular "tall tree" of Captain Flint could only be decided on the spot, and by the readings of the compass.

Yet, although that was the case, every man on board the boats had picked a favourite of his own ere we were half-way over, Long John alone shrugging his shoulders and bidding them wait till they were there.

We pulled easily, by Silver's directions, not to weary the hands prematurely, and after quite a long passage, landed at the mouth of the second river—that which runs down a woody cleft of the Spy-glass. Thence, bending to our left, we began to ascend the slope towards the plateau.

At the first outset, heavy, miry ground and a matted, marish vegetation greatly delayed our progress; but by little and little the hill began to steepen and become stony under foot, and the wood to change its character and to grow in a more open order. It was, indeed, a most pleasant portion of the island that we were now approaching. A heavy-scented broom and many flowering shrubs had almost taken the place of grass. Thickets of green nutmeg-trees were dotted here and there with the red columns and the broad shadow of the pines; and the first mingled their spice with the aroma of the others. The air, besides, was fresh and stirring, and this, under the sheer sunbeams, was a wonderful refreshment to our senses.

The party spread itself abroad, in a fan shape, shouting and leaping to and fro. About the centre, and a good way behind the rest, Silver and I followed—I tethered by my rope, he ploughing, with deep pants, among the sliding gravel. From time to time, indeed, I had to lend him a hand, or he must have missed his footing and fallen backward down the hill.

We had thus proceeded for about half a mile and were approaching the brow of the plateau when the man upon the farthest left began to cry aloud, as if in terror. Shout after shout came from him, and the others began to run in his direction.

"He can't 'a found the treasure," said old Morgan, hurrying past us from the right, "for that's clean a-top."

Indeed, as we found when we also reached the spot, it was something very different. At the foot of a pretty big pine and involved in a green creeper, which had even partly lifted some of the smaller bones, a human skeleton lay, with a few shreds of clothing, on the ground. I believe a chill struck for a moment to every heart.

"He was a seaman," said George Merry, who, bolder than the rest, had gone up close and was examining the rags of clothing. "Leastways, this is good sea-cloth."

"Aye, aye," said Silver; "like enough; you wouldn't look to find a bishop here, I reckon. But what sort of a way is that for bones to lie? 'Tain't in natur'."

Indeed, on a second glance, it seemed impossible to fancy that the body was in a natural position. But for some disarray (the work, perhaps, of the birds that had fed upon him or of the slow-growing creeper that had gradually enveloped his remains) the man lay perfectly straight—his feet pointing in one direction, his hands, raised above his head like a diver's, pointing directly in the opposite.

"I've taken a notion into my old numbskull," observed Silver. "Here's the compass; there's the tip-top p'int o' Skeleton Island, stickin' out like a tooth. Just take a bearing, will you, along the line of them bones."

It was done. The body pointed straight in the direction of the island, and the compass read duly E.S.E. and by E.

"I thought so," cried the cook; "this here is a p'inter. Right up there is our line for the Pole Star and the jolly dollars. But, by thunder! If it don't make me cold inside to think of Flint. This is one of *his* jokes, and no mistake. Him and these six was alone here; he killed 'em, every man; and this one he hauled here and laid down by compass, shiver my timbers! They're long bones, and the hair's been yellow. Aye, that would be Allardyce. You mind Allardyce, Tom Morgan?"

"Aye, aye," returned Morgan; "I mind him; he owed me money, he did, and took my knife ashore with him."

"Speaking of knives," said another, "why don't we find his'n lying round? Flint warn't the man to pick a seaman's pocket; and the birds, I guess, would leave it be."

"By the powers, and that's true!" cried Silver.

"There ain't a thing left here," said Merry, still feeling round among the bones; "not a copper doit nor a baccy box. It don't look nat'ral to me."

"No, by gum, it don't," agreed Silver; "not nat'ral, nor not nice, says you. Great guns! Messmates, but if Flint was living, this would be a hot spot for you and me. Six they were, and six are we; and bones is what they are now."

"I saw him dead with these here deadlights," said Morgan. "Billy took me in. There he laid, with penny-pieces on his eyes."

"Dead—aye, sure enough he's dead and gone below," said the fellow with the bandage; "but if ever sperrit walked, it would be Flint's. Dear heart, but he died bad, did Flint!"

"Aye, that he did," observed another; "now he raged, and now he hollered for the rum, and now he sang. 'Fifteen Men' were his only song, mates; and I tell you true, I never rightly liked to hear it since. It was main hot, and the windy was open, and I hear that old song comin' out as clear as clear—and the death-haul on the man already."

"Come, come," said Silver; "stow this talk. He's dead, and he don't walk, that I know; leastways, he won't walk by day, and you may lay to that. Care killed a cat. Fetch ahead for the doubloons."

We started, certainly; but in spite of the hot sun and the staring daylight, the pirates no longer ran separate and shouting through the wood, but kept side by side and spoke with bated breath. The terror of the dead buccaneer had fallen on their spirits.

The Treasure-hunt—The Voice Among the Trees

Partly from the damping influence of this alarm, partly to rest Silver and the sick folk, the whole party sat down as soon as they had gained the brow of the ascent.

The plateau being somewhat tilted towards the west, this spot on which we had paused commanded a wide prospect on either hand. Before us, over the tree-tops, we beheld the Cape of the Woods fringed with surf; behind, we not only looked down upon the anchorage and Skeleton Island, but saw—clear across the spit and the eastern lowlands—a great field of open sea upon the east. Sheer above us rose the Spyglass, here dotted with single pines, there black with precipices. There was no sound but that of the distant breakers, mounting from all round, and the chirp of countless insects in the brush. Not a man, not a sail, upon the sea; the very largeness of the view increased the sense of solitude.

Silver, as he sat, took certain bearings with his compass.

"There are three 'tall trees'" said he, "about in the right line from Skeleton Island. 'Spy-glass shoulder,' I take it, means that lower p'int there. It's child's play to find the stuff now. I've half a mind to dine first."

"I don't feel sharp," growled Morgan. "Thinkin' o' Flint—I think it were—as done me."

"Ah, well, my son, you praise your stars he's dead," said Silver.

"He were an ugly devil," cried a third pirate with a shudder; "that blue in the face too!"

"That was how the rum took him," added Merry. "Blue! Well, I reckon he was blue. That's a true word."

Ever since they had found the skeleton and got upon this train of thought, they had spoken lower and lower, and they had almost got to whispering by now, so that the sound of their talk hardly interrupted the silence of the wood. All of a sudden, out of the middle of the trees in front of us, a thin, high, trembling voice struck up the well-known air and words:

"Fifteen men on the dead man's chest—

Yo-ho-ho, and a bottle of rum!"

I never have seen men more dreadfully affected than the pirates. The colour went from their six faces like enchantment; some leaped to their feet, some clawed hold of others; Morgan grovelled on the ground.

"It's Flint, by ——!" cried Merry.

The song had stopped as suddenly as it began—broken off, you would have said, in the middle of a note, as though someone had laid his hand upon the singer's mouth. Coming through the clear, sunny atmosphere among the green tree-tops, I thought it had sounded airily and sweetly; and the effect on my companions was the stranger.

"Come," said Silver, struggling with his ashen lips to get the word out; "this won't do. Stand by to go about. This is a rum start, and I can't name the voice, but it's someone skylarking—someone that's flesh and blood, and you may lay to that."

His courage had come back as he spoke, and some of the colour to his face along with it. Already the others had begun to lend an ear to this encouragement and were coming a little to themselves, when the same voice broke out again—not this time singing, but in a faint distant hail that echoed yet fainter among the clefts of the Spy-glass.

"Darby M'Graw," it wailed—for that is the word that best describes the sound—"Darby M'Graw! Darby M'Graw!" again and again and again; and then rising a little higher, and with an oath that I leave out: "Fetch aft the rum, Darby!"

The buccaneers remained rooted to the ground, their eyes starting from their heads. Long after the voice had died away they still stared in silence, dreadfully, before them.

"That fixes it!" gasped one. "Let's go."

"They was his last words," moaned Morgan, "his last words above board."

Dick had his Bible out and was praying volubly. He had been well brought up, had Dick, before he came to sea and fell among bad companions.

Still Silver was unconquered. I could hear his teeth rattle in his head, but he had not yet surrendered.

"Nobody in this here island ever heard of Darby," he muttered; "not one but us that's here." And then, making a great effort: "Shipmates," he cried, "I'm here to get that stuff, and I'll not be beat by man or devil. I never was feared of Flint in his life, and, by the powers, I'll face him dead. There's seven hundred thousand pound not a quarter of a mile from here. When did ever a gentleman o' fortune show his stern to that much dollars for a boozy old seaman with a blue mug—and him dead too?"

But there was no sign of reawakening courage in his followers, rather, indeed, of growing terror at the irreverence of his words.

"Belay there, John!" said Merry. "Don't you cross a sperrit."

And the rest were all too terrified to reply. They would have run away severally had they dared; but fear kept them together, and kept them close by John, as if his daring helped them. He, on his part, had pretty well fought his weakness down.

"Sperrit? Well, maybe," he said. "But there's one thing not clear to me. There was an echo. Now, no man ever seen a sperrit with a shadow; well then, what's he doing with an echo to him, I should like to know? That ain't in natur', surely?"

This argument seemed weak enough to me. But you can never tell what will affect the superstitious, and to my wonder, George Merry was greatly relieved.

"Well, that's so," he said. "You've a head upon your shoulders, John, and no mistake. 'Bout ship, mates! This here crew is on a wrong tack, I do believe. And come to think on it, it was like Flint's voice, I grant you, but not just so clear-away like it, after all. It was liker somebody else's voice now—it was liker—"

"By the powers, Ben Gunn!" roared Silver.

"Aye, and so it were," cried Morgan, springing on his knees. "Ben Gunn it were!"

"It don't make much odds, do it, now?" asked Dick. "Ben Gunn's not here in the body any more'n Flint."

But the older hands greeted this remark with scorn.

"Why, nobody minds Ben Gunn," cried Merry; "dead or alive, nobody minds him."

It was extraordinary how their spirits had returned and how the natural colour had revived in their faces. Soon they were chatting together, with intervals of listening; and not long after, hearing no further sound, they shouldered the tools and set forth again, Merry walking first with Silver's compass to keep them on the right line with Skeleton Island. He had said the truth: dead or alive, nobody minded Ben Gunn.

Dick alone still held his Bible, and looked around him as he went, with fearful glances; but he found no sympathy, and Silver even joked him on his precautions.

"I told you," said he—"I told you you had sp'iled your Bible. If it ain't no good to swear by, what do you suppose a sperrit would give for it? Not that!" and he snapped his big fingers, halting a moment on his crutch.

But Dick was not to be comforted; indeed, it was soon plain to me that the lad was falling sick; hastened by heat, exhaustion, and the shock of his alarm, the fever, predicted by Dr. Livesey, was evidently growing swiftly higher.

It was fine open walking here, upon the summit; our way lay a little downhill, for, as I have said, the plateau tilted towards the west. The pines, great and small, grew wide apart; and even between the clumps of nutmeg and azalea, wide open spaces baked in the hot sunshine. Striking, as we did, pretty near north-west across the island, we drew, on the one hand, ever nearer under the shoulders of the Spy-glass, and on the other, looked ever wider over that western bay where I had once tossed and trembled in the coracle.

The first of the tall trees was reached, and by the bearings proved the wrong one. So with the second. The third rose nearly two hundred feet into the air above a clump of underwood—a giant of a vegetable, with a red column as big as a cottage, and a wide shadow around in which a company could have manoeuvred. It was conspicuous far to sea both on the east and west and might have been entered as a sailing mark upon the chart.

But it was not its size that now impressed my companions; it was the knowledge that seven hundred thousand pounds in gold lay somewhere buried below its spreading shadow. The thought of the money, as they drew nearer, swallowed up their previous terrors. Their eyes burned in their heads; their feet grew speedier and lighter; their whole soul was found up in that fortune, that whole lifetime of extravagance and pleasure, that lay waiting there for each of them.

Silver hobbled, grunting, on his crutch; his nostrils stood out and quivered; he cursed like a madman when the flies settled on his hot and shiny countenance; he plucked furiously at the line that held me to him and from time to time turned his eyes upon me with a deadly look. Certainly he took no pains to hide his thoughts, and certainly I read them like print. In the immediate nearness of the gold, all else had been forgotten: his promise and the doctor's warning were both things of the past, and I could not doubt that he hoped to seize upon the treasure, find and board the *Hispaniola* under cover of night, cut every honest throat about that island, and sail away as he had at first intended, laden with crimes and riches.

Shaken as I was with these alarms, it was hard for me to keep up with the rapid pace of the treasure-hunters. Now and again I stumbled, and it was then that Silver plucked so roughly at the rope and launched at me his murderous glances. Dick, who had dropped behind us and now brought up the rear, was babbling to himself both prayers and curses as his fever kept rising. This also added to my wretchedness, and to crown all, I was haunted by the thought of the tragedy that had once been acted on that plateau, when that ungodly buccaneer with the blue face—he who died at Savannah, singing and shouting for drink—had there, with his own hand, cut down his six accomplices. This grove that was now so peaceful must then have rung with cries, I thought; and even with the thought I could believe I heard it ringing still.

We were now at the margin of the thicket.

"Huzza, mates, all together!" shouted Merry; and the foremost broke into a run.

And suddenly, not ten yards further, we beheld them stop. A low cry arose. Silver doubled his pace, digging away with the foot of his crutch like one possessed; and next moment he and I had come also to a dead halt.

Before us was a great excavation, not very recent, for the sides had fallen in and grass had sprouted on the bottom. In this were the shaft of a pick broken in two and the boards of several packing-cases strewn around. On one of these boards I saw, branded with a hot iron, the name *Walrus*—the name of Flint's ship.

All was clear to probation. The *cache* had been found and rifled; the seven hundred thousand pounds were gone!

Lesson 119

1. Read chapters 33 and 34.
2. Like many action stories, just when you think all hope is lost, someone comes to the rescue. Who comes and saves Silver and Jim? (Answers)
3. Tell someone about how the book ends.
4. While the story is mostly from Jim Hawkin's point of view, what perspective is Jim telling it from? (Answers)

The Fall of a Chieftain

There never was such an overturn in this world. Each of these six men was as though he had been struck. But with Silver the blow passed almost instantly. Every thought of his soul had been set full-stretch, like a racer, on that money; well, he was brought up, in a single second, dead; and he kept his head, found his temper, and changed his plan before the others had had time to realize the disappointment.

"Jim," he whispered, "take that, and stand by for trouble."

And he passed me a double-barrelled pistol.

At the same time, he began quietly moving northward, and in a few steps had put the hollow between us two and the other five. Then he looked at me and nodded, as much as to say, "Here is a narrow corner," as, indeed, I thought it was. His looks were not quite friendly, and I was so revolted at these constant changes that I could not forbear whispering, "So you've changed sides again."

There was no time left for him to answer in. The buccaneers, with oaths and cries, began to leap, one after another, into the pit and to dig with their fingers, throwing the boards aside as they did so. Morgan found a piece of gold. He held it up with a perfect spout of oaths. It was a two-guinea piece, and it went from hand to hand among them for a quarter of a minute.

"Two guineas!" roared Merry, shaking it at Silver. "That's your seven hundred thousand pounds, is it? You're the man for bargains, ain't you? You're him that never bungled nothing, you wooden-headed lubber!"

"Dig away, boys," said Silver with the coolest insolence; "you'll find some pig-nuts and I shouldn't wonder."

"Pig-nuts!" repeated Merry, in a scream. "Mates, do you hear that? I tell you now, that man there knew it all along. Look in the face of him and you'll see it wrote there."

"Ah, Merry," remarked Silver, "standing for cap'n again? You're a pushing lad, to be sure."

But this time everyone was entirely in Merry's favour. They began to scramble out of the excavation, darting furious glances behind them. One thing I observed, which looked well for us: they all got out upon the opposite side from Silver.

Well, there we stood, two on one side, five on the other, the pit between us, and nobody screwed up high enough to offer the first blow. Silver never moved; he watched them, very upright on his crutch, and looked as cool as ever I saw him. He was brave, and no mistake.

At last Merry seemed to think a speech might help matters.

"Mates," says he, "there's two of them alone there; one's the old cripple that brought us all here and blundered us down to this; the other's that cub that I mean to have the heart of. Now, mates!"

He was raising his arm and his voice, and plainly meant to lead a charge. But just then—crack! crack! crack!—three musket-shots flashed out of the thicket. Merry tumbled head foremost into the excavation; the man with the bandage spun round like a teetotum and fell all his length upon his side, where he lay dead, but still twitching; and the other three turned and ran for it with all their might.

Before you could wink, Long John had fired two barrels of a pistol into the struggling Merry, and as the man rolled up his eyes at him in the last agony, "George," said he, "I reckon I settled you."

At the same moment, the doctor, Gray, and Ben Gunn joined us, with smoking muskets, from among the nutmeg-trees.

"Forward!" cried the doctor. "Double quick, my lads. We must head 'em off the boats."

And we set off at a great pace, sometimes plunging through the bushes to the chest.

I tell you, but Silver was anxious to keep up with us. The work that man went through, leaping on his crutch till the muscles of his chest were fit to burst, was work no sound man ever equalled; and so thinks the doctor. As it was, he was already thirty yards behind us and on the verge of strangling when we reached the brow of the slope.

"Doctor," he hailed, "see there! No hurry!"

Sure enough there was no hurry. In a more open part of the plateau, we could see the three survivors still running in the same direction as they had started, right for Mizzenmast Hill. We were already between them and the boats; and so we four sat down to breathe, while Long John, mopping his face, came slowly up with us.

"Thank ye kindly, doctor," says he. "You came in in about the nick, I guess, for me and Hawkins. And so it's you, Ben Gunn!" he added. "Well, you're a nice one, to be sure."

"I'm Ben Gunn, I am," replied the maroon, wriggling like an eel in his embarrassment. "And," he added, after a long pause, "how do, Mr. Silver? Pretty well, I thank ye, says you."

"Ben, Ben," murmured Silver, "to think as you've done me!"

The doctor sent back Gray for one of the pick-axes deserted, in their flight, by the mutineers, and then as we proceeded leisurely downhill to where the boats were lying, related in a few words what had taken place. It was a story that profoundly interested Silver; and Ben Gunn, the half-idiot maroon, was the hero from beginning to end.

Ben, in his long, lonely wanderings about the island, had found the skeleton—it was he that had rifled it; he had found the treasure; he had dug it up (it was the haft of his pick-axe that lay broken in the excavation); he had carried it on his back, in many weary journeys, from the foot of the tall pine to a cave he had on the two-pointed hill at the north-east angle of the island, and there it had lain stored in safety since two months before the arrival of the *Hispaniola*.

When the doctor had wormed this secret from him on the afternoon of the attack, and when next morning he saw the anchorage deserted, he had gone to Silver, given him the chart, which was now useless—given him the stores, for Ben Gunn's cave was well supplied with goats' meat salted by himself—given anything and everything to get a chance of moving in safety from the stockade to the two-pointed hill, there to be clear of malaria and keep a guard upon the money.

"As for you, Jim," he said, "it went against my heart, but I did what I thought best for those who had stood by their duty; and if you were not one of these, whose fault was it?"

That morning, finding that I was to be involved in the horrid disappointment he had prepared for the mutineers, he had run all the way to the cave, and leaving the squire to guard the captain, had taken Gray and the maroon and started, making the diagonal across the island to be at hand beside the pine. Soon, however, he saw that our party had the start of him; and Ben Gunn, being fleet of foot, had been dispatched in front to do his best alone. Then it had occurred to him to work upon the superstitions of his former shipmates, and he was so far successful that Gray and the doctor had come up and were already ambushed before the arrival of the treasure-hunters.

"Ah," said Silver, "it were fortunate for me that I had Hawkins here. You would have let old John be cut to bits, and never given it a thought, doctor."

"Not a thought," replied Dr. Livesey cheerily.

And by this time we had reached the gigs. The doctor, with the pick-axe, demolished one of them, and then we all got aboard the other and set out to go round by sea for North Inlet.

This was a run of eight or nine miles. Silver, though he was almost killed already with fatigue, was set to an oar, like the rest of us, and we were soon skimming swiftly over a smooth sea. Soon we passed out of the straits and doubled the south-east corner of the island, round which, four days ago, we had towed the *Hispaniola*.

As we passed the two-pointed hill, we could see the black mouth of Ben Gunn's cave and a figure standing by it, leaning on a musket. It was the squire, and we waved a handkerchief and gave him three cheers, in which the voice of Silver joined as heartily as any.

Three miles farther, just inside the mouth of North Inlet, what should we meet but the *Hispaniola*, cruising by herself? The last flood had lifted her, and had there been much wind or a strong tide current, as in the southern anchorage, we should never have found her more, or found her stranded beyond help. As it was, there was little amiss beyond the wreck of the main-sail. Another anchor was got ready and dropped in a fathom and a half of water. We all pulled round again to Rum Cove, the nearest point for Ben Gunn's treasure-house; and then Gray, single-handed, returned with the gig to the *Hispaniola*, where he was to pass the night on guard.

A gentle slope ran up from the beach to the entrance of the cave. At the top, the squire met us. To me he was cordial and kind, saying nothing of my escapade either in the way of blame or praise. At Silver's polite salute he somewhat flushed.

"John Silver," he said, "you're a prodigious villain and imposter—a monstrous imposter, sir. I am told I am not to prosecute you. Well, then, I will not. But the dead men, sir, hang about your neck like mill-stones."

"Thank you kindly, sir," replied Long John, again saluting.

"I dare you to thank me!" cried the squire. "It is a gross dereliction of my duty. Stand back."

And thereupon we all entered the cave. It was a large, airy place, with a little spring and a pool of clear water, overhung with ferns. The floor was sand. Before a big fire lay Captain Smollett; and in a far corner, only duskily flickered over by the blaze, I beheld great heaps of coin and quadrilaterals built of bars of gold. That was Flint's treasure that we had come so far to seek and that had cost already the lives of seventeen men from the *Hispaniola*. How many it had cost in the amassing, what blood and sorrow, what good ships scuttled on the deep, what brave men walking the plank blindfold, what shot of cannon, what shame and lies and cruelty, perhaps no man alive could tell. Yet there were still three upon that island—Silver, and old Morgan, and Ben Gunn—who had each taken his share in these crimes, as each had hoped in vain to share in the reward.

"Come in, Jim," said the captain. "You're a good boy in your line, Jim, but I don't think you and me'll go to sea again. You're too much of the born favourite for me. Is that you, John Silver? What brings you here, man?"

"Come back to my dooty, sir," returned Silver.

"Ah!" said the captain, and that was all he said.

What a supper I had of it that night, with all my friends around me; and what a meal it was, with Ben Gunn's salted goat and some delicacies and a bottle of old wine from the *Hispaniola*. Never, I am sure, were people gayer or happier. And there was Silver, sitting back almost out of the firelight, but eating heartily, prompt to spring forward when anything was wanted, even joining quietly in our laughter—the same bland, polite, obsequious seaman of the voyage out.

And Last

The next morning we fell early to work, for the transportation of this great mass of gold near a mile by land to the beach, and thence three miles by boat to the *Hispaniola,* was a considerable task for so small a number of workmen. The three fellows still abroad upon the island did not greatly trouble us; a single sentry on the shoulder of the hill was sufficient to ensure us against any sudden onslaught, and we thought, besides, they had had more than enough of fighting.

Therefore the work was pushed on briskly. Gray and Ben Gunn came and went with the boat, while the rest during their absences piled treasure on the beach. Two of the bars, slung in a rope's end, made a good load for a grown man—one that he was glad to walk slowly with. For my part, as I was not much use at carrying, I was kept busy all day in the cave packing the minted money into bread-bags.

It was a strange collection, like Billy Bones's hoard for the diversity of coinage, but so much larger and so much more varied that I think I never had more pleasure than in sorting them. English, French, Spanish, Portuguese, Georges, and Louises, doubloons and double guineas and moidores and sequins, the pictures of all the kings of Europe for the last hundred years, strange Oriental pieces stamped with what looked like wisps of string or bits of spider's web, round pieces and square pieces, and pieces bored through the middle, as if to wear them round your neck—nearly every variety of money in the world must, I think, have found a place in that collection; and for number, I am sure they were like autumn leaves, so that my back ached with stooping and my fingers with sorting them out.

Day after day this work went on; by every evening a fortune had been stowed aboard, but there was another fortune waiting for the morrow; and all this time we heard nothing of the three surviving mutineers.

At last—I think it was on the third night—the doctor and I were strolling on the shoulder of the hill where it overlooks the lowlands of the isle, when, from out the thick darkness below, the wind brought us a noise between shrieking and singing. It was only a snatch that reached our ears, followed by the former silence.

"Heaven forgive them," said the doctor; "'tis the mutineers!"

"All drunk, sir," struck in the voice of Silver from behind us.

Silver, I should say, was allowed his entire liberty, and in spite of daily rebuffs, seemed to regard himself once more as quite a privileged and friendly dependent. Indeed, it was remarkable how well he bore these slights and with what unwearying politeness he kept on trying to ingratiate himself with all. Yet, I think, none treated him better than a dog, unless it was Ben Gunn, who was still terribly afraid of his old quartermaster, or myself, who had really something to thank him for; although for that matter, I suppose, I had reason to think even worse of him than anybody else, for I had seen him meditating a fresh treachery upon the plateau. Accordingly, it was pretty gruffly that the doctor answered him.

"Drunk or raving," said he.

"Right you were, sir," replied Silver; "and precious little odds which, to you and me."

"I suppose you would hardly ask me to call you a humane man," returned the doctor with a sneer, "and so my feelings may surprise you, Master Silver. But if I were sure they were raving—as I am morally certain one, at least, of them is down with fever—I should leave this camp, and at whatever risk to my own carcass, take them the assistance of my skill."

"Ask your pardon, sir, you would be very wrong," quoth Silver. "You would lose your precious life, and you may lay to that. I'm on your side now, hand and glove; and I shouldn't wish for to see the party weakened, let alone yourself, seeing as I know what I owes you. But these men down there, they couldn't keep their word—no, not supposing they wished to; and what's more, they couldn't believe as you could."

"No," said the doctor. "You're the man to keep your word, we know that."

Well, that was about the last news we had of the three pirates. Only once we heard a gunshot a great way off and supposed them to be hunting. A council was held, and it was decided that we must desert them on the island—to the huge glee, I must say, of Ben Gunn, and with the strong approval of Gray. We left a good stock of powder and shot, the bulk of the salt goat, a few medicines, and some other necessaries, tools, clothing, a spare sail, a fathom or two of rope, and by the particular desire of the doctor, a handsome present of tobacco.

That was about our last doing on the island. Before that, we had got the treasure stowed and had shipped enough water and the remainder of the goat meat in case of any distress; and at last, one fine morning, we weighed anchor, which was about all that we could manage, and stood out of North Inlet, the same colours flying that the captain had flown and fought under at the palisade.

The three fellows must have been watching us closer than we thought for, as we soon had proved. For coming through the narrows, we had to lie very near the southern point, and there we saw all three of them kneeling together on a spit of sand, with their arms raised in supplication. It went to all our hearts, I think, to leave them in that wretched state; but we could not risk another mutiny; and to take them home for the gibbet would have been a cruel sort of kindness. The doctor hailed them and told them of the stores we had left, and where they were to find them. But they continued to call us by name and appeal to us, for God's sake, to be merciful and not leave them to die in such a place.

At last, seeing the ship still bore on her course and was now swiftly drawing out of earshot, one of them—I know not which it was—leapt to his feet with a hoarse cry, whipped his musket to his shoulder, and sent a shot whistling over Silver's head and through the main-sail.

After that, we kept under cover of the bulwarks, and when next I looked out they had disappeared from the spit, and the spit itself had almost melted out of sight in the growing distance. That was, at least, the end of that; and before noon, to my inexpressible joy, the highest rock of Treasure Island had sunk into the blue round of sea.

We were so short of men that everyone on board had to bear a hand—only the captain lying on a mattress in the stern and giving his orders, for though greatly recovered he was still in want of quiet. We laid her head for the nearest port in Spanish America, for we could not risk the voyage home without fresh hands; and as it was, what with baffling winds and a couple of fresh gales, we were all worn out before we reached it.

It was just at sundown when we cast anchor in a most beautiful land-locked gulf, and were immediately surrounded by shore boats full of Africans and Mexican Indians and half-bloods selling fruits and vegetables and offering to dive for bits of money. The sight of so many good-humoured faces (especially the blacks), the taste of the tropical fruits, and above all the lights that began to shine in the town made a most charming contrast to our dark and bloody sojourn on the island; and the doctor and the squire, taking me along with them, went ashore to pass the early part of the night. Here they met the captain of an English man-of-war, fell in talk with him, went on board his ship, and, in short, had so agreeable a time that day was breaking when we came alongside the *Hispaniola*.

Ben Gunn was on deck alone, and as soon as we came on board he began, with wonderful contortions, to make us a confession. Silver was gone. The maroon had connived at his escape in a shore boat some hours ago, and he now assured us he had only done so to preserve our lives, which would certainly have been forfeit if "that man with the one leg had stayed aboard." But this was not all. The sea-cook had not gone empty-handed. He had cut through a bulkhead unobserved and had removed one of the sacks of coin, worth perhaps three or four hundred guineas, to help him on his further wanderings.

I think we were all pleased to be so cheaply quit of him.

Well, to make a long story short, we got a few hands on board, made a good cruise home, and the *Hispaniola* reached Bristol just as Mr. Blandly was beginning to think of fitting out her consort. Five men only of those who had sailed returned with her. "Drink and the devil had done for the rest," with a vengeance, although, to be sure, we were not quite in so bad a case as that other ship they sang about:

With one man of her crew alive,

What put to sea with seventy-five.

All of us had an ample share of the treasure and used it wisely or foolishly, according to our natures. Captain Smollett is now retired from the sea. Gray not only saved his money, but being suddenly smit with the desire to rise, also studied his profession, and he is now mate and part owner of a fine full-rigged ship, married besides, and the father of a family. As for Ben Gunn, he got a thousand pounds, which he spent or lost in three weeks, or to be more exact, in nineteen days, for he was back begging on the twentieth. Then he was given a lodge to keep, exactly as he had feared upon the island; and he still lives, a great favourite, though something of a butt, with the country boys, and a notable singer in church on Sundays and saints' days.

Of Silver we have heard no more. That formidable seafaring man with one leg has at last gone clean out of my life; but I dare say he met his old Negress, and perhaps still lives in comfort with her and Captain Flint. It is to be hoped so, I suppose, for his chances of comfort in another world are very small.

The bar silver and the arms still lie, for all that I know, where Flint buried them; and certainly they shall lie there for me. Oxen and wain-ropes would not bring me back again to that accursed island; and the worst dreams that ever I have are when I hear the surf booming about its coasts or start upright in bed with the sharp voice of Captain Flint still ringing in my ears: "Pieces of eight! Pieces of eight!"

Lesson 120

1. Can you answer the questions about the book? (Answers)
    - Who are the narrators?
    - Name three settings from the book.
    - Name two pirates.
    - What does the parrot say over and over?
    - What flags are shown on the blockade and on the pirate ship?

Lesson 121

1. The author of your next book is Sir Walter Scott. Do you know what it means that he is called sir?
    - He was born in Scotland in 1771 and died in Scotland in 1832. He achieved international success as an author while still alive. He received the title of "Sir" after leading an expedition to recover lost crown jewels.
    - Walter Scott first wrote poetry and later prose. He used to write very early in the morning because he was a busy man. He was a sheriff and a landowner. Later in his life some of his business partners were in a great deal of debt, but Walter Scott refused to go into bankruptcy, but rather worked to pay off all the debt himself.
    - Make inferences. What do these tell you about Scott without coming right out and telling you?
2. Think about the title. What is a "talisman?" (Answers)
3. What do you imagine a story called *The Talisman* might be about?
4. The setting of the story is the Third Crusade. The Third Crusade took place over three years towards the end of the 12th century. Muslims had captured Jerusalem and the Holy Lands and European leaders vowed to reconquer it. (Third Crusade? There were others. They were all fights to control the Holy Land.) Several cities were taken, but they did not succeed in conquering Jerusalem. The two main leaders were

Saladin, for the Muslims, and Richard the Lionheart of England. He was fighting to gain Jerusalem for the Christians.

5. Do you know what chivalry is? It's the code of conduct expected of knights which included such character traits as: courage, honor, courtesy, justice, and a readiness to help the weak.
6. Knowing these things will help you understand the setting and characters.
7. This book is historical fiction. The story is made up. It's not true, but there are real life characters and real-life events in this made-up story. Sound like any other books you've read?

Vocabulary

1. Review you vocabulary from Lesson 91.

Lesson 122

1. Make a sheet to write down the characters as they are introduced. There is a war going on, again, and you can keep track of the different sides, the English and the Saracens.
2. In the first chapter we meet a lone knight, a Crusader, and he meets a Saracen, an enemy, whom he first fights and then makes peace with.
3. Unusual vocabulary:
    - Gauntlet - a long metal glove covering the wrist
    - Wristplated shoes - shoes covered with metal plates for protection
    - Falchion - a broad, short sword
    - Panoply - a protective covering
    - Hauberk - a long vest of mail, extending to the knees
    - Infidel - an unbeliever; to the Muslims Christians were infidels; to the Christians Muslims were infidels
4. Today read chapter 1.
5. The rider seems to be thinking that the land where he is riding is proof of the story that the Bible tells about Sodom. What was the punishment of Sodom? (Answers)
6. Slowly, the author reveals details about the identity of this rider? Who is he? (Answers)
7. Who does he meet in the desert? What is the result of their meeting? (Answers)

8. Draw a character sketch of the knight. Draw a picture of him and write a brief description of him.
9. If you have a question, something you are confused about, go back and try to find the answer. Don't start out confused. Every day make sure you know who's who and what they are doing. Don't read just to finish. Read to understand.

Vocabulary

1. Review the words from Lesson 36.

CHAPTER I.

They, too, retired

To the wilderness, but 'twas with arms.

PARADISE REGAINED.

The burning sun of Syria had not yet attained its highest point in the horizon, when a knight of the Red Cross, who had left his distant northern home and joined the host of the Crusaders in Palestine, was pacing slowly along the sandy deserts which lie in the vicinity of the Dead Sea, or, as it is called, the Lake Asphaltites, where the waves of the Jordan pour themselves into an inland sea, from which there is no discharge of waters.

The warlike pilgrim had toiled among cliffs and precipices during the earlier part of the morning. More lately, issuing from those rocky and dangerous defiles, he had entered upon that great plain, where the accursed cities provoked, in ancient days, the direct and dreadful vengeance of the Omnipotent.

The toil, the thirst, the dangers of the way, were forgotten, as the traveller recalled the fearful catastrophe which had converted into an arid and dismal wilderness the fair and fertile valley of Siddim, once well watered, even as the Garden of the Lord, now a parched and blighted waste, condemned to eternal sterility.

Crossing himself, as he viewed the dark mass of rolling waters, in colour as in duality unlike those of any other lake, the traveller shuddered as he remembered that beneath these sluggish waves lay the once proud cities of the plain, whose grave was dug by the thunder of the heavens, or the eruption of subterraneous fire, and whose remains were hid, even by that sea which holds no living fish in its bosom, bears no skiff on its surface, and, as if its own dreadful bed were the only fit receptacle for its sullen waters, sends not, like other lakes, a tribute to the ocean. The whole land around, as in the days of Moses, was "brimstone and salt; it is not sown, nor beareth, nor any grass groweth thereon." The land as well as the lake might be termed dead, as producing nothing having resemblance to vegetation, and even the very air was entirely devoid of its ordinary winged inhabitants, deterred probably by the odour of bitumen and sulphur which the burning sun exhaled from the waters of the lake in steaming clouds, frequently assuming the appearance of waterspouts. Masses of the slimy and sulphureous substance called naphtha, which floated idly on the sluggish and sullen waves, supplied those rolling clouds with new vapours, and afforded awful testimony to the truth of the Mosaic history.

Upon this scene of desolation the sun shone with almost intolerable splendour, and all living nature seemed to have hidden itself from the rays, excepting the solitary figure which moved through the flitting sand at a foot's pace, and appeared the sole breathing thing on the wide surface of the plain. The dress of the rider and the accoutrements of his horse were peculiarly unfit for the traveller in such a country. A coat of linked mail, with long sleeves, plated gauntlets, and a steel breastplate, had not been esteemed a sufficient weight of armour; there were also his triangular shield suspended round his neck, and his barred helmet of steel, over which he had a hood and collar of mail, which was drawn around the warrior's shoulders and throat, and filled up the vacancy between the hauberk and the headpiece. His lower limbs were sheathed, like his body, in flexible mail, securing the legs and thighs, while the feet rested in plated shoes, which corresponded with the gauntlets. A long, broad, straight-shaped, double-edged falchion, with a handle formed like a cross, corresponded with a stout poniard on the other side. The knight also bore, secured to his saddle, with one end resting on his stirrup, the long steel-headed lance, his own proper weapon, which, as he rode, projected backwards, and displayed its little pennoncelle, to dally with the faint breeze, or drop in the dead calm. To this cumbrous equipment must be added a surcoat of embroidered cloth, much frayed and worn, which was thus far useful that it excluded the burning rays of the sun from the armour, which they would otherwise have rendered intolerable to the wearer. The surcoat bore, in several places, the arms of the owner, although much defaced. These seemed to be a couchant leopard, with the motto, "I sleep; wake me not." An outline of the same device might be traced on his shield, though many a blow had almost effaced the painting. The flat top of his cumbrous cylindrical helmet was unadorned with any crest. In retaining their own unwieldy defensive armour, the Northern Crusaders seemed to set at defiance the nature of the climate and country to which they had come to war.

The accoutrements of the horse were scarcely less massive and unwieldy than those of the rider. The animal had a heavy saddle plated with steel, uniting in front with a species of breastplate, and behind with defensive armour made to cover the loins. Then there was a steel axe, or hammer, called a mace-of-arms, and which hung to the saddle-bow. The reins were secured by chain-work, and the front-stall of the bridle was a steel plate, with apertures for the eyes and nostrils, having in the midst a short, sharp pike, projecting from the forehead of the horse like the horn of the fabulous unicorn.

But habit had made the endurance of this load of panoply a second nature, both to the knight and his gallant charger. Numbers, indeed, of the Western warriors who hurried to Palestine died ere they became inured to the burning climate; but there were others to whom that climate became innocent and even friendly, and among this fortunate number was the solitary horseman who now traversed the border of the Dead Sea.

Nature, which cast his limbs in a mould of uncommon strength, fitted to wear his linked hauberk with as much ease as if the meshes had been formed of cobwebs, had endowed him with a constitution as strong as his limbs, and which bade defiance to almost all changes of climate, as well as to fatigue and privations of every kind. His disposition seemed, in some degree, to partake of the qualities of his bodily frame; and as the one possessed great strength and endurance, united with the power of violent exertion, the other, under a calm and undisturbed semblance, had much of the fiery and enthusiastic love of glory which constituted the principal attribute of the renowned Norman line, and had rendered them sovereigns in every corner of Europe where they had drawn their adventurous swords.

It was not, however, to all the race that fortune proposed such tempting rewards; and those obtained by the solitary knight during two years' campaign in Palestine had been only temporal fame, and, as he was taught to believe, spiritual privileges. Meantime, his slender stock of money had melted away, the rather that he did not pursue any of the ordinary modes by which the followers of the Crusade condescended to recruit their diminished resources at the expense of the people of Palestine—he exacted no gifts from the wretched natives for sparing their possessions when engaged in warfare with the Saracens, and he had not availed himself of any opportunity of enriching himself by the ransom of prisoners of consequence. The small train which had followed him from his native country had been gradually diminished, as the means of maintaining them disappeared, and his only remaining squire was at present on a sick-bed, and unable to attend his master, who travelled, as we have seen, singly and alone. This was of little consequence to the Crusader, who was accustomed to consider his good sword as his safest escort, and devout thoughts as his best companion.

Nature had, however, her demands for refreshment and repose even on the iron frame and patient disposition of the Knight of the Sleeping Leopard; and at noon, when the Dead Sea lay at some distance on his right, he joyfully hailed the sight of two or three palm-trees, which arose beside the well which was assigned for his mid-day station. His good horse, too, which had plodded forward with the steady endurance of his master, now lifted his head, expanded his nostrils, and quickened his pace, as if he snuffed afar off the living waters which marked the place of repose and refreshment. But labour and danger were doomed to intervene ere the horse or horseman reached the desired spot.

As the Knight of the Couchant Leopard continued to fix his eyes attentively on the yet distant cluster of palm-trees, it seemed to him as if some object was moving among them. The distant form separated itself from the trees, which partly hid its motions, and advanced towards the knight with a speed which soon showed a mounted horseman, whom his turban, long spear, and green caftan floating in the wind, on his nearer approach showed to be a Saracen cavalier. "In the desert," saith an Eastern proverb, "no man meets a friend." The Crusader was totally indifferent whether the infidel, who now approached on his gallant barb as if borne on the wings of an eagle, came as friend or foe—perhaps, as a vowed champion of the Cross, he might rather have preferred the latter. He disengaged his lance from his saddle, seized it with the right hand, placed it in rest with its point half elevated, gathered up the reins in the left, waked his horse's mettle with the spur, and prepared to encounter the stranger with the calm self-confidence belonging to the victor in many contests.

The Saracen came on at the speedy gallop of an Arab horseman, managing his steed more by his limbs and the inflection of his body than by any use of the reins, which hung loose in his left hand; so that he was enabled to wield the light, round buckler of the skin of the rhinoceros, ornamented with silver loops, which he wore on his arm, swinging it as if he meant to oppose its slender circle to the formidable thrust of the Western lance. His own long spear was not couched or levelled like that of his antagonist, but grasped by the middle with his right hand, and brandished at arm's-length above his head. As the cavalier approached his enemy at full career, he seemed to expect that the Knight of the Leopard should put his horse to the gallop to encounter him. But the Christian knight, well acquainted with the customs of Eastern warriors, did not mean to exhaust his good horse by any unnecessary exertion; and, on the contrary, made a dead halt, confident that if the enemy advanced to the actual shock, his own weight, and that of his powerful charger, would give him sufficient advantage, without the additional momentum of rapid motion. Equally sensible and apprehensive of such a probable result, the Saracen cavalier, when he had approached towards the Christian within twice the length of his lance, wheeled his steed to the left with inimitable dexterity, and rode twice around his antagonist, who, turning without quitting his ground, and presenting his front constantly to his enemy, frustrated his attempts to attack him on an unguarded point; so that the Saracen, wheeling his horse, was fain to retreat to the distance of a hundred yards. A second time, like a hawk attacking a heron, the heathen renewed the charge, and a second time was fain to retreat without coming to a close struggle. A third time he approached in the same manner, when the Christian knight, desirous to terminate this illusory warfare, in which he might at length have been worn out by the activity of his foeman, suddenly seized the mace which hung at his saddle-bow, and, with a strong hand and unerring aim, hurled it against the head of the Emir, for such and not less his enemy appeared. The Saracen was just aware of the formidable missile in time to interpose his light buckler betwixt the mace and his head; but the violence of the blow forced the buckler down on his turban, and though that defence also contributed to deaden its violence, the Saracen was beaten from his horse. Ere the Christian could avail himself of this mishap, his nimble foeman sprung from the ground, and, calling on his steed, which instantly returned to his side, he leaped into his seat without touching the stirrup, and regained all the advantage of which the Knight of the Leopard hoped to deprive him. But the latter had in the meanwhile recovered his mace, and the Eastern cavalier, who remembered the strength and dexterity with which his antagonist had aimed it, seemed to keep cautiously out of reach of that weapon of which he had so lately felt the force, while he showed his purpose of waging a distant warfare with missile weapons of his own. Planting his long spear in the sand at a distance from the scene of combat, he strung, with great address, a short bow, which he carried at his back; and putting his horse to the gallop, once more described two or three circles of a wider extent than formerly, in the course of which he discharged six arrows at the Christian with such unerring skill that the goodness of his harness alone saved him from being wounded in as many places. The seventh shaft apparently found a less perfect part of the armour, and the Christian dropped heavily from his horse. But what was the surprise of the Saracen, when, dismounting to examine the condition of his prostrate enemy, he found himself suddenly within the grasp of the European, who had had recourse to this artifice to bring his enemy within his reach! Even in this deadly grapple the Saracen was saved by his agility and presence of mind. He unloosed the sword-belt, in which the Knight of the Leopard had fixed his hold, and, thus eluding his fatal grasp, mounted his horse, which seemed to watch his motions with the intelligence of a human being, and again rode off. But in the last encounter the Saracen had lost his sword and his quiver of arrows, both of which were attached to the girdle which he was obliged to abandon. He had also lost his turban in the struggle.

These disadvantages seemed to incline the Moslem to a truce. He approached the Christian with his right hand extended, but no longer in a menacing attitude.

"There is truce betwixt our nations," he said, in the lingua franca commonly used for the purpose of communication with the Crusaders; "wherefore should there be war betwixt thee and me? Let there be peace betwixt us."

"I am well contented," answered he of the Couchant Leopard; "but what security dost thou offer that thou wilt observe the truce?"

"The word of a follower of the Prophet was never broken," answered the Emir. "It is thou, brave Nazarene, from whom I should demand security, did I not know that treason seldom dwells with courage."

The Crusader felt that the confidence of the Moslem made him ashamed of his own doubts.

"By the cross of my sword," he said, laying his hand on the weapon as he spoke, "I will be true companion to thee, Saracen, while our fortune wills that we remain in company together."

"By Mohammed, Prophet of God, and by Allah, God of the Prophet," replied his late foeman, "there is not treachery in my heart towards thee. And now wend we to yonder fountain, for the hour of rest is at hand, and the stream had hardly touched my lip when I was called to battle by thy approach."

The Knight of the Couchant Leopard yielded a ready and courteous assent; and the late foes, without an angry look or gesture of doubt, rode side by side to the little cluster of palm-trees.

Lesson 123

1. Stop and think. What has just happened? What do you think is going to happen next?
2. Read chapter 2. In this chapter, the Crusade knight and the Saracen discuss many things about their beliefs and customs as they ride.
3. The knight tells the Saracen that his horse could walk across water and not get wet. He swears that he speaks the truth. How could that happen? (It's a riddle.) (Answers)
4. Draw a character sketch of the Saracen.
5. This beautiful resting place in the middle of the desert is called an oasis.
6. These men are of different religions, Christian and Moslem (Muslim, Islam). How does each feel about drinking alcohol? Being married to one wife? (Answers)
7. Do you think that these two men like each other? Why or why not? (Answers)
8. This sentence gives a glimpse into the two religions. p. 36 "Both were courteous; but the courtesy of the Christian seemed to flow rather from a good-humored sense of what was due to others; that of the Moslem, from a high feeling of what was to be expected from himself." Christianity is others-focused; Islam is self-focused. At

times they may look the same, like both give to the poor, but the one does it out of love for God and others and the other out of love of self in order to earn righteous "points" to help him balance out the sins he's committed so that he can go to heaven.

CHAPTER II.

Times of danger have always, and in a peculiar degree, their seasons of good-will and security; and this was particularly so in the ancient feudal ages, in which, as the manners of the period had assigned war to be the chief and most worthy occupation of mankind, the intervals of peace, or rather of truce, were highly relished by those warriors to whom they were seldom granted, and endeared by the very circumstances which rendered them transitory. It is not worth while preserving any permanent enmity against a foe whom a champion has fought with to-day, and may again stand in bloody opposition to on the next morning. The time and situation afforded so much room for the ebullition of violent passions, that men, unless when peculiarly opposed to each other, or provoked by the recollection of private and individual wrongs, cheerfully enjoyed in each other's society the brief intervals of pacific intercourse which a warlike life admitted.

The distinction of religions, nay, the fanatical zeal which animated the followers of the Cross and of the Crescent against each other, was much softened by a feeling so natural to generous combatants, and especially cherished by the spirit of chivalry. This last strong impulse had extended itself gradually from the Christians to their mortal enemies the Saracens, both of Spain and of Palestine. The latter were, indeed, no longer the fanatical savages who had burst from the centre of Arabian deserts, with the sabre in one hand and the Koran in the other, to inflict death or the faith of Mohammed, or, at the best, slavery and tribute, upon all who dared to oppose the belief of the prophet of Mecca. These alternatives indeed had been offered to the unwarlike Greeks and Syrians; but in contending with the Western Christians, animated by a zeal as fiery as their own, and possessed of as unconquerable courage, address, and success in arms, the Saracens gradually caught a part of their manners, and especially of those chivalrous observances which were so well calculated to charm the minds of a proud and conquering people. They had their tournaments and games of chivalry; they had even their knights, or some rank analogous; and above all, the Saracens observed their plighted faith with an accuracy which might sometimes put to shame those who owned a better religion. Their truces, whether national or betwixt individuals, were faithfully observed; and thus it was that war, in itself perhaps the greatest of evils, yet gave occasion for display of good faith, generosity, clemency, and even kindly affections, which less frequently occur in more tranquil periods, where the passions of men, experiencing wrongs or entertaining quarrels which cannot be brought to instant decision, are apt to smoulder for a length of time in the bosoms of those who are so unhappy as to be their prey.

It was under the influence of these milder feelings which soften the horrors of warfare that the Christian and Saracen, who had so lately done their best for each other's mutual destruction, rode at a slow pace towards the fountain of palm-trees to which the Knight of the Couchant Leopard had been tending, when interrupted in mid-passage by his fleet and dangerous adversary. Each was wrapt for some time in his own reflections, and took breath after an encounter which had threatened to be fatal to one or both; and their good horses seemed no less to enjoy the interval of repose.

That of the Saracen, however, though he had been forced into much the more violent and extended sphere of motion, appeared to have suffered less from fatigue than the charger of the European knight. The sweat hung still clammy on the limbs of the latter, when those of the noble Arab were completely dried by the interval of tranquil exercise, all saving the foam-flakes which were still visible on his bridle and housings. The loose soil on which he trod so much augmented the distress of the Christian's horse, heavily loaded by his own armour and the weight of his rider, that the latter jumped from his saddle, and led his charger along the deep dust of the loamy soil, which was burnt in the sun into a substance more impalpable than the finest sand, and thus gave the faithful horse refreshment at the expense of his own additional toil; for, iron-sheathed as he was, he sunk over the mailed shoes at every step which he placed on a surface so light and unresisting.

"You are right," said the Saracen—and it was the first word that either had spoken since their truce was concluded; "your strong horse deserves your care. But what do you in the desert with an animal which sinks over the fetlock at every step as if he would plant each foot deep as the root of a date-tree?"

"Thou speakest rightly, Saracen," said the Christian knight, not delighted at the tone with which the infidel criticized his favourite steed—"rightly, according to thy knowledge and observation. But my good horse hath ere now borne me, in mine own land, over as wide a lake as thou seest yonder spread out behind us, yet not wet one hair above his hoof."

The Saracen looked at him with as much surprise as his manners permitted him to testify, which was only expressed by a slight approach to a disdainful smile, that hardly curled perceptibly the broad, thick moustache which enveloped his upper lip.

"It is justly spoken," he said, instantly composing himself to his usual serene gravity; "List to a Frank, and hear a fable."

"Thou art not courteous, misbeliever," replied the Crusader, "to doubt the word of a dubbed knight; and were it not that thou speakest in ignorance, and not in malice, our truce had its ending ere it is well begun. Thinkest thou I tell thee an untruth when I say that I, one of five hundred horsemen, armed in complete mail, have ridden—ay, and ridden for miles, upon water as solid as the crystal, and ten times less brittle?"

"What wouldst thou tell me?" answered the Moslem. "Yonder inland sea thou dost point at is peculiar in this, that, by the especial curse of God, it suffereth nothing to sink in its waves, but wafts them away, and casts them on its margin; but neither the Dead Sea, nor any of the seven oceans which environ the earth, will endure on their surface the pressure of a horse's foot, more than the Red Sea endured to sustain the advance of Pharaoh and his host."

"You speak truth after your knowledge, Saracen," said the Christian knight; "and yet, trust me, I fable not, according to mine. Heat, in this climate, converts the soil into something almost as unstable as water; and in my land cold often converts the water itself into a substance as hard as rock. Let us speak of this no longer, for the thoughts of the calm, clear, blue refulgence of a winter's lake, glimmering to stars and moonbeam, aggravate the horrors of this fiery desert, where, methinks, the very air which we breathe is like the vapour of a fiery furnace seven times heated."

The Saracen looked on him with some attention, as if to discover in what sense he was to understand words which, to him, must have appeared either to contain something of mystery or of imposition. At length he seemed determined in what manner to receive the language of his new companion.

"You are," he said, "of a nation that loves to laugh, and you make sport with yourselves, and with others, by telling what is impossible, and reporting what never chanced. Thou art one of the knights of France, who hold it for glee and pastime to GAB, as they term it, of exploits that are beyond human power. [Gaber. This French word signified a sort of sport much used among the French chivalry, which consisted in vying with each other in making the most romantic gasconades. The verb and the meaning are retained in Scottish.] I were wrong to challenge, for the time, the privilege of thy speech, since boasting is more natural to thee than truth."

"I am not of their land, neither of their fashion," said the Knight, "which is, as thou well sayest, to GAB of that which they dare not undertake—or, undertaking, cannot perfect. But in this I have imitated their folly, brave Saracen, that in talking to thee of what thou canst not comprehend, I have, even in speaking most simple truth, fully incurred the character of a braggart in thy eyes; so, I pray you, let my words pass."

They had now arrived at the knot of palm-trees and the fountain which welled out from beneath their shade in sparkling profusion.

We have spoken of a moment of truce in the midst of war; and this, a spot of beauty in the midst of a sterile desert, was scarce less dear to the imagination. It was a scene which, perhaps, would elsewhere have deserved little notice; but as the single speck, in a boundless horizon, which promised the refreshment of shade and living water, these blessings, held cheap where they are common, rendered the fountain and its neighbourhood a little paradise. Some generous or charitable hand, ere yet the evil days of Palestine began, had walled in and arched over the fountain, to preserve it from being absorbed in the earth, or choked by the flitting clouds of dust with which the least breath of wind covered the desert. The arch was now broken, and partly ruinous; but it still so far projected over and covered in the fountain that it excluded the sun in a great measure from its waters, which, hardly touched by a straggling beam, while all around was blazing, lay in a steady repose, alike delightful to the eye and the imagination. Stealing from under the arch, they were first received in a marble basin, much defaced indeed, but still cheering the eye, by showing that the place was anciently considered as a station, that the hand of man had been there and that man's accommodation had been in some measure attended to. The thirsty and weary traveller was reminded by these signs that others had suffered similar difficulties, reposed in the same spot, and, doubtless, found their way in safety to a more fertile country. Again, the scarce visible current which escaped from the basin served to nourish the few trees which surrounded the fountain, and where it sunk into the ground and disappeared, its refreshing presence was acknowledged by a carpet of velvet verdure.

In this delightful spot the two warriors halted, and each, after his own fashion, proceeded to relieve his horse from saddle, bit, and rein, and permitted the animals to drink at the basin, ere they refreshed themselves from the fountain head, which arose under the vault. They then suffered the steeds to go loose, confident that their interest, as well as their domesticated habits, would prevent their straying from the pure water and fresh grass.

Christian and Saracen next sat down together on the turf, and produced each the small allowance of store which they carried for their own refreshment. Yet, ere they severally proceeded to their scanty meal, they eyed each other with that curiosity which the close and doubtful conflict in which they had been so lately engaged was calculated to inspire. Each was desirous to measure the strength, and form some estimate of the character, of an adversary so formidable; and each was compelled to acknowledge that, had he fallen in the conflict, it had been by a noble hand.

The champions formed a striking contrast to each other in person and features, and might have formed no inaccurate representatives of their different nations. The Frank seemed a powerful man, built after the ancient Gothic cast of form, with light brown hair, which, on the removal of his helmet, was seen to curl thick and profusely over his head. His features had acquired, from the hot climate, a hue much darker than those parts of his neck which were less frequently exposed to view, or than was warranted by his full and well-opened blue eye, the colour of his hair, and of the moustaches which thickly shaded his upper lip, while his chin was carefully divested of beard, after the Norman fashion. His nose was Grecian and well formed; his mouth rather large in proportion, but filled with well-set, strong, and beautifully white teeth; his head small, and set upon the neck with much grace. His age could not exceed thirty, but if the effects of toil and climate were allowed for, might be three or four years under that period. His form was tall, powerful, and athletic, like that of a man whose strength might, in later life, become unwieldy, but which was hitherto united with lightness and activity. His hands, when he withdrew the mailed gloves, were long, fair, and well-proportioned; the wrist-bones peculiarly large and strong; and the arms remarkably well-shaped and brawny. A military hardihood and careless frankness of expression characterized his language and his motions; and his voice had the tone of one more accustomed to command than to obey, and who was in the habit of expressing his sentiments aloud and boldly, whenever he was called upon to announce them.

The Saracen Emir formed a marked and striking contrast with the Western Crusader. His stature was indeed above the middle size, but he was at least three inches shorter than the European, whose size approached the gigantic. His slender limbs and long, spare hands and arms, though well proportioned to his person, and suited to the style of his countenance, did not at first aspect promise the display of vigour and elasticity which the Emir had lately exhibited. But on looking more closely, his limbs, where exposed to view, seemed divested of all that was fleshy or cumbersome; so that nothing being left but bone, brawn, and sinew, it was a frame fitted for exertion and fatigue, far beyond that of a bulky champion, whose strength and size are counterbalanced by weight, and who is exhausted by his own exertions. The countenance of the Saracen naturally bore a general national resemblance to the Eastern tribe from whom he descended, and was as unlike as possible to the exaggerated terms in which the minstrels of the day were wont to represent the infidel champions, and the fabulous description which a sister art still presents as the Saracen's Head upon signposts. His features were small, well-formed, and delicate, though deeply embrowned by the Eastern sun, and terminated by a flowing and curled black beard, which seemed trimmed with peculiar care. The nose was straight and regular, the eyes keen, deep-set, black, and glowing, and his teeth equalled in beauty the ivory of his deserts. The person and proportions of the Saracen, in short, stretched on the turf near to his powerful antagonist, might have been compared to his sheeny and crescent-formed sabre, with its narrow and light but bright and keen Damascus blade, contrasted with the long and ponderous Gothic war-sword which was flung unbuckled on the same sod. The Emir was in the very flower of his age, and might perhaps have been termed eminently beautiful, but for the narrowness of his forehead and something of too much thinness and sharpness of feature, or at least what might have seemed such in a European estimate of beauty.

The manners of the Eastern warrior were grave, graceful, and decorous; indicating, however, in some particulars, the habitual restraint which men of warm and choleric tempers often set as a guard upon their native impetuosity of disposition, and at the same time a sense of his own dignity, which seemed to impose a certain formality of behaviour in him who entertained it.

This haughty feeling of superiority was perhaps equally entertained by his new European acquaintance, but the effect was different; and the same feeling, which dictated to the Christian knight a bold, blunt, and somewhat careless bearing, as one too conscious of his own importance to be anxious about the opinions of others, appeared to prescribe to the Saracen a style of courtesy more studiously and formally observant of ceremony. Both were courteous; but the courtesy of the Christian seemed to flow rather from a good humoured sense of what was due to others; that of the Moslem, from a high feeling of what was to be expected from himself.

The provision which each had made for his refreshment was simple, but the meal of the Saracen was abstemious. A handful of dates and a morsel of coarse barley-bread sufficed to relieve the hunger of the latter, whose education had habituated them to the fare of the desert, although, since their Syrian conquests, the Arabian simplicity of life frequently gave place to the most unbounded profusion of luxury. A few draughts from the lovely fountain by which they reposed completed his meal. That of the Christian, though coarse, was more genial. Dried hog's flesh, the abomination of the Moslemah, was the chief part of his repast; and his drink, derived from a leathern bottle, contained something better than pure element. He fed with more display of appetite, and drank with more appearance of satisfaction, than the Saracen judged it becoming to show in the performance of a mere bodily function; and, doubtless, the secret contempt which each entertained for the other, as the follower of a false religion, was considerably increased by the marked difference of their diet and manners. But each had found the weight of his opponent's arm, and the mutual respect which the bold struggle had created was sufficient to subdue other and inferior considerations. Yet the Saracen could not help remarking the circumstances which displeased him in the Christian's conduct and manners; and, after he had witnessed for some time in silence the keen appetite which protracted the knight's banquet long after his own was concluded, he thus addressed him:—

"Valiant Nazarene, is it fitting that one who can fight like a man should feed like a dog or a wolf? Even a misbelieving Jew would shudder at the food which you seem to eat with as much relish as if it were fruit from the trees of Paradise."

"Valiant Saracen," answered the Christian, looking up with some surprise at the accusation thus unexpectedly brought, "know thou that I exercise my Christian freedom in using that which is forbidden to the Jews, being, as they esteem themselves, under the bondage of the old law of Moses. We, Saracen, be it known to thee, have a better warrant for what we do—Ave Maria!—be we thankful." And, as if in defiance of his companion's scruples, he concluded a short Latin grace with a long draught from the leathern bottle.

"That, too, you call a part of your liberty," said the Saracen; "and as you feed like the brutes, so you degrade yourself to the bestial condition by drinking a poisonous liquor which even they refuse!"

"Know, foolish Saracen," replied the Christian, without hesitation, "that thou blasphemest the gifts of God, even with the blasphemy of thy father Ishmael. The juice of the grape is given to him that will use it wisely, as that which cheers the heart of man after toil, refreshes him in sickness, and comforts him in sorrow. He who so enjoyeth it may thank God for his winecup as for his daily bread; and he who abuseth the gift of Heaven is not a greater fool in his intoxication than thou in thine abstinence."

The keen eye of the Saracen kindled at this sarcasm, and his hand sought the hilt of his poniard. It was but a momentary thought, however, and died away in the recollection of the powerful champion with whom he had to deal, and the desperate grapple, the impression of which still throbbed in his limbs and veins; and he contented himself with pursuing the contest in colloquy, as more convenient for the time.

"Thy words" he said, "O Nazarene, might create anger, did not thy ignorance raise compassion. Seest thou not, O thou more blind than any who asks alms at the door of the Mosque, that the liberty thou dost boast of is restrained even in that which is dearest to man's happiness and to his household; and that thy law, if thou dost practise it, binds thee in marriage to one single mate, be she sick or healthy, be she fruitful or barren, bring she comfort and joy, or clamour and strife, to thy table and to thy bed? This, Nazarene, I do indeed call slavery; whereas, to the faithful, hath the Prophet assigned upon earth the patriarchal privileges of Abraham our father, and of Solomon, the wisest of mankind, having given us here a succession of beauty at our pleasure, and beyond the grave the black-eyed houris of Paradise."

"Now, by His name that I most reverence in heaven," said the Christian, "and by hers whom I most worship on earth, thou art but a blinded and a bewildered infidel!—That diamond signet which thou wearest on thy finger, thou holdest it, doubtless, as of inestimable value?"

"Balsora and Bagdad cannot show the like," replied the Saracen; "but what avails it to our purpose?"

"Much," replied the Frank, "as thou shalt thyself confess. Take my war-axe and dash the stone into twenty shivers: would each fragment be as valuable as the original gem, or would they, all collected, bear the tenth part of its estimation?"

"That is a child's question," answered the Saracen; "the fragments of such a stone would not equal the entire jewel in the degree of hundreds to one."

"Saracen," replied the Christian warrior, "the love which a true knight binds on one only, fair and faithful, is the gem entire; the affection thou flingest among thy enslaved wives and half-wedded slaves is worthless, comparatively, as the sparkling shivers of the broken diamond."

"Now, by the Holy Caaba," said the Emir, "thou art a madman who hugs his chain of iron as if it were of gold! Look more closely. This ring of mine would lose half its beauty were not the signet encircled and enchased with these lesser brilliants, which grace it and set it off. The central diamond is man, firm and entire, his value depending on himself alone; and this circle of lesser jewels are women, borrowing his lustre, which he deals out to them as best suits his pleasure or his convenience. Take the central stone from the signet, and the diamond itself remains as valuable as ever, while the lesser gems are comparatively of little value. And this is the true reading of thy parable; for what sayeth the poet Mansour: 'It is the favour of man which giveth beauty and comeliness to woman, as the stream glitters no longer when the sun ceaseth to shine.'"

"Saracen," replied the Crusader, "thou speakest like one who never saw a woman worthy the affection of a soldier. Believe me, couldst thou look upon those of Europe, to whom, after Heaven, we of the order of knighthood vow fealty and devotion, thou wouldst loathe for ever the poor sensual slaves who form thy haram. The beauty of our fair ones gives point to our spears and edge to our swords; their words are our law; and as soon will a lamp shed lustre when unkindled, as a knight distinguish himself by feats of arms, having no mistress of his affection."

"I have heard of this frenzy among the warriors of the West," said the Emir, "and have ever accounted it one of the accompanying symptoms of that insanity which brings you hither to obtain possession of an empty sepulchre. But yet, methinks, so highly have the Franks whom I have met with extolled the beauty of their women, I could be well contented to behold with mine own eyes those charms which can transform such brave warriors into the tools of their pleasure."

"Brave Saracen," said the Knight, "if I were not on a pilgrimage to the Holy Sepulchre, it should be my pride to conduct you, on assurance of safety, to the camp of Richard of England, than whom none knows better how to do honour to a noble foe; and though I be poor and unattended yet have I interest to secure for thee, or any such as thou seemest, not safety only, but respect and esteem. There shouldst thou see several of the fairest beauties of France and Britain form a small circle, the brilliancy of which exceeds ten-thousandfold the lustre of mines of diamonds such as thine."

"Now, by the corner-stone of the Caaba!" said the Saracen, "I will accept thy invitation as freely as it is given, if thou wilt postpone thy present intent; and, credit me, brave Nazarene, it were better for thyself to turn back thy horse's head towards the camp of thy people, for to travel towards Jerusalem without a passport is but a wilful casting-away of thy life."

"I have a pass," answered the Knight, producing a parchment, "Under Saladin's hand and signet."

The Saracen bent his head to the dust as he recognized the seal and handwriting of the renowned Soldan of Egypt and Syria; and having kissed the paper with profound respect, he pressed it to his forehead, then returned it to the Christian, saying, "Rash Frank, thou hast sinned against thine own blood and mine, for not showing this to me when we met."

"You came with levelled spear," said the Knight. "Had a troop of Saracens so assailed me, it might have stood with my honour to have shown the Soldan's pass, but never to one man."

"And yet one man," said the Saracen haughtily, "was enough to interrupt your journey."

"True, brave Moslem," replied the Christian; "but there are few such as thou art. Such falcons fly not in flocks; or, if they do, they pounce not in numbers upon one."

"Thou dost us but justice," said the Saracen, evidently gratified by the compliment, as he had been touched by the implied scorn of the European's previous boast; "from us thou shouldst have had no wrong. But well was it for me that I failed to slay thee, with the safeguard of the king of kings upon thy person. Certain it were, that the cord or the sabre had justly avenged such guilt."

"I am glad to hear that its influence shall be availing to me," said the Knight; "for I have heard that the road is infested with robber-tribes, who regard nothing in comparison of an opportunity of plunder."

"The truth has been told to thee, brave Christian," said the Saracen; "but I swear to thee, by the turban of the Prophet, that shouldst thou miscarry in any haunt of such villains, I will myself undertake thy revenge with five thousand horse. I will slay every male of them, and send their women into such distant captivity that the name of their tribe shall never again be heard within five hundred miles of Damascus. I will sow with salt the foundations of their village, and there shall never live thing dwell there, even from that time forward."

"I had rather the trouble which you design for yourself were in revenge of some other more important person than of me, noble Emir," replied the Knight; "but my vow is recorded in heaven, for good or for evil, and I must be indebted to you for pointing me out the way to my resting-place for this evening."

"That," said the Saracen, "must be under the black covering of my father's tent."

"This night," answered the Christian, "I must pass in prayer and penitence with a holy man, Theodorick of Engaddi, who dwells amongst these wilds, and spends his life in the service of God."

"I will at least see you safe thither," said the Saracen.

"That would be pleasant convoy for me," said the Christian; "yet might endanger the future security of the good father; for the cruel hand of your people has been red with the blood of the servants of the Lord, and therefore do we come hither in plate and mail, with sword and lance, to open the road to the Holy Sepulchre, and protect the chosen saints and anchorites who yet dwell in this land of promise and of miracle."

"Nazarene," said the Moslem, "in this the Greeks and Syrians have much belied us, seeing we do but after the word of Abubeker Alwakel, the successor of the Prophet, and, after him, the first commander of true believers. 'Go forth,' he said, 'Yezed Ben Sophian,' when he sent that renowned general to take Syria from the infidels; 'quit yourselves like men in battle, but slay neither the aged, the infirm, the women, nor the children. Waste not the land, neither destroy corn and fruit-trees; they are the gifts of Allah. Keep faith when you have made any covenant, even if it be to your own harm. If ye find holy men labouring with their hands, and serving God in the desert, hurt them not, neither destroy their dwellings. But when you find them with shaven crowns, they are of the synagogue of Satan! Smite with the sabre, slay, cease not till they become believers or tributaries.' As the Caliph, companion of the Prophet, hath told us, so have we done, and those whom our justice has smitten are but the priests of Satan. But unto the good men who, without stirring up nation against nation, worship sincerely in the faith of Issa Ben Mariam, we are a shadow and a shield; and such being he whom you seek, even though the light of the Prophet hath not reached him, from me he will only have love, favour, and regard."

"The anchorite whom I would now visit," said the warlike pilgrim, "is, I have heard, no priest; but were he of that anointed and sacred order, I would prove with my good lance, against paynim and infidel—"

"Let us not defy each other, brother," interrupted the Saracen; "we shall find, either of us, enough of Franks or of Moslemah on whom to exercise both sword and lance. This Theodorick is protected both by Turk and Arab; and, though one of strange conditions at intervals, yet, on the whole, he bears himself so well as the follower of his own prophet, that he merits the protection of him who was sent—"

"Now, by Our Lady, Saracen," exclaimed the Christian, "if thou darest name in the same breath the camel-driver of Mecca with—"

An electrical shock of passion thrilled through the form of the Emir; but it was only momentary, and the calmness of his reply had both dignity and reason in it, when he said, "Slander not him whom thou knowest not—the rather that we venerate the founder of thy religion, while we condemn the doctrine which your priests have spun from it. I will myself guide thee to the cavern of the hermit, which, methinks, without my help, thou wouldst find it a hard matter to reach. And, on the way, let us leave to mollahs and to monks to dispute about the divinity of our faith, and speak on themes which belong to youthful warriors—upon battles, upon beautiful women, upon sharp swords, and upon bright armour."

Lesson 124

1. Unusual vocabulary:
    - casque — his type of helmet

1. Make sure you are pronouncing chasm correctly. (Ask if you don't know.)
2. Make sure you know where Syria is.
3. Make sure you know who the Prophet is. He is the Prophet Muhammad who wrote down the Koran.
4. Read the first half of chapter 3. In this chapter the Saracen is leading the knight to find a hermit, who finds them first and attacks the Saracen but doesn't do much harm.
5. Now we know the names and countries of the knight and the Saracen. The knight is Kenneth of the Crouching Leopard, and he is from Scotland. The Saracen is

Sheerkohf, the Lion of the Mountains, and he is from Kurdistan, an area that is prominently Kurds including areas of Turkey, Iraq, Iran and Syria.

6. While you read, pay attention to how Scott develops his characters. He may tell you about the character with adjectives, or he might show you. He might reveal something about a character in how another character reacts to him or in how he acts toward another. Make inferences about characters based on their actions.

CHAPTER III.

The warriors arose from their place of brief rest and simple refreshment, and courteously aided each other while they carefully replaced and adjusted the harness from which they had relieved for the time their trusty steeds. Each seemed familiar with an employment which at that time was a part of necessary and, indeed, of indispensable duty. Each also seemed to possess, as far as the difference betwixt the animal and rational species admitted, the confidence and affection of the horse which was the constant companion of his travels and his warfare. With the Saracen this familiar intimacy was a part of his early habits; for, in the tents of the Eastern military tribes, the horse of the soldier ranks next to, and almost equal in importance with, his wife and his family; and with the European warrior, circumstances, and indeed necessity, rendered his war-horse scarcely less than his brother in arms. The steeds, therefore, suffered themselves quietly to be taken from their food and liberty, and neighed and snuffled fondly around their masters, while they were adjusting their accoutrements for further travel and additional toil. And each warrior, as he prosecuted his own task, or assisted with courtesy his companion, looked with observant curiosity at the equipments of his fellow-traveller, and noted particularly what struck him as peculiar in the fashion in which he arranged his riding accoutrements.

Ere they remounted to resume their journey, the Christian Knight again moistened his lips and dipped his hands in the living fountain, and said to his pagan associate of the journey, "I would I knew the name of this delicious fountain, that I might hold it in my grateful remembrance; for never did water slake more deliciously a more oppressive thirst than I have this day experienced."

"It is called in the Arabic language," answered the Saracen, "by a name which signifies the Diamond of the Desert."

"And well is it so named," replied the Christian. "My native valley hath a thousand springs, but not to one of them shall I attach hereafter such precious recollection as to this solitary fount, which bestows its liquid treasures where they are not only delightful, but nearly indispensable."

"You say truth," said the Saracen; "for the curse is still on yonder sea of death, and neither man nor beast drinks of its waves, nor of the river which feeds without filling it, until this inhospitable desert be passed."

They mounted, and pursued their journey across the sandy waste. The ardour of noon was now past, and a light breeze somewhat alleviated the terrors of the desert, though not without bearing on its wings an impalpable dust, which the Saracen little heeded, though his heavily-armed companion felt it as such an annoyance that he hung his iron casque at his saddle-bow, and substituted the light riding-cap, termed in the language of the time a MORTIER, from its resemblance in shape to an ordinary mortar. They rode together for some time in silence, the Saracen performing the part of director and guide of the journey, which he did by observing minute marks and bearings of the distant rocks, to a ridge of which they were gradually approaching. For a little time he seemed absorbed in the task, as a pilot when navigating a vessel through a difficult channel; but they had not proceeded half a league when he seemed secure of his route, and disposed, with more frankness than was usual to his nation, to enter into conversation.

"You have asked the name," he said, "of a mute fountain, which hath the semblance, but not the reality, of a living thing. Let me be pardoned to ask the name of the companion with whom I have this day encountered, both in danger and in repose, and which I cannot fancy unknown even here among the deserts of Palestine?"

"It is not yet worth publishing," said the Christian. "Know, however, that among the soldiers of the Cross I am called Kenneth—Kenneth of the Couching Leopard; at home I have other titles, but they would sound harsh in an Eastern ear. Brave Saracen, let me ask which of the tribes of Arabia claims your descent, and by what name you are known?"

"Sir Kenneth," said the Moslem, "I joy that your name is such as my lips can easily utter. For me, I am no Arab, yet derive my descent from a line neither less wild nor less warlike. Know, Sir Knight of the Leopard, that I am Sheerkohf, the Lion of the Mountain, and that Kurdistan, from which I derive my descent, holds no family more noble than that of Seljook."

"I have heard," answered the Christian, "that your great Soldan claims his blood from the same source?"

"Thanks to the Prophet that hath so far honoured our mountains as to send from their bosom him whose word is victory," answered the paynim. "I am but as a worm before the King of Egypt and Syria, and yet in my own land something my name may avail. Stranger, with how many men didst thou come on this warfare?"

"By my faith," said Sir Kenneth, "with aid of friends and kinsmen, I was hardly pinched to furnish forth ten well-appointed lances, with maybe some fifty more men, archers and varlets included. Some have deserted my unlucky pennon—some have fallen in battle—several have died of disease—and one trusty armour-bearer, for whose life I am now doing my pilgrimage, lies on the bed of sickness."

"Christian," said Sheerkohf, "here I have five arrows in my quiver, each feathered from the wing of an eagle. When I send one of them to my tents, a thousand warriors mount on horseback—when I send another, an equal force will arise—for the five, I can command five thousand men; and if I send my bow, ten thousand mounted riders will shake the desert. And with thy fifty followers thou hast come to invade a land in which I am one of the meanest!"

"Now, by the rood, Saracen," retorted the Western warrior, "thou shouldst know, ere thou vauntest thyself, that one steel glove can crush a whole handful of hornets."

"Ay, but it must first enclose them within its grasp," said the Saracen, with a smile which might have endangered their new alliance, had he not changed the subject by adding, "And is bravery so much esteemed amongst the Christian princes that thou, thus void of means and of men, canst offer, as thou didst of late, to be my protector and security in the camp of thy brethren?"

"Know, Saracen," said the Christian, "since such is thy style, that the name of a knight, and the blood of a gentleman, entitle him to place himself on the same rank with sovereigns even of the first degree, in so far as regards all but regal authority and dominion. Were Richard of England himself to wound the honour of a knight as poor as I am, he could not, by the law of chivalry, deny him the combat."

"Methinks I should like to look upon so strange a scene," said the Emir, "in which a leathern belt and a pair of spurs put the poorest on a level with the most powerful."

"You must add free blood and a fearless heart," said the Christian; "then, perhaps, you will not have spoken untruly of the dignity of knighthood."

"And mix you as boldly amongst the females of your chiefs and leaders?" asked the Saracen.

"God forbid," said the Knight of the Leopard, "that the poorest knight in Christendom should not be free, in all honourable service, to devote his hand and sword, the fame of his actions, and the fixed devotion of his heart, to the fairest princess who ever wore coronet on her brow!"

"But a little while since," said the Saracen, "and you described love as the highest treasure of the heart—thine hath undoubtedly been high and nobly bestowed?"

"Stranger," answered the Christian, blushing deeply as he spoke, "we tell not rashly where it is we have bestowed our choicest treasures. It is enough for thee to know that, as thou sayest, my love is highly and nobly bestowed—most highly—most nobly; but if thou wouldst hear of love and broken lances, venture thyself, as thou sayest, to the camp of the Crusaders, and thou wilt find exercise for thine ears, and, if thou wilt, for thy hands too."

The Eastern warrior, raising himself in his stirrups, and shaking aloft his lance, replied, "Hardly, I fear, shall I find one with a crossed shoulder who will exchange with me the cast of the jerrid."

"I will not promise for that," replied the Knight; "though there be in the camp certain Spaniards, who have right good skill in your Eastern game of hurling the javelin."

"Dogs, and sons of dogs!" ejaculated the Saracen; "what have these Spaniards to do to come hither to combat the true believers, who, in their own land, are their lords and taskmasters? with them I would mix in no warlike pastime."

"Let not the knights of Leon or Asturias hear you speak thus of them," said the Knight of the Leopard. "But," added he, smiling at the recollection of the morning's combat, "if, instead of a reed, you were inclined to stand the cast of a battle-axe, there are enough of Western warriors who would gratify your longing."

"By the beard of my father, sir," said the Saracen, with an approach to laughter, "the game is too rough for mere sport. I will never shun them in battle, but my head" (pressing his hand to his brow) "will not, for a while, permit me to seek them in sport."

"I would you saw the axe of King Richard," answered the Western warrior, "to which that which hangs at my saddle-bow weighs but as a feather."

"We hear much of that island sovereign," said the Saracen. "Art thou one of his subjects?"

"One of his followers I am, for this expedition," answered the Knight, "and honoured in the service; but not born his subject, although a native of the island in which he reigns."

"How mean you? " said the Eastern soldier; "have you then two kings in one poor island?"

"As thou sayest," said the Scot, for such was Sir Kenneth by birth. "It is even so; and yet, although the inhabitants of the two extremities of that island are engaged in frequent war, the country can, as thou seest, furnish forth such a body of men-at-arms as may go far to shake the unholy hold which your master hath laid on the cities of Zion."

"By the beard of Saladin, Nazarene, but that it is a thoughtless and boyish folly, I could laugh at the simplicity of your great Sultan, who comes hither to make conquests of deserts and rocks, and dispute the possession of them with those who have tenfold numbers at command, while he leaves a part of his narrow islet, in which he was born a sovereign, to the dominion of another sceptre than his. Surely, Sir Kenneth, you and the other good men of your country should have submitted yourselves to the dominion of this King Richard ere you left your native land, divided against itself, to set forth on this expedition?"

Hasty and fierce was Kenneth's answer. "No, by the bright light of Heaven! If the King of England had not set forth to the Crusade till he was sovereign of Scotland, the Crescent might, for me, and all true-hearted Scots, glimmer for ever on the walls of Zion."

Thus far he had proceeded, when, suddenly recollecting himself, he muttered, "MEA CULPA! MEA CULPA! what have I, a soldier of the Cross, to do with recollection of war betwixt Christian nations!"

The rapid expression of feeling corrected by the dictates of duty did not escape the Moslem, who, if he did not entirely understand all which it conveyed, saw enough to convince him with the assurance that Christians, as well as Moslemah, had private feelings of personal pique, and national quarrels, which were not entirely reconcilable. But the Saracens were a race, polished, perhaps, to the utmost extent which their religion permitted, and particularly capable of entertaining high ideas of courtesy and politeness; and such sentiments prevented his taking any notice of the inconsistency of Sir Kenneth's feelings in the opposite characters of a Scot and a Crusader.

Meanwhile, as they advanced, the scene began to change around them. They were now turning to the eastward, and had reached the range of steep and barren hills which binds in that quarter the naked plain, and varies the surface of the country, without changing its sterile character. Sharp, rocky eminences began to rise around them, and, in a short time, deep declivities and ascents, both formidable in height and difficult from the narrowness of the path, offered to the travellers obstacles of a different kind from those with which they had recently contended.

Dark caverns and chasms amongst the rocks—those grottoes so often alluded to in Scripture—yawned fearfully on either side as they proceeded, and the Scottish knight was informed by the

Emir that these were often the refuge of beasts of prey, or of men still more ferocious, who, driven to desperation by the constant war, and the oppression exercised by the soldiery, as well of the Cross as of the Crescent, had become robbers, and spared neither rank nor religion, neither sex nor age, in their depredations.

The Scottish knight listened with indifference to the accounts of ravages committed by wild beasts or wicked men, secure as he felt himself in his own valour and personal strength; but he was struck with mysterious dread when he recollected that he was now in the awful wilderness of the forty days' fast, and the scene of the actual personal temptation, wherewith the Evil Principle was permitted to assail the Son of Man. He withdrew his attention gradually from the light and worldly conversation of the infidel warrior beside him, and, however acceptable his gay and gallant bravery would have rendered him as a companion elsewhere, Sir Kenneth felt as if, in those wildernesses the waste and dry places in which the foul spirits were wont to wander when expelled the mortals whose forms they possessed, a bare-footed friar would have been a better associate than the gay but unbelieving paynim.

These feelings embarrassed him the rather that the Saracen's spirits appeared to rise with the journey, and because the farther he penetrated into the gloomy recesses of the mountains, the lighter became his conversation, and when he found that unanswered, the louder grew his song. Sir Kenneth knew enough of the Eastern languages to be assured that he chanted sonnets of love, containing all the glowing praises of beauty in which the Oriental poets are so fond of luxuriating, and which, therefore, were peculiarly unfitted for a serious or devotional strain of thought, the feeling best becoming the Wilderness of the Temptation. With inconsistency enough, the Saracen also sung lays in praise of wine, the liquid ruby of the Persian poets; and his gaiety at length became so unsuitable to the Christian knight's contrary train of sentiments, as, but for the promise of amity which they had exchanged, would most likely have made Sir Kenneth take measures to change his note. As it was, the Crusader felt as if he had by his side some gay, licentious fiend, who endeavoured to ensnare his soul, and endanger his immortal salvation, by inspiring loose thoughts of earthly pleasure, and thus polluting his devotion, at a time when his faith as a Christian and his vow as a pilgrim called on him for a serious and penitential state of mind. He was thus greatly perplexed, and undecided how to act; and it was in a tone of hasty displeasure that, at length breaking silence, he interrupted the lay of the celebrated Rudpiki, in which he prefers the mole on his mistress's bosom to all the wealth of Bokhara and Samarcand.

"Saracen," said the Crusader sternly, "blinded as thou art, and plunged amidst the errors of a false law, thou shouldst yet comprehend that there are some places more holy than others, and that there are some scenes also in which the Evil One hath more than ordinary power over sinful mortals. I will not tell thee for what awful reason this place—these rocks—these caverns with their gloomy arches, leading as it were to the central abyss—are held an especial haunt of Satan and his angels. It is enough that I have been long warned to beware of this place by wise and holy men, to whom the qualities of the unholy region are well known. Wherefore, Saracen, forbear thy foolish and ill-timed levity, and turn thy thoughts to things more suited to the spot—although, alas for thee! thy best prayers are but as blasphemy and sin."

The Saracen listened with some surprise, and then replied, with good-humour and gaiety, only so far repressed as courtesy required, "Good Sir Kenneth, methinks you deal unequally by your companion, or else ceremony is but indifferently taught amongst your Western tribes. I took no offence when I saw you gorge hog's flesh and drink wine, and permitted you to enjoy a treat which you called your Christian liberty, only pitying in my heart your foul pastimes. Wherefore, then, shouldst thou take scandal, because I cheer, to the best of my power, a gloomy road with a cheerful verse? What saith the poet, 'Song is like the dews of heaven on the bosom of the desert; it cools the path of the traveller.'"

"Friend Saracen," said the Christian, "I blame not the love of minstrelsy and of the GAI SCIENCE; albeit, we yield unto it even too much room in our thoughts when they should be bent on better things. But prayers and holy psalms are better fitting than LAIS of love, or of wine-cups, when men walk in this Valley of the Shadow of Death, full of fiends and demons, whom the prayers of holy men have driven forth from the haunts of humanity to wander amidst scenes as accursed as themselves."

"Speak not thus of the Genii, Christian," answered the Saracen, "for know thou speakest to one whose line and nation drew their origin from the immortal race which your sect fear and blaspheme."

"I well thought," answered the Crusader, "that your blinded race had their descent from the foul fiend, without whose aid you would never have been able to maintain this blessed land of Palestine against so many valiant soldiers of God. I speak not thus of thee in particular, Saracen, but generally of thy people and religion. Strange is it to me, however, not that you should have the descent from the Evil One, but that you should boast of it."

"From whom should the bravest boast of descending, saving from him that is bravest?" said the Saracen; "from whom should the proudest trace their line so well as from the Dark Spirit, which would rather fall headlong by force than bend the knee by his will? Eblis may be hated, stranger, but he must be feared; and such as Eblis are his descendants of Kurdistan."

Tales of magic and of necromancy were the learning of the period, and Sir Kenneth heard his companion's confession of diabolical descent without any disbelief, and without much wonder; yet not without a secret shudder at finding himself in this fearful place, in the company of one who avouched himself to belong to such a lineage. Naturally insusceptible, however, of fear, he crossed himself, and stoutly demanded of the Saracen an account of the pedigree which he had boasted. The latter readily complied.

"Know, brave stranger," he said, "that when the cruel Zohauk, one of the descendants of Giamschid, held the throne of Persia, he formed a league with the Powers of Darkness, amidst the secret vaults of Istakhar, vaults which the hands of the elementary spirits had hewn out of the living rock long before Adam himself had an existence. Here he fed, with daily oblations of human blood, two devouring serpents, which had become, according to the poets, a part of himself, and to sustain whom he levied a tax of daily human sacrifices, till the exhausted patience of his subjects caused some to raise up the scimitar of resistance, like the valiant Blacksmith and the victorious Feridoun, by whom the tyrant was at length dethroned, and imprisoned for ever in the dismal caverns of the mountain Damavend. But ere that deliverance had taken place, and whilst the power of the bloodthirsty tyrant was at its height, the band of ravening slaves whom he had sent forth to purvey victims for his daily sacrifice brought to the vaults of the palace of

Istakhar seven sisters so beautiful that they seemed seven houris. These seven maidens were the daughters of a sage, who had no treasures save those beauties and his own wisdom. The last was not sufficient to foresee this misfortune, the former seemed ineffectual to prevent it. The eldest exceeded not her twentieth year, the youngest had scarce attained her thirteenth; and so like were they to each other that they could not have been distinguished but for the difference of height, in which they gradually rose in easy gradation above each other, like the ascent which leads to the gates of Paradise. So lovely were these seven sisters when they stood in the darksome vault, disrobed of all clothing saving a cymar of white silk, that their charms moved the hearts of those who were not mortal. Thunder muttered, the earth shook, the wall of the vault was rent, and at the chasm entered one dressed like a hunter, with bow and shafts, and followed by six others, his brethren. They were tall men, and, though dark, yet comely to behold; but their eyes had more the glare of those of the dead than the light which lives under the eyelids of the living. 'Zeineb,' said the leader of the band—and as he spoke he took the eldest sister by the hand, and his voice was soft, low, and melancholy—'I am Cothrob, king of the subterranean world, and supreme chief of Ginnistan. I and my brethren are of those who, created out of the pure elementary fire, disdained, even at the command of Omnipotence, to do homage to a clod of earth, because it was called Man. Thou mayest have heard of us as cruel, unrelenting, and persecuting. It is false. We are by nature kind and generous; only vengeful when insulted, only cruel when affronted. We are true to those who trust us; and we have heard the invocations of thy father, the sage Mithrasp, who wisely worships not alone the Origin of Good, but that which is called the Source of Evil. You and your sisters are on the eve of death; but let each give to us one hair from your fair tresses, in token of fealty, and we will carry you many miles from hence to a place of safety, where you may bid defiance to Zohauk and his ministers.' The fear of instant death, saith the poet, is like the rod of the prophet Haroun, which devoured all other rods when transformed into snakes before the King of Pharaoh; and the daughters of the Persian sage were less apt than others to be afraid of the addresses of a spirit. They gave the tribute which Cothrob demanded, and in an instant the sisters were transported to an enchanted castle on the mountains of Tugrut, in Kurdistan, and were never again seen by mortal eye. But in process of time seven youths, distinguished in the war and in the chase, appeared in the environs of the castle of the demons. They were darker, taller, fiercer, and more resolute than any of the scattered inhabitants of the valleys of Kurdistan; and they took to themselves wives, and became fathers of the seven tribes of the Kurdmans, whose valour is known throughout the universe."

The Christian knight heard with wonder the wild tale, of which Kurdistan still possesses the traces, and, after a moment's thought, replied, "Verily, Sir Knight, you have spoken well—your genealogy may be dreaded and hated, but it cannot be contemned. Neither do I any longer wonder at your obstinacy in a false faith, since, doubtless, it is part of the fiendish disposition which hath descended from your ancestors, those infernal huntsmen, as you have described them, to love falsehood rather than truth; and I no longer marvel that your spirits become high and exalted, and vent themselves in verse and in tunes, when you approach to the places encumbered by the haunting of evil spirits, which must excite in you that joyous feeling which others experience when approaching the land of their human ancestry."

"By my father's beard, I think thou hast the right," said the Saracen, rather amused than offended by the freedom with which the Christian had uttered his reflections; "for, though the

Prophet (blessed be his name!) hath sown amongst us the seed of a better faith than our ancestors learned in the ghostly halls of Tugrut, yet we are not willing, like other Moslemah, to pass hasty doom on the lofty and powerful elementary spirits from whom we claim our origin. These Genii, according to our belief and hope, are not altogether reprobate, but are still in the way of probation, and may hereafter be punished or rewarded. Leave we this to the mollahs and the imauns. Enough that with us the reverence for these spirits is not altogether effaced by what we have learned from the Koran, and that many of us still sing, in memorial of our fathers' more ancient faith, such verses as these."

So saying, he proceeded to chant verses, very ancient in the language and structure, which some have thought derive their source from the worshippers of Arimanes, the Evil Principle.

Lesson 125

1. Unusual vocabulary:
    - "hirsute" means "hairy"
1. Finish reading chapter 3.
2. A new character enters the story. Add him to your character list and include a description of who he is.
3. Why does the new character attack the Saracen? (Answers)
4. What's one Bible verse tells what's wrong with his attacking the Saracen? (Answers)
5. Who is the real enemy of the cross?
6. I feel that the author's tone in telling this story so far is a little humorous. Would you agree or disagree? Why? (Answers–my opinion)

AHRIMAN.

Dark Ahriman, whom Irak still
Holds origin of woe and ill!
When, bending at thy shrine,
We view the world with troubled eye,
Where see we 'neath the extended sky,
An empire matching thine!

If the Benigner Power can yield
A fountain in the desert field,
Where weary pilgrims drink;
Thine are the waves that lash the rock,
Thine the tornado's deadly shock,
Where countless navies sink!

Or if he bid the soil dispense
Balsams to cheer the sinking sense,
How few can they deliver
From lingering pains, or pang intense,
Red Fever, spotted Pestilence,
The arrows of thy quiver!

Chief in Man's bosom sits thy sway,
And frequent, while in words we pray
Before another throne,
Whate'er of specious form be there,
The secret meaning of the prayer
Is, Ahriman, thine own.

Say, hast thou feeling, sense, and form,
Thunder thy voice, thy garments storm,
As Eastern Magi say;
With sentient soul of hate and wrath,
And wings to sweep thy deadly path,
And fangs to tear thy prey?

Or art thou mix'd in Nature's source,
An ever-operating force,
Converting good to ill;
An evil principle innate,
Contending with our better fate,
And, oh! victorious still?

Howe'er it be, dispute is vain.
On all without thou hold'st thy reign,
Nor less on all within;
Each mortal passion's fierce career,
Love, hate, ambition, joy, and fear,
Thou goadest into sin.

Whene'er a sunny gleam appears,
To brighten up our vale of tears,
Thou art not distant far;
'Mid such brief solace of our lives,
Thou whett'st our very banquet-knives
To tools of death and war.

Thus, from the moment of our birth,
Long as we linger on the earth,
Thou rulest the fate of men;
Thine are the pangs of life's last hour,
And—who dare answer?—is thy power,
Dark Spirit! ended THEN?

[The worthy and learned clergyman by whom this species of hymn has been translated desires, that, for fear of misconception, we should warn the reader to recollect that it is composed by a heathen, to whom the real causes of moral and physical evil are unknown, and who views their predominance in the system of the universe as all must view that appalling fact who have not the benefit of the Christian revelation. On our own part, we beg to add, that we understand the style of the translator is more paraphrastic than can be approved by those who are acquainted with the singularly curious original. The translator seems to have despaired of rendering into English verse the flights of Oriental poetry; and, possibly, like many learned and ingenious men, finding it impossible to discover the sense of the original, he may have tacitly substituted his own.]

These verses may perhaps have been the not unnatural effusion of some half-enlightened philosopher, who, in the fabled deity, Arimanes, saw but the prevalence of moral and physical evil; but in the ears of Sir Kenneth of the Leopard they had a different effect, and, sung as they were by one who had just boasted himself a descendant of demons, sounded very like an address of worship to the arch-fiend himself. He weighed within himself whether, on hearing such blasphemy in the very desert where Satan had stood rebuked for demanding homage, taking an abrupt leave of the Saracen was sufficient to testify his abhorrence; or whether he was not rather constrained by his vow as a Crusader to defy the infidel to combat on the spot, and leave him food for the beasts of the wilderness, when his attention was suddenly caught by an unexpected apparition.

The light was now verging low, yet served the knight still to discern that they two were no longer alone in the desert, but were closely watched by a figure of great height and very thin, which skipped over rocks and bushes with so much agility as, added to the wild and hirsute appearance of the individual, reminded him of the fauns and silvans, whose images he had seen in the ancient temples of Rome. As the single-hearted Scottishman had never for a moment doubted these gods of the ancient Gentiles to be actually devils, so he now hesitated not to believe that the blasphemous hymn of the Saracen had raised up an infernal spirit.

"But what recks it?" said stout Sir Kenneth to himself; "down with the fiend and his worshippers!"

He did not, however, think it necessary to give the same warning of defiance to two enemies as he would unquestionably have afforded to one. His hand was upon his mace, and perhaps the unwary Saracen would have been paid for his Persian poetry by having his brains dashed out on the spot, without any reason assigned for it; but the Scottish Knight was spared from committing what would have been a sore blot in his shield of arms. The apparition, on which his eyes had been fixed for some time, had at first appeared to dog their path by concealing itself behind rocks and shrubs, using those advantages of the ground with great address, and surmounting its irregularities with surprising agility. At length, just as the Saracen paused in his song, the figure, which was that of a tall man clothed in goat-skins, sprung into the midst of the path, and seized a rein of the Saracen's bridle in either hand, confronting thus and bearing back the noble horse, which, unable to endure the manner in which this sudden assailant pressed the long-armed bit, and the severe curb, which, according to the Eastern fashion, was a solid ring of iron, reared upright, and finally fell backwards on his master, who, however, avoided the peril of the fall by lightly throwing himself to one side.

The assailant then shifted his grasp from the bridle of the horse to the throat of the rider, flung himself above the struggling Saracen, and, despite of his youth and activity kept him undermost, wreathing his long arms above those of his prisoner, who called out angrily, and yet half-laughing at the same time—"Hamako—fool—unloose me—this passes thy privilege—unloose me, or I will use my dagger."

"Thy dagger!—infidel dog!" said the figure in the goat-skins, "hold it in thy gripe if thou canst!" and in an instant he wrenched the Saracen's weapon out of its owner's hand, and brandished it over his head.

"Help, Nazarene!" cried Sheerkohf, now seriously alarmed; "help, or the Hamako will slay me."

"Slay thee!" replied the dweller of the desert; "and well hast thou merited death, for singing thy blasphemous hymns, not only to the praise of thy false prophet, who is the foul fiend's harbinger, but to that of the Author of Evil himself."

The Christian Knight had hitherto looked on as one stupefied, so strangely had this rencontre contradicted, in its progress and event, all that he had previously conjectured. He felt, however, at length, that it touched his honour to interfere in behalf of his discomfited companion, and therefore addressed himself to the victorious figure in the goat-skins.

"Whosoe'er thou art," he said, "and whether of good or of evil, know that I am sworn for the time to be true companion to the Saracen whom thou holdest under thee; therefore, I pray thee to let him arise, else I will do battle with thee in his behalf."

"And a proper quarrel it were," answered the Hamako, "for a Crusader to do battle in—for the sake of an unbaptized dog, to combat one of his own holy faith! Art thou come forth to the wilderness to fight for the Crescent against the Cross? A goodly soldier of God art thou to listen to those who sing the praises of Satan!"

Yet, while he spoke thus, he arose himself, and, suffering the Saracen to rise also, returned him his cangiar, or poniard.

"Thou seest to what a point of peril thy presumption hath brought thee," continued he of the goat-skins, now addressing Sheerkohf, "and by what weak means thy practised skill and boasted agility can be foiled, when such is Heaven's pleasure. Wherefore, beware, O Ilderim! for know that, were there not a twinkle in the star of thy nativity which promises for thee something that is good and gracious in Heaven's good time, we two had not parted till I had torn asunder the throat which so lately trilled forth blasphemies."

"Hamako," said the Saracen, without any appearance of resenting the violent language and yet more violent assault to which he had been subjected, "I pray thee, good Hamako, to beware how thou dost again urge thy privilege over far; for though, as a good Moslem, I respect those whom Heaven hath deprived of ordinary reason, in order to endow them with the spirit of prophecy, yet I like not other men's hands on the bridle of my horse, neither upon my own person. Speak, therefore, what thou wilt, secure of any resentment from me; but gather so much sense as to apprehend that if thou shalt again proffer me any violence, I will strike thy shagged head from thy meagre shoulders.—and to thee, friend Kenneth," he added, as he remounted his steed, "I must needs say, that in a companion through the desert, I love friendly deeds better than fair words. Of the last thou hast given me enough; but it had been better to have aided me more speedily in my struggle with this Hamako, who had well-nigh taken my life in his frenzy."

"By my faith," said the Knight, "I did somewhat fail—was somewhat tardy in rendering thee instant help; but the strangeness of the assailant, the suddenness of the scene—it was as if thy wild and wicked lay had raised the devil among us—and such was my confusion, that two or three minutes elapsed ere I could take to my weapon."

"Thou art but a cold and considerate friend," said the Saracen; "and, had the Hamako been one grain more frantic, thy companion had been slain by thy side, to thy eternal dishonour, without thy stirring a finger in his aid, although thou satest by, mounted, and in arms."

"By my word, Saracen," said the Christian, "if thou wilt have it in plain terms, I thought that strange figure was the devil; and being of thy lineage, I knew not what family secret you might be communicating to each other, as you lay lovingly rolling together on the sand."

"Thy gibe is no answer, brother Kenneth," said the Saracen; "for know, that had my assailant been in very deed the Prince of Darkness, thou wert bound not the less to enter into combat with him in thy comrade's behalf. Know, also, that whatever there may be of foul or of fiendish about the Hamako belongs more to your lineage than to mine—this Hamako being, in truth, the anchorite whom thou art come hither to visit."

"This!" said Sir Kenneth, looking at the athletic yet wasted figure before him—"this! Thou mockest, Saracen—this cannot be the venerable Theodorick!"

"Ask himself, if thou wilt not believe me," answered Sheerkohf; and ere the words had left his mouth, the hermit gave evidence in his own behalf.

"I am Theodorick of Engaddi," he said—"I am the walker of the desert—I am friend of the Cross, and flail of all infidels, heretics, and devil-worshippers. Avoid ye, avoid ye! Down with Mahound, Termagaunt, and all their adherents!"—So saying, he pulled from under his shaggy garment a sort of flail or jointed club, bound with iron, which he brandished round his head with singular dexterity.

"Thou seest thy saint," said the Saracen, laughing, for the first time, at the unmitigated astonishment with which Sir Kenneth looked on the wild gestures and heard the wayward muttering of Theodorick, who, after swinging his flail in every direction, apparently quite reckless whether it encountered the head of either of his companions, finally showed his own strength, and the soundness of the weapon, by striking into fragments a large stone which lay near him.

"This is a madman," said Sir Kenneth.

"Not the worse saint," returned the Moslem, speaking according to the well-known Eastern belief, that madmen are under the influence of immediate inspiration. "Know, Christian, that when one eye is extinguished, the other becomes more keen; when one hand is cut off, the other becomes more powerful; so, when our reason in human things is disturbed or destroyed, our view heavenward becomes more acute and perfect."

Here the voice of the Saracen was drowned in that of the hermit, who began to hollo aloud in a wild, chanting tone, "I am Theodorick of Engaddi—I am the torch-brand of the desert—I am the flail of the infidels! The lion and the leopard shall be my comrades, and draw nigh to my cell for shelter; neither shall the goat be afraid of their fangs. I am the torch and the lantern—Kyrie Eleison!"

He closed his song by a short race, and ended that again by three forward bounds, which would have done him great credit in a gymnastic academy, but became his character of hermit so indifferently that the Scottish Knight was altogether confounded and bewildered.

The Saracen seemed to understand him better. "You see," he said, "that he expects us to follow him to his cell, which, indeed, is our only place of refuge for the night. You are the leopard, from the portrait on your shield; I am the lion, as my name imports; and by the goat, alluding to his garb of goat-skins, he means himself. We must keep him in sight, however, for he is as fleet as a dromedary."

In fact, the task was a difficult one, for though the reverend guide stopped from time to time, and waved his hand, as if to encourage them to come on, yet, well acquainted with all the winding dells and passes of the desert, and gifted with uncommon activity, which, perhaps, an unsettled state of mind kept in constant exercise, he led the knights through chasms and along footpaths where even the light-armed Saracen, with his well-trained barb, was in considerable risk, and where the iron-sheathed European and his over-burdened steed found themselves in such imminent peril as the rider would gladly have exchanged for the dangers of a general action. Glad he was when, at length, after this wild race, he beheld the holy man who had led it standing in front of a cavern, with a large torch in his hand, composed of a piece of wood dipped in bitumen, which cast a broad and flickering light, and emitted a strong sulphureous smell.

Undeterred by the stifling vapour, the knight threw himself from his horse and entered the cavern, which afforded small appearance of accommodation. The cell was divided into two parts, in the outward of which were an altar of stone and a crucifix made of reeds: this served the anchorite for his chapel. On one side of this outward cave the Christian knight, though not without scruple, arising from religious reverence to the objects around, fastened up his horse, and arranged him for the night, in imitation of the Saracen, who gave him to understand that such was the custom of the place. The hermit, meanwhile, was busied putting his inner apartment in order to receive his guests, and there they soon joined him. At the bottom of the outer cave, a small aperture, closed with a door of rough plank, led into the sleeping apartment of the hermit, which was more commodious. The floor had been brought to a rough level by the labour of the inhabitant, and then strewed with white sand, which he daily sprinkled with water from a small fountain which bubbled out of the rock in one corner, affording in that stifling climate, refreshment alike to the ear and the taste. Mattresses, wrought of twisted flags, lay by the side of the cell; the sides, like the floor, had been roughly brought to shape, and several herbs and flowers were hung around them. Two waxen torches, which the hermit lighted, gave a cheerful air to the place, which was rendered agreeable by its fragrance and coolness.

There were implements of labour in one corner of the apartment, in another was a niche for a rude statue of the Virgin. A table and two chairs showed that they must be the handiwork of the anchorite, being different in their form from Oriental accommodations. The former was covered, not only with reeds and pulse, but also with dried flesh, which Theodorick assiduously placed in such arrangement as should invite the appetite of his guests. This appearance of courtesy, though mute, and expressed by gestures only, seemed to Sir Kenneth something entirely irreconcilable with his former wild and violent demeanour. The movements of the hermit were now become composed, and apparently it was only a sense of religious humiliation which prevented his features, emaciated as they were by his austere mode of life, from being majestic and noble. He trod his cell as one who seemed born to rule over men, but who had abdicated his empire to become the servant of Heaven. Still, it must be allowed that his gigantic size, the length of his unshaven locks and beard, and the fire of a deep-set and wild eye were rather attributes of a soldier than of a recluse.

Even the Saracen seemed to regard the anchorite with some veneration, while he was thus employed, and he whispered in a low tone to Sir Kenneth, "The Hamako is now in his better mind, but he will not speak until we have eaten—such is his vow."

It was in silence, accordingly, that Theodorick motioned to the Scot to take his place on one of the low chairs, while Sheerkohf placed himself, after the custom of his nation, upon a cushion of mats. The hermit then held up both hands, as if blessing the refreshment which he had placed before his guests, and they proceeded to eat in silence as profound as his own. To the Saracen this gravity was natural; and the Christian imitated his taciturnity, while he employed his thoughts on the singularity of his own situation, and the contrast betwixt the wild, furious gesticulations, loud cries, and fierce actions of Theodorick, when they first met him, and the demure, solemn, decorous assiduity with which he now performed the duties of hospitality.

When their meal was ended, the hermit, who had not himself eaten a morsel, removed the fragments from the table, and placing before the Saracen a pitcher of sherbet, assigned to the Scot a flask of wine.

"Drink," he said, "my children"—they were the first words he had spoken—"the gifts of God are to be enjoyed, when the Giver is remembered."

Having said this, he retired to the outward cell, probably for performance of his devotions, and left his guests together in the inner apartment; when Sir Kenneth endeavoured, by various questions, to draw from Sheerkohf what that Emir knew concerning his host. He was interested by more than mere curiosity in these inquiries. Difficult as it was to reconcile the outrageous demeanour of the recluse at his first appearance with his present humble and placid behaviour, it seemed yet more impossible to think it consistent with the high consideration in which, according to what Sir Kenneth had learned, this hermit was held by the most enlightened divines of the Christian world. Theodorick, the hermit of Engaddi, had, in that character, been the correspondent of popes and councils; to whom his letters, full of eloquent fervour, had described the miseries imposed by the unbelievers upon the Latin Christians in the Holy Land, in colours scarce inferior to those employed at the Council of Clermont by the Hermit Peter, when he preached the first Crusade. To find, in a person so reverend and so much revered, the frantic gestures of a mad fakir, induced the Christian knight to pause ere he could resolve to communicate to him certain important matters, which he had in charge from some of the leaders of the Crusade.

It had been a main object of Sir Kenneth's pilgrimage, attempted by a route so unusual, to make such communications; but what he had that night seen induced him to pause and reflect ere he proceeded to the execution of his commission. From the Emir he could not extract much information, but the general tenor was as follows:—That, as he had heard, the hermit had been once a brave and valiant soldier, wise in council and fortunate in battle, which last he could easily believe from the great strength and agility which he had often seen him display; that he had appeared at Jerusalem in the character not of a pilgrim, but in that of one who had devoted himself to dwell for the remainder of his life in the Holy Land. Shortly afterwards, he fixed his residence amid the scenes of desolation where they now found him, respected by the Latins for his austere devotion, and by the Turks and Arabs on account of the symptoms of insanity which he displayed, and which they ascribed to inspiration. It was from them he had the name of Hamako, which expresses such a character in the Turkish language. Sheerkohf himself seemed at a loss how to rank their host. He had been, he said, a wise man, and could often for many hours together speak lessons of virtue or wisdom, without the slightest appearance of inaccuracy. At other times he was wild and violent, but never before had he seen him so mischievously disposed as he had that day appeared to be. His rage was chiefly provoked by any affront to his religion; and there was a story of some wandering Arabs, who had insulted his worship and defaced his altar, and whom he had on that account attacked and slain with the short flail which he carried with him in lieu of all other weapons. This incident had made a great noise, and it was as much the fear of the hermit's iron flail as regard for his character as a Hamako which caused the roving tribes to respect his dwelling and his chapel. His fame had spread so far that Saladin had issued particular orders that he should be spared and protected. He himself, and other Moslem lords of rank, had visited the cell more than once, partly from curiosity, partly that they expected from a man so learned as the

Christian Hamako some insight into the secrets of futurity. "He had," continued the Saracen, "a rashid, or observatory, of great height, contrived to view the heavenly bodies, and particularly the planetary system—by whose movements and influences, as both Christian and Moslem believed, the course of human events was regulated, and might be predicted."

This was the substance of the Emir Sheerkohf's information, and it left Sir Kenneth in doubt whether the character of insanity arose from the occasional excessive fervour of the hermit's zeal, or whether it was not altogether fictitious, and assumed for the sake of the immunities which it afforded. Yet it seemed that the infidels had carried their complaisance towards him to an uncommon length, considering the fanaticism of the followers of Mohammed, in the midst of whom he was living, though the professed enemy of their faith. He thought also there was more intimacy of acquaintance betwixt the hermit and the Saracen than the words of the latter had induced him to anticipate; and it had not escaped him that the former had called the latter by a name different from that which he himself had assumed. All these considerations authorized caution, if not suspicion. He determined to observe his host closely, and not to be over-hasty in communicating with him on the important charge entrusted to him.

"Beware, Saracen," he said; "methinks our host's imagination wanders as well on the subject of names as upon other matters. Thy name is Sheerkohf, and he called thee but now by another."

"My name, when in the tent of my father," replied the Kurdman, "was Ilderim, and by this I am still distinguished by many. In the field, and to soldiers, I am known as the Lion of the Mountain, being the name my good sword hath won for me. But hush, the Hamako comes—it is to warn us to rest. I know his custom; none must watch him at his vigils."

The anchorite accordingly entered, and folding his arms on his bosom as he stood before them, said with a solemn voice, "Blessed be His name, who hath appointed the quiet night to follow the busy day, and the calm sleep to refresh the wearied limbs and to compose the troubled spirit!"

Both warriors replied "Amen!" and, arising from the table, prepared to betake themselves to the couches, which their host indicated by waving his hand, as, making a reverence to each, he again withdrew from the apartment.

The Knight of the Leopard then disarmed himself of his heavy panoply, his Saracen companion kindly assisting him to undo his buckler and clasps, until he remained in the close dress of chamois leather, which knights and men-at-arms used to wear under their harness. The Saracen, if he had admired the strength of his adversary when sheathed in steel, was now no less struck with the accuracy of proportion displayed in his nervous and well-compacted figure. The knight, on the other hand, as, in exchange of courtesy, he assisted the Saracen to disrobe himself of his upper garments, that he might sleep with more convenience, was, on his side, at a loss to conceive how such slender proportions and slimness of figure could be reconciled with the vigour he had displayed in personal contest.

Each warrior prayed ere he addressed himself to his place of rest. The Moslem turned towards his KEBLAH, the point to which the prayer of each follower of the Prophet was to be addressed, and murmured his heathen orisons; while the Christian, withdrawing from the contamination of the infidel's neighbourhood, placed his huge cross-handled sword upright, and kneeling before it as the sign of salvation, told his rosary with a devotion which was enhanced by the recollection of the scenes through which he had passed, and the dangers from which he had been rescued, in the course of the day. Both warriors, worn by toil and travel, were soon fast asleep, each on his separate pallet.

Lesson 126

1. Unusual Vocabulary:
    - votaresses — women who are zealous worshippers
2. Read chapter 4. In this chapter the hermit secretly takes the knight to some places of worship in his cave monastery where the knight sees his lady love.
3. Where does the hermit take the knight first? Second? (Answers)
4. What does the knight see? (Answers)
5. How is the knight feeling? Why? (Answers)
6. Who is Edith? (Answers)
7. How does Sir Walter Scott reveal his characters? Can you think of ways he's revealed through his speech, through his wardrobe, through his actions, through his thoughts...Don't forget to add to your character sheet too as you read each day.

CHAPTER IV.

Kenneth the Scot was uncertain how long his senses had been lost in profound repose, when he was roused to recollection by a sense of oppression on his chest, which at first suggested a flirting dream of struggling with a powerful opponent, and at length recalled him fully to his senses. He was about to demand who was there, when, opening his eyes, he beheld the figure of the anchorite, wild and savage-looking as we have described him, standing by his bedside, and pressing his right hand upon his breast, while he held a small silver lamp in the other.

"Be silent," said the hermit, as the prostrate knight looked up in surprise; "I have that to say to you which yonder infidel must not hear."

These words he spoke in the French language, and not in the lingua franca, or compound of Eastern and European dialects, which had hitherto been used amongst them.

"Arise," he continued, "put on thy mantle; speak not, but tread lightly, and follow me."

Sir Kenneth arose, and took his sword.

"It needs not," answered the anchorite, in a whisper; "we are going where spiritual arms avail much, and fleshly weapons are but as the reed and the decayed gourd."

The knight deposited his sword by the bedside as before, and, armed only with his dagger, from which in this perilous country he never parted, prepared to attend his mysterious host.

The hermit then moved slowly forwards, and was followed by the knight, still under some uncertainty whether the dark form which glided on before to show him the path was not, in fact, the creation of a disturbed dream. They passed, like shadows, into the outer apartment, without disturbing the paynim Emir, who lay still buried in repose. Before the cross and altar, in the outward room, a lamp was still burning, a missal was displayed, and on the floor lay a discipline, or penitential scourge of small cord and wire, the lashes of which were recently stained with blood—a token, no doubt, of the severe penance of the recluse. Here Theodorick kneeled down, and pointed to the knight to take his place beside him upon the sharp flints, which seemed placed for the purpose of rendering the posture of reverential devotion as uneasy as possible. He read many prayers of the Catholic Church, and chanted, in a low but earnest voice, three of the penitential psalms. These last he intermixed with sighs, and tears, and convulsive throbs, which bore witness how deeply he felt the divine poetry which he recited. The Scottish knight assisted with profound sincerity at these acts of devotion, his opinion of his host beginning, in the meantime, to be so much changed, that he doubted whether, from the severity of his penance and the ardour of his prayers, he ought not to regard him as a saint; and when they arose from the ground, he stood with reverence before him, as a pupil before an honoured master. The hermit was, on his side, silent and abstracted for the space of a few minutes.

"Look into yonder recess, my son," he said, pointing to the farther corner of the cell; "there thou wilt find a veil—bring it hither."

The knight obeyed, and in a small aperture cut out of the wall, and secured with a door of wicker, he found the veil inquired for. When he brought it to the light, he discovered that it was torn, and soiled in some places with some dark substance. The anchorite looked at it with a deep but smothered emotion, and ere he could speak to the Scottish knight, was compelled to vent his feelings in a convulsive groan.

"Thou art now about to look upon the richest treasure that the earth possesses," he at length said; "woe is me, that my eyes are unworthy to be lifted towards it! Alas! I am but the vile and despised sign, which points out to the wearied traveller a harbour of rest and security, but must itself remain for ever without doors. In vain have I fled to the very depths of the rocks, and the very bosom of the thirsty desert. Mine enemy hath found me—even he whom I have denied has pursued me to my fortresses."

He paused again for a moment, and turning to the Scottish knight, said, in a firmer tone of voice, "You bring me a greeting from Richard of England?"

"I come from the Council of Christian Princes," said the knight; "but the King of England being indisposed, I am not honoured with his Majesty's commands."

"Your token?" demanded the recluse.

Sir Kenneth hesitated. Former suspicions, and the marks of insanity which the hermit had formerly exhibited, rushed suddenly on his thoughts; but how suspect a man whose manners were so saintly? "My password," he said at length, "is this—Kings begged of a beggar."

"It is right," said the hermit, while he paused. "I know you well; but the sentinel upon his post—and mine is an important one—challenges friend as well as foe."

He then moved forward with the lamp, leading the way into the room which they had left. The Saracen lay on his couch, still fast asleep. The hermit paused by his side, and looked down on him.

"He sleeps," he said, "in darkness, and must not be awakened."

The attitude of the Emir did indeed convey the idea of profound repose. One arm, flung across his body, as he lay with his face half turned to the wall, concealed, with its loose and long sleeve, the greater part of his face; but the high forehead was yet visible. Its nerves, which during his waking hours were so uncommonly active, were now motionless, as if the face had been composed of dark marble, and his long silken eyelashes closed over his piercing and hawklike eyes. The open and relaxed hand, and the deep, regular, and soft breathing, all gave tokens of the most profound repose. The slumberer formed a singular group along with the tall forms of the hermit in his shaggy dress of goat-skins, bearing the lamp, and the knight in his close leathern coat—the former with an austere expression of ascetic gloom, the latter with anxious curiosity deeply impressed on his manly features.

"He sleeps soundly," said the hermit, in the same low tone as before; and repeating the words, though he had changed the meaning from that which is literal to a metaphorical sense—"he sleeps in darkness, but there shall be for him a dayspring.—O Ilderim, thy waking thoughts are yet as vain and wild as those which are wheeling their giddy dance through thy sleeping brain; but the trumpet shall be heard, and the dream shall be dissolved."

So saying, and making the knight a sign to follow him, the hermit went towards the altar, and passing behind it, pressed a spring, which, opening without noise, showed a small iron door wrought in the side of the cavern, so as to be almost imperceptible, unless upon the most severe scrutiny. The hermit, ere he ventured fully to open the door, dropped some oil on the hinges, which the lamp supplied. A small staircase, hewn in the rock, was discovered, when the iron door was at length completely opened.

"Take the veil which I hold," said the hermit, in a melancholy tone, "and blind mine eyes; For I may not look on the treasure which thou art presently to behold, without sin and presumption."

Without reply, the knight hastily muffled the recluse's head in the veil, and the latter began to ascend the staircase as one too much accustomed to the way to require the use of light, while at the same time he held the lamp to the Scot, who followed him for many steps up the narrow ascent. At length they rested in a small vault of irregular form, in one nook of which the staircase terminated, while in another corner a corresponding stair was seen to continue the ascent. In a third angle was a Gothic door, very rudely ornamented with the usual attributes of clustered columns and carving, and defended by a wicket, strongly guarded with iron, and studded with large nails. To this last point the hermit directed his steps, which seemed to falter as he approached it.

"Put off thy shoes," he said to his attendant; "the ground on which thou standest is holy. Banish from thy innermost heart each profane and carnal thought, for to harbour such while in this place were a deadly impiety."

The knight laid aside his shoes as he was commanded, and the hermit stood in the meanwhile as if communing with his soul in secret prayer, and when he again moved, commanded the knight to knock at the wicket three times. He did so. The door opened spontaneously—at least Sir Kenneth beheld no one—and his senses were at once assailed by a stream of the purest light, and by a strong and almost oppressive sense of the richest perfumes. He stepped two or three paces back, and it was the space of a minute ere he recovered the dazzling and overpowering effects of the sudden change from darkness to light.

When he entered the apartment in which this brilliant lustre was displayed, he perceived that the light proceeded from a combination of silver lamps, fed with purest oil, and sending forth the richest odours, hanging by silver chains from the roof of a small Gothic chapel, hewn, like most part of the hermit's singular mansion, out of the sound and solid rock. But whereas, in every other place which Sir Kenneth had seen, the labour employed upon the rock had been of the simplest and coarsest description, it had in this chapel employed the invention and the chisels of the most able architects. The groined roofs rose from six columns on each side, carved with the rarest skill; and the manner in which the crossings of the concave arches were bound together, as it were, with appropriate ornaments, were all in the finest tone of the architecture of the age. Corresponding to the line of pillars, there were on each side six richly-wrought niches, each of which contained the image of one of the twelve apostles.

At the upper and eastern end of the chapel stood the altar, behind which a very rich curtain of Persian silk, embroidered deeply with gold, covered a recess, containing, unquestionably, some image or relic of no ordinary sanctity, in honour of which this singular place of worship had been erected, Under the persuasion that this must be the case, the knight advanced to the shrine, and kneeling down before it, repeated his devotions with fervency, during which his attention was disturbed by the curtain being suddenly raised, or rather pulled aside, how or by whom he saw not; but in the niche which was thus disclosed he beheld a cabinet of silver and ebony, with a double folding-door, the whole formed into the miniature resemblance of a Gothic church.

As he gazed with anxious curiosity on the shrine, the two folding-doors also flew open, discovering a large piece of wood, on which were blazoned the words, VERA CRUX; at the same time a choir of female voices sung GLORIA PATRI. The instant the strain had ceased, the shrine was closed, and the curtain again drawn, and the knight who knelt at the altar might now continue his devotions undisturbed, in honour of the holy relic which had been just disclosed to his view. He did this under the profound impression of one who had witnessed, with his own eyes, an awful evidence of the truth of his religion; and it was some time ere, concluding his orisons, he arose, and ventured to look around him for the hermit, who had guided him to this sacred and mysterious spot. He beheld him, his head still muffled in the veil which he had himself wrapped around it, crouching, like a rated hound, upon the threshold of the chapel; but, apparently, without venturing to cross it—the holiest reverence, the most penitential remorse, was expressed by his posture, which seemed that of a man borne down and crushed to the earth by the burden of his inward feelings. It seemed to the Scot that only the sense of the deepest penitence, remorse, and humiliation could have thus prostrated a frame so strong and a spirit so fiery.

He approached him as if to speak; but the recluse anticipated his purpose, murmuring in stifled tones, from beneath the fold in which his head was muffled, and which sounded like a voice proceeding from the cerements of a corpse,—"Abide, abide—happy thou that mayest—the vision is not yet ended." So saying, he reared himself from the ground, drew back from the threshold on which he had hitherto lain prostrate, and closed the door of the chapel, which, secured by a spring bolt within, the snap of which resounded through the place, appeared so much like a part of the living rock from which the cavern was hewn, that Kenneth could hardly discern where the aperture had been. He was now alone in the lighted chapel which contained the relic to which he had lately rendered his homage, without other arms than his dagger, or other companion than his pious thoughts and dauntless courage.

Uncertain what was next to happen, but resolved to abide the course of events, Sir Kenneth paced the solitary chapel till about the time of the earliest cock-crowing. At this dead season, when night and morning met together, he heard, but from what quarter he could not discover, the sound of such a small silver bell as is rung at the elevation of the host in the ceremony, or sacrifice, as it has been called, of the mass. The hour and the place rendered the sound fearfully solemn, and, bold as he was, the knight withdrew himself into the farther nook of the chapel, at the end opposite to the altar, in order to observe, without interruption, the consequences of this unexpected signal.

He did not wait long ere the silken curtain was again withdrawn, and the relic again presented to his view. As he sunk reverentially on his knee, he heard the sound of the lauds, or earliest office of the Catholic Church, sung by female voices, which united together in the performance as they had done in the former service. The knight was soon aware that the voices were no longer stationary in the distance, but approached the chapel and became louder, when a door, imperceptible when closed, like that by which he had himself entered, opened on the other side of the vault, and gave the tones of the choir more room to swell along the ribbed arches of the roof.

The knight fixed his eyes on the opening with breathless anxiety, and, continuing to kneel in the attitude of devotion which the place and scene required, expected the consequence of these preparations. A procession appeared about to issue from the door. First, four beautiful boys, whose arms, necks, and legs were bare, showing the bronze complexion of the East, and contrasting with the snow-white tunics which they wore, entered the chapel by two and two. The first pair bore censers, which they swung from side to side, adding double fragrance to the odours with which the chapel already was impregnated. The second pair scattered flowers.

After these followed, in due and majestic order, the females who composed the choir—six, who from their black scapularies, and black veils over their white garments, appeared to be professed nuns of the order of Mount Carmel; and as many whose veils, being white, argued them to be novices, or occasional inhabitants in the cloister, who were not as yet bound to it by vows. The former held in their hands large rosaries, while the younger and lighter figures who followed carried each a chaplet of red and white roses. They moved in procession around the chapel, without appearing to take the slightest notice of Kenneth, although passing so near him that their robes almost touched him, while they continued to sing. The knight doubted not that he was in one of those cloisters where the noble Christian maidens had formerly openly devoted themselves to the services of the church. Most of them had been suppressed since the Mohammedans had reconquered Palestine, but many, purchasing connivance by presents, or receiving it from the clemency or contempt of the victors, still continued to observe in private the ritual to which their vows had consecrated them. Yet, though Kenneth knew this to be the case, the solemnity of the place and hour, the surprise at the sudden appearance of these votaresses, and the visionary manner in which they moved past him, had such influence on his imagination that he could scarce conceive that the fair procession which he beheld was formed of creatures of this world, so much did they resemble a choir of supernatural beings, rendering homage to the universal object of adoration.

Such was the knight's first idea, as the procession passed him, scarce moving, save just sufficiently to continue their progress; so that, seen by the shadowy and religious light which the lamps shed through the clouds of incense which darkened the apartment, they appeared rather to glide than to walk.

But as a second time, in surrounding the chapel, they passed the spot on which he kneeled, one of the white-stoled maidens, as she glided by him, detached from the chaplet which she carried a rosebud, which dropped from her fingers, perhaps unconsciously, on the foot of Sir Kenneth. The knight started as if a dart had suddenly struck his person; for, when the mind is wound up to a high pitch of feeling and expectation, the slightest incident, if unexpected, gives fire to the train which imagination has already laid. But he suppressed his emotion, recollecting how easily an incident so indifferent might have happened, and that it was only the uniform monotony of the movement of the choristers which made the incident in the slightest degree remarkable.

Still, while the procession, for the third time, surrounded the chapel, the thoughts and the eyes of Kenneth followed exclusively the one among the novices who had dropped the rosebud. Her step, her face, her form were so completely assimilated to the rest of the choristers that it was impossible to perceive the least marks of individuality; and yet Kenneth's heart throbbed like a bird that would burst from its cage, as if to assure him, by its sympathetic suggestions, that the female who held the right file on the second rank of the novices was dearer to him, not only than all the rest that were present, but than the whole sex besides. The romantic passion of love, as it was cherished, and indeed enjoined, by the rules of chivalry, associated well with the no less romantic feelings of devotion; and they might be said much more to enhance than to counteract each other. It was, therefore, with a glow of expectation that had something even of a religious character that Sir Kenneth, his sensations thrilling from his heart to the ends of his fingers, expected some second sign of the presence of one who, he strongly fancied, had already bestowed on him the first. Short as the space was during which the procession again completed a third perambulation of the chapel, it seemed an eternity to Kenneth. At length the form which he had watched with such devoted attention drew nigh. There was no difference betwixt that shrouded figure and the others, with whom it moved in concert and in unison, until, just as she passed for the third time the kneeling Crusader, a part of a little and well-proportioned hand, so beautifully formed as to give the highest idea of the perfect proportions of the form to which it belonged, stole through the folds of the gauze, like a moonbeam through the fleecy cloud of a summer night, and again a rosebud lay at the feet of the Knight of the Leopard.

This second intimation could not be accidental—-it could not be fortuitous, the resemblance of that half-seen but beautiful female hand with one which his lips had once touched, and, while they touched it, had internally sworn allegiance to the lovely owner. Had further proof been wanting, there was the glimmer of that matchless ruby ring on that snow-white finger, whose invaluable worth Kenneth would yet have prized less than the slightest sign which that finger could have made; and, veiled too, as she was, he might see, by chance or by favour, a stray curl of the dark tresses, each hair of which was dearer to him a hundred times than a chain of massive gold. It was the lady of his love! But that she should be here—in the savage and sequestered desert—among vestals, who rendered themselves habitants of wilds and of caverns, that they might perform in secret those Christian rites which they dared not assist in openly; that this should be so, in truth and in reality, seemed too incredible—it must be a dream—a delusive trance of the imagination. While these thoughts passed through the mind of Kenneth, the same passage, by which the procession had entered the chapel, received them on their return. The young sacristans, the sable nuns, vanished successively through the open door. At length she from whom he had received this double intimation passed also; yet, in passing, turned her head, slightly indeed, but perceptibly, towards the place where he remained fixed as an image. He marked the last wave of her veil—it was gone—and a darkness sunk upon his soul, scarce less palpable than that which almost immediately enveloped his external sense; for the last chorister had no sooner crossed the threshold of the door than it shut with a loud sound, and at the same instant the voices of the choir were silent, the lights of the chapel were at once extinguished, and Sir Kenneth remained solitary and in total darkness. But to Kenneth, solitude, and darkness, and the uncertainty of his mysterious situation were as nothing—he thought not of them—cared not for them—cared for nought in the world save the flitting vision which had just glided past him, and the tokens of her favour which she had bestowed. To grope on the floor for the buds which she had dropped—to press them to his lips, to his bosom, now alternately, now together—to rivet his lips to the cold stones on which, as near as he could judge, she had so lately stepped—to play all the extravagances which strong affection suggests and vindicates to those who yield themselves up to it, were but the tokens of passionate love common to all ages. But it was peculiar to the times of chivalry that, in his wildest rapture, the knight imagined of no attempt to follow or to trace the object of such romantic attachment; that he thought of her as of a deity, who, having deigned to show herself for an instant to her devoted worshipper, had again returned to the darkness of her sanctuary—or as an influential planet, which, having darted in some auspicious minute one favourable ray, wrapped itself again in its veil of mist. The motions of the lady of his love were to him those of a superior being, who was to move without watch or control, rejoice him by her appearance, or depress him by her absence, animate him by her kindness, or drive him to despair by her cruelty—all at her own free will, and without other importunity or remonstrance than that expressed by the most devoted services of the heart and sword of the champion, whose sole object in life was to fulfil her commands, and, by the splendour of his own achievements, to exalt her fame.

Such were the rules of chivalry, and of the love which was its ruling principle. But Sir Kenneth's attachment was rendered romantic by other and still more peculiar circumstances. He had never even heard the sound of his lady's voice, though he had often beheld her beauty with rapture. She moved in a circle which his rank of knighthood permitted him indeed to approach, but not to mingle with; and highly as he stood distinguished for warlike skill and enterprise, still the poor Scottish soldier was compelled to worship his divinity at a distance almost as great as divides the Persian from the sun which he adores. But when was the pride of woman too lofty to overlook the passionate devotion of a lover, however inferior in degree? Her eye had been on him in the tournament, her ear had heard his praises in the report of the battles which were daily fought; and while count, duke, and lord contended for her grace, it flowed, unwillingly perhaps at first, or even unconsciously, towards the poor Knight of the Leopard, who, to support his rank, had little besides his sword. When she looked, and when she listened, the lady saw and heard enough to encourage her in a partiality which had at first crept on her unawares. If a knight's personal beauty was praised, even the most prudish dames of the military court of England would make an exception in favour of the Scottish Kenneth; and it oftentimes happened that, notwithstanding the very considerable largesses which princes and peers bestowed on the minstrels, an impartial spirit of independence would seize the poet, and the harp was swept to the heroism of one who had neither palfreys nor garments to bestow in guerdon of his applause.

The moments when she listened to the praises of her lover became gradually more and more dear to the high-born Edith, relieving the flattery with which her ear was weary, and presenting to her a subject of secret contemplation, more worthy, as he seemed by general report, than those who surpassed him in rank and in the gifts of fortune. As her attention became constantly, though cautiously, fixed on Sir Kenneth, she grew more and more convinced of his personal devotion to herself and more and more certain in her mind that in Kenneth of Scotland she beheld the fated knight doomed to share with her through weal and woe—and the prospect looked gloomy and dangerous—the passionate attachment to which the poets of the age ascribed such universal dominion, and which its manners and morals placed nearly on the same rank with devotion itself.

Let us not disguise the truth from our readers. When Edith became aware of the state of her own sentiments, chivalrous as were her sentiments, becoming a maiden not distant from the throne of England—gratified as her pride must have been with the mute though unceasing homage rendered to her by the knight whom she had distinguished, there were moments when the feelings of the woman, loving and beloved, murmured against the restraints of state and form by which she was surrounded, and when she almost blamed the timidity of her lover, who seemed resolved not to infringe them. The etiquette, to use a modern phrase, of birth and rank, had drawn around her a magical circle, beyond which Sir Kenneth might indeed bow and gaze, but within which he could no more pass than an evoked spirit can transgress the boundaries prescribed by the rod of a powerful enchanter. The thought involuntarily pressed on her that she herself must venture, were it but the point of her fairy foot, beyond the prescribed boundary, if she ever hoped to give a lover so reserved and bashful an opportunity of so slight a favour as but to salute her shoe-tie. There was an example—the noted precedent of the "King's daughter of Hungary," who thus generously encouraged the "squire of low degree;" and Edith, though of kingly blood, was no king's daughter, any more than her lover was of low degree—fortune had put no such extreme barrier in obstacle to their affections. Something, however, within the maiden's bosom—that modest pride which throws fetters even on love itself forbade her, notwithstanding the superiority of her condition, to make those advances, which, in every case, delicacy assigns to the other sex; above all, Sir Kenneth was a knight so gentle and honourable, so highly accomplished, as her imagination at least suggested, together with the strictest feelings of what was due to himself and to her, that however constrained her attitude might be while receiving his adorations, like the image of some deity, who is neither supposed to feel nor to reply to the homage of its votaries, still the idol feared that to step prematurely from her pedestal would be to degrade herself in the eyes of her devoted worshipper.

Yet the devout adorer of an actual idol can even discover signs of approbation in the rigid and immovable features of a marble image; and it is no wonder that something, which could be as favourably interpreted, glanced from the bright eye of the lovely Edith, whose beauty, indeed, consisted rather more in that very power of expression, than an absolute regularity of contour or brilliancy of complexion. Some slight marks of distinction had escaped from her, notwithstanding her own jealous vigilance, else how could Sir Kenneth have so readily and so undoubtingly recognized the lovely hand, of which scarce two fingers were visible from under the veil, or how could he have rested so thoroughly assured that two flowers, successively dropped on the spot, were intended as a recognition on the part of his lady-love? By what train of observation—by what secret signs, looks, or gestures—by what instinctive freemasonry of love, this degree of intelligence came to subsist between Edith and her lover, we cannot attempt to trace; for we are old, and such slight vestiges of affection, quickly discovered by younger eyes, defy the power of ours. Enough that such affection did subsist between parties who had never even spoken to one another—though, on the side of Edith, it was checked by a deep sense of the difficulties and dangers which must necessarily attend the further progress of their attachment; and upon that of the knight by a thousand doubts and fears lest he had overestimated the slight tokens of the lady's notice, varied, as they necessarily were, by long intervals of apparent coldness, during which either the fear of exciting the observation of others, and thus drawing danger upon her lover, or that of sinking in his esteem by seeming too willing to be won, made her behave with indifference, and as if unobservant of his presence.

This narrative, tedious perhaps, but which the story renders necessary, may serve to explain the state of intelligence, if it deserves so strong a name, betwixt the lovers, when Edith's unexpected appearance in the chapel produced so powerful an effect on the feelings of her knight.

Lesson 127

1. Read chapter 5. In this chapter still in the upper level of the rustic monastery, the knight encounters two strange dwarfs and puzzles over why the hermit seems to feel so guilty.
2. Who are Nectabanus and Guenevra? (Answers)
3. How does the knight meet them? (Answers)
4. The knight wonders what the hermit could have done to make him feel so guilty. Do you have any ideas?
5. The knight associates the dwarfs with gnomes and thinks of them as supernatural. Of course we know that dwarfs are just people. Personally, our family keeps away from all kinds of gnomey things because they ARE associated with the supernatural.

CHAPTER V.

Their necromantic forms in vain

Haunt us on the tented plain;

We bid these spectre shapes avaunt,

Ashtaroth and Termagaunt.

WARTON.

The most profound silence, the deepest darkness, continued to brood for more than an hour over the chapel in which we left the Knight of the Leopard still kneeling, alternately expressing thanks to Heaven and gratitude to his lady for the boon which had been vouchsafed to him. His own safety, his own destiny, for which he was at all times little anxious, had not now the weight of a grain of dust in his reflections. He was in the neighbourhood of Lady Edith; he had received tokens of her grace; he was in a place hallowed by relics of the most awful sanctity. A Christian soldier, a devoted lover, could fear nothing, think of nothing, but his duty to Heaven and his devoir to his lady.

At the lapse of the space of time which we have noticed, a shrill whistle, like that with which a falconer calls his hawk, was heard to ring sharply through the vaulted chapel. It was a sound ill suited to the place, and reminded Sir Kenneth how necessary it was he should be upon his guard. He started from his knee, and laid his hand upon his poniard. A creaking sound, as of a screw or pulleys, succeeded, and a light streaming upwards, as from an opening in the floor, showed that a trap-door had been raised or depressed. In less than a minute a long, skinny arm, partly naked, partly clothed in a sleeve of red samite, arose out of the aperture, holding a lamp as high as it could stretch upwards, and the figure to which the arm belonged ascended step by step to the level of the chapel floor. The form and face of the being who thus presented himself were those of a frightful dwarf, with a large head, a cap fantastically adorned with three peacock feathers, a dress of red samite, the richness of which rendered his ugliness more conspicuous, distinguished by gold bracelets and armlets, and a white silk sash, in which he wore a gold-hilted dagger. This singular figure had in his left hand a kind of broom. So soon as he had stepped from the aperture through which he arose, he stood still, and, as if to show himself more distinctly, moved the lamp which he held slowly over his face and person, successively illuminating his wild and fantastic features, and his misshapen but nervous limbs. Though disproportioned in person, the dwarf was not so distorted as to argue any want of strength or activity. While Sir Kenneth gazed on this disagreeable object, the popular creed occurred to his remembrance concerning the gnomes or earthly spirits which make their abode in the caverns of the earth; and so much did this figure correspond with ideas he had formed of their appearance, that he looked on it with disgust, mingled not indeed with fear, but that sort of awe which the presence of a supernatural creature may infuse into the most steady bosom.

The dwarf again whistled, and summoned from beneath a companion. This second figure ascended in the same manner as the first; but it was a female arm in this second instance which upheld the lamp from the subterranean vault out of which these presentments arose, and it was a female form, much resembling the first in shape and proportions, which slowly emerged from the floor. Her dress was also of red samite, fantastically cut and flounced, as if she had been dressed for some exhibition of mimes or jugglers; and with the same minuteness which her predecessor had exhibited, she passed the lamp over her face and person, which seemed to rival the male's in ugliness. But with all this most unfavourable exterior, there was one trait in the features of both which argued alertness and intelligence in the most uncommon degree. This arose from the brilliancy of their eyes, which, deep-set beneath black and shaggy brows, gleamed with a lustre which, like that in the eye of the toad, seemed to make some amends for the extreme ugliness of countenance and person.

Sir Kenneth remained as if spellbound, while this unlovely pair, moving round the chapel close to each other, appeared to perform the duty of sweeping it, like menials; but as they used only one hand, the floor was not much benefited by the exercise, which they plied with such oddity of gestures and manner as befitted their bizarre and fantastic appearance. When they approached near to the knight in the course of their occupation, they ceased to use their brooms; and placing themselves side by side, directly opposite to Sir Kenneth, they again slowly shifted the lights which they held, so as to allow him distinctly to survey features which were not rendered more agreeable by being brought nearer, and to observe the extreme quickness and keenness with which their black and glittering eyes flashed back the light of the lamps. They then turned the gleam of both lights upon the knight, and having accurately surveyed him, turned their faces to each other, and set up a loud, yelling laugh, which resounded in his ears. The sound was so ghastly that Sir Kenneth started at hearing it, and hastily demanded, in the name of God, who they were who profaned that holy place with such antic gestures and elritch exclamations.

"I am the dwarf Nectabanus," said the abortion-seeming male, in a voice corresponding to his figure, and resembling the voice of the night-crow more than any sound which is heard by daylight.

"And I am Guenevra, his lady and his love," replied the female, in tones which, being shriller, were yet wilder than those of her companion.

"Wherefore are you here?" again demanded the knight, scarcely yet assured that they were human beings which he saw before him.

"I am," replied the male dwarf, with much assumed gravity and dignity, "the twelfth Imaum. I am Mohammed Mohadi, the guide and the conductor of the faithful. A hundred horses stand ready saddled for me and my train at the Holy City, and as many at the City of Refuge. I am he who shall bear witness, and this is one of my houris."

"Thou liest!" answered the female, interrupting her companion, in tones yet shriller than his own; "I am none of thy houris, and thou art no such infidel trash as the Mohammed of whom thou speakest. May my curse rest upon his coffin! I tell thee, thou ass of Issachar, thou art King Arthur of Britain, whom the fairies stole away from the field of Avalon; and I am Dame Guenevra, famed for her beauty."

"But in truth, noble sir," said the male, "we are distressed princes, dwelling under the wing of King Guy of Jerusalem, until he was driven out from his own nest by the foul infidels—Heaven's bolts consume them!"

"Hush," said a voice from the side upon which the knight had entered—"hush, fools, and begone; your ministry is ended."

The dwarfs had no sooner heard the command than, gibbering in discordant whispers to each other, they blew out their lights at once, and left the knight in utter darkness, which, when the pattering of their retiring feet had died away, was soon accompanied by its fittest companion, total silence.

The knight felt the departure of these unfortunate creatures a relief. He could not, from their language, manners, and appearance, doubt that they belonged to the degraded class of beings whom deformity of person and weakness of intellect recommended to the painful situation of appendages to great families, where their personal appearance and imbecility were food for merriment to the household. Superior in no respect to the ideas and manners of his time, the Scottish knight might, at another period, have been much amused by the mummery of these poor effigies of humanity; but now their appearance, gesticulations, and language broke the train of deep and solemn feeling with which he was impressed, and he rejoiced in the disappearance of the unhappy objects.

A few minutes after they had retired, the door at which he had entered opened slowly, and remaining ajar, discovered a faint light arising from a lantern placed upon the threshold. Its doubtful and wavering gleam showed a dark form reclined beside the entrance, but without its precincts, which, on approaching it more nearly, he recognized to be the hermit, crouching in the same humble posture in which he had at first laid himself down, and which, doubtless, he had retained during the whole time of his guest's continuing in the chapel.

"All is over," said the hermit, as he heard the knight approaching, "and the most wretched of earthly sinners, with him who should think himself most honoured and most happy among the race of humanity, must retire from this place. Take the light, and guide me down the descent, for I must not uncover my eyes until I am far from this hallowed spot."

The Scottish knight obeyed in silence, for a solemn and yet ecstatic sense of what he had seen had silenced even the eager workings of curiosity. He led the way, with considerable accuracy, through the various secret passages and stairs by which they had ascended, until at length they found themselves in the outward cell of the hermit's cavern.

"The condemned criminal is restored to his dungeon, reprieved from one miserable day to another, until his awful Judge shall at length appoint the well-deserved sentence to be carried into execution."

As the hermit spoke these words, he laid aside the veil with which his eyes had been bound, and looked at it with a suppressed and hollow sigh. No sooner had he restored it to the crypt from which he had caused the Scot to bring it, than he said hastily and sternly to his companion; "Begone, begone—to rest, to rest. You may sleep—you can sleep—I neither can nor may."

Respecting the profound agitation with which this was spoken, the knight retired into the inner cell; but casting back his eye as he left the exterior grotto, he beheld the anchorite stripping his shoulders with frantic haste of their shaggy mantle, and ere he could shut the frail door which separated the two compartments of the cavern, he heard the clang of the scourge and the groans of the penitent under his self-inflicted penance. A cold shudder came over the knight as he reflected what could be the foulness of the sin, what the depth of the remorse, which, apparently, such severe penance could neither cleanse nor assuage. He told his beads devoutly, and flung himself on his rude couch, after a glance at the still sleeping Moslem, and, wearied by the various scenes of the day and the night, soon slept as sound as infancy. Upon his awaking in the morning, he held certain conferences with the hermit upon matters of importance, and the result of their intercourse induced him to remain for two days longer in the grotto. He was regular, as became a pilgrim, in his devotional exercises, but was not again admitted to the chapel in which he had seen such wonders.

Lesson 128

1. Unusual vocabulary:
    - halberd — weapon with an ax-like head
2. Read chapter 6.
3. We meet Richard the Lion Heart, King of England. Write three words to describe his character/personality. (Answers)
4. Why is Richard so frustrated? (Answers)
5. Why do you think Thomas de Vaux is able to take care of the King when everyone else is afraid to do that job? (Answers)
6. Walter Scott is a very fine story teller. He takes his time to introduce his characters gradually and shows them in actions that reveal their character. Good writers always say, "Showing is better than telling." Is there anything else you can add to your character development sheet?

CHAPTER VI.

Now change the scene—and let the trumpets sound,

For we must rouse the lion from his lair.

OLD PLAY.

The scene must change, as our programme has announced, from the mountain wilderness of Jordan to the camp of King Richard of England, then stationed betwixt Jean d'Acre and Ascalon, and containing that army with which he of the lion heart had promised himself a triumphant march to Jerusalem, and in which he would probably have succeeded, if not hindered by the jealousies of the Christian princes engaged in the same enterprise, and the offence taken by them at the uncurbed haughtiness of the English monarch, and Richard's unveiled contempt for his brother sovereigns, who, his equals in rank, were yet far his inferiors in courage, hardihood, and military talents. Such discords, and particularly those betwixt Richard and Philip of France, created disputes and obstacles which impeded every active measure proposed by the heroic though impetuous Richard, while the ranks of the Crusaders were daily thinned, not only by the desertion of individuals, but of entire bands, headed by their respective feudal leaders, who withdrew from a contest in which they had ceased to hope for success.

The effects of the climate became, as usual, fatal to soldiers from the north, and the more so that the dissolute license of the Crusaders, forming a singular contrast to the principles and purpose of their taking up arms, rendered them more easy victims to the insalubrious influence of burning heat and chilling dews. To these discouraging causes of loss was to be added the sword of the enemy. Saladin, than whom no greater name is recorded in Eastern history, had learned, to his fatal experience, that his light-armed followers were little able to meet in close encounter with the iron-clad Franks, and had been taught, at the same time, to apprehend and dread the adventurous character of his antagonist Richard. But if his armies were more than once routed with great slaughter, his numbers gave the Saracen the advantage in those lighter skirmishes, of which many were inevitable.

As the army of his assailants decreased, the enterprises of the Sultan became more numerous and more bold in this species of petty warfare. The camp of the Crusaders was surrounded, and almost besieged, by clouds of light cavalry, resembling swarms of wasps, easily crushed when they are once grasped, but furnished with wings to elude superior strength, and stings to inflict harm and mischief. There was perpetual warfare of posts and foragers, in which many valuable lives were lost, without any corresponding object being gained; convoys were intercepted, and communications were cut off. The Crusaders had to purchase the means of sustaining life, by life itself; and water, like that of the well of Bethlehem, longed for by King David, one of its ancient monarchs, was then, as before, only obtained by the expenditure of blood.

These evils were in a great measure counterbalanced by the stern resolution and restless activity of King Richard, who, with some of his best knights, was ever on horseback, ready to repair to any point where danger occurred, and often not only bringing unexpected succour to the Christians, but discomfiting the infidels when they seemed most secure of victory. But even the iron frame of Coeur de Lion could not support without injury the alternations of the unwholesome climate, joined to ceaseless exertions of body and mind. He became afflicted with one of those slow and wasting fevers peculiar to Asia, and in despite of his great strength and still greater courage, grew first unfit to mount on horseback, and then unable to attend the councils of war which were from time to time held by the Crusaders. It was difficult to say whether this state of personal inactivity was rendered more galling or more endurable to the English monarch by the resolution of the council to engage in a truce of thirty days with the Sultan Saladin; for on the one hand, if he was incensed at the delay which this interposed to the progress of the great enterprise, he was, on the other, somewhat consoled by knowing that others were not acquiring laurels while he remained inactive upon a sick-bed.

That, however, which Coeur de Lion could least excuse was the general inactivity which prevailed in the camp of the Crusaders so soon as his illness assumed a serious aspect; and the reports which he extracted from his unwilling attendants gave him to understand that the hopes of the host had abated in proportion to his illness, and that the interval of truce was employed, not in recruiting their numbers, reanimating their courage, fostering their spirit of conquest, and preparing for a speedy and determined advance upon the Holy City, which was the object of their expedition, but in securing the camp occupied by their diminished followers with trenches, palisades, and other fortifications, as if preparing rather to repel an attack from a powerful enemy so soon as hostilities should recommence, than to assume the proud character of conquerors and assailants.

The English king chafed under these reports, like the imprisoned lion viewing his prey from the iron barriers of his cage. Naturally rash and impetuous, the irritability of his temper preyed on itself. He was dreaded by his attendants and even the medical assistants feared to assume the necessary authority which a physician, to do justice to his patient, must needs exercise over him. One faithful baron, who, perhaps, from the congenial nature of his disposition, was devoutly attached to the King's person, dared alone to come between the dragon and his wrath, and quietly, but firmly, maintained a control which no other dared assume over the dangerous invalid, and which Thomas de Multon only exercised because he esteemed his sovereign's life and honour more than he did the degree of favour which he might lose, or even the risk which he might incur, in nursing a patient so intractable, and whose displeasure was so perilous.

Sir Thomas was the Lord of Gilsland, in Cumberland, and in an age when surnames and titles were not distinctly attached, as now, to the individuals who bore them, he was called by the Normans the Lord de Vaux; and in English by the Saxons, who clung to their native language, and were proud of the share of Saxon blood in this renowned warrior's veins, he was termed Thomas, or, more familiarly, Thom of the Gills, or Narrow Valleys, from which his extensive domains derived their well-known appellation.

This chief had been exercised in almost all the wars, whether waged betwixt England and Scotland, or amongst the various domestic factions which then tore the former country asunder, and in all had been distinguished, as well from his military conduct as his personal prowess. He was, in other respects, a rude soldier, blunt and careless in his bearing, and taciturn—nay, almost sullen—in his habits of society, and seeming, at least, to disclaim all knowledge of policy and of courtly art. There were men, however, who pretended to look deeply into character, who asserted that the Lord de Vaux was not less shrewd and aspiring than he was blunt and bold, and who thought that, while he assimilated himself to the king's own character of blunt hardihood, it was, in some degree at least, with an eye to establish his favour, and to gratify his own hopes of deep-laid ambition. But no one cared to thwart his schemes, if such he had, by rivalling him in the dangerous occupation of daily attendance on the sick-bed of a patient whose disease was pronounced infectious, and more especially when it was remembered that the patient was Coeur de Lion, suffering under all the furious impatience of a soldier withheld from battle, and a sovereign sequestered from authority; and the common soldiers, at least in the English army, were generally of opinion that De Vaux attended on the King like comrade upon comrade, in the honest and disinterested frankness of military friendship contracted between the partakers of daily dangers.

It was on the decline of a Syrian day that Richard lay on his couch of sickness, loathing it as much in mind as his illness made it irksome to his body. His bright blue eye, which at all times shone with uncommon keenness and splendour, had its vivacity augmented by fever and mental impatience, and glanced from among his curled and unshorn locks of yellow hair as fitfully and as vividly as the last gleams of the sun shoot through the clouds of an approaching thunderstorm, which still, however, are gilded by its beams. His manly features showed the progress of wasting illness, and his beard, neglected and untrimmed, had overgrown both lips and chin. Casting himself from side to side, now clutching towards him the coverings, which at the next moment he flung as impatiently from him, his tossed couch and impatient gestures showed at once the energy and the reckless impatience of a disposition whose natural sphere was that of the most active exertion.

Beside his couch stood Thomas de Vaux, in face, attitude, and manner the strongest possible contrast to the suffering monarch. His stature approached the gigantic, and his hair in thickness might have resembled that of Samson, though only after the Israelitish champion's locks had passed under the shears of the Philistines, for those of De Vaux were cut short, that they might be enclosed under his helmet. The light of his broad, large hazel eye resembled that of the autumn morn; and it was only perturbed for a moment, when from time to time it was attracted by Richard's vehement marks of agitation and restlessness. His features, though massive like his person, might have been handsome before they were defaced with scars; his upper lip, after the fashion of the Normans, was covered with thick moustaches, which grew so long and luxuriantly as to mingle with his hair, and, like his hair, were dark brown, slightly brindled with grey. His frame seemed of that kind which most readily defies both toil and climate, for he was thin-flanked, broad-chested, long-armed, deep-breathed, and strong-limbed. He had not laid aside his buff-coat, which displayed the cross cut on the shoulder, for more than three nights, enjoying but such momentary repose as the warder of a sick monarch's couch might by snatches indulge. This Baron rarely changed his posture, except to administer to Richard the medicine or refreshments which none of his less favoured attendants could persuade the impatient monarch to take; and there was something affecting in the kindly yet awkward manner in which he discharged offices so strangely contrasted with his blunt and soldierly habits and manners.

The pavilion in which these personages were, had, as became the time, as well as the personal character of Richard, more of a warlike than a sumptuous or royal character. Weapons offensive and defensive, several of them of strange and newly-invented construction, were scattered about the tented apartment, or disposed upon the pillars which supported it. Skins of animals slain in the chase were stretched on the ground, or extended along the sides of the pavilion; and upon a heap of these silvan spoils lay three ALANS, as they were then called (wolf-greyhounds, that is), of the largest size, and as white as snow. Their faces, marked with many a scar from clutch and fang, showed their share in collecting the trophies upon which they reposed; and their eyes, fixed from time to time with an expressive stretch and yawn upon the bed of Richard, evinced how much they marvelled at and regretted the unwonted inactivity which they were compelled to share. These were but the accompaniments of the soldier and huntsman; but on a small table close by the bed was placed a shield of wrought steel, of triangular form, bearing the three lions passant first assumed by the chivalrous monarch, and before it the golden circlet, resembling much a ducal coronet, only that it was higher in front than behind, which, with the purple velvet and embroidered tiara that lined it, formed then the emblem of England's sovereignty. Beside it, as if prompt for defending the regal symbol, lay a mighty curtal-axe, which would have wearied the arm of any other than Coeur de Lion.

In an outer partition of the pavilion waited two or three officers of the royal household, depressed, anxious for their master's health, and not less so for their own safety, in case of his decease. Their gloomy apprehensions spread themselves to the warders without, who paced about in downcast and silent contemplation, or, resting on their halberds, stood motionless on their post, rather like armed trophies than living warriors.

"So thou hast no better news to bring me from without, Sir Thomas!" said the King, after a long and perturbed silence, spent in the feverish agitation which we have endeavoured to describe. "All our knights turned women, and our ladies become devotees, and neither a spark of valour nor of gallantry to enlighten a camp which contains the choicest of Europe's chivalry—ha!"

"The truce, my lord," said De Vaux, with the same patience with which he had twenty times repeated the explanation—"the truce prevents us bearing ourselves as men of action; and for the ladies, I am no great reveller, as is well known to your Majesty, and seldom exchange steel and buff for velvet and gold—but thus far I know, that our choicest beauties are waiting upon the Queen's Majesty and the Princess, to a pilgrimage to the convent of Engaddi, to accomplish their vows for your Highness's deliverance from this trouble."

"And is it thus," said Richard, with the impatience of indisposition, "that royal matrons and maidens should risk themselves, where the dogs who defile the land have as little truth to man as they have faith towards God?"

"Nay, my lord," said De Vaux, "they have Saladin's word for their safety."

"True, true!" replied Richard; "and I did the heathen Soldan injustice—I owe him reparation for it. Would God I were but fit to offer it him upon my body between the two hosts—Christendom and heathenesse both looking on!"

As Richard spoke, he thrust his right arm out of bed naked to the shoulder, and painfully raising himself in his couch, shook his clenched hand, as if it grasped sword or battle-axe, and was then brandished over the jewelled turban of the Soldan. It was not without a gentle degree of violence, which the King would scarce have endured from another, that De Vaux, in his character of sick-nurse, compelled his royal master to replace himself in the couch, and covered his sinewy arm, neck, and shoulders with the care which a mother bestows upon an impatient child.

"Thou art a rough nurse, though a willing one, De Vaux," said the King, laughing with a bitter expression, while he submitted to the strength which he was unable to resist; "methinks a coif would become thy lowering features as well as a child's biggin would beseem mine. We should be a babe and nurse to frighten girls with."

"We have frightened men in our time, my liege," said De Vaux; "and, I trust, may live to frighten them again. What is a fever-fit, that we should not endure it patiently, in order to get rid of it easily?"

"Fever-fit!" exclaimed Richard impetuously; "thou mayest think, and justly, that it is a fever-fit with me; but what is it with all the other Christian princes—with Philip of France, with that dull Austrian, with him of Montserrat, with the Hospitallers, with the Templars—what is it with all them? I will tell thee. It is a cold palsy, a dead lethargy, a disease that deprives them of speech and action, a canker that has eaten into the heart of all that is noble, and chivalrous, and virtuous among them—that has made them false to the noblest vow ever knights were sworn to—has made them indifferent to their fame, and forgetful of their God!"

"For the love of Heaven, my liege," said De Vaux, "take it less violently—you will be heard without doors, where such speeches are but too current already among the common soldiery, and engender discord and contention in the Christian host. Bethink you that your illness mars the mainspring of their enterprise; a mangonel will work without screw and lever better than the Christian host without King Richard."

"Thou flatterest me, De Vaux," said Richard, and not insensible to the power of praise, he reclined his head on the pillow with a more deliberate attempt to repose than he had yet exhibited. But Thomas de Vaux was no courtier; the phrase which had offered had risen spontaneously to his lips, and he knew not how to pursue the pleasing theme so as to soothe and prolong the vein which he had excited. He was silent, therefore, until, relapsing into his moody contemplations, the King demanded of him sharply, "Despardieux! This is smoothly said to soothe a sick man; but does a league of monarchs, an assemblage or nobles, a convocation of all the chivalry of Europe, droop with the sickness of one man, though he chances to be King of England? Why should Richard's illness, or Richard's death, check the march of thirty thousand men as brave as himself? When the master stag is struck down, the herd do not disperse upon his fall; when the falcon strikes the leading crane, another takes the guidance of the phalanx. Why do not the powers assemble and choose some one to whom they may entrust the guidance of the host?"

"Forsooth, and if it please your Majesty," said De Vaux, "I hear consultations have been held among the royal leaders for some such purpose."

"Ha!" exclaimed Richard, his jealousy awakened, giving his mental irritation another direction, "am I forgot by my allies ere I have taken the last sacrament? Do they hold me dead already? But no, no, they are right. And whom do they select as leader of the Christian host?"

"Rank and dignity," said De Vaux, "point to the King of France."

"Oh, ay," answered the English monarch, "Philip of France and Navarre—Denis Mountjoie—his most Christian Majesty! Mouth-filling words these! There is but one risk—that he might mistake the words EN ARRIERE for EN AVANT, and lead us back to Paris, instead of marching to Jerusalem. His politic head has learned by this time that there is more to be gotten by oppressing his feudatories, and pillaging his allies, than fighting with the Turks for the Holy Sepulchre."

"They might choose the Archduke of Austria," said De Vaux.

"What! because he is big and burly like thyself, Thomas—nearly as thick-headed, but without thy indifference to danger and carelessness of offence? I tell thee that Austria has in all that mass of flesh no bolder animation than is afforded by the peevishness of a wasp and the courage of a wren. Out upon him! He a leader of chivalry to deeds of glory! Give him a flagon of Rhenish to drink with his besmirched baaren-hauters and lance-knechts."

"There is the Grand Master of the Templars," continued the baron, not sorry to keep his master's attention engaged on other topics than his own illness, though at the expense of the characters of prince and potentate. "There is the Grand Master of the Templars," he continued, "undaunted, skilful, brave in battle, and sage in council, having no separate kingdoms of his own to divert his exertions from the recovery of the Holy Land—what thinks your Majesty of the Master as a general leader of the Christian host?"

"Ha, Beau-Seant?" answered the King. "Oh, no exception can be taken to Brother Giles Amaury; he understands the ordering of a battle, and the fighting in front when it begins. But, Sir Thomas, were it fair to take the Holy Land from the heathen Saladin, so full of all the virtues which may distinguish unchristened man, and give it to Giles Amaury, a worse pagan than himself, an idolater, a devil-worshipper, a necromancer, who practises crimes the most dark and unnatural in the vaults and secret places of abomination and darkness?"

"The Grand Master of the Hospitallers of St. John of Jerusalem is not tainted by fame, either with heresy or magic," said Thomas de Vaux.

"But is he not a sordid miser?" said Richard hastily; "has he not been suspected—ay, more than suspected—of selling to the infidels those advantages which they would never have won by fair force? Tush, man, better give the army to be made merchandise of by Venetian skippers and Lombardy pedlars, than trust it to the Grand Master of St. John."

"Well, then, I will venture but another guess," said the Baron de Vaux. "What say you to the gallant Marquis of Montserrat, so wise, so elegant, such a good man-at-arms?"

"Wise?—cunning, you would say," replied Richard; "elegant in a lady's chamber, if you will. Oh, ay, Conrade of Montserrat—who knows not the popinjay? Politic and versatile, he will change you his purposes as often as the trimmings of his doublet, and you shall never be able to guess the hue of his inmost vestments from their outward colours. A man-at-arms? Ay, a fine figure on horseback, and can bear him well in the tilt-yard, and at the barriers, when swords are blunted at point and edge, and spears are tipped with trenchers of wood instead of steel pikes. Wert thou not with me when I said to that same gay Marquis, 'Here we be, three good Christians, and on yonder plain there pricks a band of some threescore Saracens—what say you to charge them briskly? There are but twenty unbelieving miscreants to each true knight."

"I recollect the Marquis replied," said De Vaux, "that his limbs were of flesh, not of iron, and that he would rather bear the heart of a man than of a beast, though that beast were the lion, But I see how it is—we shall end where we began, without hope of praying at the Sepulchre until Heaven shall restore King Richard to health."

At this grave remark Richard burst out into a hearty fit of laughter, the first which he had for some time indulged in. "Why what a thing is conscience," he said, "that through its means even such a thick-witted northern lord as thou canst bring thy sovereign to confess his folly! It is true that, did they not propose themselves as fit to hold my leading-staff, little should I care for plucking the silken trappings off the puppets thou hast shown me in succession. What concerns it me what fine tinsel robes they swagger in, unless when they are named as rivals in the glorious enterprise to which I have vowed myself? Yes, De Vaux, I confess my weakness, and the wilfulness of my ambition. The Christian camp contains, doubtless, many a better knight than Richard of England, and it would be wise and worthy to assign to the best of them the leading of the host. But," continued the warlike monarch, raising himself in his bed, and shaking the cover from his head, while his eyes sparkled as they were wont to do on the eve of battle, "were such a knight to plant the banner of the Cross on the Temple of Jerusalem while I was unable to bear my share in the noble task, he should, so soon as I was fit to lay lance in rest, undergo my challenge to mortal combat, for having diminished my fame, and pressed in before to the object of my enterprise. But hark, what trumpets are those at a distance?"

"Those of King Philip, as I guess, my liege," said the stout Englishman.

"Thou art dull of ear, Thomas," said the King, endeavouring to start up; "hearest thou not that clash and clang? By Heaven, the Turks are in the camp—I hear their LELIES." [The war-cries of the Moslemah.]

He again endeavoured to get out of bed, and De Vaux was obliged to exercise his own great strength, and also to summon the assistance of the chamberlains from the inner tent, to restrain him.

"Thou art a false traitor, De Vaux," said the incensed monarch, when, breathless and exhausted with struggling, he was compelled to submit to superior strength, and to repose in quiet on his couch. "I would I were—I would I were but strong enough to dash thy brains out with my battle-axe!"

"I would you had the strength, my liege," said De Vaux, "and would even take the risk of its being so employed. The odds would be great in favour of Christendom were Thomas Multon dead and Coeur de Lion himself again."

"Mine honest faithful servant," said Richard, extending his hand, which the baron reverentially saluted, "forgive thy master's impatience of mood. It is this burning fever which chides thee, and not thy kind master, Richard of England. But go, I prithee, and bring me word what strangers are in the camp, for these sounds are not of Christendom."

De Vaux left the pavilion on the errand assigned, and in his absence, which he had resolved should be brief, he charged the chamberlains, pages, and attendants to redouble their attention on their sovereign, with threats of holding them to responsibility, which rather added to than diminished their timid anxiety in the discharge of their duty; for next, perhaps, to the ire of the monarch himself, they dreaded that of the stern and inexorable Lord of Gilsland. [Sir Thomas Multon of Gilsland.]

Lesson 129

1. Unusual vocabulary:
    - equerries — officer/noble in charge of the stables (where the horses are kept) (equestrian comes from the same root, right?)
2. Read chapter 7. Sir Kenneth has arrived in camp with a Muslim physician who says he can cure King Richard, but de Vaux is skeptical. The army of the Crusaders seems to be very dis-united, lots of jealousies and suspicions of one another.
3. How does de Vaux feel about Scotsmen? (Answers)
4. Why does Sir Kenneth want to see King Richard? (Answers)

5. If you were de Vaux, would you allow a Muslim physician to give medicine to the King of England? Why or why not? (Answers)
6. Do you have any characters to add to your character list?

CHAPTER VII.

There never was a time on the march parts yet,

When Scottish with English met,

But it was marvel if the red blood ran not

As the rain does in the street.

—BATTLE OF OTTERBOURNE.

A considerable band of Scottish warriors had joined the Crusaders, and had naturally placed themselves under the command of the English monarch, being, like his native troops, most of them of Saxon and Norman descent, speaking the same languages, possessed, some of them, of English as well as Scottish demesnes, and allied in some cases by blood and intermarriage. The period also preceded that when the grasping ambition of Edward I. gave a deadly and envenomed character to the wars betwixt the two nations—the English fighting for the subjugation of Scotland, and the Scottish, with all the stern determination and obstinacy which has ever characterized their nation, for the defence of their independence, by the most violent means, under the most disadvantageous circumstances, and at the most extreme hazard. As yet, wars betwixt the two nations, though fierce and frequent, had been conducted on principles of fair hostility, and admitted of those softening shades by which courtesy and the respect for open and generous foemen qualify and mitigate the horrors of war. In time of peace, therefore, and especially when both, as at present, were engaged in war, waged in behalf of a common cause, and rendered dear to them by their ideas of religion, the adventurers of both countries frequently fought side by side, their national emulation serving only to stimulate them to excel each other in their efforts against the common enemy.

The frank and martial character of Richard, who made no distinction betwixt his own subjects and those of William of Scotland, excepting as they bore themselves in the field of battle, tended much to conciliate the troops of both nations. But upon his illness, and the disadvantageous circumstances in which the Crusaders were placed, the national disunion between the various bands united in the Crusade, began to display itself, just as old wounds break out afresh in the human body when under the influence of disease or debility.

The Scottish and English, equally jealous and high-spirited, and apt to take offence—the former the more so, because the poorer and the weaker nation—began to fill up by internal dissension the period when the truce forbade them to wreak their united vengeance on the Saracens. Like the contending Roman chiefs of old, the Scottish would admit no superiority, and their southern neighbours would brook no equality. There were charges and recriminations, and both the common soldiery and their leaders and commanders, who had been good comrades in time of victory, lowered on each other in the period of adversity, as if their union had not been then more essential than ever, not only to the success of their common cause, but to their joint safety. The same disunion had begun to show itself betwixt the French and English, the Italians and the Germans, and even between the Danes and Swedes; but it is only that which divided the two nations whom one island bred, and who seemed more animated against each other for the very reason, that our narrative is principally concerned with.

Of all the English nobles who had followed their King to Palestine, De Vaux was most prejudiced against the Scottish. They were his near neighbours, with whom he had been engaged during his whole life in private or public warfare, and on whom he had inflicted many calamities, while he had sustained at their hands not a few. His love and devotion to the King was like the vivid affection of the old English mastiff to his master, leaving him churlish and inaccessible to all others even towards those to whom he was indifferent—and rough and dangerous to any against whom he entertained a prejudice. De Vaux had never observed without jealousy and displeasure his King exhibit any mark of courtesy or favour to the wicked, deceitful, and ferocious race born on the other side of a river, or an imaginary line drawn through waste and wilderness; and he even doubted the success of a Crusade in which they were suffered to bear arms, holding them in his secret soul little better than the Saracens whom he came to combat. It may be added that, as being himself a blunt and downright Englishman, unaccustomed to conceal the slightest movement either of love or of dislike, he accounted the fair-spoken courtesy which the Scots had learned, either from imitation of their frequent allies, the French, or which might have arisen from their own proud and reserved character, as a false and astucious mark of the most dangerous designs against their neighbours, over whom he believed, with genuine English confidence, they could, by fair manhood, never obtain any advantage.

Yet, though De Vaux entertained these sentiments concerning his Northern neighbours, and extended them, with little mitigation, even to such as had assumed the Cross, his respect for the King, and a sense of the duty imposed by his vow as a Crusader, prevented him from displaying them otherwise than by regularly shunning all intercourse with his Scottish brethren-at-arms as far as possible, by observing a sullen taciturnity when compelled to meet them occasionally, and by looking scornfully upon them when they encountered on the march and in camp. The Scottish barons and knights were not men to bear his scorn unobserved or unreplied to; and it came to that pass that he was regarded as the determined and active enemy of a nation, whom, after all, he only disliked, and in some sort despised. Nay, it was remarked by close observers that, if he had not towards them the charity of Scripture, which suffereth long, and judges kindly, he was by no means deficient in the subordinate and limited virtue, which alleviates and relieves the wants of others. The wealth of Thomas of Gilsland procured supplies of provisions and medicines, and some of these usually flowed by secret channels into the quarters of the Scottish—his surly benevolence proceeding on the principle that, next to a man's friend, his foe was of most importance to him, passing over all the intermediate relations as too indifferent to merit even a thought. This explanation is necessary, in order that the reader may fully understand what we are now to detail.

Thomas de Vaux had not made many steps beyond the entrance of the royal pavilion when he was aware of what the far more acute ear of the English monarch—no mean proficient in the art of minstrelsy—had instantly discovered, that the musical strains, namely, which had reached their ears, were produced by the pipes, shalms, and kettle-drums of the Saracens; and at the bottom of an avenue of tents, which formed a broad access to the pavilion of Richard, he could see a crowd of idle soldiers assembled around the spot from which the music was heard, almost in the centre of the camp; and he saw, with great surprise, mingled amid the helmets of various forms worn by the Crusaders of different nations, white turbans and long pikes, announcing the presence of armed Saracens, and the huge deformed heads of several camels or dromedaries, overlooking the multitude by aid of their long, disproportioned necks.

Wondering, and displeased at a sight so unexpected and singular—for it was customary to leave all flags of truce and other communications from the enemy at an appointed place without the barriers—the baron looked eagerly round for some one of whom he might inquire the cause of this alarming novelty.

The first person whom he met advancing to him he set down at once, by his grave and haughty step, as a Spaniard or a Scot; and presently after muttered to himself, "And a Scot it is—he of the Leopard. I have seen him fight indifferently well, for one of his country."

Loath to ask even a passing question, he was about to pass Sir Kenneth, with that sullen and lowering port which seems to say, "I know thee, but I will hold no communication with thee." But his purpose was defeated by the Northern Knight, who moved forward directly to him, and accosting him with formal courtesy, said, "My Lord de Vaux of Gilsland, I have in charge to speak with you."

"Ha!" returned the English baron, "with me? But say your pleasure, so it be shortly spoken—I am on the King's errand."

"Mine touches King Richard yet more nearly," answered Sir Kenneth; "I bring him, I trust, health."

The Lord of Gilsland measured the Scot with incredulous eyes, and replied, "Thou art no leech, I think, Sir Scot; I had as soon thought of your bringing the King of England wealth."

Sir Kenneth, though displeased with the manner of the baron's reply, answered calmly, "Health to Richard is glory and wealth to Christendom.—But my time presses; I pray you, may I see the King?"

"Surely not, fair sir," said the baron, "until your errand be told more distinctly. The sick chambers of princes open not to all who inquire, like a northern hostelry."

"My lord," said Kenneth, "the cross which I wear in common with yourself, and the importance of what I have to tell, must, for the present, cause me to pass over a bearing which else I were unapt to endure. In plain language, then, I bring with me a Moorish physician, who undertakes to work a cure on King Richard."

"A Moorish physician!" said De Vaux; "and who will warrant that he brings not poisons instead of remedies?"

"His own life, my lord—his head, which he offers as a guarantee."

"I have known many a resolute ruffian," said De Vaux, "who valued his own life as little as it deserved, and would troop to the gallows as merrily as if the hangman were his partner in a dance."

"But thus it is, my lord," replied the Scot. "Saladin, to whom none will deny the credit of a generous and valiant enemy, hath sent this leech hither with an honourable retinue and guard, befitting the high estimation in which El Hakim [The Physician] is held by the Soldan, and with fruits and refreshments for the King's private chamber, and such message as may pass betwixt honourable enemies, praying him to be recovered of his fever, that he may be the fitter to receive a visit from the Soldan, with his naked scimitar in his hand, and a hundred thousand cavaliers at his back. Will it please you, who are of the King's secret council, to cause these camels to be discharged of their burdens, and some order taken as to the reception of the learned physician?"

"Wonderful!" said De Vaux, as speaking to himself.—"And who will vouch for the honour of Saladin, in a case when bad faith would rid him at once of his most powerful adversary?"

"I myself," replied Sir Kenneth, "will be his guarantee, with honour, life, and fortune."

"Strange!" again ejaculated De Vaux; "the North vouches for the South—the Scot for the Turk! May I crave of you, Sir Knight, how you became concerned in this affair?"

"I have been absent on a pilgrimage, in the course of which," replied Sir Kenneth "I had a message to discharge towards the holy hermit of Engaddi."

"May I not be entrusted with it, Sir Kenneth, and with the answer of the holy man?"

"It may not be, my lord," answered the Scot.

"I am of the secret council of England," said the Englishman haughtily.

"To which land I owe no allegiance," said Kenneth. "Though I have voluntarily followed in this war the personal fortunes of England's sovereign, I was dispatched by the General Council of the kings, princes, and supreme leaders of the army of the Blessed Cross, and to them only I render my errand."

"Ha! sayest thou?" said the proud Baron de Vaux. "But know, messenger of the kings and princes as thou mayest be, no leech shall approach the sick-bed of Richard of England without the consent of him of Gilsland; and they will come on evil errand who dare to intrude themselves against it."

He was turning loftily away, when the Scot, placing himself closer, and more opposite to him, asked, in a calm voice, yet not without expressing his share of pride, whether the Lord of Gilsland esteemed him a gentleman and a good knight.

"All Scots are ennobled by their birthright," answered Thomas de Vaux, something ironically; but sensible of his own injustice, and perceiving that Kenneth's colour rose, he added, "For a good knight it were sin to doubt you, in one at least who has seen you well and bravely discharge your devoir."

"Well, then," said the Scottish knight, satisfied with the frankness of the last admission, "and let me swear to you, Thomas of Gilsland, that, as I am true Scottish man, which I hold a privilege equal to my ancient gentry, and as sure as I am a belted knight, and come hither to acquire LOS [Los—laus, praise, or renown] and fame in this mortal life, and forgiveness of my sins in that which is to come—so truly, and by the blessed Cross which I wear, do I protest unto you that I desire but the safety of Richard Coeur de Lion, in recommending the ministry of this Moslem physician."

The Englishman was struck with the solemnity of the obtestation, and answered with more cordiality than he had yet exhibited, "Tell me, Sir Knight of the Leopard, granting (which I do not doubt) that thou art thyself satisfied in this matter, shall I do well, in a land where the art of poisoning is as general as that of cooking, to bring this unknown physician to practise with his drugs on a health so valuable to Christendom?"

"My lord," replied the Scot, "thus only can I reply—that my squire, the only one of my retinue whom war and disease had left in attendance on me, has been of late suffering dangerously under this same fever, which, in valiant King Richard, has disabled the principal limb of our holy enterprise. This leech, this El Hakim, hath ministered remedies to him not two hours since, and already he hath fallen into a refreshing sleep. That he can cure the disorder, which has proved so fatal, I nothing doubt; that he hath the purpose to do it is, I think, warranted by his mission from the royal Soldan, who is true-hearted and loyal, so far as a blinded infidel may be called so; and for his eventual success, the certainty of reward in case of succeeding, and punishment in case of voluntary failure, may be a sufficient guarantee."

The Englishman listened with downcast looks, as one who doubted, yet was not unwilling to receive conviction. At length he looked up and said, "May I see your sick squire, fair sir?"

The Scottish knight hesitated and coloured, yet answered at last, "Willingly, my Lord of Gilsland. But you must remember, when you see my poor quarter, that the nobles and knights of Scotland feed not so high, sleep not so soft, and care not for the magnificence of lodgment which is Proper to their southern neighbours. I am POORLY lodged, my Lord of Gilsland," he added, with a haughty emphasis on the word, while, with some unwillingness, he led the way to his temporary place of abode.

Whatever were the prejudices of De Vaux against the nation of his new acquaintance, and though we undertake not to deny that some of these were excited by its proverbial poverty, he had too much nobleness of disposition to enjoy the mortification of a brave individual thus compelled to make known wants which his pride would gladly have concealed.

"Shame to the soldier of the Cross," he said, "who thinks of worldly splendour, or of luxurious accommodation, when pressing forward to the conquest of the Holy City. Fare as hard as we may, we shall yet be better than the host of martyrs and of saints, who, having trod these scenes before us, now hold golden lamps and evergreen palms."

This was the most metaphorical speech which Thomas of Gilsland was ever known to utter, the rather, perhaps (as will sometimes happen), that it did not entirely express his own sentiments, being somewhat a lover of good cheer and splendid accommodation. By this time they reached the place of the camp where the Knight of the Leopard had assumed his abode.

Appearances here did indeed promise no breach of the laws of mortification, to which the Crusaders, according to the opinion expressed by him of Gilsland, ought to subject themselves. A space of ground, large enough to accommodate perhaps thirty tents, according to the Crusaders' rules of castrametation, was partly vacant—because, in ostentation, the knight had demanded ground to the extent of his original retinue—partly occupied by a few miserable huts, hastily constructed of boughs, and covered with palm-leaves. These habitations seemed entirely deserted, and several of them were ruinous. The central hut, which represented the pavilion of the leader, was distinguished by his swallow-tailed pennon, placed on the point of a spear, from which its long folds dropped motionless to the ground, as if sickening under the scorching rays of the Asiatic sun. But no pages or squires—not even a solitary warder—was placed by the emblem of feudal power and knightly degree. If its reputation defended it not from insult, it had no other guard.

Sir Kenneth cast a melancholy look around him, but suppressing his feelings, entered the hut, making a sign to the Baron of Gilsland to follow. He also cast around a glance of examination, which implied pity not altogether unmingled with contempt, to which, perhaps, it is as nearly akin as it is said to be to love. He then stooped his lofty crest, and entered a lowly hut, which his bulky form seemed almost entirely to fill.

The interior of the hut was chiefly occupied by two beds. One was empty, but composed of collected leaves, and spread with an antelope's hide. It seemed, from the articles of armour laid beside it, and from a crucifix of silver, carefully and reverentially disposed at the head, to be the couch of the knight himself. The other contained the invalid, of whom Sir Kenneth had spoken, a strong-built and harsh-featured man, past, as his looks betokened, the middle age of life. His couch was trimmed more softly than his master's, and it was plain that the more courtly garments of the latter, the loose robe in which the knights showed themselves on pacific occasions, and the other little spare articles of dress and adornment, had been applied by Sir Kenneth to the accommodation of his sick domestic. In an outward part of the hut, which yet was within the range of the English baron's eye, a boy, rudely attired with buskins of deer's hide, a blue cap or bonnet, and a doublet, whose original finery was much tarnished, sat on his knees by a chafing-dish filled with charcoal, cooking upon a plate of iron the cakes of barley-bread, which were then, and still are, a favourite food with the Scottish people. Part of an antelope was suspended against one of the main props of the hut. Nor was it difficult to know how it had been procured; for a large stag greyhound, nobler in size and appearance than those even which guarded King Richard's sick-bed, lay eyeing the process of baking the cake. The sagacious animal, on their first entrance, uttered a stifled growl, which sounded from his deep chest like distant thunder. But he saw his master, and acknowledged his presence by wagging his tail and couching his head, abstaining from more tumultuous or noisy greeting, as if his noble instinct had taught him the propriety of silence in a sick man's chamber.

Beside the couch sat on a cushion, also composed of skins, the Moorish physician of whom Sir Kenneth had spoken, cross-legged, after the Eastern fashion. The imperfect light showed little of him, save that the lower part of his face was covered with a long, black beard, which descended over his breast; that he wore a high TOLPACH, a Tartar cap of the lamb's wool manufactured at Astracan, bearing the same dusky colour; and that his ample caftan, or Turkish robe, was also of a dark hue. Two piercing eyes, which gleamed with unusual lustre, were the only lineaments of his visage that could be discerned amid the darkness in which he was enveloped.

The English lord stood silent with a sort of reverential awe; for notwithstanding the roughness of his general bearing, a scene of distress and poverty, firmly endured without complaint or murmur, would at any time have claimed more reverence from Thomas de Vaux than would all the splendid formalities of a royal presence-chamber, unless that presence-chamber were King Richard's own. Nothing was for a time heard but the heavy and regular breathings of the invalid, who seemed in profound repose.

"He hath not slept for six nights before," said Sir Kenneth, "as I am assured by the youth, his attendant."

"Noble Scot," said Thomas de Vaux, grasping the Scottish knight's hand, with a pressure which had more of cordiality than he permitted his words to utter, "this gear must be amended. Your esquire is but too evil fed and looked to."

In the latter part of this speech he naturally raised his voice to its usual decided tone, The sick man was disturbed in his slumbers.

"My master," he said, murmuring as in a dream, "noble Sir Kenneth, taste not, to you as to me, the waters of the Clyde cold and refreshing after the brackish springs of Palestine?"

"He dreams of his native land, and is happy in his slumbers," whispered Sir Kenneth to De Vaux; but had scarce uttered the words, when the physician, arising from the place which he had taken near the couch of the sick, and laying the hand of the patient, whose pulse he had been carefully watching, quietly upon the couch, came to the two knights, and taking them each by the arm, while he intimated to them to remain silent, led them to the front of the hut.

"In the name of Issa Ben Mariam," he said, "whom we honour as you, though not with the same blinded superstition, disturb not the effect of the blessed medicine of which he hath partaken. To awaken him now is death or deprivation of reason; but return at the hour when the muezzin calls from the minaret to evening prayer in the mosque, and if left undisturbed until then, I promise you this same Frankish soldier shall be able, without prejudice to his health, to hold some brief converse with you on any matters on which either, and especially his master, may have to question him."

The knights retreated before the authoritative commands of the leech, who seemed fully to comprehend the importance of the Eastern proverb that the sick chamber of the patient is the kingdom of the physician.

They paused, and remained standing together at the door of the hut—Sir Kenneth with the air of one who expected his visitor to say farewell, and De Vaux as if he had something on his mind which prevented him from doing so. The hound, however, had pressed out of the tent after them, and now thrust his long, rough countenance into the hand of his master, as if modestly soliciting some mark of his kindness. He had no sooner received the notice which he desired, in the shape of a kind word and slight caress, than, eager to acknowledge his gratitude and joy for his master's return, he flew off at full speed, galloping in full career, and with outstretched tail, here and there, about and around, cross-ways and endlong, through the decayed huts and the esplanade we have described, but never transgressing those precincts which his sagacity knew were protected by his master's pennon. After a few gambols of this kind, the dog, coming close up to his master, laid at once aside his frolicsome mood, relapsed into his usual gravity and slowness of gesture and deportment, and looked as if he were ashamed that anything should have moved him to depart so far out of his sober self-control.

Both knights looked on with pleasure; for Sir Kenneth was justly proud of his noble hound, and the northern English baron was, of course, an admirer of the chase, and a judge of the animal's merits.

"A right able dog," he said. "I think, fair sir, King Richard hath not an ALAN which may match him, if he be as stanch as he is swift. But let me pray you—speaking in all honour and kindness—have you not heard the proclamation that no one under the rank of earl shall keep hunting dogs within King Richard's camp without the royal license, which, I think, Sir Kenneth, hath not been issued to you? I speak as Master of the Horse."

"And I answer as a free Scottish knight," said Kenneth sternly. "For the present I follow the banner of England, but I cannot remember that I have ever subjected myself to the forest-laws of that kingdom, nor have I such respect for them as would incline me to do so. When the trumpet sounds to arms, my foot is in the stirrup as soon as any—when it clangs for the charge, my lance has not yet been the last laid in the rest. But for my hours of liberty or of idleness King Richard has no title to bar my recreation."

"Nevertheless," said De Vaux, "it is a folly to disobey the King's ordinance; so, with your good leave, I, as having authority in that matter, will send you a protection for my friend here."

"I thank you," said the Scot coldly; "but he knows my allotted quarters, and within these I can protect him myself.—And yet," he said, suddenly changing his manner, "this is but a cold return for a well-meant kindness. I thank you, my lord, most heartily. The King's equerries or prickers might find Roswal at disadvantage, and do him some injury, which I should not, perhaps, be slow in returning, and so ill might come of it. You have seen so much of my house-keeping, my lord," he added, with a smile, "that I need not shame to say that Roswal is our principal purveyor, and well I hope our Lion Richard will not be like the lion in the minstrel fable, that went a-hunting, and kept the whole booty to himself. I cannot think he would grudge a poor gentleman, who follows him faithfully, his hour of sport and his morsel of game, more especially when other food is hard enough to come by."

"By my faith, you do the King no more than justice; and yet," said the baron, "there is something in these words, vert and venison, that turns the very brains of our Norman princes."

"We have heard of late," said the Scot, "by minstrels and pilgrims, that your outlawed yeomen have formed great bands in the shires of York and Nottingham, having at their head a most stout archer, called Robin Hood, with his lieutenant, Little John. Methinks it were better that Richard relaxed his forest-code in England, than endeavour to enforce it in the Holy Land."

"Wild work, Sir Kenneth," replied De Vaux, shrugging his shoulders, as one who would avoid a perilous or unpleasing topic—"a mad world, sir. I must now bid you adieu, having presently to return to the King's pavilion. At vespers I will again, with your leave, visit your quarters, and speak with this same infidel physician. I would, in the meantime, were it no offence, willingly send you what would somewhat mend your cheer."

"I thank you, sir," said Sir Kenneth, "but it needs not. Roswal hath already stocked my larder for two weeks, since the sun of Palestine, if it brings diseases, serves also to dry venison."

The two warriors parted much better friends than they had met; but ere they separated, Thomas de Vaux informed himself at more length of the circumstances attending the mission of the Eastern physician, and received from the Scottish knight the credentials which he had brought to King Richard on the part of Saladin.

Lesson 130

1. Unusual vocabulary:
    - prelate — high ranking member of the clergy
2. Read chapter 8. De Vaux goes to see how the physician's cure has worked on Sir Kenneth's servant before he allows the physician to visit the King and a bishop of the church decides to accompany him.
3. Who has sent this Muslim physician to bring a cure to King Richard? (Answers)
4. What does King Richard say he plans to do after he is well? (Answers)
5. What does de Vaux do to try to judge whether or not this physician's cure will work? (Answers)
6. Who accompanies him? What is your impression of this churchman? Why? (Answers)

CHAPTER VIII.

A wise physician, skilled our wounds to heal,

Is more than armies to the common weal.

POPE'S ILLIAD.

"This is a strange tale, Sir Thomas," said the sick monarch, when he had heard the report of the trusty Baron of Gilsland. "Art thou sure this Scottish man is a tall man and true?"

"I cannot say, my lord," replied the jealous Borderer. "I live a little too near the Scots to gather much truth among them, having found them ever fair and false. But this man's bearing is that of a true man, were he a devil as well as a Scot; that I must needs say for him in conscience."

"And for his carriage as a knight, how sayest thou, De Vaux?" demanded the King.

"It is your Majesty's business more than mine to note men's bearings; and I warrant you have noted the manner in which this man of the Leopard hath borne himself. He hath been full well spoken of."

"And justly, Thomas," said the King. "We have ourselves witnessed him. It is indeed our purpose in placing ourselves ever in the front of battle, to see how our liegemen and followers acquit themselves, and not from a desire to accumulate vainglory to ourselves, as some have supposed. We know the vanity of the praise of man, which is but a vapour, and buckle on our armour for other purposes than to win it."

De Vaux was alarmed when he heard the King make a declaration so inconsistent with his nature, and believed at first that nothing short of the approach of death could have brought him to speak in depreciating terms of military renown, which was the very breath of his nostrils. But recollecting he had met the royal confessor in the outer pavilion, he was shrewd enough to place this temporary self-abasement to the effect of the reverend man's lesson, and suffered the King to proceed without reply.

"Yes," continued Richard, "I have indeed marked the manner in which this knight does his devoir. My leading-staff were not worth a fool's bauble had he escaped my notice; and he had ere now tasted of our bounty, but that I have also marked his overweening and audacious presumption."

"My liege," said the Baron of Gilsland, observing the King's countenance change, "I fear I have transgressed your pleasure in lending some countenance to his transgression."

"How, De Multon, thou?" said the King, contracting his brows, and speaking in a tone of angry surprise. "Thou countenance his insolence? It cannot be."

"Nay, your Majesty will pardon me to remind you that I have by mine office right to grant liberty to men of gentle blood to keep them a hound or two within camp, just to cherish the noble art of venerie; and besides, it were a sin to have maimed or harmed a thing so noble as this gentleman's dog."

"Has he, then, a dog so handsome?" said the King.

"A most perfect creature of Heaven," said the baron, who was an enthusiast in field-sports—"of the noblest Northern breed—deep in the chest, strong in the stern—black colour, and brindled on the breast and legs, not spotted with white, but just shaded into grey—strength to pull down a bull, swiftness to cote an antelope."

The King laughed at his enthusiasm. "Well, thou hast given him leave to keep the hound, so there is an end of it. Be not, however, liberal of your licenses among those knights adventurers who have no prince or leader to depend upon; they are ungovernable, and leave no game in Palestine.—But to this piece of learned heathenesse—sayest thou the Scot met him in the desert?"

"No, my liege; the Scot's tale runs thus. He was dispatched to the old hermit of Engaddi, of whom men talk so much—"

"'Sdeath and hell!" said Richard, starting up. "By whom dispatched, and for what? Who dared send any one thither, when our Queen was in the Convent of Engaddi, upon her pilgrimage for our recovery?"

"The Council of the Crusade sent him, my lord," answered the Baron de Vaux; "for what purpose, he declined to account to me. I think it is scarce known in the camp that your royal consort is on a pilgrimage; and even the princes may not have been aware, as the Queen has been sequestered from company since your love prohibited her attendance in case of infection."

"Well, it shall be looked into," said Richard. "So this Scottish man, this envoy, met with a wandering physician at the grotto of Engaddi—ha?"

"Not so my liege," replied De Vaux? "but he met, I think, near that place, with a Saracen Emir with whom he had some MELEE in the way of proof of valour, and finding him worthy to bear brave men company, they went together, as errant knights are wont, to the grotto of Engaddi."

Here De Vaux stopped, for he was not one of those who can tell a long story in a sentence.

"And did they there meet the physician?" demanded the King impatiently.

"No, my liege," replied De Vaux; "but the Saracen, learning your Majesty's grievous illness, undertook that Saladin should send his own physician to you, and with many assurances of his eminent skill; and he came to the grotto accordingly, after the Scottish knight had tarried a day for him and more. He is attended as if he were a prince, with drums and atabals, and servants on horse and foot, and brings with him letters of credence from Saladin."

"Have they been examined by Giacomo Loredani?"

"I showed them to the interpreter ere bringing them hither, and behold their contents in English."

Richard took a scroll, in which were inscribed these words: The blessing of Allah and his Prophet Mohammed ["Out upon the hound!" said Richard, spitting in contempt, by way of interjection], Saladin, king of kings, Saldan of Egypt and of Syria, the light and refuge of the earth, to the great Melech Ric, Richard of England, greeting. Whereas, we have been informed that the hand of sickness hath been heavy upon thee, our royal brother, and that thou hast with thee only such Nazarene and Jewish mediciners as work without the blessing of Allah and our holy Prophet ["Confusion on his head!" again muttered the English monarch], we have therefore sent to tend and wait upon thee at this time the physician to our own person, Adonbec el Hakim, before whose face the angel Azrael [The Angel of Death] spreads his wings and departs from the sick chamber; who knows the virtues of herbs and stones, the path of the sun, moon, and stars, and can save man from all that is not written on his forehead. And this we do, praying you heartily to honour and make use of his skill; not only that we may do service to thy worth and valour, which is the glory of all the nations of Frangistan, but that we may bring the controversy which is at present between us to an end, either by honourable agreement, or by open trial thereof with our weapons, in a fair field—seeing that it neither becomes thy place and courage to die the death of a slave who hath been overwrought by his taskmaster, nor befits it our fame that a brave adversary be snatched from our weapon by such a disease. And, therefore, may the holy—"

"Hold, hold," said Richard, "I will have no more of his dog of a prophet! It makes me sick to think the valiant and worthy Soldan should believe in a dead dog. Yes, I will see his physician. I will put myself into the charge of this Hakim—I will repay the noble Soldan his generosity—I will meet Saladin in the field, as he so worthily proposes, and he shall have no cause to term Richard of England ungrateful. I will strike him to the earth with my battle-axe—I will convert him to Holy Church with such blows as he has rarely endured. He shall recant his errors before my good cross-handled sword, and I will have him baptized on the battle-field, from my own helmet, though the cleansing waters were mixed with the blood of us both.—Haste, De Vaux, why dost thou delay a conclusion so pleasing? Fetch the Hakim hither."

"My lord," said the baron, who perhaps saw some accession of fever in this overflow of confidence, "bethink you, the Soldan is a pagan, and that you are his most formidable enemy—"

"For which reason he is the more bound to do me service in this matter, lest a paltry fever end the quarrel betwixt two such kings. I tell thee he loves me as I love him—as noble adversaries ever love each other. By my honour, it were sin to doubt his good faith!"

"Nevertheless, my lord, it were well to wait the issue of these medicines upon the Scottish squire," said the Lord of Gilsland. "My own life depends upon it, for worthy were I to die like a dog did I proceed rashly in this matter, and make shipwreck of the weal of Christendom."

"I never knew thee before hesitate for fear of life," said Richard upbraidingly.

"Nor would I now, my liege," replied the stout-hearted baron, "save that yours lies at pledge as well as my own."

"Well, thou suspicious mortal," answered Richard, "begone then, and watch the progress of this remedy. I could almost wish it might either cure or kill me, for I am weary of lying here like an ox dying of the murrain, when tambours are beating, horses stamping, and trumpets sounding without."

The baron hastily departed, resolved, however, to communicate his errand to some churchman, as he felt something burdened in conscience at the idea of his master being attended by an unbeliever.

The Archbishop of Tyre was the first to whom he confided his doubts, knowing his interest with his master, Richard, who both loved and honoured that sagacious prelate. The bishop heard the doubts which De Vaux stated, with that acuteness of intelligence which distinguishes the Roman Catholic clergy. The religious scruples of De Vaux he treated with as much lightness as propriety permitted him to exhibit on such a subject to a layman.

"Mediciners," he said, "like the medicines which they employed, were often useful, though the one were by birth or manners the vilest of humanity, as the others are, in many cases, extracted from the basest materials. Men may use the assistance of pagans and infidels," he continued, "in their need, and there is reason to think that one cause of their being permitted to remain on earth is that they might minister to the convenience of true Christians. Thus we lawfully make slaves of heathen captives. Again," proceeded the prelate, "there is no doubt that the primitive Christians used the services of the unconverted heathen. Thus in the ship of Alexandria, in which the blessed Apostle Paul sailed to Italy, the sailors were doubtless pagans; yet what said the holy saint when their ministry was needful?—'NISI HI IN NAVI MANSERINT, VOS SALVI FIERI NON POTESTIS'—Unless these men abide in the ship, ye cannot be saved. Again, Jews are infidels to

Christianity, as well as Mohammedans. But there are few physicians in the camp excepting Jews, and such are employed without scandal or scruple. Therefore, Mohammedans may be used for their service in that capacity—QUOD ERAT DEMONSTRANDUM."

This reasoning entirely removed the scruples of Thomas de Vaux, who was particularly moved by the Latin quotation, as he did not understand a word of it.

But the bishop proceeded with far less fluency when he considered the possibility of the Saracen's acting with bad faith; and here he came not to a speedy decision. The baron showed him the letters of credence. He read and re-read them, and compared the original with the translation.

"It is a dish choicely cooked," he said, "to the palate of King Richard, and I cannot but have my suspicions of the wily Saracen. They are curious in the art of poisons, and can so temper them that they shall be weeks in acting upon the party, during which time the perpetrator has leisure to escape. They can impregnate cloth and leather, nay, even paper and parchment, with the most subtle venom. Our Lady forgive me! And wherefore, knowing this, hold I these letters of credence so close to my face? Take them, Sir Thomas—take them speedily!"

Here he gave them at arm's-length, and with some appearance of haste, to the baron. "But come, my Lord de Vaux," he continued, "wend we to the tent of this sick squire, where we shall learn whether this Hakim hath really the art of curing which he professeth, ere we consider whether there be safety in permitting him to exercise his art upon King Richard.—Yet, hold! let me first take my pouncet-box, for these fevers spread like an infection. I would advise you to use dried rosemary steeped in vinegar, my lord. I, too, know something of the healing art."

"I thank your reverend lordship," replied Thomas of Gilsland; "but had I been accessible to the fever, I had caught it long since by the bed of my master."

The Bishop of Tyre blushed, for he had rather avoided the presence of the sick monarch; and he bid the baron lead on.

As they paused before the wretched hut in which Kenneth of the Leopard and his follower abode, the bishop said to De Vaux, "Now, of a surety, my lord, these Scottish Knights have worse care of their followers than we of our dogs. Here is a knight, valiant, they say, in battle, and thought fitting to be graced with charges of weight in time of truce, whose esquire of the body is lodged worse than in the worst dog-kennel in England. What say you of your neighbours?"

"That a master doth well enough for his servant when he lodgeth him in no worse dwelling than his own," said De Vaux, and entered the hut.

The bishop followed, not without evident reluctance; for though he lacked not courage in some respects, yet it was tempered with a strong and lively regard for his own safety. He recollected, however, the necessity there was for judging personally of the skill of the Arabian physician, and entered the hut with a stateliness of manner calculated, as he thought, to impose respect on the stranger.

The prelate was, indeed, a striking and commanding figure. In his youth he had been eminently handsome, and even in age was unwilling to appear less so. His episcopal dress was of the richest fashion, trimmed with costly fur, and surrounded by a cope of curious needlework. The rings on his fingers were worth a goodly barony, and the hood which he wore, though now unclasped and thrown back for heat, had studs of pure gold to fasten it around his throat and under his chin when he so inclined. His long beard, now silvered with age, descended over his breast. One of two youthful acolytes who attended him created an artificial shade, peculiar then to the East, by bearing over his head an umbrella of palmetto leaves, while the other refreshed his reverend master by agitating a fan of peacock-feathers.

When the Bishop of Tyre entered the hut of the Scottish knight, the master was absent, and the Moorish physician, whom he had come to see, sat in the very posture in which De Vaux had left him several hours before, cross-legged upon a mat made of twisted leaves, by the side of the patient, who appeared in deep slumber, and whose pulse he felt from time to time. The bishop remained standing before him in silence for two or three minutes, as if expecting some honourable salutation, or at least that the Saracen would seem struck with the dignity of his appearance. But Adonbec el Hakim took no notice of him beyond a passing glance, and when the prelate at length saluted him in the lingua franca current in the country, he only replied by the ordinary Oriental greeting, "SALAM ALICUM—Peace be with you."

"Art thou a physician, infidel?" said the bishop, somewhat mortified at this cold reception. "I would speak with thee on that art."

"If thou knewest aught of medicine," answered El Hakim, "thou wouldst be aware that physicians hold no counsel or debate in the sick chamber of their patient. Hear," he added, as the low growling of the staghound was heard from the inner hut, "even the dog might teach thee reason, Ulemat. His instinct teaches him to suppress his barking in the sick man's hearing. Come without the tent," said he, rising and leading the way, "if thou hast ought to say with me."

Notwithstanding the plainness of the Saracen leech's dress, and his inferiority of size when contrasted with the tall prelate and gigantic English baron, there was something striking in his manner and countenance, which prevented the Bishop of Tyre from expressing strongly the displeasure he felt at this unceremonious rebuke. When without the hut, he gazed upon Adonbec in silence for several minutes before he could fix on the best manner to renew the conversation. No locks were seen under the high bonnet of the Arabian, which hid also part of a brow that seemed lofty and expanded, smooth, and free from wrinkles, as were his cheeks, where they were seen under the shade of his long beard. We have elsewhere noticed the piercing quality of his dark eyes.

The prelate, struck with his apparent youth, at length broke a pause, which the other seemed in no haste to interrupt, by demanding of the Arabian how old he was?

"The years of ordinary men," said the Saracen, "are counted by their wrinkles; those of sages by their studies. I dare not call myself older than a hundred revolutions of the Hegira." [Meaning that his attainments were those which might have been made in a hundred years.]

The Baron of Gilsland, who took this for a literal assertion that he was a century old, looked doubtfully upon the prelate, who, though he better understood the meaning of El Hakim, answered his glance by mysteriously shaking his head. He resumed an air of importance when he again authoritatively demanded what evidence Adonbec could produce of his medical proficiency.

"Ye have the word of the mighty Saladin," said the sage, touching his cap in sign of reverence—"a word which was never broken towards friend or foe. What, Nazarene, wouldst thou demand more?"

"I would have ocular proof of thy skill," said the baron, "and without it thou approachest not to the couch of King Richard."

"The praise of the physician," said the Arabian, "is in the recovery of his patient. Behold this sergeant, whose blood has been dried up by the fever which has whitened your camp with skeletons, and against which the art of your Nazarene leeches hath been like a silken doublet against a lance of steel. Look at his fingers and arms, wasted like the claws and shanks of the crane. Death had this morning his clutch on him; but had Azrael been on one side of the couch, I being on the other, his soul should not have been left from his body. Disturb me not with further questions, but await the critical minute, and behold in silent wonder the marvellous event."

The physician had then recourse to his astrolabe, the oracle of Eastern science, and watching with grave precision until the precise time of the evening prayer had arrived, he sunk on his knees, with his face turned to Mecca, and recited the petitions which close the Moslemah's day of toil. The bishop and the English baron looked on each other, meanwhile, with symptoms of contempt and indignation, but neither judged it fit to interrupt El Hakim in his devotions, unholy as they considered them to be.

The Arab arose from the earth, on which he had prostrated himself, and walking into the hut where the patient lay extended, he drew a sponge from a small silver box, dipped perhaps in some aromatic distillation, for when he put it to the sleeper's nose, he sneezed, awoke, and looked wildly around. He was a ghastly spectacle as he sat up almost naked on his couch, the bones and cartilages as visible through the surface of his skin as if they had never been clothed with flesh. His face was long, and furrowed with wrinkles; but his eye, though it wandered at first, became gradually more settled. He seemed to be aware of the presence of his dignified visitors, for he attempted feebly to pull the covering from his head in token of reverence, as he inquired, in a subdued and submissive voice, for his master.

"Do you know us, vassal?" said the Lord of Gilsland.

"Not perfectly, my lord," replied the squire faintly. "My sleep has been long and full of dreams. Yet I know that you are a great English lord, as seemeth by the red cross, and this a holy prelate, whose blessing I crave on me a poor sinner."

"Thou hast it—BENEDICTIO DOMINI SIT VOBISCUM," said the prelate, making the sign of the cross, but without approaching nearer to the patient's bed.

"Your eyes witness," said the Arabian, "the fever hath been subdued. He speaks with calmness and recollection—his pulse beats composedly as yours—try its pulsations yourself."

The prelate declined the experiment; but Thomas of Gilsland, more determined on making the trial, did so, and satisfied himself that the fever was indeed gone.

"This is most wonderful," said the knight, looking to the bishop; "the man is assuredly cured. I must conduct this mediciner presently to King Richard's tent. What thinks your reverence?"

"Stay, let me finish one cure ere I commence another," said the Arab; "I will pass with you when I have given my patient the second cup of this most holy elixir."

So saying he pulled out a silver cup, and filling it with water from a gourd which stood by the bedside, he next drew forth a small silken bag made of network, twisted with silver, the contents of which the bystanders could not discover, and immersing it in the cup, continued to watch it in silence during the space of five minutes. It seemed to the spectators as if some effervescence took place during the operation; but if so, it instantly subsided.

"Drink," said the physician to the sick man—"sleep, and awaken free from malady."

"And with this simple-seeming draught thou wilt undertake to cure a monarch?" said the Bishop of Tyre.

"I have cured a beggar, as you may behold," replied the sage. "Are the Kings of Frangistan made of other clay than the meanest of their subjects?"

"Let us have him presently to the King," said the Baron of Gilsland. "He hath shown that he possesses the secret which may restore his health. If he fails to exercise it, I will put himself past the power of medicine."

As they were about to leave the hut, the sick man, raising his voice as much as his weakness permitted, exclaimed, "Reverend father, noble knight, and you, kind leech, if you would have me sleep and recover, tell me in charity what is become of my dear master?"

"He is upon a distant expedition, friend," replied the prelate—"on an honourable embassy, which may detain him for some days."

"Nay," said the Baron of Gilsland, "why deceive the poor fellow?—Friend, thy master has returned to the camp, and you will presently see him."

The invalid held up, as if in thankfulness, his wasted hands to Heaven, and resisting no longer the soporiferous operation of the elixir, sunk down in a gentle sleep.

"You are a better physician than I, Sir Thomas," said the prelate—"a soothing falsehood is fitter for a sick-room than an unpleasing truth."

"How mean you, my reverend lord?" said De Vaux hastily. "Think you I would tell a falsehood to save the lives of a dozen such as he?"

"You said," replied the bishop, with manifest symptoms of alarm—"you said the esquire's master was returned—he, I mean, of the Couchant Leopard."

"And he IS returned," said De Vaux. "I spoke with him but a few hours since. This learned leech came in his company."

"Holy Virgin! why told you not of his return to me?" said the bishop, in evident perturbation.

"Did I not say that this same Knight of the Leopard had returned in company with the physician? I thought I had," replied De Vaux carelessly. "But what signified his return to the skill of the physician, or the cure of his Majesty?"

"Much, Sir Thomas—it signified much," said the bishop, clenching his hands, pressing his foot against the earth, and giving signs of impatience, as if in an involuntary manner. "But where can he be gone now, this same knight? God be with us—here may be some fatal errors!"

"Yonder serf in the outer space," said De Vaux, not without wonder at the bishop's emotion, "can probably tell us whither his master has gone."

The lad was summoned, and in a language nearly incomprehensible to them, gave them at length to understand that an officer had summoned his master to the royal tent some time before their arrival at that of his master. The anxiety of the bishop appeared to rise to the highest, and became evident to De Vaux, though, neither an acute observer nor of a suspicious temper. But with his anxiety seemed to increase his wish to keep it subdued and unobserved. He took a hasty leave of De Vaux, who looked after him with astonishment, and after shrugging his shoulders in silent wonder, proceeded to conduct the Arabian physician to the tent of King Richard.

Lesson 131

1. Stop and think. What has just happened in the book? What do you think is going to happen next?
2. Read chapter 9. As King Richard waits for the physician, he hears some disturbing news about his allies from Sir Kenneth.
3. While King Richard waits for the physician to come, he sends for Sir Kenneth. He discovers that Sir Kenneth had been sent on an errand. Who sent him? What was the errand? How does King Richard react to this news? (Answers)
4. Who visits King Richard next? What is their purpose? Do you trust them? Why or why not? (Answers)
5. Finally, the King meets the physician and takes the medicine. Do you think it will work? Why? (Answers)

Vocabulary

1. Make sure that you know that an "infidel" is someone who doesn't adhere to your religion. Someone who is an infidel to a Christian is a believer to another and visa versa.
2. I haven't given you vocabulary words from *The Talisman*. Have you been figuring out any new words as you read? Do you look them up? Make sure you understand what you are reading. If you need to, stop to look up a word or to ask what it means.

CHAPTER IX.

This is the prince of leeches; fever, plague,

Cold rheum, and hot podagra, do but look on him,

And quit their grasp upon the tortured sinews.

ANONYMOUS.

The Baron of Gilsland walked with slow step and an anxious countenance towards the royal pavilion. He had much diffidence of his own capacity, except in a field of battle, and conscious of no very acute intellect, was usually contented to wonder at circumstances which a man of livelier imagination would have endeavoured to investigate and understand, or at least would have made the subject of speculation. But it seemed very extraordinary, even to him, that the attention of the bishop should have been at once abstracted from all reflection on the marvellous cure which they had witnessed, and upon the probability it afforded of Richard being restored to health, by what seemed a very trivial piece of information announcing the motions of a beggardly Scottish knight, than whom Thomas of Gilsland knew nothing within the circle of gentle blood more unimportant or contemptible; and despite his usual habit of passively beholding passing events, the baron's spirit toiled with unwonted attempts to form conjectures on the cause.

At length the idea occurred at once to him that the whole might be a conspiracy against King Richard, formed within the camp of the allies, and to which the bishop, who was by some represented as a politic and unscrupulous person, was not unlikely to have been accessory. It was true that, in his own opinion, there existed no character so perfect as that of his master; for Richard being the flower of chivalry, and the chief of Christian leaders, and obeying in all points the commands of Holy Church, De Vaux's ideas of perfection went no further. Still, he knew that, however unworthily, it had been always his master's fate to draw as much reproach and dislike as honour and attachment from the display of his great qualities; and that in the very camp, and amongst those princes bound by oath to the Crusade, were many who would have sacrificed all hope of victory over the Saracens to the pleasure of ruining, or at least of humbling, Richard of England.

"Wherefore," said the baron to himself, "it is in no sense impossible that this El Hakim, with this his cure, or seeming cure, wrought on the body of the Scottish squire, may mean nothing but a trick, to which he of the Leopard may be accessory, and wherein the Bishop of Tyre, prelate as he is, may have some share."

This hypothesis, indeed, could not be so easily reconciled with the alarm manifested by the bishop on learning that, contrary to his expectation, the Scottish knight had suddenly returned to the Crusaders' camp. But De Vaux was influenced only by his general prejudices, which dictated to him the assured belief that a wily Italian priest, a false-hearted Scot, and an infidel physician, formed a set of ingredients from which all evil, and no good, was likely to be extracted. He resolved, however, to lay his scruples bluntly before the King, of whose judgment he had nearly as high an opinion as of his valour.

Meantime, events had taken place very contrary to the suppositions which Thomas de Vaux had entertained. Scarce had he left the royal pavilion, when, betwixt the impatience of the fever, and that which was natural to his disposition, Richard began to murmur at his delay, and express an earnest desire for his return. He had seen enough to try to reason himself out of this irritation, which greatly increased his bodily malady. He wearied his attendants by demanding from them amusements, and the breviary of the priest, the romance of the clerk, even the harp of his favourite minstrel, were had recourse to in vain. At length, some two hours before sundown, and long, therefore, ere he could expect a satisfactory account of the process of the cure which the Moor or Arabian had undertaken, he sent, as we have already heard, a messenger commanding the attendance of the Knight of the Leopard, determined to soothe his impatience by obtaining from Sir Kenneth a more particular account of the cause of his absence from the camp, and the circumstances of his meeting with this celebrated physician.

The Scottish knight, thus summoned, entered the royal presence as one who was no stranger to such scenes. He was scarcely known to the King of England, even by sight, although, tenacious of his rank, as devout in the adoration of the lady of his secret heart, he had never been absent on those occasions when the munificence and hospitality of England opened the Court of its monarch to all who held a certain rank in chivalry. The King gazed fixedly on Sir Kenneth approaching his bedside, while the knight bent his knee for a moment, then arose, and stood before him in a posture of deference, but not of subservience or humility, as became an officer in the presence of his sovereign.

"Thy name," said the King, "is Kenneth of the Leopard—from whom hadst thou degree of knighthood?"

"I took it from the sword of William the Lion, King of Scotland," replied the Scot.

"A weapon," said the King, "well worthy to confer honour; nor has it been laid on an undeserving shoulder. We have seen thee bear thyself knightly and valiantly in press of battle, when most need there was; and thou hadst not been yet to learn that thy deserts were known to us, but that thy presumption in other points has been such that thy services can challenge no better reward than that of pardon for thy transgression. What sayest thou—ha?"

Kenneth attempted to speak, but was unable to express himself distinctly; the consciousness of his too ambitious love, and the keen, falcon glance with which Coeur de Lion seemed to penetrate his inmost soul, combining to disconcert him.

"And yet," said the King, "although soldiers should obey command, and vassals be respectful towards their superiors, we might forgive a brave knight greater offence than the keeping a simple hound, though it were contrary to our express public ordinance."

Richard kept his eye fixed on the Scot's face, beheld and beholding, smiling inwardly at the relief produced by the turn he had given to his general accusation.

"So please you, my lord," said the Scot, "your majesty must be good to us poor gentlemen of Scotland in this matter. We are far from home, scant of revenues, and cannot support ourselves as your wealthy nobles, who have credit of the Lombards. The Saracens shall feel our blows the harder that we eat a piece of dried venison from time to time with our herbs and barley-cakes."

"It skills not asking my leave," said Richard, "since Thomas de Vaux, who doth, like all around me, that which is fittest in his own eyes, hath already given thee permission for hunting and hawking."

"For hunting only, and please you," said the Scot. "But if it please your Majesty to indulge me with the privilege of hawking also, and you list to trust me with a falcon on fist, I trust I could supply your royal mess with some choice waterfowl."

"I dread me, if thou hadst but the falcon," said the King, "thou wouldst scarce wait for the permission. I wot well it is said abroad that we of the line of Anjou resent offence against our forest-laws as highly as we would do treason against our crown. To brave and worthy men, however, we could pardon either misdemeanour.—But enough of this. I desire to know of you, Sir Knight, wherefore, and by whose authority, you took this recent journey to the wilderness of the Dead Sea and Engaddi?"

"By order," replied the knight, "of the Council of Princes of the Holy Crusade."

"And how dared any one to give such an order, when I—not the least, surely, in the league—was unacquainted with it?"

"It was not my part, please your highness," said the Scot, "to inquire into such particulars. I am a soldier of the Cross—serving, doubtless, for the present, under your highness's banner, and proud of the permission to do so, but still one who hath taken on him the holy symbol for the rights of Christianity and the recovery of the Holy Sepulchre, and bound, therefore, to obey without question the orders of the princes and chiefs by whom the blessed enterprise is directed. That indisposition should seclude, I trust for but a short time, your highness from their councils, in which you hold so potential a voice, I must lament with all Christendom; but, as a soldier, I must obey those on whom the lawful right of command devolves, or set but an evil example in the Christian camp."

"Thou sayest well," said King Richard; "and the blame rests not with thee, but with those with whom, when it shall please Heaven to raise me from this accursed bed of pain and inactivity, I hope to reckon roundly. What was the purport of thy message?"

"Methinks, and please your highness," replied Sir Kenneth, "that were best asked of those who sent me, and who can render the reasons of mine errand; whereas I can only tell its outward form and purport."

"Palter not with me, Sir Scot—it were ill for thy safety," said the irritable monarch.

"My safety, my lord," replied the knight firmly, "I cast behind me as a regardless thing when I vowed myself to this enterprise, looking rather to my immortal welfare than to that which concerns my earthly body."

"By the mass," said King Richard, "thou art a brave fellow! Hark thee, Sir Knight, I love the Scottish people; they are hardy, though dogged and stubborn, and, I think, true men in the main, though the necessity of state has sometimes constrained them to be dissemblers. I deserve some love at their hand, for I have voluntarily done what they could not by arms have extorted from me any more than from my predecessors, I have re-established the fortresses of Roxburgh and

Berwick, which lay in pledge to England; I have restored your ancient boundaries; and, finally, I have renounced a claim to homage upon the crown of England, which I thought unjustly forced on you. I have endeavoured to make honourable and independent friends, where former kings of England attempted only to compel unwilling and rebellious vassals."

"All this you have done, my Lord King," said Sir Kenneth, bowing—"all this you have done, by your royal treaty with our sovereign at Canterbury. Therefore have you me, and many better Scottish men, making war against the infidels, under your banners, who would else have been ravaging your frontiers in England. If their numbers are now few, it is because their lives have been freely waged and wasted."

"I grant it true," said the King; "and for the good offices I have done your land I require you to remember that, as a principal member of the Christian league, I have a right to know the negotiations of my confederates. Do me, therefore, the justice to tell me what I have a title to be acquainted with, and which I am certain to know more truly from you than from others."

"My lord," said the Scot, "thus conjured, I will speak the truth; for I well believe that your purposes towards the principal object of our expedition are single-hearted and honest, and it is more than I dare warrant for others of the Holy League. Be pleased, therefore, to know my charge was to propose, through the medium of the hermit of Engaddi—a holy man, respected and protected by Saladin himself—"

"A continuation of the truce, I doubt not," said Richard, hastily interrupting him.

"No, by Saint Andrew, my liege," said the Scottish knight; "but the establishment of a lasting peace, and the withdrawing our armies from Palestine."

"Saint George!" said Richard, in astonishment. "Ill as I have justly thought of them, I could not have dreamed they would have humbled themselves to such dishonour. Speak, Sir Kenneth, with what will did you carry such a message?"

"With right good will, my lord," said Kenneth; "because, when we had lost our noble leader, under whose guidance alone I hoped for victory, I saw none who could succeed him likely to lead us to conquest, and I accounted it well in such circumstances to avoid defeat."

"And on what conditions was this hopeful peace to be contracted?" said King Richard, painfully suppressing the passion with which his heart was almost bursting.

"These were not entrusted to me, my lord," answered the Knight of the Couchant Leopard. "I delivered them sealed to the hermit."

"And for what hold you this reverend hermit—for fool, madman, traitor, or saint?" said Richard.

"His folly, sire," replied the shrewd Scottish man, "I hold to be assumed to win favour and reverence from the Paynimrie, who regard madmen as the inspired of Heaven—at least it seemed to me as exhibited only occasionally, and not as mixing, like natural folly, with the general tenor of his mind."

"Shrewdly replied," said the monarch, throwing himself back on his couch, from which he had half-raised himself. "Now of his penitence?"

"His penitence," continued Kenneth, "appears to me sincere, and the fruits of remorse for some dreadful crime, for which he seems, in his own opinion, condemned to reprobation."

"And for his policy?" said King Richard.

"Methinks, my lord," said the Scottish knight, "he despairs of the security of Palestine, as of his own salvation, by any means short of a miracle—at least, since the arm of Richard of England hath ceased to strike for it."

"And, therefore, the coward policy of this hermit is like that of these miserable princes, who, forgetful of their knighthood and their faith, are only resolved and determined when the question is retreat, and rather than go forward against an armed Saracen, would trample in their flight over a dying ally!"

"Might I so far presume, my Lord King," said the Scottish knight, "this discourse but heats your disease, the enemy from which Christendom dreads more evil than from armed hosts of infidels."

The countenance of King Richard was, indeed, more flushed, and his action became more feverishly vehement, as, with clenched hand, extended arm, and flashing eyes, he seemed at once to suffer under bodily pain, and at the same time under vexation of mind, while his high spirit led him to speak on, as if in contempt of both.

"You can flatter, Sir Knight," he said, "but you escape me not. I must know more from you than you have yet told me. Saw you my royal consort when at Engaddi?"

"To my knowledge—no, my lord," replied Sir Kenneth, with considerable perturbation, for he remembered the midnight procession in the chapel of the rocks.

"I ask you," said the King, in a sterner voice, "whether you were not in the chapel of the Carmelite nuns at Engaddi, and there saw Berengaria, Queen of England, and the ladies of her Court, who went thither on pilgrimage?"

"My lord," said Sir Kenneth, "I will speak the truth as in the confessional. In a subterranean chapel, to which the anchorite conducted me, I beheld a choir of ladies do homage to a relic of the highest sanctity; but as I saw not their faces, nor heard their voices, unless in the hymns which they chanted, I cannot tell whether the Queen of England was of the bevy."

"And was there no one of these ladies known to you?"

Sir Kenneth stood silent.

"I ask you," said Richard, raising himself on his elbow, "as a knight and a gentleman—and I shall know by your answer how you value either character—did you, or did you not, know any lady amongst that band of worshippers?"

"My lord," said Kenneth, not without much hesitation, "I might guess."

"And I also may guess," said the King, frowning sternly; "but it is enough. Leopard as you are, Sir Knight, beware tempting the lion's paw. Hark ye—to become enamoured of the moon would be but an act of folly; but to leap from the battlements of a lofty tower, in the wild hope of coming within her sphere, were self-destructive madness."

At this moment some bustling was heard in the outer apartment, and the King, hastily changing to his more natural manner, said, "Enough—begone—speed to De Vaux, and send him hither with the Arabian physician. My life for the faith of the Soldan! Would he but abjure his false law, I would aid him with my sword to drive this scum of French and Austrians from his dominions, and think Palestine as well ruled by him as when her kings were anointed by the decree of Heaven itself."

The Knight of the Leopard retired, and presently afterwards the chamberlain announced a deputation from the Council, who had come to wait on the Majesty of England.

"It is well they allow that I am living yet," was his reply. "Who are the reverend ambassadors?"

"The Grand Master of the Templars and the Marquis of Montserrat."

"Our brother of France loves not sick-beds," said Richard; "yet, had Philip been ill, I had stood by his couch long since.—Jocelyn, lay me the couch more fairly—it is tumbled like a stormy sea. Reach me yonder steel mirror—pass a comb through my hair and beard. They look, indeed, liker a lion's mane than a Christian man's locks. Bring water."

"My lord," said the trembling chamberlain, "the leeches say that cold water may be fatal."

"To the foul fiend with the leeches!" replied the monarch; "if they cannot cure me, think you I will allow them to torment me?—There, then," he said, after having made his ablutions, "admit the worshipful envoys; they will now, I think, scarcely see that disease has made Richard negligent of his person."

The celebrated Master of the Templars was a tall, thin, war-worn man, with a slow yet penetrating eye, and a brow on which a thousand dark intrigues had stamped a portion of their obscurity. At the head of that singular body, to whom their order was everything, and their individuality nothing—seeking the advancement of its power, even at the hazard of that very religion which the fraternity were originally associated to protect—accused of heresy and witchcraft, although by their character Christian priests—suspected of secret league with the Soldan, though by oath devoted to the protection of the Holy Temple, or its recovery—the whole order, and the whole personal character of its commander, or Grand Master, was a riddle, at the exposition of which most men shuddered. The Grand Master was dressed in his white robes of solemnity, and he bore the ABACUS, a mystic staff of office, the peculiar form of which has given rise to such singular conjectures and commentaries, leading to suspicions that this celebrated fraternity of Christian knights were embodied under the foulest symbols of paganism.

Conrade of Montserrat had a much more pleasing exterior than the dark and mysterious priest-soldier by whom he was accompanied. He was a handsome man, of middle age, or something past that term, bold in the field, sagacious in council, gay and gallant in times of festivity; but, on the other hand, he was generally accused of versatility, of a narrow and selfish ambition, of a desire to extend his own principality, without regard to the weal of the Latin kingdom of Palestine, and of seeking his own interest, by private negotiations with Saladin, to the prejudice of the Christian leaguers.

When the usual salutations had been made by these dignitaries, and courteously returned by King Richard, the Marquis of Montserrat commenced an explanation of the motives of their visit, sent, as he said they were, by the anxious kings and princes who composed the Council of the Crusaders, "to inquire into the health of their magnanimous ally, the valiant King of England."

"We know the importance in which the princes of the Council hold our health," replied the English King; "and are well aware how much they must have suffered by suppressing all curiosity concerning it for fourteen days, for fear, doubtless, of aggravating our disorder, by showing their anxiety regarding the event."

The flow of the Marquis's eloquence being checked, and he himself thrown into some confusion by this reply, his more austere companion took up the thread of the conversation, and with as much dry and brief gravity as was consistent with the presence which he addressed, informed the King that they came from the Council, to pray, in the name of Christendom, "that he would not suffer his health to be tampered with by an infidel physician, said to be dispatched by Saladin, until the Council had taken measures to remove or confirm the suspicion which they at present conceived did attach itself to the mission of such a person."

"Grand Master of the Holy and Valiant Order of Knights Templars, and you, most noble Marquis of Montserrat," replied Richard, "if it please you to retire into the adjoining pavilion, you shall presently see what account we make of the tender remonstrances of our royal and princely colleagues in this religious warfare."

The Marquis and Grand Master retired accordingly; nor had they been many minutes in the outward pavilion when the Eastern physician arrived, accompanied by the Baron of Gilsland and Kenneth of Scotland. The baron, however, was a little later of entering the tent than the other two, stopping, perchance, to issue some orders to the warders without.

As the Arabian physician entered, he made his obeisance, after the Oriental fashion, to the Marquis and Grand Master, whose dignity was apparent, both from their appearance and their bearing. The Grand Master returned the salutation with an expression of disdainful coldness, the Marquis with the popular courtesy which he habitually practised to men of every rank and nation. There was a pause, for the Scottish knight, waiting for the arrival of De Vaux, presumed not, of his own authority, to enter the tent of the King of England; and during this interval the Grand Master sternly demanded of the Moslem, "Infidel, hast thou the courage to practise thine art upon the person of an anointed sovereign of the Christian host?"

"The sun of Allah," answered the sage, "shines on the Nazarene as well as on the true believer, and His servant dare make no distinction betwixt them when called on to exercise the art of healing."

"Misbelieving Hakim," said the Grand Master, "or whatsoever they call thee for an unbaptized slave of darkness, dost thou well know that thou shalt be torn asunder by wild horses should King Richard die under thy charge?"

"That were hard justice," answered the physician, "seeing that I can but use human means, and that the issue is written in the book of light."

"Nay, reverend and valiant Grand Master," said the Marquis of Montserrat, "consider that this learned man is not acquainted with our Christian order, adopted in the fear of God, and for the safety of His anointed.—Be it known to thee, grave physician, whose skill we doubt not, that your wisest course is to repair to the presence of the illustrious Council of our Holy League, and there to give account and reckoning to such wise and learned leeches as they shall nominate, concerning your means of process and cure of this illustrious patient; so shall you escape all the danger which, rashly taking such a high matter upon your sole answer, you may else most likely incur."

"My lords," said El Hakim, "I understand you well. But knowledge hath its champions as well as your military art—nay, hath sometimes had its martyrs as well as religion. I have the command of my sovereign, the Soldan Saladin, to heal this Nazarene King, and, with the blessing of the Prophet, I will obey his commands. If I fail, ye wear swords thirsting for the blood of the faithful, and I proffer my body to your weapons. But I will not reason with one uncircumcised upon the virtue of the medicines of which I have obtained knowledge through the grace of the Prophet, and I pray you interpose no delay between me and my office."

"Who talks of delay?" said the Baron de Vaux, hastily entering the tent; "we have had but too much already. I salute you, my Lord of Montserrat, and you, valiant Grand Master. But I must presently pass with this learned physician to the bedside of my master."

"My lord," said the Marquis, in Norman-French, or the language of Ouie, as it was then called, "are you well advised that we came to expostulate, on the part of the Council of the Monarchs and Princes of the Crusade, against the risk of permitting an infidel and Eastern physician to tamper with a health so valuable as that of your master, King Richard?"

"Noble Lord Marquis," replied the Englishman bluntly, "I can neither use many words, nor do I delight in listening to them; moreover, I am much more ready to believe what my eyes have seen than what my ears have heard. I am satisfied that this heathen can cure the sickness of King Richard, and I believe and trust he will labour to do so. Time is precious. If Mohammed—may God's curse be on him! stood at the door of the tent, with such fair purpose as this Adonbec el Hakim entertains, I would hold it sin to delay him for a minute. So, give ye God'en, my lords."

"Nay, but," said Conrade of Montserrat, "the King himself said we should be present when this same physician dealt upon him."

The baron whispered the chamberlain, probably to know whether the Marquis spoke truly, and then replied, "My lords, if you will hold your patience, you are welcome to enter with us; but if you interrupt, by action or threat, this accomplished physician in his duty, be it known that, without respect to your high quality, I will enforce your absence from Richard's tent; for know, I am so well satisfied of the virtue of this man's medicines, that were Richard himself to refuse them, by our Lady of Lanercost, I think I could find in my heart to force him to take the means of his cure whether he would or no.—Move onward, El Hakim."

The last word was spoken in the lingua franca, and instantly obeyed by the physician. The Grand Master looked grimly on the unceremonious old soldier, but, on exchanging a glance with the Marquis, smoothed his frowning brow as well as he could, and both followed De Vaux and the Arabian into the inner tent, where Richard lay expecting them, with that impatience with which the sick man watches the step of his physician. Sir Kenneth, whose attendance seemed neither asked nor prohibited, felt himself, by the circumstances in which he stood, entitled to follow these high dignitaries; but, conscious of his inferior power and rank, remained aloof during the scene which took place.

Richard, when they entered his apartment, immediately exclaimed, "So ho! a goodly fellowship come to see Richard take his leap in the dark. My noble allies, I greet you as the representatives of our assembled league; Richard will again be amongst you in his former fashion, or ye shall bear to the grave what is left of him.—De Vaux, lives he or dies he, thou hast the thanks of thy prince. There is yet another—but this fever hath wasted my eyesight. What, the bold Scot, who would climb heaven without a ladder! He is welcome too.—Come, Sir Hakim, to the work, to the work!"

The physician, who had already informed himself of the various symptoms of the King's illness, now felt his pulse for a long time, and with deep attention, while all around stood silent, and in breathless expectation. The sage next filled a cup with spring water, and dipped into it the small red purse, which, as formerly, he took from his bosom. When he seemed to think it sufficiently medicated, he was about to offer it to the sovereign, who prevented him by saying, "Hold an instant. Thou hast felt my pulse—let me lay my finger on thine. I too, as becomes a good knight, know something of thine art."

The Arabian yielded his hand without hesitation, and his long, slender dark fingers were for an instant enclosed, and almost buried, in the large enfoldment of King Richard's hand.

"His blood beats calm as an infant's," said the King; "so throbs not theirs who poison princes. De Vaux, whether we live or die, dismiss this Hakim with honour and safety.—Commend us, friend, to the noble Saladin. Should I die, it is without doubt of his faith; should I live, it will be to thank him as a warrior would desire to be thanked."

He then raised himself in bed, took the cup in his hand, and turning to the Marquis and the Grand Master—"Mark what I say, and let my royal brethren pledge me in Cyprus wine, 'To the immortal honour of the first Crusader who shall strike lance or sword on the gate of Jerusalem; and to the shame and eternal infamy of whomsoever shall turn back from the plough on which he hath laid his hand!'"

He drained the cup to the bottom, resigned it to the Arabian, and sunk back, as if exhausted, upon the cushions which were arranged to receive him. The physician then, with silent but expressive signs, directed that all should leave the tent excepting himself and De Vaux, whom no remonstrance could induce to withdraw. The apartment was cleared accordingly.

Lesson 132

1. Stop and think. What has just happened in the book? What do you think is going to happen next?
2. Read chapter 10. The author reveals that the Marquis and the Grand Master have good plans for themselves and very bad plans for King Richard.
3. We learn more about the Marquis of Montserrat and the Grand Master of the Knights Templar. How do they really feel about King Richard? (Answers)
4. What are their ambitions? How do they plan to achieve them? (Answers)
5. Are you concerned for King Richard's welfare? (Answers)
6. Add to your character sheet.

CHAPTER X.

And now I will unclasp a secret book,

And, to your quick-conceiving discontent,

I'll read you matter deep and dangerous.

HENRY IV., PART I.

The Marquis of Montserrat and the Grand Master of the Knights Templars stood together in the front of the royal pavilion, within which this singular scene had passed, and beheld a strong guard of bills and bows drawn out to form a circle around it, and keep at distance all which might disturb the sleeping monarch. The soldiers wore the downcast, silent, and sullen looks with which they trail their arms at a funeral, and stepped with such caution that you could not hear a buckler ring or a sword clatter, though so many men in armour were moving around the tent. They lowered their weapons in deep reverence as the dignitaries passed through their files, but with the same profound silence.

"There is a change of cheer among these island dogs," said the Grand Master to Conrade, when they had passed Richard's guards. "What hoarse tumult and revel used to be before this pavilion!—nought but pitching the bar, hurling the ball, wrestling, roaring of songs, clattering of wine pots, and quaffing of flagons among these burly yeomen, as if they were holding some country wake, with a Maypole in the midst of them instead of a royal standard."

"Mastiffs are a faithful race," said Conrade; "and the King their Master has won their love by being ready to wrestle, brawl, or revel amongst the foremost of them, whenever the humour seized him."

"He is totally compounded of humours," said the Grand Master. "Marked you the pledge he gave us! instead of a prayer, over his grace-cup yonder."

"He would have felt it a grace-cup, and a well-spiced one too," said the Marquis, "were Saladin like any other Turk that ever wore turban, or turned him to Mecca at call of the muezzin. But he affects faith, and honour, and generosity, as if it were for an unbaptized dog like him to practise the virtuous bearing of a Christian knight. It is said he hath applied to Richard to be admitted within the pale of chivalry."

"By Saint Bernard!" exclaimed the Grand Master, "it were time then to throw off our belts and spurs, Sir Conrade, deface our armorial bearings, and renounce our burgonets, if the highest honour of Christianity were conferred on an unchristened Turk of tenpence."

"You rate the Soldan cheap," replied the Marquis; "yet though he be a likely man, I have seen a better heathen sold for forty pence at the bagnio."

They were now near their horses, which stood at some distance from the royal tent, prancing among the gallant train of esquires and pages by whom they were attended, when Conrade, after a moment's pause, proposed that they should enjoy the coolness of the evening breeze which had arisen, and, dismissing their steeds and attendants, walk homewards to their own quarters through the lines of the extended Christian camp. The Grand Master assented, and they proceeded to walk together accordingly, avoiding, as if by mutual consent, the more inhabited parts of the canvas city, and tracing the broad esplanade which lay between the tents and the external defences, where they could converse in private, and unmarked, save by the sentinels as they passed them.

They spoke for a time upon the military points and preparations for defence; but this sort of discourse, in which neither seemed to take interest, at length died away, and there was a long pause, which terminated by the Marquis of Montserrat stopping short, like a man who has formed a sudden resolution, and gazing for some moments on the dark, inflexible countenance of the Grand Master, he at length addressed him thus: "Might it consist with your valour and sanctity, reverend Sir Giles Amaury, I would pray you for once to lay aside the dark visor which you wear, and to converse with a friend barefaced."

The Templar half smiled.

"There are light-coloured masks," he said, "as well as dark visors, and the one conceals the natural features as completely as the other."

"Be it so," said the Marquis, putting his hand to his chin, and withdrawing it with the action of one who unmasks himself; "there lies my disguise. And now, what think you, as touching the interests of your own order, of the prospects of this Crusade?"

"This is tearing the veil from my thoughts rather than exposing your own," said the Grand Master; "yet I will reply with a parable told to me by a santon of the desert. 'A certain farmer prayed to Heaven for rain, and murmured when it fell not at his need. To punish his impatience, Allah,' said the santon, 'sent the Euphrates upon his farm, and he was destroyed, with all his possessions, even by the granting of his own wishes.'"

"Most truly spoken," said the Marquis Conrade. "Would that the ocean had swallowed up nineteen parts of the armaments of these Western princes! What remained would better have served the purpose of the Christian nobles of Palestine, the wretched remnant of the Latin kingdom of Jerusalem. Left to ourselves, we might have bent to the storm; or, moderately supported with money and troops, we might have compelled Saladin to respect our valour, and grant us peace and protection on easy terms. But from the extremity of danger with which this powerful Crusade threatens the Soldan, we cannot suppose, should it pass over, that the Saracen will suffer any one of us to hold possessions or principalities in Syria, far less permit the existence of the Christian military fraternities, from whom they have experienced so much mischief."

"Ay, but," said the Templar, "these adventurous Crusaders may succeed, and again plant the Cross on the bulwarks of Zion."

"And what will that advantage either the Order of the Templars, or Conrade of Montserrat?" said the Marquis.

"You it may advantage," replied the Grand Master. "Conrade of Montserrat might become Conrade King of Jerusalem."

"That sounds like something," said the Marquis, "and yet it rings but hollow. Godfrey of Bouillon might well choose the crown of thorns for his emblem. Grand Master, I will confess to you I have caught some attachment to the Eastern form of government—a pure and simple monarchy should consist but of king and subjects. Such is the simple and primitive structure—a shepherd and his flock. All this internal chain of feudal dependance is artificial and sophisticated; and I would rather hold the baton of my poor marquisate with a firm gripe, and wield it after my pleasure, than the sceptre of a monarch, to be in effect restrained and curbed by the will of as many proud feudal barons as hold land under the Assizes of Jerusalem. [The Assises de Jerusalem were the digest of feudal law, composed by Godfrey of Boulogne, for the government of the Latin kingdom of Palestine, when reconquered from the Saracens. "It was composed with advice of the patriarch and barons, the clergy and laity, and is," says the historian Gibbon, "a precious monument of feudatory jurisprudence, founded upon those principles of freedom which were essential to the system."] A king should tread freely, Grand Master, and should not be controlled by here a ditch, and there a fence-here a feudal privilege, and there a mail-clad baron with his sword in his hand to maintain it. To sum the whole, I am aware that Guy de Lusignan's claims to the throne would be preferred to mine, if Richard recovers, and has aught to say in the choice."

"Enough," said the Grand Master; "thou hast indeed convinced me of thy sincerity. Others may hold the same opinions, but few, save Conrade of Montserrat, dared frankly avow that he desires not the restitution of the kingdom of Jerusalem, but rather prefers being master of a portion of its fragments—like the barbarous islanders, who labour not for the deliverance of a goodly vessel from the billows, expecting rather to enrich themselves at the expense of the wreck."

"Thou wilt not betray my counsel?" said Conrade, looking sharply and suspiciously. "Know, for certain, that my tongue shall never wrong my head, nor my hand forsake the defence of either. Impeach me if thou wilt—I am prepared to defend myself in the lists against the best Templar who ever laid lance in rest."

"Yet thou start'st somewhat suddenly for so bold a steed," said the Grand Master. "However, I swear to thee by the Holy Temple, which our Order is sworn to defend, that I will keep counsel with thee as a true comrade."

"By which Temple?" said the Marquis of Montserrat, whose love of sarcasm often outran his policy and discretion; "swearest thou by that on the hill of Zion, which was built by King Solomon, or by that symbolical, emblematical edifice, which is said to be spoken of in the councils held in the vaults of your Preceptories, as something which infers the aggrandizement of thy valiant and venerable Order?"

The Templar scowled upon him with an eye of death, but answered calmly, "By whatever Temple I swear, be assured, Lord Marquis, my oath is sacred. I would I knew how to bind THEE by one of equal obligation."

"I will swear truth to thee," said the Marquis, laughing, "by the earl's coronet, which I hope to convert, ere these wars are over, into something better. It feels cold on my brow, that same slight coronal; a duke's cap of maintenance were a better protection against such a night-breeze as now blows, and a king's crown more preferable still, being lined with comfortable ermine and velvet. In a word, our interests bind us together; for think not, Lord Grand Master, that, were these allied princes to regain Jerusalem, and place a king of their own choosing there, they would suffer your Order, any more than my poor marquisate, to retain the independence which we now hold. No, by Our Lady! In such case, the proud Knights of Saint John must again spread plasters and dress plague sores in the hospitals; and you, most puissant and venerable Knights of the Temple, must return to your condition of simple men-at-arms, sleep three on a pallet, and mount two upon one horse, as your present seal still expresses to have been your ancient most simple custom."

"The rank, privileges, and opulence of our Order prevent so much degradation as you threaten," said the Templar haughtily.

"These are your bane," said Conrade of Montserrat; "and you, as well as I, reverend Grand Master, know that, were the allied princes to be successful in Palestine, it would be their first point of policy to abate the independence of your Order, which, but for the protection of our holy father the Pope, and the necessity of employing your valour in the conquest of Palestine, you would long since have experienced. Give them complete success, and you will be flung aside, as the splinters of a broken lance are tossed out of the tilt-yard."

"There may be truth in what you say," said the Templar, darkly smiling. "But what were our hopes should the allies withdraw their forces, and leave Palestine in the grasp of Saladin?"

"Great and assured," replied Conrade. "The Soldan would give large provinces to maintain at his behest a body of well-appointed Frankish lances. In Egypt, in Persia, a hundred such auxiliaries, joined to his own light cavalry, would turn the battle against the most fearful odds. This dependence would be but for a time—perhaps during the life of this enterprising Soldan; but in the East empires arise like mushrooms. Suppose him dead, and us strengthened with a constant succession of fiery and adventurous spirits from Europe, what might we not hope to achieve, uncontrolled by these monarchs, whose dignity throws us at present into the shade—and, were they to remain here, and succeed in this expedition, would willingly consign us for ever to degradation and dependence?"

"You say well, my Lord Marquis," said the Grand Master, "and your words find an echo in my bosom. Yet must we be cautious—Philip of France is wise as well as valiant."

"True, and will be therefore the more easily diverted from an expedition to which, in a moment of enthusiasm, or urged by his nobles, he rashly bound himself. He is jealous of King Richard, his natural enemy, and longs to return to prosecute plans of ambition nearer to Paris than Palestine.

Any fair pretence will serve him for withdrawing from a scene in which he is aware he is wasting the force of his kingdom."

"And the Duke of Austria?" said the Templar.

"Oh, touching the Duke," returned Conrade, "his self-conceit and folly lead him to the same conclusions as do Philip's policy and wisdom. He conceives himself, God help the while, ungratefully treated, because men's mouths—even those of his own MINNE-SINGERS [The German minstrels were so termed.]—are filled with the praises of King Richard, whom he fears and hates, and in whose harm he would rejoice, like those unbred, dastardly curs, who, if the foremost of the pack is hurt by the gripe of the wolf, are much more likely to assail the sufferer from behind than to come to his assistance. But wherefore tell I this to thee, save to show that I am in sincerity in desiring that this league be broken up, and the country freed of these great monarchs with their hosts? And thou well knowest, and hast thyself seen, how all the princes of influence and power, one alone excepted, are eager to enter into treaty with the Soldan."

"I acknowledge it," said the Templar; "he were blind that had not seen this in their last deliberations. But lift yet thy mask an inch higher, and tell me thy real reason for pressing upon the Council that Northern Englishman, or Scot, or whatever you call yonder Knight of the Leopard, to carry their proposals for a treaty?"

"There was a policy in it," replied the Italian. "His character of native of Britain was sufficient to meet what Saladin required, who knew him to belong to the band of Richard; while his character of Scot, and certain other personal grudges which I wot of, rendered it most unlikely that our envoy should, on his return, hold any communication with the sick-bed of Richard, to whom his presence was ever unacceptable."

"Oh, too finespun policy," said the Grand Master; "trust me, that Italian spiders' webs will never bind this unshorn Samson of the Isle—well if you can do it with new cords, and those of the toughest. See you not that the envoy whom you have selected so carefully hath brought us, in this physician, the means of restoring the lion-hearted, bull-necked Englishman to prosecute his Crusading enterprise. And so soon as he is able once more to rush on, which of the princes dare hold back? They must follow him for very shame, although they would march under the banner of Satan as soon."

"Be content," said Conrade of Montserrat; "ere this physician, if he work by anything short of miraculous agency, can accomplish Richard's cure, it may be possible to put some open rupture betwixt the Frenchman—at least the Austrian—and his allies of England, so that the breach shall be irreconcilable; and Richard may arise from his bed, perhaps to command his own native troops, but never again, by his sole energy, to wield the force of the whole Crusade."

"Thou art a willing archer," said the Templar; "but, Conrade of Montserrat, thy bow is over-slack to carry an arrow to the mark."

He then stopped short, cast a suspicious glance to see that no one overheard him, and taking Conrade by the hand, pressed it eagerly as he looked the Italian in the face, and repeated slowly, "Richard arise from his bed, sayest thou? Conrade, he must never arise!"

The Marquis of Montserrat started. "What! spoke you of Richard of England—of Coeur de Lion—the champion of Christendom?"

His cheek turned pale and his knees trembled as he spoke. The Templar looked at him, with his iron visage contorted into a smile of contempt.

"Knowest thou what thou look'st like, Sir Conrade, at this moment? Not like the politic and valiant Marquis of Montserrat, not like him who would direct the Council of Princes and determine the fate of empires—but like a novice, who, stumbling upon a conjuration in his master's book of gramarye, has raised the devil when he least thought of it, and now stands terrified at the spirit which appears before him."

"I grant you," said Conrade, recovering himself, "that—unless some other sure road could be discovered—thou hast hinted at that which leads most direct to our purpose. But, blessed Mary! we shall become the curse of all Europe, the malediction of every one, from the Pope on his throne to the very beggar at the church gate, who, ragged and leprous, in the last extremity of human wretchedness, shall bless himself that he is neither Giles Amaury nor Conrade of Montserrat."

"If thou takest it thus," said the Grand Master, with the same composure which characterized him all through this remarkable dialogue, "let us hold there has nothing passed between us—that we have spoken in our sleep—have awakened, and the vision is gone."

"It never can depart," answered Conrade.

"Visions of ducal crowns and kingly diadems are, indeed, somewhat tenacious of their place in the imagination," replied the Grand Master.

"Well," answered Conrade, "let me but first try to break peace between Austria and England."

They parted. Conrade remained standing still upon the spot, and watching the flowing white cloak of the Templar as he stalked slowly away, and gradually disappeared amid the fast-sinking darkness of the Oriental night. Proud, ambitious, unscrupulous, and politic, the Marquis of Montserrat was yet not cruel by nature. He was a voluptuary and an epicurean, and, like many who profess this character, was averse, even upon selfish motives, from inflicting pain or witnessing acts of cruelty; and he retained also a general sense of respect for his own reputation, which sometimes supplies the want of the better principle by which reputation is to be maintained.

"I have," he said, as his eyes still watched the point at which he had seen the last slight wave of the Templar's mantle—"I have, in truth, raised the devil with a vengeance! Who would have thought this stern, ascetic Grand Master, whose whole fortune and misfortune is merged in that of his order, would be willing to do more for its advancement than I who labour for my own interest? To check this wild Crusade was my motive, indeed, but I durst not think on the ready mode which this determined priest has dared to suggest. Yet it is the surest—perhaps even the safest."

Such were the Marquis's meditations, when his muttered soliloquy was broken by a voice from a little distance, which proclaimed with the emphatic tone of a herald, "Remember the Holy Sepulchre!"

The exhortation was echoed from post to post, for it was the duty of the sentinels to raise this cry from time to time upon their periodical watch, that the host of the Crusaders might always have in their remembrance the purpose of their being in arms. But though Conrade was familiar with the custom, and had heard the warning voice on all former occasions as a matter of habit, yet it came at the present moment so strongly in contact with his own train of thought, that it seemed a voice from Heaven warning him against the iniquity which his heart meditated. He looked around anxiously, as if, like the patriarch of old, though from very different circumstances, he was expecting some ram caught in a thicket some substitution for the sacrifice which his comrade proposed to offer, not to the Supreme Being, but to the Moloch of their own ambition. As he looked, the broad folds of the ensign of England, heavily distending itself to the failing night-breeze, caught his eye. It was displayed upon an artificial mound, nearly in the midst of the camp, which perhaps of old some Hebrew chief or champion had chosen as a memorial of his place of rest. If so, the name was now forgotten, and the Crusaders had christened it Saint George's Mount, because from that commanding height the banner of England was supereminently displayed, as if an emblem of sovereignty over the many distinguished, noble, and even royal ensigns, which floated in lower situations.

A quick intellect like that of Conrade catches ideas from the glance of a moment. A single look on the standard seemed to dispel the uncertainty of mind which had affected him. He walked to his pavilion with the hasty and determined step of one who has adopted a plan which he is resolved to achieve, dismissed the almost princely train who waited to attend him, and, as he committed himself to his couch, muttered his amended resolution, that the milder means are to be tried before the more desperate are resorted to.

"To-morrow," he said, "I sit at the board of the Archduke of Austria. We will see what can be done to advance our purpose before prosecuting the dark suggestions of this Templar."

Lesson 133

1. Read chapter 11. (This is a long chapter. Sorry. Get a drink. Get comfy.) The Marquis is successful in stirring up trouble between King Richard and the Archduke of Austria, which King Phillip of France manages to stop before it gets out of hand.
2. Compare the Archduke of Austria with King Richard of England. (Answers)
3. What mischief does the Marquis get started? (Answers)
4. What does King Richard do when he learns what is happening? (Answers)
5. How does King Phillip of France calm the situation? (Answers)
6. The author says, "The present seemed one of those occasions in which prudence and calmness might reasonably expect to triumph over obstinacy and impetuous violence." Who is prudent and calm? Who is impetuous and violent? (Answers)
7. It is also interesting to learn about the importance of the jester and the wise man in the Austrian court.

CHAPTER XI.

One thing is certain in our Northern land—

Allow that birth or valour, wealth or wit,

Give each precedence to their possessor,

Envy, that follows on such eminence,

As comes the lyme-hound on the roebuck's trace,

Shall pull them down each one.

SIR DAVID LINDSAY.

Leopold, Grand Duke of Austria, was the first possessor of that noble country to whom the princely rank belonged. He had been raised to the ducal sway in the German Empire on account of his near relationship to the Emperor, Henry the Stern, and held under his government the finest provinces which are watered by the Danube. His character has been stained in history on account of one action of violence and perfidy, which arose out of these very transactions in the Holy Land; and yet the shame of having made Richard a prisoner when he returned through his dominions; unattended and in disguise, was not one which flowed from Leopold's natural disposition. He was rather a weak and a vain than an ambitious or tyrannical prince. His mental powers resembled the qualities of his person. He was tall, strong, and handsome, with a complexion in which red and white were strongly contrasted, and had long flowing locks of fair hair. But there was an awkwardness in his gait which seemed as if his size was not animated by energy sufficient to put in motion such a mass; and in the same manner, wearing the richest dresses, it always seemed as if they became him not. As a prince, he appeared too little familiar with his own dignity; and being often at a loss how to assert his authority when the occasion demanded it, he frequently thought himself obliged to recover, by acts and expressions of ill-timed violence, the ground which might have been easily and gracefully maintained by a little more presence of mind in the beginning of the controversy.

Not only were these deficiencies visible to others, but the Archduke himself could not but sometimes entertain a painful consciousness that he was not altogether fit to maintain and assert the high rank which he had acquired; and to this was joined the strong, and sometimes the just, suspicion that others esteemed him lightly accordingly.

When he first joined the Crusade, with a most princely attendance, Leopold had desired much to enjoy the friendship and intimacy of Richard, and had made such advances towards cultivating his regard as the King of England ought, in policy, to have received and answered. But the Archduke, though not deficient in bravery, was so infinitely inferior to Coeur de Lion in that ardour of mind which wooed danger as a bride, that the King very soon held him in a certain degree of contempt. Richard, also, as a Norman prince, a people with whom temperance was habitual, despised the inclination of the German for the pleasures of the table, and particularly his liberal indulgence in the use of wine. For these, and other personal reasons, the King of England very soon looked upon the Austrian Prince with feelings of contempt, which he was at no pains to conceal or modify, and which, therefore, were speedily remarked, and returned with deep hatred, by the suspicious Leopold. The discord between them was fanned by the secret and politic arts of Philip of France, one of the most sagacious monarchs of the time, who, dreading the fiery and overbearing character of Richard, considering him as his natural rival, and feeling offended, moreover, at the dictatorial manner in which he, a vassal of France for his Continental domains, conducted himself towards his liege lord, endeavoured to strengthen his own party, and weaken that of Richard, by uniting the Crusading princes of inferior degree in resistance to what he termed the usurping authority of the King of England. Such was the state of politics and opinions entertained by the Archduke of Austria, when Conrade of Montserrat resolved upon employing his jealousy of England as the means of dissolving, or loosening at least, the league of the Crusaders.

The time which he chose for his visit was noon; and the pretence, to present the Archduke with some choice Cyprus wine which had lately fallen into his hands, and discuss its comparative merits with those of Hungary and of the Rhine. An intimation of his purpose was, of course, answered by a courteous invitation to partake of the Archducal meal, and every effort was used to render it fitting the splendour of a sovereign prince. Yet the refined taste of the Italian saw more cumbrous profusion than elegance or splendour in the display of provisions under which the board groaned.

The Germans, though still possessing the martial and frank character of their ancestors—who subdued the Roman Empire—had retained withal no slight tinge of their barbarism. The practices and principles of chivalry were not carried to such a nice pitch amongst them as amongst the French and English knights, nor were they strict observers of the prescribed rules of society, which among those nations were supposed to express the height of civilization. Sitting at the table of the Archduke, Conrade was at once stunned and amused with the clang of Teutonic sounds assaulting his ears on all sides, notwithstanding the solemnity of a princely banquet. Their dress seemed equally fantastic to him, many of the Austrian nobles retaining their long beards, and almost all of them wearing short jerkins of various colours, cut, and flourished, and fringed in a manner not common in Western Europe.

Numbers of dependants, old and young, attended in the pavilion, mingled at times in the conversation, received from their masters the relics of the entertainment, and devoured them as they stood behind the backs of the company. Jesters, dwarfs, and minstrels were there in unusual numbers, and more noisy and intrusive than they were permitted to be in better regulated society. As they were allowed to share freely in the wine, which flowed round in large quantities, their licensed tumult was the more excessive.

All this while, and in the midst of a clamour and confusion which would better have become a German tavern during a fair than the tent of a sovereign prince, the Archduke was waited upon with a minuteness of form and observance which showed how anxious he was to maintain rigidly the state and character to which his elevation had entitled him. He was served on the knee, and only by pages of noble blood, fed upon plate of silver, and drank his Tokay and Rhenish wines from a cup of gold. His ducal mantle was splendidly adorned with ermine, his coronet might have equalled in value a royal crown, and his feet, cased in velvet shoes (the length of which, peaks included, might be two feet), rested upon a footstool of solid silver. But it served partly to intimate the character of the man, that, although desirous to show attention to the Marquis of Montserrat, whom he had courteously placed at his right hand, he gave much more of his attention to his SPRUCH-SPRECHER—that is, his man of conversation, or SAYER-OF-SAYINGS—who stood behind the Duke's right shoulder.

This personage was well attired in a cloak and doublet of black velvet, the last of which was decorated with various silver and gold coins stitched upon it, in memory of the munificent princes who had conferred them, and bearing a short staff to which also bunches of silver coins were attached by rings, which he jingled by way of attracting attention when he was about to say anything which he judged worthy of it. This person's capacity in the household of the Archduke was somewhat betwixt that of a minstrel and a counsellor. He was by turns a flatterer, a poet, and an orator; and those who desired to be well with the Duke generally studied to gain the good-will of the SPRUCH-SPRECHER.

Lest too much of this officer's wisdom should become tiresome, the Duke's other shoulder was occupied by his HOFF-NARR, or court-jester, called Jonas Schwanker, who made almost as much noise with his fool's cap, bells, and bauble, as did the orator, or man of talk, with his jingling baton.

These two personages threw out grave and comic nonsense alternately; while their master, laughing or applauding them himself, yet carefully watched the countenance of his noble guest, to discern what impressions so accomplished a cavalier received from this display of Austrian eloquence and wit. It is hard to say whether the man of wisdom or the man of folly contributed most to the amusement of the party, or stood highest in the estimation of their princely master; but the sallies of both seemed excellently well received. Sometimes they became rivals for the conversation, and clanged their flappers in emulation of each other with a most alarming contention; but, in general, they seemed on such good terms, and so accustomed to support each other's play, that the SPRUCH-SPRECHER often condescended to follow up the jester's witticisms with an explanation, to render them more obvious to the capacity of the audience, so that his wisdom became a sort of commentary on the buffoon's folly. And sometimes, in requital, the HOFF-NARR, with a pithy jest, wound up the conclusion of the orator's tedious harangue.

Whatever his real sentiments might be, Conrade took especial care that his countenance should express nothing but satisfaction with what he heard, and smiled or applauded as zealously, to all appearance, as the Archduke himself at the solemn folly of the SPRUCH-SPRECHER and the gibbering wit of the fool. In fact, he watched carefully until the one or other should introduce some topic favourable to the purpose which was uppermost in his mind.

It was not long ere the King of England was brought on the carpet by the jester, who had been accustomed to consider Dickon of the Broom (which irreverent epithet he substituted for Richard Plantagenet) as a subject of mirth, acceptable and inexhaustible. The orator, indeed, was silent, and it was only when applied to by Conrade that he observed, "The GENISTA, or broom-plant, was an emblem of humility; and it would be well when those who wore it would remember the warning."

The allusion to the illustrious badge of Plantagenet was thus rendered sufficiently manifest, and Jonas Schwanker observed that they who humbled themselves had been exalted with a vengeance. "Honour unto whom honour is due," answered the Marquis of Montserrat. "We have all had some part in these marches and battles, and methinks other princes might share a little in the renown which Richard of England engrosses amongst minstrels and MINNE-SINGERS. Has no one of the joyeuse science here present a song in praise of the royal Archduke of Austria, our princely entertainer?"

Three minstrels emulously stepped forward with voice and harp. Two were silenced with difficulty by the SPRUCH-SPRECHER, who seemed to act as master of the revels, and a hearing was at length procured for the poet preferred, who sung, in high German, stanzas which may be thus translated:—

"What brave chief shall head the forces, Where the red-cross legions gather? Best of horsemen, best of horses, Highest head and fairest feather."

Here the orator, jingling his staff, interrupted the bard to intimate to the party—what they might not have inferred from the description—that their royal host was the party indicated, and a full-crowned goblet went round to the acclamation, HOCH LEBE DER HERZOG LEOPOLD! Another stanza followed:—

"Ask not Austria why, 'midst princes, Still her banner rises highest; Ask as well the strong-wing'd eagle, Why to heaven he soars the highest."

"The eagle," said the expounder of dark sayings, "is the cognizance of our noble lord the Archduke—of his royal Grace, I would say—and the eagle flies the highest and nearest to the sun of all the feathered creation."

"The lion hath taken a spring above the eagle," said Conrade carelessly.

The Archduke reddened, and fixed his eyes on the speaker, while the SPRUCH-SPRECHER answered, after a minute's consideration, "The Lord Marquis will pardon me—a lion cannot fly above an eagle, because no lion hath got wings."

"Except the lion of Saint Mark," responded the jester.

"That is the Venetian's banner," said the Duke; "but assuredly that amphibious race, half nobles, half merchants, will not dare to place their rank in comparison with ours."

"Nay, it was not of the Venetian lion that I spoke," said the Marquis of Montserrat, "but of the three lions passant of England. Formerly, it is said, they were leopards; but now they are become lions at all points, and must take precedence of beast, fish, or fowl, or woe worth the gainstander."

"Mean you seriously, my lord?" said the Austrian, now considerably flushed with wine. "Think you that Richard of England asserts any pre-eminence over the free sovereigns who have been his voluntary allies in this Crusade?"

"I know not but from circumstances," answered Conrade. "Yonder hangs his banner alone in the midst of our camp, as if he were king and generalissimo of our whole Christian army."

"And do you endure this so patiently, and speak of it so coldly?" said the Archduke.

"Nay, my lord," answered Conrade, "it cannot concern the poor Marquis of Montserrat to contend against an injury patiently submitted to by such potent princes as Philip of France and Leopold of Austria. What dishonour you are pleased to submit to cannot be a disgrace to me."

Leopold closed his fist, and struck on the table with violence.

"I have told Philip of this," he said. "I have often told him that it was our duty to protect the inferior princes against the usurpation of this islander; but he answers me ever with cold respects of their relations together as suzerain and vassal, and that it were impolitic in him to make an open breach at this time and period."

"The world knows that Philip is wise," said Conrade, "and will judge his submission to be policy. Yours, my lord, you can yourself alone account for; but I doubt not you have deep reasons for submitting to English domination."

"I submit!" said Leopold indignantly—"I, the Archduke of Austria, so important and vital a limb of the Holy Roman Empire—I submit myself to this king of half an island, this grandson of a Norman bastard! No, by Heaven! The camp and all Christendom shall see that I know how to right myself, and whether I yield ground one inch to the English bandog.—Up, my lieges and merry men; up and follow me! We will—and that without losing one instant—place the eagle of Austria where she shall float as high as ever floated the cognizance of king or kaiser."

With that he started from his seat, and amidst the tumultuous cheering of his guests and followers, made for the door of the pavilion, and seized his own banner, which stood pitched before it.

"Nay, my lord," said Conrade, affecting to interfere, "it will blemish your wisdom to make an affray in the camp at this hour; and perhaps it is better to submit to the usurpation of England a little longer than to—"

"Not an hour, not a moment longer," vociferated the Duke; and with the banner in his hand, and followed by his shouting guests and attendants, marched hastily to the central mount, from which the banner of England floated, and laid his hand on the standard-spear, as if to pluck it from the ground.

"My master, my dear master!" said Jonas Schwanker, throwing his arms about the Duke, "take heed—lions have teeth—"

"And eagles have claws," said the Duke, not relinquishing his hold on the banner-staff, yet hesitating to pull it from the ground.

The speaker of sentences, notwithstanding such was his occupation, had nevertheless some intervals of sound sense. He clashed his staff loudly, and Leopold, as if by habit, turned his head towards his man of counsel.

"The eagle is king among the fowls of the air," said the SPRUCH-SPRECHER, "as is the lion among the beasts of the field—each has his dominion, separated as wide as England and Germany. Do thou, noble eagle, no dishonour to the princely lion, but let your banners remain floating in peace side by side."

Leopold withdrew his hand from the banner-spear, and looked round for Conrade of Montserrat, but he saw him not; for the Marquis, so soon as he saw the mischief afoot, had withdrawn himself from the crowd, taking care, in the first place, to express before several neutral persons his regret that the Archduke should have chosen the hours after dinner to avenge any wrong of which he might think he had a right to complain. Not seeing his guest, to whom he wished more particularly to have addressed himself, the Archduke said aloud that, having no wish to breed dissension in the army of the Cross, he did but vindicate his own privileges and right to stand upon an equality with the King of England, without desiring, as he might have done, to advance his banner—which he derived from emperors, his progenitors—above that of a mere descendant of the Counts of Anjou; and in the meantime he commanded a cask of wine to be brought hither and pierced, for regaling the bystanders, who, with tuck of drum and sound of music, quaffed many a carouse round the Austrian standard.

This disorderly scene was not acted without a degree of noise, which alarmed the whole camp.

The critical hour had arrived at which the physician, according to the rules of his art, had predicted that his royal patient might be awakened with safety, and the sponge had been applied for that purpose; and the leech had not made many observations ere he assured the Baron of Gilsland that the fever had entirely left his sovereign, and that, such was the happy strength of his constitution, it would not be even necessary, as in most cases, to give a second dose of the powerful medicine. Richard himself seemed to be of the same opinion, for, sitting up and rubbing his eyes, he demanded of De Vaux what present sum of money was in the royal coffers.

The baron could not exactly inform him of the amount.

"It matters not," said Richard; "be it greater or smaller, bestow it all on this learned leech, who hath, I trust, given me back again to the service of the Crusade. If it be less than a thousand byzants, let him have jewels to make it up."

"I sell not the wisdom with which Allah has endowed me," answered the Arabian physician; "and be it known to you, great Prince, that the divine medicine of which you have partaken would lose its effects in my unworthy hands did I exchange its virtues either for gold or diamonds."

"The Physician refuseth a gratuity!" said De Vaux to himself. "This is more extraordinary than his being a hundred years old."

"Thomas de Vaux," said Richard, "thou knowest no courage but what belongs to the sword, no bounty and virtue but what are used in chivalry. I tell thee that this Moor, in his independence, might set an example to them who account themselves the flower of knighthood."

"It is reward enough for me," said the Moor, folding his arms on his bosom, and maintaining an attitude at once respectful and dignified, "that so great a king as the Melech Ric [Richard was thus called by the Eastern nations.] should thus speak of his servant.—But now let me pray you again to compose yourself on your couch; for though I think there needs no further repetition of the divine draught, yet injury might ensue from any too early exertion ere your strength be entirely restored."

"I must obey thee, Hakim," said the King; "yet believe me, my bosom feels so free from the wasting fire which for so many days hath scorched it, that I care not how soon I expose it to a brave man's lance.—But hark! what mean these shouts, and that distant music, in the camp? Go, Thomas de Vaux, and make inquiry."

"It is the Archduke Leopold," said De Vaux, returning after a minute's absence, "who makes with his pot-companions some procession through the camp."

"The drunken fool!" exclaimed King Richard; "can he not keep his brutal inebriety within the veil of his pavilion, that he must needs show his shame to all Christendom?—What say you, Sir Marquis?" he added, addressing himself to Conrade of Montserrat, who at that moment entered the tent.

"Thus much, honoured Prince," answered the Marquis, "that I delight to see your Majesty so well, and so far recovered; and that is a long speech for any one to make who has partaken of the Duke of Austria's hospitality."

"What! you have been dining with the Teutonic wine-skin!" said the monarch. "And what frolic has he found out to cause all this disturbance? Truly, Sir Conrade, I have still held you so good a reveller that I wonder at your quitting the game."

De Vaux, who had got a little behind the King, now exerted himself by look and sign to make the Marquis understand that he should say nothing to Richard of what was passing without. But Conrade understood not, or heeded not, the prohibition.

"What the Archduke does," he said, "is of little consequence to any one, least of all to himself, since he probably knows not what he is acting; yet, to say truth, it is a gambol I should not like to share in, since he is pulling down the banner of England from Saint George's Mount, in the centre of the camp yonder, and displaying his own in its stead."

"WHAT sayest thou?" exclaimed the King, in a tone which might have waked the dead.

"Nay," said the Marquis, "let it not chafe your Highness that a fool should act according to his folly—"

"Speak not to me," said Richard, springing from his couch, and casting on his clothes with a dispatch which seemed marvellous—"Speak not to me, Lord Marquis!—De Multon, I command thee speak not a word to me—he that breathes but a syllable is no friend to Richard Plantagenet.—Hakim, be silent, I charge thee!"

All this while the King was hastily clothing himself, and, with the last word, snatched his sword from the pillar of the tent, and without any other weapon, or calling any attendance, he rushed out of his pavilion. Conrade, holding up his hands as if in astonishment, seemed willing to enter into conversation with De Vaux; but Sir Thomas pushed rudely past him, and calling to one of the royal equerries, said hastily, "Fly to Lord Salisbury's quarters, and let him get his men together and follow me instantly to Saint George's Mount. Tell him the King's fever has left his blood and settled in his brain."

Imperfectly heard, and still more imperfectly comprehended, by the startled attendant whom De Vaux addressed thus hastily, the equerry and his fellow-servants of the royal chamber rushed hastily into the tents of the neighbouring nobility, and quickly spread an alarm, as general as the cause seemed vague, through the whole British forces. The English soldiers, waked in alarm from that noonday rest which the heat of the climate had taught them to enjoy as a luxury, hastily asked each other the cause of the tumult, and without waiting an answer, supplied by the force of their own fancy the want of information. Some said the Saracens were in the camp, some that the King's life was attempted, some that he had died of the fever the preceding night, many that he was assassinated by the Duke of Austria. The nobles and officers, at an equal loss with the common men to ascertain the real cause of the disorder, laboured only to get their followers under arms and under authority, lest their rashness should occasion some great misfortune to the Crusading army. The English trumpets sounded loud, shrill, and continuously. The alarm-cry of "Bows and bills, bows and bills!" was heard from quarter to quarter, again and again shouted, and again and again answered by the presence of the ready warriors, and their national invocation, "Saint George for merry England!"

The alarm went through the nearest quarter of the camp, and men of all the various nations assembled, where, perhaps, every people in Christendom had their representatives, flew to arms, and drew together under circumstances of general confusion, of which they knew neither the cause nor the object. It was, however, lucky, amid a scene so threatening, that the Earl of Salisbury, while he hurried after De Vaux's summons with a few only of the readiest English men-at-arms, directed the rest of the English host to be drawn up and kept under arms, to advance to Richard's succour if necessity should require, but in fit array and under due command, and not with the tumultuary haste which their own alarm and zeal for the King's safety might have dictated.

In the meanwhile, without regarding for one instant the shouts, the cries, the tumult which began to thicken around him, Richard, with his dress in the last disorder, and his sheathed blade under his arm, pursued his way with the utmost speed, followed only by De Vaux and one or two household servants, to Saint George's Mount.

He outsped even the alarm which his impetuosity only had excited, and passed the quarter of his own gallant troops of Normandy, Poitou, Gascony, and Anjou before the disturbance had reached them, although the noise accompanying the German revel had induced many of the soldiery to get on foot to listen. The handful of Scots were also quartered in the vicinity, nor had they been disturbed by the uproar. But the King's person and his haste were both remarked by the Knight of the Leopard, who, aware that danger must be afoot, and hastening to share in it, snatched his shield and sword, and united himself to De Vaux, who with some difficulty kept pace with his impatient and fiery master. De Vaux answered a look of curiosity, which the Scottish knight directed towards him, with a shrug of his broad shoulders, and they continued, side by side, to pursue Richard's steps.

The King was soon at the foot of Saint George's Mount, the sides as well as platform of which were now surrounded and crowded, partly by those belonging to the Duke of Austria's retinue, who were celebrating, with shouts of jubilee, the act which they considered as an assertion of national honour; partly by bystanders of different nations, whom dislike to the English, or mere curiosity, had assembled together to witness the end of these extraordinary proceedings. Through this disorderly troop Richard burst his way, like a goodly ship under full sail, which cleaves her forcible passage through the rolling billows, and heeds not that they unite after her passage and roar upon her stern.

The summit of the eminence was a small level space, on which were pitched the rival banners, surrounded still by the Archduke's friends and retinue. In the midst of the circle was Leopold himself, still contemplating with self-satisfaction the deed he had done, and still listening to the shouts of applause which his partisans bestowed with no sparing breath. While he was in this state of self-gratulation, Richard burst into the circle, attended, indeed, only by two men, but in his own headlong energies an irresistible host.

"Who has dared," he said, laying his hands upon the Austrian standard, and speaking in a voice like the sound which precedes an earthquake—"Who has dared to place this paltry rag beside the banner of England?"

The Archduke wanted not personal courage, and it was impossible he could hear this question without reply. Yet so much was he troubled and surprised by the unexpected arrival of Richard, and affected by the general awe inspired by his ardent and unyielding character, that the demand was twice repeated, in a tone which seemed to challenge heaven and earth, ere the Archduke replied, with such firmness as he could command, "It was I, Leopold of Austria."

"Then shall Leopold of Austria," replied Richard, "presentry see the rate at which his banner and his pretensions are held by Richard of England."

So saying, he pulled up the standard-spear, splintered it to pieces, threw the banner itself on the ground, and placed his foot upon it.

"Thus," said he, "I trample on the banner of Austria. Is there a knight among your Teutonic chivalry dare impeach my deed?"

There was a momentary silence; but there are no braver men than the Germans.

"I," and "I," and "I," was heard from several knights of the Duke's followers; and he himself added his voice to those which accepted the King of England's defiance.

"Why do we dally thus?" said the Earl Wallenrode, a gigantic warrior from the frontiers of Hungary. "Brethren and noble gentlemen, this man's foot is on the honour of your country—let us rescue it from violation, and down with the pride of England!"

So saying, he drew his sword, and struck at the King a blow which might have proved fatal, had not the Scot intercepted and caught it upon his shield.

"I have sworn," said King Richard—and his voice was heard above all the tumult, which now waxed wild and loud—"never to strike one whose shoulder bears the cross; therefore live, Wallenrode—but live to remember Richard of England."

As he spoke, he grasped the tall Hungarian round the waist, and, unmatched in wrestling, as in other military exercises, hurled him backwards with such violence that the mass flew as if discharged from a military engine, not only through the ring of spectators who witnessed the extraordinary scene, but over the edge of the mount itself, down the steep side of which Wallenrode rolled headlong, until, pitching at length upon his shoulder, he dislocated the bone, and lay like one dead. This almost supernatural display of strength did not encourage either the Duke or any of his followers to renew a personal contest so inauspiciously commenced. Those who stood farthest back did, indeed, clash their swords, and cry out, "Cut the island mastiff to pieces!" but those who were nearer veiled, perhaps, their personal fears under an affected regard for order, and cried, for the most part, "Peace! Peace! the peace of the Cross—the peace of Holy Church and our Father the Pope!"

These various cries of the assailants, contradicting each other, showed their irresolution; while Richard, his foot still on the archducal banner, glared round him with an eye that seemed to seek an enemy, and from which the angry nobles shrunk appalled, as from the threatened grasp of a lion. De Vaux and the Knight of the Leopard kept their places beside him; and though the swords which they held were still sheathed, it was plain that they were prompt to protect Richard's person to the very last, and their size and remarkable strength plainly showed the defence would be a desperate one.

Salisbury and his attendants were also now drawing near, with bills and partisans brandished, and bows already bended.

At this moment King Philip of France, attended by one or two of his nobles, came on the platform to inquire the cause of the disturbance, and made gestures of surprise at finding the King of England raised from his sick-bed, and confronting their common ally, the Duke of Austria, in such a menacing and insulting posture. Richard himself blushed at being discovered by Philip, whose sagacity he respected as much as he disliked his person, in an attitude neither becoming his character as a monarch, nor as a Crusader; and it was observed that he withdrew his foot, as if accidentally, from the dishonoured banner, and exchanged his look of violent emotion for one of affected composure and indifference. Leopold also struggled to attain some degree of calmness, mortified as he was by having been seen by Philip in the act of passively submitting to the insults of the fiery King of England.

Possessed of many of those royal qualities for which he was termed by his subjects the August, Philip might be termed the Ulysses, as Richard was indisputably the Achilles, of the Crusade. The King of France was sagacious, wise, deliberate in council, steady and calm in action, seeing clearly, and steadily pursuing, the measures most for the interest of his kingdom—dignified and royal in his deportment, brave in person, but a politician rather than a warrior. The Crusade would have been no choice of his own; but the spirit was contagious, and the expedition was enforced upon him by the church, and by the unanimous wish of his nobility. In any other situation, or in a milder age, his character might have stood higher than that of the adventurous Coeur de Lion. But in the Crusade, itself an undertaking wholly irrational, sound reason was the quality of all others least estimated, and the chivalric valour which both the age and the enterprise demanded was considered as debased if mingled with the least touch of discretion. So that the merit of Philip, compared with that of his haughty rival, showed like the clear but minute flame of a lamp placed near the glare of a huge, blazing torch, which, not possessing half the utility, makes ten times more impression on the eye. Philip felt his inferiority in public opinion with the pain natural to a high-spirited prince; and it cannot be wondered at if he took such opportunities as offered for placing his own character in more advantageous contrast with that of his rival. The present seemed one of those occasions in which prudence and calmness might reasonably expect to triumph over obstinacy and impetuous violence.

"What means this unseemly broil betwixt the sworn brethren of the Cross—the royal Majesty of England and the princely Duke Leopold? How is it possible that those who are the chiefs and pillars of this holy expedition—"

"A truce with thy remonstrance, France," said Richard, enraged inwardly at finding himself placed on a sort of equality with Leopold, yet not knowing how to resent it. "This duke, or prince, or pillar, if you will, hath been insolent, and I have chastised him—that is all. Here is a coil, forsooth, because of spurning a hound!"

"Majesty of France," said the Duke, "I appeal to you and every sovereign prince against the foul indignity which I have sustained. This King of England hath pulled down my banner-torn and trampled on it."

"Because he had the audacity to plant it beside mine," said Richard.

"My rank as thine equal entitled me," replied the Duke, emboldened by the presence of Philip.

"Assert such equality for thy person," said King Richard, "and, by Saint George, I will treat thy person as I did thy broidered kerchief there, fit but for the meanest use to which kerchief may be put."

"Nay, but patience, brother of England," said Philip, "and I will presently show Austria that he is wrong in this matter.—Do not think, noble Duke," he continued, "that, in permitting the standard of England to occupy the highest point in our camp, we, the independent sovereigns of the Crusade, acknowledge any inferiority to the royal Richard. It were inconsistent to think so, since even the Oriflamme itself—the great banner of France, to which the royal Richard himself, in respect of his French possessions, is but a vassal—holds for the present an inferior place to the Lions of England. But as sworn brethren of the Cross, military pilgrims, who, laying aside the pomp and pride of this world, are hewing with our swords the way to the Holy Sepulchre, I myself, and the other princes, have renounced to King Richard, from respect to his high renown and great feats of arms, that precedence which elsewhere, and upon other motives, would not have been yielded. I am satisfied that, when your royal grace of Austria shall have considered this, you will express sorrow for having placed your banner on this spot, and that the royal Majesty of England will then give satisfaction for the insult he has offered."

The SPRUCH-SPRECHER and the jester had both retired to a safe distance when matters seemed coming to blows; but returned when words, their own commodity, seemed again about to become the order of the day.

The man of proverbs was so delighted with Philip's politic speech that he clashed his baton at the conclusion, by way of emphasis, and forgot the presence in which he was, so far as to say aloud that he himself had never said a wiser thing in his life.

"It may be so," whispered Jonas Schwanker, "but we shall be whipped if you speak so loud."

The Duke answered sullenly that he would refer his quarrel to the General Council of the Crusade—a motion which Philip highly applauded, as qualified to take away a scandal most harmful to Christendom.

Richard, retaining the same careless attitude, listened to Philip until his oratory seemed exhausted, and then said aloud, "I am drowsy—this fever hangs about me still. Brother of France, thou art acquainted with my humour, and that I have at all times but few words to spare. Know, therefore, at once, I will submit a matter touching the honour of England neither to Prince, Pope, nor Council. Here stands my banner—whatsoever pennon shall be reared within three butts' length of it—ay, were it the Oriflamme, of which you were, I think, but now speaking—shall be treated as that dishonoured rag; nor will I yield other satisfaction than that which these poor limbs can render in the lists to any bold challenge—ay, were it against five champions instead of one."

"Now," said the jester, whispering his companion, "that is as complete a piece of folly as if I myself had said it; but yet, I think, there may be in this matter a greater fool than Richard yet."

"And who may that be?" asked the man of wisdom.

"Philip," said the jester, "or our own Royal Duke, should either accept the challenge. But oh, most sage SPRUCH-SPECHER, what excellent kings wouldst thou and I have made, since those on whose heads these crowns have fallen can play the proverb-monger and the fool as completely as ourselves!"

While these worthies plied their offices apart, Philip answered calmly to the almost injurious defiance of Richard, "I came not hither to awaken fresh quarrels, contrary to the oath we have sworn, and the holy cause in which we have engaged. I part from my brother of England as brothers should part, and the only strife between the Lions of England and the Lilies of France shall be which shall be carried deepest into the ranks of the infidels."

"It is a bargain, my royal brother," said Richard, stretching out his hand with all the frankness which belonged to his rash but generous disposition; "and soon may we have the opportunity to try this gallant and fraternal wager."

"Let this noble Duke also partake in the friendship of this happy moment," said Philip; and the Duke approached half-sullenly, half-willing to enter into some accommodation.

"I think not of fools, nor of their folly," said Richard carelessly; and the Archduke, turning his back on him, withdrew from the ground.

Richard looked after him as he retired.

"There is a sort of glow-worm courage," he said, "that shows only by night. I must not leave this banner unguarded in darkness; by daylight the look of the Lions will alone defend it. Here, Thomas of Gilsland, I give thee the charge of the standard—watch over the honour of England."

"Her safety is yet more dear to me," said De Vaux, "and the life of Richard is the safety of England. I must have your Highness back to your tent, and that without further tarriance."

"Thou art a rough and peremptory nurse, De Vaux," said the king, smiling; and then added, addressing Sir Kenneth, "Valiant Scot, I owe thee a boon, and I will pay it richly. There stands the banner of England! Watch it as novice does his armour on the night before he is dubbed. Stir not from it three spears' length, and defend it with thy body against injury or insult. Sound thy bugle if thou art assailed by more than three at once. Dost thou undertake the charge?"

"Willingly," said Kenneth; "and will discharge it upon penalty of my head. I will but arm me, and return hither instantly."

The Kings of France and England then took formal leave of each other, hiding, under an appearance of courtesy, the grounds of complaint which either had against the other—Richard against Philip, for what he deemed an officious interference betwixt him and Austria, and Philip against Coeur de Lion, for the disrespectful manner in which his mediation had been received. Those whom this disturbance had assembled now drew off in different directions, leaving the contested mount in the same solitude which had subsisted till interrupted by the Austrian bravado. Men judged of the events of the day according to their partialities, and while the English charged the Austrian with having afforded the first ground of quarrel, those of other nations concurred in casting the greater blame upon the insular haughtiness and assuming character of Richard.

"Thou seest," said the Marquis of Montserrat to the Grand Master of the Templars, "that subtle courses are more effective than violence. I have unloosed the bonds which held together this bunch of sceptres and lances—thou wilt see them shortly fall asunder."

"I would have called thy plan a good one," said the Templar, "had there been but one man of courage among yonder cold-blooded Austrians to sever the bonds of which you speak with his sword. A knot that is unloosed may again be fastened, but not so the cord which has been cut to pieces."

Lesson 134

1. Stop and think. What has just happened in the book? What do you think is going to happen next? (You're not supposed to know what happens next. You're just supposed to think!)
2. Read chapter 12. Sir Kenneth is tempted to leave his post guarding the banner of England through the night when he receives what seems to be an invitation from the love of his dreams, Edith, delivered by that strange dwarf.
3. What is Sir Kenneth thinking about as he stands guard over the English banner? (Answers)
4. Who appears in the darkness and why has he come? (Answers)
5. Sir Kenneth has a tough choice - stay at his post or go to see his lady, whom he has probably never even spoken to before. What do you think he should do? (Answers)

CHAPTER XII.

'Tis woman that seduces all mankind.

GAY.

In the days of chivalry, a dangerous post or a perilous adventure was a reward frequently assigned to military bravery as a compensation for its former trials; just as, in ascending a precipice, the surmounting one crag only lifts the climber to points yet more dangerous.

It was midnight, and the moon rode clear and high in heaven, when Kenneth of Scotland stood upon his watch on Saint George's Mount, beside the banner of England, a solitary sentinel, to protect the emblem of that nation against the insults which might be meditated among the thousands whom Richard's pride had made his enemies. High thoughts rolled, one after each other, upon the mind of the warrior. It seemed to him as if he had gained some favour in the eyes of the chivalrous monarch, who till now had not seemed to distinguish him among the crowds of brave men whom his renown had assembled under his banner, and Sir Kenneth little recked that the display of royal regard consisted in placing him upon a post so perilous. The devotion of his ambitious and high-placed affection inflamed his military enthusiasm. Hopeless as that attachment was in almost any conceivable circumstances, those which had lately occurred had, in some degree, diminished the distance between Edith and himself. He upon whom Richard had conferred the distinction of guarding his banner was no longer an adventurer of slight note, but placed within the regard of a princess, although he was as far as ever from her level. An unknown and obscure fate could not now be his. If he was surprised and slain on the post which had been assigned him, his death—and he resolved it should be glorious—must deserve the praises as well as call down the vengeance of Coeur de Lion, and be followed by the regrets, and even the tears, of the high-born beauties of the English Court. He had now no longer reason to fear that he should die as a fool dieth.

Sir Kenneth had full leisure to enjoy these and similar high-souled thoughts, fostered by that wild spirit of chivalry, which, amid its most extravagant and fantastic flights, was still pure from all selfish alloy—generous, devoted, and perhaps only thus far censurable, that it proposed objects and courses of action inconsistent with the frailties and imperfections of man. All nature around him slept in calm moon-shine or in deep shadow. The long rows of tents and pavilions, glimmering or darkening as they lay in the moonlight or in the shade, were still and silent as the streets of a deserted city. Beside the banner-staff lay the large staghound already mentioned, the sole companion of Kenneth's watch, on whose vigilance he trusted for early warning of the approach of any hostile footstep. The noble animal seemed to understand the purpose of their watch; for he looked from time to time at the rich folds of the heavy pennon, and, when the cry of the sentinels came from the distant lines and defences of the camp, he answered them with one deep and reiterated bark, as if to affirm that he too was vigilant in his duty. From time to time, also, he lowered his lofty head, and wagged his tail, as his master passed and repassed him in the short turns which he took upon his post; or, when the knight stood silent and abstracted leaning on his lance, and looking up towards heaven, his faithful attendant ventured sometimes, in the phrase of romance, "to disturb his thoughts," and awaken him from his reverie, by thrusting his large rough snout into the knight's gauntleted hand, to solicit a transitory caress.

Thus passed two hours of the knight's watch without anything remarkable occurring. At length, and upon a sudden, the gallant staghound bayed furiously, and seemed about to dash forward where the shadow lay the darkest, yet waited, as if in the slips, till he should know the pleasure of his master.

"Who goes there?" said Sir Kenneth, aware that there was something creeping forward on the shadowy side of the mount.

"In the name of Merlin and Maugis," answered a hoarse, disagreeable voice, "tie up your fourfooted demon there, or I come not at you."

"And who art thou that would approach my post?" said Sir Kenneth, bending his eyes as keenly as he could on some object, which he could just observe at the bottom of the ascent, without being able to distinguish its form. "Beware—I am here for death and life."

"Take up thy long-fanged Sathanas," said the voice, "or I will conjure him with a bolt from my arblast."

At the same time was heard the sound of a spring or check, as when a crossbow is bent.

"Unbend thy arblast, and come into the moonlight," said the Scot, "or, by Saint Andrew, I will pin thee to the earth, be what or whom thou wilt!"

As he spoke he poised his long lance by the middle, and, fixing his eye upon the object, which seemed to move, he brandished the weapon, as if meditating to cast it from his hand—a use of the weapon sometimes, though rarely, resorted to when a missile was necessary. But Sir Kenneth was ashamed of his purpose, and grounded his weapon, when there stepped from the shadow into the moonlight, like an actor entering upon the stage, a stunted, decrepit creature, whom, by his fantastic dress and deformity, he recognized, even at some distance, for the male of the two dwarfs whom he had seen in the chapel at Engaddi. Recollecting, at the same moment, the other and far different visions of that extraordinary night, he gave his dog a signal, which he instantly understood, and, returning to the standard, laid himself down beside it with a stifled growl.

The little, distorted miniature of humanity, assured of his safety from an enemy so formidable, came panting up the ascent, which the shortness of his legs rendered laborious, and, when he arrived on the platform at the top, shifted to his left hand the little crossbow, which was just such a toy as children at that period were permitted to shoot small birds with, and, assuming an attitude of great dignity, gracefully extended his right hand to Sir Kenneth, in an attitude as if he expected he would salute it. But such a result not following, he demanded, in a sharp and angry tone of voice, "Soldier, wherefore renderest thou not to Nectabanus the homage due to his dignity? Or is it possible that thou canst have forgotten him?"

"Great Nectabanus," answered the knight, willing to soothe the creature's humour, "that were difficult for any one who has ever looked upon thee. Pardon me, however, that, being a soldier upon my post, with my lance in my hand, I may not give to one of thy puissance the advantage of coming within my guard, or of mastering my weapon. Suffice it that I reverence thy dignity, and submit myself to thee as humbly as a man-at-arms in my place may."

"It shall suffice," said Nectabanus, "so that you presently attend me to the presence of those who have sent me hither to summon you."

"Great sir," replied the knight, "neither in this can I gratify thee, for my orders are to abide by this banner till daybreak—so I pray you to hold me excused in that matter also."

So saying, he resumed his walk upon the platform; but the dwarf did not suffer him so easily to escape from his importunity.

"Look you," he said, placing himself before Sir Kenneth, so as to interrupt his way, "either obey me, Sir Knight, as in duty bound, or I will lay the command upon thee, in the name of one whose beauty could call down the genii from their sphere, and whose grandeur could command the immortal race when they had descended."

A wild and improbable conjecture arose in the knight's mind, but he repelled it. It was impossible, he thought, that the lady of his love should have sent him such a message by such a messenger; yet his voice trembled as he said, "Go to, Nectabanus. Tell me at once, and as a true man, whether this sublime lady of whom thou speakest be other than the houri with whose assistance I beheld thee sweeping the chapel at Engaddi?"

"How! presumptuous Knight," replied the dwarf, "think'st thou the mistress of our own royal affections, the sharer of our greatness, and the partner of our comeliness, would demean herself by laying charge on such a vassal as thou? No; highly as thou art honoured, thou hast not yet deserved the notice of Queen Guenevra, the lovely bride of Arthur, from whose high seat even princes seem but pigmies. But look thou here, and as thou knowest or disownest this token, so obey or refuse her commands who hath deigned to impose them on thee."

So saying, he placed in the knight's hand a ruby ring, which, even in the moonlight, he had no difficulty to recognize as that which usually graced the finger of the high-born lady to whose service he had devoted himself. Could he have doubted the truth of the token, he would have been convinced by the small knot of carnation-coloured ribbon which was fastened to the ring. This was his lady's favourite colour, and more than once had he himself, assuming it for that of his own liveries, caused the carnation to triumph over all other hues in the lists and in the battle.

Sir Kenneth was struck nearly mute by seeing such a token in such hands.

"In the name of all that is sacred, from whom didst thou receive this witness?" said the knight. "Bring, if thou canst, thy wavering understanding to a right settlement for a minute or two, and tell me the person by whom thou art sent, and the real purpose of thy message, and take heed what thou sayest, for this is no subject for buffoonery."

"Fond and foolish Knight," said the dwarf, "wouldst thou know more of this matter than that thou art honoured with commands from a princess, delivered to thee by a king? We list not to parley with thee further than to command thee, in the name and by the power of that ring, to follow us to her who is the owner of the ring. Every minute that thou tarriest is a crime against thy allegiance."

"Good Nectabanus, bethink thyself," said the knight. "Can my lady know where and upon what duty I am this night engaged? Is she aware that my life—pshaw, why should I speak of life—but that my honour depends on my guarding this banner till daybreak; and can it be her wish that I should leave it even to pay homage to her? It is impossible—the princess is pleased to be merry with her servant in sending him such a message; and I must think so the rather that she hath chosen such a messenger."

"Oh, keep your belief," said Nectabanus, turning round as if to leave the platform; "it is little to me whether you be traitor or true man to this royal lady—so fare thee well."

"Stay, stay—I entreat you stay," said Sir Kenneth. "Answer me but one question: is the lady who sent thee near to this place?"

"What signifies it?" said the dwarf. "Ought fidelity to reckon furlongs, or miles, or leagues—like the poor courier, who is paid for his labour by the distance which he traverses? Nevertheless, thou soul of suspicion, I tell thee, the fair owner of the ring now sent to so unworthy a vassal, in whom there is neither truth nor courage, is not more distant from this place than this arblast can send a bolt."

The knight gazed again on that ring, as if to ascertain that there was no possible falsehood in the token. "Tell me," he said to the dwarf, "is my presence required for any length of time?"

"Time!" answered Nectabanus, in his flighty manner; "what call you time? I see it not—I feel it not—it is but a shadowy name—a succession of breathings measured forth by night by the clank of a bell, by day by a shadow crossing along a dial-stone. Knowest thou not a true knight's time should only be reckoned by the deeds that he performs in behalf of God and his lady?"

"The words of truth, though in the mouth of folly," said the knight. "And doth my lady really summon me to some deed of action, in her name and for her sake?—and may it not be postponed for even the few hours till daybreak?"

"She requires thy presence instantly," said the dwarf, "and without the loss of so much time as would be told by ten grains of the sandglass. Hearken, thou cold-blooded and suspicious knight, these are her very words—Tell him that the hand which dropped roses can bestow laurels."

This allusion to their meeting in the chapel of Engaddi sent a thousand recollections through Sir Kenneth's brain, and convinced him that the message delivered by the dwarf was genuine. The rosebuds, withered as they were, were still treasured under his cuirass, and nearest to his heart. He paused, and could not resolve to forego an opportunity, the only one which might ever offer, to gain grace in her eyes whom he had installed as sovereign of his affections. The dwarf, in the meantime, augmented his confusion by insisting either that he must return the ring or instantly attend him.

"Hold, hold, yet a moment hold," said the knight, and proceeded to mutter to himself, "Am I either the subject or slave of King Richard, more than as a free knight sworn to the service of the Crusade? And whom have I come hither to honour with lance and sword? Our holy cause and my transcendent lady!"

"The ring! the ring!" exclaimed the dwarf impatiently; "false and slothful knight, return the ring, which thou art unworthy to touch or to look upon."

"A moment, a moment, good Nectabanus," said Sir Kenneth; "disturb not my thoughts.—What if the Saracens were just now to attack our lines? Should I stay here like a sworn vassal of England, watching that her king's pride suffered no humiliation; or should I speed to the breach, and fight for the Cross? To the breach, assuredly; and next to the cause of God come the commands of my liege lady. And yet, Coeur de Lion's behest—my own promise! Nectabanus, I conjure thee once more to say, are you to conduct me far from hence?"

"But to yonder pavilion; and, since you must needs know," replied Nectabanus, "the moon is glimmering on the gilded ball which crowns its roof, and which is worth a king's ransom."

"I can return in an instant," said the knight, shutting his eyes desperately to all further consequences, "I can hear from thence the bay of my dog if any one approaches the standard. I will throw myself at my lady's feet, and pray her leave to return to conclude my watch.—Here, Roswal" (calling his hound, and throwing down his mantle by the side of the standard-spear), "watch thou here, and let no one approach."

The majestic dog looked in his master's face, as if to be sure that he understood his charge, then sat down beside the mantle, with ears erect and head raised, like a sentinel, understanding perfectly the purpose for which he was stationed there.

"Come now, good Nectabanus," said the knight, "let us hasten to obey the commands thou hast brought."

"Haste he that will," said the dwarf sullenly; "thou hast not been in haste to obey my summons, nor can I walk fast enough to follow your long strides—you do not walk like a man, but bound like an ostrich in the desert."

There were but two ways of conquering the obstinacy of Nectabanus, who, as he spoke, diminished his walk into a snail's pace. For bribes Sir Kenneth had no means—for soothing no time; so in his impatience he snatched the dwarf up from the ground, and bearing him along, notwithstanding his entreaties and his fear, reached nearly to the pavilion pointed out as that of the Queen. In approaching it, however, the Scot observed there was a small guard of soldiers sitting on the ground, who had been concealed from him by the intervening tents. Wondering that the clash of his own armour had not yet attracted their attention, and supposing that his motions might, on the present occasion, require to be conducted with secrecy, he placed the little panting guide upon the ground to recover his breath, and point out what was next to be done. Nectabanus was both frightened and angry; but he had felt himself as completely in the power of the robust knight as an owl in the claws of an eagle, and therefore cared not to provoke him to any further display of his strength.

He made no complaints, therefore, of the usage he had received; but, turning amongst the labyrinth of tents, he led the knight in silence to the opposite side of the pavilion, which thus screened them from the observation of the warders, who seemed either too negligent or too sleepy to discharge their duty with much accuracy. Arrived there, the dwarf raised the under part of the canvas from the ground, and made signs to Sir Kenneth that he should introduce himself to the inside of the tent, by creeping under it. The knight hesitated. There seemed an indecorum in thus privately introducing himself into a pavilion pitched, doubtless, for the accommodation of noble ladies; but he recalled to remembrance the assured tokens which the dwarf had exhibited, and concluded that it was not for him to dispute his lady's pleasure.

He stooped accordingly, crept beneath the canvas enclosure of the tent, and heard the dwarf whisper from without, "Remain here until I call thee."

Lesson 135

1. Stop and think. What has just happened in the book? What do you think is going to happen next?
2. Read chapter 13. Sir Kenneth discovers that he has been tricked into thinking that Edith had summoned him, and by the time he returns to his post, the banner of England has been stolen and his beloved dog injured.
3. Where is Sir Kenneth when he hears the Queen and her maidens laughing at him? (Answers)
4. What trick had the Queen and her maidens and the dwarf played on the knight? Why? (Answers)
5. Why does it take Sir Kenneth so long to return to his post? (Answers)

CHAPTER XIII.

You talk of Gaiety and Innocence!

The moment when the fatal fruit was eaten,

They parted ne'er to meet again; and Malice

Has ever since been playmate to light Gaiety,

From the first moment when the smiling infant

Destroys the flower or butterfly he toys with,

To the last chuckle of the dying miser,

Who on his deathbed laughs his last to hear

His wealthy neighbour has become a bankrupt.

OLD PLAY.

Sir Kenneth was left for some minutes alone and in darkness. Here was another interruption which must prolong his absence from his post, and he began almost to repent the facility with which he had been induced to quit it. But to return without seeing the Lady Edith was now not to be thought of. He had committed a breach of military discipline, and was determined at least to prove the reality of the seductive expectations which had tempted him to do so. Meanwhile his situation was unpleasant. There was no light to show him into what sort of apartment he had been led—the Lady Edith was in immediate attendance on the Queen of England—and the discovery of his having introduced himself thus furtively into the royal pavilion might, were it discovered; lead to much and dangerous suspicion. While he gave way to these unpleasant reflections, and began almost to wish that he could achieve his retreat unobserved, he heard a noise of female voices, laughing, whispering, and speaking, in an adjoining apartment, from which, as the sounds gave him reason to judge, he could only be separated by a canvas partition. Lamps were burning, as he might perceive by the shadowy light which extended itself even to his side of the veil which divided the tent, and he could see shades of several figures sitting and moving in the adjoining apartment. It cannot be termed discourtesy in Sir Kenneth that, situated as he was, he overheard a conversation in which he found himself deeply interested.

"Call her—call her, for Our Lady's sake," said the voice of one of these laughing invisibles. "Nectabanus, thou shalt be made ambassador to Prester John's court, to show them how wisely thou canst discharge thee of a mission."

The shrill tone of the dwarf was heard, yet so much subdued that Sir Kenneth could not understand what he said, except that he spoke something of the means of merriment given to the guard.

"But how shall we rid us of the spirit which Nectabanus hath raised, my maidens?"

"Hear me, royal madam," said another voice. "If the sage and princely Nectabanus be not over-jealous of his most transcendent bride and empress, let us send her to get us rid of this insolent knight-errant, who can be so easily persuaded that high-born dames may need the use of his insolent and overweening valour."

"It were but justice, methinks," replied another, "that the Princess Guenever should dismiss, by her courtesy, him whom her husband's wisdom has been able to entice hither."

Struck to the heart with shame and resentment at what he had heard, Sir Kenneth was about to attempt his escape from the tent at all hazards, when what followed arrested his purpose.

"Nay, truly," said the first speaker, "our cousin Edith must first learn how this vaunted wight hath conducted himself, and we must reserve the power of giving her ocular proof that he hath failed in his duty. It may be a lesson will do good upon her; for, credit me, Calista, I have sometimes thought she has let this Northern adventurer sit nearer her heart than prudence would sanction."

One of the other voices was then heard to mutter something of the Lady Edith's prudence and wisdom.

"Prudence, wench!" was the reply. "It is mere pride, and the desire to be thought more rigid than any of us. Nay, I will not quit my advantage. You know well that when she has us at fault no one can, in a civil way, lay your error before you more precisely than can my Lady Edith. But here she comes."

A figure, as if entering the apartment, cast upon the partition a shade, which glided along slowly until it mixed with those which already clouded it. Despite of the bitter disappointment which he had experienced—despite the insult and injury with which it seemed he had been visited by the malice, or, at best, by the idle humour of Queen Berengaria (for he already concluded that she who spoke loudest, and in a commanding tone, was the wife of Richard), the knight felt something so soothing to his feelings in learning that Edith had been no partner to the fraud practised on him, and so interesting to his curiosity in the scene which was about to take place, that, instead of prosecuting his more prudent purpose of an instant retreat, he looked anxiously, on the contrary, for some rent or crevice by means of which he might be made eye as well as ear witness to what was to go forward.

"Surely," said he to himself, "the Queen, who hath been pleased for an idle frolic to endanger my reputation, and perhaps my life, cannot complain if I avail myself of the chance which fortune seems willing to afford me to obtain knowledge of her further intentions."

It seemed, in the meanwhile, as if Edith were waiting for the commands of the Queen, and as if the other were reluctant to speak for fear of being unable to command her laughter and that of her companions; for Sir Kenneth could only distinguish a sound as of suppressed tittering and merriment.

"Your Majesty," said Edith at last, "seems in a merry mood, though, methinks, the hour of night prompts a sleepy one. I was well disposed bedward when I had your Majesty's commands to attend you."

"I will not long delay you, cousin, from your repose," said the Queen, "though I fear you will sleep less soundly when I tell you your wager is lost."

"Nay, royal madam," said Edith, "this, surely, is dwelling on a jest which has rather been worn out, I laid no wager, however it was your Majesty's pleasure to suppose, or to insist, that I did so."

"Nay, now, despite our pilgrimage, Satan is strong with you, my gentle cousin, and prompts thee to leasing. Can you deny that you gaged your ruby ring against my golden bracelet that yonder Knight of the Libbard, or how call you him, could not be seduced from his post?"

"Your Majesty is too great for me to gainsay you," replied Edith, "but these ladies can, if they will, bear me witness that it was your Highness who proposed such a wager, and took the ring from my finger, even while I was declaring that I did not think it maidenly to gage anything on such a subject."

"Nay, but, my Lady Edith," said another voice, "you must needs grant, under your favour, that you expressed yourself very confident of the valour of that same Knight of the Leopard."

"And if I did, minion," said Edith angrily, "is that a good reason why thou shouldst put in thy word to flatter her Majesty's humour? I spoke of that knight but as all men speak who have seen him in the field, and had no more interest in defending than thou in detracting from him. In a camp, what can women speak of save soldiers and deeds of arms?"

"The noble Lady Edith," said a third voice, "hath never forgiven Calista and me, since we told your Majesty that she dropped two rosebuds in the chapel."

"If your Majesty," said Edith, in a tone which Sir Kenneth could judge to be that of respectful remonstrance, "have no other commands for me than to hear the gibes of your waiting-women, I must crave your permission to withdraw."

"Silence, Florise," said the Queen, "and let not our indulgence lead you to forget the difference betwixt yourself and the kinswoman of England.—But you, my dear cousin," she continued, resuming her tone of raillery, "how can you, who are so good-natured, begrudge us poor wretches a few minutes' laughing, when we have had so many days devoted to weeping and gnashing of teeth?"

"Great be your mirth, royal lady," said Edith; "yet would I be content not to smile for the rest of my life, rather than—"

She stopped, apparently out of respect; but Sir Kenneth could hear that she was in much agitation.

"Forgive me," said Berengaria, a thoughtless but good-humoured princess of the House of Navarre; "but what is the great offence, after all? A young knight has been wiled hither—has stolen, or has been stolen, from his post, which no one will disturb in his absence—for the sake of a fair lady; for, to do your champion justice, sweet one, the wisdom of Nectabanus could conjure him hither in no name but yours."

"Gracious Heaven! your Majesty does not say so?" said Edith, in a voice of alarm quite different from the agitation she had previously evinced,—"you cannot say so consistently with respect for your own honour and for mine, your husband's kinswoman! Say you were jesting with me, my royal mistress, and forgive me that I could, even for a moment, think it possible you could be in earnest!"

"The Lady Edith," said the Queen, in a displeased tone of voice, "regrets the ring we have won of her. We will restore the pledge to you, gentle cousin; only you must not grudge us in turn a little triumph over the wisdom which has been so often spread over us, as a banner over a host."

"A triumph!" exclaimed Edith indignantly—"a triumph! The triumph will be with the infidel, when he hears that the Queen of England can make the reputation of her husband's kinswoman the subject of a light frolic."

"You are angry, fair cousin, at losing your favourite ring," said the Queen. "Come, since you grudge to pay your wager, we will renounce our right; it was your name and that pledge brought him hither, and we care not for the bait after the fish is caught."

"Madam," replied Edith impatiently, "you know well that your Grace could not wish for anything of mine but it becomes instantly yours. But I would give a bushel of rubies ere ring or name of mine had been used to bring a brave man into a fault, and perhaps to disgrace and punishment."

"Oh, it is for the safety of our true knight that we fear!" said the Queen. "You rate our power too low, fair cousin, when you speak of a life being lost for a frolic of ours. O Lady Edith, others have influence on the iron breasts of warriors as well as you—the heart even of a lion is made of flesh, not of stone; and, believe me, I have interest enough with Richard to save this knight, in whose fate Lady Edith is so deeply concerned, from the penalty of disobeying his royal commands."

"For the love of the blessed Cross, most royal lady," said Edith—and Sir Kenneth, with feelings which it were hard to unravel, heard her prostrate herself at the Queen's feet—"for the love of our blessed Lady, and of every holy saint in the calendar, beware what you do! You know not King Richard—you have been but shortly wedded to him. Your breath might as well combat the west wind when it is wildest, as your words persuade my royal kinsman to pardon a military offence. Oh, for God's sake, dismiss this gentleman, if indeed you have lured him hither! I could almost be content to rest with the shame of having invited him, did I know that he was returned again where his duty calls him!"

"Arise, cousin, arise," said Queen Berengaria, "and be assured all will be better than you think. Rise, dear Edith. I am sorry I have played my foolery with a knight in whom you take such deep interest. Nay, wring not thy hands; I will believe thou carest not for him—believe anything rather than see thee look so wretchedly miserable. I tell thee I will take the blame on myself with King Richard in behalf of thy fair Northern friend—thine acquaintance, I would say, since thou own'st him not as a friend. Nay, look not so reproachfully. We will send Nectabanus to dismiss this Knight of the Standard to his post; and we ourselves will grace him on some future day, to make amends for his wild-goose chase. He is, I warrant, but lying perdu in some neighbouring tent."

"By my crown of lilies, and my sceptre of a specially good water-reed," said Nectabanus, "your Majesty is mistaken, He is nearer at hand than you wot—he lieth ensconced there behind that canvas partition."

"And within hearing of each word we have said!" exclaimed the Queen, in her turn violently surprised and agitated. "Out, monster of folly and malignity!"

As she uttered these words, Nectabanus fled from the pavilion with a yell of such a nature as leaves it still doubtful whether Berengaria had confined her rebuke to words, or added some more emphatic expression of her displeasure.

"What can now be done?" said the Queen to Edith, in a whisper of undisguised uneasiness.

"That which must," said Edith firmly. "We must see this gentleman and place ourselves in his mercy."

So saying, she began hastily to undo a curtain, which at one place covered an entrance or communication.

"For Heaven's sake, forbear—consider," said the Queen—"my apartment—our dress—the hour—my honour!"

But ere she could detail her remonstrances, the curtain fell, and there was no division any longer betwixt the armed knight and the party of ladies. The warmth of an Eastern night occasioned the undress of Queen Berengaria and her household to be rather more simple and unstudied than their station, and the presence of a male spectator of rank, required. This the Queen remembered, and with a loud shriek fled from the apartment where Sir Kenneth was disclosed to view in a compartment of the ample pavilion, now no longer separated from that in which they stood. The grief and agitation of the Lady Edith, as well as the deep interest she felt in a hasty explanation with the Scottish knight, perhaps occasioned her forgetting that her locks were more dishevelled and her person less heedfully covered than was the wont of high-born damsels, in an age which was not, after all, the most prudish or scrupulous period of the ancient time. A thin, loose garment of pink-coloured silk made the principal part of her vestments, with Oriental slippers, into which she had hastily thrust her bare feet, and a scarf hurriedly and loosely thrown about her shoulders. Her head had no other covering than the veil of rich and dishevelled locks falling round it on every side, that half hid a countenance which a mingled sense of modesty and of resentment, and other deep and agitated feelings, had covered with crimson.

But although Edith felt her situation with all that delicacy which is her sex's greatest charm, it did not seem that for a moment she placed her own bashfulness in comparison with the duty which, as she thought, she owed to him who had been led into error and danger on her account. She drew, indeed, her scarf more closely over her neck and bosom, and she hastily laid from her hand a lamp which shed too much lustre over her figure; but, while Sir Kenneth stood motionless on the same spot in which he was first discovered, she rather stepped towards than retired from him, as she exclaimed, "Hasten to your post, valiant knight!—you are deceived in being trained hither—ask no questions."

"I need ask none," said the knight, sinking upon one knee, with the reverential devotion of a saint at the altar, and bending his eyes on the ground, lest his looks should increase the lady's embarrassment.

"Have you heard all?" said Edith impatiently. "Gracious saints! then wherefore wait you here, when each minute that passes is loaded with dishonour!"

"I have heard that I am dishonoured, lady, and I have heard it from you," answered Kenneth. "What reck I how soon punishment follows? I have but one petition to you; and then I seek, among the sabres of the infidels, whether dishonour may not be washed out with blood."

"Do not so, neither," said the lady. "Be wise—dally not here; all may yet be well, if you will but use dispatch."

"I wait but for your forgiveness," said the knight, still kneeling, "for my presumption in believing that my poor services could have been required or valued by you."

"I do forgive you—oh, I have nothing to forgive! have been the means of injuring you. But oh, begone! I will forgive—I will value you—that is, as I value every brave Crusader—if you will but begone!"

"Receive, first, this precious yet fatal pledge," said the knight, tendering the ring to Edith, who now showed gestures of impatience.

"Oh, no, no " she said, declining to receive it. "Keep it—keep it as a mark of my regard—my regret, I would say. Oh, begone, if not for your own sake, for mine!"

Almost recompensed for the loss even of honour, which her voice had denounced to him, by the interest which she seemed to testify in his safety, Sir Kenneth rose from his knee, and, casting a momentary glance on Edith, bowed low, and seemed about to withdraw. At the same instant, that maidenly bashfulness, which the energy of Edith's feelings had till then triumphed over, became conqueror in its turn, and she hastened from the apartment, extinguishing her lamp as she went, and leaving, in Sir Kenneth's thoughts, both mental and natural gloom behind her.

She must be obeyed, was the first distinct idea which waked him from his reverie, and he hastened to the place by which he had entered the pavilion. To pass under the canvas in the manner he had entered required time and attention, and he made a readier aperture by slitting the canvas wall with his poniard. When in the free air, he felt rather stupefied and overpowered by a conflict of sensations, than able to ascertain what was the real import of the whole. He was obliged to spur himself to action by recollecting that the commands of the Lady Edith had required haste. Even then, engaged as he was amongst tent-ropes and tents, he was compelled to move with caution until he should regain the path or avenue, aside from which the dwarf had led him, in order to escape the observation of the guards before the Queen's pavilion; and he was obliged also to move slowly, and with precaution, to avoid giving an alarm, either by falling or by the clashing of his armour. A thin cloud had obscured the moon, too, at the very instant of his leaving the tent, and Sir Kenneth had to struggle with this inconvenience at a moment when the dizziness of his head and the fullness of his heart scarce left him powers of intelligence sufficient to direct his motions.

But at once sounds came upon his ear which instantly recalled him to the full energy of his faculties. These proceeded from the Mount of Saint George. He heard first a single, fierce, angry, and savage bark, which was immediately followed by a yell of agony. No deer ever bounded with a wilder start at the voice of Roswal than did Sir Kenneth at what he feared was the death-cry of that noble hound, from whom no ordinary injury could have extracted even the slightest acknowledgment of pain. He surmounted the space which divided him from the avenue, and, having attained it, began to run towards the mount, although loaded with his mail, faster than most men could have accompanied him even if unarmed, relaxed not his pace for the steep sides of the artificial mound, and in a few minutes stood on the platform upon its summit.

The moon broke forth at this moment, and showed him that the Standard of England was vanished, that the spear on which it had floated lay broken on the ground, and beside it was his faithful hound, apparently in the agonies of death.

Lesson 136

1. Stop and think. What has just happened in the book? What do you think is going to happen next?
2. Read chapter 14. The mysterious Muslim physician, Hakim, offers healing for Sir Kenneth's dog and some advice to Sir Kenneth, "Get out of here and go to the Saracens to save your life," as well as revealing some secret plans for a marriage between Saladin and Edith.
3. As Sir Kenneth weeps for his wounded dog, who appears out of the darkness? What does that person offer to do? (Answers)
4. What advice does he give Sir Kenneth? (Answers)
5. What else does Sir Kenneth learn from Hakim? (Answers)

6. What do you think Sir Kenneth is going to do? (Answers)

Vocabulary

1. Review the words from Lesson 131.

CHAPTER XIV.

All my long arrear of honour lost,
Heap'd up in youth, and hoarded up for age.
Hath Honour's fountain then suck'd up the stream?
He hath—and hooting boys may barefoot pass,
And gather pebbles from the naked ford!
DON SEBASTIAN.

After a torrent of afflicting sensations, by which he was at first almost stunned and confounded, Sir Kenneth's first thought was to look for the authors of this violation of the English banner; but in no direction could he see traces of them. His next, which to some persons, but scarce to any who have made intimate acquaintances among the canine race, may appear strange, was to examine the condition of his faithful Roswal, mortally wounded, as it seemed, in discharging the duty which his master had been seduced to abandon. He caressed the dying animal, who, faithful to the last, seemed to forget his own pain in the satisfaction he received from his master's presence, and continued wagging his tail and licking his hand, even while by low moanings he expressed that his agony was increased by the attempts which Sir Kenneth made to withdraw from the wound the fragment of the lance or javelin with which it had been inflicted; then redoubled his feeble endearments, as if fearing he had offended his master by showing a sense of the pain to which his interference had subjected him. There was something in the display of the dying creature's attachment which mixed as a bitter ingredient with the sense of disgrace and desolation by which Sir Kenneth was oppressed. His only friend seemed removed from him, just when he had incurred the contempt and hatred of all besides. The knight's strength of mind gave way to a burst of agonized distress, and he groaned and wept aloud.

While he thus indulged his grief, a clear and solemn voice, close beside him, pronounced these words in the sonorous tone of the readers of the mosque, and in the lingua franca mutually understood by Christians and Saracens:—

"Adversity is like the period of the former and of the latter rain—cold, comfortless, unfriendly to man and to animal; yet from that season have their birth the flower and the fruit, the date, the rose, and the pomegranate."

Sir Kenneth of the Leopard turned towards the speaker, and beheld the Arabian physician, who, approaching unheard, had seated himself a little behind him cross-legged, and uttered with gravity, yet not without a tone of sympathy, the moral sentences of consolation with which the Koran and its commentators supplied him; for, in the East, wisdom is held to consist less in a display of the sage's own inventive talents, than in his ready memory and happy application of and reference to "that which is written."

Ashamed at being surprised in a womanlike expression of sorrow, Sir Kenneth dashed his tears indignantly aside, and again busied himself with his dying favourite.

"The poet hath said," continued the Arab, without noticing the knight's averted looks and sullen deportment, "the ox for the field, and the camel for the desert. Were not the hand of the leech fitter than that of the soldier to cure wounds, though less able to inflict them?"

"This patient, Hakim, is beyond thy help," said Sir Kenneth; "and, besides, he is, by thy law, an unclean animal."

"Where Allah hath deigned to bestow life, and a sense of pain and pleasure," said the physician, "it were sinful pride should the sage, whom He has enlightened, refuse to prolong existence or assuage agony. To the sage, the cure of a miserable groom, of a poor dog and of a conquering monarch, are events of little distinction. Let me examine this wounded animal."

Sir Kenneth acceded in silence, and the physician inspected and handled Roswal's wound with as much care and attention as if he had been a human being. He then took forth a case of instruments, and, by the judicious and skilful application of pincers, withdrew from the wounded shoulder the fragment of the weapon, and stopped with styptics and bandages the effusion of blood which followed; the creature all the while suffering him patiently to perform these kind offices, as if he had been aware of his kind intentions.

"The animal may be cured," said El Hakim, addressing himself to Sir Kenneth, "if you will permit me to carry him to my tent, and treat him with the care which the nobleness of his nature deserves. For know, that thy servant Adonbec is no less skilful in the race and pedigree and distinctions of good dogs and of noble steeds than in the diseases which afflict the human race."

"Take him with you," said the knight. "I bestow him on you freely, if he recovers. I owe thee a reward for attendance on my squire, and have nothing else to pay it with. For myself, I will never again wind bugle or halloo to hound!"

The Arabian made no reply, but gave a signal with a clapping of his hands, which was instantly answered by the appearance of two black slaves. He gave them his orders in Arabic, received the answer that "to hear was to obey," when, taking the animal in their arms, they removed him, without much resistance on his part; for though his eyes turned to his master, he was too weak to struggle.

"Fare thee well, Roswal, then," said Sir Kenneth—"fare thee well, my last and only friend—thou art too noble a possession to be retained by one such as I must in future call myself!—I would," he said, as the slaves retired, "that, dying as he is, I could exchange conditions with that noble animal!"

"It is written," answered the Arabian, although the exclamation had not been addressed to him, "that all creatures are fashioned for the service of man; and the master of the earth speaketh folly when he would exchange, in his impatience, his hopes here and to come for the servile condition of an inferior being."

"A dog who dies in discharging his duty," said the knight sternly, "is better than a man who survives the desertion of it. Leave me, Hakim; thou hast, on this side of miracle, the most wonderful science which man ever possessed, but the wounds of the spirit are beyond thy power."

"Not if the patient will explain his calamity, and be guided by the physician," said Adonbec el Hakim.

"Know, then," said Sir Kenneth, "since thou art so importunate, that last night the Banner of England was displayed from this mound—I was its appointed guardian—morning is now breaking—there lies the broken banner-spear, the standard itself is lost, and here sit I a living man!"

"How!" said El Hakim, examining him; "thy armour is whole—there is no blood on thy weapons, and report speaks thee one unlikely to return thus from fight. Thou hast been trained from thy post—ay, trained by the rosy cheek and black eye of one of those houris, to whom you Nazarenes vow rather such service as is due to Allah, than such love as may lawfully be rendered to forms of clay like our own. It has been thus assuredly; for so hath man ever fallen, even since the days of Sultan Adam."

"And if it were so, physician," said Sir Kenneth sullenly, "what remedy?"

"Knowledge is the parent of power," said El Hakim, "as valour supplies strength. Listen to me. Man is not as a tree, bound to one spot of earth; nor is he framed to cling to one bare rock, like the scarce animated shell-fish. Thine own Christian writings command thee, when persecuted in one city, to flee to another; and we Moslem also know that Mohammed, the Prophet of Allah, driven forth from the holy city of Mecca, found his refuge and his helpmates at Medina."

"And what does this concern me?" said the Scot.

"Much," answered the physician. "Even the sage flies the tempest which he cannot control. Use thy speed, therefore, and fly from the vengeance of Richard to the shadow of Saladin's victorious banner."

"I might indeed hide my dishonour," said Sir Kenneth ironically, "in a camp of infidel heathens, where the very phrase is unknown. But had I not better partake more fully in their reproach? Does not thy advice stretch so far as to recommend me to take the turban? Methinks I want but apostasy to consummate my infamy."

"Blaspheme not, Nazarene," said the physician sternly. "Saladin makes no converts to the law of the Prophet, save those on whom its precepts shall work conviction. Open thine eyes to the light, and the great Soldan, whose liberality is as boundless as his power, may bestow on thee a kingdom; remain blinded if thou will, and, being one whose second life is doomed to misery, Saladin will yet, for this span of present time, make thee rich and happy. But fear not that thy brows shall be bound with the turban, save at thine own free choice."

"My choice were rather," said the knight, "that my writhen features should blacken, as they are like to do, in this evening's setting sun."

"Yet thou art not wise, Nazarene," said El Hakim, "to reject this fair offer; for I have power with Saladin, and can raise thee high in his grace. Look you, my son—this Crusade, as you call your wild enterprise, is like a large dromond [The largest sort of vessels then known were termed dromond's, or dromedaries.] parting asunder in the waves. Thou thyself hast borne terms of truce from the kings and princes, whose force is here assembled, to the mighty Soldan, and knewest not, perchance, the full tenor of thine own errand."

"I knew not, and I care not," said the knight impatiently. "What avails it to me that I have been of late the envoy of princes, when, ere night, I shall be a gibbeted and dishonoured corpse?"

"Nay, I speak that it may not be so with thee," said the physician. "Saladin is courted on all sides. The combined princes of this league formed against him have made such proposals of composition and peace, as, in other circumstances, it might have become his honour to have granted to them. Others have made private offers, on their own separate account, to disjoin their forces from the camp of the Kings of Frangistan, and even to lend their arms to the defence of the standard of the Prophet. But Saladin will not be served by such treacherous and interested defection. The king of kings will treat only with the Lion King. Saladin will hold treaty with none but the Melech Ric, and with him he will treat like a prince, or fight like a champion. To Richard he will yield such conditions of his free liberality as the swords of all Europe could never compel from him by force or terror. He will permit a free pilgrimage to Jerusalem, and all the places where the Nazarenes list to worship; nay, he will so far share even his empire with his brother Richard, that he will allow Christian garrisons in the six strongest cities of Palestine, and one in Jerusalem itself, and suffer them to be under the immediate command of the officers of Richard, who, he consents, shall bear the name of King Guardian of Jerusalem. Yet further, strange and incredible as you may think it, know, Sir Knight—for to your honour I can commit even that almost incredible secret—know that Saladin will put a sacred seal on this happy union betwixt the bravest and noblest of Frangistan and Asia, by raising to the rank of his royal spouse a Christian damsel, allied in blood to King Richard, and known by the name of the Lady Edith of Plantagenet." [This may appear so extraordinary and improbable a proposition that it is necessary to say such a one was actually made. The historians, however, substitute the widowed Queen of Naples, sister of Richard, for the bride, and Saladin's brother for the bridegroom. They appear to have been ignorant of the existence of Edith of Plantagenet.—See MILL'S History of the Crusades, vol. ii., p. 61.]

"Ha!—sayest thou?" exclaimed Sir Kenneth, who, listening with indifference and apathy to the preceding part of El Hakim's speech, was touched by this last communication, as the thrill of a nerve, unexpectedly jarred, will awaken the sensation of agony, even in the torpor of palsy. Then, moderating his tone, by dint of much effort he restrained his indignation, and, veiling it under the appearance of contemptuous doubt, he prosecuted the conversation, in order to get as much knowledge as possible of the plot, as he deemed it, against the honour and happiness of her whom he loved not the less that his passion had ruined, apparently, his fortunes, at once, and his honour.—"And what Christian," he said, With tolerable calmness, "would sanction a union so unnatural as that of a Christian maiden with an unbelieving Saracen?"

"Thou art but an ignorant, bigoted Nazarene," said the Hakim. "Seest thou not how the Mohammedan princes daily intermarry with the noble Nazarene maidens in Spain, without scandal either to Moor or Christian? And the noble Soldan will, in his full confidence in the blood of Richard, permit the English maid the freedom which your Frankish manners have assigned to women. He will allow her the free exercise of her religion, seeing that, in very truth, it signifies but little to which faith females are addicted; and he will assign her such place and rank over all the women of his zenana, that she shall be in every respect his sole and absolute queen."

"What!" said Sir Kenneth, "darest thou think, Moslem, that Richard would give his kinswoman—a high-born and virtuous princess—to be, at best, the foremost concubine in the haram of a misbeliever? Know, Hakim, the meanest free Christian noble would scorn, on his child's behalf, such splendid ignominy."

"Thou errest," said the Hakim. "Philip of France, and Henry of Champagne, and others of Richard's principal allies, have heard the proposal without starting, and have promised, as far as they may, to forward an alliance that may end these wasteful wars; and the wise arch-priest of Tyre hath undertaken to break the proposal to Richard, not doubting that he shall be able to bring the plan to good issue. The Soldan's wisdom hath as yet kept his proposition secret from others, such as he of Montserrat, and the Master of the Templars, because he knows they seek to thrive by Richard's death or disgrace, not by his life or honour. Up, therefore, Sir Knight, and to horse. I will give thee a scroll which shall advance thee highly with the Soldan; and deem not that you are leaving your country, or her cause, or her religion, since the interest of the two monarchs will speedily be the same. To Saladin thy counsel will be most acceptable, since thou canst make him aware of much concerning the marriages of the Christians, the treatment of their wives, and other points of their laws and usages, which, in the course of such treaty, it much concerns him that he should know. The right hand of the Soldan grasps the treasures of the East, and it is the fountain or generosity. Or, if thou desirest it, Saladin, when allied with England, can have but little difficulty to obtain from Richard, not only thy pardon and restoration to favour, but an honourable command in the troops which may be left of the King of England's host, to maintain their joint government in Palestine. Up, then, and mount—there lies a plain path before thee."

"Hakim," said the Scottish knight, "thou art a man of peace; also thou hast saved the life of Richard of England—and, moreover, of my own poor esquire, Strauchan. I have, therefore, heard to an end a matter which, being propounded by another Moslem than thyself, I would have cut short with a blow of my dagger! Hakim, in return for thy kindness, I advise thee to see that the Saracen who shall propose to Richard a union betwixt the blood of Plantagenet and that of his accursed race do put on a helmet which is capable to endure such a blow of a battle-axe as that which struck down the gate of Acre. Certes, he will be otherwise placed beyond the reach even of thy skill."

"Thou art, then, wilfully determined not to fly to the Saracen host?" said the physician. "Yet, remember, thou stayest to certain destruction; and the writings of thy law, as well as ours, prohibit man from breaking into the tabernacle of his own life."

"God forbid!" replied the Scot, crossing himself; "but we are also forbidden to avoid the punishment which our crimes have deserved. And since so poor are thy thoughts of fidelity, Hakim, it grudges me that I have bestowed my good hound on thee, for, should he live, he will have a master ignorant of his value."

"A gift that is begrudged is already recalled," said El Hakim; "only we physicians are sworn not to send away a patient uncured. If the dog recover, he is once more yours."

"Go to, Hakim," answered Sir Kenneth; "men speak not of hawk and hound when there is but an hour of day-breaking betwixt them and death. Leave me to recollect my sins, and reconcile myself to Heaven."

"I leave thee in thine obstinacy," said the physician; "the mist hides the precipice from those who are doomed to fall over it."

He withdrew slowly, turning from time to time his head, as if to observe whether the devoted knight might not recall him either by word or signal. At last his turbaned figure was lost among the labyrinth of tents which lay extended beneath, whitening in the pale light of the dawning, before which the moonbeam had now faded away.

But although the physician Adonbec's words had not made that impression upon Kenneth which the sage desired, they had inspired the Scot with a motive for desiring life, which, dishonoured as he conceived himself to be, he was before willing to part from as from a sullied vestment no longer becoming his wear. Much that had passed betwixt himself and the hermit, besides what he had observed between the anchorite and Sheerkohf (or Ilderim), he now recalled to recollection, and tended to confirm what the Hakim had told him of the secret article of the treaty.

"The reverend impostor!" he exclaimed to himself; "the hoary hypocrite! He spoke of the unbelieving husband converted by the believing wife; and what do I know but that the traitor exhibited to the Saracen, accursed of God, the beauties of Edith Plantagenet, that the hound might judge if the princely Christian lady were fit to be admitted into the haram of a misbeliever? If I had yonder infidel Ilderim, or whatsoever he is called, again in the gripe with which I once held him fast as ever hound held hare, never again should HE at least come on errand disgraceful to the honour of Christian king or noble and virtuous maiden. But I—my hours are fast dwindling into minutes—yet, while I have life and breath, something must be done, and speedily."

He paused for a few minutes, threw from him his helmet, then strode down the hill, and took the road to King Richard's pavilion.

Lesson 137

1. Read chapter 15. King Richard sentences Sir Kenneth to death for deserting his post, and de Vaux discovers that he has some sympathy for the knight even though he is a Scot.
2. Why is King Richard so angry with his Scottish knight? (Answers)
3. Why do you think Sir Kenneth did not tell de Vaux the truth about why he left his post? (Answers)
4. Do you think Sir Kenneth will be executed? If you say no, how do you think he might escape? (Answers)

CHAPTER XV.

The feather'd songster, chanticleer,
Had wound his bugle-horn,
And told the early villager
The coming of the morn.
King Edward saw the ruddy streaks
Of light eclipse the grey,
And heard the raven's croaking throat
Proclaim the fated day.
"Thou'rt right," he said, "for, by the God
That sits enthron'd on high,
Charles Baldwin, and his fellows twain,
This day shall surely die."

CHATTERTON.

On the evening on which Sir Kenneth assumed his post, Richard, after the stormy event which disturbed its tranquillity, had retired to rest in the plenitude of confidence inspired by his unbounded courage and the superiority which he had displayed in carrying the point he aimed at in presence of the whole Christian host and its leaders, many of whom, he was aware, regarded in their secret souls the disgrace of the Austrian Duke as a triumph over themselves; so that his pride felt gratified, that in prostrating one enemy he had mortified a hundred.

Another monarch would have doubled his guards on the evening after such a scene, and kept at least a part of his troops under arms. But Coeur de Lion dismissed, upon the occasion, even his ordinary watch, and assigned to his soldiers a donative of wine to celebrate his recovery, and to drink to the Banner of Saint George; and his quarter of the camp would have assumed a character totally devoid of vigilance and military preparation, but that Sir Thomas de Vaux, the Earl of Salisbury, and other nobles, took precautions to preserve order and discipline among the revellers.

The physician attended the King from his retiring to bed till midnight was past, and twice administered medicine to him during that period, always previously observing the quarter of heaven occupied by the full moon, whose influences he declared to be most sovereign, or most baleful, to the effect of his drugs. It was three hours after midnight ere El Hakim withdrew from the royal tent, to one which had been pitched for himself and his retinue. In his way thither he visited the tent of Sir Kenneth of the Leopard, in order to see the condition of his first patient in the Christian camp, old Strauchan, as the knight's esquire was named. Inquiring there for Sir Kenneth himself, El Hakim learned on what duty he was employed, and probably this information led him to Saint George's Mount, where he found him whom he sought in the disastrous circumstances alluded to in the last chapter.

It was about the hour of sunrise, when a slow, armed tread was heard approaching the King's pavilion; and ere De Vaux, who slumbered beside his master's bed as lightly as ever sleep sat upon the eyes of a watch-dog, had time to do more than arise and say, "Who comes?" the Knight of the Leopard entered the tent, with a deep and devoted gloom seated upon his manly features.

"Whence this bold intrusion, Sir Knight?" said De Vaux sternly, yet in a tone which respected his master's slumbers.

"Hold! De Vaux," said Richard, awaking on the instant; "Sir Kenneth cometh like a good soldier to render an account of his guard. To such the general's tent is ever accessible." Then rising from his slumbering posture, and leaning on his elbow, he fixed his large bright eye upon the warrior—"Speak, Sir Scot; thou comest to tell me of a vigilant, safe, and honourable watch, dost thou not? The rustling of the folds of the Banner of England were enough to guard it, even without the body of such a knight as men hold thee."

"As men will hold me no more," said Sir Kenneth. "My watch hath neither been vigilant, safe, nor honourable. The Banner of England has been carried off."

"And thou alive to tell it!" said Richard, in a tone of derisive incredulity. "Away, it cannot be. There is not even a scratch on thy face. Why dost thou stand thus mute? Speak the truth—it is ill jesting with a king; yet I will forgive thee if thou hast lied."

"Lied, Sir King!" returned the unfortunate knight, with fierce emphasis, and one glance of fire from his eye, bright and transient as the flash from the cold and stony flint. "But this also must be endured. I have spoken the truth."

"By God and by Saint George!" said the King, bursting into fury, which, however, he instantly checked. "De Vaux, go view the spot. This fever has disturbed his brain. This cannot be. The man's courage is proof. It CANNOT be! Go speedily—or send, if thou wilt not go."

The King was interrupted by Sir Henry Neville, who came, breathless, to say that the banner was gone, and the knight who guarded it overpowered, and most probably murdered, as there was a pool of blood where the banner-spear lay shivered.

"But whom do I see here?" said Neville, his eyes suddenly resting upon Sir Kenneth.

"A traitor," said the King, starting to his feet, and seizing the curtal-axe, which was ever near his bed—"a traitor! whom thou shalt see die a traitor's death." And he drew back the weapon as in act to strike.

Colourless, but firm as a marble statue, the Scot stood before him, with his bare head uncovered by any protection, his eyes cast down to the earth, his lips scarcely moving, yet muttering probably in prayer. Opposite to him, and within the due reach for a blow, stood King Richard, his large person wrapt in the folds of his camiscia, or ample gown of linen, except where the violence of his action had flung the covering from his right arm, shoulder, and a part of his breast, leaving to view a specimen of a frame which might have merited his Saxon predecessor's epithet of Ironside.

He stood for an instant, prompt to strike; then sinking the head of the weapon towards the ground, he exclaimed, "But there was blood, Neville—there was blood upon the place. Hark thee, Sir Scot—brave thou wert once, for I have seen thee fight. Say thou hast slain two of the thieves in defence of the Standard—say but one—say thou hast struck but a good blow in our behalf, and get thee out of the camp with thy life and thy infamy!"

"You have called me liar, my Lord King," replied Kenneth firmly; "and therein, at least, you have done me wrong. Know that there was no blood shed in defence of the Standard save that of a poor hound, which, more faithful than his master, defended the charge which he deserted."

"Now, by Saint George!" said Richard, again heaving up his arm. But De Vaux threw himself between the King and the object of his vengeance, and spoke with the blunt truth of his character, "My liege, this must not be—here, nor by your hand. It is enough of folly for one night and day to have entrusted your banner to a Scot. Said I not they were ever fair and false?" [Such were the terms in which the English used to speak of their poor northern neighbours, forgetting that their own encroachments upon the independence of Scotland obliged the weaker nation to defend themselves by policy as well as force. The disgrace must be divided between Edward I. and Edward III., who enforced their domination over a free country, and the Scots, who were compelled to take compulsory oaths, without any purpose of keeping them.]

"Thou didst, De Vaux; thou wast right, and I confess it," said Richard. "I should have known him better—I should have remembered how the fox William deceived me touching this Crusade."

"My lord," said Sir Kenneth, "William of Scotland never deceived; but circumstances prevented his bringing his forces."

"Peace, shameless!" said the King; "thou sulliest the name of a prince, even by speaking it.—And yet, De Vaux, it is strange," he added, "to see the bearing of the man. Coward or traitor he must be, yet he abode the blow of Richard Plantagenet as our arm had been raised to lay knighthood on his shoulder. Had he shown the slightest sign of fear, had but a joint trembled or an eyelid quivered, I had shattered his head like a crystal goblet. But I cannot strike where there is neither fear nor resistance."

There was a pause.

"My lord," said Kenneth—

"Ha!" replied Richard, interrupting him, "hast thou found thy speech? Ask grace from Heaven, but none from me; for England is dishonoured through thy fault, and wert thou mine own and only brother, there is no pardon for thy fault."

"I speak not to demand grace of mortal man," said the Scot; "it is in your Grace's pleasure to give or refuse me time for Christian shrift—if man denies it, may God grant me the absolution which I would otherwise ask of His church! But whether I die on the instant, or half an hour hence, I equally beseech your Grace for one moment's opportunity to speak that to your royal person which highly concerns your fame as a Christian king."

"Say on," said the King, making no doubt that he was about to hear some confession concerning the loss of the Banner.

"What I have to speak," said Sir Kenneth, "touches the royalty of England, and must be said to no ears but thine own."

"Begone with yourselves, sirs," said the King to Neville and De Vaux.

The first obeyed, but the latter would not stir from the King's presence.

"If you said I was in the right," replied De Vaux to his sovereign, "I will be treated as one should be who hath been found to be right—that is, I will have my own will. I leave you not with this false Scot."

"How! De Vaux," said Richard angrily, and stamping slightly, "darest thou not venture our person with one traitor?"

"It is in vain you frown and stamp, my lord," said De Vaux; "I venture not a sick man with a sound one, a naked man with one armed in proof."

"It matters not," said the Scottish knight; "I seek no excuse to put off time. I will speak in presence of the Lord of Gilsland. He is good lord and true."

"But half an hour since," said De Vaux, with a groan, implying a mixture of sorrow and vexation, "and I had said as much for thee!"

"There is treason around you, King of England," continued Sir Kenneth.

"It may well be as thou sayest," replied Richard; "I have a pregnant example."

"Treason that will injure thee more deeply than the loss of a hundred banners in a pitched field. The—the—" Sir Kenneth hesitated, and at length continued, in a lower tone, "The Lady Edith--"

"Ha!" said the King, drawing himself suddenly into a state of haughty attention, and fixing his eye firmly on the supposed criminal; "what of her? what of her? What has she to do with this matter?"

"My lord," said the Scot, "there is a scheme on foot to disgrace your royal lineage, by bestowing the hand of the Lady Edith on the Saracen Soldan, and thereby to purchase a peace most dishonourable to Christendom, by an alliance most shameful to England."

This communication had precisely the contrary effect from that which Sir Kenneth expected. Richard Plantagenet was one of those who, in Iago's words, would not serve God because it was the devil who bade him; advice or information often affected him less according to its real import, than through the tinge which it took from the supposed character and views of those by whom it was communicated. Unfortunately, the mention of his relative's name renewed his recollection of what he had considered as extreme presumption in the Knight of the Leopard, even when he stood high in the roll of chivalry, but which, in his present condition, appeared an insult sufficient to drive the fiery monarch into a frenzy of passion.

"Silence," he said, "infamous and audacious! By Heaven, I will have thy tongue torn out with hot pincers, for mentioning the very name of a noble Christian damsel! Know, degenerate traitor, that I was already aware to what height thou hadst dared to raise thine eyes, and endured it, though it were insolence, even when thou hadst cheated us—for thou art all a deceit—into holding thee as of some name and fame. But now, with lips blistered with the confession of thine own dishonour—that thou shouldst NOW dare to name our noble kinswoman as one in whose fate thou hast part or interest! What is it to thee if she marry Saracen or Christian? What is it to thee if, in a camp where princes turn cowards by day and robbers by night—where brave knights turn to paltry deserters and traitors—what is it, I say, to thee, or any one, if I should please to ally myself to truth and to valour, in the person of Saladin?"

"Little to me, indeed, to whom all the world will soon be as nothing," answered Sir Kenneth boldly; "but were I now stretched on the rack, I would tell thee that what I have said is much to thine own conscience and thine own fame. I tell thee, Sir King, that if thou dost but in thought entertain the purpose of wedding thy kinswoman, the Lady Edith—"

"Name her not—and for an instant think not of her," said the King, again straining the curtal-axe in his gripe, until the muscles started above his brawny arm, like cordage formed by the ivy around the limb of an oak.

"Not name—not think of her!" answered Sir Kenneth, his spirits, stunned as they were by self-depression, beginning to recover their elasticity from this species of controversy. "Now, by the Cross, on which I place my hope, her name shall be the last word in my mouth, her image the last thought in my mind. Try thy boasted strength on this bare brow, and see if thou canst prevent my purpose."

"He will drive me mad!" said Richard, who, in his despite, was once more staggered in his purpose by the dauntless determination of the criminal.

Ere Thomas of Gilsland could reply, some bustle was heard without, and the arrival of the Queen was announced from the outer part of the pavilion.

"Detain her—detain her, Neville," cried the King; "this is no sight for women.—Fie, that I have suffered such a paltry traitor to chafe me thus!—Away with him, De Vaux," he whispered, "through the back entrance of our tent; coop him up close, and answer for his safe custody with your life. And hark ye—he is presently to die—let him have a ghostly father—we would not kill soul and body. And stay—hark thee—we will not have him dishonoured—he shall die knightlike, in his belt and spurs; for if his treachery be as black as hell, his boldness may match that of the devil himself."

De Vaux, right glad, if the truth may be guessed, that the scene ended without Richard's descending to the unkingly act of himself slaying an unresisting prisoner, made haste to remove Sir Kenneth by a private issue to a separate tent, where he was disarmed, and put in fetters for security. De Vaux looked on with a steady and melancholy attention, while the provost's officers, to whom Sir Kenneth was now committed, took these severe precautions.

When they were ended, he said solemnly to the unhappy criminal, "It is King Richard's pleasure that you die undegraded—without mutilation of your body, or shame to your arms—and that your head be severed from the trunk by the sword of the executioner."

"It is kind," said the knight, in a low and rather submissive tone of voice, as one who received an unexpected favour; "my family will not then hear the worst of the tale. Oh, my father—my father!"

This muttered invocation did not escape the blunt but kindly-natured Englishman, and he brushed the back of his large hand over his rough features ere he could proceed.

"It is Richard of England's further pleasure," he said at length, "that you have speech with a holy man; and I have met on the passage hither with a Carmelite friar, who may fit you for your passage. He waits without, until you are in a frame of mind to receive him."

"Let it be instantly," said the knight. "In this also Richard is kind. I cannot be more fit to see the good father at any time than now; for life and I have taken farewell, as two travellers who have arrived at the crossway, where their roads separate."

"It is well," said De Vaux slowly and solemnly; "for it irks me somewhat to say that which sums my message. It is King Richard's pleasure that you prepare for instant death."

"God's pleasure and the King's be done," replied the knight patiently. "I neither contest the justice of the sentence, nor desire delay of the execution."

De Vaux began to leave the tent, but very slowly—paused at the door, and looked back at the Scot, from whose aspect thoughts of the world seemed banished, as if he was composing himself into deep devotion. The feelings of the stout English baron were in general none of the most acute, and yet, on the present occasion, his sympathy overpowered him in an unusual manner. He came hastily back to the bundle of reeds on which the captive lay, took one of his fettered hands, and said, with as much softness as his rough voice was capable of expressing, "Sir Kenneth, thou art yet young—thou hast a father. My Ralph, whom I left training his little galloway nag on the banks of the Irthing, may one day attain thy years, and, but for last night, would to God I saw his youth bear such promise as thine! Can nothing be said or done in thy behalf?"

"Nothing," was the melancholy answer. "I have deserted my charge—the banner entrusted to me is lost. When the headsman and block are prepared, the head and trunk are ready to part company."

"Nay, then, God have mercy!" said De Vaux. "Yet would I rather than my best horse I had taken that watch myself. There is mystery in it, young man, as a plain man may descry, though he cannot see through it. Cowardice? Pshaw! No coward ever fought as I have seen thee do. Treachery? I cannot think traitors die in their treason so calmly. Thou hast been trained from thy post by some deep guile—some well-devised stratagem—the cry of some distressed maiden has caught thine ear, or the laughful look of some merry one has taken thine eye. Never blush for it; we have all been led aside by such gear. Come, I pray thee, make a clean conscience of it to me, instead of the priest. Richard is merciful when his mood is abated. Hast thou nothing to entrust to me?"

The unfortunate knight turned his face from the kind warrior, and answered, "NOTHING."

And De Vaux, who had exhausted his topics of persuasion, arose and left the tent, with folded arms, and in melancholy deeper than he thought the occasion merited—even angry with himself to find that so simple a matter as the death of a Scottish man could affect him so nearly.

"Yet," as he said to himself, "though the rough-footed knaves be our enemies in Cumberland, in Palestine one almost considers them as brethren."

Lesson 138

1. Read chapter 16. The Queen and her ladies learn of the terrible consequences of their little trick on Sir Kenneth, and the Queen is urged by her attendants to go to King Richard and plead for him to pardon the knight.
2. Draw a picture of Queen Berengaria. How old is she? (Answers)
3. What color would you not wear if you were going to try to please King Richard? (Answers)
4. Why is the Queen a little jealous of Lady Edith? (Answers)
5. Do you think that the Queen will be successful? (Answers)

Vocabulary

2. Review the words from Lesson 131.

CHAPTER XVI.

'Tis not her sense, for sure in that

There's nothing more than common;

And all her wit is only chat,

Like any other woman.

SONG.

The high-born Berengaria, daughter of Sanchez, King of Navarre, and the Queen-Consort of the heroic Richard, was accounted one of the most beautiful women of the period. Her form was slight, though exquisitely moulded. She was graced with a complexion not common in her country, a profusion of fair hair, and features so extremely juvenile as to make her look several years younger than she really was, though in reality she was not above one-and-twenty. Perhaps it was under the consciousness of this extremely juvenile appearance that she affected, or at least practised, a little childish petulance and wilfulness of manner, not unbefitting, she might suppose, a youthful bride, whose rank and age gave her a right to have her fantasies indulged and attended to. She was by nature perfectly good-humoured, and if her due share of admiration and homage (in her opinion a very large one) was duly resigned to her, no one could possess better temper or a more friendly disposition; but then, like all despots, the more power that was voluntarily yielded to her, the more she desired to extend her sway. Sometimes, even when all her ambition was gratified, she chose to be a little out of health, and a little out of spirits; and physicians had to toil their wits to invent names for imaginary maladies, while her ladies racked their imagination for new games, new head-gear, and new court-scandal, to pass away those unpleasant hours, during which their own situation was scarce to be greatly envied. Their most frequent resource for diverting this malady was some trick or piece of mischief practised upon each other; and the good Queen, in the buoyancy of her reviving spirits, was, to speak truth, rather too indifferent whether the frolics thus practised were entirely befitting her own dignity, or whether the pain which those suffered upon whom they were inflicted was not beyond the proportion of pleasure which she herself derived from them. She was confident in her husband's favour, in her high rank, and in her supposed power to make good whatever such pranks might cost others. In a word, she gambolled with the freedom of a young lioness, who is unconscious of the weight of her own paws when laid on those whom she sports with.

The Queen Berengaria loved her husband passionately, but she feared the loftiness and roughness of his character; and as she felt herself not to be his match in intellect, was not much pleased to see that he would often talk with Edith Plantagenet in preference to herself, simply because he found more amusement in her conversation, a more comprehensive understanding, and a more noble cast of thoughts and sentiments, than his beautiful consort exhibited. Berengaria did not hate Edith on this account, far less meditate her any harm; for, allowing for some selfishness, her character was, on the whole, innocent and generous. But the ladies of her train, sharpsighted in such matters, had for some time discovered that a poignant jest at the expense of the Lady Edith was a specific for relieving her Grace of England's low spirits, and the discovery saved their imagination much toil.

There was something ungenerous in this, because the Lady Edith was understood to be an orphan; and though she was called Plantagenet, and the fair Maid of Anjou, and admitted by Richard to certain privileges only granted to the royal family, and held her place in the circle accordingly, yet few knew, and none acquainted with the Court of England ventured to ask, in what exact degree of relationship she stood to Coeur de Lion. She had come with Eleanor, the celebrated Queen Mother of England, and joined Richard at Messina, as one of the ladies destined to attend on Berengaria, whose nuptials then approached. Richard treated his kinswoman with much respectful observance, and the Queen made her her most constant attendant, and, even in despite of the petty jealousy which we have observed, treated her, generally, with suitable respect.

The ladies of the household had, for a long time, no further advantage over Edith than might be afforded by an opportunity of censuring a less artfully disposed head attire or an unbecoming robe; for the lady was judged to be inferior in these mysteries. The silent devotion of the Scottish knight did not, indeed, pass unnoticed; his liveries, his cognizances, his feats of arms, his mottoes and devices, were nearly watched, and occasionally made the subject of a passing jest. But then came the pilgrimage of the Queen and her ladies to Engaddi, a journey which the Queen had undertaken under a vow for the recovery of her husband's health, and which she had been encouraged to carry into effect by the Archbishop of Tyre for a political purpose. It was then, and in the chapel at that holy place, connected from above with a Carmelite nunnery, from beneath with the cell of the anchorite, that one of the Queen's attendants remarked that secret sign of intelligence which Edith had made to her lover, and failed not instantly to communicate it to her Majesty. The Queen returned from her pilgrimage enriched with this admirable recipe against dullness or ennui; and her train was at the same time augmented by a present of two wretched dwarfs from the dethroned Queen of Jerusalem, as deformed and as crazy (the excellence of that unhappy species) as any Queen could have desired. One of Berengaria's idle amusements had been to try the effect of the sudden appearance of such ghastly and fantastic forms on the nerves of the Knight when left alone in the chapel; but the jest had been lost by the composure of the Scot and the interference of the anchorite. She had now tried another, of which the consequences promised to be more serious.

The ladies again met after Sir Kenneth had retired from the tent, and the Queen, at first little moved by Edith's angry expostulations, only replied to her by upbraiding her prudery, and by indulging her wit at the expense of the garb, nation, and, above all the poverty of the Knight of the Leopard, in which she displayed a good deal of playful malice, mingled with some humour, until Edith was compelled to carry her anxiety to her separate apartment. But when, in the morning, a female whom Edith had entrusted to make inquiry brought word that the Standard was missing, and its champion vanished, she burst into the Queen's apartment, and implored her to rise and proceed to the King's tent without delay, and use her powerful mediation to prevent the evil consequences of her jest.

The Queen, frightened in her turn, cast, as is usual, the blame of her own folly on those around her, and endeavoured to comfort Edith's grief, and appease her displeasure, by a thousand inconsistent arguments. She was sure no harm had chanced—the knight was sleeping, she fancied, after his night-watch. What though, for fear of the King's displeasure, he had deserted with the Standard—it was but a piece of silk, and he but a needy adventurer; or if he was put under warding for a time, she would soon get the King to pardon him—it was but waiting to let Richard's mood pass away.

Thus she continued talking thick and fast, and heaping together all sorts of inconsistencies, with the vain expectation of persuading both Edith and herself that no harm could come of a frolic which in her heart she now bitterly repented. But while Edith in vain strove to intercept this torrent of idle talk, she caught the eye of one of the ladies who entered the Queen's apartment. There was death in her look of affright and horror, and Edith, at the first glance of her countenance, had sunk at once on the earth, had not strong necessity and her own elevation of character enabled her to maintain at least external composure.

"Madam," she said to the Queen, "lose not another word in speaking, but save life—if, indeed," she added, her voice choking as she said it, "life may yet be saved."

"It may, it may," answered the Lady Calista. "I have just heard that he has been brought before the King. It is not yet over—but," she added, bursting into a vehement flood of weeping, in which personal apprehensions had some share, "it will soon, unless some course be taken."

"I will vow a golden candlestick to the Holy Sepulchre, a shrine of silver to our Lady of Engaddi, a pall, worth one hundred byzants, to Saint Thomas of Orthez," said the Queen in extremity.

"Up, up, madam!" said Edith; "call on the saints if you list, but be your own best saint."

"Indeed, madam," said the terrified attendant, "the Lady Edith speaks truth. Up, madam, and let us to King Richard's tent and beg the poor gentleman's life."

"I will go—I will go instantly," said the Queen, rising and trembling excessively; while her women, in as great confusion as herself, were unable to render her those duties which were indispensable to her levee. Calm, composed, only pale as death, Edith ministered to the Queen with her own hand, and alone supplied the deficiencies of her numerous attendants.

"How you wait, wenches!" said the Queen, not able even then to forget frivolous distinctions. "Suffer ye the Lady Edith to do the duties of your attendance? Seest thou, Edith, they can do nothing; I shall never be attired in time. We will send for the Archbishop of Tyre, and employ him as a mediator."

"Oh, no, no!" exclaimed Edith. "Go yourself madam; you have done the evil, do you confer the remedy."

"I will go—I will go," said the Queen; "but if Richard be in his mood, I dare not speak to him—he will kill me!"

"Yet go, gracious madam," said the Lady Calista, who best knew her mistress's temper; "not a lion, in his fury, could look upon such a face and form, and retain so much as an angry thought, far less a love-true knight like the royal Richard, to whom your slightest word would be a command."

"Dost thou think so, Calista?" said the Queen. "Ah, thou little knowest yet I will go. But see you here, what means this? You have bedizened me in green, a colour he detests. Lo you! let me have a blue robe, and—search for the ruby carcanet, which was part of the King of Cyprus's ransom; it is either in the steel casket, or somewhere else."

"This, and a man's life at stake!" said Edith indignantly; "it passes human patience. Remain at your ease, madam; I will go to King Richard. I am a party interested. I will know if the honour of a poor maiden of his blood is to be so far tampered with that her name shall be abused to train a brave gentleman from his duty, bring him within the compass of death and infamy, and make, at the same time, the glory of England a laughing-stock to the whole Christian army."

At this unexpected burst of passion, Berengaria listened with an almost stupefied look of fear and wonder. But as Edith was about to leave the tent, she exclaimed, though faintly, "Stop her, stop her!"

"You must indeed stop, noble Lady Edith," said Calista, taking her arm gently; "and you, royal madam, I am sure, will go, and without further dallying. If the Lady Edith goes alone to the King, he will be dreadfully incensed, nor will it be one life that will stay his fury."

"I will go—I will go," said the Queen, yielding to necessity; and Edith reluctantly halted to wait her movements.

They were now as speedy as she could have desired. The Queen hastily wrapped herself in a large loose mantle, which covered all inaccuracies of the toilet. In this guise, attended by Edith and her women, and preceded and followed by a few officers and men-at-arms, she hastened to the tent of her lionlike husband.

Lesson 139

1. Read chapter 17. The Queen, Lady Edith and the hermit of Engaddi try to persuade Richard to pardon Sir Kenneth, but nothing works.
2. Look back at your list of character traits for King Richard. (Chapter 6) Would you add any or subtract any based on how you have seen him behave over the last few chapters? (Answers)
3. The hermit tells King Richard that he has learned a secret from Sir Kenneth in the confessional that would persuade the King to spare his life. What is a confessional? What is the responsibility of a priest as a confessor? (Answers)
4. Why are the other ladies waiting on the Queen surprised by Lady Edith's demeanor? (Answers)
5. Draw a picture of the executioner. The author says he is "misanthropic." What does that mean? Is that a good trait for an executioner to have? (Answers)

CHAPTER XVII.

Were every hair upon his head a life,
And every life were to be supplicated
By numbers equal to those hairs quadrupled,
Life after life should out like waning stars
Before the daybreak—or as festive lamps,
Which have lent lustre to the midnight revel,
Each after each are quench'd when guests depart!

OLD PLAY

The entrance of Queen Berengaria into the interior of Richard's pavilion was withstood—in the most respectful and reverential manner indeed, but still withstood—by the chamberlains who watched in the outer tent. She could hear the stern command of the King from within, prohibiting their entrance.

"You see," said the Queen, appealing to Edith, as if she had exhausted all means of intercession in her power; "I knew it—the King will not receive us."

At the same time, they heard Richard speak to some one within:—"Go, speed thine office quickly, sirrah, for in that consists thy mercy—ten byzants if thou dealest on him at one blow. And hark thee, villain, observe if his cheek loses colour, or his eye falters; mark me the smallest twitch of the features, or wink of the eyelid. I love to know how brave souls meet death."

"If he sees my blade waved aloft without shrinking, he is the first ever did so," answered a harsh, deep voice, which a sense of unusual awe had softened into a sound much lower than its usual coarse tones.

Edith could remain silent no longer. "If your Grace," she said to the Queen, "make not your own way, I make it for you; or if not for your Majesty, for myself at least.—Chamberlain, the Queen demands to see King Richard—the wife to speak with her husband."

"Noble lady," said the officer, lowering his wand of office, "it grieves me to gainsay you, but his Majesty is busied on matters of life and death."

"And we seek also to speak with him on matters of life and death," said Edith. "I will make entrance for your Grace." And putting aside the chamberlain with one hand, she laid hold on the curtain with the other.

"I dare not gainsay her Majesty's pleasure," said the chamberlain, yielding to the vehemence of the fair petitioner; and as he gave way, the Queen found herself obliged to enter the apartment of Richard.

The Monarch was lying on his couch, and at some distance, as awaiting his further commands, stood a man whose profession it was not difficult to conjecture. He was clothed in a jerkin of red cloth, which reached scantly below the shoulders, leaving the arms bare from about half way above the elbow; and as an upper garment, he wore, when about as at present to betake himself to his dreadful office, a coat or tabard without sleeves, something like that of a herald, made of dressed bull's hide, and stained in the front with many a broad spot and speckle of dull crimson. The jerkin, and the tabard over it, reached the knee; and the nether stocks, or covering of the legs, were of the same leather which composed the tabard. A cap of rough shag served to hide the upper part of a visage which, like that of a screech owl, seemed desirous to conceal itself from light, the lower part of the face being obscured by a huge red beard, mingling with shaggy locks of the same colour. What features were seen were stern and misanthropical. The man's figure was short, strongly made, with a neck like a bull, very broad shoulders, arms of great and disproportioned length, a huge square trunk, and thick bandy legs. This truculent official leant on a sword, the blade of which was nearly four feet and a half in length, while the handle of twenty inches, surrounded by a ring of lead plummets to counterpoise the weight of such a blade, rose considerably above the man's head as he rested his arm upon its hilt, waiting for King Richard's further directions.

On the sudden entrance of the ladies, Richard, who was then lying on his couch with his face towards the entrance, and resting on his elbow as he spoke to his grisly attendant, flung himself hastily, as if displeased and surprised, to the other side, turning his back to the Queen and the females of her train, and drawing around him the covering of his couch, which, by his own choice, or more probably the flattering selection of his chamberlains, consisted of two large lions' skins, dressed in Venice with such admirable skill that they seemed softer than the hide of the deer.

Berengaria, such as we have described her, knew well—what woman knows not?—her own road to victory. After a hurried glance of undisguised and unaffected terror at the ghastly companion of her husband's secret counsels, she rushed at once to the side of Richard's couch, dropped on her knees, flung her mantle from her shoulders, showing, as they hung down at their full length, her beautiful golden tresses, and while her countenance seemed like the sun bursting through a cloud, yet bearing on its pallid front traces that its splendours have been obscured, she seized upon the right hand of the King, which, as he assumed his wonted posture, had been employed in dragging the covering of his couch, and gradually pulling it to her with a force which was resisted, though but faintly, she possessed herself of that arm, the prop of Christendom and the dread of Heathenesse, and imprisoning its strength in both her little fairy hands, she bent upon it her brow, and united to it her lips.

"What needs this, Berengaria?" said Richard, his head still averted, but his hand remaining under her control.

"Send away that man, his look kills me!" muttered Berengaria.

"Begone, sirrah," said Richard, still without looking round, "What wait'st thou for? art thou fit to look on these ladies?"

"Your Highness's pleasure touching the head," said the man.

"Out with thee, dog!" answered Richard—"a Christian burial!" The man disappeared, after casting a look upon the beautiful Queen, in her deranged dress and natural loveliness, with a smile of admiration more hideous in its expression than even his usual scowl of cynical hatred against humanity.

"And now, foolish wench, what wishest thou?" said Richard, turning slowly and half reluctantly round to his royal suppliant.

But it was not in nature for any one, far less an admirer of beauty like Richard, to whom it stood only in the second rank to glory, to look without emotion on the countenance and the tremor of a creature so beautiful as Berengaria, or to feel, without sympathy, that her lips, her brow, were on his hand, and that it was wetted by her tears. By degrees, he turned on her his manly countenance, with the softest expression of which his large blue eye, which so often gleamed with insufferable light, was capable. Caressing her fair head, and mingling his large fingers in her beautiful and dishevelled locks, he raised and tenderly kissed the cherub countenance which seemed desirous to hide itself in his hand. The robust form, the broad, noble brow and majestic looks, the naked arm and shoulder, the lions' skins among which he lay, and the fair, fragile feminine creature that kneeled by his side, might have served for a model of Hercules reconciling himself, after a quarrel, to his wife Dejanira.

"And, once more, what seeks the lady of my heart in her knight's pavilion at this early and unwonted hour?"

"Pardon, my most gracious liege—pardon!" said the Queen, whose fears began again to unfit her for the duty of intercessor.

"Pardon—for what?" asked the King.

"First, for entering your royal presence too boldly and unadvisedly—"

She stopped.

"THOU too boldly!—the sun might as well ask pardon because his rays entered the windows of some wretch's dungeon. But I was busied with work unfit for thee to witness, my gentle one; and I was unwilling, besides, that thou shouldst risk thy precious health where sickness had been so lately rife."

"But thou art now well?" said the Queen, still delaying the communication which she feared to make.

"Well enough to break a lance on the bold crest of that champion who shall refuse to acknowledge thee the fairest dame in Christendom."

"Thou wilt not then refuse me one boon—only one—only a poor life?"

"Ha!—proceed," said King Richard, bending his brows.

"This unhappy Scottish knight—" murmured the Queen.

"Speak not of him, madam," exclaimed Richard sternly; "he dies—his doom is fixed."

"Nay, my royal liege and love, 'tis but a silken banner neglected. Berengaria will give thee another broidered with her own hand, and rich as ever dallied with the wind. Every pearl I have shall go to bedeck it, and with every pearl I will drop a tear of thankfulness to my generous knight."

"Thou knowest not what thou sayest," said the King, interrupting her in anger. "Pearls! can all the pearls of the East atone for a speck upon England's honour—all the tears that ever woman's eye wept wash away a stain on Richard's fame? Go to, madam, know your place, and your time, and your sphere. At present we have duties in which you cannot be our partner."

"Thou hearest, Edith," whispered the Queen; "we shall but incense him."

"Be it so," said Edith, stepping forward.—"My lord, I, your poor kinswoman, crave you for justice rather than mercy; and to the cry of justice the ears of a monarch should be open at every time, place, and circumstance."

"Ha! our cousin Edith?" said Richard, rising and sitting upright on the side of his couch, covered with his long camiscia. "She speaks ever kinglike, and kinglike will I answer her, so she bring no request unworthy herself or me."

The beauty of Edith was of a more intellectual and less voluptuous cast than that of the Queen; but impatience and anxiety had given her countenance a glow which it sometimes wanted, and her mien had a character of energetic dignity that imposed silence for a moment even on Richard himself, who, to judge by his looks, would willingly have interrupted her.

"My lord," she said, "this good knight, whose blood you are about to spill, hath done, in his time, service to Christendom. He has fallen from his duty through a snare set for him in mere folly and idleness of spirit. A message sent to him in the name of one who—why should I not speak it?—it was in my own—induced him for an instant to leave his post. And what knight in the Christian camp might not have thus far transgressed at command of a maiden, who, poor howsoever in other qualities, hath yet the blood of Plantagenet in her veins?"

"And you saw him, then, cousin?" replied the King, biting his lips to keep down his passion.

"I did, my liege," said Edith. "It is no time to explain wherefore. I am here neither to exculpate myself nor to blame others."

"And where did you do him such a grace?"

"In the tent of her Majesty the Queen."

"Of our royal consort!" said Richard. "Now by Heaven, by Saint George of England, and every other saint that treads its crystal floor, this is too audacious! I have noticed and overlooked this warrior's insolent admiration of one so far above him, and I grudged him not that one of my blood should shed from her high-born sphere such influence as the sun bestows on the world beneath. But, heaven and earth! that you should have admitted him to an audience by night, in the very tent of our royal consort!—and dare to offer this as an excuse for his disobedience and desertion! By my father's soul, Edith, thou shalt rue this thy life long in a monastery!"

"My liege," said Edith, "your greatness licenses tyranny. My honour, Lord King, is as little touched as yours, and my Lady the Queen can prove it if she think fit. But I have already said I am not here to excuse myself or inculpate others. I ask you but to extend to one, whose fault was committed under strong temptation, that mercy, which even you yourself, Lord King, must one day supplicate at a higher tribunal, and for faults, perhaps, less venial."

"Can this be Edith Plantagenet?" said the King bitterly—"Edith Plantagenet, the wise and the noble? Or is it some lovesick woman who cares not for her own fame in comparison of the life of her paramour? Now, by King Henry's soul! little hinders but I order thy minion's skull to be brought from the gibbet, and fixed as a perpetual ornament by the crucifix in thy cell!"

"And if thou dost send it from the gibbet to be placed for ever in my sight," said Edith, "I will say it is a relic of a good knight, cruelly and unworthily done to death by" (she checked herself)—"by one of whom I shall only say, he should have known better how to reward chivalry. Minion callest thou him?" she continued, with increasing vehemence. "He was indeed my lover, and a most true one; but never sought he grace from me by look or word—contented with such humble observance as men pay to the saints. And the good—the valiant—the faithful must die for this!"

"Oh, peace, peace, for pity's sake," whispered the Queen, "you do but offend him more!"

"I care not," said Edith; "the spotless virgin fears not the raging lion. Let him work his will on this worthy knight. Edith, for whom he dies, will know how to weep his memory. To me no one shall speak more of politic alliances to be sanctioned with this poor hand. I could not—I would not—have been his bride living—our degrees were too distant. But death unites the high and the low—I am henceforward the spouse of the grave."

The King was about to answer with much anger, when a Carmelite monk entered the apartment hastily, his head and person muffled in the long mantle and hood of striped cloth of the coarsest texture which distinguished his order, and, flinging himself on his knees before the King, conjured him, by every holy word and sign, to stop the execution.

"Now, by both sword and sceptre," said Richard, "the world is leagued to drive me mad!—fools, women, and monks cross me at every step. How comes he to live still?"

"My gracious liege," said the monk, "I entreated of the Lord of Gilsland to stay the execution until I had thrown myself at your royal—"

"And he was wilful enough to grant thy request," said the King; "but it is of a piece with his wonted obstinacy. And what is it thou hast to say? Speak, in the fiend's name!"

"My lord, there is a weighty secret, but it rests under the seal of confession. I dare not tell or even whisper it; but I swear to thee by my holy order, by the habit which I wear, by the blessed Elias, our founder, even him who was translated without suffering the ordinary pangs of mortality, that this youth hath divulged to me a secret, which, if I might confide it to thee, would utterly turn thee from thy bloody purpose in regard to him."

"Good father," said Richard, "that I reverence the church, let the arms which I now wear for her sake bear witness. Give me to know this secret, and I will do what shall seem fitting in the matter. But I am no blind Bayard, to take a leap in the dark under the stroke of a pair of priestly spurs."

"My lord," said the holy man, throwing back his cowl and upper vesture, and discovering under the latter a garment of goatskin, and from beneath the former a visage so wildly wasted by climate, fast, and penance, as to resemble rather the apparition of an animated skeleton than a human face, "for twenty years have I macerated this miserable body in the caverns of Engaddi, doing penance for a great crime. Think you I, who am dead to the world, would contrive a falsehood to endanger my own soul; or that one, bound by the most sacred oaths to the contrary—one such as I, who have but one longing wish connected with earth, to wit, the rebuilding of our Christian Zion—would betray the secrets of the confessional? Both are alike abhorrent to my very soul."

"So," answered the King, "thou art that hermit of whom men speak so much? Thou art, I confess, like enough to those spirits which walk in dry places; but Richard fears no hobgoblins. And thou art he, too, as I bethink me, to whom the Christian princes sent this very criminal to open a communication with the Soldan, even while I, who ought to have been first consulted, lay on my sick-bed? Thou and they may content themselves—I will not put my neck into the loop of a Carmelite's girdle. And, for your envoy, he shall die the rather and the sooner that thou dost entreat for him."

"Now God be gracious to thee, Lord King!" said the hermit, with much emotion; "thou art setting that mischief on foot which thou wilt hereafter wish thou hadst stopped, though it had cost thee a limb. Rash, blinded man, yet forbear!"

"Away, away," cried the King, stamping; "the sun has risen on the dishonour of England, and it is not yet avenged.—Ladies and priest, withdraw, if you would not hear orders which would displease you; for, by St. George, I swear—"

"Swear NOT!" said the voice of one who had just then entered the pavilion.

"Ha! my learned Hakim," said the King, "come, I hope, to tax our generosity."

"I come to request instant speech with you—instant—and touching matters of deep interest."

"First look on my wife, Hakim, and let her know in you the preserver of her husband."

"It is not for me," said the physician, folding his arms with an air of Oriental modesty and reverence, and bending his eyes on the ground—"it is not for me to look upon beauty unveiled, and armed in its splendours."

"Retire, then, Berengaria," said the Monarch; "and, Edith, do you retire also;—nay, renew not your importunities! This I give to them that the execution shall not be till high noon. Go and be pacified—dearest Berengaria, begone.—Edith," he added, with a glance which struck terror even into the courageous soul of his kinswoman, "go, if you are wise."

The females withdrew, or rather hurried from the tent, rank and ceremony forgotten, much like a flock of wild-fowl huddled together, against whom the falcon has made a recent stoop.

They returned from thence to the Queen's pavilion to indulge in regrets and recriminations, equally unavailing. Edith was the only one who seemed to disdain these ordinary channels of sorrow. Without a sigh, without a tear, without a word of upbraiding, she attended upon the Queen, whose weak temperament showed her sorrow in violent hysterical ecstasies and passionate hypochondriacal effusions, in the course of which Edith sedulously and even affectionately attended her.

"It is impossible she can have loved this knight," said Florise to Calista, her senior in attendance upon the Queen's person. "We have been mistaken; she is but sorry for his fate, as for a stranger who has come to trouble on her account."

"Hush, hush," answered her more experienced and more observant comrade; "she is of that proud house of Plantagenet who never own that a hurt grieves them. While they have themselves been bleeding to death, under a mortal wound, they have been known to bind up the scratches sustained by their more faint-hearted comrades. Florise, we have done frightfully wrong, and, for my own part, I would buy with every jewel I have that our fatal jest had remained unacted."

Lesson 140

1. Read chapter 18 (The hermit was once a rich and powerful knight who fell in love with a person of low station, but he caused her great harm and he has felt guilty ever since.) In this chapter, King Richard is finally persuaded to spare the life of the Scottish knight by the arguments of his Muslim physician, Hakim, but he banishes Sir Kenneth from his sight forever.
2. What do we learn about the talisman in this chapter? (Answers)
3. How does Hakim use the story of the talisman to persuade King Richard to spare the life of Sir Kenneth? (Answers)
4. King Richard is sure that the Archduke of Austria stole his banner and he starts to send de Vaux to accuse him. Who prevents de Vaux from leaving the King's tent? What message does he deliver? (Answers)

CHAPTER XVIII.

This work desires a planetary intelligence

Of Jupiter and Sol; and those great spirits

Are proud, fantastical. It asks great charges

To entice them from the guiding of their spheres,

To wait on mortals.

ALBUMAZAR.

The hermit followed the ladies from the pavilion of Richard, as shadow follows a beam of sunshine when the clouds are driving over the face of the sun. But he turned on the threshold, and held up his hand towards the King in a warning, or almost a menacing posture, as he said, "Woe to him who rejects the counsel of the church, and betaketh himself to the foul divan of the infidel! King Richard, I do not yet shake the dust from my feet and depart from thy encampment; the sword falls not—but it hangs but by a hair. Haughty monarch, we shall meet again."

"Be it so, haughty priest," returned Richard, "prouder in thy goatskins than princes in purple and fine linen."

The hermit vanished from the tent, and the King continued, addressing the Arabian, "Do the dervises of the East, wise Hakim, use such familiarity with their princes?"

"The dervise," replied Adonbec, "should be either a sage or a madman; there is no middle course for him who wears the khirkhah, [Literally, the torn robe. The habit of the dervises is so called.] who watches by night, and fasts by day. Hence hath he either wisdom enough to bear himself discreetly in the presence of princes; or else, having no reason bestowed on him, he is not responsible for his own actions."

"Methinks our monks have adopted chiefly the latter character," said Richard. "But to the matter. In what can I pleasure you, my learned physician?"

"Great King," said El Hakim, making his profound Oriental obeisance, "let thy servant speak one word, and yet live. I would remind thee that thou owest—not to me, their humble instrument—but to the Intelligences, whose benefits I dispense to mortals, a life—"

"And I warrant me thou wouldst have another in requital, ha?" interrupted the King.

"Such is my humble prayer," said the Hakim, "to the great Melech Ric—even the life of this good knight, who is doomed to die, and but for such fault as was committed by the Sultan Adam, surnamed Aboulbeschar, or the father of all men."

"And thy wisdom might remind thee, Hakim, that Adam died for it," said the King, somewhat sternly, and then began to pace the narrow space of his tent with some emotion, and to talk to himself. "Why, God-a-mercy, I knew what he desired as soon as ever he entered the pavilion! Here is one poor life justly condemned to extinction, and I, a king and a soldier, who have slain thousands by my command, and scores with my own hand, am to have no power over it, although the honour of my arms, of my house, of my very Queen, hath been attainted by the culprit. By Saint George, it makes me laugh! By Saint Louis, it reminds me of Blondel's tale of an enchanted castle, where the destined knight was withstood successively in his purpose of entrance by forms and figures the most dissimilar, but all hostile to his undertaking! No sooner one sunk than another appeared! Wife—kinswoman—hermit—Hakim-each appears in the lists as soon as the other is defeated! Why, this is a single knight fighting against the whole MELEE of the tournament—ha! ha! ha!" And Richard laughed aloud; for he had, in fact, begun to change his mood, his resentment being usually too violent to be of long endurance.

The physician meanwhile looked on him with a countenance of surprise, not unmingled with contempt; for the Eastern people make no allowance for these mercurial changes in the temper, and consider open laughter, upon almost any account, as derogatory to the dignity of man, and becoming only to women and children. At length the sage addressed the King when he saw him more composed:—

"A doom of death should not issue from laughing lips. Let thy servant hope that thou hast granted him this man's life."

"Take the freedom of a thousand captives instead," said Richard; "restore so many of thy countrymen to their tents and families, and I will give the warrant instantly. This man's life can avail thee nothing, and it is forfeited."

"All our lives are forfeited," said the Hakim, putting his hand to his cap. "But the great Creditor is merciful, and exacts not the pledge rigorously nor untimely."

"Thou canst show me," said Richard, "no special interest thou hast to become intercessor betwixt me and the execution of justice, to which I am sworn as a crowned king."

"Thou art sworn to the dealing forth mercy as well as justice," said El Hakim; "but what thou seekest, great King, is the execution of thine own will. And for the concern I have in this request, know that many a man's life depends upon thy granting this boon."

"Explain thy words," said Richard; "but think not to impose upon me by false pretexts."

"Be it far from thy servant!" said Adonbec. "Know, then, that the medicine to which thou, Sir King, and many one besides, owe their recovery, is a talisman, composed under certain aspects of the heavens, when the Divine Intelligences are most propitious. I am but the poor administrator of its virtues. I dip it in a cup of water, observe the fitting hour to administer it to the patient, and the potency of the draught works the cure."

"A most rare medicine," said the King, "and a commodious! and, as it may be carried in the leech's purse, would save the whole caravan of camels which they require to convey drugs and physic stuff; I marvel there is any other in use."

"It is written," answered the Hakim, with imperturbable gravity, "'Abuse not the steed which hath borne thee from the battle.' Know that such talismans might indeed be framed, but rare has been the number of adepts who have dared to undertake the application of their virtue. Severe restrictions, painful observances, fasts, and penance, are necessary on the part of the sage who uses this mode of cure; and if, through neglect of these preparations, by his love of ease, or his indulgence of sensual appetite, he omits to cure at least twelve persons within the course of each moon, the virtue of the divine gift departs from the amulet, and both the last patient and the physician will be exposed to speedy misfortune, neither will they survive the year. I require yet one life to make up the appointed number."

"Go out into the camp, good Hakim, where thou wilt find a-many," said the King, "and do not seek to rob my headsman of HIS patients; it is unbecoming a mediciner of thine eminence to interfere with the practice of another. Besides, I cannot see how delivering a criminal from the death he deserves should go to make up thy tale of miraculous cures."

"When thou canst show why a draught of cold water should have cured thee when the most precious drugs failed," said the Hakim, "thou mayest reason on the other mysteries attendant on this matter. For myself, I am inefficient to the great work, having this morning touched an unclean animal. Ask, therefore, no further questions; it is enough that, by sparing this man's life at my request, you will deliver yourself, great King, and thy servant, from a great danger."

"Hark thee, Adonbec," replied the King, "I have no objection that leeches should wrap their words in mist, and pretend to derive knowledge from the stars; but when you bid Richard Plantagenet fear that a danger will fall upon HIM from some idle omen, or omitted ceremonial, you speak to no ignorant Saxon, or doting old woman, who foregoes her purpose because a hare crosses the path, a raven croaks, or a cat sneezes."

"I cannot hinder your doubt of my words," said Adonbec; "but yet let my Lord the King grant that truth is on the tongue of his servant—will he think it just to deprive the world, and every wretch who may suffer by the pains which so lately reduced him to that couch, of the benefit of this most virtuous talisman, rather than extend his forgiveness to one poor criminal? Bethink you, Lord King, that, though thou canst slay thousands, thou canst not restore one man to health. Kings have the power of Satan to torment, sages that of Allah to heal—beware how thou hinderest the good to humanity which thou canst not thyself render. Thou canst cut off the head, but not cure the aching tooth."

"This is over-insolent," said the King, hardening himself, as the Hakim assumed a more lofty and almost a commanding tone. "We took thee for our leech, not for our counsellor or conscience-keeper."

"And is it thus the most renowned Prince of Frangistan repays benefit done to his royal person?" said El Hakim, exchanging the humble and stooping posture in which he had hitherto solicited the King, for an attitude lofty and commanding. "Know, then," he said, "that: through every court of Europe and Asia—to Moslem and Nazarene—to knight and lady—wherever harp is heard and sword worn—wherever honour is loved and infamy detested—to every quarter of the world—will I denounce thee, Melech Ric, as thankless and ungenerous; and even the lands—if there be any such—that never heard of thy renown shall yet be acquainted with thy shame!"

"Are these terms to me, vile infidel?" said Richard, striding up to him in fury. "Art weary of thy life?"

"Strike!" said El Hakim; "thine own deed shall then paint thee more worthless than could my words, though each had a hornet's sting."

Richard turned fiercely from him, folded his arms, traversed the tent as before, and then exclaimed, "Thankless and ungenerous!—as well be termed coward and infidel! Hakim, thou hast chosen thy boon; and though I had rather thou hadst asked my crown jewels, yet I may not, kinglike, refuse thee. Take this Scot, therefore, to thy keeping; the provost will deliver him to thee on this warrant."

He hastily traced one or two lines, and gave them to the physician. "Use him as thy bond-slave, to be disposed of as thou wilt—only, let him beware how he comes before the eyes of Richard. Hark thee—thou art wise—he hath been over-bold among those in whose fair looks and weak judgments we trust our honour, as you of the East lodge your treasures in caskets of silver wire, as fine and as frail as the web of a gossamer."

"Thy servant understands the words of the King," said the sage, at once resuming the reverent style of address in which he had commenced. "When the rich carpet is soiled, the fool pointeth to the stain—the wise man covers it with his mantle. I have heard my lord's pleasure, and to hear is to obey."

"It is well," said the King; "let him consult his own safety, and never appear in my presence more. Is there aught else in which I may do thee pleasure?"

"The bounty of the King hath filled my cup to the brim," said the sage—"yea, it hath been abundant as the fountain which sprung up amid the camp of the descendants of Israel when the rock was stricken by the rod of Moussa Ben Amram."

"Ay, but," said the King, smiling, "it required, as in the desert, a hard blow on the rock ere it yielded its treasures. I would that I knew something to pleasure thee, which I might yield as freely as the natural fountain sends forth its waters."

"Let me touch that victorious hand," said the sage, "in token that if Adonbec el Hakim should hereafter demand a boon of Richard of England, he may do so, yet plead his command."

"Thou hast hand and glove upon it, man," replied Richard; "only, if thou couldst consistently make up thy tale of patients without craving me to deliver from punishment those who have deserved it, I would more willingly discharge my debt in some other form."

"May thy days be multiplied!" answered the Hakim, and withdrew from the apartment after the usual deep obeisance.

King Richard gazed after him as he departed, like one but half-satisfied with what had passed.

"Strange pertinacity," he said, "in this Hakim, and a wonderful chance to interfere between that audacious Scot and the chastisement he has merited so richly. Yet let him live! there is one brave man the more in the world. And now for the Austrian. Ho! is the Baron of Gilsland there without?"

Sir Thomas de Vaux thus summoned, his bulky form speedily darkened the opening of the pavilion, while behind him glided as a spectre, unannounced, yet unopposed, the savage form of the hermit of Engaddi, wrapped in his goatskin mantle.

Richard, without noticing his presence, called in a loud tone to the baron, "Sir Thomas de Vaux, of Lanercost and Gilsland, take trumpet and herald, and go instantly to the tent of him whom they call Archduke of Austria, and see that it be when the press of his knights and vassals is greatest around him, as is likely at this hour, for the German boar breakfasts ere he hears mass—enter his presence with as little reverence as thou mayest, and impeach him, on the part of Richard of England, that he hath this night, by his own hand, or that of others, stolen from its staff the Banner of England. Wherefore say to him our pleasure that within an hour from the time of my speaking he restore the said banner with all reverence—he himself and his principal barons waiting the whilst with heads uncovered, and without their robes of honour. And that, moreover, he pitch beside it, on the one hand, his own Banner of Austria reversed, as that which hath been dishonoured by theft and felony, and on the other, a lance, bearing the bloody head of him who was his nearest counsellor, or assistant, in this base injury. And say, that such our behests being punctually discharged we will, for the sake of our vow and the weal of the Holy Land, forgive his other forfeits."

"And how if the Duke of Austria deny all accession to this act of wrong and of felony?" said Thomas de Vaux.

"Tell him," replied the King, "we will prove it upon his body—ay, were he backed with his two bravest champions. Knightlike will we prove it, on foot or on horse, in the desert or in the field, time, place, and arms all at his own choice."

"Bethink you of the peace of God and the church, my liege lord," said the Baron of Gilsland, "among those princes engaged in this holy Crusade."

"Bethink you how to execute my commands, my liege vassal," answered Richard impatiently. "Methinks men expect to turn our purpose by their breath, as boys blow feathers to and fro. Peace of the church! Who, I prithee, minds it? The peace of the church, among Crusaders, implies war with the Saracens, with whom the princes have made truce; and the one ends with the other. And besides, see you not how every prince of them is seeking his own several ends? I will seek mine also—and that is honour. For honour I came hither; and if I may not win it upon the Saracens, at least I will not lose a jot from any respect to this paltry Duke, though he were bulwarked and buttressed by every prince in the Crusade."

De Vaux turned to obey the King's mandate, shrugging his shoulders at the same time, the bluntness of his nature being unable to conceal that its tenor went against his judgment. But the hermit of Engaddi stepped forward, and assumed the air of one charged with higher commands than those of a mere earthly potentate. Indeed, his dress of shaggy skins, his uncombed and untrimmed hair and beard, his lean, wild, and contorted features, and the almost insane fire which gleamed from under his bushy eyebrows, made him approach nearly to our idea of some seer of Scripture, who, charged with high mission to the sinful Kings of Judah or Israel, descended from the rocks and caverns in which he dwelt in abstracted solitude, to abash earthly tyrants in the midst of their pride, by discharging on them the blighting denunciations of Divine Majesty, even as the cloud discharges the lightnings with which it is fraught on the pinnacles and towers of castles and palaces. In the midst of his most wayward mood, Richard respected the church and its ministers; and though offended at the intrusion of the hermit into his tent, he greeted him with respect—at the same time, however, making a sign to Sir Thomas de Vaux to hasten on his message.

But the hermit prohibited the baron, by gesture, look, and word, to stir a yard on such an errand; and holding up his bare arm, from which the goatskin mantle fell back in the violence of his action, he waved it aloft, meagre with famine, and wealed with the blows of the discipline.

"In the name of God, and of the most holy Father, the vicegerent of the Christian Church upon earth, I prohibit this most profane, bloodthirsty, and brutal defiance betwixt two Christian princes, whose shoulders are signed with the blessed mark under which they swore brotherhood. Woe to him by whom it is broken!—Richard of England, recall the most unhallowed message thou hast given to that baron. Danger and death are nigh thee! The dagger is glancing at thy very throat!--"

"Danger and death are playmates to Richard," answered the Monarch proudly; "and he hath braved too many swords to fear a dagger."

"Danger and death are near," replied the seer, and sinking his voice to a hollow, unearthly tone, he added, "And after death the judgment!"

"Good and holy father," said Richard, "I reverence thy person and thy sanctity—"

"Reverence not me!" interrupted the hermit; "reverence sooner the vilest insect that crawls by the shores of the Dead Sea, and feeds upon its accursed slime. But reverence Him whose commands I speak—reverence Him whose sepulchre you have vowed to rescue—revere the oath of concord which you have sworn, and break not the silver cord of union and fidelity with which you have bound yourself to your princely confederates."

"Good father," said the King, "you of the church seem to me to presume somewhat, if a layman may say so much, upon the dignity of your holy character. Without challenging your right to take charge of our conscience, methinks you might leave us the charge of our own honour."

"Presume!" repeated the hermit. "Is it for me to presume, royal Richard, who am but the bell obeying the hand of the sexton—but the senseless and worthless trumpet carrying the command of him who sounds it? See, on my knees I throw myself before thee, imploring thee to have mercy on Christendom, on England, and on thyself!"

"Rise, rise," said Richard, compelling him to stand up; "it beseems not that knees which are so frequently bended to the Deity should press the ground in honour of man. What danger awaits us, reverend father? and when stood the power of England so low that the noisy bluster of this new-made Duke's displeasure should alarm her or her monarch?"

"I have looked forth from my mountain turret upon the starry host of heaven, as each in his midnight circuit uttered wisdom to another, and knowledge to the few who can understand their voice. There sits an enemy in thy House of Life, Lord King, malign at once to thy fame and thy prosperity—an emanation of Saturn, menacing thee with instant and bloody peril, and which, but thou yield thy proud will to the rule of thy duty, will presently crush thee even in thy pride."

"Away, away—this is heathen science," said the King. "Christians practise it not—wise men believe it not. Old man, thou dotest."

"I dote not, Richard," answered the hermit—"I am not so happy. I know my condition, and that some portion of reason is yet permitted me, not for my own use, but that of the Church and the advancement of the Cross. I am the blind man who holds a torch to others, though it yields no light to himself. Ask me touching what concerns the weal of Christendom, and of this Crusade, and I will speak with thee as the wisest counsellor on whose tongue persuasion ever sat. Speak to me of my own wretched being, and my words shall be those of the maniac outcast which I am."

"I would not break the bands of unity asunder among the princes of the Crusade," said Richard, with a mitigated tone and manner; "but what atonement can they render me for the injustice and insult which I have sustained?"

"Even of that I am prepared and commissioned to speak by the Council, which, meeting hastily at the summons of Philip of France, have taken measures for that effect."

"Strange," replied Richard, "that others should treat of what is due to the wounded majesty of England!"

"They are willing to anticipate your demands, if it be possible," answered the hermit. "In a body, they consent that the Banner of England be replaced on Saint George's Mount; and they lay under ban and condemnation the audacious criminal, or criminals, by whom it was outraged, and will announce a princely reward to any who shall denounce the delinquent's guilt, and give his flesh to the wolves and ravens."

"And Austria," said Richard, "upon whom rest such strong presumptions that he was the author of the deed?"

"To prevent discord in the host," replied the hermit, "Austria will clear himself of the suspicion by submitting to whatsoever ordeal the Patriarch of Jerusalem shall impose."

"Will he clear himself by the trial by combat?" said King Richard.

"His oath prohibits it," said the hermit; "and, moreover, the Council of the Princes—"

"Will neither authorize battle against the Saracens," interrupted Richard, "nor against any one else. But it is enough, father—thou hast shown me the folly of proceeding as I designed in this matter. You shall sooner light your torch in a puddle of rain than bring a spark out of a cold-blooded coward. There is no honour to be gained on Austria, and so let him pass. I will have him perjure himself, however; I will insist on the ordeal. How I shall laugh to hear his clumsy fingers hiss, as he grasps the red-hot globe of iron! Ay, or his huge mouth riven, and his gullet swelling to suffocation, as he endeavours to swallow the consecrated bread!"

"Peace, Richard," said the hermit—"oh, peace, for shame, if not for charity! Who shall praise or honour princes who insult and calumniate each other? Alas! that a creature so noble as thou art—so accomplished in princely thoughts and princely daring—so fitted to honour Christendom by thy actions, and, in thy calmer mood, to rule her by thy wisdom, should yet have the brute and wild fury of the lion mingled with the dignity and courage of that king of the forest!"

He remained an instant musing with his eyes fixed on the ground, and then proceeded—"But Heaven, that knows our imperfect nature, accepts of our imperfect obedience, and hath delayed, though not averted, the bloody end of thy daring life. The destroying angel hath stood still, as of old by the threshing-floor of Araunah the Jebusite, and the blade is drawn in his hand, by which, at no distant date, Richard, the lion-hearted, shall be as low as the meanest peasant."

"Must it, then, be so soon?" said Richard. "Yet, even so be it. May my course be bright, if it be but brief!"

"Alas! noble King," said the solitary, and it seemed as if a tear (unwonted guest) were gathering in his dry and glazened eye, "short and melancholy, marked with mortification, and calamity, and captivity, is the span that divides thee from the grave which yawns for thee—a grave in which thou shalt be laid without lineage to succeed thee—without the tears of a people, exhausted by thy ceaseless wars, to lament thee—without having extended the knowledge of thy subjects—without having done aught to enlarge their happiness."

"But not without renown, monk—not without the tears of the lady of my love! These consolations, which thou canst neither know nor estimate, await upon Richard to his grave."

"DO I not know, CAN I not estimate the value of minstrel's praise and of lady's love?" retorted the hermit, in a tone which for a moment seemed to emulate the enthusiasm of Richard himself. "King of England," he continued, extending his emaciated arm, "the blood which boils in thy blue veins is not more noble than that which stagnates in mine. Few and cold as the drops are, they still are of the blood of the royal Lusignan—of the heroic and sainted Godfrey. I am—that is, I was when in the world—Alberick Mortemar—"

"Whose deeds," said Richard, "have so often filled Fame's trumpet! Is it so?—can it be so? Could such a light as thine fall from the horizon of chivalry, and yet men be uncertain where its embers had alighted?"

"He raves," said Richard, turning from the solitary to De Vaux, as one who felt some pain from a sarcasm which yet he could not resent; then turned him calmly, and somewhat scornfully, to the anchoret, as he replied, "Thou hast found a fair bevy of daughters, reverend father, to one who hath been but few months married; but since I must put them from my roof, it were but like a father to provide them with suitable matches. Therefore, I will part with my pride to the noble canons of the church—my luxury, as thou callest it, to the monks of the rule—and my bloodthirstiness to the Knights of the Temple."

"O heart of steel, and hand of iron," said the anchoret, "upon whom example, as well as advice, is alike thrown away! Yet shalt thou be spared for a season, in case it so be thou shouldst turn, and do that which is acceptable in the sight of Heaven. For me I must return to my place. Kyrie Eleison! I am he through whom the rays of heavenly grace dart like those of the sun through a burning-glass, concentrating them on other objects, until they kindle and blaze, while the glass itself remains cold and uninfluenced. Kyrie Eleison!—the poor must be called, for the rich have refused the banquet—Kyrie Eleison!"

So saying, he burst from the tent, uttering loud cries.

"A mad priest!" said Richard, from whose mind the frantic exclamations of the hermit had partly obliterated the impression produced by the detail of his personal history and misfortunes.

"After him, De Vaux, and see he comes to no harm; for, Crusaders as we are, a juggler hath more reverence amongst our varlets than a priest or a saint, and they may, perchance, put some scorn upon him."

The knight obeyed, and Richard presently gave way to the thoughts which the wild prophecy of the monk had inspired. "To die early—without lineage—without lamentation! A heavy sentence, and well that it is not passed by a more competent judge. Yet the Saracens, who are accomplished in mystical knowledge, will often maintain that He, in whose eyes the wisdom of the sage is but as folly, inspires wisdom and prophecy into the seeming folly of the madman. Yonder hermit is said to read the stars, too, an art generally practised in these lands, where the heavenly host was of yore the object of idolatry. I would I had asked him touching the loss of my banner; for not the blessed Tishbite, the founder of his order, could seem more wildly rapt out of himself, or speak with a tongue more resembling that of a prophet.—How now, De Vaux, what news of the mad priest?"

"Mad priest, call you him, my lord?" answered De Vaux. "Methinks he resembles more the blessed Baptist himself, just issued from the wilderness. He has placed himself on one of the military engines, and from thence he preaches to the soldiers as never man preached since the time of Peter the Hermit. The camp, alarmed by his cries, crowd around him in thousands; and breaking off every now and then from the main thread of his discourse, he addresses the several nations, each in their own language, and presses upon each the arguments best qualified to urge them to perseverance in the delivery of Palestine."

"By this light, a noble hermit!" said King Richard. "But what else could come from the blood of Godfrey? HE despair of safety, because he hath in former days lived PAR AMOURS? I will have the Pope send him an ample remission, and I would not less willingly be intercessor had his BELLE AMIE been an abbess."

As he spoke, the Archbishop of Tyre craved audience, for the purpose of requesting Richard's attendance, should his health permit, on a secret conclave of the chiefs of the Crusade, and to explain to him the military and political incidents which had occurred during his illness.

Lesson 141

1. Read chapter 19. Richard is urged by the Archbishop of Tyre, who also informs him of the possible marriage of the Soldan to his cousin Edith, to attend a meeting of the council of the Crusaders where he makes amends with most of the other leaders and somehow persuades them to give the Crusade one more chance.
2. Unusual vocabulary:
    - Paynim - a pagan, a non-Christian
    - Paternoster - our Father, the Lord's prayer
3. Who comes to visit King Richard? What is his errand? (Answers)
4. What does the Master of the Templars accuse Richard of? (Answers)
5. How does King Richard respond? (Answers)

6. How does King Richard hold onto his temper? (Answers)
7. What are the plans of the Marquis and the Templar for King Richard? (Answers)
8. "Yet and but," said the Templar, "are words for fools; wise men neither hesitate nor retract - they resolve and they execute." What does this mean? What do wise men do and not do? (Answers)

CHAPTER XIX.

Must we then sheathe our still victorious sword;
Turn back our forward step, which ever trod
O'er foemen's necks the onward path of glory;
Unclasp the mail, which with a solemn vow,
In God's own house, we hung upon our shoulders—
That vow, as unaccomplish'd as the promise
Which village nurses make to still their children,
And after think no more of?
THE CRUSADE, A TRAGEDY.

The Archbishop of Tyre was an emissary well chosen to communicate to Richard tidings, which from another voice the lion-hearted King would not have brooked to hear without the most unbounded explosions of resentment. Even this sagacious and reverend prelate found difficulty in inducing him to listen to news which destroyed all his hopes of gaining back the Holy Sepulchre by force of arms, and acquiring the renown which the universal all-hail of Christendom was ready to confer upon him as the Champion of the Cross.

But, by the Archbishop's report, it appeared that Saladin was assembling all the force of his hundred tribes, and that the monarchs of Europe, already disgusted from various motives with the expedition, which had proved so hazardous, and was daily growing more so, had resolved to abandon their purpose. In this they were countenanced by the example of Philip of France, who, with many protestations of regard, and assurances that he would first see his brother of England in safety, declared his intention to return to Europe. His great vassal, the Earl of Champagne, had adopted the same resolution; and it could not excite surprise that Leopold of Austria, affronted as he had been by Richard, was glad to embrace an opportunity of deserting a cause in which his haughty opponent was to be considered as chief. Others announced the same purpose; so that it was plain that the King of England was to be left, if he chose to remain, supported only by such volunteers as might, under such depressing circumstances, join themselves to the English army, and by the doubtful aid of Conrade of Montserrat and the military orders of the Temple and of Saint John, who, though they were sworn to wage battle against the Saracens, were at least equally jealous of any European monarch achieving the conquest of Palestine, where, with shortsighted and selfish policy, they proposed to establish independent dominions of their own.

It needed not many arguments to show Richard the truth of his situation; and indeed, after his first burst of passion, he sat him calmly down, and with gloomy looks, head depressed, and arms folded on his bosom, listened to the Archbishop's reasoning on the impossibility of his carrying on the Crusade when deserted by his companions. Nay, he forbore interruption, even when the prelate ventured, in measured terms, to hint that Richard's own impetuosity had been one main cause of disgusting the princes with the expedition.

"CONFITEOR," answered Richard, with a dejected look, and something of a melancholy smile—"I confess, reverend father, that I ought on some accounts to sing CULPA MEA. But is it not hard that my frailties of temper should be visited with such a penance—that, for a burst or two of natural passion, I should be doomed to see fade before me ungathered such a rich harvest of glory to God and honour to chivalry? But it shall NOT fade. By the soul of the Conqueror, I will plant the Cross on the towers of Jerusalem, or it shall be planted over Richard's grave!"

"Thou mayest do it," said the prelate, "yet not another drop of Christian blood be shed in the quarrel."

"Ah, you speak of compromise, Lord Prelate; but the blood of the infidel hounds must also cease to flow," said Richard.

"There will be glory enough," replied the Archbishop, "in having extorted from Saladin, by force of arms, and by the respect inspired by your fame, such conditions as at once restore the Holy Sepulchre, open the Holy Land to pilgrims, secure their safety by strong fortresses, and, stronger than all, assure the safety of the Holy City, by conferring on Richard the title of King Guardian of Jerusalem."

"How!" said Richard, his eyes sparkling with unusual light. "I—I—I the King Guardian of the Holy City! Victory itself, but that it is victory, could not gain more—scarce so much, when won with unwilling and disunited forces. But Saladin still proposes to retain his interest in the Holy Land?"

"As a joint sovereign, the sworn ally," replied the prelate, "of the mighty Richard—his relative, if it may be permitted, by marriage."

"By marriage!" said Richard, surprised, yet less so than the prelate had expected. "Ha!—ay—Edith Plantagenet. Did I dream this? or did some one tell me? My head is still weak from this fever, and has been agitated. Was it the Scot, or the Hakim, or yonder holy hermit, that hinted such a wild bargain?"

"The hermit of Engaddi, most likely," said the Archbishop, "for he hath toiled much in this matter; and since the discontent of the princes has became apparent, and a separation of their forces unavoidable, he hath had many consultations, both with Christian and pagan, for arranging such a pacification as may give to Christendom, at least in part, the objects of this holy warfare."

"My kinswoman to an infidel—ha!" exclaimed Richard, as his eyes began to sparkle.

The prelate hastened to avert his wrath.

"The Pope's consent must doubtless be first attained, and the holy hermit, who is well known at Rome, will treat with the holy Father."

"How?—without our consent first given?" said the King.

"Surely no," said the Bishop, in a quieting and insinuating tone of voice—"only with and under your especial sanction."

"My sanction to marry my kinswoman to an infidel!" said Richard; yet he spoke rather in a tone of doubt than as distinctly reprobating the measure proposed. "Could I have dreamed of such a composition when I leaped upon the Syrian shore from the prow of my galley, even as a lion springs on his prey! And now—But proceed—I will hear with patience."

Equally delighted and surprised to find his task so much easier than he had apprehended, the Archbishop hastened to pour forth before Richard the instances of such alliances in Spain—not without countenance from the Holy See; the incalculable advantages which all Christendom would derive from the union of Richard and Saladin by a bond so sacred; and, above all, he spoke with great vehemence and unction on the probability that Saladin would, in case of the proposed alliance, exchange his false faith for the true one.

"Hath the Soldan shown any disposition to become Christian?" said Richard. "If so, the king lives not on earth to whom I would grant the hand of a kinswoman, ay, or sister, sooner than to my noble Saladin—ay, though the one came to lay crown and sceptre at her feet, and the other had nothing to offer but his good sword and better heart!"

"Saladin hath heard our Christian teachers," said the Bishop, somewhat evasively—"my unworthy self, and others—and as he listens with patience, and replies with calmness, it can hardly be but that he be snatched as a brand from the burning. MAGNA EST VERITAS, ET PREVALEBIT! moreover, the hermit of Engaddi, few of whose words have fallen fruitless to the ground, is possessed fully with the belief that there is a calling of the Saracens and the other heathen approaching, to which this marriage shall be matter of induction. He readeth the course of the stars; and dwelling, with maceration of the flesh, in those divine places which the saints have trodden of old, the spirit of Elijah the Tishbite, the founder of his blessed order, hath been with him as it was with the prophet Elisha, the son of Shaphat, when he spread his mantle over him."

King Richard listened to the Prelate's reasoning with a downcast brow and a troubled look.

"I cannot tell," he said, "How, it is with me, but methinks these cold counsels of the Princes of Christendom have infected me too with a lethargy of spirit. The time hath been that, had a layman proposed such alliance to me, I had struck him to earth—if a churchman, I had spit at him as a renegade and priest of Baal; yet now this counsel sounds not so strange in mine ear. For why should I not seek for brotherhood and alliance with a Saracen, brave, just, generous—who loves and honours a worthy foe, as if he were a friend—whilst the Princes of Christendom shrink from the side of their allies, and forsake the cause of Heaven and good knighthood? But I will possess my patience, and will not think of them. Only one attempt will I make to keep this gallant brotherhood together, if it be possible; and if I fail, Lord Archbishop, we will speak together of thy counsel, which, as now, I neither accept nor altogether reject. Wend we to the Council, my lord—the hour calls us. Thou sayest Richard is hasty and proud—thou shalt see him humble himself like the lowly broom-plant from which he derives his surname."

With the assistance of those of his privy chamber, the King then hastily robed himself in a doublet and mantle of a dark and uniform colour; and without any mark of regal dignity, excepting a ring of gold upon his head, he hastened with the Archbishop of Tyre to attend the Council, which waited but his presence to commence its sitting.

The pavilion of the Council was an ample tent, having before it the large Banner of the Cross displayed, and another, on which was portrayed a female kneeling, with dishevelled hair and disordered dress, meant to represent the desolate and distressed Church of Jerusalem, and bearing the motto, AFFLICTAE SPONSAE NE OBLIVISCARIS. Warders, carefully selected, kept every one at a distance from the neighbourhood of this tent, lest the debates, which were sometimes of a loud and stormy character, should reach other ears than those they were designed for.

Here, therefore, the princes of the Crusade were assembled awaiting Richard's arrival. And even the brief delay which was thus interposed was turned to his disadvantage by his enemies, various instances being circulated of his pride and undue assumption of superiority, of which even the necessity of the present short pause was quoted as an instance. Men strove to fortify each other in their evil opinion of the King of England, and vindicated the offence which each had taken, by putting the most severe construction upon circumstances the most trifling; and all this, perhaps, because they were conscious of an instinctive reverence for the heroic monarch, which it would require more than ordinary efforts to overcome.

They had settled, accordingly, that they should receive him on his entrance with slight notice, and no more respect than was exactly necessary to keep within the bounds of cold ceremonial. But when they beheld that noble form, that princely countenance, somewhat pale from his late illness—the eye which had been called by minstrels the bright star of battle and victory—when his feats, almost surpassing human strength and valour, rushed on their recollection, the Council of Princes simultaneously arose—even the jealous King of France and the sullen and offended Duke of Austria—arose with one consent, and the assembled princes burst forth with one voice in the acclamation, "God save King Richard of England! Long life to the valiant Lion's-heart!"

With a countenance frank and open as the summer sun when it rises, Richard distributed his thanks around, and congratulated himself on being once more among his royal brethren of the Crusade.

"Some brief words he desired to say," such was his address to the assembly, "though on a subject so unworthy as himself, even at the risk of delaying for a few minutes their consultations for the weal of Christendom and the advancement of their holy enterprise."

The assembled princes resumed their seats, and there was a profound silence.

"This day," continued the King of England, "is a high festival of the church, and it well becomes Christian men, at such a tide, to reconcile themselves with their brethren, and confess their faults to each other. Noble princes and fathers of this holy expedition, Richard is a soldier—his hand is ever readier than his tongue—and his tongue is but too much used to the rough language of his trade. But do not, for Plantagenet's hasty speeches and ill-considered actions, forsake the noble cause of the redemption of Palestine—do not throw away earthly renown and eternal salvation, to be won here if ever they can be won by man, because the act of a soldier may have been hasty, and his speech as hard as the iron which he has worn from childhood. Is Richard in default to any of you, Richard will make compensation both by word and action.—Noble brother of France, have I been so unlucky as to offend you?"

"The Majesty of France has no atonement to seek from that of England," answered Philip, with kingly dignity, accepting, at the same time, the offered hand of Richard; "and whatever opinion I may adopt concerning the prosecution of this enterprise will depend on reasons arising out of the state of my own kingdom—certainly on no jealousy or disgust at my royal and most valorous brother."

"Austria," said Richard, walking up to the Archduke, with a mixture of frankness and dignity, while Leopold arose from his seat, as if involuntarily, and with the action of an automaton, whose motions depended upon some external impulse—"Austria thinks he hath reason to be offended with England; England, that he hath cause to complain of Austria. Let them exchange forgiveness, that the peace of Europe and the concord of this host may remain unbroken. We are now joint supporters of a more glorious banner than ever blazed before an earthly prince, even the Banner of Salvation. Let not, therefore, strife be betwixt us for the symbol of our more worldly dignities; but let Leopold restore the pennon of England, if he has it in his power, and Richard will say, though from no motive save his love for Holy Church, that he repents him of the hasty mood in which he did insult the standard of Austria."

The Archduke stood still, sullen and discontented, with his eyes fixed on the floor, and his countenance lowering with smothered displeasure, which awe, mingled with awkwardness, prevented his giving vent to in words.

The Patriarch of Jerusalem hastened to break the embarrassing silence, and to bear witness for the Archduke of Austria that he had exculpated himself, by a solemn oath, from all knowledge, direct or indirect, of the aggression done to the Banner of England.

"Then we have done the noble Archduke the greater wrong," said Richard; "and craving his pardon for imputing to him an outrage so cowardly, we extend our hand to him in token of renewed peace and amity. But how is this? Austria refuses our uncovered hand, as he formerly refused our mailed glove? What! are we neither to be his mate in peace nor his antagonist in war? Well, let it be so. We will take the slight esteem in which he holds us as a penance for aught which we may have done against him in heat of blood, and will therefore hold the account between us cleared."

So saying, he turned from the Archduke with an air rather of dignity than scorn, leaving the Austrian apparently as much relieved by the removal of his eye as is a sullen and truant schoolboy when the glance of his severe pedagogue is withdrawn.

"Noble Earl of Champagne—princely Marquis of Montserrat—valiant Grand Master of the Templars—I am here a penitent in the confessional. Do any of you bring a charge or claim amends from me?"

"I know not on what we could ground any," said the smooth-tongued Conrade, "unless it were that the King of England carries off from his poor brothers of the war all the fame which they might have hoped to gain in the expedition."

"My charge, if I am called on to make one," said the Master of the Templars, "is graver and deeper than that of the Marquis of Montserrat. It may be thought ill to beseem a military monk such as I to raise his voice where so many noble princes remain silent; but it concerns our whole host, and not least this noble King of England, that he should hear from some one to his face those charges which there are enow to bring against him in his absence. We laud and honour the courage and high achievements of the King of England; but we feel aggrieved that he should on all occasions seize and maintain a precedence and superiority over us, which it becomes not independent princes to submit to. Much we might yield of our free will to his bravery, his zeal, his wealth, and his power; but he who snatches all as matter of right, and leaves nothing to grant out of courtesy and favour, degrades us from allies into retainers and vassals, and sullies in the eyes of our soldiers and subjects the lustre of our authority, which is no longer independently exercised. Since the royal Richard has asked the truth from us, he must neither be surprised nor angry when he hears one, to whom worldly pomp is prohibited, and secular authority is nothing, saving so far as it advances the prosperity of God's Temple, and the prostration of the lion which goeth about seeking whom he may devour—when he hears, I say, such a one as I tell him the truth in reply to his question; which truth, even while I speak it, is, I know, confirmed by the heart of every one who hears me, however respect may stifle their voices."

Richard coloured very highly while the Grand Master was making this direct and unvarnished attack upon his conduct, and the murmur of assent which followed it showed plainly that almost all who were present acquiesced in the justice of the accusation. Incensed, and at the same time mortified, he yet foresaw that to give way to his headlong resentment would be to give the cold and wary accuser the advantage over him which it was the Templar's principal object to obtain. He therefore, with a strong effort, remained silent till he had repeated a pater noster, being the course which his confessor had enjoined him to pursue when anger was likely to obtain dominion over him. The King then spoke with composure, though not without an embittered tone, especially at the outset:—

"And is it even so? And are our brethren at such pains to note the infirmities of our natural temper, and the rough precipitance of our zeal, which may sometimes have urged us to issue commands when there was little time to hold council? I could not have thought that offences, casual and unpremeditated like mine, could find such deep root in the hearts of my allies in this most holy cause; that for my sake they should withdraw their hands from the plough when the furrow was near the end—for my sake turn aside from the direct path to Jerusalem, which their swords have opened. I vainly thought that my small services might have outweighed my rash errors—that if it were remembered that I pressed to the van in an assault, it would not be forgotten that I was ever the last in the retreat—that, if I elevated my banner upon conquered fields of battle, it was all the advantage that I sought, while others were dividing the spoil. I may have called the conquered city by my name, but it was to others that I yielded the dominion. If I have been headstrong in urging bold counsels, I have not, methinks, spared my own blood or my people's in carrying them into as bold execution; or if I have, in the hurry of march or battle, assumed a command over the soldiers of others, such have been ever treated as my own when my wealth purchased the provisions and medicines which their own sovereigns could not procure. But it shames me to remind you of what all but myself seem to have forgotten. Let us rather look forward to our future measures; and believe me, brethren," he continued, his face kindling with eagerness, "you shall not find the pride, or the wrath, or the ambition of Richard a stumbling-block of offence in the path to which religion and glory summon you as with the trumpet of an archangel. Oh, no, no! never would I survive the thought that my frailties and infirmities had been the means to sever this goodly fellowship of assembled princes. I would cut off my left hand with my right, could my doing so attest my sincerity. I will yield up, voluntarily, all right to command in the host—even mine own liege subjects. They shall be led by such sovereigns as you may nominate; and their King, ever but too apt to exchange the leader's baton for the adventurer's lance, will serve under the banner of Beau-Seant among the Templars—ay, or under that of Austria, if Austria will name a brave man to lead his forces. Or if ye are yourselves a-weary of this war, and feel your armour chafe your tender bodies, leave but with Richard some ten or fifteen thousand of your soldiers to work out the accomplishment of your vow; and when Zion is won," he exclaimed, waving his hand aloft, as if displaying the standard of the Cross over Jerusalem—"when Zion is won, we will write upon her gates, NOT the name of Richard Plantagenet, but of those generous princes who entrusted him with the means of conquest!"

The rough eloquence and determined expression of the military monarch at once roused the drooping spirits of the Crusaders, reanimated their devotion, and, fixing their attention on the principal object of the expedition, made most of them who were present blush for having been moved by such petty subjects of complaint as had before engrossed them. Eye caught fire from eye, voice lent courage to voice. They resumed, as with one accord, the war-cry with which the sermon of Peter the Hermit was echoed back, and shouted aloud, "Lead us on, gallant Lion's-heart; none so worthy to lead where brave men follow. Lead us on—to Jerusalem—to Jerusalem! It is the will of God—it is the will of God! Blessed is he who shall lend an arm to its fulfilment!"

The shout, so suddenly and generally raised, was heard beyond the ring of sentinels who guarded the pavilion of Council, and spread among the soldiers of the host, who, inactive and dispirited by disease and climate, had begun, like their leaders, to droop in resolution; but the reappearance of Richard in renewed vigour, and the well-known shout which echoed from the assembly of the princes, at once rekindled their enthusiasm, and thousands and tens of thousands answered with the same shout of "Zion, Zion! War, war! Instant battle with the infidels! It is the will of God—it is the will of God!"

The acclamations from without increased in their turn the enthusiasm which prevailed within the pavilion. Those who did not actually catch the flame were afraid—at least for the time—to seem colder than others. There was no more speech except of a proud advance towards Jerusalem upon the expiry of the truce, and the measures to be taken in the meantime for supplying and recruiting the army. The Council broke up, all apparently filled with the same enthusiastic purpose—which, however, soon faded in the bosom of most, and never had an existence in that of others.

Of the latter class were the Marquis Conrade and the Grand Master of the Templars, who retired together to their quarters ill at ease, and malcontent with the events of the day.

"I ever told it to thee," said the latter, with the cold, sardonic expression peculiar to him, "that Richard would burst through the flimsy wiles you spread for him, as would a lion through a spider's web. Thou seest he has but to speak, and his breath agitates these fickle fools as easily as the whirlwind catcheth scattered straws, and sweeps them together, or disperses them at its pleasure."

"When the blast has passed away," said Conrade, "the straws, which it made dance to its pipe, will settle to earth again."

"But knowest thou not besides," said the Templar, "that it seems, if this new purpose of conquest shall be abandoned and pass away, and each mighty prince shall again be left to such guidance as his own scanty brain can supply, Richard may yet probably become King of Jerusalem by compact, and establish those terms of treaty with the Soldan which thou thyself thought'st him so likely to spurn at?"

"Now, by Mahound and Termagaunt, for Christian oaths are out of fashion," said Conrade, "sayest thou the proud King of England would unite his blood with a heathen Soldan? My policy threw in that ingredient to make the whole treaty an abomination to him. As bad for us that he become our master by an agreement, as by victory."

"Thy policy hath ill calculated Richard's digestion," answered the Templar; "I know his mind by a whisper from the Archbishop. And then thy master-stroke respecting yonder banner—it has passed off with no more respect than two cubits of embroidered silk merited. Marquis Conrade, thy wit begins to halt; I will trust thy finespun measures no longer, but will try my own. Knowest thou not the people whom the Saracens call Charegites?"

"Surely," answered the Marquis; "they are desperate and besotted enthusiasts, who devote their lives to the advancement of religion—-somewhat like Templars, only they are never known to pause in the race of their calling."

"Jest not," answered the scowling monk. "Know that one of these men has set down in his bloody vow the name of the Island Emperor yonder, to be hewn down as the chief enemy of the Moslem faith."

"A most judicious paynim," said Conrade. "May Mohammed send him his paradise for a reward!"

"He was taken in the camp by one of our squires, and in private examination frankly avowed his fixed and determined purpose to me," said the Grand Master.

"Now the heavens pardon them who prevented the purpose of this most judicious Charegite!" answered Conrade.

"He is my prisoner," added the Templar, "and secluded from speech with others, as thou mayest suppose; but prisons have been broken—"

"Chains left unlocked, and captives have escaped," answered the Marquis. "It is an ancient saying, no sure dungeon but the grave."

"When loose, he resumes his quest," continued the military priest; "for it is the nature of this sort of blood hound never to quit the suit of the prey he has once scented."

"Say no more of it," said the Marquis; "I see thy policy—it is dreadful, but the emergency is imminent."

"I only told thee of it," said the Templar, "that thou mayest keep thyself on thy guard; for the uproar will be dreadful, and there is no knowing on whom the English may vent their rage. Ay, and there is another risk. My page knows the counsels of this Charegite," he continued; "and, moreover, he is a peevish, self-willed fool, whom I would I were rid of, as he thwarts me by presuming to see with his own eyes, not mine. But our holy order gives me power to put a remedy to such inconvenience. Or stay—the Saracen may find a good dagger in his cell, and I warrant you he uses it as he breaks forth, which will be of a surety so soon as the page enters with his food."

"It will give the affair a colour," said Conrade; "and yet—"

"YET and BUT," said the Templar, "are words for fools; wise men neither hesitate nor retract—they resolve and they execute."

Lesson 142

1. Read chapter 20. After King Richard has visited the Queen and her ladies, he returns to his tent to find that the Soldan has sent him a Nubian slave, who appears to be mute, to attend him; meanwhile, King Richard's guards are being entertained by a marabout, who dances and does many foolish things.
2. Unusual Vocabulary:
    - Soldan - We generally use the word Sultan, the leader of the Muslims; at this time his name was Saladin.
    - Marabout - a Muslim hermit or holy man
    - Nubian - a black-skinned African
3. Why does Queen Beregania say she is angry with the King. (Answers)
4. Why does the Soldan say that he has sent Richard this slave? (Answers)
5. Richard's guards persuade the marabout to drink alcohol. Why is this disrespectful? What does the marabout do? (Answers)
6. How are you feeling about this marabout? (Answers)

CHAPTER XX.

When beauty leads the lion in her toils,
Such are her charms, he dare not raise his mane,
Far less expand the terror of his fangs.

So great Alcides made his club a distaff,

And spun to please fair Omphale.

ANONYMOUS.

Richard, the unsuspicious object of the dark treachery detailed in the closing part of the last chapter, having effected, for the present at least, the triumphant union of the Crusading princes in a resolution to prosecute the war with vigour, had it next at heart to establish tranquillity in his own family; and, now that he could judge more temperately, to inquire distinctly into the circumstances leading to the loss of his banner, and the nature and the extent of the connection betwixt his kinswoman Edith and the banished adventurer from Scotland.

Accordingly, the Queen and her household were startled with a visit from Sir Thomas de Vaux, requesting the present attendance of the Lady Calista of Montfaucon, the Queen's principal bower-woman, upon King Richard.

"What am I to say, madam?" said the trembling attendant to the Queen, "He will slay us all."

"Nay, fear not, madam," said De Vaux. "His Majesty hath spared the life of the Scottish knight, who was the chief offender, and bestowed him upon the Moorish physician. He will not be severe upon a lady, though faulty."

"Devise some cunning tale, wench," said Berengaria. "My husband hath too little time to make inquiry into the truth."

"Tell the tale as it really happened," said Edith, "lest I tell it for thee."

"With humble permission of her Majesty," said De Vaux, "I would say Lady Edith adviseth well; for although King Richard is pleased to believe what it pleases your Grace to tell him, yet I doubt his having the same deference for the Lady Calista, and in this especial matter."

"The Lord of Gilsland is right," said the Lady Calista, much agitated at the thoughts of the investigation which was to take place; "and besides, if I had presence of mind enough to forge a plausible story, beshrew me if I think I should have the courage to tell it."

In this candid humour, the Lady Calista was conducted by De Vaux to the King, and made, as she had proposed, a full confession of the decoy by which the unfortunate Knight of the Leopard had been induced to desert his post; exculpating the Lady Edith, who, she was aware, would not fail to exculpate herself, and laying the full burden on the Queen, her mistress, whose share of the frolic, she well knew, would appear the most venial in the eyes of Coeur de Lion. In truth, Richard was a fond, almost a uxorious husband. The first burst of his wrath had long since passed away, and he was not disposed severely to censure what could not now be amended. The wily Lady Calista, accustomed from her earliest childhood to fathom the intrigues of a court, and watch the indications of a sovereign's will, hastened back to the Queen with the speed of a lapwing, charged with the King's commands that she should expect a speedy visit from him; to which the bower-lady added a commentary founded on her own observation, tending to show that Richard meant just to preserve so much severity as might bring his royal consort to repent of her frolic, and then to extend to her and all concerned his gracious pardon.

"Sits the wind in that corner, wench?" said the Queen, much relieved by this intelligence. "Believe me that, great commander as he is, Richard will find it hard to circumvent us in this matter, and that, as the Pyrenean shepherds are wont to say in my native Navarre, Many a one comes for wool, and goes back shorn."

Having possessed herself of all the information which Calista could communicate, the royal Berengaria arrayed herself in her most becoming dress, and awaited with confidence the arrival of the heroic Richard.

He arrived, and found himself in the situation of a prince entering an offending province, in the confidence that his business will only be to inflict rebuke, and receive submission, when he unexpectedly finds it in a state of complete defiance and insurrection. Berengaria well knew the power of her charms and the extent of Richard's affection, and felt assured that she could make her own terms good, now that the first tremendous explosion of his anger had expended itself without mischief. Far from listening to the King's intended rebuke, as what the levity of her conduct had justly deserved, she extenuated, nay, defended as a harmless frolic, that which she was accused of. She denied, indeed, with many a pretty form of negation, that she had directed Nectabanus absolutely to entice the knight farther than the brink of the Mount on which he kept watch—and, indeed, this was so far true, that she had not designed Sir Kenneth to be introduced into her tent—and then, eloquent in urging her own defence, the Queen was far more so in pressing upon Richard the charge of unkindness, in refusing her so poor a boon as the life of an unfortunate knight, who, by her thoughtless prank, had been brought within the danger of martial law. She wept and sobbed while she enlarged on her husband's obduracy on this score, as a rigour which had threatened to make her unhappy for life, whenever she should reflect that she had given, unthinkingly, the remote cause for such a tragedy. The vision of the slaughtered victim would have haunted her dreams—nay, for aught she knew, since such things often happened, his actual spectre might have stood by her waking couch. To all this misery of the mind was she exposed by the severity of one who, while he pretended to dote upon her slightest glance, would not forego one act of poor revenge, though the issue was to render her miserable.

All this flow of female eloquence was accompanied with the usual arguments of tears and sighs, and uttered with such tone and action as seemed to show that the Queen's resentment arose neither from pride nor sullenness, but from feelings hurt at finding her consequence with her husband less than she had expected to possess.

The good King Richard was considerably embarrassed. He tried in vain to reason with one whose very jealousy of his affection rendered her incapable of listening to argument, nor could he bring himself to use the restraint of lawful authority to a creature so beautiful in the midst of her unreasonable displeasure. He was therefore reduced to the defensive, endeavoured gently to chide her suspicions and soothe her displeasure, and recalled to her mind that she need not look back upon the past with recollections either of remorse or supernatural fear, since Sir Kenneth was alive and well, and had been bestowed by him upon the great Arabian physician, who, doubtless, of all men, knew best how to keep him living. But this seemed the unkindest cut of all, and the Queen's sorrow was renewed at the idea of a Saracen—a mediciner—obtaining a boon for which, with bare head and on bended knee, she had petitioned her husband in vain. At this new charge Richard's patience began rather to give way, and he said, in a serious tone of voice,

"Berengaria, the physician saved my life. If it is of value in your eyes, you will not grudge him a higher recompense than the only one I could prevail on him to accept."

The Queen was satisfied she had urged her coquettish displeasure to the verge of safety.

"My Richard," she said, "why brought you not that sage to me, that England's Queen might show how she esteemed him who could save from extinction the lamp of chivalry, the glory of England, and the light of poor Berengaria's life and hope?"

In a word, the matrimonial dispute was ended; but, that some penalty might be paid to justice, both King and Queen accorded in laying the whole blame on the agent Nectabanus, who (the Queen being by this time well weary of the poor dwarf's humour) was, with his royal consort Guenevra, sentenced to be banished from the Court; and the unlucky dwarf only escaped a supplementary whipping, from the Queen's assurances that he had already sustained personal chastisement. It was decreed further that, as an envoy was shortly to be dispatched to Saladin, acquainting him with the resolution of the Council to resume hostilities so soon as the truce was ended, and as Richard proposed to send a valuable present to the Soldan, in acknowledgment of the high benefit he had derived from the services of El Hakim, the two unhappy creatures should be added to it as curiosities, which, from their extremely grotesque appearance, and the shattered state of their intellect, were gifts that might well pass between sovereign and sovereign.

Richard had that day yet another female encounter to sustain; but he advanced to it with comparative indifference, for Edith, though beautiful and highly esteemed by her royal relative—nay, although she had from his unjust suspicions actually sustained the injury of which Berengaria only affected to complain—still was neither Richard's wife nor mistress, and he feared her reproaches less, although founded in reason, than those of the Queen, though unjust and fantastical. Having requested to speak with her apart, he was ushered into her apartment, adjoining that of the Queen, whose two female Coptish slaves remained on their knees in the most remote corner during the interview. A thin black veil extended its ample folds over the tall and graceful form of the high-born maiden, and she wore not upon her person any female ornament of what kind soever. She arose and made a low reverence when Richard entered, resumed her seat at his command, and, when he sat down beside her, waited, without uttering a syllable, until he should communicate his pleasure.

Richard, whose custom it was to be familiar with Edith, as their relationship authorized, felt this reception chilling, and opened the conversation with some embarrassment.

"Our fair cousin," he at length said, "is angry with us; and we own that strong circumstances have induced us, without cause, to suspect her of conduct alien to what we have ever known in her course of life. But while we walk in this misty valley of humanity, men will mistake shadows for substances. Can my fair cousin not forgive her somewhat vehement kinsman Richard?"

"Who can refuse forgiveness to RICHARD," answered Edith, "provided Richard can obtain pardon of the KING?"

"Come, my kinswoman," replied Coeur de Lion, "this is all too solemn. By Our Lady, such a melancholy countenance, and this ample sable veil, might make men think thou wert a new-made widow, or had lost a betrothed lover, at least. Cheer up! Thou hast heard, doubtless, that there is no real cause for woe; why, then, keep up the form of mourning?"

"For the departed honour of Plantagenet—for the glory which hath left my father's house."

Richard frowned. "Departed honour! glory which hath left our house!" he repeated angrily. "But my cousin Edith is privileged. I have judged her too hastily; she has therefore a right to deem of me too harshly. But tell me at least in what I have faulted."

"Plantagenet," said Edith, "should have either pardoned an offence, or punished it. It misbecomes him to assign free men, Christians, and brave knights, to the fetters of the infidels. It becomes him not to compromise and barter, or to grunt life under the forfeiture of liberty. To have doomed the unfortunate to death might have been severity, but had a show of justice; to condemn him to slavery and exile was barefaced tyranny."

"I see, my fair cousin," said Richard, "you are of those pretty ones who think an absent lover as bad as none, or as a dead one. Be patient; half a score of light horsemen may yet follow and redeem the error, if thy gallant have in keeping any secret which might render his death more convenient than his banishment."

"Peace with thy scurrile jests!" answered Edith, colouring deeply. "Think, rather, that for the indulgence of thy mood thou hast lopped from this great enterprise one goodly limb, deprived the Cross of one of its most brave supporters, and placed a servant of the true God in the hands of the heathen; hast given, too, to minds as suspicious as thou hast shown thine own in this matter, some right to say that Richard Coeur de Lion banished the bravest soldier in his camp lest his name in battle might match his own."

"I—I!" exclaimed Richard, now indeed greatly moved—"am I one to be jealous of renown? I would he were here to profess such an equality! I would waive my rank and my crown, and meet him, manlike, in the lists, that it might appear whether Richard Plantagenet had room to fear or to envy the prowess of mortal man. Come, Edith, thou think'st not as thou sayest. Let not anger or grief for the absence of thy lover make thee unjust to thy kinsman, who, notwithstanding all thy techiness, values thy good report as high as that of any one living."

"The absence of my lover?" said the Lady Edith, "But yes, he may be well termed my lover, who hath paid so dear for the title. Unworthy as I might be of such homage, I was to him like a light, leading him forward in the noble path of chivalry; but that I forgot my rank, or that he presumed beyond his, is false, were a king to speak it."

"My fair cousin," said Richard, "do not put words in my mouth which I have not spoken. I said not you had graced this man beyond the favour which a good knight may earn, even from a princess, whatever be his native condition. But, by Our Lady, I know something of this love-gear. It begins with mute respect and distant reverence; but when opportunities occur, familiarity increases, and so—But it skills not talking with one who thinks herself wiser than all the world."

"My kinsman's counsels I willingly listen to, when they are such," said Edith, "as convey no insult to my rank and character."

"Kings, my fair cousin, do not counsel, but rather command," said Richard.

"Soldans do indeed command," said Edith, "but it is because they have slaves to govern."

"Come, you might learn to lay aside this scorn of Soldanrie, when you hold so high of a Scot," said the King. "I hold Saladin to be truer to his word than this William of Scotland, who must needs be called a Lion, forsooth; he hath foully faulted towards me in failing to send the auxiliary aid he promised. Let me tell thee, Edith, thou mayest live to prefer a true Turk to a false Scot."

"No—never!" answered Edith—"not should Richard himself embrace the false religion, which he crossed the seas to expel from Palestine."

"Thou wilt have the last word," said Richard, "and thou shalt have it. Even think of me what thou wilt, pretty Edith. I shall not forget that we are near and dear cousins."

So saying, he took his leave in fair fashion, but very little satisfied with the result of his visit.

It was the fourth day after Sir Kenneth had been dismissed from the camp, and King Richard sat in his pavilion, enjoying an evening breeze from the west, which, with unusual coolness on her wings, seemed breathed from merry England for the refreshment of her adventurous Monarch, as he was gradually recovering the full strength which was necessary to carry on his gigantic projects. There was no one with him, De Vaux having been sent to Ascalon to bring up reinforcements and supplies of military munition, and most of his other attendants being occupied in different departments, all preparing for the re-opening of hostilities, and for a grand preparatory review of the army of the Crusaders, which was to take place the next day. The King sat listening to the busy hum among the soldiery, the clatter from the forges, where horseshoes were preparing, and from the tents of the armourers, who were repairing harness. The voice of the soldiers, too, as they passed and repassed, was loud and cheerful, carrying with its very tone an assurance of high and excited courage, and an omen of approaching victory. While Richard's ear drank in these sounds with delight, and while he yielded himself to the visions of conquest and of glory which they suggested, an equerry told him that a messenger from Saladin waited without.

"Admit him instantly," said the King, "and with due honour, Josceline."

The English knight accordingly introduced a person, apparently of no higher rank than a Nubian slave, whose appearance was nevertheless highly interesting. He was of superb stature and nobly formed, and his commanding features, although almost jet-black, showed nothing of African descent. He wore over his coal-black locks a milk-white turban, and over his shoulders a short mantle of the same colour, open in front and at the sleeves, under which appeared a doublet of dressed leopard's skin reaching within a handbreadth of the knee. The rest of his muscular limbs, both legs and arms, were bare, excepting that he had sandals on his feet, and wore a collar and bracelets of silver. A straight broadsword, with a handle of box-wood and a sheath covered with snakeskin, was suspended from his waist. In his right hand he held a short javelin, with a broad, bright steel head, of a span in length, and in his left he led by a leash of twisted silk and gold a large and noble staghound.

The messenger prostrated himself, at the same time partially uncovering his shoulders, in sign of humiliation, and having touched the earth with his forehead, arose so far as to rest on one knee, while he delivered to the King a silken napkin, enclosing another of cloth of gold, within which was a letter from Saladin in the original Arabic, with a translation into Norman-English, which may be modernized thus:—

"Saladin, King of Kings, to Melech Ric, the Lion of England. Whereas, we are informed by thy last message that thou hast chosen war rather than peace, and our enmity rather than our friendship, we account thee as one blinded in this matter, and trust shortly to convince thee of thine error, by the help of our invincible forces of the thousand tribes, when Mohammed, the Prophet of God, and Allah, the God of the Prophet, shall judge the controversy betwixt us. In what remains, we make noble account of thee, and of the gifts which thou hast sent us, and of the two dwarfs, singular in their deformity as Ysop, and mirthful as the lute of Isaack. And in requital of these tokens from the treasure-house of thy bounty, behold we have sent thee a Nubian slave, named Zohauk, of whom judge not by his complexion, according to the foolish ones of the earth, in respect the dark-rinded fruit hath the most exquisite flavour. Know that he is strong to execute the will of his master, as Rustan of Zablestan; also he is wise to give counsel when thou shalt learn to hold communication with him, for the Lord of Speech hath been stricken with silence betwixt the ivory walls of his palace. We commend him to thy care, hoping the hour may not be distant when he may render thee good service. And herewith we bid thee farewell; trusting that our most holy Prophet may yet call thee to a sight of the truth, failing which illumination, our desire is for the speedy restoration of thy royal health, that Allah may judge between thee and us in a plain field of battle."

And the missive was sanctioned by the signature and seal of the Soldan.

Richard surveyed the Nubian in silence as he stood before him, his looks bent upon the ground, his arms folded on his bosom, with the appearance of a black marble statue of the most exquisite workmanship, waiting life from the touch of a Prometheus. The King of England, who, as it was emphatically said of his successor Henry the Eighth, loved to look upon A MAN, was well pleased with the thews, sinews, and symmetry of him whom he now surveyed, and questioned him in the lingua franca, "Art thou a pagan?"

The slave shook his head, and raising his finger to his brow, crossed himself in token of his Christianity, then resumed his posture of motionless humility.

"A Nubian Christian, doubtless," said Richard, "and mutilated of the organ of speech by these heathen dogs?"

The mute again slowly shook his head, in token of negative, pointed with his forefinger to Heaven, and then laid it upon his own lips.

"I understand thee," said Richard; "thou dost suffer under the infliction of God, not by the cruelty of man. Canst thou clean an armour and belt, and buckle it in time of need?"

The mute nodded, and stepping towards the coat of mail, which hung with the shield and helmet of the chivalrous monarch upon the pillar of the tent, he handled it with such nicety of address as sufficiently to show that he fully understood the business of an armour-bearer.

"Thou art an apt, and wilt doubtless be a useful knave. Thou shalt wait in my chamber, and on my person," said the King, "to show how much I value the gift of the royal Soldan. If thou hast no tongue, it follows thou canst carry no tales, neither provoke me to be sudden by any unfit reply."

The Nubian again prostrated himself till his brow touched the earth, then stood erect, at some paces distant, as waiting for his new master's commands.

"Nay, thou shalt commence thy office presently," said Richard, "for I see a speck of rust darkening on that shield; and when I shake it in the face of Saladin, it should be bright and unsullied as the Soldan's honour and mine own."

A horn was winded without, and presently Sir Henry Neville entered with a packet of dispatches. "From England, my lord," he said, as he delivered it.

"From England—our own England!" repeated Richard, in a tone of melancholy enthusiasm. "Alas! they little think how hard their Sovereign has been beset by sickness and sorrow—faint friends and forward enemies." Then opening the dispatches, he said hastily, "Ha! this comes from no peaceful land—they too have their feuds. Neville, begone; I must peruse these tidings alone, and at leisure."

Neville withdrew accordingly, and Richard was soon absorbed in the melancholy details which had been conveyed to him from England, concerning the factions that were tearing to pieces his native dominions—the disunion of his brothers John and Geoffrey, and the quarrels of both with the High Justiciary Longchamp, Bishop of Ely—the oppressions practised by the nobles upon the peasantry, and rebellion of the latter against their masters, which had produced everywhere scenes of discord, and in some instances the effusion of blood. Details of incidents mortifying to his pride, and derogatory from his authority, were intermingled with the earnest advice of his wisest and most attached counsellors that he should presently return to England, as his presence offered the only hope of saving the Kingdom from all the horrors of civil discord, of which France and Scotland were likely to avail themselves. Filled with the most painful anxiety, Richard read, and again read, the ill-omened letters; compared the intelligence which some of them contained with the same facts as differently stated in others; and soon became totally insensible to whatever was passing around him, although seated, for the sake of coolness, close to the entrance of his tent, and having the curtains withdrawn, so that he could see and be seen by the guards and others who were stationed without.

Deeper in the shadow of the pavilion, and busied with the task his new master had imposed, sat the Nubian slave, with his back rather turned towards the King. He had finished adjusting and cleaning the hauberk and brigandine, and was now busily employed on a broad pavesse, or buckler, of unusual size, and covered with steel-plating, which Richard often used in reconnoitring, or actually storming fortified places, as a more effectual protection against missile weapons than the narrow triangular shield used on horseback. This pavesse bore neither the royal lions of England, nor any other device, to attract the observation of the defenders of the walls against which it was advanced; the care, therefore, of the armourer was addressed to causing its surface to shine as bright as crystal, in which he seemed to be peculiarly successful. Beyond the Nubian, and scarce visible from without, lay the large dog, which might be termed his brother slave, and which, as if he felt awed by being transferred to a royal owner, was couched close to the side of the mute, with head and ears on the ground, and his limbs and tail drawn close around and under him.

While the Monarch and his new attendant were thus occupied, another actor crept upon the scene, and mingled among the group of English yeomen, about a score of whom, respecting the unusually pensive posture and close occupation of their Sovereign, were, contrary to their wont, keeping a silent guard in front of his tent. It was not, however, more vigilant than usual. Some were playing at games of hazard with small pebbles, others spoke together in whispers of the approaching day of battle, and several lay asleep, their bulky limbs folded in their green mantles.

Amid these careless warders glided the puny form of a little old Turk, poorly dressed like a marabout or santon of the desert—a sort of enthusiasts, who sometimes ventured into the camp of the Crusaders, though treated always with contumely, and often with violence. Indeed, the luxury and profligate indulgence of the Christian leaders had occasioned a motley concourse in their tents of musicians, courtesans, Jewish merchants, Copts, Turks, and all the varied refuse of the Eastern nations; so that the caftan and turban, though to drive both from the Holy Land was the professed object of the expedition, were, nevertheless, neither an uncommon nor an alarming sight in the camp of the Crusaders. When, however, the little insignificant figure we have described approached so nigh as to receive some interruption from the warders, he dashed his dusky green turban from his head, showed that his beard and eyebrows were shaved like those of a professed buffoon, and that the expression of his fantastic and writhen features, as well as of his little black eyes, which glittered like jet, was that of a crazed imagination.

"Dance, marabout," cried the soldiers, acquainted with the manners of these wandering enthusiasts, "dance, or we will scourge thee with our bow-strings till thou spin as never top did under schoolboy's lash." Thus shouted the reckless warders, as much delighted at having a subject to tease as a child when he catches a butterfly, or a schoolboy upon discovering a bird's nest.

The marabout, as if happy to do their behests, bounded from the earth, and spun his giddy round before them with singular agility, which, when contrasted with his slight and wasted figure, and diminutive appearance, made him resemble a withered leaf twirled round and round at the pleasure of the winter's breeze. His single lock of hair streamed upwards from his bald and shaven head, as if some genie upheld him by it; and indeed it seemed as if supernatural art were necessary to the execution of the wild, whirling dance, in which scarce the tiptoe of the performer was seen to touch the ground. Amid the vagaries of his performance he flew here and there, from one spot to another, still approaching, however, though almost imperceptibly, to the entrance of the royal tent; so that, when at length he sunk exhausted on the earth, after two or three bounds still higher than those which he had yet executed, he was not above thirty yards from the King's person.

"Give him water," said one yeoman; "they always crave a drink after their merry-go-round."

"Aha, water, sayest thou, Long Allen?" exclaimed another archer, with a most scornful emphasis on the despised element; "how wouldst like such beverage thyself, after such a morrice dancing?"

"The devil a water-drop he gets here," said a third. "We will teach the light-footed old infidel to be a good Christian, and drink wine of Cyprus."

"Ay, ay," said a fourth; "and in case he be restive, fetch thou Dick Hunter's horn, that he drenches his mare withal."

A circle was instantly formed around the prostrate and exhausted dervise, and while one tall yeoman raised his feeble form from the ground, another presented to him a huge flagon of wine. Incapable of speech, the old man shook his head, and waved away from him with his hand the liquor forbidden by the Prophet. But his tormentors were not thus to be appeased.

"The horn, the horn!" exclaimed one. "Little difference between a Turk and a Turkish horse, and we will use him conforming."

"By Saint George, you will choke him!" said Long Allen; "and besides, it is a sin to throw away upon a heathen dog as much wine as would serve a good Christian for a treble night-cap."

"Thou knowest not the nature of these Turks and pagans, Long Allen," replied Henry Woodstall. "I tell thee, man, that this flagon of Cyprus will set his brains a-spinning, just in the opposite direction that they went whirling in the dancing, and so bring him, as it were, to himself again. Choke? He will no more choke on it than Ben's black bitch on the pound of butter."

"And for grudging it," said Tomalin Blacklees, "why shouldst thou grudge the poor paynim devil a drop of drink on earth, since thou knowest he is not to have a drop to cool the tip of his tongue through a long eternity?"

"That were hard laws, look ye," said Long Allen, "only for being a Turk, as his father was before him. Had he been Christian turned heathen, I grant you the hottest corner had been good winter quarters for him."

"Hold thy peace, Long Allen," said Henry Woodstall. "I tell thee that tongue of thine is not the shortest limb about thee, and I prophesy that it will bring thee into disgrace with Father Francis, as once about the black-eyed Syrian wench. But here comes the horn. Be active a bit, man, wilt thou, and just force open his teeth with the haft of thy dudgeon-dagger."

"Hold, hold—he is conformable," said Tomalin; "see, see, he signs for the goblet—give him room, boys! OOP SEY ES, quoth the Dutchman—down it goes like lamb's-wool! Nay, they are true topers when once they begin—your Turk never coughs in his cup, or stints in his liquoring."

In fact, the dervise, or whatever he was, drank—or at least seemed to drink—the large flagon to the very bottom at a single pull; and when he took it from his lips after the whole contents were exhausted, only uttered, with a deep sigh, the words, ALLAH KERIM, or God is merciful. There was a laugh among the yeomen who witnessed this pottle-deep potation, so obstreperous as to rouse and disturb the King, who, raising his finger, said angrily, "How, knaves, no respect, no observance?"

All were at once hushed into silence, well acquainted with the temper of Richard, which at some times admitted of much military familiarity, and at others exacted the most precise respect, although the latter humour was of much more rare occurrence. Hastening to a more reverent distance from the royal person, they attempted to drag along with them the marabout, who, exhausted apparently by previous fatigue, or overpowered by the potent draught he had just swallowed, resisted being moved from the spot, both with struggles and groans.

"Leave him still, ye fools," whispered Long Allen to his mates; "by Saint Christopher, you will make our Dickon go beside himself, and we shall have his dagger presently fly at our costards. Leave him alone; in less than a minute he will sleep like a dormouse."

At the same moment the Monarch darted another impatient glance to the spot, and all retreated in haste, leaving the dervise on the ground, unable, as it seemed, to stir a single limb or joint of his body. In a moment afterward all was as still and quiet as it had been before the intrusion.

Lesson 143

1. Read chapter 21. The marabout tries to assassinate King Richard, but the Nubian saves his life and later informs King Richard in writing that he can help him identify the person who had taken the English banner.
2. Unusual Vocabulary:
    - Carrion – dead body
    - Chattel – a slave
    - Changier/poniard – a small, slender dagger
3. How is the Nubian able to see the marabout's evil intentions? (Answers)
4. Why did Richard's guards disobey his orders to suck the poison from the Nubian's wound? (Answers)
5. What message does the Nubian bring from the Sultan? (Answers)
6. What is mysterious about the Nubian? (Answers)

CHAPTER XXI

—and wither'd Murder,

Alarum'd by his sentinel, the wolf,

Whose howl's his watch, thus with his stealthy pace,

With Tarquin's ravishing strides, towards his design

Moves like a ghost.

MACBETH.

For the space of a quarter of an hour, or longer, after the incident related, all remained perfectly quiet in the front of the royal habitation. The King read and mused in the entrance of his pavilion; behind, and with his back turned to the same entrance, the Nubian slave still burnished the ample pavesse; in front of all, at a hundred paces distant, the yeomen of the guard stood, sat, or lay extended on the grass, attentive to their own sports, but pursuing them in silence, while on the esplanade betwixt them and the front of the tent lay, scarcely to be distinguished from a bundle of rags, the senseless form of the marabout.

But the Nubian had the advantage of a mirror from the brilliant reflection which the surface of the highly-polished shield now afforded, by means of which he beheld, to his alarm and surprise, that the marabout raised his head gently from the ground, so as to survey all around him, moving with a well-adjusted precaution which seemed entirely inconsistent with a state of ebriety. He couched his head instantly, as if satisfied he was unobserved, and began, with the slightest possible appearance of voluntary effort, to drag himself, as if by chance, ever nearer and nearer to the King, but stopping and remaining fixed at intervals, like the spider, which, moving towards her object, collapses into apparent lifelessness when she thinks she is the subject of observation. This species of movement appeared suspicious to the Ethiopian, who, on his part, prepared himself, as quietly as possible, to interfere, the instant that interference should seem to be necessary.

The marabout, meanwhile, glided on gradually and imperceptibly, serpent-like, or rather snail-like, till he was about ten yards distant from Richard's person, when, starting on his feet, he sprung forward with the bound of a tiger, stood at the King's back in less than an instant, and brandished aloft the cangiar, or poniard, which he had hidden in his sleeve. Not the presence of his whole army could have saved their heroic Monarch; but the motions of the Nubian had been as well calculated as those of the enthusiast, and ere the latter could strike, the former caught his uplifted arm. Turning his fanatical wrath upon what thus unexpectedly interposed betwixt him and his object, the Charegite, for such was the seeming marabout, dealt the Nubian a blow with the dagger, which, however, only grazed his arm, while the far superior strength of the Ethiopian easily dashed him to the ground. Aware of what had passed, Richard had now arisen, and with little more of surprise, anger, or interest of any kind in his countenance than an ordinary man would show in brushing off and crushing an intrusive wasp, caught up the stool on which he had been sitting, and exclaiming only, "Ha, dog!" dashed almost to pieces the skull of the assassin, who uttered twice, once in a loud, and once in a broken tone, the words ALLAH ACKBAR!—God is victorious—and expired at the King's feet.

"Ye are careful warders," said Richard to his archers, in a tone of scornful reproach, as, aroused by the bustle of what had passed, in terror and tumult they now rushed into his tent; "watchful sentinels ye are, to leave me to do such hangman's work with my own hand. Be silent, all of you, and cease your senseless clamour!—saw ye never a dead Turk before? Here, cast that carrion out of the camp, strike the head from the trunk, and stick it on a lance, taking care to turn the face to Mecca, that he may the easier tell the foul impostor on whose inspiration he came hither how he has sped on his errand.—For thee, my swart and silent friend," he added, turning to the Ethiopian—"but how's this? Thou art wounded—and with a poisoned weapon, I warrant me, for by force of stab so weak an animal as that could scarce hope to do more than raze the lion's hide.—Suck the poison from his wound one of you—the venom is harmless on the lips, though fatal when it mingles with the blood."

The yeomen looked on each other confusedly and with hesitation, the apprehension of so strange a danger prevailing with those who feared no other.

"How now, sirrahs," continued the King, "are you dainty-lipped, or do you fear death, that you daily thus?"

"Not the death of a man," said Long Allen, to whom the King looked as he spoke; "but methinks I would not die like a poisoned rat for the sake of a black chattel there, that is bought and sold in a market like a Martlemas ox."

"His Grace speaks to men of sucking poison," muttered another yeoman, "as if he said, 'Go to, swallow a gooseberry!'"

"Nay," said Richard, "I never bade man do that which I would not do myself."

And without further ceremony, and in spite of the general expostulations of those around, and the respectful opposition of the Nubian himself, the King of England applied his lips to the wound of the black slave, treating with ridicule all remonstrances, and overpowering all resistance. He had no sooner intermitted his singular occupation, than the Nubian started from him, and casting a scarf over his arm, intimated by gestures, as firm in purpose as they were respectful in manner, his determination not to permit the Monarch to renew so degrading an employment. Long Allen also interposed, saying that, if it were necessary to prevent the King engaging again in a treatment of this kind, his own lips, tongue, and teeth were at the service of the Ethiopian, and that he would eat him up bodily, rather than King Richard's mouth should again approach him.

Neville, who entered with other officers, added his remonstrances.

"Nay, nay, make not a needless halloo about a hart that the hounds have lost, or a danger when it is over," said the King. "The wound will be a trifle, for the blood is scarce drawn—an angry cat had dealt a deeper scratch. And for me, I have but to take a drachm of orvietan by way of precaution, though it is needless."

Thus spoke Richard, a little ashamed, perhaps, of his own condescension, though sanctioned both by humanity and gratitude. But when Neville continued to make remonstrances on the peril to his royal person, the King imposed silence on him.

"Peace, I prithee—make no more of it. I did it but to show these ignorant, prejudiced knaves how they might help each other when these cowardly caitiffs come against us with sarbacanes and poisoned shafts. But," he added, "take thee this Nubian to thy quarters, Neville—I have changed my mind touching him—let him be well cared for. But hark in thine ear; see that he escapes thee not—there is more in him than seems. Let him have all liberty, so that he leave not the camp.—And you, ye beef-devouring, wine-swilling English mastiffs, get ye to your guard again, and be sure you keep it more warily. Think not you are now in your own land of fair play, where men speak before they strike, and shake hands ere they cut throats. Danger in our land walks openly, and with his blade drawn, and defies the foe whom he means to assault; but here he challenges you with a silk glove instead of a steel gauntlet, cuts your throat with the feather of a turtle-dove, stabs you with the tongue of a priest's brooch, or throttles you with the lace of my lady's boddice. Go to—keep your eyes open and your mouths shut—drink less, and look sharper about you; or I will place your huge stomachs on such short allowance as would pinch the stomach of a patient Scottish man."

The yeomen, abashed and mortified, withdrew to their post, and Neville was beginning to remonstrate with his master upon the risk of passing over thus slightly their negligence upon their duty, and the propriety of an example in a case so peculiarly aggravated as the permitting one so suspicious as the marabout to approach within dagger's length of his person, when Richard interrupted him with, "Speak not of it, Neville—wouldst thou have me avenge a petty risk to myself more severely than the loss of England's banner? It has been stolen—stolen by a thief, or delivered up by a traitor, and no blood has been shed for it.—My sable friend, thou art an expounder of mysteries, saith the illustrious Soldan—now would I give thee thine own weight in gold, if, by raising one still blacker than thyself or by what other means thou wilt, thou couldst show me the thief who did mine honour that wrong. What sayest thou, ha?"

The mute seemed desirous to speak, but uttered only that imperfect sound proper to his melancholy condition; then folded his arms, looked on the King with an eye of intelligence, and nodded in answer to his question.

"How!" said Richard, with joyful impatience. "Wilt thou undertake to make discovery in this matter?"

The Nubian slave repeated the same motion.

"But how shall we understand each other?" said the King. "Canst thou write, good fellow?"

The slave again nodded in assent.

"Give him writing-tools," said the King. "They were readier in my father's tent than mine; but they be somewhere about, if this scorching climate have not dried up the ink.—Why, this fellow is a jewel—a black diamond, Neville."

"So please you, my liege," said Neville, "if I might speak my poor mind, it were ill dealing in this ware. This man must be a wizard, and wizards deal with the Enemy, who hath most interest to sow tares among the wheat, and bring dissension into our councils, and—"

"Peace, Neville," said Richard. "Hello to your northern hound when he is close on the haunch of the deer, and hope to recall him, but seek not to stop Plantagenet when he hath hope to retrieve his honour."

The slave, who during this discussion had been writing, in which art he seemed skilful, now arose, and pressing what he had written to his brow, prostrated himself as usual, ere he delivered it into the King's hands. The scroll was in French, although their intercourse had hitherto been conducted by Richard in the lingua franca.

"To Richard, the conquering and invincible King of England, this from the humblest of his slaves. Mysteries are the sealed caskets of Heaven, but wisdom may devise means to open the lock. Were your slave stationed where the leaders of the Christian host were made to pass before him in order, doubt nothing that if he who did the injury whereof my King complains shall be among the number, he may be made manifest in his iniquity, though it be hidden under seven veils."

"Now, by Saint George!" said King Richard, "thou hast spoken most opportunely.—Neville, thou knowest that when we muster our troops to-morrow the princes have agreed that, to expiate the affront offered to England in the theft of her banner, the leaders should pass our new standard as it floats on Saint George's Mount, and salute it with formal regard. Believe me, the secret traitor will not dare to absent himself from an expurgation so solemn, lest his very absence should be matter of suspicion. There will we place our sable man of counsel, and if his art can detect the villain, leave me to deal with him."

"My liege," said Neville, with the frankness of an English baron, "beware what work you begin. Here is the concord of our holy league unexpectedly renewed—will you, upon such suspicion as a slave can instil, tear open wounds so lately closed? Or will you use the solemn procession, adopted for the reparation of your honour and establishment of unanimity amongst the discording princes, as the means of again finding out new cause of offence, or reviving ancient quarrels? It were scarce too strong to say this were a breach of the declaration your Grace made to the assembled Council of the Crusade."

"Neville," said the King, sternly interrupting him, "thy zeal makes thee presumptuous and unmannerly. Never did I promise to abstain from taking whatever means were most promising to discover the infamous author of the attack on my honour. Ere I had done so, I would have renounced my kingdom, my life. All my declarations were under this necessary and absolute qualification;—only, if Austria had stepped forth and owned the injury like a man, I proffered, for the sake of Christendom, to have forgiven HIM."

"But," continued the baron anxiously, "what hope that this juggling slave of Saladin will not palter with your Grace?"

"Peace, Neville," said the King; "thou thinkest thyself mighty wise, and art but a fool. Mind thou my charge touching this fellow; there is more in him than thy Westmoreland wit can fathom.—And thou, smart and silent, prepare to perform the feat thou hast promised, and, by the word of a King, thou shalt choose thine own recompense.—Lo, he writes again."

The mute accordingly wrote and delivered to the King, with the same form as before, another slip of paper, containing these words, "The will of the King is the law to his slave; nor doth it become him to ask guerdon for discharge of his devoir."

"GUERDON and DEVOIR!" said the King, interrupting himself as he read, and speaking to Neville in the English tongue with some emphasis on the words. "These Eastern people will profit by the Crusaders—they are acquiring the language of chivalry! And see, Neville, how discomposed that fellow looks! were it not for his colour he would blush. I should not think it strange if he understood what I say—they are perilous linguists."

"The poor slave cannot endure your Grace's eye," said Neville; "it is nothing more."

"Well, but," continued the King, striking the paper with his finger as he proceeded, "this bold scroll proceeds to say that our trusty mute is charged with a message from Saladin to the Lady Edith Plantagenet, and craves means and opportunity to deliver it. What thinkest thou of a request so modest—ha, Neville?"

"I cannot say," said Neville, "how such freedom may relish with your Grace; but the lease of the messenger's neck would be a short one, who should carry such a request to the Soldan on the part of your Majesty."

"Nay, I thank Heaven that I covet none of his sunburnt beauties," said Richard; "and for punishing this fellow for discharging his master's errand, and that when he has just saved my life—methinks it were something too summary. I'll tell thee, Neville, a secret; for although our sable and mute minister be present, he cannot, thou knowest, tell it over again, even if he should chance to understand us. I tell thee that, for this fortnight past, I have been under a strange spell, and I would I were disenchanted. There has no sooner any one done me good service, but, lo you, he cancels his interest in me by some deep injury; and, on the other hand, he who hath deserved death at my hands for some treachery or some insult, is sure to be the very person of all others who confers upon me some obligation that overbalances his demerits, and renders respite of his sentence a debt due from my honour. Thus, thou seest, I am deprived of the best part of my royal function, since I can neither punish men nor reward them. Until the influence of this disqualifying planet be passed away, I will say nothing concerning the request of this our sable attendant, save that it is an unusually bold one, and that his best chance of finding grace in our eyes will be to endeavour to make the discovery which he proposes to achieve in our behalf. Meanwhile, Neville, do thou look well to him, and let him be honourably cared for. And hark thee once more," he said, in a low whisper, "seek out yonder hermit of Engaddi, and bring him to me forthwith, be he saint or savage, madman or sane. Let me see him privately."

Neville retired from the royal tent, signing to the Nubian to follow him, and much surprised at what he had seen and heard, and especially at the unusual demeanour of the King. In general, no task was so easy as to discover Richard's immediate course of sentiment and feeling, though it might, in some cases, be difficult to calculate its duration; for no weathercock obeyed the changing wind more readily than the King his gusts of passion. But on the present occasion his manner seemed unusually constrained and mysterious; nor was it easy to guess whether displeasure or kindness predominated in his conduct towards his new dependant, or in the looks with which, from time to time, he regarded him. The ready service which the King had rendered to counteract the bad effects of the Nubian's wound might seem to balance the obligation conferred on him by the slave when he intercepted the blow of the assassin; but it seemed, as a much longer account remained to be arranged between them, that the Monarch was doubtful whether the settlement might leave him, upon the whole, debtor or creditor, and that, therefore, he assumed in the meantime a neutral demeanour, which might suit with either character. As for the Nubian, by whatever means he had acquired the art of writing the European languages, the King remained convinced that the English tongue at least was unknown to him, since, having watched him closely during the last part of the interview, he conceived it impossible for any one understanding a conversation, of which he was himself the subject, to have so completely avoided the appearance of taking an interest in it.

Lesson 144

1. Read chapter 22. This chapter is a "flashback;" it discusses something that happened in an earlier time than the recent action. Sir Kenneth leaves the camp of the Crusaders under his new "master," Hakim the physician and learns the value of the Arabian horses and later receives some medicine from Hakim to help him sleep.

2. How does the author show that Sir Kenneth was paying more attention to his own thoughts and feelings than he was to the details of his journey? (Answers)
3. How do the Muslims pass the time on their long journey? (Answers)
4. What disturbs their pleasant ride? How does Hakim feel about the interruption? (Answers)
5. How does Hakim solve this problem? (Answers)
6. Where do they end their journey? (Answers)

CHAPTER XXII.

Who's there!—Approach—'tis kindly done—

My learned physician and a friend.

SIR EUSTACE GREY.

Our narrative retrogrades to a period shortly previous to the incidents last mentioned, when, as the reader must remember, the unfortunate Knight of the Leopard, bestowed upon the Arabian physician by King Richard, rather as a slave than in any other capacity, was exiled from the camp of the Crusaders, in whose ranks he had so often and so brilliantly distinguished himself. He followed his new master—for so he must now term the Hakim—to the Moorish tents which contained his retinue and his property, with the stupefied feelings of one who, fallen from the summit of a precipice, and escaping unexpectedly with life, is just able to drag himself from the fatal spot, but without the power of estimating the extent of the damage which he has sustained. Arrived at the tent, he threw himself, without speech of any kind, upon a couch of dressed buffalo's hide, which was pointed out to him by his conductor, and hiding his face betwixt his hands, groaned heavily, as if his heart were on the point of bursting. The physician heard him, as he was giving orders to his numerous domestics to prepare for their departure the next morning before daybreak, and, moved with compassion, interrupted his occupation to sit down, cross-legged, by the side of his couch, and administer comfort according to the Oriental manner.

"My friend," he said, "be of good comfort; for what saith the poet—it is better that a man should be the servant of a kind master than the slave of his own wild passions. Again, be of good courage; because, whereas Ysouf Ben Yagoube was sold to a king by his brethren, even to Pharaoh, King of Egypt, thy king hath, on the other hand, bestowed thee on one who will be to thee as a brother."

Sir Kenneth made an effort to thank the Hakim, but his heart was too full, and the indistinct sounds which accompanied his abortive attempts to reply induced the kind physician to desist from his premature endeavours at consolation. He left his new domestic, or guest, in quiet, to indulge his sorrows, and having commanded all the necessary preparations for their departure on the morning, sat down upon the carpet of the tent, and indulged himself in a moderate repast. After he had thus refreshed himself, similar viands were offered to the Scottish knight; but though the slaves let him understand that the next day would be far advanced ere they would halt for the purpose of refreshment, Sir Kenneth could not overcome the disgust which he felt against swallowing any nourishment, and could be prevailed upon to taste nothing, saving a draught of cold water.

He was awake long after his Arab host had performed his usual devotions and betaken himself to his repose; nor had sleep visited him at the hour of midnight, when a movement took place among the domestics, which, though attended with no speech, and very little noise, made him aware they were loading the camels and preparing for departure. In the course of these preparations, the last person who was disturbed, excepting the physician himself, was the knight of Scotland, whom, about three in the morning, a sort of major-domo, or master of the household, acquainted that he must arise. He did so, without further answer, and followed him into the moonlight, where stood the camels, most of which were already loaded, and one only remained kneeling until its burden should be completed.

A little apart from the camels stood a number of horses ready bridled and saddled, and the Hakim himself, coming forth, mounted on one of them with as much agility as the grave decorum of his character permitted, and directed another, which he pointed out, to be led towards Sir Kenneth. An English officer was in attendance, to escort them through the camp of the Crusaders, and to ensure their leaving it in safety; and all was ready for their departure. The pavilion which they had left was, in the meanwhile, struck with singular dispatch, and the tent-poles and coverings composed the burden of the last camel—when the physician, pronouncing solemnly the verse of the Koran, "God be our guide, and Mohammed our protector, in the desert as in the watered field," the whole cavalcade was instantly in motion.

In traversing the camp, they were challenged by the various sentinels who maintained guard there, and suffered to proceed in silence, or with a muttered curse upon their prophet, as they passed the post of some more zealous Crusader. At length the last barriers were left behind them, and the party formed themselves for the march with military precaution. Two or three horsemen advanced in front as a vanguard; one or two remained a bow-shot in the rear; and, wherever the ground admitted, others were detached to keep an outlook on the flanks. In this manner they proceeded onward; while Sir Kenneth, looking back on the moonlit camp, might now indeed seem banished, deprived at once of honour and of liberty, from the glimmering banners under which he had hoped to gain additional renown, and the tented dwellings of chivalry, of Christianity, and—of Edith Plantagenet.

The Hakim, who rode by his side, observed, in his usual tone of sententious consolation, "It is unwise to look back when the journey lieth forward;" and as he spoke, the horse of the knight made such a perilous stumble as threatened to add a practical moral to the tale.

The knight was compelled by this hint to give more attention to the management of his steed, which more than once required the assistance and support of the check-bridle, although, in other respects, nothing could be more easy at once, and active, than the ambling pace at which the animal (which was a mare) proceeded.

"The conditions of that horse," observed the sententious physician, "are like those of human fortune—seeing that, amidst his most swift and easy pace, the rider must guard himself against a fall, and that it is when prosperity is at the highest that our prudence should be awake and vigilant to prevent misfortune."

The overloaded appetite loathes even the honeycomb, and it is scarce a wonder that the knight, mortified and harassed with misfortunes and abasement, became something impatient of hearing his misery made, at every turn, the ground of proverbs and apothegms, however just and apposite.

"Methinks," he said, rather peevishly, "I wanted no additional illustration of the instability of fortune though I would thank thee, Sir Hakim, for the choice of a steed for me, would the jade but stumble so effectually as at once to break my neck and her own."

"My brother," answered the Arab sage, with imperturbable gravity, "thou speakest as one of the foolish. Thou sayest in thy heart that the sage should have given you, as his guest, the younger and better horse, and reserved the old one for himself. But know that the defects of the older steed may be compensated by the energies of the young rider, whereas the violence of the young horse requires to be moderated by the cold temper of the older."

So spoke the sage; but neither to this observation did Sir Kenneth return any answer which could lead to a continuance of their conversation, and the physician, wearied, perhaps, of administering comfort to one who would not be comforted, signed to one of his retinue.

"Hassan," he said, "hast thou nothing wherewith to beguile the way?"

Hassan, story-teller and poet by profession, spurred up, upon this summons, to exercise his calling. "Lord of the palace of life," he said, addressing the physician, "thou, before whom the angel Azrael spreadeth his wings for flight—thou, wiser than Solimaun Ben Daoud, upon whose signet was inscribed the REAL NAME which controls the spirits of the elements—forbid it, Heaven, that while thou travellest upon the track of benevolence, bearing healing and hope wherever thou comest, thine own course should be saddened for lack of the tale and of the song. Behold, while thy servant is at thy side, he will pour forth the treasures of his memory, as the fountain sendeth her stream beside the pathway, for the refreshment or him that walketh thereon."

After this exordium, Hassan uplifted his voice, and began a tale of love and magic, intermixed with feats of warlike achievement, and ornamented with abundant quotations from the Persian poets, with whose compositions the orator seemed familiar. The retinue of the physician, such excepted as were necessarily detained in attendance on the camels, thronged up to the narrator, and pressed as close as deference for their master permitted, to enjoy the delight which the inhabitants of the East have ever derived from this species of exhibition.

At another time, notwithstanding his imperfect knowledge of the language, Sir Kenneth might have been interested in the recitation, which, though dictated by a more extravagant imagination, and expressed in more inflated and metaphorical language, bore yet a strong resemblance to the romances of chivalry then so fashionable in Europe. But as matters stood with him, he was scarcely even sensible that a man in the centre of the cavalcade recited and sung, in a low tone, for nearly two hours, modulating his voice to the various moods of passion introduced into the tale, and receiving, in return, now low murmurs of applause, now muttered expressions of wonder, now sighs and tears, and sometimes, what it was far more difficult to extract from such an audience, a tribute of smiles, and even laughter.

During the recitation, the attention of the exile, however abstracted by his own deep sorrow, was occasionally awakened by the low wail of a dog, secured in a wicker enclosure suspended on one of the camels, which, as an experienced woodsman, he had no hesitation in recognizing to be that of his own faithful hound; and from the plaintive tone of the animal, he had no doubt that he was sensible of his master's vicinity, and, in his way, invoking his assistance for liberty and rescue.

"Alas! poor Roswal," he said, "thou callest for aid and sympathy upon one in stricter bondage than thou thyself art. I will not seem to heed thee or return thy affection, since it would serve but to load our parting with yet more bitterness."

Thus passed the hours of night and the space of dim hazy dawn which forms the twilight of a Syrian morning. But when the very first line of the sun's disk began to rise above the level horizon, and when the very first level ray shot glimmering in dew along the surface of the desert, which the travellers had now attained, the sonorous voice of El Hakim himself overpowered and cut short the narrative of the tale-teller, while he caused to resound along the sands the solemn summons, which the muezzins thunder at morning from the minaret of every mosque.

"To prayer—to prayer! God is the one God.—To prayer—to prayer! Mohammed is the Prophet of God.—To prayer—to prayer! Time is flying from you.—To prayer—to prayer! Judgment is drawing nigh to you."

In an instant each Moslem cast himself from his horse, turned his face towards Mecca, and performed with sand an imitation of those ablutions, which were elsewhere required to be made with water, while each individual, in brief but fervent ejaculations, recommended himself to the care, and his sins to the forgiveness, of God and the Prophet.

Even Sir Kenneth, whose reason at once and prejudices were offended by seeing his companions in that which he considered as an act of idolatry, could not help respecting the sincerity of their misguided zeal, and being stimulated by their fervour to apply supplications to Heaven in a purer form, wondering, meanwhile, what new-born feelings could teach him to accompany in prayer, though with varied invocation, those very Saracens, whose heathenish worship he had conceived a crime dishonourable to the land in which high miracles had been wrought, and where the day-star of redemption had arisen.

The act of devotion, however, though rendered in such strange society, burst purely from his natural feelings of religious duty, and had its usual effect in composing the spirits which had been long harassed by so rapid a succession of calamities. The sincere and earnest approach of the Christian to the throne of the Almighty teaches the best lesson of patience under affliction; since wherefore should we mock the Deity with supplications, when we insult him by murmuring under His decrees? or how, while our prayers have in every word admitted the vanity and nothingness of the things of time in comparison to those of eternity, should we hope to deceive the Searcher of Hearts, by permitting the world and worldly passions to reassume the reins even immediately after a solemn address to Heaven! But Sir Kenneth was not of these. He felt himself comforted and strengthened, and better prepared to execute or submit to whatever his destiny might call upon him to do or to suffer.

Meanwhile, the party of Saracens regained their saddles, and continued their route, and the tale-teller, Hassan, resumed the thread of his narrative; but it was no longer to the same attentive audience. A horseman, who had ascended some high ground on the right hand of the little column, had returned on a speedy gallop to El Hakim, and communicated with him. Four or five more cavaliers had then been dispatched, and the little band, which might consist of about twenty or thirty persons, began to follow them with their eyes, as men from whose gestures, and advance or retreat, they were to augur good or evil. Hassan, finding his audience inattentive, or being himself attracted by the dubious appearances on the flank, stinted in his song; and the march became silent, save when a camel-driver called out to his patient charge, or some anxious follower of the Hakim communicated with his next neighbour in a hurried and low whisper.

This suspense continued until they had rounded a ridge, composed of hillocks of sand, which concealed from their main body the object that had created this alarm among their scouts. Sir Kenneth could now see, at the distance of a mile or more, a dark object moving rapidly on the bosom of the desert, which his experienced eye recognized for a party of cavalry, much superior to their own in numbers, and, from the thick and frequent flashes which flung back the level beams of the rising sun, it was plain that these were Europeans in their complete panoply.

The anxious looks which the horsemen of El Hakim now cast upon their leader seemed to indicate deep apprehension; while he, with gravity as undisturbed as when he called his followers to prayer, detached two of his best-mounted cavaliers, with instructions to approach as closely as prudence permitted to these travellers of the desert, and observe more minutely their numbers, their character, and, if possible, their purpose. The approach of danger, or what was feared as such, was like a stimulating draught to one in apathy, and recalled Sir Kenneth to himself and his situation.

"What fear you from these Christian horsemen, for such they seem?" he said to the Hakim.

"Fear!" said El Hakim, repeating the word disdainfully. "The sage fears nothing but Heaven, but ever expects from wicked men the worst which they can do."

"They are Christians," said Sir Kenneth, "and it is the time of truce—why should you fear a breach of faith?"

"They are the priestly soldiers of the Temple," answered El Hakim, "whose vow limits them to know neither truce nor faith with the worshippers of Islam. May the Prophet blight them, both root, branch, and twig! Their peace is war, and their faith is falsehood. Other invaders of Palestine have their times and moods of courtesy. The lion Richard will spare when he has conquered, the eagle Philip will close his wing when he has stricken a prey, even the Austrian bear will sleep when he is gorged; but this horde of ever-hungry wolves know neither pause nor satiety in their rapine. Seest thou not that they are detaching a party from their main body, and that they take an eastern direction? Yon are their pages and squires, whom they train up in their accursed mysteries, and whom, as lighter mounted, they send to cut us off from our watering-place. But they will be disappointed. I know the war of the desert yet better than they."

He spoke a few words to his principal officer, and his whole demeanour and countenance was at once changed from the solemn repose of an Eastern sage accustomed more to contemplation than to action, into the prompt and proud expression of a gallant soldier whose energies are roused by the near approach of a danger which he at once foresees and despises.

To Sir Kenneth's eyes the approaching crisis had a different aspect, and when Adonbec said to him, "Thou must tarry close by my side," he answered solemnly in the negative.

"Yonder," he said, "are my comrades in arms—the men in whose society I have vowed to fight or fall. On their banner gleams the sign of our most blessed redemption—I cannot fly from the Cross in company with the Crescent."

"Fool!" said the Hakim; "their first action would be to do thee to death, were it only to conceal their breach of the truce."

"Of that I must take my chance," replied Sir Kenneth; "but I wear not the bonds of the infidels an instant longer than I can cast them from me."

"Then will I compel thee to follow me," said El Hakim.

"Compel!" answered Sir Kenneth angrily. "Wert thou not my benefactor, or one who has showed will to be such, and were it not that it is to thy confidence I owe the freedom of these hands, which thou mightst have loaded with fetters, I would show thee that, unarmed as I am, compulsion would be no easy task."

"Enough, enough," replied the Arabian physician, "we lose time even when it is becoming precious."

So saying, he threw his arm aloft, and uttered a loud and shrill cry, as a signal to his retinue, who instantly dispersed themselves on the face of the desert, in as many different directions as a chaplet of beads when the string is broken. Sir Kenneth had no time to note what ensued; for, at the same instant, the Hakim seized the rein of his steed, and putting his own to its mettle, both sprung forth at once with the suddenness of light, and at a pitch of velocity which almost deprived the Scottish knight of the power of respiration, and left him absolutely incapable, had he been desirous, to have checked the career of his guide. Practised as Sir Kenneth was in horsemanship from his earliest youth, the speediest horse he had ever mounted was a tortoise in comparison to those of the Arabian sage. They spurned the sand from behind them; they seemed to devour the desert before them; miles flew away with minutes—and yet their strength seemed unabated, and their respiration as free as when they first started upon the wonderful race. The motion, too, as easy as it was swift, seemed more like flying through the air than riding on the earth, and was attended with no unpleasant sensation, save the awe naturally felt by one who is moving at such astonishing speed, and the difficulty of breathing occasioned by their passing through the air so rapidly.

It was not until after an hour of this portentous motion, and when all human pursuit was far, far behind, that the Hakim at length relaxed his speed, and, slackening the pace of the horses into a hand-gallop, began, in a voice as composed and even as if he had been walking for the last hour, a descant upon the excellence of his coursers to the Scot, who, breathless, half blind, half deaf, and altogether giddy; from the rapidity of this singular ride, hardly comprehended the words which flowed so freely from his companion.

"These horses," he said, "are of the breed called the Winged, equal in speed to aught excepting the Borak of the Prophet. They are fed on the golden barley of Yemen, mixed with spices and with a small portion of dried sheep's flesh. Kings have given provinces to possess them, and their age is active as their youth. Thou, Nazarene, art the first, save a true believer, that ever had beneath his loins one of this noble race, a gift of the Prophet himself to the blessed Ali, his kinsman and lieutenant, well called the Lion of God. Time lays his touch so lightly on these generous steeds, that the mare on which thou now sittest has seen five times five years pass over her, yet retains her pristine speed and vigour, only that in the career the support of a bridle, managed by a hand more experienced than thine, hath now become necessary. May the Prophet be blessed, who hath bestowed on the true believers the means of advance and retreat, which causeth their iron-clothed enemies to be worn out with their own ponderous weight! How the horses of yonder dog Templars must have snorted and blown, when they had toiled fetlock-deep in the desert for one-twentieth part of the space which these brave steeds have left behind them, without one thick pant, or a drop of moisture upon their sleek and velvet coats!"

The Scottish knight, who had now begun to recover his breath and powers of attention, could not help acknowledging in his heart the advantage possessed by these Eastern warriors in a race of animals, alike proper for advance or retreat, and so admirably adapted to the level and sandy deserts of Arabia and Syria. But he did not choose to augment the pride of the Moslem by acquiescing in his proud claim of superiority, and therefore suffered the conversation to drop, and, looking around him, could now, at the more moderate pace at which they moved, distinguish that he was in a country not unknown to him.

The blighted borders and sullen waters of the Dead Sea, the ragged and precipitous chain of mountains arising on the left, the two or three palms clustered together, forming the single green speck on the bosom of the waste wilderness—objects which, once seen, were scarcely to be forgotten—showed to Sir Kenneth that they were approaching the fountain called the Diamond of the Desert, which had been the scene of his interview on a former occasion with the Saracen Emir Sheerkohf, or Ilderim. In a few minutes they checked their horses beside the spring, and the Hakim invited Sir Kenneth to descend from horseback and repose himself as in a place of safety. They unbridled their steeds, El Hakim observing that further care of them was unnecessary, since they would be speedily joined by some of the best mounted among his slaves, who would do what further was needful.

"Meantime," he said, spreading some food on the grass, "eat and drink, and be not discouraged. Fortune may raise up or abase the ordinary mortal, but the sage and the soldier should have minds beyond her control."

The Scottish knight endeavoured to testify his thanks by showing himself docile; but though he strove to eat out of complaisance, the singular contrast between his present situation and that which he had occupied on the same spot when the envoy of princes and the victor in combat, came like a cloud over his mind, and fasting, lassitude, and fatigue oppressed his bodily powers. El Hakim examined his hurried pulse, his red and inflamed eye, his heated hand, and his shortened respiration.

"The mind," he said, "grows wise by watching, but her sister the body, of coarser materials, needs the support of repose. Thou must sleep; and that thou mayest do so to refreshment, thou must take a draught mingled with this elixir."

He drew from his bosom a small crystal vial, cased in silver filigree-work, and dropped into a little golden drinking-cup a small portion of a dark-coloured fluid.

"This," he said, "is one of those productions which Allah hath sent on earth for a blessing, though man's weakness and wickedness have sometimes converted it into a curse. It is powerful as the wine-cup of the Nazarene to drop the curtain on the sleepless eye, and to relieve the burden of the overloaded bosom; but when applied to the purposes of indulgence and debauchery, it rends the nerves, destroys the strength, weakens the intellect, and undermines life. But fear not thou to use its virtues in the time of need, for the wise man warms him by the same firebrand with which the madman burneth the tent." [Some preparation of opium seems to be intimated.]

"I have seen too much of thy skill, sage Hakim," said Sir Kenneth, "to debate thine hest;" and swallowed the narcotic, mingled as it was with some water from the spring, then wrapped him in the haik, or Arab cloak, which had been fastened to his saddle-pommel, and, according to the directions of the physician, stretched himself at ease in the shade to await the promised repose. Sleep came not at first, but in her stead a train of pleasing yet not rousing or awakening sensations. A state ensued in which, still conscious of his own identity and his own condition, the knight felt enabled to consider them not only without alarm and sorrow, but as composedly as he might have viewed the story of his misfortunes acted upon a stage—or rather as a disembodied spirit might regard the transactions of its past existence. From this state of repose, amounting almost to apathy respecting the past, his thoughts were carried forward to the future, which, in spite of all that existed to overcloud the prospect, glittered with such hues as, under much happier auspices, his unstimulated imagination had not been able to produce, even in its most exalted state. Liberty, fame, successful love, appeared to be the certain and not very distant prospect of the enslaved exile, the dishonoured knight, even of the despairing lover who had placed his hopes of happiness so far beyond the prospect of chance, in her wildest possibilities, serving to countenance his wishes. Gradually as the intellectual sight became overclouded, these gay visions became obscure, like the dying hues of sunset, until they were at last lost in total oblivion; and Sir Kenneth lay extended at the feet of El Hakim, to all appearance, but for his deep respiration, as inanimate a corpse as if life had actually departed.

Lesson 145

1. Read chapter 23. Sir Kenneth awakes and unexpectedly meets an old friend, Ilderim, and they nearly have a fight over what Sir Kenneth thinks is disrespect to King Richard's wife and her attendants.
2. What surprise awaits Sir Kenneth when he wakes up? (Answers)
3. What reason does Ilderim give for having sneaked into the Crusaders' camp? How does Sir Kenneth react? (Answers)
4. Ilderim has some plans for Sir Kenneth. What are they? (Answers)

CHAPTER XXIII.

'Mid these wild scenes Enchantment waves her hand,

To change the face of the mysterious land;

Till the bewildering scenes around us seem

The Vain productions of a feverish dream.

ASTOLPHO, A ROMANCE.

When the Knight of the Leopard awoke from his long and profound repose, he found himself in circumstances so different from those in which he had lain down to sleep, that he doubted whether he was not still dreaming, or whether the scene had not been changed by magic. Instead of the damp grass, he lay on a couch of more than Oriental luxury; and some kind hands had, during his repose, stripped him of the cassock of chamois which he wore under his armour, and substituted a night-dress of the finest linen and a loose gown of silk. He had been canopied only by the palm-trees of the desert, but now he lay beneath a silken pavilion, which blazed with the richest colours of the Chinese loom, while a slight curtain of gauze, displayed around his couch, was calculated to protect his repose from the insects, to which he had, ever since his arrival in these climates, been a constant and passive prey. He looked around, as if to convince himself that he was actually awake; and all that fell beneath his eye partook of the splendour of his dormitory. A portable bath of cedar, lined with silver, was ready for use, and steamed with the odours which had been used in preparing it. On a small stand of ebony beside the couch stood a silver vase, containing sherbet of the most exquisite quality, cold as snow, and which the thirst that followed the use of the strong narcotic rendered peculiarly delicious. Still further to dispel the dregs of intoxication which it had left behind, the knight resolved to use the bath, and experienced in doing so a delightful refreshment. Having dried himself with napkins of the Indian wool, he would willingly have resumed his own coarse garments, that he might go forth to see whether the world was as much changed without as within the place of his repose. These, however, were nowhere to be seen, but in their place he found a Saracen dress of rich materials, with sabre and poniard, and all befitting an emir of distinction. He was able to suggest no motive to himself for this exuberance of care, excepting a suspicion that these attentions were intended to shake him in his religious profession—as indeed it was well known that the high esteem of the European knowledge and courage made the Soldan unbounded in his gifts to those who, having become his prisoners, had been induced to take the turban. Sir Kenneth, therefore, crossing himself devoutly, resolved to set all such snares at defiance; and that he might do so the more firmly, conscientiously determined to avail himself as moderately as possible of the attentions and luxuries thus liberally heaped upon him. Still, however, he felt his head oppressed and sleepy; and aware, too, that his undress was not fit for appearing abroad, he reclined upon the couch, and was again locked in the arms of slumber.

But this time his rest was not unbroken, for he was awakened by the voice of the physician at the door of the tent, inquiring after his health, and whether he had rested sufficiently. "May I enter your tent?" he concluded, "for the curtain is drawn before the entrance."

"The master," replied Sir Kenneth, determined to show that he was not surprised into forgetfulness of his own condition, "need demand no permission to enter the tent of the slave."

"But if I come not as a master?" said El Hakim, still without entering.

"The physician," answered the knight, "hath free access to the bedside of his patient."

"Neither come I now as a physician," replied El Hakim; "and therefore I still request permission, ere I come under the covering of thy tent."

"Whoever comes as a friend," said Sir Kenneth, "and such thou hast hitherto shown thyself to me, the habitation of the friend is ever open to him."

"Yet once again," said the Eastern sage, after the periphrastical manner of his countrymen, "supposing that I come not as a friend?"

"Come as thou wilt," said the Scottish knight, somewhat impatient of this circumlocution; "be what thou wilt—thou knowest well it is neither in my power nor my inclination to refuse thee entrance."

"I come, then," said El Hakim, "as your ancient foe, but a fair and a generous one."

He entered as he spoke; and when he stood before the bedside of Sir Kenneth, the voice continued to be that of Adonbec, the Arabian physician, but the form, dress, and features were those of Ilderim of Kurdistan, called Sheerkohf. Sir Kenneth gazed upon him as if he expected the vision to depart, like something created by his imagination.

"Doth it so surprise thee," said Ilderim, "and thou an approved warrior, to see that a soldier knows somewhat of the art of healing? I say to thee, Nazarene, that an accomplished cavalier should know how to dress his steed, as well as how to ride him; how to forge his sword upon the stithy, as well as how to use it in battle; how to burnish his arms, as well as how to wear them; and, above all, how to cure wounds, as well as how to inflict them."

As he spoke, the Christian knight repeatedly shut his eyes, and while they remained closed, the idea of the Hakim, with his long, flowing dark robes, high Tartar cap, and grave gestures was present to his imagination; but so soon as he opened them, the graceful and richly-gemmed turban, the light hauberk of steel rings entwisted with silver, which glanced brilliantly as it obeyed every inflection of the body, the features freed from their formal expression, less swarthy, and no longer shadowed by the mass of hair (now limited to a well-trimmed beard), announced the soldier and not the sage.

"Art thou still so much surprised," said the Emir, "and hast thou walked in the world with such little observance, as to wonder that men are not always what they seem? Thou thyself—art thou what thou seemest?"

"No, by Saint Andrew!" exclaimed the knight; "for to the whole Christian camp I seem a traitor, and I know myself to be a true though an erring man."

"Even so I judged thee," said Ilderim; "and as we had eaten salt together, I deemed myself bound to rescue thee from death and contumely. But wherefore lie you still on your couch, since the sun is high in the heavens? or are the vestments which my sumpter-camels have afforded unworthy of your wearing?"

"Not unworthy, surely, but unfitting for it," replied the Scot. "Give me the dress of a slave, noble Ilderim, and I will don it with pleasure; but I cannot brook to wear the habit of the free Eastern warrior with the turban of the Moslem."

"Nazarene," answered the Emir, "thy nation so easily entertain suspicion that it may well render themselves suspected. Have I not told thee that Saladin desires no converts saving those whom the holy Prophet shall dispose to submit themselves to his law? violence and bribery are alike alien to his plan for extending the true faith. Hearken to me, my brother. When the blind man was miraculously restored to sight, the scales dropped from his eyes at the Divine pleasure. Think'st thou that any earthly leech could have removed them? No. Such mediciner might have tormented the patient with his instruments, or perhaps soothed him with his balsams and cordials, but dark as he was must the darkened man have remained; and it is even so with the blindness of the understanding. If there be those among the Franks who, for the sake of worldly lucre, have assumed the turban of the Prophet, and followed the laws of Islam, with their own consciences be the blame. Themselves sought out the bait; it was not flung to them by the Soldan. And when they shall hereafter be sentenced, as hypocrites, to the lowest gulf of hell, below Christian and Jew, magician and idolater, and condemned to eat the fruit of the tree Yacoun, which is the heads of demons, to themselves, not to the Soldan, shall their guilt and their punishment be attributed. Wherefore wear, without doubt or scruple, the vesture prepared for you, since, if you proceed to the camp of Saladin, your own native dress will expose you to troublesome observation, and perhaps to insult."

"IF I go to the camp of Saladin?" said Sir Kenneth, repeating the words of the Emir; "alas! am I a free agent, and rather must I NOT go wherever your pleasure carries me?"

"Thine own will may guide thine own motions," said the Emir, "as freely as the wind which moveth the dust of the desert in what direction it chooseth. The noble enemy who met and well-nigh mastered my sword cannot become my slave like him who has crouched beneath it. If wealth and power would tempt thee to join our people, I could ensure thy possessing them; but the man who refused the favours of the Soldan when the axe was at his head, will not, I fear, now accept them, when I tell him he has his free choice."

"Complete your generosity, noble Emir," said Sir Kenneth, "by forbearing to show me a mode of requital which conscience forbids me to comply with. Permit me rather to express, as bound in courtesy, my gratitude for this most chivalrous bounty, this undeserved generosity."

"Say not undeserved," replied the Emir Ilderim. "Was it not through thy conversation, and thy account of the beauties which grace the court of the Melech Ric, that I ventured me thither in disguise, and thereby procured a sight the most blessed that I have ever enjoyed—that I ever shall enjoy, until the glories of Paradise beam on my eyes?"

"I understand you not," said Sir Kenneth, colouring alternately, and turning pale, as one who felt that the conversation was taking a tone of the most painful delicacy.

"Not understand me!" exclaimed the Emir. "If the sight I saw in the tent of King Richard escaped thine observation, I will account it duller than the edge of a buffoon's wooden falchion. True, thou wert under sentence of death at the time; but, in my case, had my head been dropping from the trunk, the last strained glances of my eyeballs had distinguished with delight such a vision of loveliness, and the head would have rolled itself towards the incomparable houris, to kiss with its quivering lips the hem of their vestments. Yonder royalty of England, who for her superior loveliness deserves to be Queen of the universe—what tenderness in her blue eye, what lustre in her tresses of dishevelled gold! By the tomb of the Prophet, I scarce think that the houri who shall present to me the diamond cup of immortality will deserve so warm a caress!"

"Saracen," said Sir Kenneth sternly, "thou speakest of the wife of Richard of England, of whom men think not and speak not as a woman to be won, but as a Queen to be revered."

"I cry you mercy," said the Saracen. "I had forgotten your superstitious veneration for the sex, which you consider rather fit to be wondered at and worshipped than wooed and possessed. I warrant, since thou exactest such profound respect to yonder tender piece of frailty, whose every motion, step, and look bespeaks her very woman, less than absolute adoration must not be yielded to her of the dark tresses and nobly speaking eye. SHE indeed, I will allow, hath in her noble port and majestic mien something at once pure and firm; yet even she, when pressed by opportunity and a forward lover, would, I warrant thee, thank him in her heart rather for treating her as a mortal than as a goddess."

"Respect the kinswoman of Coeur de Lion!" said Sir Kenneth, in a tone of unrepressed anger.

"Respect her!" answered the Emir in scorn; "by the Caaba, and if I do, it shall be rather as the bride of Saladin."

"The infidel Soldan is unworthy to salute even a spot that has been pressed by the foot of Edith Plantagenet!" exclaimed the Christian, springing from his couch.

"Ha! what said the Giaour?" exclaimed the Emir, laying his hand on his poniard hilt, while his forehead glowed like glancing copper, and the muscles of his lips and cheeks wrought till each curl of his beard seemed to twist and screw itself, as if alive with instinctive wrath. But the Scottish knight, who had stood the lion-anger of Richard, was unappalled at the tigerlike mood of the chafed Saracen.

"What I have said," continued Sir Kenneth, with folded arms and dauntless look, "I would, were my hands loose, maintain on foot or horseback against all mortals; and would hold it not the most memorable deed of my life to support it with my good broadsword against a score of these sickles and bodkins," pointing at the curved sabre and small poniard of the Emir.

The Saracen recovered his composure as the Christian spoke, so far as to withdraw his hand from his weapon, as if the motion had been without meaning, but still continued in deep ire.

"By the sword of the Prophet," he said, "which is the key both of heaven and hell, he little values his own life, brother, who uses the language thou dost! Believe me, that were thine hands loose, as thou term'st it, one single true believer would find them so much to do that thou wouldst soon wish them fettered again in manacles of iron."

"Sooner would I wish them hewn off by the shoulder-blades!" replied Sir Kenneth.

"Well. Thy hands are bound at present," said the Saracen, in a more amicable tone—"bound by thine own gentle sense of courtesy; nor have I any present purpose of setting them at liberty. We have proved each other's strength and courage ere now, and we may again meet in a fair field—and shame befall him who shall be the first to part from his foeman! But now we are friends, and I look for aid from thee rather than hard terms or defiances."

"We ARE friends," repeated the knight; and there was a pause, during which the fiery Saracen paced the tent, like the lion, who, after violent irritation, is said to take that method of cooling the distemperature of his blood, ere he stretches himself to repose in his den. The colder European remained unaltered in posture and aspect; yet he, doubtless, was also engaged in subduing the angry feelings which had been so unexpectedly awakened.

"Let us reason of this calmly," said the Saracen. "I am a physician, as thou knowest, and it is written that he who would have his wound cured must not shrink when the leech probes and tests it. Seest thou, I am about to lay my finger on the sore. Thou lovest this kinswoman of the Melech Ric. Unfold the veil that shrouds thy thoughts—or unfold it not if thou wilt, for mine eyes see through its coverings."

"I LOVED her," answered Sir Kenneth, after a pause, "as a man loves Heaven's grace, and sued for her favour like a sinner for Heaven's pardon."

"And you love her no longer?" said the Saracen.

"Alas," answered Sir Kenneth, "I am no longer worthy to love her. I pray thee cease this discourse—thy words are poniards to me."

"Pardon me but a moment," continued Ilderim. "When thou, a poor and obscure soldier, didst so boldly and so highly fix thine affection, tell me, hadst thou good hope of its issue?"

"Love exists not without hope," replied the knight; "but mine was as nearly allied to despair as that of the sailor swimming for his life, who, as he surmounts billow after billow, catches by intervals some gleam of the distant beacon, which shows him there is land in sight, though his sinking heart and wearied limbs assure him that he shall never reach it."

"And now," said Ilderim, "these hopes are sunk—that solitary light is quenched for ever?"

"For ever," answered Sir Kenneth, in the tone of an echo from the bosom of a ruined sepulchre.

"Methinks," said the Saracen, "if all thou lackest were some such distant meteoric glimpse of happiness as thou hadst formerly, thy beacon-light might be rekindled, thy hope fished up from the ocean in which it has sunk, and thou thyself, good knight, restored to the exercise and amusement of nourishing thy fantastic fashion upon a diet as unsubstantial as moonlight; for, if thou stood'st tomorrow fair in reputation as ever thou wert, she whom thou lovest will not be less the daughter of princes and the elected bride of Saladin."

"I would it so stood," said the Scot, "and if I did not—"

He stopped short, like a man who is afraid of boasting under circumstances which did not permit his being put to the test. The Saracen smiled as he concluded the sentence.

"Thou wouldst challenge the Soldan to single combat?" said he.

"And if I did," said Sir Kenneth haughtily, "Saladin's would neither be the first nor the best turban that I have couched lance at."

"Ay, but methinks the Soldan might regard it as too unequal a mode of perilling the chance of a royal bride and the event of a great war," said the Emir.

"He may be met with in the front of battle," said the knight, his eyes gleaming with the ideas which such a thought inspired.

"He has been ever found there," said Ilderim; "nor is it his wont to turn his horse's head from any brave encounter. But it was not of the Soldan that I meant to speak. In a word, if it will content thee to be placed in such reputation as may be attained by detection of the thief who stole the Banner of England, I can put thee in a fair way of achieving this task—that is, if thou wilt be governed; for what says Lokman, 'If the child would walk, the nurse must lead him; if the ignorant would understand, the wise must instruct.'"

"And thou art wise, Ilderim," said the Scot—"wise though a Saracen, and generous though an infidel. I have witnessed that thou art both. Take, then, the guidance of this matter; and so thou ask nothing of me contrary to my loyalty and my Christian faith, I, will obey thee punctually. Do what thou hast said, and take my life when it is accomplished."

"Listen thou to me, then," said the Saracen. "Thy noble hound is now recovered, by the blessing of that divine medicine which healeth man and beast; and by his sagacity shall those who assailed him be discovered."

"Ha!" said the knight, "methinks I comprehend thee. I was dull not to think of this!"

"But tell me," added the Emir, "hast thou any followers or retainers in the camp by whom the animal may be known?"

"I dismissed," said Sir Kenneth, "my old attendant, thy patient, with a varlet that waited on him, at the time when I expected to suffer death, giving him letters for my friends in Scotland; there are none other to whom the dog is familiar. But then my own person is well known—my very speech will betray me, in a camp where I have played no mean part for many months."

"Both he and thou shalt be disguised, so as to escape even close examination. I tell thee," said the Saracen, "that not thy brother in arms—not thy brother in blood—shall discover thee, if thou be guided by my counsels. Thou hast seen me do matters more difficult—he that can call the dying from the darkness of the shadow of death can easily cast a mist before the eyes of the living. But mark me: there is still the condition annexed to this service—that thou deliver a letter of Saladin to the niece of the Melech Ric, whose name is as difficult to our Eastern tongue and lips, as her beauty is delightful to our eyes."

Sir Kenneth paused before he answered, and the Saracen observing his hesitation, demanded of him, "if he feared to undertake this message?"

"Not if there were death in the execution," said Sir Kenneth. "I do but pause to consider whether it consists with my honour to bear the letter of the Soldan, or with that of the Lady Edith to receive it from a heathen prince."

"By the head of Mohammed, and by the honour of a soldier—by the tomb at Mecca, and by the soul of my father," said the Emir, "I swear to thee that the letter is written in all honour and respect. The song of the nightingale will sooner blight the rose-bower she loves than will the words of the Soldan offend the ears of the lovely kinswoman of England."

"Then," said the knight, "I will bear the Soldan's letter faithfully, as if I were his born vassal—understanding, that beyond this simple act of service, which I will render with fidelity, from me of all men he can least expect mediation or advice in this his strange love-suit."

"Saladin is noble," answered the Emir, "and will not spur a generous horse to a leap which he cannot achieve. Come with me to my tent," he added, "and thou shalt be presently equipped with a disguise as unsearchable as midnight, so thou mayest walk the camp of the Nazarenes as if thou hadst on thy finger the signet of Giaougi." [Perhaps the same with Gyges.]

Lesson 146

1. Read chapter 24. When during a procession of all the Crusaders, the Nubian's dog attacks Conrade, the Marquis de Montserrat, revealing him to be the one who stole the King's banner, King Richard challenges him to combat to determine the truth of this accusation, but others persuade Richard to send a substitute to battle in his name.
2. Unusual Vocabulary:
    - Morion - an open helmet
    - Sagacity - wisdom
3. When you read, "the reader can now have little doubt who the Ethiopian slave really was . . . ," what did you think? (Answers)
4. Who is the Nubian? When did you figure that out? (Answers)
5. Why won't the other Crusaders accept King Richard's willingness to defend his own honor in Conrade's challenge? (Answers)
6. Where will the challenge be carried out? (Answers)

CHAPTER XXIV

A grain of dust

Soiling our cup, will make our sense reject

Fastidiously the draught which we did thirst for;

A rusted nail, placed near the faithful compass,

Will sway it from the truth, and wreck the argosy.

Even this small cause of anger and disgust

Will break the bonds of amity 'mongst princes,

And wreck their noblest purposes.

THE CRUSADE.

The reader can now have little doubt who the Ethiopian slave really was, with what purpose he had sought Richard's camp, and wherefore and with what hope he now stood close to the person of that Monarch, as, surrounded by his valiant peers of England and Normandy, Coeur de Lion stood on the summit of Saint George's Mount, with the Banner of England by his side, borne by the most goodly person in the army, being his own natural brother, William with the Long Sword, Earl of Salisbury, the offspring of Henry the Second's amour with the celebrated Rosamond of Woodstock.

From several expressions in the King's conversation with Neville on the preceding day, the Nubian was left in anxious doubt whether his disguise had not been penetrated, especially as that the King seemed to be aware in what manner the agency of the dog was expected to discover the thief who stole the banner, although the circumstance of such an animal's having been wounded on the occasion had been scarce mentioned in Richard's presence. Nevertheless, as the King continued to treat him in no other manner than his exterior required, the Nubian remained uncertain whether he was or was not discovered, and determined not to throw his disguise aside voluntarily.

Meanwhile, the powers of the various Crusading princes, arrayed under their royal and princely leaders, swept in long order around the base of the little mound; and as those of each different country passed by, their commanders advanced a step or two up the hill, and made a signal of courtesy to Richard and to the Standard of England, "in sign of regard and amity," as the protocol of the ceremony heedfully expressed it, "not of subjection or vassalage." The spiritual dignitaries, who in those days veiled not their bonnets to created being, bestowed on the King and his symbol of command their blessing instead of rendering obeisance.

Thus the long files marched on, and, diminished as they were by so many causes, appeared still an iron host, to whom the conquest of Palestine might seem an easy task. The soldiers, inspired by the consciousness of united strength, sat erect in their steel saddles; while it seemed that the trumpets sounded more cheerfully shrill, and the steeds, refreshed by rest and provender, chafed on the bit, and trod the ground more proudly. On they passed, troop after troop, banners waving, spears glancing, plumes dancing, in long perspective—a host composed of different nations, complexions, languages, arms, and appearances, but all fired, for the time, with the holy yet romantic purpose of rescuing the distressed daughter of Zion from her thraldom, and redeeming the sacred earth, which more than mortal had trodden, from the yoke of the unbelieving pagan. And it must be owned that if, in other circumstances, the species of courtesy rendered to the King of England by so many warriors, from whom he claimed no natural allegiance, had in it something that might have been thought humiliating, yet the nature and cause of the war was so fitted to his pre-eminently chivalrous character and renowned feats in arms, that claims which might elsewhere have been urged were there forgotten, and the brave did willing homage to the bravest, in an expedition where the most undaunted and energetic courage was necessary to success.

The good King was seated on horseback about half way up the mount, a morion on his head, surmounted by a crown, which left his manly features exposed to public view, as, with cool and considerate eye, he perused each rank as it passed him, and returned the salutation of the leaders. His tunic was of sky-coloured velvet, covered with plates of silver, and his hose of crimson silk, slashed with cloth of gold. By his side stood the seeming Ethiopian slave, holding the noble dog in a leash, such as was used in woodcraft. It was a circumstance which attracted no notice, for many of the princes of the Crusade had introduced black slaves into their household, in imitation of the barbarous splendour of the Saracens. Over the King's head streamed the large folds of the banner, and, as he looked to it from time to time, he seemed to regard a ceremony, indifferent to himself personally, as important, when considered as atoning an indignity offered to the kingdom which he ruled. In the background, and on the very summit of the Mount, a wooden turret, erected for the occasion, held the Queen Berengaria and the principal ladies of the Court. To this the King looked from time to time; and then ever and anon his eyes were turned on the Nubian and the dog, but only when such leaders approached, as, from circumstances of previous ill-will, he suspected of being accessory to the theft of the standard, or whom he judged capable of a crime so mean.

Thus, he did not look in that direction when Philip Augustus of France approached at the head of his splendid troops of Gallic chivalry—-nay, he anticipated the motions of the French King, by descending the Mount as the latter came up the ascent, so that they met in the middle space, and blended their greetings so gracefully that it appeared they met in fraternal equality. The sight of the two greatest princes in Europe, in rank at once and power, thus publicly avowing their concord, called forth bursts of thundering acclaim from the Crusading host at many miles distance, and made the roving Arab scouts of the desert alarm the camp of Saladin with intelligence that the army of the Christians was in motion. Yet who but the King of kings can read the hearts of monarchs? Under this smooth show of courtesy, Richard nourished displeasure and suspicion against Philip, and Philip meditated withdrawing himself and his host from the army of the Cross, and leaving Richard to accomplish or fail in the enterprise with his own unassisted forces.

Richard's demeanour was different when the dark-armed knights and squires of the Temple chivalry approached—men with countenances bronzed to Asiatic blackness by the suns of Palestine, and the admirable state of whose horses and appointments far surpassed even that of the choicest troops of France and England. The King cast a hasty glance aside; but the Nubian stood quiet, and his trusty dog sat at his feet, watching, with a sagacious yet pleased look, the ranks which now passed before them. The King's look turned again on the chivalrous Templars, as the Grand Master, availing himself of his mingled character, bestowed his benediction on Richard as a priest, instead of doing him reverence as a military leader.

"The misproud and amphibious caitiff puts the monk upon me," said Richard to the Earl of Salisbury. "But, Longsword, we will let it pass. A punctilio must not lose Christendom the services of these experienced lances, because their victories have rendered them overweening. Lo you, here comes our valiant adversary, the Duke of Austria. Mark his manner and bearing,

Longsword—and thou, Nubian, let the hound have full view of him. By Heaven, he brings his buffoons along with him!"

In fact, whether from habit, or, which is more likely, to intimate contempt of the ceremonial he was about to comply with, Leopold was attended by his SPRUCH-SPRECHER and his jester; and as he advanced towards Richard, he whistled in what he wished to be considered as an indifferent manner, though his heavy features evinced the sullenness, mixed with the fear, with which a truant schoolboy may be seen to approach his master. As the reluctant dignitary made, with discomposed and sulky look, the obeisance required, the SPRUCH-SPRECHER shook his baton, and proclaimed, like a herald, that, in what he was now doing, the Archduke of Austria was not to be held derogating from the rank and privileges of a sovereign prince; to which the jester answered with a sonorous AMEN, which provoked much laughter among the bystanders.

King Richard looked more than once at the Nubian and his dog; but the former moved not, nor did the latter strain at the leash, so that Richard said to the slave with some scorn, "Thy success in this enterprise, my sable friend, even though thou hast brought thy hound's sagacity to back thine own, will not, I fear, place thee high in the rank of wizards, or much augment thy merits towards our person."

The Nubian answered, as usual, only by a lowly obeisance.

Meantime the troops of the Marquis of Montserrat next passed in order before the King of England. That powerful and wily baron, to make the greater display of his forces, had divided them into two bodies. At the head of the first, consisting of his vassals and followers, and levied from his Syrian possessions, came his brother Enguerrand; and he himself followed, leading on a gallant band of twelve hundred Stradiots, a kind of light cavalry raised by the Venetians in their Dalmatian possessions, and of which they had entrusted the command to the Marquis, with whom the republic had many bonds of connection. These Stradiots were clothed in a fashion partly European, but partaking chiefly of the Eastern fashion. They wore, indeed, short hauberks, but had over them party-coloured tunics of rich stuffs, with large wide pantaloons and half-boots. On their heads were straight upright caps, similar to those of the Greeks; and they carried small round targets, bows and arrows, scimitars, and poniards. They were mounted on horses carefully selected, and well maintained at the expense of the State of Venice; their saddles and appointments resembled those of the Turks, and they rode in the same manner, with short stirrups and upon a high seat. These troops were of great use in skirmishing with the Arabs, though unable to engage in close combat, like the iron-sheathed men-at-arms of Western and Northern Europe.

Before this goodly band came Conrade, in the same garb with the Stradiots, but of such rich stuff that he seemed to blaze with gold and silver, and the milk-white plume fastened in his cap by a clasp of diamonds seemed tall enough to sweep the clouds. The noble steed which he reined bounded and caracoled, and displayed his spirit and agility in a manner which might have troubled a less admirable horseman than the Marquis, who gracefully ruled him with the one hand, while the other displayed the baton, whose predominancy over the ranks which he led seemed equally absolute. Yet his authority over the Stradiots was more in show than in substance; for there paced beside him, on an ambling palfrey of soberest mood, a little old man, dressed entirely in black, without beard or moustaches, and having an appearance altogether mean and insignificant when compared with the blaze of splendour around him. But this mean-looking old man was one of those deputies whom the Venetian government sent into camps to overlook the conduct of the generals to whom the leading was consigned, and to maintain that jealous system of espial and control which had long distinguished the policy of the republic.

Conrade, who, by cultivating Richard's humour, had attained a certain degree of favour with him, no sooner was come within his ken than the King of England descended a step or two to meet him, exclaiming, at the same time, "Ha, Lord Marquis, thou at the head of the fleet Stradiots, and thy black shadow attending thee as usual, whether the sun shines or not! May not one ask thee whether the rule of the troops remains with the shadow or the substance?"

Conrade was commencing his reply with a smile, when Roswal, the noble hound, uttering a furious and savage yell, sprung forward. The Nubian, at the same time, slipped the leash, and the hound, rushing on, leapt upon Conrade's noble charger, and, seizing the Marquis by the throat, pulled him down from the saddle. The plumed rider lay rolling on the sand, and the frightened horse fled in wild career through the camp.

"Thy hound hath pulled down the right quarry, I warrant him," said the King to the Nubian, "and I vow to Saint George he is a stag of ten tynes! Pluck the dog off; lest he throttle him."

The Ethiopian, accordingly, though not without difficulty, disengaged the dog from Conrade, and fastened him up, still highly excited, and struggling in the leash. Meanwhile many crowded to the spot, especially followers of Conrade and officers of the Stradiots, who, as they saw their leader lie gazing wildly on the sky, raised him up amid a tumultuary cry of "Cut the slave and his hound to pieces!"

But the voice of Richard, loud and sonorous, was heard clear above all other exclamations. "He dies the death who injures the hound! He hath but done his duty, after the sagacity with which God and nature have endowed the brave animal.—Stand forward for a false traitor, thou Conrade, Marquis of Montserrat! I impeach thee of treason."

Several of the Syrian leaders had now come up, and Conrade—vexation, and shame, and confusion struggling with passion in his manner and voice—exclaimed, "What means this? With what am I charged? Why this base usage and these reproachful terms? Is this the league of concord which England renewed but so lately?"

"Are the Princes of the Crusade turned hares or deers in the eyes of King Richard that he should slip hounds on them?" said the sepulchral voice of the Grand Master of the Templars.

"It must be some singular accident—some fatal mistake," said Philip of France, who rode up at the same moment.

"Some deceit of the Enemy," said the Archbishop of Tyre.

"A stratagem of the Saracens," cried Henry of Champagne. "It were well to hang up the dog, and put the slave to the torture."

"Let no man lay hand upon them," said Richard, "as he loves his own life! Conrade, stand forth, if thou darest, and deny the accusation which this mute animal hath in his noble instinct brought against thee, of injury done to him, and foul scorn to England!"

"I never touched the banner," said Conrade hastily.

"Thy words betray thee, Conrade!" said Richard, "for how didst thou know, save from conscious guilt, that the question is concerning the banner?"

"Hast thou then not kept the camp in turmoil on that and no other score?" answered Conrade; "and dost thou impute to a prince and an ally a crime which, after all, was probably committed by some paltry felon for the sake of the gold thread? Or wouldst thou now impeach a confederate on the credit of a dog?"

By this time the alarm was becoming general, so that Philip of France interposed.

"Princes and nobles," he said, "you speak in presence of those whose swords will soon be at the throats of each other if they hear their leaders at such terms together. In the name of Heaven, let us draw off each his own troops into their separate quarters, and ourselves meet an hour hence in the Pavilion of Council to take some order in this new state of confusion."

"Content," said King Richard, "though I should have liked to have interrogated that caitiff while his gay doublet was yet besmirched with sand. But the pleasure of France shall be ours in this matter."

The leaders separated as was proposed, each prince placing himself at the head of his own forces; and then was heard on all sides the crying of war-cries and the sounding of gathering-notes upon bugles and trumpets, by which the different stragglers were summoned to their prince's banner, and the troops were shortly seen in motion, each taking different routes through the camp to their own quarters. But although any immediate act of violence was thus prevented, yet the accident which had taken place dwelt on every mind; and those foreigners who had that morning hailed Richard as the worthiest to lead their army, now resumed their prejudices against his pride and intolerance, while the English, conceiving the honour of their country connected with the quarrel, of which various reports had gone about, considered the natives of other countries jealous of the fame of England and her King, and disposed to undermine it by the meanest arts of intrigue. Many and various were the rumours spread upon the occasion, and there was one which averred that the Queen and her ladies had been much alarmed by the tumult, and that one of them had swooned.

The Council assembled at the appointed hour. Conrade had in the meanwhile laid aside his dishonoured dress, and with it the shame and confusion which, in spite of his talents and promptitude, had at first overwhelmed him, owing to the strangeness of the accident and suddenness of the accusation. He was now robed like a prince; and entered the council-chamber attended by the Archduke of Austria, the Grand Masters both of the Temple and of the Order of Saint John, and several other potentates, who made a show of supporting him and defending his cause, chiefly perhaps from political motives, or because they themselves nourished a personal enmity against Richard.

This appearance of union in favour of Conrade was far from influencing the King of England. He entered the Council with his usual indifference of manner, and in the same dress in which he had just alighted from horseback. He cast a careless and somewhat scornful glance on the leaders, who had with studied affectation arranged themselves around Conrade as if owning his cause, and in the most direct terms charged Conrade of Montserrat with having stolen the Banner of England, and wounded the faithful animal who stood in its defence.

Conrade arose boldly to answer, and in despite, as he expressed himself, of man and brute, king or dog, avouched his innocence of the crime charged.

"Brother of England," said Philip, who willingly assumed the character of moderator of the assembly, "this is an unusual impeachment. We do not hear you avouch your own knowledge of this matter, further than your belief resting upon the demeanour of this hound towards the Marquis of Montserrat. Surely the word of a knight and a prince should bear him out against the barking of a cur?"

"Royal brother," returned Richard, "recollect that the Almighty, who gave the dog to be companion of our pleasures and our toils, hath invested him with a nature noble and incapable of deceit. He forgets neither friend nor foe—remembers, and with accuracy, both benefit and injury. He hath a share of man's intelligence, but no share of man's falsehood. You may bribe a soldier to slay a man with his sword, or a witness to take life by false accusation; but you cannot make a hound tear his benefactor. He is the friend of man, save when man justly incurs his enmity. Dress yonder marquis in what peacock-robes you will, disguise his appearance, alter his complexion with drugs and washes, hide him amidst a hundred men,—I will yet pawn my sceptre that the hound detects him, and expresses his resentment, as you have this day beheld. This is no new incident, although a strange one. Murderers and robbers have been ere now convicted, and suffered death under such evidence, and men have said that the finger of God was in it. In thine own land, royal brother, and upon such an occasion, the matter was tried by a solemn duel betwixt the man and the dog, as appellant and defendant in a challenge of murder. The dog was victorious, the man was punished, and the crime was confessed. Credit me, royal brother, that hidden crimes have often been brought to light by the testimony even of inanimate substances, not to mention animals far inferior in instinctive sagacity to the dog, who is the friend and companion of our race."

"Such a duel there hath indeed been, royal brother," answered Philip, "and that in the reign of one of our predecessors, to whom God be gracious. But it was in the olden time, nor can we hold it a precedent fitting for this occasion. The defendant in that case was a private gentleman of small rank or respect; his offensive weapons were only a club, his defensive a leathern jerkin. But we cannot degrade a prince to the disgrace of using such rude arms, or to the ignominy of such a combat."

"I never meant that you should," said King Richard; "it were foul play to hazard the good hound's life against that of such a double-faced traitor as this Conrade hath proved himself. But there lies our own glove; we appeal him to the combat in respect of the evidence we brought forth against him. A king, at least, is more than the mate of a marquis."

Conrade made no hasty effort to seize on the pledge which Richard cast into the middle of the assembly, and King Philip had time to reply ere the marquis made a motion to lift the glove.

"A king," said he of France, "is as much more than a match for the Marquis Conrade as a dog would be less. Royal Richard, this cannot be permitted. You are the leader of our expedition—the sword and buckler of Christendom."

"I protest against such a combat," said the Venetian proveditore, "until the King of England shall have repaid the fifty thousand byzants which he is indebted to the republic. It is enough to be threatened with loss of our debt, should our debtor fall by the hands of the pagans, without the additional risk of his being slain in brawls amongst Christians concerning dogs and banners."

"And I," said William with the Long Sword, Earl of Salisbury, "protest in my turn against my royal brother perilling his life, which is the property of the people of England, in such a cause. Here, noble brother, receive back your glove, and think only as if the wind had blown it from your hand. Mine shall lie in its stead. A king's son, though with the bar sinister on his shield, is at least a match for this marmoset of a marquis."

"Princes and nobles," said Conrade, "I will not accept of King Richard's defiance. He hath been chosen our leader against the Saracens, and if his conscience can answer the accusation of provoking an ally to the field on a quarrel so frivolous, mine, at least, cannot endure the reproach of accepting it. But touching his bastard brother, William of Woodstock, or against any other who shall adopt or shall dare to stand godfather to this most false charge, I will defend my honour in the lists, and prove whosoever impeaches it a false liar."

"The Marquis of Montserrat," said the Archbishop of Tyre, "hath spoken like a wise and moderate gentleman; and methinks this controversy might, without dishonour to any party, end at this point."

"Methinks it might so terminate," said the King of France, "provided King Richard will recall his accusation as made upon over-slight grounds."

"Philip of France," answered Coeur de Lion, "my words shall never do my thoughts so much injury. I have charged yonder Conrade as a thief, who, under cloud of night, stole from its place the emblem of England's dignity. I still believe and charge him to be such; and when a day is appointed for the combat, doubt not that, since Conrade declines to meet us in person, I will find a champion to appear in support of my challenge—for thou, William, must not thrust thy long sword into this quarrel without our special license."

"Since my rank makes me arbiter in this most unhappy matter," said Philip of France, "I appoint the fifth day from hence for the decision thereof, by way of combat, according to knightly usage—Richard, King of England, to appear by his champion as appellant, and Conrade, Marquis of Montserrat, in his own person, as defendant. Yet I own I know not where to find neutral ground where such a quarrel may be fought out; for it must not be in the neighbourhood of this camp, where the soldiers would make faction on the different sides."

"It were well," said Richard, "to apply to the generosity of the royal Saladin, since, heathen as he is, I have never known knight more fulfilled of nobleness, or to whose good faith we may so peremptorily entrust ourselves. I speak thus for those who may be doubtful of mishap; for myself, wherever I see my foe, I make that spot my battle-ground."

"Be it so," said Philip; "we will make this matter known to Saladin, although it be showing to an enemy the unhappy spirit of discord which we would willingly hide from even ourselves, were it possible. Meanwhile, I dismiss this assembly, and charge you all, as Christian men and noble knights, that ye let this unhappy feud breed no further brawling in the camp, but regard it as a thing solemnly referred to the judgment of God, to whom each of you should pray that He will dispose of victory in the combat according to the truth of the quarrel; and therewith may His will be done!"

"Amen, amen!" was answered on all sides; while the Templar whispered the Marquis, "Conrade, wilt thou not add a petition to be delivered from the power of the dog, as the Psalmist hath it?"

"Peace, thou—!" replied the Marquis; "there is a revealing demon abroad which may report, amongst other tidings, how far thou dost carry the motto of thy order—'FERIATUR LEO'."

"Thou wilt stand the brunt of challenge?" said the Templar.

"Doubt me not," said Conrade. "I would not, indeed, have willingly met the iron arm of Richard himself, and I shame not to confess that I rejoice to be free of his encounter; but, from his bastard brother downward, the man breathes not in his ranks whom I fear to meet."

"It is well you are so confident," continued the Templar; "and, in that case, the fangs of yonder hound have done more to dissolve this league of princes than either thy devices or the dagger of the Charegite. Seest thou how, under a brow studiously overclouded, Philip cannot conceal the satisfaction which he feels at the prospect of release from the alliance which sat so heavy on him? Mark how Henry of Champagne smiles to himself, like a sparkling goblet of his own wine; and see the chuckling delight of Austria, who thinks his quarrel is about to be avenged without risk or trouble of his own. Hush! he approaches.—A most grievous chance, most royal Austria, that these breaches in the walls of our Zion—"

"If thou meanest this Crusade," replied the Duke, "I would it were crumbled to pieces, and each were safe at home! I speak this in confidence."

"But," said the Marquis of Montserrat, "to think this disunion should be made by the hands of King Richard, for whose pleasure we have been contented to endure so much, and to whom we have been as submissive as slaves to a master, in hopes that he would use his valour against our enemies, instead of exercising it upon our friends!"

"I see not that he is so much more valorous than others," said the Archduke. "I believe, had the noble Marquis met him in the lists, he would have had the better; for though the islander deals heavy blows with the pole-axe, he is not so very dexterous with the lance. I should have cared little to have met him myself on our old quarrel, had the weal of Christendom permitted to sovereign princes to breathe themselves in the lists; and if thou desirest it, noble Marquis, I will myself be your godfather in this combat."

"And I also," said the Grand Master.

"Come, then, and take your nooning in our tent, noble sirs," said the Duke, "and we'll speak of this business over some right NIERENSTEIN."

They entered together accordingly.

"What said our patron and these great folks together?" said Jonas Schwanker to his companion, the SPRUCH-SPRECHER, who had used the freedom to press nigh to his master when the Council was dismissed, while the jester waited at a more respectful distance.

"Servant of Folly," said the SPRUCH-SPRECHER, "moderate thy curiosity; it beseems not that I should tell to thee the counsels of our master."

"Man of wisdom, you mistake," answered Jonas. "We are both the constant attendants on our patron, and it concerns us alike to know whether thou or I—Wisdom or Folly—have the deeper interest in him."

"He told to the Marquis," answered the SPRUCH-SPRECHER, "and to the Grand Master, that he was aweary of these wars, and would be glad he was safe at home."

"That is a drawn cast, and counts for nothing in the game," said the jester; "it was most wise to think thus, but great folly to tell it to others—proceed."

"Ha, hem!" said the SPRUCH-SPRECHER; "he next said to them that Richard was not more valorous than others, or over-dexterous in the tilt-yard."

"Woodcock of my side," said Schwanker, "this was egregious folly. What next?"

"Nay, I am something oblivious," replied the man of wisdom—"he invited them to a goblet of NIERENSTEIN."

"That hath a show of wisdom in it," said Jonas. "Thou mayest mark it to thy credit in the meantime; but an he drink too much, as is most likely, I will have it pass to mine. Anything more?"

"Nothing worth memory," answered the orator; "only he wished he had taken the occasion to meet Richard in the lists."

"Out upon it—out upon it!" said Jonas; "this is such dotage of folly that I am well-nigh ashamed of winning the game by it. Ne'ertheless, fool as he is, we will follow him, most sage SPRUCH-SPRECHER, and have our share of the wine of NIERENSTEIN."

Lesson 147

1. Read chapter 25. The Nubian/Ethiopian/Sir Kenneth meets briefly with King Richard and then takes his message from Saladin to Edith, but although she recognizes him, he refuses to break out of his character and speak to her, frustrating her. Minstrel - a medieval traveling entertainer
2. Sir Kenneth, the Nubian aka the Ethiopian, says in his thoughts that Richard is "liberal, generous, and truly noble." Did you have any of those words in your

character trait list for Richard? Do you agree with Sir Kenneth? Why or why not? If you do agree, add these character traits to your list. (Answers)

3. Sir Kenneth carries two messages. What are they? (Answers)
4. What happens when the Nubian meets Edith? (Answers)
5. Why does she become angry with him? (Answers)

CHAPTER XXV.

Yet this inconstancy is such,

As thou, too, shalt adore;

I could not love thee, love so much,

Loved I not honour more.

MONTROSE'S LINES.

When King Richard returned to his tent, he commanded the Nubian to be brought before him. He entered with his usual ceremonial reverence, and having prostrated himself, remained standing before the King in the attitude of a slave awaiting the orders of his master. It was perhaps well for him that the preservation of his character required his eyes to be fixed on the ground, since the keen glance with which Richard for some time surveyed him in silence would, if fully encountered, have been difficult to sustain.

"Thou canst well of woodcraft," said the King, after a pause, "and hast started thy game and brought him to bay as ably as if Tristrem himself had taught thee. [A universal tradition ascribed to Sir Tristrem, famous for his love of the fair Queen Yseult, the laws concerning the practice of woodcraft, or VENERIE, as it was called, being those that related to the rules of the chase, which were deemed of much consequence during the Middle Ages.] But this is not all—he must be brought down at force. I myself would have liked to have levelled my hunting-spear at him. There are, it seems, respects which prevent this. Thou art about to return to the camp of the Soldan, bearing a letter, requiring of his courtesy to appoint neutral ground for the deed of chivalry, and should it consist with his pleasure, to concur with us in witnessing it. Now, speaking conjecturally, we think thou mightst find in that camp some cavalier who, for the love of truth and his own augmentation of honour, will do battle with this same traitor of Montserrat."

The Nubian raised his eyes and fixed them on the King with a look of eager ardour; then raised them to Heaven with such solemn gratitude that the water soon glistened in them; then bent his head, as affirming what Richard desired, and resumed his usual posture of submissive attention.

"It is well," said the King; "and I see thy desire to oblige me in this matter. And herein, I must needs say, lies the excellence of such a servant as thou, who hast not speech either to debate our purpose or to require explanation of what we have determined. An English serving man in thy place had given me his dogged advice to trust the combat with some good lance of my household, who, from my brother Longsword downwards, are all on fire to do battle in my cause; and a chattering Frenchman had made a thousand attempts to discover wherefore I look for a champion from the camp of the infidels. But thou, my silent agent, canst do mine errand without questioning or comprehending it; with thee to hear is to obey."

A bend of the body and a genuflection were the appropriate answer of the Ethiopian to these observations.

"And now to another point," said the King, and speaking suddenly and rapidly—"have you yet seen Edith Plantagenet?"

The mute looked up as in the act of being about to speak—nay, his lips had begun to utter a distinct negative—when the abortive attempt died away in the imperfect murmurs of the dumb.

"Why, lo you there!" said the King, "the very sound of the name of a royal maiden of beauty so surpassing as that of our lovely cousin seems to have power enough well-nigh to make the dumb speak. What miracles then might her eye work upon such a subject! I will make the experiment, friend slave. Thou shalt see this choice beauty of our Court, and do the errand of the princely Soldan."

Again a joyful glance—again a genuflection—but, as he arose, the King laid his hand heavily on his shoulder, and proceeded with stern gravity thus: "Let me in one thing warn you, my sable envoy. Even if thou shouldst feel that the kindly influence of her whom thou art soon to behold should loosen the bonds of thy tongue, presently imprisoned, as the good Soldan expresses it, within the ivory walls of its castle, beware how thou changest thy taciturn character, or speakest a word in her presence, even if thy powers of utterance were to be miraculously restored. Believe me that I should have thy tongue extracted by the roots, and its ivory palace—that is, I presume, its range of teeth—drawn out one by one. Wherefore, be wise and silent still."

The Nubian, so soon as the King had removed his heavy grasp from his shoulder, bent his head, and laid his hand on his lips, in token of silent obedience.

But Richard again laid his hand on him more gently, and added, "This behest we lay on thee as on a slave. Wert thou knight and gentleman, we would require thine honour in pledge of thy silence, which is one especial condition of our present trust."

The Ethiopian raised his body proudly, looked full at the King, and laid his right hand on his heart.

Richard then summoned his chamberlain.

"Go, Neville," he said, "with this slave to the tent of our royal consort, and say it is our pleasure that he have an audience—a private audience—of our cousin Edith. He is charged with a commission to her. Thou canst show him the way also, in case he requires thy guidance, though thou mayst have observed it is wonderful how familiar he already seems to be with the purlieus of our camp.—And thou, too, friend Ethiop," the King continued, "what thou dost do quickly, and return hither within the half-hour."

"I stand discovered," thought the seeming Nubian, as, with downcast looks and folded arms, he followed the hasty stride of Neville towards the tent of Queen Berengaria—"I stand undoubtedly discovered and unfolded to King Richard; yet I cannot perceive that his resentment is hot against me. If I understand his words—and surely it is impossible to misinterpret them—he gives me a noble chance of redeeming my honour upon the crest of this false Marquis, whose guilt I read in his craven eye and quivering lip when the charge was made against him.—Roswal, faithfully hast thou served thy master, and most dearly shall thy wrong be avenged!—But what is the meaning of my present permission to look upon her whom I had despaired ever to see again? And why, or how, can the royal Plantagenet consent that I should see his divine kinswoman, either as the messenger of the heathen Saladin, or as the guilty exile whom he so lately expelled from his camp—his audacious avowal of the affection which is his pride being the greatest enhancement of his guilt? That Richard should consent to her receiving a letter from an infidel lover by the hands of one of such disproportioned rank are either of them circumstances equally incredible, and, at the same time, inconsistent with each other. But Richard, when unmoved by his heady passions, is liberal, generous, and truly noble; and as such I will deal with him, and act according to his instructions, direct or implied, seeking to know no more than may gradually unfold itself without my officious inquiry. To him who has given me so brave an opportunity to vindicate my tarnished honour, I owe acquiescence and obedience; and painful as it may be, the debt shall be paid. And yet"—thus the proud swelling of his heart further suggested—"Coeur de Lion, as he is called, might have measured the feelings of others by his own. I urge an address to his kinswoman! I, who never spoke word to her when I took a royal prize from her hand—when I was accounted not the lowest in feats of chivalry among the defenders of the Cross! I approach her when in a base disguise, and in a servile habit—and, alas! when my actual condition is that of a slave, with a spot of dishonour on that which was once my shield! I do this! He little knows me. Yet I thank him for the opportunity which may make us all better acquainted with each other."

As he arrived at this conclusion, they paused before the entrance of the Queen's pavilion.

They were of course admitted by the guards, and Neville, leaving the Nubian in a small apartment, or antechamber, which was but too well remembered by him, passed into that which was used as the Queen's presence-chamber. He communicated his royal master's pleasure in a low and respectful tone of voice, very different from the bluntness of Thomas de Vaux, to whom Richard was everything and the rest of the Court, including Berengaria herself, was nothing. A burst of laughter followed the communication of his errand.

"And what like is the Nubian slave who comes ambassador on such an errand from the Soldan?—an African, De Neville, is he not?" said a female voice, easily recognized for that of Berengaria. "An African, is he not, De Neville, with black skin—ha, worthy Sir Henry?"

"Let not your Grace forget the shin-bones," said another voice, "bent outwards like the edge of a Saracen scimitar."

"Rather like the bow of a Cupid, since he comes upon a lover's errand," said the Queen.—"Gentle Neville, thou art ever prompt to pleasure us poor women, who have so little to pass away our idle moments. We must see this messenger of love. Turks and Moors have I seen many, but Africans never."

"I am created to obey your Grace's commands, so you will bear me out with my Sovereign for doing so," answered the debonair knight. "Yet, let me assure your Grace you will see something different from what you expect."

"So much the better—uglier yet than our imaginations can fancy, yet the chosen love-messenger of this gallant Soldan!"

"Gracious madam," said the Lady Calista, "may I implore you would permit the good knight to carry this messenger straight to the Lady Edith, to whom his credentials are addressed? We have already escaped hardly for such a frolic."

"Escaped?" repeated the Queen scornfully. "Yet thou mayest be right, Calista, in thy caution. Let this Nubian, as thou callest him, first do his errand to our cousin—besides, he is mute too, is he not?"

"He is, gracious madam," answered the knight.

"Royal sport have these Eastern ladies," said Berengaria, "attended by those before whom they may say anything, yet who can report nothing. Whereas in our camp, as the Prelate of Saint Jude's is wont to say, a bird of the air will carry the matter."

"Because," said De Neville, "your Grace forgets that you speak within canvas walls."

The voices sunk on this observation, and after a little whispering, the English knight again returned to the Ethiopian, and made him a sign to follow. He did so, and Neville conducted him to a pavilion, pitched somewhat apart from that of the Queen, for the accommodation, it seemed, of the Lady Edith and her attendants. One of her Coptic maidens received the message communicated by Sir Henry Neville, and in the space of a very few minutes the Nubian was ushered into Edith's presence, while Neville was left on the outside of the tent. The slave who introduced him withdrew on a signal from her mistress, and it was with humiliation, not of the posture only but of the very inmost soul, that the unfortunate knight, thus strangely disguised, threw himself on one knee, with looks bent on the ground and arms folded on his bosom, like a criminal who expects his doom. Edith was clad in the same manner as when she received King Richard, her long, transparent dark veil hanging around her like the shade of a summer night on a beautiful landscape, disguising and rendering obscure the beauties which it could not hide. She held in her hand a silver lamp, fed with some aromatic spirit, which burned with unusual brightness.

When Edith came within a step of the kneeling and motionless slave, she held the light towards his face, as if to peruse his features more attentively, then turned from him, and placed her lamp so as to throw the shadow of his face in profile upon the curtain which hung beside. She at length spoke in a voice composed, yet deeply sorrowful,

"Is it you? It is indeed you, brave Knight of the Leopard—gallant Sir Kenneth of Scotland; is it indeed you?—thus servilely disguised—thus surrounded by a hundred dangers."

At hearing the tones of his lady's voice thus unexpectedly addressed to him, and in a tone of compassion approaching to tenderness, a corresponding reply rushed to the knight's lips, and scarce could Richard's commands and his own promised silence prevent his answering that the sight he saw, the sounds he just heard, were sufficient to recompense the slavery of a life, and dangers which threatened that life every hour. He did recollect himself, however, and a deep and impassioned sigh was his only reply to the high-born Edith's question.

"I see—I know I have guessed right," continued Edith. "I marked you from your first appearance near the platform on which I stood with the Queen. I knew, too, your valiant hound. She is no true lady, and is unworthy of the service of such a knight as thou art, from whom disguises of dress or hue could conceal a faithful servant. Speak, then, without fear to Edith Plantagenet. She knows how to grace in adversity the good knight who served, honoured, and did deeds of arms in her name, when fortune befriended him.—Still silent! Is it fear or shame that keeps thee so! Fear should be unknown to thee; and for shame, let it remain with those who have wronged thee."

The knight, in despair at being obliged to play the mute in an interview so interesting, could only express his mortification by sighing deeply, and laying his finger upon his lips. Edith stepped back, as if somewhat displeased.

"What!" she said, "the Asiatic mute in very deed, as well as in attire? This I looked not for. Or thou mayest scorn me, perhaps, for thus boldly acknowledging that I have heedfully observed the homage thou hast paid me? Hold no unworthy thoughts of Edith on that account. She knows well the bounds which reserve and modesty prescribe to high-born maidens, and she knows when and how far they should give place to gratitude—to a sincere desire that it were in her power to repay services and repair injuries arising from the devotion which a good knight bore towards her. Why fold thy hands together, and wring them with so much passion? Can it be," she added, shrinking back at the idea, "that their cruelty has actually deprived thee of speech? Thou shakest thy head. Be it a spell—be it obstinacy, I question thee no further, but leave thee to do thine errand after thine own fashion. I also can be mute."

The disguised knight made an action as if at once lamenting his own condition and deprecating her displeasure, while at the same time he presented to her, wrapped, as usual, in fine silk and cloth of gold, the letter of the Soldan. She took it, surveyed it carelessly, then laid it aside, and bending her eyes once more on the knight, she said in a low tone, "Not even a word to do thine errand to me?"

He pressed both his hands to his brow, as if to intimate the pain which he felt at being unable to obey her; but she turned from him in anger.

"Begone!" she said. "I have spoken enough—too much—to one who will not waste on me a word in reply. Begone!—and say, if I have wronged thee, I have done penance; for if I have been the unhappy means of dragging thee down from a station of honour, I have, in this interview, forgotten my own worth, and lowered myself in thy eyes and in my own."

She covered her eyes with her hands, and seemed deeply agitated. Sir Kenneth would have approached, but she waved him back.

"Stand off! thou whose soul Heaven hath suited to its new station! Aught less dull and fearful than a slavish mute had spoken a word of gratitude, were it but to reconcile me to my own degradation. Why pause you?—begone!"

The disguised knight almost involuntarily looked towards the letter as an apology for protracting his stay. She snatched it up, saying in a tone of irony and contempt, "I had forgotten—the dutiful slave waits an answer to his message. How's this—from the Soldan!"

She hastily ran over the contents, which were expressed both in Arabic and French, and when she had done, she laughed in bitter anger.

"Now this passes imagination!" she said; "no jongleur can show so deft a transmutation! His legerdemain can transform zechins and byzants into doits and maravedis; but can his art convert a Christian knight, ever esteemed among the bravest of the Holy Crusade, into the dust-kissing slave of a heathen Soldan—the bearer of a paynim's insolent proposals to a Christian maiden—nay, forgetting the laws of honourable chivalry, as well as of religion? But it avails not talking to the willing slave of a heathen hound. Tell your master, when his scourge shall have found thee a tongue, that which thou hast seen me do"—so saying, she threw the Soldan's letter on the ground, and placed her foot upon it—"and say to him, that Edith Plantagenet scorns the homage of an unchristened pagan."

With these words she was about to shoot from the knight, when, kneeling at her feet in bitter agony, he ventured to lay his hand upon her robe and oppose her departure.

"Heard'st thou not what I said, dull slave?" she said, turning short round on him, and speaking with emphasis. "Tell the heathen Soldan, thy master, that I scorn his suit as much as I despise the prostration of a worthless renegade to religion and chivalry—to God and to his lady!"

So saying, she burst from him, tore her garment from his grasp, and left the tent.

The voice of Neville, at the same time, summoned him from without. Exhausted and stupefied by the distress he had undergone during this interview, from which he could only have extricated himself by breach of the engagement which he had formed with King Richard, the unfortunate knight staggered rather than walked after the English baron, till they reached the royal pavilion, before which a party of horsemen had just dismounted. There were light and motion within the tent, and when Neville entered with his disguised attendant, they found the King, with several of his nobility, engaged in welcoming those who were newly arrived.

Lesson 148

1. Read chapter 26. King Richard's favorite minstrel, Blondel, arrives with Richard's friend de Vaux, and sings a tale for the King and Queen and their attendants, including Edith, whom Richard later privately asks about her willingness to marry Saladin.
2. What is the song that Blondel sings? What is it about? (Answers)
3. Why is the song significant? (Answers)
4. What does Edith say when King Richard asks her about Saladin's proposal? (Answers)
5. What is the prophecy about the proposed marriage of Edith and Saladin made by the hermit of Engeddi? (Answers)

CHAPTER XXVI.

"The tears I shed must ever fall.

I weep not for an absent swain;

For time may happier hours recall,
And parted lovers meet again.

"I weep not for the silent dead.
Their pains are past, their sorrows o'er;
And those that loved their steps must tread,
When death shall join to part no more."

But worse than absence, worse than death,
She wept her lover's sullied fame,
And, fired with all the pride of birth,
She wept a soldier's injured name.
BALLAD.

The frank and bold voice of Richard was heard in joyous gratulation.

"Thomas de Vaux! stout Tom of the Gills! by the head of King Henry, thou art welcome to me as ever was flask of wine to a jolly toper! I should scarce have known how to order my battle-array, unless I had thy bulky form in mine eye as a landmark to form my ranks upon. We shall have blows anon, Thomas, if the saints be gracious to us; and had we fought in thine absence, I would have looked to hear of thy being found hanging upon an elder-tree."

"I should have borne my disappointment with more Christian patience, I trust," said Thomas de Vaux, "than to have died the death of an apostate. But I thank your Grace for my welcome, which is the more generous, as it respects a banquet of blows, of which, saving your pleasure, you are ever too apt to engross the larger share. But here have I brought one to whom your Grace will, I know, give a yet warmer welcome."

The person who now stepped forward to make obeisance to Richard was a young man of low stature and slight form. His dress was as modest as his figure was unimpressive; but he bore on his bonnet a gold buckle, with a gem, the lustre of which could only be rivalled by the brilliancy of the eye which the bonnet shaded. It was the only striking feature in his countenance; but when once noticed, it ever made a strong impression on the spectator. About his neck there hung in a scarf of sky-blue silk a WREST as it was called—that is, the key with which a harp is tuned, and which was of solid gold.

This personage would have kneeled reverently to Richard, but the Monarch raised him in joyful haste, pressed him to his bosom warmly, and kissed him on either side of the face.

"Blondel de Nesle!" he exclaimed joyfully—"welcome from Cyprus, my king of minstrels!—welcome to the King of England, who rates not his own dignity more highly than he does thine. I have been sick, man, and, by my soul, I believe it was for lack of thee; for, were I half way to the gate of heaven, methinks thy strains could call me back. And what news, my gentle master, from the land of the lyre? Anything fresh from the TROUVEURS of Provence? Anything from the minstrels of merry Normandy? Above all, hast thou thyself been busy? But I need not ask thee—thou canst not be idle if thou wouldst; thy noble qualities are like a fire burning within, and compel thee to pour thyself out in music and song."

"Something I have learned, and something I have done, noble King," answered the celebrated Blondel, with a retiring modesty which all Richard's enthusiastic admiration of his skill had been unable to banish.

"We will hear thee, man—we will hear thee instantly," said the King. Then, touching Blondel's shoulder kindly, he added, "That is, if thou art not fatigued with thy journey; for I would sooner ride my best horse to death than injure a note of thy voice."

"My voice is, as ever, at the service of my royal patron," said Blondel; "but your Majesty," he added, looking at some papers on the table, "seems more importantly engaged, and the hour waxes late."

"Not a whit, man, not a whit, my dearest Blondel. I did but sketch an array of battle against the Saracens, a thing of a moment, almost as soon done as the routing of them."

"Methinks, however," said Thomas de Vaux, "it were not unfit to inquire what soldiers your Grace hath to array. I bring reports on that subject from Ascalon."

"Thou art a mule, Thomas," said the King—"a very mule for dullness and obstinacy! Come, nobles—a hall—a hall—range ye around him! Give Blondel the tabouret. Where is his harp-bearer?—or, soft, lend him my harp, his own may be damaged by the journey."

"I would your Grace would take my report," said Thomas de Vaux. "I have ridden far, and have more list to my bed than to have my ears tickled."

"THY ears tickled!" said the King; "that must be with a woodcock's feather, and not with sweet sounds. Hark thee, Thomas, do thine ears know the singing of Blondel from the braying of an ass?"

"In faith, my liege," replied Thomas, "I cannot well say; but setting Blondel out of the question, who is a born gentleman, and doubtless of high acquirements, I shall never, for the sake of your Grace's question, look on a minstrel but I shall think upon an ass."

"And might not your manners," said Richard, "have excepted me, who am a gentleman born as well as Blondel, and, like him, a guild-brother of the joyeuse science?"

"Your Grace should remember," said De Vaux, smiling, "that 'tis useless asking for manners from a mule."

"Most truly spoken," said the King; "and an ill-conditioned animal thou art. But come hither, master mule, and be unloaded, that thou mayest get thee to thy litter, without any music being wasted on thee. Meantime do thou, good brother of Salisbury, go to our consort's tent, and tell her that Blondel has arrived, with his budget fraught with the newest minstrelsy. Bid her come hither instantly, and do thou escort her, and see that our cousin, Edith Plantagenet, remain not behind."

His eye then rested for a moment on the Nubian, with that expression of doubtful meaning which his countenance usually displayed when he looked at him.

"Ha, our silent and secret messenger returned?—Stand up, slave, behind the back of De Neville, and thou shalt hear presently sounds which will make thee bless God that He afflicted thee rather with dumbness than deafness."

So saying, he turned from the rest of the company towards De Vaux, and plunged instantly into the military details which that baron laid before him.

About the time that the Lord of Gilsland had finished his audience, a messenger announced that the Queen and her attendants were approaching the royal tent.—"A flask of wine, ho!" said the King; "of old King Isaac's long-saved Cyprus, which we won when we stormed Famagosta. Fill to the stout Lord of Gilsland, gentles—a more careful and faithful servant never had any prince."

"I am glad," said Thomas de Vaux, "that your Grace finds the mule a useful slave, though his voice be less musical than horse-hair or wire."

"What, thou canst not yet digest that quip of the mule?" said Richard. "Wash it down with a brimming flagon, man, or thou wilt choke upon it. Why, so—well pulled!—and now I will tell thee, thou art a soldier as well as I, and we must brook each other's jests in the hall as each other's blows in the tourney, and love each other the harder we hit. By my faith, if thou didst not hit me as hard as I did thee in our late encounter! thou gavest all thy wit to the thrust. But here lies the difference betwixt thee and Blondel. Thou art but my comrade—I might say my pupil—in the art of war; Blondel is my master in the science of minstrelsy and music. To thee I permit the freedom of intimacy; to him I must do reverence, as to my superior in his art. Come, man, be not peevish, but remain and hear our glee."

"To see your Majesty in such cheerful mood," said the Lord of Gilsland, "by my faith, I could remain till Blondel had achieved the great romance of King Arthur, which lasts for three days."

"We will not tax your patience so deeply," said the King. "But see, yonder glare of torches without shows that our consort approaches. Away to receive her, man, and win thyself grace in the brightest eyes of Christendom. Nay, never stop to adjust thy cloak. See, thou hast let Neville come between the wind and the sails of thy galley."

"He was never before me in the field of battle," said De Vaux, not greatly pleased to see himself anticipated by the more active service of the chamberlain.

"No, neither he nor any one went before thee there, my good Tom of the Gills," said the King, "unless it was ourself, now and then."

"Ay, my liege," said De Vaux, "and let us do justice to the unfortunate. The unhappy Knight of the Leopard hath been before me too, at a season; for, look you, he weighs less on horseback, and so—"

"Hush!" said the King, interrupting him in a peremptory tone, "not a word of him," and instantly stepped forward to greet his royal consort; and when he had done so, he presented to her Blondel, as king of minstrelsy and his master in the gay science. Berengaria, who well knew that her royal husband's passion for poetry and music almost equalled his appetite for warlike fame, and that Blondel was his especial favourite, took anxious care to receive him with all the flattering distinctions due to one whom the King delighted to honour. Yet it was evident that, though Blondel made suitable returns to the compliments showered on him something too abundantly by the royal beauty, he owned with deeper reverence and more humble gratitude the simple and graceful welcome of Edith, whose kindly greeting appeared to him, perhaps, sincere in proportion to its brevity and simplicity.

Both the Queen and her royal husband were aware of this distinction, and Richard, seeing his consort somewhat piqued at the preference assigned to his cousin, by which perhaps he himself did not feel much gratified, said in the hearing of both, "We minstrels, Berengaria, as thou mayest see by the bearing of our master Blondel, pay more reverence to a severe judge like our kinswoman than to a kindly, partial friend like thyself, who is willing to take our worth upon trust."

Edith was moved by this sarcasm of her royal kinsman, and hesitated not to reply that, "To be a harsh and severe judge was not an attribute proper to her alone of all the Plantagenets."

She had perhaps said more, having some touch of the temper of that house, which, deriving their name and cognizance from the lowly broom (PLANTA GENISTA), assumed as an emblem of humility, were perhaps one of the proudest families that ever ruled in England; but her eye, when kindling in her reply, suddenly caught those of the Nubian, although he endeavoured to conceal himself behind the nobles who were present, and she sunk upon a seat, turning so pale that Queen Berengaria deemed herself obliged to call for water and essences, and to go through the other ceremonies appropriate to a lady's swoon. Richard, who better estimated Edith's strength of mind, called to Blondel to assume his seat and commence his lay, declaring that minstrelsy was worth every other recipe to recall a Plantagenet to life. "Sing us," he said, "that song of the Bloody Vest, of which thou didst formerly give me the argument ere I left Cyprus. Thou must be perfect in it by this time, or, as our yeomen say, thy bow is broken."

The anxious eye of the minstrel, however, dwelt on Edith, and it was not till he observed her returning colour that he obeyed the repeated commands of the King. Then, accompanying his voice with the harp, so as to grace, but yet not drown, the sense of what he sung, he chanted in a sort of recitative one of those ancient adventures of love and knighthood which were wont of yore to win the public attention. So soon as he began to prelude, the insignificance of his personal appearance seemed to disappear, and his countenance glowed with energy and inspiration. His full, manly, mellow voice, so absolutely under command of the purest taste, thrilled on every ear and to every heart. Richard, rejoiced as after victory, called out the appropriate summons for silence, "Listen, lords, in bower and hall"; while, with the zeal of a patron at once and a pupil, he arranged the circle around, and hushed them into silence; and he himself sat down with an air of expectation and interest, not altogether unmixed with the gravity of the professed critic. The courtiers turned their eyes on the King, that they might be ready to trace and imitate the emotions his features should express, and Thomas de Vaux yawned tremendously, as one who submitted unwillingly to a wearisome penance. The song of Blondel was of course in the Norman language, but the verses which follow express its meaning and its manner.

THE BLOODY VEST.

'Twas near the fair city of Benevent,
When the sun was setting on bough and bent,
And knights were preparing in bower and tent,
On the eve of the Baptist's tournament;
When in Lincoln green a stripling gent,
Well seeming a page by a princess sent,
Wander'd the camp, and, still as he went,
Inquired for the Englishman, Thomas a Kent.

Far hath he far'd, and farther must fare,
Till he finds his pavilion nor stately nor rare,—
Little save iron and steel was there;
And, as lacking the coin to pay armourer's care,
With his sinewy arms to the shoulders bare,
The good knight with hammer and file did repair
The mail that to-morrow must see him wear,
For the honour of Saint John and his lady fair.

"Thus speaks my lady," the page said he,
And the knight bent lowly both head and knee,
"She is Benevent's Princess so high in degree,
And thou art as lowly as knight may well be—
He that would climb so lofty a tree,
Or spring such a gulf as divides her from thee,
Must dare some high deed, by which all men may see
His ambition is back'd by his hie chivalrie.

"Therefore thus speaks my lady," the fair page he said,
And the knight lowly louted with hand and with head,
"Fling aside the good armour in which thou art clad,
And don thou this weed of her night-gear instead,
For a hauberk of steel, a kirtle of thread;
And charge, thus attir'd, in the tournament dread,
And fight as thy wont is where most blood is shed,
And bring honour away, or remain with the dead."

Untroubled in his look, and untroubled in his breast, The knight the weed hath taken, and reverently hath kiss'd. "Now blessed be the moment, the messenger be blest! Much honour'd do I hold me in my lady's high behest; And say unto my lady, in this dear night-weed dress'd, To the best armed champion I will not veil my crest; But if I live and bear me well 'tis her turn to take the test." Here, gentles, ends the foremost fytte of the Lay of the Bloody Vest.

"Thou hast changed the measure upon us unawares in that last couplet, my Blondel," said the King.

"Most true, my lord," said Blondel. "I rendered the verses from the Italian of an old harper whom I met in Cyprus, and not having had time either to translate it accurately or commit it to memory, I am fain to supply gaps in the music and the verse as I can upon the spur of the moment, as you see boors mend a quickset fence with a fagot."

"Nay, on my faith," said the King, "I like these rattling, rolling Alexandrines. Methinks they come more twangingly off to the music than that briefer measure."

"Both are licensed, as is well known to your Grace," answered Blondel.

"They are so, Blondel," said Richard, "yet methinks the scene where there is like to be fighting will go best on in these same thundering Alexandrines, which sound like the charge of cavalry, while the other measure is but like the sidelong amble of a lady's palfrey."

"It shall be as your Grace pleases," replied Blondel, and began again to prelude.

"Nay, first cherish thy fancy with a cup of fiery Chios wine," said the King. "And hark thee, I would have thee fling away that new-fangled restriction of thine, of terminating in accurate and similar rhymes. They are a constraint on thy flow of fancy, and make thee resemble a man dancing in fetters."

"The fetters are easily flung off, at least," said Blondel, again sweeping his fingers over the strings, as one who would rather have played than listened to criticism.

"But why put them on, man?" continued the King. "Wherefore thrust thy genius into iron bracelets? I marvel how you got forward at all. I am sure I should not have been able to compose a stanza in yonder hampered measure."

Blondel looked down, and busied himself with the strings of his harp, to hide an involuntary smile which crept over his features; but it escaped not Richard's observation.

"By my faith, thou laughest at me, Blondel," he said; "and, in good truth, every man deserves it who presumes to play the master when he should be the pupil. But we kings get bad habits of self-opinion. Come, on with thy lay, dearest Blondel—on after thine own fashion, better than aught that we can suggest, though we must needs be talking."

Blondel resumed the lay; but as extemporaneous composition was familiar to him, he failed not to comply with the King's hints, and was perhaps not displeased to show with how much ease he could new-model a poem, even while in the act of recitation.

THE BLOODY VEST.
FYTTE SECOND.

The Baptist's fair morrow beheld gallant feats—
There was winning of honour and losing of seats;
There was hewing with falchions and splintering of staves—
The victors won glory, the vanquish'd won graves.
Oh, many a knight there fought bravely and well,
Yet one was accounted his peers to excel,
And 'twas he whose sole armour on body and breast
Seem'd the weed of a damsel when bouned for her rest.

There were some dealt him wounds that were bloody and sore,
But others respected his plight, and forbore.
"It is some oath of honour," they said, "and I trow,
'Twere unknightly to slay him achieving his vow."
Then the Prince, for his sake, bade the tournament cease—
He flung down his warder, the trumpets sung peace;
And the judges declare, and competitors yield,
That the Knight of the Night-gear was first in the field.

The feast it was nigh, and the mass it was nigher,
When before the fair Princess low looted a squire,
And deliver'd a garment unseemly to view,
With sword-cut and spear-thrust, all hack'd and pierc'd through;
All rent and all tatter'd, all clotted with blood,
With foam of the horses, with dust, and with mud;
Not the point of that lady's small finger, I ween,
Could have rested on spot was unsullied and clean.

"This token my master, Sir Thomas a Kent,
Restores to the Princess of fair Benevent;
He that climbs the tall tree has won right to the fruit,
He that leaps the wide gulf should prevail in his suit;
Through life's utmost peril the prize I have won,
And now must the faith of my mistress be shown:
For she who prompts knights on such danger to run
Must avouch his true service in front of the sun.

"'I restore,' says my master, 'the garment I've worn,
And I claim of the Princess to don it in turn;
For its stains and its rents she should prize it the more,
Since by shame 'tis unsullied, though crimson'd with gore.'"
Then deep blush'd the Princess—yet kiss'd she and press'd

The blood-spotted robes to her lips and her breast.
"Go tell my true knight, church and chamber shall show
If I value the blood on this garment or no."

And when it was time for the nobles to pass,
In solemn procession to minster and mass,
The first walk'd the Princess in purple and pall,
But the blood-besmear'd night-robe she wore over all;
And eke, in the hall, where they all sat at dine,
When she knelt to her father and proffer'd the wine,
Over all her rich robes and state jewels she wore
That wimple unseemly bedabbled with gore.

Then lords whisper'd ladies, as well you may think,
And ladies replied with nod, titter, and wink;
And the Prince, who in anger and shame had look'd down,
Turn'd at length to his daughter, and spoke with a frown:
"Now since thou hast publish'd thy folly and guilt,
E'en atone with thy hand for the blood thou hast spilt;
Yet sore for your boldness you both will repent,
When you wander as exiles from fair Benevent."

Then out spoke stout Thomas, in hall where he stood,
Exhausted and feeble, but dauntless of mood:
"The blood that I lost for this daughter of thine,
I pour'd forth as freely as flask gives its wine;
And if for my sake she brooks penance and blame,
Do not doubt I will save her from suffering and shame;
And light will she reck of thy princedom and rent,
When I hail her, in England, the Countess of Kent."

A murmur of applause ran through the assembly, following the example of Richard himself, who loaded with praises his favourite minstrel, and ended by presenting him with a ring of considerable value. The Queen hastened to distinguish the favourite by a rich bracelet, and many of the nobles who were present followed the royal example.

"Is our cousin Edith," said the King, "become insensible to the sound of the harp she once loved?"

"She thanks Blondel for his lay," replied Edith, "but doubly the kindness of the kinsman who suggested it."

"Thou art angry, cousin," said the King; "angry because thou hast heard of a woman more wayward than thyself. But you escape me not. I will walk a space homeward with you towards the Queen's pavilion. We must have conference together ere the night has waned into morning."

The Queen and her attendants were now on foot, and the other guests withdrew from the royal tent. A train with blazing torches, and an escort of archers, awaited Berengaria without the pavilion, and she was soon on her way homeward. Richard, as he had proposed, walked beside his kinswoman, and compelled her to accept of his arm as her support, so that they could speak to each other without being overheard.

"What answer, then, am I to return to the noble Soldan?" said Richard. "The kings and princes are falling from me, Edith; this new quarrel hath alienated them once more. I would do something for the Holy Sepulchre by composition, if not by victory; and the chance of my doing this depends, alas, on the caprice of a woman. I would lay my single spear in the rest against ten of the best lances in Christendom, rather than argue with a wilful wench who knows not what is for her own good. What answer, coz, am I to return to the Soldan? It must be decisive."

"Tell him," said Edith, "that the poorest of the Plantagenets will rather wed with misery than with misbelief."

"Shall I say with slavery, Edith?" said the King. "Methinks that is nearer thy thoughts."

"There is no room," said Edith, "for the suspicion you so grossly insinuate. Slavery of the body might have been pitied, but that of the soul is only to be despised. Shame to thee, King of merry England. Thou hast enthralled both the limbs and the spirit of a knight, one scarce less famed than thyself."

"Should I not prevent my kinswoman from drinking poison, by sullying the vessel which contained it, if I saw no other means of disgusting her with the fatal liquor?" replied the King.

"It is thyself," answered Edith, "that would press me to drink poison, because it is proffered in a golden chalice."

"Edith," said Richard, "I cannot force thy resolution; but beware you shut not the door which Heaven opens. The hermit of Engaddi—he whom Popes and Councils have regarded as a prophet—hath read in the stars that thy marriage shall reconcile me with a powerful enemy, and that thy husband shall be Christian, leaving thus the fairest ground to hope that the conversion of the Soldan, and the bringing in of the sons of Ishmael to the pale of the church, will be the consequence of thy wedding with Saladin. Come, thou must make some sacrifice rather than mar such happy prospects."

"Men may sacrifice rams and goats," said Edith, "but not honour and conscience. I have heard that it was the dishonour of a Christian maiden which brought the Saracens into Spain; the shame of another is no likely mode of expelling them from Palestine."

"Dost thou call it shame to become an empress?" said the King.

"I call it shame and dishonour to profane a Christian sacrament by entering into it with an infidel whom it cannot bind; and I call it foul dishonour that I, the descendant of a Christian princess, should become of free will the head of a haram of heathen concubines."

"Well, kinswoman," said the King, after a pause, "I must not quarrel with thee, though I think thy dependent condition might have dictated more compliance."

"My liege," replied Edith, "your Grace hath worthily succeeded to all the wealth, dignity, and dominion of the House of Plantagenet—do not, therefore, begrudge your poor kinswoman some small share of their pride."

"By my faith, wench," said the King, "thou hast unhorsed me with that very word, so we will kiss and be friends. I will presently dispatch thy answer to Saladin. But after all, coz, were it not better to suspend your answer till you have seen him? Men say he is pre-eminently handsome."

"There is no chance of our meeting, my lord," said Edith.

"By Saint George, but there is next to a certainty of it," said the King; "for Saladin will doubtless afford us a free field for the doing of this new battle of the Standard, and will witness it himself. Berengaria is wild to behold it also; and I dare be sworn not a feather of you, her companions and attendants, will remain behind—least of all thou thyself, fair coz. But come, we have reached the pavilion, and must part; not in unkindness thou, oh—nay, thou must seal it with thy lip as well as thy hand, sweet Edith—it is my right as a sovereign to kiss my pretty vassals."

He embraced her respectfully and affectionately, and returned through the moonlit camp, humming to himself such snatches of Blondel's lay as he could recollect.

On his arrival he lost no time in making up his dispatches for Saladin, and delivered them to the Nubian, with a charge to set out by peep of day on his return to the Soldan.

Lesson 149

1. Read chapter 27. (This chapter and the last are long ones.) After a day's journey across the desert, King Richard and his entourage are welcomed rather wildly by Saladin's troups and then by Saladin himself, who reveals that he is also Hakim the physician who brought the cure to King Richard when he was ill.
2. Unusual Vocabulary:
    - Foibles - a minor weakness of character
    - Scimitar - a curved, single-edged sword of the Orient
3. Where is the battle for honor between the two Crusader champions going to be fought? (Answers)
4. How is it possible that Saladin and King Richard, sworn enemies in the battle for Jerusalem, can "embrace one another as brothers and equals?" (Answers)
5. Saladin compares weapons with King Richard. How are they different? (Answers)
6. What does it mean when de Vaux says, "there are so many surprises and changes in this land, that my poor brain turns." (Answers)
7. What does Edith say when King Richard challenges her about what she will do if Sir Kenneth wins the battle and regains his honor? (Answers)
8. What has happened to the rest of the Crusader's army? (Answers)

CHAPTER XXVII.

We heard the Techir—so these Arabs call

Their shout of onset, when, with loud acclaim,

They challenge Heaven to give them victory.

SIEGE OF DAMASCUS.

On the subsequent morning Richard was invited to a conference by Philip of France, in which the latter, with many expressions of his high esteem for his brother of England, communicated to him in terms extremely courteous, but too explicit to be misunderstood, his positive intention to return to Europe, and to the cares of his kingdom, as entirely despairing of future success in their undertaking, with their diminished forces and civil discords. Richard remonstrated, but in vain; and when the conference ended he received without surprise a manifesto from the Duke of Austria, and several other princes, announcing a resolution similar to that of Philip, and in no modified terms, assigning, for their defection from the cause of the Cross, the inordinate ambition and arbitrary domination of Richard of England. All hopes of continuing the war with any prospect of ultimate success were now abandoned; and Richard, while he shed bitter tears over his disappointed hopes of glory, was little consoled by the recollection that the failure was in some degree to be imputed to the advantages which he had given his enemies by his own hasty and imprudent temper.

"They had not dared to have deserted my father thus," he said to De Vaux, in the bitterness of his resentment. "No slanders they could have uttered against so wise a king would have been believed in Christendom; whereas—fool that I am!—I have not only afforded them a pretext for deserting me, but even a colour for casting all the blame of the rupture upon my unhappy foibles."

These thoughts were so deeply galling to the King, that De Vaux was rejoiced when the arrival of an ambassador from Saladin turned his reflections into a different channel.

This new envoy was an Emir much respected by the Soldan, whose name was Abdallah el Hadgi. He derived his descent from the family of the Prophet, and the race or tribe of Hashem, in witness of which genealogy he wore a green turban of large dimensions. He had also three times performed the journey to Mecca, from which he derived his epithet of El Hadgi, or the Pilgrim. Notwithstanding these various pretensions to sanctity, Abdallah was (for an Arab) a boon companion, who enjoyed a merry tale, and laid aside his gravity so far as to quaff a blithe flagon when secrecy ensured him against scandal. He was likewise a statesman, whose abilities had been used by Saladin in various negotiations with the Christian princes, and particularly with Richard, to whom El Hadgi was personally known and acceptable. Animated by the cheerful acquiescence with which the envoy of Saladin afforded a fair field for the combat, a safe conduct for all who might choose to witness it, and offered his own person as a guarantee of his fidelity, Richard soon forgot his disappointed hopes, and the approaching dissolution of the Christian league, in the interesting discussions preceding a combat in the lists.

The station called the Diamond of the Desert was assigned for the place of conflict, as being nearly at an equal distance betwixt the Christian and Saracen camps. It was agreed that Conrade of Montserrat, the defendant, with his godfathers, the Archduke of Austria and the Grand Master of the Templars, should appear there on the day fixed for the combat, with a hundred armed followers, and no more; that Richard of England and his brother Salisbury, who supported the accusation, should attend with the same number, to protect his champion; and that the Soldan should bring with him a guard of five hundred chosen followers, a band considered as not more than equal to the two hundred Christian lances. Such persons of consideration as either party chose to invite to witness the contest were to wear no other weapons than their swords, and to come without defensive armour. The Soldan undertook the preparation of the lists, and to provide accommodations and refreshments of every kind for all who were to assist at the solemnity; and his letters expressed with much courtesy the pleasure which he anticipated in the prospect of a personal and peaceful meeting with the Melech Ric, and his anxious desire to render his reception as agreeable as possible.

All preliminaries being arranged and communicated to the defendant and his godfathers, Abdullah the Hadgi was admitted to a more private interview, where he heard with delight the strains of Blondel. Having first carefully put his green turban out of sight, and assumed a Greek cap in its stead, he requited the Norman minstrel's music with a drinking song from the Persian, and quaffed a hearty flagon of Cyprus wine, to show that his practice matched his principles. On the next day, grave and sober as the water-drinker Mirglip, he bent his brow to the ground before Saladin's footstool, and rendered to the Soldan an account of his embassy.

On the day before that appointed for the combat Conrade and his friends set off by daybreak to repair to the place assigned, and Richard left the camp at the same hour and for the same purpose; but, as had been agreed upon, he took his journey by a different route—a precaution which had been judged necessary, to prevent the possibility of a quarrel betwixt their armed attendants.

The good King himself was in no humour for quarrelling with any one. Nothing could have added to his pleasurable anticipations of a desperate and bloody combat in the lists, except his being in his own royal person one of the combatants; and he was half in charity again even with Conrade of Montserrat. Lightly armed, richly dressed, and gay as a bridegroom on the eve of his nuptials, Richard caracoled along by the side of Queen Berengaria's litter, pointing out to her the various scenes through which they passed, and cheering with tale and song the bosom of the inhospitable wilderness. The former route of the Queen's pilgrimage to Engaddi had been on the other side of the chain of mountains, so that the ladies were strangers to the scenery of the desert; and though Berengaria knew her husband's disposition too well not to endeavour to seem interested in what he was pleased either to say or to sing, she could not help indulging some female fears when she found herself in the howling wilderness with so small an escort, which seemed almost like a moving speck on the bosom of the plain, and knew at the same time they were not so distant from the camp of Saladin, but what they might be in a moment surprised and swept off by an overpowering host of his fiery-footed cavalry, should the pagan be faithless enough to embrace an opportunity thus tempting. But when she hinted these suspicions to Richard he repelled them with displeasure and disdain. "It were worse than ingratitude," he said, "to doubt the good faith of the generous Soldan."

Yet the same doubts and fears recurred more than once, not to the timid mind of the Queen alone, but to the firmer and more candid soul of Edith Plantagenet, who had no such confidence in the faith of the Moslem as to render her perfectly at ease when so much in their power; and her surprise had been far less than her terror, if the desert around had suddenly resounded with the shout of ALLAH HU! and a band of Arab cavalry had pounced on them like vultures on their prey. Nor were these suspicions lessened when, as evening approached, they were aware of a single Arab horseman, distinguished by his turban and long lance, hovering on the edge of a small eminence like a hawk poised in the air, and who instantly, on the appearance of the royal retinue, darted off with the speed of the same bird when it shoots down the wind and disappears from the horizon.

"We must be near the station," said King Richard; "and yonder cavalier is one of Saladin's outposts—methinks I hear the noise of the Moorish horns and cymbals. Get you into order, my hearts, and form yourselves around the ladies soldierlike and firmly."

As he spoke, each knight, squire, and archer hastily closed in upon his appointed ground, and they proceeded in the most compact order, which made their numbers appear still smaller. And to say the truth, though there might be no fear, there was anxiety as well as curiosity in the attention with which they listened to the wild bursts of Moorish music, which came ever and anon more distinctly from the quarter in which the Arab horseman had been seen to disappear.

De Vaux spoke in a whisper to the King. "Were it not well, my liege, to send a page to the top of that sand-bank? Or would it stand with your pleasure that I prick forward? Methinks, by all yonder clash and clang, if there be no more than five hundred men beyond the sand-hills, half of the Soldan's retinue must be drummers and cymbal-tossers. Shall I spur on?"

The baron had checked his horse with the bit, and was just about to strike him with the spurs when the King exclaimed, "Not for the world. Such a caution would express suspicion, and could do little to prevent surprise, which, however, I apprehend not."

They advanced accordingly in close and firm order till they surmounted the line of low sand-hills, and came in sight of the appointed station, when a splendid, but at the same time a startling, spectacle awaited them.

The Diamond of the Desert, so lately a solitary fountain, distinguished only amid the waste by solitary groups of palm-trees, was now the centre of an encampment, the embroidered flags and gilded ornaments of which glittered far and wide, and reflected a thousand rich tints against the setting sun. The coverings of the large pavilions were of the gayest colours—scarlet, bright yellow, pale blue, and other gaudy and gleaming hues—and the tops of their pillars, or tent-poles, were decorated with golden pomegranates and small silken flags. But besides these distinguished pavilions, there were what Thomas de Vaux considered as a portentous number of the ordinary black tents of the Arabs, being sufficient, as he conceived, to accommodate, according to the Eastern fashion, a host of five thousand men. A number of Arabs and Kurds, fully corresponding to the extent of the encampment, were hastily assembling, each leading his horse in his hand, and their muster was accompanied by an astonishing clamour of their noisy instruments of martial music, by which, in all ages, the warfare of the Arabs has been animated.

They soon formed a deep and confused mass of dismounted cavalry in front of their encampment, when, at the signal of a shrill cry, which arose high over the clangour of the music, each cavalier sprung to his saddle. A cloud of dust arising at the moment of this manoeuvre hid from Richard and his attendants the camp, the palm-trees, and the distant ridge of mountains, as well as the troops whose sudden movement had raised the cloud, and, ascending high over their heads, formed itself into the fantastic forms of writhed pillars, domes, and minarets. Another shrill yell was heard from the bosom of this cloudy tabernacle. It was the signal for the cavalry to advance, which they did at full gallop, disposing themselves as they came forward so as to come in at once on the front, flanks, and rear of Richard's little bodyguard, who were thus surrounded, and almost choked by the dense clouds of dust enveloping them on each side, through which were seen alternately, and lost, the grim forms and wild faces of the Saracens, brandishing and tossing their lances in every possible direction with the wildest cries and halloos, and frequently only reining up their horses when within a spear's length of the Christians, while those in the rear discharged over the heads of both parties thick volleys of arrows. One of these struck the litter in which the Queen was seated, who loudly screamed, and the red spot was on Richard's brow in an instant.

"Ha! Saint George," he exclaimed, "we must take some order with this infidel scum!"

But Edith, whose litter was near, thrust her head out, and with her hand holding one of the shafts, exclaimed, "Royal Richard, beware what you do! see, these arrows are headless!"

"Noble, sensible wench!" exclaimed Richard; "by Heaven, thou shamest us all by thy readiness of thought and eye.—Be not moved, my English hearts," he exclaimed to his followers; "their arrows have no heads—and their spears, too, lack the steel points. It is but a wild welcome, after their savage fashion, though doubtless they would rejoice to see us daunted or disturbed. Move onward, slow and steady."

The little phalanx moved forward accordingly, accompanied on all sides by the Arabs, with the shrillest and most piercing cries, the bowmen, meanwhile, displaying their agility by shooting as near the crests of the Christians as was possible, without actually hitting them, while the lancers charged each other with such rude blows of their blunt weapons that more than one of them lost his saddle, and well-nigh his life, in this rough sport. All this, though designed to express welcome, had rather a doubtful appearance in the eyes of the Europeans.

As they had advanced nearly half way towards the camp, King Richard and his suite forming, as it were, the nucleus round which this tumultuary body of horsemen howled, whooped, skirmished, and galloped, creating a scene of indescribable confusion, another shrill cry was heard, on which all these irregulars, who were on the front and upon the flanks of the little body of Europeans, wheeled off; and forming themselves into a long and deep column, followed with comparative order and silence in the rear of Richard's troops. The dust began now to dissipate in their front, when there advanced to meet them through that cloudy veil a body of cavalry of a different and more regular description, completely armed with offensive and defensive weapons, and who might well have served as a bodyguard to the proudest of Eastern monarchs. This splendid troop consisted of five hundred men and each horse which it contained was worth an earl's ransom. The riders were Georgian and Circassian slaves in the very prime of life. Their helmets and hauberks were formed of steel rings, so bright that they shone like silver; their vestures were of the gayest colours, and some of cloth of gold or silver; the sashes were twisted with silk and gold, their rich turbans were plumed and jewelled, and their sabres and poniards, of Damascene steel, were adorned with gold and gems on hilt and scabbard.

This splendid array advanced to the sound of military music, and when they met the Christian body they opened their files to the right and left, and let them enter between their ranks. Richard now assumed the foremost place in his troop, aware that Saladin himself was approaching. Nor was it long when, in the centre of his bodyguard, surrounded by his domestic officers and those hideous servants who guard the Eastern haram, and whose misshapen forms were rendered yet more frightful by the richness of their attire, came the Soldan, with the look and manners of one on whose brow Nature had written, This is a King! In his snow-white turban, vest, and wide Eastern trousers, wearing a sash of scarlet silk, without any other ornament, Saladin might have seemed the plainest-dressed man in his own guard. But closer inspection discerned in his turban that inestimable gem which was called by the poets the Sea of Light; the diamond on which his signet was engraved, and which he wore in a ring, was probably worth all the jewels of the English crown; and a sapphire which terminated the hilt of his cangiar was not of much inferior value. It should be added that, to protect himself from the dust, which in the vicinity of the Dead Sea resembles the finest ashes, or, perhaps, out of Oriental pride, the Soldan wore a sort of veil attached to his turban, which partly obscured the view of his noble features. He rode a milk-white Arabian, which bore him as if conscious and proud of his noble burden.

There was no need of further introduction. The two heroic monarchs—for such they both were—threw themselves at once from horseback, and the troops halting and the music suddenly ceasing, they advanced to meet each other in profound silence, and after a courteous inclination on either side they embraced as brethren and equals. The pomp and display upon both sides attracted no further notice—no one saw aught save Richard and Saladin, and they too beheld nothing but each other. The looks with which Richard surveyed Saladin were, however, more intently curious than those which the Soldan fixed upon him; and the Soldan also was the first to break silence.

"The Melech Ric is welcome to Saladin as water to this desert. I trust he hath no distrust of this numerous array. Excepting the armed slaves of my household, those who surround you with eyes of wonder and of welcome are—even the humblest of them—the privileged nobles of my thousand tribes; for who that could claim a title to be present would remain at home when such a Prince was to be seen as Richard, with the terrors of whose name, even on the sands of Yemen, the nurse stills her child, and the free Arab subdues his restive steed!"

"And these are all nobles of Araby?" said Richard, looking around on wild forms with their persons covered with haiks, their countenance swart with the sunbeams, their teeth as white as ivory, their black eyes glancing with fierce and preternatural lustre from under the shade of their turbans, and their dress being in general simple even to meanness.

"They claim such rank," said Saladin; "but though numerous, they are within the conditions of the treaty, and bear no arms but the sabre—even the iron of their lances is left behind."

"I fear," muttered De Vaux in English, "they have left them where they can be soon found. A most flourishing House of Peers, I confess, and would find Westminster Hall something too narrow for them."

"Hush, De Vaux," said Richard, "I command thee.—Noble Saladin," he said, "suspicion and thou cannot exist on the same ground. Seest thou," pointing to the litters, "I too have brought some champions with me, though armed, perhaps, in breach of agreement; for bright eyes and fair features are weapons which cannot be left behind."

The Soldan, turning to the litters, made an obeisance as lowly as if looking towards Mecca, and kissed the sand in token of respect.

"Nay," said Richard, "they will not fear a closer encounter, brother; wilt thou not ride towards their litters, and the curtains will be presently withdrawn?"

"That may Allah prohibit!" said Saladin, "since not an Arab looks on who would not think it shame to the noble ladies to be seen with their faces uncovered."

"Thou shalt see them, then, in private, brother," answered Richard.

"To what purpose?" answered Saladin mournfully. "Thy last letter was, to the hopes which I had entertained, like water to fire; and wherefore should I again light a flame which may indeed consume, but cannot cheer me? But will not my brother pass to the tent which his servant hath prepared for him? My principal black slave hath taken order for the reception of the Princesses, the officers of my household will attend your followers, and ourself will be the chamberlain of the royal Richard."

He led the way accordingly to a splendid pavilion, where was everything that royal luxury could devise. De Vaux, who was in attendance, then removed the chappe (CAPA), or long riding-cloak, which Richard wore, and he stood before Saladin in the close dress which showed to advantage the strength and symmetry of his person, while it bore a strong contrast to the flowing robes which disguised the thin frame. of the Eastern monarch. It was Richard's two-handed sword that chiefly attracted the attention of the Saracen—a broad, straight blade, the seemingly unwieldy length of which extended well-nigh from the shoulder to the heel of the wearer.

"Had I not," said Saladin, "seen this brand flaming in the front of battle, like that of Azrael, I had scarce believed that human arm could wield it. Might I request to see the Melech Ric strike one blow with it in peace, and in pure trial of strength?"

"Willingly, noble Saladin," answered Richard; and looking around for something whereon to exercise his strength, he saw a steel mace held by one of the attendants, the handle being of the same metal, and about an inch and a half in diameter. This he placed on a block of wood.

The anxiety of De Vaux for his master's honour led him to whisper in English, "For the blessed Virgin's sake, beware what you attempt, my liege! Your full strength is not as yet returned—give no triumph to the infidel."

"Peace, fool!" said Richard, standing firm on his ground, and casting a fierce glance around; "thinkest thou that I can fail in HIS presence?"

The glittering broadsword, wielded by both his hands, rose aloft to the King's left shoulder, circled round his head, descended with the sway of some terrific engine, and the bar of iron rolled on the ground in two pieces, as a woodsman would sever a sapling with a hedging-bill.

"By the head of the Prophet, a most wonderful blow!" said the Soldan, critically and accurately examining the iron bar which had been cut asunder; and the blade of the sword was so well tempered as to exhibit not the least token of having suffered by the feat it had performed. He then took the King's hand, and looking on the size and muscular strength which it exhibited, laughed as he placed it beside his own, so lank and thin, so inferior in brawn and sinew.

"Ay, look well," said De Vaux in English, "it will be long ere your long jackanape's fingers do such a feat with your fine gilded reaping-hook there."

"Silence, De Vaux," said Richard; "by Our Lady, he understands or guesses thy meaning—be not so broad, I pray thee."

The Soldan, indeed, presently said, "Something I would fain attempt—though wherefore should the weak show their inferiority in presence of the strong? Yet each land hath its own exercises, and this may be new to the Melech Ric." So saying, he took from the floor a cushion of silk and down, and placed it upright on one end. "Can thy weapon, my brother, sever that cushion?" he said to King Richard.

"No, surely," replied the King; "no sword on earth, were it the Excalibur of King Arthur, can cut that which opposes no steady resistance to the blow."

"Mark, then," said Saladin; and tucking up the sleeve of his gown, showed his arm, thin indeed and spare, but which constant exercise had hardened into a mass consisting of nought but bone, brawn, and sinew. He unsheathed his scimitar, a curved and narrow blade, which glittered not like the swords of the Franks, but was, on the contrary, of a dull blue colour, marked with ten millions of meandering lines, which showed how anxiously the metal had been welded by the armourer. Wielding this weapon, apparently so inefficient when compared to that of Richard, the Soldan stood resting his weight upon his left foot, which was slightly advanced; he balanced himself a little, as if to steady his aim; then stepping at once forward, drew the scimitar across the cushion, applying the edge so dexterously, and with so little apparent effort, that the cushion seemed rather to fall asunder than to be divided by violence.

"It is a juggler's trick," said De Vaux, darting forward and snatching up the portion of the cushion which had been cut off, as if to assure himself of the reality of the feat; "there is gramarye in this."

The Soldan seemed to comprehend him, for he undid the sort of veil which he had hitherto worn, laid it double along the edge of his sabre, extended the weapon edgeways in the air, and drawing it suddenly through the veil, although it hung on the blade entirely loose, severed that also into two parts, which floated to different sides of the tent, equally displaying the extreme temper and sharpness of the weapon, and the exquisite dexterity of him who used it.

"Now, in good faith, my brother," said Richard, "thou art even matchless at the trick of the sword, and right perilous were it to meet thee! Still, however, I put some faith in a downright

English blow, and what we cannot do by sleight we eke out by strength. Nevertheless, in truth thou art as expert in inflicting wounds as my sage Hakim in curing them. I trust I shall see the learned leech. I have much to thank him for, and had brought some small present."

As he spoke, Saladin exchanged his turban for a Tartar cap. He had no sooner done so, than De Vaux opened at once his extended mouth and his large, round eyes, and Richard gazed with scarce less astonishment, while the Soldan spoke in a grave and altered voice: "The sick man, saith the poet, while he is yet infirm, knoweth the physician by his step; but when he is recovered, he knoweth not even his face when he looks upon him."

"A miracle!—a miracle!" exclaimed Richard.

"Of Mahound's working, doubtless," said Thomas de Vaux.

"That I should lose my learned Hakim," said Richard, "merely by absence of his cap and robe, and that I should find him again in my royal brother Saladin!"

"Such is oft the fashion of the world," answered the Soldan; "the tattered robe makes not always the dervise."

"And it was through thy intercession," said Richard, "that yonder Knight of the Leopard was saved from death, and by thy artifice that he revisited my camp in disguise?"

"Even so," replied Saladin. "I was physician enough to know that, unless the wounds of his bleeding honour were stanched, the days of his life must be few. His disguise was more easily penetrated than I had expected from the success of my own."

"An accident," said King Richard (probably alluding to the circumstance of his applying his lips to the wound of the supposed Nubian), "let me first know that his skin was artificially discoloured; and that hint once taken, detection became easy, for his form and person are not to be forgotten. I confidently expect that he will do battle on the morrow."

"He is full in preparation, and high in hope," said the Soldan. "I have furnished him with weapons and horse, thinking nobly of him from what I have seen under various disguises."

"Knows he now," said Richard, "to whom he lies under obligation?"

"He doth," replied the Saracen. "I was obliged to confess my person when I unfolded my purpose."

"And confessed he aught to you?" said the King of England.

"Nothing explicit," replied the Soldan; "but from much that passed between us, I conceive his love is too highly placed to be happy in its issue."

"And thou knowest that his daring and insolent passion crossed thine own wishes?" said Richard.

"I might guess so much," said Saladin; "but his passion had existed ere my wishes had been formed—and, I must now add, is likely to survive them. I cannot, in honour, revenge me for my disappointment on him who had no hand in it. Or, if this high-born dame loved him better than myself, who can say that she did not justice to a knight of her own religion, who is full of nobleness?"

"Yet of too mean lineage to mix with the blood of Plantagenet," said Richard haughtily.

"Such may be your maxims in Frangistan," replied the Soldan. "Our poets of the Eastern countries say that a valiant camel-driver is worthy to kiss the lip of a fair Queen, when a cowardly prince is not worthy to salute the hem of her garment. But with your permission, noble brother, I must take leave of thee for the present, to receive the Duke of Austria and yonder Nazarene knight, much less worthy of hospitality, but who must yet be suitably entreated, not for their sakes, but for mine own honour—for what saith the sage Lokman? 'Say not that the food is lost unto thee which is given to the stranger; for if his body be strengthened and fattened therewithal, not less is thine own worship and good name cherished and augmented.'"

The Saracen Monarch departed from King Richard's tent, and having indicated to him, rather with signs than with speech, where the pavilion of the Queen and her attendants was pitched, he went to receive the Marquis of Montserrat and his attendants, for whom, with less goodwill, but with equal splendour, the magnificent Soldan had provided accommodations. The most ample refreshments, both in the Oriental and after the European fashion, were spread before the royal and princely guests of Saladin, each in their own separate pavilion; and so attentive was the Soldan to the habits and taste of his visitors, that Grecian slaves were stationed to present them with the goblet, which is the abomination of the sect of Mohammed. Ere Richard had finished his meal, the ancient Omrah, who had brought the Soldan's letter to the Christian camp, entered with a plan of the ceremonial to be observed on the succeeding day of combat. Richard, who knew the taste of his old acquaintance, invited him to pledge him in a flagon of wine of Shiraz; but Abdallah gave him to understand, with a rueful aspect, that self-denial in the present circumstances was a matter in which his life was concerned, for that Saladin, tolerant in many respects, both observed and enforced by high penalties the laws of the Prophet.

"Nay, then," said Richard, "if he loves not wine, that lightener of the human heart, his conversion is not to be hoped for, and the prediction of the mad priest of Engaddi goes like chaff down the wind."

The King then addressed himself to settle the articles of combat, which cost a considerable time, as it was necessary on some points to consult with the opposite parties, as well as with the Soldan.

They were at length finally agreed upon, and adjusted by a protocol in French and in Arabian, which was subscribed by Saladin as umpire of the field, and by Richard and Leopold as guarantees for the two combatants. As the Omrah took his final leave of King Richard for the evening, De Vaux entered.

"The good knight," he said, "who is to do battle tomorrow requests to know whether he may not to-night pay duty to his royal godfather!"

"Hast thou seen him, De Vaux?" said the King, smiling; "and didst thou know an ancient acquaintance?"

"By our Lady of Lanercost," answered De Vaux, "there are so many surprises and changes in this land that my poor brain turns. I scarce knew Sir Kenneth of Scotland, till his good hound, that had been for a short while under my care, came and fawned on me; and even then I only knew the tyke by the depth of his chest, the roundness of his foot, and his manner of baying, for the poor gazehound was painted like any Venetian courtesan."

"Thou art better skilled in brutes than men, De Vaux," said the King.

"I will not deny," said De Vaux, "I have found them ofttimes the honester animals. Also, your Grace is pleased to term me sometimes a brute myself; besides that, I serve the Lion, whom all men acknowledge the king of brutes."

"By Saint George, there thou brokest thy lance fairly on my brow," said the King. "I have ever said thou hast a sort of wit, De Vaux; marry, one must strike thee with a sledge-hammer ere it can be made to sparkle. But to the present gear—is the good knight well armed and equipped?"

"Fully, my liege, and nobly," answered De Vaux. "I know the armour well; it is that which the Venetian commissary offered your highness, just ere you became ill, for five hundred byzants."

"And he hath sold it to the infidel Soldan, I warrant me, for a few ducats more, and present payment. These Venetians would sell the Sepulchre itself!"

"The armour will never be borne in a nobler cause," said De Vaux.

"Thanks to the nobleness of the Saracen," said the King, "not to the avarice of the Venetians."

"I would to God your Grace would be more cautious," said the anxious De Vaux. "Here are we deserted by all our allies, for points of offence given to one or another; we cannot hope to prosper upon the land; and we have only to quarrel with the amphibious republic, to lose the means of retreat by sea!"

"I will take care," said Richard impatiently; "but school me no more. Tell me rather, for it is of interest, hath the knight a confessor?"

"He hath," answered De Vaux; "the hermit of Engaddi, who erst did him that office when preparing for death, attends him on the present occasion, the fame of the duel having brought him hither."

"'Tis well," said Richard; "and now for the knight's request. Say to him, Richard will receive him when the discharge of his devoir beside the Diamond of the Desert shall have atoned for his fault beside the Mount of Saint George; and as thou passest through the camp, let the Queen know I will visit her pavilion—and tell Blondel to meet me there."

De Vaux departed, and in about an hour afterwards, Richard, wrapping his mantle around him, and taking his ghittern in his hand, walked in the direction of the Queen's pavilion. Several Arabs passed him, but always with averted heads and looks fixed upon the earth, though he could observe that all gazed earnestly after him when he was past. This led him justly to conjecture that his person was known to them; but that either the Soldan's commands, or their own Oriental politeness, forbade them to seem to notice a sovereign who desired to remain incognito.

When the King reached the pavilion of his Queen he found it guarded by those unhappy officials whom Eastern jealousy places around the zenana. Blondel was walking before the door, and touched his rote from time to time in a manner which made the Africans show their ivory teeth, and bear burden with their strange gestures and shrill, unnatural voices.

"What art thou after with this herd of black cattle, Blondel?" said the King; "wherefore goest thou not into the tent?"

"Because my trade can neither spare the head nor the fingers," said Blondel, "and these honest blackamoors threatened to cut me joint from joint if I pressed forward."

"Well, enter with me," said the King, "and I will be thy safeguard."

The blacks accordingly lowered pikes and swords to King Richard, and bent their eyes on the ground, as if unworthy to look upon him. In the interior of the pavilion they found Thomas de Vaux in attendance on the Queen. While Berengaria welcomed Blondel, King Richard spoke for some time secretly and apart with his fair kinswoman.

At length, "Are we still foes, my fair Edith?" he said, in a whisper.

"No, my liege," said Edith, in a voice just so low as not to interrupt the music; "none can bear enmity against King Richard when he deigns to show himself, as he really is, generous and noble, as well as valiant and honourable."

So saying, she extended her hand to him. The King kissed it in token of reconciliation, and then proceeded.

"You think, my sweet cousin, that my anger in this matter was feigned; but you are deceived. The punishment I inflicted upon this knight was just; for he had betrayed—no matter for how tempting a bribe, fair cousin—the trust committed to him. But I rejoice, perchance as much as you, that to-morrow gives him a chance to win the field, and throw back the stain which for a time clung to him upon the actual thief and traitor. No!—future times may blame Richard for impetuous folly, but they shall say that in rendering judgment he was just when he should and merciful when he could."

"Laud not thyself, cousin King," said Edith. "They may call thy justice cruelty, thy mercy caprice."

"And do not thou pride thyself," said the King, "as if thy knight, who hath not yet buckled on his armour, were unbelting it in triumph—Conrade of Montserrat is held a good lance. What if the Scot should lose the day?"

"It is impossible!" said Edith firmly. "My own eyes saw yonder Conrade tremble and change colour like a base thief; he is guilty, and the trial by combat is an appeal to the justice of God. I myself, in such a cause, would encounter him without fear."

"By the mass, I think thou wouldst, wench," said the King, "and beat him to boot, for there never breathed a truer Plantagenet than thou."

He paused, and added in a very serious tone, "See that thou continue to remember what is due to thy birth."

"What means that advice, so seriously given at this moment?" said Edith. "Am I of such light nature as to forget my name—my condition?"

"I will speak plainly, Edith," answered the King, "and as to a friend. What will this knight be to you, should he come off victor from yonder lists?"

"To me?" said Edith, blushing deep with shame and displeasure. "What can he be to me more than an honoured knight, worthy of such grace as Queen Berengaria might confer on him, had he selected her for his lady, instead of a more unworthy choice? The meanest knight may devote himself to the service of an empress, but the glory of his choice," she said proudly, "must be his reward."

"Yet he hath served and suffered much for you," said the King.

"I have paid his services with honour and applause, and his sufferings with tears," answered Edith. "Had he desired other reward, he would have done wisely to have bestowed his affections within his own degree."

"You would not, then, wear the bloody night-gear for his sake?" said King Richard.

"No more," answered Edith, "than I would have required him to expose his life by an action in which there was more madness than honour."

"Maidens talk ever thus," said the King; "but when the favoured lover presses his suit, she says, with a sigh, her stars had decreed otherwise."

"Your Grace has now, for the second time, threatened me with the influence of my horoscope," Edith replied, with dignity. "Trust me, my liege, whatever be the power of the stars, your poor kinswoman will never wed either infidel or obscure adventurer. Permit me that I listen to the music of Blondel, for the tone of your royal admonitions is scarce so grateful to the ear."

The conclusion of the evening offered nothing worthy of notice.

Lesson 150

1. Finish the book! Sir Kenneth wins the battle and marries his love, Edith Plantagenet, when it is revealed that he is actually the Prince of Scotland, the villainous Grand Master is punished, and King Richard reluctantly concedes Jerusalem to Saladin and his people.
2. Why would the champions who are going to battle each other need to see a confessor? (Answers)
3. Why does the Grand Master of the Templars interrupt Conrade's confession to the hermit of Engeddi? What does the Grand Master do later in the chapter? Then what happens to the Grand Master? (Answers)

4. Who wins the battle? What is the new surprise revealed about the champion? How is this possible? (Answers)
5. What was the mix-up about the conversion prophecy of the hermit? How does the hermit feel about his mistake? (Answers)
6. Why does Richard envy Sir Kenneth? What does he want to do? (Answers)
7. What wedding present does Saladin give Edith and Kenneth/David, Prince of Scotland? (Answers)
8. Sir Walter Scott was a Christian man, but I don't feel that he told this story in terms of good guys (Crusaders) and bad guys (Saracens). Do you agree or disagree? What do you think he wants us to feel about the Saracens? The Crusaders? (Answers)

CHAPTER XXVIII.

Heard ye the din of battle bray,

Lance to lance, and horse to horse?

GRAY.

It had been agreed, on account of the heat of the climate, that the judicial combat which was the cause of the present assemblage of various nations at the Diamond of the Desert should take place at one hour after sunrise. The wide lists, which had been constructed under the inspection of the Knight of the Leopard, enclosed a space of hard sand, which was one hundred and twenty yards long by forty in width. They extended in length from north to south, so as to give both parties the equal advantage of the rising sun. Saladin's royal seat was erected on the western side of the enclosure, just in the centre, where the combatants were expected to meet in mid encounter. Opposed to this was a gallery with closed casements, so contrived that the ladies, for whose accommodation it was erected, might see the fight without being themselves exposed to view. At either extremity of the lists was a barrier, which could be opened or shut at pleasure. Thrones had been also erected, but the Archduke, perceiving that his was lower than King Richard's, refused to occupy it; and Coeur de Lion, who would have submitted to much ere any formality should have interfered with the combat, readily agreed that the sponsors, as they were called, should remain on horseback during the fight. At one extremity of the lists were placed the followers of Richard, and opposed to them were those who accompanied the defender Conrade. Around the throne destined for the Soldan were ranged his splendid Georgian Guards, and the rest of the enclosure was occupied by Christian and Mohammedan spectators.

Long before daybreak the lists were surrounded by even a larger number of Saracens than Richard had seen on the preceding evening. When the first ray of the sun's glorious orb arose above the desert, the sonorous call, "To prayer—to prayer!" was poured forth by the Soldan himself, and answered by others, whose rank and zeal entitled them to act as muezzins. It was a striking spectacle to see them all sink to earth, for the purpose of repeating their devotions, with their faces turned to Mecca. But when they arose from the ground, the sun's rays, now strengthening fast, seemed to confirm the Lord of Gilsland's conjecture of the night before. They were flashed back from many a spearhead, for the pointless lances of the preceding day were certainly no longer such. De Vaux pointed it out to his master, who answered with impatience that he had perfect confidence in the good faith of the Soldan; but if De Vaux was afraid of his bulky body, he might retire.

Soon after this the noise of timbrels was heard, at the sound of which the whole Saracen cavaliers threw themselves from their horses, and prostrated themselves, as if for a second morning prayer. This was to give an opportunity to the Queen, with Edith and her attendants, to pass from the pavilion to the gallery intended for them. Fifty guards of Saladin's seraglio escorted them with naked sabres, whose orders were to cut to pieces whomsoever, were he prince or peasant, should venture to gaze on the ladies as they passed, or even presume to raise his head until the cessation of the music should make all men aware that they were lodged in their gallery, not to be gazed on by the curious eye.

This superstitious observance of Oriental reverence to the fair sex called forth from Queen Berengaria some criticisms very unfavourable to Saladin and his country. But their den, as the royal fair called it, being securely closed and guarded by their sable attendants, she was under the necessity of contenting herself with seeing, and laying aside for the present the still more exquisite pleasure of being seen.

Meantime the sponsors of both champions went, as was their duty, to see that they were duly armed and prepared for combat. The Archduke of Austria was in no hurry to perform this part of the ceremony, having had rather an unusually severe debauch upon wine of Shiraz the preceding evening. But the Grand Master of the Temple, more deeply concerned in the event of the combat, was early before the tent of Conrade of Montserrat. To his great surprise, the attendants refused him admittance.

"Do you not know me, ye knaves?" said the Grand Master, in great anger.

"We do, most valiant and reverend," answered Conrade's squire; "but even you may not at present enter—the Marquis is about to confess himself."

"Confess himself!" exclaimed the Templar, in a tone where alarm mingled with surprise and scorn—"and to whom, I pray thee?"

"My master bid me be secret," said the squire; on which the Grand Master pushed past him, and entered the tent almost by force.

The Marquis of Montserrat was kneeling at the feet of the hermit of Engaddi, and in the act of beginning his confession.

"What means this, Marquis?" said the Grand Master; "up, for shame—or, if you must needs confess, am not I here?"

"I have confessed to you too often already," replied Conrade, with a pale cheek and a faltering voice. "For God's sake, Grand Master, begone, and let me unfold my conscience to this holy man."

"In what is he holier than I am?" said the Grand Master.—"Hermit, prophet, madman—say, if thou darest, in what thou excellest me?"

"Bold and bad man," replied the hermit, "know that I am like the latticed window, and the divine light passes through to avail others, though, alas! it helpeth not me. Thou art like the iron stanchions, which neither receive light themselves, nor communicate it to any one."

"Prate not to me, but depart from this tent," said the Grand Master; "the Marquis shall not confess this morning, unless it be to me, for I part not from his side."

"Is this YOUR pleasure?" said the hermit to Conrade; "for think not I will obey that proud man, if you continue to desire my assistance."

"Alas," said Conrade irresolutely, "what would you have me say? Farewell for a while—-we will speak anon."

"O procrastination!" exclaimed the hermit, "thou art a soul-murderer!—Unhappy man, farewell—not for a while, but until we shall both meet no matter where. And for thee," he added, turning to the Grand Master, "TREMBLE!"

"Tremble!" replied the Templar contemptuously, "I cannot if I would."

The hermit heard not his answer, having left the tent.

"Come! to this gear hastily," said the Grand Master, "since thou wilt needs go through the foolery. Hark thee—I think I know most of thy frailties by heart, so we may omit the detail, which may be somewhat a long one, and begin with the absolution. What signifies counting the spots of dirt that we are about to wash from our hands?"

"Knowing what thou art thyself," said Conrade, "it is blasphemous to speak of pardoning another."

"That is not according to the canon, Lord Marquis," said the Templar; "thou art more scrupulous than orthodox. The absolution of the wicked priest is as effectual as if he were himself a saint—otherwise, God help the poor penitent! What wounded man inquires whether the surgeon that tends his gashes has clean hands or no? Come, shall we to this toy?"

"No," said Conrade, "I will rather die unconfessed than mock the sacrament."

"Come, noble Marquis," said the Templar, "rouse up your courage, and speak not thus. In an hour's time thou shalt stand victorious in the lists, or confess thee in thy helmet, like a valiant knight."

"Alas, Grand Master," answered Conrade, "all augurs ill for this affair, the strange discovery by the instinct of a dog—the revival of this Scottish knight, who comes into the lists like a spectre—all betokens evil."

"Pshaw," said the Templar, "I have seen thee bend thy lance boldly against him in sport, and with equal chance of success. Think thou art but in a tournament, and who bears him better in the tilt-yard than thou?—Come, squires and armourers, your master must be accoutred for the field."

The attendants entered accordingly, and began to arm the Marquis.

"What morning is without?" said Conrade.

"The sun rises dimly," answered a squire.

"Thou seest, Grand Master," said Conrade, "nought smiles on us."

"Thou wilt fight the more coolly, my son," answered the Templar; "thank Heaven, that hath tempered the sun of Palestine to suit thine occasion."

Thus jested the Grand Master. But his jests had lost their influence on the harassed mind of the Marquis, and notwithstanding his attempts to seem gay, his gloom communicated itself to the Templar.

"This craven," he thought, "will lose the day in pure faintness and cowardice of heart, which he calls tender conscience. I, whom visions and auguries shake not—-who am firm in my purpose as the living rock—I should have fought the combat myself. Would to God the Scot may strike him dead on the spot; it were next best to his winning the victory. But come what will, he must have no other confessor than myself—our sins are too much in common, and he might confess my share with his own."

While these thoughts passed through his mind, he continued to assist the Marquis in arming, but it was in silence.

The hour at length arrived; the trumpets sounded; the knights rode into the lists armed at all points, and mounted like men who were to do battle for a kingdom's honour. They wore their visors up, and riding around the lists three times, showed themselves to the spectators. Both were goodly persons, and both had noble countenances. But there was an air of manly confidence on the brow of the Scot—a radiancy of hope, which amounted even to cheerfulness; while, although pride and effort had recalled much of Conrade's natural courage, there lowered still on his brow a cloud of ominous despondence. Even his steed seemed to tread less lightly and blithely to the trumpet-sound than the noble Arab which was bestrode by Sir Kenneth; and the SPRUCH-SPRECHER shook his head while he observed that, while the challenger rode around the lists in the course of the sun—that is, from right to left—the defender made the same circuit WIDDERSINS—that is, from left to right—which is in most countries held ominous.

A temporary altar was erected just beneath the gallery occupied by the Queen, and beside it stood the hermit in the dress of his order as a Carmelite friar. Other churchmen were also present. To this altar the challenger and defender were successively brought forward, conducted by their respective sponsors. Dismounting before it, each knight avouched the justice of his cause by a solemn oath on the Evangelists, and prayed that his success might be according to the truth or falsehood of what he then swore. They also made oath that they came to do battle in knightly guise, and with the usual weapons, disclaiming the use of spells, charms, or magical devices to incline victory to their side. The challenger pronounced his vow with a firm and manly voice, and a bold and cheerful countenance. When the ceremony was finished, the Scottish Knight looked at the gallery, and bent his head to the earth, as if in honour of those invisible beauties which were enclosed within; then, loaded with armour as he was, sprung to the saddle without the use of the stirrup, and made his courser carry him in a succession of caracoles to his station at the eastern extremity of the lists. Conrade also presented himself before the altar with boldness enough; but his voice as he took the oath sounded hollow, as if drowned in his helmet. The lips with which he appealed to Heaven to adjudge victory to the just quarrel grew white as they uttered the impious mockery. As he turned to remount his horse, the Grand Master approached him closer, as if to rectify something about the sitting of his gorget, and whispered, "Coward and fool! recall thy senses, and do me this battle bravely, else, by Heaven, shouldst thou escape him, thou escapest not ME!"

The savage tone in which this was whispered perhaps completed the confusion of the Marquis's nerves, for he stumbled as he made to horse; and though he recovered his feet, sprung to the saddle with his usual agility, and displayed his address in horsemanship as he assumed his position opposite to the challenger's, yet the accident did not escape those who were on the watch for omens which might predict the fate of the day.

The priests, after a solemn prayer that God would show the rightful quarrel, departed from the lists. The trumpets of the challenger then rung a flourish, and a herald-at-arms proclaimed at the eastern end of the lists—"Here stands a good knight, Sir Kenneth of Scotland, champion for the royal King Richard of England, who accuseth Conrade, Marquis of Montserrat, of foul treason and dishonour done to the said King."

When the words Kenneth of Scotland announced the name and character of the champion, hitherto scarce generally known, a loud and cheerful acclaim burst from the followers of King Richard, and hardly, notwithstanding repeated commands of silence, suffered the reply of the defendant to be heard. He, of course, avouched his innocence, and offered his body for battle. The esquires of the combatants now approached, and delivered to each his shield and lance, assisting to hang the former around his neck, that his two hands might remain free, one for the management of the bridle, the other to direct the lance.

The shield of the Scot displayed his old bearing, the leopard, but with the addition of a collar and broken chain, in allusion to his late captivity. The shield of the Marquis bore, in reference to his title, a serrated and rocky mountain. Each shook his lance aloft, as if to ascertain the weight and toughness of the unwieldy weapon, and then laid it in the rest. The sponsors, heralds, and squires now retired to the barriers, and the combatants sat opposite to each other, face to face, with couched lance and closed visor, the human form so completely enclosed, that they looked more like statues of molten iron than beings of flesh and blood. The silence of suspense was now general. Men breathed thicker, and their very souls seemed seated in their eyes; while not a sound was to be heard save the snorting and pawing of the good steeds, who, sensible of what was about to happen, were impatient to dash into career. They stood thus for perhaps three minutes, when, at a signal given by the Soldan, a hundred instruments rent the air with their brazen clamours, and each champion striking his horse with the spurs, and slacking the rein, the horses started into full gallop, and the knights met in mid space with a shock like a thunderbolt. The victory was not in doubt—no, not one moment. Conrade, indeed, showed himself a practised warrior; for he struck his antagonist knightly in the midst of his shield, bearing his lance so straight and true that it shivered into splinters from the steel spear-head up to the very gauntlet. The horse of Sir Kenneth recoiled two or three yards and fell on his haunches; but the rider easily raised him with hand and rein. But for Conrade there was no recovery. Sir Kenneth's lance had pierced through the shield, through a plated corselet of Milan steel, through a SECRET, or coat of linked mail, worn beneath the corselet, had wounded him deep in the bosom, and borne him from his saddle, leaving the truncheon of the lance fixed in his wound. The sponsors, heralds, and Saladin himself, descending from his throne, crowded around the wounded man; while Sir Kenneth, who had drawn his sword ere yet he discovered his antagonist was totally helpless, now commanded him to avow his guilt. The helmet was hastily unclosed, and the wounded man, gazing wildly on the skies, replied, "What would you more? God hath decided justly—I am guilty; but there are worse traitors in the camp than I. In pity to my soul, let me have a confessor!"

He revived as he uttered these words.

"The talisman—the powerful remedy, royal brother!" said King Richard to Saladin.

"The traitor," answered the Soldan, "is more fit to be dragged from the lists to the gallows by the heels, than to profit by its virtues. And some such fate is in his look," he added, after gazing fixedly upon the wounded man; "for though his wound may be cured, yet Azrael's seal is on the wretch's brow."

"Nevertheless," said Richard, "I pray you do for him what you may, that he may at least have time for confession. Slay not soul and body! To him one half hour of time may be worth more, by ten thousandfold, than the life of the oldest patriarch."

"My royal brother's wish shall be obeyed," said Saladin.—"Slaves, bear this wounded man to our tent."

"Do not so," said the Templar, who had hitherto stood gloomily looking on in silence. "The royal Duke of Austria and myself will not permit this unhappy Christian prince to be delivered over to the Saracens, that they may try their spells upon him. We are his sponsors, and demand that he be assigned to our care."

"That is, you refuse the certain means offered to recover him?" said Richard.

"Not so," said the Grand Master, recollecting himself. "If the Soldan useth lawful medicines, he may attend the patient in my tent."

"Do so, I pray thee, good brother," said Richard to Saladin, "though the permission be ungraciously yielded.—But now to a more glorious work. Sound, trumpets—shout, England—in honour of England's champion!"

Drum, clarion, trumpet, and cymbal rung forth at once, and the deep and regular shout, which for ages has been the English acclamation, sounded amidst the shrill and irregular yells of the Arabs, like the diapason of the organ amid the howling of a storm. There was silence at length.

"Brave Knight of the Leopard," resumed Coeur de Lion, "thou hast shown that the Ethiopian may change his skin, and the leopard his spots, though clerks quote Scripture for the impossibility. Yet I have more to say to you when I have conducted you to the presence of the ladies, the best judges and best rewarders of deeds of chivalry."

The Knight of the Leopard bowed assent.

"And thou, princely Saladin, wilt also attend them. I promise thee our Queen will not think herself welcome, if she lacks the opportunity to thank her royal host for her most princely reception."

Saladin bent his head gracefully, but declined the invitation.

"I must attend the wounded man," he said. "The leech leaves not his patient more than the champion the lists, even if he be summoned to a bower like those of Paradise. And further, royal Richard, know that the blood of the East flows not so temperately in the presence of beauty as that of your land. What saith the Book itself?—Her eye is as the edge of the sword of the Prophet, who shall look upon it? He that would not be burnt avoideth to tread on hot embers—wise men spread not the flax before a flickering torch. He, saith the sage, who hath forfeited a treasure, doth not wisely to turn back his head to gaze at it."

Richard, it may be believed, respected the motives of delicacy which flowed from manners so different from his own, and urged his request no further.

"At noon," said the Soldan, as he departed, "I trust ye will all accept a collation under the black camel-skin tent of a chief of Kurdistan."

The same invitation was circulated among the Christians, comprehending all those of sufficient importance to be admitted to sit at a feast made for princes.

"Hark!" said Richard, "the timbrels announce that our Queen and her attendants are leaving their gallery—and see, the turbans sink on the ground, as if struck down by a destroying angel. All lie prostrate, as if the glance of an Arab's eye could sully the lustre of a lady's cheek! Come, we will to the pavilion, and lead our conqueror thither in triumph. How I pity that noble Soldan, who knows but of love as it is known to those of inferior nature!"

Blondel tuned his harp to his boldest measure, to welcome the introduction of the victor into the pavilion of Queen Berengaria. He entered, supported on either side by his sponsors, Richard and Thomas Longsword, and knelt gracefully down before the Queen, though more than half the homage was silently rendered to Edith, who sat on her right hand.

"Unarm him, my mistresses," said the King, whose delight was in the execution of such chivalrous usages; "let Beauty honour Chivalry! Undo his spurs, Berengaria; Queen though thou be, thou owest him what marks of favour thou canst give.—Unlace his helmet, Edith;—by this hand thou shalt, wert thou the proudest Plantagenet of the line, and he the poorest knight on earth!"

Both ladies obeyed the royal commands—Berengaria with bustling assiduity, as anxious to gratify her husband's humour, and Edith blushing and growing pale alternately, as, slowly and awkwardly, she undid, with Longsword's assistance, the fastenings which secured the helmet to the gorget.

"And what expect you from beneath this iron shell?" said Richard, as the removal of the casque gave to view the noble countenance of Sir Kenneth, his face glowing with recent exertion, and not less so with present emotion. "What think ye of him, gallants and beauties?" said Richard. "Doth he resemble an Ethiopian slave, or doth he present the face of an obscure and nameless adventurer? No, by my good sword! Here terminate his various disguises. He hath knelt down before you unknown, save by his worth; he arises equally distinguished by birth and by fortune. The adventurous knight, Kenneth, arises David, Earl of Huntingdon, Prince Royal of Scotland!"

There was a general exclamation of surprise, and Edith dropped from her hand the helmet which she had just received.

"Yes, my masters," said the King, "it is even so. Ye know how Scotland deceived us when she proposed to send this valiant Earl, with a bold company of her best and noblest, to aid our arms in this conquest of Palestine, but failed to comply with her engagements. This noble youth, under whom the Scottish Crusaders were to have been arrayed, thought foul scorn that his arm should be withheld from the holy warfare, and joined us at Sicily with a small train of devoted and faithful attendants, which was augmented by many of his countrymen to whom the rank of their leader was unknown. The confidants of the Royal Prince had all, save one old follower, fallen by death, when his secret, but too well kept, had nearly occasioned my cutting off, in a Scottish adventurer, one of the noblest hopes of Europe.—Why did you not mention your rank, noble Huntingdon, when endangered by my hasty and passionate sentence? Was it that you thought Richard capable of abusing the advantage I possessed over the heir of a King whom I have so often found hostile?"

"I did you not that injustice, royal Richard," answered the Earl of Huntingdon; "but my pride brooked not that I should avow myself Prince of Scotland in order to save my life, endangered for default of loyalty. And, moreover, I had made my vow to preserve my rank unknown till the Crusade should be accomplished; nor did I mention it save IN ARTICULO MORTIS, and under the seal of confession, to yonder reverend hermit."

"It was the knowledge of that secret, then, which made the good man so urgent with me to recall my severe sentence?" said Richard. "Well did he say that, had this good knight fallen by my mandate, I should have wished the deed undone though it had cost me a limb. A limb! I should have wished it undone had it cost me my life—-since the world would have said that Richard had abused the condition in which the heir of Scotland had placed himself by his confidence in his generosity."

"Yet, may we know of your Grace by what strange and happy chance this riddle was at length read?" said the Queen Berengaria.

"Letters were brought to us from England," said the King, "in which we learned, among other unpleasant news, that the King of Scotland had seized upon three of our nobles, when on a pilgrimage to Saint Ninian, and alleged, as a cause, that his heir, being supposed to be fighting in the ranks of the Teutonic Knights against the heathen of Borussia, was, in fact, in our camp, and in our power; and, therefore, William proposed to hold these nobles as hostages for his safety. This gave me the first light on the real rank of the Knight of the Leopard; and my suspicions were confirmed by De Vaux, who, on his return from Ascalon, brought back with him the Earl of Huntingdon's sole attendant, a thick-skulled slave, who had gone thirty miles to unfold to De Vaux a secret he should have told to me."

"Old Strauchan must be excused," said the Lord of Gilsland. "He knew from experience that my heart is somewhat softer than if I wrote myself Plantagenet."

"Thy heart soft? thou commodity of old iron and Cumberland flint, that thou art!" exclaimed the King.—"It is we Plantagenets who boast soft and feeling hearts. Edith," turning to his cousin with an expression which called the blood into her cheek, "give me thy hand, my fair cousin, and, Prince of Scotland, thine."

"Forbear, my lord," said Edith, hanging back, and endeavouring to hide her confusion under an attempt to rally her royal kinsman's credulity. "Remember you not that my hand was to be the signal of converting to the Christian faith the Saracen and Arab, Saladin and all his turbaned host?"

"Ay, but the wind of prophecy hath chopped about, and sits now in another corner," replied Richard.

"Mock not, lest your bonds be made strong," said the hermit stepping forward. "The heavenly host write nothing but truth in their brilliant records. It is man's eyes which are too weak to read their characters aright. Know, that when Saladin and Kenneth of Scotland slept in my grotto, I read in the stars that there rested under my roof a prince, the natural foe of Richard, with whom the fate of Edith Plantagenet was to be united. Could I doubt that this must be the Soldan, whose rank was well known to me, as he often visited my cell to converse on the revolutions of the heavenly bodies? Again, the lights of the firmament proclaimed that this prince, the husband of Edith Plantagenet, should be a Christian; and I—weak and wild interpreter!—argued thence the conversion of the noble Saladin, whose good qualities seemed often to incline him towards the better faith. The sense of my weakness hath humbled me to the dust; but in the dust I have found comfort! I have not read aright the fate of others—who can assure me but that I may have miscalculated mine own? God will not have us break into His council-house, or spy out His hidden mysteries. We must wait His time with watching and prayer—with fear and with hope. I came hither the stern seer—the proud prophet—skilled, as I thought, to instruct princes, and gifted even with supernatural powers, but burdened with a weight which I deemed no shoulders but mine could have borne. But my bands have been broken! I go hence humble in mine ignorance, penitent—and not hopeless."

With these words he withdrew from the assembly; and it is recorded that from that period his frenzy fits seldom occurred, and his penances were of a milder character, and accompanied with better hopes of the future. So much is there of self-opinion, even in insanity, that the conviction of his having entertained and expressed an unfounded prediction with so much vehemence seemed to operate like loss of blood on the human frame, to modify and lower the fever of the brain.

It is needless to follow into further particulars the conferences at the royal tent, or to inquire whether David, Earl of Huntingdon, was as mute in the presence of Edith Plantagenet as when he was bound to act under the character of an obscure and nameless adventurer. It may be well believed that he there expressed with suitable earnestness the passion to which he had so often before found it difficult to give words.

The hour of noon now approached, and Saladin waited to receive the Princes of Christendom in a tent, which, but for its large size, differed little from that of the ordinary shelter of the common Kurdman, or Arab; yet beneath its ample and sable covering was prepared a banquet after the most gorgeous fashion of the East, extended upon carpets of the richest stuffs, with cushions laid for the guests. But we cannot stop to describe the cloth of gold and silver—the superb embroidery in arabesque—the shawls of Kashmere and the muslins of India, which were here unfolded in all their splendour; far less to tell the different sweetmeats, ragouts edged with rice coloured in various manners, with all the other niceties of Eastern cookery. Lambs roasted whole, and game and poultry dressed in pilaus, were piled in vessels of gold, and silver, and porcelain, and intermixed with large mazers of sherbet, cooled in snow and ice from the caverns of Mount Lebanon. A magnificent pile of cushions at the head of the banquet seemed prepared for the master of the feast, and such dignitaries as he might call to share that place of distinction; while from the roof of the tent in all quarters, but over this seat of eminence in particular, waved many a banner and pennon, the trophies of battles won and kingdoms overthrown. But amongst and above them all, a long lance displayed a shroud, the banner of Death, with this impressive inscription—"SALADIN, KING OF KINGS—SALADIN, VICTOR OF VICTORS—SALADIN MUST DIE." Amid these preparations, the slaves who had arranged the refreshments stood with drooped heads and folded arms, mute and motionless as monumental statuary, or as automata, which waited the touch of the artist to put them in motion.

Expecting the approach of his princely guests, the Soldan, imbued, as most were, with the superstitions of his time, paused over a horoscope and corresponding scroll, which had been sent to him by the hermit of Engaddi when he departed from the camp.

"Strange and mysterious science," he muttered to himself, "which, pretending to draw the curtain of futurity, misleads those whom it seems to guide, and darkens the scene which it pretends to illuminate! Who would not have said that I was that enemy most dangerous to Richard, whose enmity was to be ended by marriage with his kinswoman? Yet it now appears that a union betwixt this gallant Earl and the lady will bring about friendship betwixt Richard and Scotland, an enemy more dangerous than I, as a wildcat in a chamber is more to be dreaded than a lion in a distant desert. But then," he continued to mutter to himself, "the combination intimates that this husband was to be Christian.—Christian!" he repeated, after a pause. "That gave the insane fanatic star-gazer hopes that I might renounce my faith! But me, the faithful follower of our Prophet—me it should have undeceived. Lie there, mysterious scroll," he added, thrusting it under the pile of cushions; "strange are thy bodements and fatal, since, even when true in themselves, they work upon those who attempt to decipher their meaning all the effects of falsehood.—How now! what means this intrusion?"

He spoke to the dwarf Nectabanus, who rushed into the tent fearfully agitated, with each strange and disproportioned feature wrenched by horror into still more extravagant ugliness—his mouth open, his eyes staring, his hands, with their shrivelled and deformed fingers, wildly expanded.

"What now?" said the Soldan sternly.

"ACCIPE HOC!" groaned out the dwarf.

"Ha! sayest thou?" answered Saladin.

"ACCIPE HOC!" replied the panic-struck creature, unconscious, perhaps, that he repeated the same words as before.

"Hence, I am in no vein for foolery," said the Emperor.

"Nor am I further fool," said the dwarf, "than to make my folly help out my wits to earn my bread, poor, helpless wretch! Hear, hear me, great Soldan!"

"Nay, if thou hast actual wrong to complain of," said Saladin, "fool or wise, thou art entitled to the ear of a King. Retire hither with me;" and he led him into the inner tent.

Whatever their conference related to, it was soon broken off by the fanfare of the trumpets announcing the arrival of the various Christian princes, whom Saladin welcomed to his tent with a royal courtesy well becoming their rank and his own; but chiefly he saluted the young Earl of Huntingdon, and generously congratulated him upon prospects which seemed to have interfered with and overclouded those which he had himself entertained.

"But think not," said the Soldan, "thou noble youth, that the Prince of Scotland is more welcome to Saladin than was Kenneth to the solitary Ilderim when they met in the desert, or the distressed Ethiop to the Hakim Adonbec. A brave and generous disposition like thine hath a value independent of condition and birth, as the cool draught, which I here proffer thee, is as delicious from an earthen vessel as from a goblet of gold."

The Earl of Huntingdon made a suitable reply, gratefully acknowledging the various important services he had received from the generous Soldan; but when he had pledged Saladin in the bowl of sherbet which the Soldan had proffered to him, he could not help remarking with a smile, "The brave cavalier Ilderim knew not of the formation of ice, but the munificent Soldan cools his sherbet with snow."

"Wouldst thou have an Arab or a Kurdman as wise as a Hakim?" said the Soldan. "He who does on a disguise must make the sentiments of his heart and the learning of his head accord with the dress which he assumes. I desired to see how a brave and single-hearted cavalier of Frangistan would conduct himself in debate with such a chief as I then seemed; and I questioned the truth of a well-known fact, to know by what arguments thou wouldst support thy assertion."

While they were speaking, the Archduke of Austria, who stood a little apart, was struck with the mention of iced sherbet, and took with pleasure and some bluntness the deep goblet, as the Earl of Huntingdon was about to replace it.

"Most delicious!" he exclaimed, after a deep draught, which the heat of the weather, and the feverishness following the debauch of the preceding day, had rendered doubly acceptable. He sighed as he handed the cup to the Grand Master of the Templars. Saladin made a sign to the dwarf, who advanced and pronounced, with a harsh voice, the words, ACCIPE HOC! The Templar started, like a steed who sees a lion under a bush beside the pathway; yet instantly recovered, and to hide, perhaps, his confusion, raised the goblet to his lips. But those lips never touched that goblet's rim. The sabre of Saladin left its sheath as lightning leaves the cloud. It was waved in the air, and the head of the Grand Master rolled to the extremity of the tent, while the trunk remained for a second standing, with the goblet still clenched in its grasp, then fell, the liquor mingling with the blood that spurted from the veins.

There was a general exclamation of treason, and Austria, nearest to whom Saladin stood with the bloody sabre in his hand, started back as if apprehensive that his turn was to come next. Richard and others laid hand on their swords.

"Fear nothing, noble Austria," said Saladin, as composedly as if nothing had happened,—"nor you, royal England, be wroth at what you have seen. Not for his manifold treasons—not for the attempt which, as may be vouched by his own squire, he instigated against King Richard's life—not that he pursued the Prince of Scotland and myself in the desert, reducing us to save our lives by the speed of our horses—not that he had stirred up the Maronites to attack us upon this very occasion, had I not brought up unexpectedly so many Arabs as rendered the scheme abortive—not for any or all of these crimes does he now lie there, although each were deserving such a doom—but because, scarce half an hour ere he polluted our presence, as the simoom empoisons the atmosphere, he poniarded his comrade and accomplice, Conrade of Montserrat, lest he should confess the infamous plots in which they had both been engaged."

"How! Conrade murdered?—And by the Grand Master, his sponsor and most intimate friend!" exclaimed Richard. "Noble Soldan, I would not doubt thee; yet this must be proved, otherwise-"

"There stands the evidence," said Saladin, pointing to the terrified dwarf. "Allah, who sends the fire-fly to illuminate the night season, can discover secret crimes by the most contemptible means."

The Soldan proceeded to tell the dwarf's story, which amounted to this. In his foolish curiosity, or, as he partly confessed, with some thoughts of pilfering, Nectabanus had strayed into the tent of Conrade, which had been deserted by his attendants, some of whom had left the encampment to carry the news of his defeat to his brother, and others were availing themselves of the means which Saladin had supplied for revelling. The wounded man slept under the influence of Saladin's wonderful talisman, so that the dwarf had opportunity to pry about at pleasure until he was frightened into concealment by the sound of a heavy step. He skulked behind a curtain, yet could see the motions, and hear the words, of the Grand Master, who entered, and carefully secured the covering of the pavilion behind him. His victim started from sleep, and it would appear that he instantly suspected the purpose of his old associate, for it was in a tone of alarm that he demanded wherefore he disturbed him.

"I come to confess and to absolve thee," answered the Grand Master.

Of their further speech the terrified dwarf remembered little, save that Conrade implored the Grand Master not to break a wounded reed, and that the Templar struck him to the heart with a Turkish dagger, with the words ACCIPE HOC!—words which long afterwards haunted the terrified imagination of the concealed witness.

"I verified the tale," said Saladin, "by causing the body to be examined; and I made this unhappy being, whom Allah hath made the discoverer of the crime, repeat in your own presence the words which the murderer spoke; and you yourselves saw the effect which they produced upon his conscience!"

The Soldan paused, and the King of England broke silence.

"If this be true, as I doubt not, we have witnessed a great act of justice, though it bore a different aspect. But wherefore in this presence? wherefore with thine own hand?"

"I had designed otherwise," said Saladin. "But had I not hastened his doom, it had been altogether averted, since, if I had permitted him to taste of my cup, as he was about to do, how could I, without incurring the brand of inhospitality, have done him to death as he deserved? Had he murdered my father, and afterwards partaken of my food and my bowl, not a hair of his head could have been injured by me. But enough of him—let his carcass and his memory be removed from amongst us."

The body was carried away, and the marks of the slaughter obliterated or concealed with such ready dexterity, as showed that the case was not altogether so uncommon as to paralyze the assistants and officers of Saladin's household.

But the Christian princes felt that the scene which they had beheld weighed heavily on their spirits, and although, at the courteous invitation of the Soldan, they assumed their seats at the banquet, yet it was with the silence of doubt and amazement. The spirits of Richard alone surmounted all cause for suspicion or embarrassment. Yet he too seemed to ruminate on some proposition, as if he were desirous of making it in the most insinuating and acceptable manner which was possible. At length he drank off a large bowl of wine, and addressing the Soldan, desired to know whether it was not true that he had honoured the Earl of Huntingdon with a personal encounter.

Saladin answered with a smile that he had proved his horse and his weapons with the heir of Scotland, as cavaliers are wont to do with each other when they meet in the desert; and modestly added that, though the combat was not entirely decisive, he had not on his part much reason to pride himself on the event. The Scot, on the other hand, disclaimed the attributed superiority, and wished to assign it to the Soldan.

"Enough of honour thou hast had in the encounter," said Richard, "and I envy thee more for that than for the smiles of Edith Plantagenet, though one of them might reward a bloody day's work.—But what say you, noble princes? Is it fitting that such a royal ring of chivalry should break up without something being done for future times to speak of? What is the overthrow and death of a traitor to such a fair garland of honour as is here assembled, and which ought not to part without witnessing something more worthy of their regard?—How say you, princely Soldan? What if we two should now, and before this fair company, decide the long-contended question for this land of Palestine, and end at once these tedious wars? Yonder are the lists ready, nor can Paynimrie ever hope a better champion than thou. I, unless worthier offers, will lay down my gauntlet in behalf of Christendom, and in all love and honour we will do mortal battle for the possession of Jerusalem."

There was a deep pause for the Soldan's answer. His cheek and brow coloured highly, and it was the opinion of many present that he hesitated whether he should accept the challenge. At length he said, "Fighting for the Holy City against those whom we regard as idolaters and worshippers of stocks and stones and graven images, I might confide that Allah would strengthen my arm; or if I fell beneath the sword of the Melech Ric, I could not pass to Paradise by a more glorious death. But Allah has already given Jerusalem to the true believers, and it were a tempting the God of the Prophet to peril, upon my own personal strength and skill, that which I hold securely by the superiority of my forces."

"If not for Jerusalem, then," said Richard, in the tone of one who would entreat a favour of an intimate friend, "yet, for the love of honour, let us run at least three courses with grinded lances?"

"Even this," said Saladin, half smiling at Coeur de Lion's affectionate earnestness for the combat—"even this I may not lawfully do. The master places the shepherd over the flock not for the shepherd's own sake, but for the sake of the sheep. Had I a son to hold the sceptre when I fell, I might have had the liberty, as I have the will, to brave this bold encounter; but your own Scripture saith that when the herdsman is smitten, the sheep are scattered."

"Thou hast had all the fortune," said Richard, turning to the Earl of Huntingdon with a sigh. "I would have given the best year in my life for that one half hour beside the Diamond of the Desert!"

The chivalrous extravagance of Richard awakened the spirits of the assembly, and when at length they arose to depart Saladin advanced and took Coeur de Lion by the hand.

"Noble King of England," he said, "we now part, never to meet again. That your league is dissolved, no more to be reunited, and that your native forces are far too few to enable you to prosecute your enterprise, is as well known to me as to yourself. I may not yield you up that Jerusalem which you so much desire to hold—it is to us, as to you, a Holy City. But whatever other terms Richard demands of Saladin shall be as willingly yielded as yonder fountain yields its waters. Ay and the same should be as frankly afforded by Saladin if Richard stood in the desert with but two archers in his train!"

The next day saw Richard's return to his own camp, and in a short space afterwards the young Earl of Huntingdon was espoused by Edith Plantagenet. The Soldan sent, as a nuptial present on this occasion, the celebrated TALISMAN. But though many cures were wrought by means of it in Europe, none equalled in success and celebrity those which the Soldan achieved. It is still in existence, having been bequeathed by the Earl of Huntingdon to a brave knight of Scotland, Sir Simon of the Lee, in whose ancient and highly honoured family it is still preserved; and although charmed stones have been dismissed from the modern Pharmacopoeia, its virtues are still applied to for stopping blood, and in cases of canine madness.

Our Story closes here, as the terms on which Richard relinquished his conquests are to be found in every history of the period.

Lesson 151

1. Write a paragraph about one of the following themes in the book. (Yes, this is your *reading* assignment.) Make sure you start with a thesis statement that says specifically what you will be talking about. In the body of your paragraph use at least three specific examples from the book. It would be excellent if you could use a quote

from the book. Your body should have at least six sentences. Finish with a conclusion sentence.

- Men are not always what they seem
- Friendship
- Honor
- Faith/religion
- The Crusaders and the Saracens (weapons, faith, military uniforms, ideas about women, chivalry and the law of hospitality)

Lesson 152

1. Read chapter 1 of the *The King Will Make a Way*. (I wrote this book. It has been professionally edited, so I trust it to use as an example. I want to show you that you can write your own novel!)
2. Why does Gabe call himself "croakless?" (Answers)
3. Why do you think Gabe compares himself to a toad? Why not a lion without a roar? (Answers)
4. What's Phineas' relationship to Vulpine? (Answers)
5. I used a motif of golden vs. wooden in the book to represent the things of God and the things of this world.

"We'll tell them the King is dead."

"But the people will still remember him."

"We'll make them forget, simply stop mentioning him. He won't exist to the children. He just stays up there on that hill of his, never to be seen. It will be easy."

The discussion was one of hushed excitement, rather than heated debate. Vulpine, the elected leader of the village assembly and the self-appointed leader of the Brothers and Sons, answered everyone's qualms. He spoke with such certitude that those around him often quickly acquiesced, though he considered it a bother to always have to explain himself. Tall and dark, he used his size to stare down his competitors and used his quick mind to silence them. His piercing eyes appeared black against the contrasting whites, which lent to the aura of the man.

"Good doctor, would you be obliged to help us in the matter?" Vulpine turned everyone's attention toward the village physician.

"You mean something along the lines of...." the good doctor cleared his throat, "Upon examination, it is my conclusion that the King died peacefully in his sleep from nothing other than ripe old age." He practiced the diagnosis in his most professional voice.

"Something along those lines would do splendidly,"

Vulpine said smirking and suggested a drink.

“Gabe!” he bellowed, pausing the clandestine meeting. “Why does a guest have to holler for a drink?” he growled toward the kitchen.

Gabe, a small boy for ten, came out cautiously with a tray of drinks, taking one step at a time as if checking to make sure the floorboards were solid before putting his weight down. The windowless kitchen door swung back and forth behind him while he made his way across the wooden floor without a misstep, even though his golden hair threatened to block his view and cause a catastrophe. He relieved himself of his load, transferring the burden to the heavy oak table. Gabe made an about-face as if under a general’s orders and headed straight back to the kitchen.

Behind closed doors, he asked his mother again why Father let those men use their family’s inn for meetings.

“I’ve answered you already” was all she responded, without taking her eyes off the pie crust she was rolling out. She was always at work, an ant in an apron. This is where Gabe saw her most often, in the kitchen. The room showed signs of her handiwork: the drying herbs hanging from the rafters, the pot of stew bubbling on the hearth, and, of course, the round pie dough growing ever thinner. Gabe watched her pause to brush brown wisps of hair from her face. People often teased her that her food must not be any good since she was so slender, but she never took offense because it was widely known no one could bake a pie or season a stew like Mother. Wiping the flour off her hands, she looked at Gabe, who seemed to be hanging there as if out to dry. She sighed and smiled. “Why don’t you ask your father?” she suggested and set back to work.

Gabe knew just where to find his father in the evenings, and from the kitchen he climbed the creaky stairs that led to the bed chambers. The largest was their family quarters. There were two beds in it—as long as the inn wasn’t crowded and an extra bed wasn’t needed elsewhere. The room also held Father’s small table and chair. Here he sat with the inn’s books, recording the day’s accounts, meticulously adding and subtracting, keeping the inn prospering, if modestly.

Gabe was often told he looked like his father, but Gabe didn’t believe that. Apart from their shared heritage of golden hair and green eyes with flecks of brown, Gabe didn’t think it was possible that he could grow into his father’s image.

“Father?” Gabe’s father turned his head to see his son standing inside the door. Father straightened and warmly welcomed Gabe to his side. Gabe repeated the question he had just asked Mother.

“Because I love you,” his father began, “and because I love your mother and your sisters. I want to take care of you all the best I can. I know you aren’t used to serving in the dining hall, but they want you to be the only one to come into the room during their meetings. Gabe, they are paying customers. The inn is mostly empty now that it is fall. You understand, right?” Gabe nodded. With a smile and a pat, his father turned back to his books under the flicker of the candle flame.

Gabe flopped down the stairs and, seeing he wasn’t in demand in the kitchen, he slipped out of the inn into the cool night air. He knew he might be needed inside, but he made a roaming retreat back to the kitchen, circling first around the inn. Shuffling his feet, he paused to look at the well-weathered sign in front of their two-story inn. It simply read,

"There Is Always Room."

There was plenty of room now that traveling season was over and fall had arrived. Gabe wondered if there was another way he could help make money for the family so those brusque men wouldn't have to be welcomed anymore.

Gabe leaned against the wooden frame of the inn and looked at the hill, which was their nearest neighbor to the east. He stood there wondering how one went about finding work and shrunk back as he realized he'd have to ask someone if they needed a boy. He imagined himself frozen in front of someone's stables while a man stood before him demanding to know why he'd come. He pictured his mouth ajar, the words caught in his throat. A croakless toad, that's what I am. Why is it so hard to spit out that first word? He shook his head as if to knock the thoughts out of his mind, wanting to leave them out there in the dirt to be trampled on, and entered through the side door back to safety at his mother's side.

Waiting for his next order, Gabe leaned against the wall just next to the double-hinged door in order to hear the men. This was hardly necessary for though the men spoke mostly in faint tones, they were quick to raise the rafters with their shouts for him. As he rested against the wall, soaking in the scent of freshly grated cinnamon, he heard one voice above the others. What he heard made his eyes stretch wide and his mouth pop open as if his chin had just dropped anchor.

"The King is dead!" Vulpine raised his glass in a toast, and the phrase echoed around the plain wooden room.

****

The King sat in his resplendent hilltop abode, very much alive. King's Hill, as it was known, lay on the village's eastern boundary. No one ever set foot on it. For as long as anyone in his family remembered, there had always been a guard on duty at the foot of the hill, and everyone grew up knowing King's Hill was off limits to the villagers.

Although not by any means an imposing mountain, its name did stretch its definition, and it towered over the village. One side of the hill was always dressed in forest green, ranks of conifers acting as a shield between the King and the village. Luscious green covered the base where the pines didn't conceal it from the sun, and the meadow grass always danced in the breeze which rolled down the hill like a giggling child. Wild flowers, violet and gold, stood in defiance of the falling temperatures. The trees which filled out the rest of the hill embraced the cool air and were as golden as the sun reflecting off the King's crown.

Approaching the pinnacle, the greens and golds gave way to gray as the hill became solid rock at its summit. It was there at the peak the King's home had been hewn from the side of the hill. In the center of this stony alcove, inlaid with gold, stood the throne. Over the throne a white banner hung, waving its message of the King's love for the village.

Under the banner the King sat, watching over the village, always knowing everything that happened. He knew exactly what had been said at the meeting and hadn't been surprised—he was never surprised by anything.

It was there in his throne room at the top of the village that the King listened to his song, which the trees and streams and flowers and even the rocks sang toward his throne continuously. Vulpine had decided it would be sung in the village only once more—at the King's funeral.

****

Vulpine's right-hand man, Phineas Tract, was more than an assistant; he acted as Vulpine's mouthpiece to the public. Vulpine spoke to Phineas and Phineas parroted the words to the villagers. He lacked in hair as much as he lacked in height, and he was a good foot shorter than his master. Though not a slave, he was certainly obedient to Vulpine. His gift lay not in an appealing appearance but in his smooth voice that calmed jittery crowds. The friendly, reassuring voice he used when explaining things made people feel as if everything were under control, even if they didn't understand what he was saying.

To talk with the villagers, he would stroll down to the square, which was the center of village life. People congregated around the well in the middle of the square to hear the latest gossip, or they walked along the shops which walled in the square on two sides. There was the tailor, butcher, shoemaker, doctor and candy man. There was also the metalsmith, who could make metal pour, and the glass blower, who could make glass bend.

While some shops sold cloth, tools and other household wares, there was also a daily market that began where the square ended. The only dividing marker was a bell tower, which held the copper bell that beckoned the villagers to the square for important events and announcements. Beyond the tower were brightly painted wooden stalls full of every kind of sight and scent: pies, licorice, rum, pickles, birds, canes, toys, rugs. Any villager in need of something could find it in the market or at least someone willing to make it for them, at a price.

Children would beg a peppermint stick and then run ahead, weaving through the shoppers to play in the lake which formed the western boundary of the village. Each evening the sun dipped into the lake, setting it on fire. The village children, however, didn't come for its beauty. They liked the cool tickle on their toes as they dangled their feet in the water, sending ripples gliding over its surface. Later, the children returned home heading in every direction, leaving muddy footprints along the roads which lead out of each corner of the square, some passing the school where the wealthier families sent their children to study.

It seemed as if everyone visited the square at least once every day, and Phineas was no exception. Almost every day he sauntered into the open area like the Pied Piper, and curious villagers would follow him. They trooped together to the east end of the Square where the impressive government building, the Assembly Hall, stood, its pillars proclaiming its importance. Phineas would climb the steps that lined the front of the Hall, as it was commonly known and, positioning himself on its porch, he would deliver the daily digest.

The day the King's death was announced was no different. Phineas reported how the King had died peacefully in his sleep and announced his funeral would take place the following day. Step by step, everything had been carefully orchestrated—by Vulpine.

Lesson 153

1. Read chapter 2 of the *The King Will Make a Way.*
2. What does Gabe's father find? (Answers) What do you think it represents?
3. Why is Gabe so bothered? (Answers)
4. What is Vulpine's ultimate goal? (Answers)
5. Author's Note: Remember the motif of golden vs. wooden? Who has golden hair? Who has brown hair?
6. Make a list of the all of the characters so far. What do you know about them? Gabe, our main character, you will see grow and mature and change throughout the novel. Some things about a character will never change, but every character, and person, is always growing and changing and learning. Don't forget to have your characters learn something along the way.
7. What do the character names tell us about them? How do they fit their names? Any guesses on who they represent in the metaphor?
    - Gabriel means man of God.
    - Angela means angelic (in the book it says she has an angelic name).
    - Vulpine literally means cunning or crafty. (I picked this name by looking up crafty in the thesaurus. It just sounded villainous.)
    - Phineas Tract: Phineas means oracle. Tract is short for tractable meaning easily managed or controlled.
8. I used ancestry.com to check to see if these last names existed. I did A LOT of research throughout the writing of the book even though it is fiction. At one point I was looking up melting points because there is a fire and I was trying to figure out if something would survive the fire. You have Google. Use it!

No one worked on the day of the funeral. Fog misted over the village as the King's song was sung by his grave. After the ceremony, Gabe plodded home with his family, thinking through all he knew about the King. He knew the King had founded the village about a hundred years before and set as its foundation, a book of laws he had written himself. He didn't know anything about the book or its laws and nor could he think of anything else he knew about the King.

Back at home, Gabe's family sat around the table together. They lived at the inn but ate in the kitchen, the large room being reserved for guests only. Eating a cold meal and discussing the King, Gabe inundated his parents with questions.

Gabe's two sisters, who sat side by side holding hands under the table, were listening. The older one could have been Gabe's identical twin if she hadn't been born a girl. Not only did both have Father's golden hair, but also his eyes. Whenever they asked their father what color their eyes were, he'd say, "The color of muddy grass."

Five-year-old Tabitha, with her brown curls and equally dark wide eyes, adored everything about her big sister and stuck to her like the freckles on her nose. Living up to her angelic name, Angela never seemed bothered by her little sidekick. She patiently explained to her why cows needed milking and why the sun went to sleep every night. Though just ten like Gabe, Angela always seemed to know the answer to anything. Now she seemed content just to listen.

"Did you ever see the King?" Gabe wanted to know. "Why didn't the King ever come down? Why didn't he ever talk to us?"

Gabe's father was a wise and humble man, slow to speak and slow to anger. He took Gabe's questions seriously and pondered on each a bit before answering.

"I never did get a chance to see the King, but I know that he used to visit the villagers. My grandfather used to talk about it. He was just a young boy at the time. He said the King was a majestic sight, wearing a golden crown and his royal robe. My grandfather said everyone flocked to be near him because he was full of wisdom and grace.

"No one is quite sure what happened to make the King leave or why he never returned. But my father once told me that he suspected the leaders of our village one day asked him not to return. He thought they were jealous the people adored the King and hung on his words and not theirs. The King left peacefully. At least that's what my father told me. "People have different ideas about it all, but one thing is sure. When the King left, he told the villagers he would see them again. He said that he hoped it would be a pleasant encounter, but he feared many would not welcome his return."

"But he never did return, right, Father?" "No, he never did."

"Why would the King say he would come back and not keep his word?" The question had pestered Gabe for days.

He and Angela, with Tabitha in her shadow, were lugging water from the family's well out back to Betty, their milk cow.

"He didn't know he was going to die, Gabe. He just didn't get back in time. He wasn't trying to break his word. It just happened." Angela thought it was a reasonable explanation.

"I don't know. If he really just slipped away in his sleep, he must have known he was getting close to the end of his life. Why wouldn't he keep his promise before he died?"

Gabe was more airing his thoughts than searching for answers from his sister. "If he was as wonderful as some people think, he would have come back before he died."

"Why is this bothering you?" Angela didn't understand what Gabe was feeling. "So he didn't come back. What's the big deal? We lived without him. Our parents have lived without him.

Things are okay. We didn't need him to come back. He never did anything. We're okay without him."

Gabe wasn't feeling okay but he kept quiet. Morning chores were soon finished and the children joined their parents at the table for breakfast. After warm bowls of sloppy mush, or at least as Gabe was eating his, Father produced an intricately carved wooden box and laid it carefully on the table. "What is it, Father?" Tabitha asked, wiggling with impatience.

"This box was my grandfather's. Then it was my father's. Then it was mine."

"What's inside of it?" Tabitha pressed, not satisfied with his answer.

Father smiled and leaned back a bit. "After our discussion about the King, I remembered this old box. I admit it has just sat neglected, stashed away for years. I guess I put it away to keep it from damage since it was so old and beautiful. But in putting it aside, I forgot about it. I spent the last few days trying to find it."

Tabitha didn't understand why Father was telling them about the box he had put away so well he had forgotten all about it. And she couldn't understand why the box was remembered and on the table now. "But what is it, Father?" she couldn't help but ask again.

Without a word, he opened the box. It was full of old papers, yellowed and wrinkled with age. Father laughed at Tabitha, who looked as if she expected a new doll to be buried under the stack.

This time Angela spoke up. "Are they old letters? Maybe great-grandfather's love letters to his wife." Angela was pleased with the thought.

"No, Angela, but they are written by my grandfather; at least, written in his hand. It's a copy of the King's law.

Today, the law book is just considered an historical book.

You know it's kept locked in a glass case in the Assembly Hall. But years ago, it was the law of the village, and my grandfather used to go with his family to hear the King's law read aloud daily in the Hall. His father must have had him write down what he heard as part of his education."

Gabe's interest was piqued, and he moved to the edge of his seat. He was sure that this would make all the uncertainty go away. Gabe's father had been watching his reaction and speaking to Gabe, he said, "And as part of your education, today you may be excused to read through all these papers."

In a flash, Gabe gathered up the box and raced out to the animal shed to be alone with his great-grandfather's work, the King's words.

Vulpine was sure no one knew any of the King's words anymore and moved to erase from the village all memory of the King. The Brothers and Sons had met and decided to hold a competition to distract the villagers from the King's funeral and to get rid of what current ties to the King—his banner and his song. Phineas announced that in just two weeks, the winning banner and song would be revealed to the public.

The village artisans got right to work, and the village filled with excited chatter over the competitors' creations.

The only rule they worked under was this: the banner or song had to be completely new and different in order to lead the village into the future.

Gabe, however, wasn't thinking about the competition; his thoughts were always on the King. He was keen to report what he had learned from reading the King's law and felt confirmed in his suspicion that something was amiss. He was literally bouncing in his seat, waiting for his family to settle in for the evening meal.

As soon as he had the chance, he poured out all that he had bottled up. "He said in the book of law that he would come back. It's in there! It also says that all the words of the law are sure and true, that the King's word cannot fail. He couldn't have died without coming back to the village!"

Gabe spilled his words, his mouth trying to keep pace with his mind.

"I still don't see how that matters." Angela didn't find Gabe's excitement contagious. "He died. He couldn't help it that he died before he came back."

Gabe deflated and looked to his father. "Gabe," Father began, "thanks for reading through those for us. I'm sure there are some other interesting things you could share with us." Gabe nodded and abandoned his attempt to convince them that the King had to still be alive. He told them other tidbits of the law but didn't stop believing the King was still living on the hill.

Two weeks passed quickly. As Gabe read and reread the King's law, artists brought their banners and presented them to the Assembly, the men elected to lead the village. Vulpine easily swayed the majority to his opinion. With mere comments, he led the Assemblymen to choose the banner that would serve his plans best.

The new banner was green to symbolize the fertile farm lands that ran the length of the road between the inn and the square and stretched back more than half a mile from the farm houses on each side. On the wide end of the banner was a depiction of the Assembly Hall, honoring its preeminence in the village. The banner came to a point where there was a picture of the well, symbolizing life. Vulpine approved the banner's meaning: the Assembly pointed the villagers to life.

Vulpine was just as pleased with the winning song. The bell beckoned to the villagers, and the crowd gathered for the unveiling of the winners. The Assemblymen huddled on the porch on that windy, gray day when the new banner was unfurled and the new village song was sung. The villagers were sure their leaders had chosen well as the song stirred their spirits just to hear it, and they were happy to sing its pledge to serve the village.

That evening at the inn, Vulpine snickered with Phineas over drinks about how easily the villagers had their minds taken off the King. "Our fathers got that old man to stay up on King's Hill and locked up his law book. Now, the Assembly has voted out his song and banner and replaced them with ones of our own choosing. Sometimes it's too easy, Phineas. The villagers elected me a member of the Assembly. The other members elected me lord of the

Assembly," Vulpine crowed. "There is only one title left for me to attain." Vulpine reveled in the thought. "I'm practically already the king myself."

Lesson 154

1. Read chapter 3 of the *The King Will Make a Way*.
2. Why does Gabe fall when he's climbing the mountain? (hint: It's not because he tripped.) (Answers)
3. What is Gabe's invitation to visit the King? (Answers)
4. Author's note: The toad Gabe catches escapes "without a sound." He's a croakless toad, just like Gabe. But, this toad saved the day and helped Gabe get to the King, and it was also obeying the King's orders in doing so. Similarity to Gabe?

Gabe's mind was still on the King, and he again reasoned with his family why the King had to still be living. Gabe looked at his father with pleading eyes. His father took a deep breath and conceded. "I propose you go on a hike, Gabe. Climb King's Hill. See if the King is there. Is that what you want?"

The boy's eyes brightened and his back straightened. "Yes, sir."

"Good then. If the King is dead, he won't be there. Then we'll know that the law was a nice idea thought up by the King who gave us our village, and he just died before he could do what he wrote there. If the King is there…well, that's unlikely, as he's dead, but I understand your need to put the question to rest for yourself."

"No one goes up King's Hill. Ever. It's always been off limits." Mother's flustered words revealed her concern over the planned adventure. "It was set apart for the King's use. I heard Phineas Tract declare that the hill would be kept forever as a monument for the King, and it was to be undisturbed. You know they keep it guarded."

"If the guard won't let him past, well, at least he tried," Father offered as consolation.

"I'll go in the morning." It was decided.

Gabe was awake before dawn, trying to decide what qualified as morning so that he could get up and begin his expedition. He napped fitfully, listening for the sounds that would announce the day, but it was a smell that roused him. Mother's sleep had flitted away as well, and she arose extra early to prepare a raisin loaf for her son. She didn't like the idea of her son going off into the unknown. She always felt best when her family was all under the protective roof of their inn. She wrestled with her thoughts as she wrestled with the dough. "Worrying won't help a thing," she kept telling herself, the repetition soothing her.

Gabe followed the scent trail to the kitchen and eagerly gathered up the warm bread and hard cheese his mother set before him. "I'll eat on the path. I need to get going." His mother made no response, a statue gracing their kitchen. "I won't be long. I can be to the top in an hour if I go quickly," he added, trying to assuage her concerns. She nodded, slightly. He nodded back.

Gabe struck out east on the dirt road that ran from the village square to King's Hill. Even though the hill was just a few stone throws away from the inn, he felt like a pioneer— adventurous and alone. He had been alone before, but it felt different this time; it felt brave and unsure. Overriding his paradoxical emotions was just one thought, *If I see the King, what will I say to him?*

He reached the foot of the hill without having prepared an opening line. A toad landed on his left foot, distracting him from his thoughts. The toad hopped off just beyond him, and the natural impulse of a ten-year-old boy to try and catch it overpowered him. He lunged for it. Missed. Again. Drat. He crouched down low like a lioness ready to pounce. He waited until the toad was least suspecting. *Gotcha!*

"King's Hill is off limits. What are you doing here?" The guard demanded answers from the boy sprawled on the ground. Gabe held up the toad.

"Just trying to catch my toad." The reply slipped off his tongue. *Well, it is my toad now. I caught him*, he assured himself of the truth of the statement. The toad, without a sound, made a desperate attempt for escape and leapt to freedom. As if by reflex, Gabe again launched himself toward the toad. The guard snorted and retreated to his post. Gabe kept up the maneuvers until the guard was safely settled back in his guard box, comfortably seated on his stool. Gabe thanked the toad for his help and made his way into the cover of the pines.

The encounter with the toad had relaxed him, and instead of trying to figure out what to say to the King, he explored his surroundings. Hidden among the dense needles of the pines, Gabe felt safe. He crouched and examined mushrooms, pine cones, rocks and beetles. Finding himself at the foot of an evergreen with low sweeping branches, he ducked underneath. Next to the trunk, he was able to stand up and move around. Imagining himself barricaded inside a fort, he opened his pack and dug into his rations.

Tasting the sweet raisins his mother had folded into his bread—a special treat for a special occasion—reminded him of his word to her that he wouldn't be long. He refocused on his task. *Climb the hill. Find the King's home.And...* He didn't know what came next. *Okay. One step at a time.* On his feet again, he raised his eyes and started to climb purposefully.

It was cold in the cover of the forest; the sun still low in the sky as Gabe walked through the trees. His eyes leapt to each movement in the forest. The animals, not accustomed to humans, bolted before Gabe, who couldn't catch a glimpse of any of them. He saw branches bend and heard leaves rustle, but the animals remained hidden.

The sun climbed higher, matching Gabe's achievement. Gabe soon came out of the pine forest and for the first time, laid eyes on the summit. He wasn't sure what he had thought.

He realized he had no idea what to expect. He had heard the King lived in a golden palace.

A deer appeared from among the pines, and Gabe froze, hoping not to scare it away so he could watch it. The forest animals never dared to visit the village, and he was fascinated by this unusual sight. With minute movements, he slowly slipped down onto one knee in the dewy grass. The buck moved regally toward him. Closer. Closer. Gabe was astonished, electrified by this steadily approaching Creature. Closer. Closer. He wasn't sure if he should be scared, except that he didn't feel fear. He felt awe. The buck stopped next to him, his powerful antlers declaring his dominance on the hill. Gabe gradually stretched his legs and straightened until he reached his full height and found himself looking into the eyes of the buck.

The magnificent creature turned and advanced across the hill. He paused. His towering trophy turned, and the buck looked again into the boy's eyes. He gave his antlers a shake and was off again, crossing and climbing the hillside. Gabe began to follow. *Is this buck escorting me?* The procession led in and out of bushes and other trees, but this time the animals didn't run. Rabbits, foxes, squirrels, mice, beavers, badgers…the animals came out from hiding and lined the parade route. A hawk settled on a tree. A cardinal in another. A nightingale. The boy gaped as a great brown bear lumbered out.

Gabe, the pioneer, the adventurer, the explorer, was certainly in uncharted waters now. He wasn't afraid though. It was exhilarating. Some of the animals began to fall in line and trail behind Gabe. With each step, Gabe grew taller, more confident; he felt like he was king of the forest, king of the hill.

All at once, the procession halted. Gabe tripped on the buck's left hind leg and fell. No matter. All of the animals had their heads on the ground—bowing. What is happening? Gabe peeled his face off the ground and looked up. The King stood before him.

Gabe scrambled to his feet and then froze. *The King. The King.* They were the only words spinning through his mind. *The King. The King.* Only seconds passed before the magnitude of the moment struck him. He sank to the ground and bowed, following the animals' example, and trembled.

"Welcome, Gabe. I've been waiting for you. I'm glad to see the toad and buck have done their jobs well." The King's voice was strong and calm, a kind voice but one that demanded respect. Gabe's body remained unmoving, but his mind raced. *He knows my name. The toad and buck did their jobs? The toad from this morning? What job?*

The King *s*miled and turned his back to Gabe. The animals raised themselves and frolicked and frisked their way back to their homes. "Join me." Gabe recognized the King's invitation as a command. He lifted his head and saw the King moving steadily toward a cave. Gabe jumped to his feet and walked in the King's footsteps.

Gabe gawked as they approached the King's home, amazed the King lived in a cave, but as he entered, his surprise grew further. The King took his place on the throne, and Gabe stood before him, twisting and turning to take in the glittering eyeful. The King sat quietly and let the boy have his fill of the room. Gabe's gaze found its way back to the King, and he hung his head in shame for staring so intently at everything. He could hear his mother scolding him for being so nosy.

"Why don't you look around? Feel free to touch anything you like and to ask questions if you find something interesting." The King seemed to know just what Gabe had been feeling and his shame lifted. He moved uneasily at first, afraid he'd be clumsy and break something, but soon his worries evaporated like the morning dew on the hill, and he explored the cave freely.

It didn't seem like a cave, though. Gabe touched the wall. *This isn't rock. It looks like gold.* "The walls of the cave are covered with gold," the King responded to his ponderings. Gabe nodded, astonished again at the King's ability to know just what he was thinking. Fixed in the wall were twelve jewels, forming a semi-circle around the throne, which stood in the center of the room. Gabe fingered one. *I might as well ask. He probably already knows I want to.* Gabe cleared his throat. The King patiently waited. Gabe cleared his throat again.

"What type of stone is this?" Gabe held his breath.

"Emerald. And that's sapphire. Ruby. Diamond." The King pointed to the different precious stones and named them all. "The throne is made from gold, so are the steps leading up to the throne."

Gabe just nodded. What could he say? He lived in a wooden house with wooden tables and chairs. He ate out of a wooden bowl with a wooden spoon. Here, his surroundings were surreal.

He made his way around the back of the throne and saw that there was one wooden object there, a cabinet. Examining it up close, Gabe realized the carvings in the wood were scenes from the village. He ran his finger through the crevices, tracing the square, the Hall, the school yard, the inn. It was all there. Inside the cabinet was a single dish, a plate of pearl circumscribed with gold.

This time it was easier to ask. "Why is there only one plate here?" All at once, he felt foolish. *Only one person lives here. Why would there be more than one plate? Stupid.*

The King answered gently. "That plate has been reserved for a special guest."

"Oh."

"A guest from the village." The King was smiling broadly. "Why don't you take it out and have a closer look?" The King was enjoying himself.

Gabe delicately lifted the latch on the door, and it swung open. With extreme caution, he lifted the brittle looking plate off its stand. It was more elegant than fancy, holding no design apart from its trim. Gabe cautiously turned it over in his hands. Etched in gold on the back was his name, Gabriel. "My name." The whispered words escaped in his astonishment.

The King began to laugh now. "You're the special guest. I had the plate prepared for you."

He cradled the plate in his arms, just as he had Tabitha when she was first born. They felt the same -smooth and fragile. He gingerly made his way around the throne. He stood again before the King, and then, without being conscious of making a decision, decided to sit and stay awhile. He folded his knees beneath him and sat at the King's feet. The plate rested in his lap. His eyes rested on the plate. Finally, he blurted out his question. "Why?"

"I'm always prepared to feed those who seek me." The King's answer was an enigma to Gabe, but he decided not to ask any further questions. In the wonder of the morning, Gabe had forgotten entirely his original purpose in coming. As he sat silently before the King, it all started to come back to him.

"They said you were dead." He plunged into his story, and the rest flowed as steady as a river into the sea. The King listened patiently. "And, I don't know, I just couldn't rest until I found you. They didn't think I would find you, but somehow I just knew you would be here. No one else believes you are alive, but I knew you just had to be." Gabe had been talking to the floor. He looked up and his heart melted. *He understands me. He loves me.*

Unthinking, he flung himself at the King's feet. The plate crashed to the floor and fractured into three pieces. Gabe wrapped his arms around the King's legs, and crying, he clung fast, sure he would never let go.

The King let him stay there, wet and clingy. Finally, Gabe, quieted and calmed, released his vice grip and sat up. He stared at the plate and felt ashamed again. The King stood and walked down the steps that led to his throne. He bent and picked up the pieces, held them together for a moment and then handed the plate to Gabe, whole.

This time Gabe was speechless for a whole new reason; he was flabbergasted. Stunned, he stammered, "I…I…I'm sorry I broke the plate."

"Already fixed and forgotten." The King's light remark removed Gabe's shame. "Now, let me tell you more about this plate." The King spoke as he took his place again on his throne. Gabe settled in once more at the King's feet with the plate, this time, on the floor beside him. "This plate is my invitation to you to come and sup with me, anytime." Gabe smiled. "Sup with us" was just how his mother would say it, inviting in friends or strangers for a meal. "Come to me whenever you like, and I will see that you are never hungry."

Gabe felt full. "Could I come back tomorrow?" The King smiled and nodded.

Gabe placed his plate back onto its stand, his sign that he was always welcome to visit the King. He scuttled toward the door but stopped short of it. "Thank you," he said simply and ducked out the door without saying goodbye. He hadn't felt a need to. He'd be back tomorrow.

Lesson 155

1. Read chapter 4 of the *The King Will Make a Way.*
2. What is Gabe learning from the King? (Answers)
3. Why doesn't the King go down to the village? (Answers)
4. What has Gabe gained from the King? (Answers)
5. Think about it: How does knowing Jesus (the King) mean sacrifice, privilege and responsibility?

Gabe stopped in front of the inn and tried to brush the dirt from his trousers. He removed his right shoe and shook a pebble from it. *How can I explain what just happened? What am I—* He didn't get to finish the thought. Angela had spotted him and ran out to greet him. Tabitha skipped along behind.

"What happened?" Angela asked. "I found him."

"What?"

"I found the King. I…I…" His lips couldn't form the words. His tongue flapped uselessly, making odd monosyllabic noises. He didn't know how to begin.

"You found the King? How do you know? There was someone living on the hill? How do you know it wasn't someone else?"

"Impossible." Gabe found that question easy to answer. "There's no one like him. He knew my name. He knew what I was thinking. He answered my questions before I asked them. He somehow fixed a plate I had broken by just holding it. He loved me." His voice dropped off, but the words didn't fall; they floated in the breeze and carried their warmth with them. Angela could almost feel the warmth of the King's love as the words washed over her face.

Butterflies began flitting around in Angela's stomach. "Mother's at the market. Father's paying a visit to Percy Katrid. Will you tell me all about the King?"

They sat on the ground, leaning their backs on the hard wood of the inn. He started at the beginning from when his first shoe hit the path until he had thanked the King. He told her every detail he could describe. He even confessed to clinging to the King and crying. Angela remained transfixed the whole time. When all was told, he sat quietly and imagined himself again at the King's feet. Finding the King alive should have raised more questions than it settled, but he was content. No more questions raged in him. He was at peace like the lake at sunrise on a cloudless winter day.

Tabitha twirled and watched her skirts fly out. Angela let Gabe sit in peace while she thoughtfully studied his face and determined something was different. She was sure something had happened to him up on the hill that morning.

"I believe you."

Gabe's thoughts were interrupted. "What?"

"I believe you."

It hadn't occurred to Gabe that his words could be unbelievable, but as he thought about it, he realized it all sounded crazy. He started to giggle at the absurd story of the dead King who's alive and reads minds and fixes plates and who actually only has one plate which happens to have his name on it. He realized the significance of his sister's affirmation.

"Thank you."

Angela smiled.

"Do you think anyone else will believe me?"

Angela shook her head. "It's a tall tale." She began laughing herself. "Do you think I could meet him?"

"I don't know. I'll ask him tomorrow. I'm going back. I'm going to go every day."

"Father's not going to let you skip your chores and learning to go climb that hill every day."

"I have to go. I don't know. The King has a way of helping me come to him. He'll help me get there."

Angela remembered the toad and the buck. "Right, I forgot. I'll help you too. I don't need to go. I can stay home and do your morning chores. You can meet with the King, and then you can tell me everything he—"

"Oh, Gabe, you're home." Their mother was barreling toward them, the bounty in her satchel threatening an avalanche. "Now don't you try that again. Only so much a mother's heart can take."

"Gabe met the King, and he did magic tricks." Tabitha's summary of his morning was not what he had expected to share with his mother. He began to object, but his mother spoke first.

"Telling your sister stories, I see. Anyhow, it's a good thing you are back here now. I just heard Lord Vulpine wants to hold another meeting tonight. We need to fix up a stew and get the room set." She blustered past them and set straight to work.

Gabe stood dumbfounded. *Make-believe stories. That's what she thinks. She doesn't know the truth. Does she want to know what really happened?* He realized his parents didn't consider for a moment that the King might still be alive. It wasn't a possibility to them. *How can I convince them he's alive?*

"Let's go help." Angela's words cut into his distressing thoughts but didn't cut loose their weight. He carried the burden as he trudged after his sister.

When Gabe's father returned home, events imitated those earlier with his mother. Neither had heard the truth, but neither asked for it.

That evening, while Vulpine commanded the audience of the Brothers and Sons, Gabe sought an audience with his father. He found him again hunched over his books. "Father, I want to go every day to King's Hill."

"What?" Gabe's father had been interrupted and his mind was elsewhere.

"I want to go up King's Hill every day. I want to see the King."

"The King? What do you mean?"

"I met the King today. He invited me back, and I want to go."

"Gabe, I don't know what you are talking about. The King is dead. If you enjoyed your hike, then fine, it would be good exercise for you to climb for a bit each day if the guard doesn't mind it. You'd have to go early in the morning and be back in time for chores and breakfast. But no talking with strangers."

"Yes, sir." His father had been quicker to respond than usual. He wasn't willing to ponder the possibility of the King living on the hill. Gabe withdrew from the room sullenly.

The next morning, Gabe was up and out before the sun had thrown off nighttime's cloak. He returned in time for breakfast but ate in silence. Afterward, as they plucked the apples from their family's trees and gathered them into bushels, he shared with Angela all the King had told him. Gabe was fast asleep before the candles in the inn had been blown out.

And so began a daily ritual of rising early, racing up the hill, sitting at the King's feet, and retracing his steps, usually in time for breakfast. Angela took up more and more of his chores and became a diligent disciple, taking in every word of the King as reported by Gabe.

The snows came, and Gabe rose in the dark when the shrill shrieking of scavenging rats could still be heard. Huddled in his cloak, he plowed his way down the road and up the hill. He never missed a chance to meet with the King. The King taught him the words of the book of law, explained the meanings behind the words and answered Gabe's questions.

"Are there others who come daily to visit you?"

"No. Sometimes there is someone who wanders up the hill a bit, seeking one thing or another, but only those who truly seek me are able to find me."

"Why don't they seek you?"

"They aren't willing to make the necessary sacrifices."

Gabe reflected over the past months: the early hours and lack of sleep, the long climb, the risk of being caught by the guard, the feeling of separation from all the other kids who had no interest in the King, his family not understanding his new life.

"Maybe it's a sacrifice," he conceded, "but it feels like a privilege."

"It's both, and it is also a responsibility."

Gabe didn't ask for an explanation. He was thinking of another question.

"What about Angela?" Gabe knew he didn't need to explain who she was. "She has sacrificed to get to know you, but she hasn't seen you."

"You're right. She has sacrificed her time and energy, and even though she hasn't seen me, do you think she has received some of the privileges of finding me?"

"Yes," Gabe answered simply; he knew it was true. He and Angela both had something that others lacked. They had peace and joy and both felt the King's love. They were gaining knowledge and wisdom about the world that even the leaders of the village wouldn't be able to match.

"Maybe if you would come down to the village, then people would know you are alive and would want to be with you. Why don't you come to the village?"

"The first day you came, I showed you your plate. It was your invitation to visit me as often as you like. The village withdrew their invitation to me. Not everyone is willing to make the sacrifices you have made to be with me, nor are they willing to accept the responsibility of knowing me and my law. But even so, I said I would come back one day, and I will."

Lesson 156

1. Read chapter 5 of the *The King Will Make a Way.*
2. How does the King help Gabe warn his family about the storm? (Answers)
3. What is the "rampaging drunk"? (Answers)
4. Father realizes Vulpine wants to be king. Knowing the King represents Jesus, who does Vulpine represent? (Answers)

"Gabe, I want you to know something." Gabe was again at the King's feet and saw sadness in his eyes. He sat up straighter.

"A very severe hailstorm is going to strike the village. I'm telling you so you won't be frightened. People won't be suspecting it when the winds pick up. They'll think it is just an April shower. It will be coming soon. On a sunny day, when the winds suddenly pick up and a dark cloud covers the sun, I want you to go to your kitchen and stay there until the storm passes."

"When is it coming?" Gabe felt uneasy all of a sudden.

"Soon. Watch for the signs, and you'll be prepared."

"Yes, sir, but how will I convince my family? My parents don't even believe you exist."

"I'll make a way. Your family will be safe."

He had done it again, lifted the burden off Gabe. When Gabe returned home that day, he mentioned the storm to no one but Angela. Over the next few days, the King didn't mention it again, so neither did Gabe.

Then one night, Gabe had a nightmare. He thrashed and sweated and cried out. Angela sat up with a start. She could almost feel Gabe's heart pounding as he sat up, panting. Tabitha was sleeping peacefully next to Angela when Mother rushed to his bedside.

"It's okay. It's okay." Mother tried to calm him. She stroked his hair to soothe her nerves as much as his.

"I had a dream. Mother, you can't go out today. There's going to be a hail storm. I saw it. A terrible storm. Hail big enough to knock a man down. The winds tore the banner off the Hall, and hail put holes in its roof. I saw roofs collapse and animals killed. You can't go out today."

"Gabe, what are you talking about? It was a dream. Relax. Let me go get you a warm cup of milk." She shuffled through the dark doorway and disappeared.

"Do you really think it will come today?" Angela asked.

Gabe tried to see Angela's form in the dark. "I think it might. He didn't tell me when, but he said he would help me make Mother and Father believe so they would be safe. Maybe that's why I had the dream. It was awful. I don't want to think about it anymore."

"Okay. It will be okay. The King will help us. Think about him. Think about King's Hill. You'll be able to go back to sleep."

He followed Angela's advice, relaxed and was asleep before Mother returned with the milk.

When the family gathered for breakfast, Mother told Father about their eventful night. He, like Tabitha, always did a good impersonation of a hibernating animal, sleeping no matter what was happening in the outside world. He listened to Mother and noticed the concern written in the wrinkles on Gabe's forehead.

"I'm glad it was just a dream. Don't worry about it." His father spoke nonchalantly. When his advice didn't soften the lines on Gabe's face, he added, "We can't just stop our lives because of a dream."

"It's not just the dream," Gabe said softly. "The King told me a terrible hailstorm was coming. He said when the winds picked up and the clouds blocked the sun, we were to go to our kitchen and wait out the storm." Gabe didn't dare look at anything above his toes.

"What?" His father was perplexed by what he was hearing.

Gabe didn't answer.

"What did you say?" Gabe's father never raised his voice, but there were times when Gabe felt like Father was yelling at him, and this was one of them.

"The King told me." The words fell to the floor.

"What are you saying?" The subject of the King had been dropped by the family months ago. His parents knew he went up the hill daily but that was all.

"The King told me." This time Gabe looked his father in the eyes and spoke each word deliberately.

His father was taken aback by his forthrightness and spoke softly in return. "When did you speak with the King?"

Gabe looked directly at his father. "I speak with the King every day. The King is alive and lives on the hill. You and Mother didn't believe me when I first went, so I've kept quiet about it."

"He's told me everything about the King," Angela added. "And I believe him. It's true."

"I have no idea what you are talking about." Mother's vexation was evident. She busied herself cleaning to avoid the conversation.

Father, however, was carried to a world away by Gabe's words. He watched his grandfather as he scrolled the words of the King's law. He flew to the summit of the hill, heavy laden with a King's golden throne. He heard the King's song and his banner flap in the breeze. He was remembering the King. His world had faded away, and the reality of the King engulfed him. Taking in a gulp of air, Gabe's astonished father came to his senses and asked, "He lives?"

"He lives," Gabe answered authoritatively.

"He lives," Angela assured him, beaming.

Gabe and Angela watched the transformation come over their father with gleeful hearts. They knew the experience well. Gratefulness overwhelmed Gabe. Months of wishing for this moment, and here he was, a witness to it. Angela sighed a happy sigh and said, "This is the perfect day."

"When will you tell me about the King?" Gabe's father realized he was an infant in his knowledge.

"When we're huddled in the kitchen during the storm," Gabe decided. "The King has a way of—" Gabe started in but was promptly interrupted.

Mother's skirts brushed against the table as she swept past the others, fixing a scarf over her dark brown hair. "I'm going to market. I'm not staying home because of someone's imagination. Besides, what will everyone eat if I don't go?" She was out the door.

Father was worried. Angela set out to console him. "Gabe, didn't the King say your family would be safe during the storm?"

Gabe nodded toward Angela.

"Well," said Angela, "let's not worry. You taught me the King's word is always true."

"That's right." Father's memory was jolted. "You told us that right after you read the King's law. 'The King's words are sure and true.' I believe that's what you said. Don't know how I can remember that, but I'm glad I do. Let's believe the King's words and not worry."

"Yes, sir!" Gabe was feeling giddy, a rubber ball set loose from a great height. He felt like anything was possible. No fears were lurking inside. *The King will keep Mother safe.*

Mother had already left the inn, but Father, along with Gabe and Angela, agreed to stay home for the rest of the day. Keeping Tabitha with them would not present a problem.

There was no sign of a storm. The sun was a golden medallion adorning a cloudless blue sky. The family busied themselves with chores around the inn. Gabe chopped and stacked firewood which would be needed for the stove, even when the weather warmed. Angela swept the floors and peeled potatoes. They worked silently, but they knew what the other was thinking. *When's the storm going to come?*

Crash! Tabitha shrieked. Bang! "Tabitha, go sit at the kitchen table and don't leave." Tabitha was so surprised by Angela's commanding tone that she quickly obeyed the order. Gabe had dashed out the front door of the inn and skidded to a halt. Angela quickly fell in behind him. The landscape was staggering, even though they had been warned. The sun was gone, swallowed whole by the threatening mass of a cumulonimbus, hovering, dwarfing the village like a giant boot about to squash a bug.

The inn's sign was knocking against the eave, its metal chains jangling. In a pine just in front of the inn, a red crossbill wrapped protective wings around her eggs and braced to defend her nest against the storm. Gabe's gaze turned to King's Hill. It seemed the storm skirted along its edges; the peak was reaching up to the clear blue heavens. *The King was somehow in control of this storm.* Gabe didn't understand the thought, but it was a comforting one anyway.

The dusty road had become more whirlpool than walkway, dirt fiercely swirling, not caring who was pummeled by its pebbles. Their next-door neighbor passed by. "Can you believe this wind?"

Gabe hollered back, "Get inside, Mr. Bollix, and stay there! This is going to be a bad storm!"

"I've seen worse. Funny how suddenly the wind picked up. I'm on my way home now. We'll be seeing you." He shielded his eyes from the onslaught of dust.

Gabe was startled by the man's composure. Gabe wanted to tear through the streets telling everyone to take cover. Thinking of Mother, he felt helpless. The vanished fears were slowly creeping back.

Father rushed to the door and herded his children away from the whipping winds. He had brought Betty inside. The incongruous sight made Gabe laugh out loud. "What would Mother say if she saw a cow in the dining hall?" The laughter left his lips with the words. *Mother.* The three of them stood in silence. Then it began.

Thud. Thud. Thud. A heavy fist was pounding the roof. They looked up at the ceiling and then at each other. *Hail.* "Let's get into the kitchen." Their father shepherded the children to the kitchen where Tabitha was waiting at the table. Inside, the only movement was the kitchen door swinging back and forth. Outside, the storm was a rampaging drunk, toppling everything within its reach, its fury crashing and splintering all it touched.

Thump. Rattle. The three tried to ignore the percussion symphony playing for them outside, especially the hail which was using the inn as a kettle drum. They distracted themselves with talk of the King.

Father looked to Gabe. "I don't know where to begin, what to ask. What do you want to tell me about the King?"

Apart from having his mother sitting across from him right then asking the same question, there was nothing more Gabe wanted. "Remember the old village song? The line, *His love's a banner waving over all of us.*"

"Of course, *His love's a banner waving over all of us, a beacon leading us out of our darkest night.*" Tabitha didn't recognize the words.

"Well, that song was about the King, right?" Gabe was enjoying his role as teacher. "It tells us about him. He is love. When you are with him, you feel loved. I don't know how to describe it, except I think we all feel it right now."

It was true. They all looked at each other and loved each other. It was more than the requisite love of family bonds. It was deeper and purer and more unalterable than any of them could describe.

"Why does the village have a new song now?" Angela asked. "The old one was so beautiful. Why did they change it?"

"I think I know," Father answered with a sigh. "I'm realizing it all right now. I was blind to it before. Obviously if the King is alive, we were lied to by our leaders. They were also the ones behind taking away the song that taught us about the King. It's just as before. I bet my father was right that the village leaders asked the King not to return. They didn't want to compete with him for authority over the village. They are doing the same now. They want to get rid of the King so they can rule."

"But Father, they already rule the village. The King hasn't been involved in years and years. I don't understand."

"Angela, there's a difference between elected officials making laws and rulers who usurp power and abuse authority." Father's gaze was fixed hard at the far wall. "I couldn't see it before."

"I don't understand what you're talking about." "Lord Vulpine."

"What?" Angela couldn't follow her father's thinking. "Lord Vulpine wants to be king."

"I'm lost, Father. What are you talking about?"

"I'm sorry, Angela. I'm just realizing it all and still trying to put the pieces together. Lord Vulpine convinced everyone the King is dead. They changed the village banner and song to erase any memory of the King. Vulpine has been working through the Assembly, but somehow I bet he's going to figure out a way around them so that he alone holds power over the village."

"What's he going to do?" Angela asked, worried.

"I have no idea. But it is obvious he wants the King dead. Then he could be sure there wouldn't be any opposition from the outside to his taking power."

"We don't have to worry about the King." Gabe interrupted the discussion. "There's no way they could kill him. He's untouchable. Even today, his throne sits above the clouds. If this storm can't touch him, Vulpine can't either."

Everyone's focus was brought back to the storm. "Where do you think Mother is?" Angela asked what was now on everyone's mind.

Lesson 157

1. Read chapter 6 of the *The King Will Make a Way.*
2. What happened when Gabe tried to tell Mrs. Bollix about the King? (Answers)
3. What does this sentence mean? "By seeding comments here and there, he found others similarly disaffected." (Answers) (hint: disaffected means dissatisfied with authority and no longer willing to support them)
4. Why do you think Vulpine picked up the King's law book right away? (Answers)

It took almost half an hour for the drunken man to plunge into a stupor. The village lay deathly still. Taking Tabitha by the hand, Father led the way outside, removing his family from the protection of the inn. They were aghast. The village looked like a forest after loggers had come through. It had been ripped, torn, tossed, tumbled, shaken, crushed, knocked down, as if it had been a bowling pin and the hail had rolled a strike.

"I'm going to take a look around the inn. You three just stay here." Father began inspecting their property and disappeared around a corner.

"Where's Mother?" Tabitha whined.

"She'll be home in a minute." Angela tried to sound confident.

A woman screamed. Three heads snapped in the direction of their neighbors. "I'm going to help." Gabe sprinted past the edge of the inn and leapt over the wood pile which used to be the fence surrounding the Bollix property. The fence had been built to keep out danger, but it had failed to thwart the storm.

"Mrs. Bollix? Where are you? What's wrong?" He stopped to listen. Sobs. Gabe took off toward the barn. One glance through the open door told the story. He went numb. Mrs. Bollix rocked back and forth; her body convulsed with sobbing. Mr. Bollix lay motionless under heavy rafters, a portion of the barn roof now missing where it had once used its strength to shelter. Light poured in from the collapsed roof; the sun went on shining, acting as if nothing had happened.

"Mrs. Bollix, I…" Gabe's words caught in his throat. What could he say? "I'm sorry" was all he could manage.

Some help I'm being.

Mrs. Bollix slowed her rocking and for the first time acknowledged her company. "There's nothing you could have done to help. He was dead by the time I found him." A torrent of tears started up again.

Gabe was at a loss. *What can I do? What could I have done? I warned him it would be a bad storm and told him to stay inside.* Guilt crept up from the base of his spine until the weight of it caused his head to hang in shame. He could have told him about the King and his words.

"Mrs. Bollix?" She didn't respond. Gabe went to her and knelt at her side. "Mrs. Bollix?" She slowly calmed herself again and turned and looked at him with vacant eyes.

"Mrs. Bollix, I'm sorry because I knew the storm was coming, and I knew it would be bad, and I didn't tell your husband and warn him ahead of time. It's my fault."

"What are you talking about? No one knew a hailstorm was coming. You saw how fast it came on. You couldn't have done anything."

"I did know. The King told me. The King, the King of our village is alive, and he knew, and he told me."

"I don't know what you're talking about. Leave me in peace here. My head is throbbing, and you're talking like a madman."

Unsure of what to say or do, he started toward the door. "I'll ask my father to come help." He spoke to the hay and ducked outside. He ran back to the inn. No one was waiting out front anymore. He went inside trying to find someone. Betty was no longer in the dining hall. He heard a voice in the kitchen. *Mother*?

He pushed forcefully on the door causing it to slap back hard in the opposite direction. His mother was at the table pouring out her story.

"The wind was blowing strong, and I had my bag full of vegetables. I thought of Gabe and decided to come right home. But I wasn't fast enough, and hail started to rain down while I was still in the square. Did you see the hail? They were huge balls. I was running and running to get to the Hall. I saw the wind rip the banner right off the roof before I ducked inside. I waited there for the storm to end, but after a bit, a hail stone the size of a melon came crashing through the roof! I'm not exaggerating. It's the truth. It broke through the roof, but not only that, it landed right on the glass case that holds the King's law book. It shattered the case, completely destroyed it. Lord Vulpine was there, and he picked up the law book right away, which I thought showed a lot of care, and he told me to have the inn ready for another meeting tonight."

Gabe shot his father a distressed look. Father spoke up. "They can't have their meetings here anymore. Something has come up. I'll explain later. I'll go tell him myself. You stay here and recover."

Gabe and Angela excused themselves with Father, leaving Tabitha behind to keep Mother company.

"Father, I know you are on an errand, but I told Mrs. Bollix that you would help her. Mr. Bollix was killed by the storm. Part of his barn roof fell on him." Angela gasped in disbelief.

Father looked at the ground, shaking his head. "I wonder what else has happened. I'll send his brother over. I don't know what else has happened out there. Maybe you two should stay home."

Angela was distraught over her friend's loss and requested, "Please let me go check on Sally and stay with her and Mrs. Bollix until her uncle comes."

Gabe asked too. "Please let me go and see who needs help. What if we are the only ones who were safe?"

"Not only safe, but the inn didn't really suffer much damage. I don't know how, but the King really took care of us. Okay you two, go see if you can help."

Father set off to speak with Vulpine and Mrs. Bollix's brother-in-law. Angela retraced Gabe's steps to their neighbors. Gabe remained a moment surveying the scene; the backdrop was the same, but the props were all different. The road was littered with branches and fence posts. Trees were now stumps, fences kindling, roofs floors. The hail had been cannonballs fired upon an unsuspecting enemy. Several shots had struck down animals left out to pasture.

Gabe headed across the road, picking up debris as he went and calling out to see if anyone needed help. He worked cleaning up yards the rest of the day. In the evening, Father sat with a block of wood whittling while Gabe told him about the King. Father now joined Angela as a disciple, learning everything the King had told Gabe.

Gabe asked his father, "Do you want to come up and meet the King?"

Father took a deep breath and looked up at the ceiling. He shook his head slowly, one time left then right. "No, Gabe. I couldn't. I don't know. Honestly, I feel almost scared to meet him. It doesn't seem my place. We can learn from you. The King gave you an invitation to come whenever you wanted. You should be the one going."

Gabe nodded. He loved having an invitation to visit the King, but now he began to realize the responsibility that came with it.

Mother came into the dining hall where they were sitting together. "What are you doing, lollygagging around? Doesn't anyone have work to do?"

Father answered her. "We are working. We are learning. Why don't you sit and listen to Gabe tell us about his visits with the King?"

"Nonsense. Someone has to work around here. There's always work to be done." Mother was off in a huff.

The three looked at each other but didn't speak until Gabe continued teaching about the King. The scene was repeated the next day.

"Why are you pretending to work at that whittling? You use that as an excuse to sit around. We have enough of your creations gathering dust. Do we really need more?"

Father patiently responded, "You never know. Maybe someday we'll sell them, and they will be valuable to us. Why don't you take a break and sit with us? Gabe has some fascinating lessons to teach us."

"I don't need my son teaching me lessons. Where's the dignity in having your son for a teacher?" Father didn't take offense at Mother's words because he knew it wasn't really him that she was upset with, just the talk of the King. Mother's frustration grew as the days passed.

The spring rain showered. The summer heat scorched. The fall apples ripened. The lake froze. The flowers bloomed. The corn was knee high. The harvest was gathered. Snow drifted; eggs hatched; bees buzzed; leaves tumbled. The seasons and years flew by as Gabe faithfully visited the King. Angela was well versed in the King's law and was becoming a lady.

For three years Gabe sat still at the King's feet, but Vulpine was on the move. He prowled around the village, watching, observing, making sure he had his finger on the pulse of the villagers in order to steer them in the direction of his choosing. He was certain the key to controlling the villagers was to direct their gossip, the talk of the village, what was on everyone's mind.

To achieve this end, he often fed words to Phineas which he then regurgitated in the square. "Lord Vulpine won a great victory for our village in the Assembly yesterday." "Lord Vulpine makes sure the prices are fair at the market." "Lord Vulpine is always working for what's best for our village."

The members of the Brothers and Sons secret society would repeat Phineas' words or, more accurately, Vulpine's, as they milled about the well, while they shopped in the market and when they welcomed guests into their homes. Most villagers were unwittingly dutiful in repeating the platitudes until they were branded onto their minds, and at that point, they became truth no matter their accuracy.

One day, Phineas carefully left out Vulpine's name from the announcement. Vulpine had easily convinced the other elected village leaders that elections weren't in the best interest of the village. Assemblyman Stone, never without his pipe, was the first to shake Vulpine's hand to congratulate him on the new law. Phineas explained the ruling to the villagers from the porch that ran the front length of the Hall. "Today, the Assembly has voted to end the village's annual elections. In order to maintain continuity within the village, your current elected leaders will serve until death." He assured the crowd gathered in the square that this was for peace and unity within the village. Everyone agreed that peace and unity were desirable and welcomed the new law.

Percy Katrid, a friend of Gabe's father, took notice of Vulpine's maneuvers. A handsome man, tall and broad, he won the admiration of many just by standing there. He may have been past his prime in strength and agility, but his physique maintained its powerful presence. His mind hadn't lost its edge either. It didn't escape Percy how Vulpine always managed to find a way for his name to be mentioned, or how Vulpine always took credit for any positive change in the village. Vulpine seemed to be praised even for the weather, when it was good. When the weather turned sour, or just plain strange as it often had over those few years, Phineas would keep force feeding lines to the villagers.

"Lord Vulpine wants to see the drought end quickly!" The crowd would cheer their agreement. Percy Katrid thought the comment and the crowd's reaction inane. "Imbeciles, everyone wants the drought to end," he would mutter to no one. By seeding comments here and there, he found others similarly disaffected. But none of them, not even Percy, had an inkling of what Vulpine was planning for the coming winter.

Lesson 158

1. Read chapter 7 of the *The King Will Make a Way.*
2. How did the virus get started? I did research on this. This was a way biological warfare has actually been carried out in history. (Answers)
3. What does Gabe notice about Angela's change in demeanor? (Answers)
4. What is one way Gabe is realizing the responsibility of knowing the King? (Answers)

The harvest had been gathered and stored, and the time Vulpine had been patiently waiting for was fast approaching. He knew the rewards of delaying gratification and took pains not to move too soon.

The Brothers and Sons had gathered and heard Vulpine's instructions. They were each to store up in their homes one month's worth of food and supplies by midwinter. The rain had been sparse that summer, so the harvest was as well, and they were to all buy their bulk now while the farmers still felt amply supplied. They were told to anticipate the markets being closed during the winter, so they wouldn't be able to rely, as they normally would, on the farmers selling food in the stalls. Although there were men of many trades among the Brothers and Sons, including other Assemblymen, not one was a farmer, and so none had their own stores of food.

They weren't told why the market would close. In the whispered sessions, only the broad aspects of Vulpine's plans were shared. The details were told only to those who needed to know. This time it would again be the village doctor who would be assisting Vulpine. As a member of the Brothers and Sons, he was obliged to use all that was in his power to serve Vulpine and help him become king. Years of work had gone into the planning and maneuvering. The doctor's help would now bring him one step closer to what he had long desired.

Vulpine had asked the doctor if he could prepare a plague. Vulpine explained the practicality of the request. The villagers needed to feel weak and scared so they would embrace a leader—a king. The summer drought had helped but hadn't been enough. He wanted a sickness that would spread easily and be serious enough to kill, not the entire village, just enough to create the fear he needed to harness for his own ends. The village doctor, though employed to save lives, fulfilled the request.

He figured he could meet Vulpine's requirements by dipping an arrow into the decomposing bodies of villagers who had died of their illnesses and then causing someone to be "accidentally" shot with the poisoned arrow. It was planned that the virus would be unleashed midwinter.

Phineas crunched through the autumn leaves on his way to the square and from the Hall announced that over the winter months, when the farm work was slow, the men of the village were to take part in military training. The village had never before had any sort of army, nor had they ever been attacked by enemies, but Vulpine had convinced the Assembly of the need for a trained force.

Gabe would turn fourteen over the winter and was too young to be considered man enough to join in the training. His father, however, took part in the daily drills. He marched, practiced sword play, shot arrows and learned to fire a cannon. Percy Katrid also trained with the others and played the part of a submitted soldier. While he felt devotion to the village in which he was born and raised, he felt none towards Vulpine, who presided over the training exercises.

As lord of the Assembly, Vulpine took it upon himself to name a general for the village defenses. He named a Jeremy Writ, one of the members of the Brothers and Sons. He was a lanky man, an intellectual who saw the profit in serving Vulpine. General Writ was appointed not for his expertise but for quite another reason. He would do Vulpine's bidding without question.

Vulpine was pleased with how this new phase of his plan was progressing and gave the doctor the nod in midwinter. Just as had been planned, one of the Brothers and Sons accidently shot one of his fellow soldiers in the leg with an infected arrow. Soon a virus began to spread. Men were falling ill, experiencing delirium from unusually high fevers and weakness from vomiting. The illness lasted five whole days at a time. The drills were halted after one of the sick soldiers died, and the men were sent home to rest, which resulted in bringing the virus to their families.

As a result, the village effectually shut down as the villagers fell prey to the sickness. The virus made its way through the village like locusts, devouring all the life in its path. Panic started to set in as several children died from the sudden illness. Vulpine suspended the regular meetings of the Assembly and went into hiding.

Gabe's father had returned home sick, and Tabitha and Angela had taken ill along with him. Gabe nursed them back to health. Mother stayed away but prepared broths for them to sip while they still lay in bed. Gabe constantly toted water from the well behind the inn, through the kitchen, up the stairs and into the family quarters in order to sponge the victims with cool water to bring down their temperatures and to wash their clothes and bedding after their stomachs wretched violently. Gabe had never seen Angela so quietly submissive as during those days when he would ask her to sit or roll over or whatever was necessary for his nursing care.

Gabe still sneaked away each day in the quiet of the morning when everyone was finally settled and sleeping peacefully. The King had reassured him that his father and sisters would all live through the sickness and that he and his mother would not succumb to it. He believed the King, and he never hesitated to be at their sick beds, ready to help in any way he could. In a week's time they had come through safely, and in another week's time they were out of bed, fully recovered.

As Father and the girls were gaining back their full strength, the King had some questions for Gabe. "What would you want someone to do for you if you were sick, or if your parents were sick?" The King had a plan and was gently leading Gabe on the right path.

Gabe thought it over. "I would want someone to take care of me, to help me, to do my chores, to cook my meals and to tell me that I was going to be okay."

In a teacherly fashion, the King asked, "What does my law say about the things we would want others to do for us?" Gabe knew the answer. "It says that we should do to others what we would want them to do to us."

"So what are you going to do?" The King nudged Gabe toward applying his knowledge.

"I'm going to help others."

"How?" the King asked encouragingly.

"I'll help people take care of their work in their homes and do my best to comfort them."

"Good." The King approved Gabe's plan, which had been the King's plan all along, and Gabe grew eager to get started.

He had one big hurdle to overcome before he could follow through on his word to the King; he had to convince his parents to let him go into the homes of the sick. Most people avoided all contact with others and shut themselves into their homes. The square now echoed in emptiness instead of vibrating with life. The villagers lived in fear and looked out only for themselves. Some villagers even refused to care for their sick family members and quarantined them in rooms in their own homes, leaving them to suffer alone.

Only two weeks had passed since Father had fallen ill and had been sent home to recuperate. The virus had spread like a juicy bit of gossip and had paid a visit to most homes in the village. Shops were closed and the market was bare, both for fear of the contagion and for lack of sellers and shoppers since the majority of the village was sick or had been sick with the violent virus. Only the families of the members of the Brothers and Sons had been conveniently shut safely in their homes at the beginning of the outbreak.

No one else in the village was tending to the sick outside of their own families, but Gabe persuaded his parents that he was immune to the sickness as he had been exposed to it during their family's bout with the plague and hadn't caught it. Angela took up the cause and suggested that Gabe might be able to bring home some food other than the family's stored apples and staples they had been forced to begin living on. Their parents saw both their points and relented to let Gabe go alone. They were unsure of how desperate people were and how they would act, and they wanted to keep Angela safe at home.

Gabe and Angela were bursting with excitement to begin helping. They had decided they would start with their nearest neighbors and work house to house down the road for as long as they were needed. Angela would be in charge of preparing food for Gabe to take to neighbors. It wouldn't be an easy task as Mother wouldn't allow Angela to use anything from their stock other than flour and salt for the job. Mother wanted to be sure the family had all they needed to last through the plague, for which there was no end in sight. It was like an unwelcome houseguest taking up residence without any mention of when he will be moving on.

Angela tied Mother's apron around her waist and, taking a wooden cup from the cupboard, she dug it into the flour barrel. Four times she dumped its contents into a large bowl. With her hands she squeezed in a hunk of butter she had made herself. She was thankful for the constant supply of milk, butter and cheese Betty provided the family. She rolled the butter and flour between her fingers until each had disappeared into the other. A little at a time, she added water and stirred it sparingly until the dough would hold together. Dusting the table with flour, she used the surface to roll the dough out as thin as she dared. She sprinkled on salt and slid it into the oven. It would make a crispy cracker, a perfect complement to the soup she was preparing.

Next Angela turned to the pot on the stove. She salted the water and begged a bit of seasoning from Mother. On the stovetop next to the simmering water, Angela heated a pan and poured in a cup of oil, dredged from Mother's cooking pots. When the oil had been heated, its fragrance wafted through the air, telling Angela it was time to add in a cup of flour. Stirring vigorously, Angela watched the flour bubble in the oil and turn a rich brown, the aroma of roasted wheat filling the kitchen. With one movement she lifted the pan and poured it into bubbling broth. It hissed and spat as the oil and water quarreled. Angela briskly stirred them together and ended the dispute. The flour thickened the broth so that it would cling to the crisping crackers.

Gabe filled two jars with the soup, wrapped a napkin around some crackers and headed out the door. He stood in the chill of the afternoon and let the sun warm his cheeks. How could such a beautiful day hold death in its air?

Lesson 159

1. Read chapter 8 of the *The King Will Make a Way.*
2. Who was really behind the virus? (Answers)
3. What law did he remind Gabe of? (Answers)
4. How did the King use the plague to help Angela? (Answers)

5. What do you think the doctor was feeling when Gabe found him? Do you really think he was just tired?
6. If you struggle with the concept of the King being behind the plague, wait and see the King's love at work through the plague. Also, consider the numerous Old Testament examples of God directly killing someone, Korah for example in Numbers 16. Also look at Revelation 16 and how the seven plagues come from God. Read Deuteronomy 32 for an example of God promising to send all sorts of disaster and terror on the Israelites.

Gabe knocked on the door of the Bollix family farmhouse. Angela's friend Sally answered the door.

"Gabe, welcome. Is everything okay? How is your family?"

Gabe smiled, thinking he had come to ask the same questions. "We're okay. Do you need any food?" Gabe held out his offering of warm soup and crackers.

Sally reached out and took the jars and napkin. "Thank you, Gabe. My mother is sick, and I'm taking care of my brothers and sisters myself. We have our harvest stored up here if you need some food, but this meal will help me. I appreciate it."

"If you could spare some food for us, we could really use it."

"Of course." Sally helped him home with bags of potatoes and carrots.

"Thank you so much," Gabe said, expressing his gratitude. "We'll be sure to use some of this to make food for other families as well."

"I'm glad to help. Thanks for coming, Gabe. I'm glad you came to check on us." Sally headed back into her home and closed the door.

Gabe's parents were pleased with Gabe's first attempt at helping and didn't stop him from going out again. Gabe approached the next house and knocked on the door while balancing soup and crackers in one hand.

A small boy opened the door. Gabe asked where his mother and father were. He just stared at Gabe, not answering. He still made no sound when Gabe entered the house to look around.

"Hello?" Gabe called repeatedly, shivering in the chill of the house. The little boy tagged along as Gabe went in search of someone, anyone in the house.

Gabe found a room with a woman lying in bed with a baby. He stood frozen, not knowing if he should enter. Gabe continued calling out, but he received no answer. He looked again at the little boy and asked, "Is this your mother?" The boy nodded. "Where is your father?" The boy only shook his head no.

Gabe swallowed hard, hoping that didn't mean the boy's father was dead. Is his mother alive? He looked once more at the still bodies in the room and swallowed hard again.

Grimacing, he moved haltingly across the room to the bed. He called out his timid greeting again. There was no response. He tried one last time, and the mother stirred and mumbled.

Gabe backed away to the room entrance. "I brought some food." Gabe felt foolish saying the words, but he had no idea what to do. He looked at the little boy and added, "I'll keep your little boy with me until you are better." The woman gave Gabe no recognition. Gabe was at a loss and stood there in silence.

Gabe shivered again and came to his senses. He quickly started a fire in the fireplace and taking the boy by the hand, left the house. The boy made no objection to following Gabe home, and Mother recognized him immediately when Gabe entered the inn.

Everyone agreed something had to be done. Mother wanted to help the woman, but she didn't want to risk getting sick. Angela and Father, immune from having been sick, went together to take back the broth and see how they could help. It didn't take them long to discover that the woman was very ill and the baby was dead. Father had the morose chore of burying her baby.

The little boy remained with Mother as Gabe went to the next farmhouse. This time he was met by shouts to go away. Gabe's enthusiasm for helping was waning, and he carried on only out of his love for the King and his desire to please him. At the next farmhouse, he was greeted by the matriarch of the family. "My name is Emily. I would be grateful if you would help us."

She told Gabe how their youngest son had died from the virus, and John, their only other son, was now in bed with the fiendish fever. She was concerned her husband was trying to work too hard when he himself was recovering from illness.

"We are reliant on John for so much," his mother confessed. "We would be so thankful if you could spare a bit of time to help some." Gabe lent his services in chopping wood and milking cows before heading to the next farm.

At the next home, he carried water and moved a mattress. Some of the farmers gave Gabe food for his own family, but at other homes he wasn't welcome at all.

To go to the shopkeepers' homes, he borrowed a cart from the Bollix family to carry Angela's soup pot. He pulled the cart slowly over the road to the square. At first glance, he thought that all the shops in the Square were closed, but as he walked along one row, he saw the village doctor through a window. He was sitting with his head in his hands.

Gabe pushed open the door, and the doctor quickly looked up like a child caught with his hand in the cookie jar. He cleared his throat and asked Gabe how he could help him.

"Actually, I came to help," Gabe answered. "Do you need food?" Gabe pointed to the pot.

"Yes, thank you. It's impossible to buy any food these days." The doctor found a bowl, and Gabe ladled in the potato soup which Angela had prepared from Sally's gift. Gabe handed him a cracker and apologized there wasn't more.

"No, it's wonderful," the doctor insisted. "It's been a tough few weeks for me. I'm afraid you caught me hiding out. Everyone thinks the square is empty. I just wanted a moment's rest."

Gabe smiled and nodded. “I should go see if I can find anyone else needing food.”

“That’s very good of you,” the doctor said in farewell.

Gabe didn’t reply and pulled open the door. He looked back at the doctor, who had resumed the position Gabe had found him in, slumped over with his head in his hands. Gabe looked at him sadly and then pushed on across the square.

Door to door like a desperate salesman, Gabe offered his soup until the pot was scooped clean and dry. Even without the soup, he continued to offer help and to ask what people needed. He told some he would try to return the next day with more food.

He eventually came to a row of tall, fine houses. He knocked on the door of one of the beautiful homes. A servant opened the door and curtly asked Gabe his business. He offered help meekly, as he’d done at so many other homes, but his proffer was met with a gruff reply.

“The good doctor has servants to help him and a stock room full of food and supplies. He doesn’t need help from someone like you.” He shut the door in Gabe’s face. Gabe stepped back and shook his head in confusion. He backed away and decided it was time to return home.

That night Gabe shared his mattress on the floor with the neighbor boy. His mother had been brought over to the inn as well and was settled into one of the empty guest rooms where she was recovering from her illness and the shock of losing her husband and baby.

When morning came, Angela prepared more soup and crackers, and Gabe returned as promised to the homes on the far side of the square. The inn quickly became known as a place of refuge and help. Over the next few weeks as the virus took its final toll on the village, people would sometimes make their way to the inn, looking for food, shelter or a helping hand. Everyone who came found all three.

As winter’s sharp edge softened and spring breezes started to blow across the village, hopes began to rise that the wind was sweeping the virus away. Slowly, life began returning to the village. Windows, shuttered for weeks, opened to air out the stale homes. Villagers breathed easy again and fear was disappearing along with the winter frosts.

Gabe sloshed through the mud at the base of the mountain on his way again to meet with the King. He would finally ask his burning question.

“Why?” Gabe was sitting at the King’s feet, talking with him about the plague of sickness that had paralyzed the village. “Why did the whole village suffer? Why did my family get sick, and I didn’t?”

The King looked sympathetically at Gabe. He knew he couldn’t comprehend the full answer, but he wanted to help him understand what he could.

“Did the virus harm your family?” The King put the question to Gabe.

Gabe didn’t answer right away. His sisters throwing up seemed like being harmed, but now he knew they were no worse off than before. He also knew that Angela was allowed to help others because of her immunity and that since her illness, a sort of quietness had come over her. She didn't always have an answer ready; it made her seem more gentle. "I guess not," he ventured to answer.

"Did the virus harm the village?" The King looked kindly at his pupil.

Gabe was sure the answer was yes. "It did harm the village. They say close to two hundred people died. Many were children. That's harm."

"Did the village deserve the harm that came to it?" The King's eyes were serious.

Gabe didn't know how to answer that one. He thought of his neighbor's lifeless baby and replied, "How could a little baby deserve to be killed? It didn't even know right from wrong. How could it deserve to be harmed?"

"Not the baby, Gabe. The village. Did the village deserve the harm that came to it?"

Gabe shook his head. "I don't know. I know the village doesn't follow your laws. Does that mean the villagers deserve to be harmed?"

"What does my law say is the penalty for not obeying it?"

The King forced Gabe to look directly into his eyes.

Gabe thought through all he had been taught and knew the consequences of disobedience were great. "Just about everything that could go wrong is a penalty: not having enough food, sickness, being killed, drought and fierce weather in the village."

The King nodded. "I know you don't fully understand why the village has to suffer the penalty and not just the individual, but the individual matters too. I knew and told you that you would not catch the illness, and maybe those children who died were being spared something worse. Remember that I'm always just. I am the only one who really knows what judgments and punishments are right and necessary. And never forget my song. I love the village. The villagers need to know that things are not all right the way they are."

Gabe nodded and felt like he understood a little better, except for one more thing.

"How do you do it? How do you judge what people are doing from here? How do you punish those not obeying your law from your throne room? How do you control something like a sickness?" Gabe's question multiplied into many on his tongue.

The King gently replied, "That's not something I can explain, but you can find comfort in knowing that however I do it, I can."

Gabe nodded and knew the King was right. Some things about the King were just too mysterious for someone like him to understand.

Lesson 160

1. Read chapter 9 of the *The King Will Make a Way*.
2. How did the King use the virus for the good of the village? (Answers)
3. Who finds out that people are talking about the King being alive? (Answers)
4. What are some of the responsibilities that Gabe has faced because he knows the King? (Answers)

The village returned somewhat to normal. The loss of lives left many gaps unfilled in homes and hearts. Vulpine was pleased with the results of his experiment with the doctor and prepared to make his final move to become king.

Gabe, unaware he would never again climb the hill to meet the King, sat in front of the throne like every other day before the sun had the chance to warm the village.

The King had a question for Gabe. "When you were younger and your father disciplined you for disobedience, what did you do after you received your discipline?"

Gabe was used to the King leading him to a lesson in this way and was anxious to find out what the King was getting at. "I obeyed whatever I hadn't before."

"Of course, that's the purpose of discipline. Do you remember our talk about the village disobeying my laws and receiving what was just in return?" Gabe nodded. "They disobeyed my laws. Do you think any learned their lesson from the discipline of the plague?"

A hint of a smile showed on Gabe's face. He understood. "You do love the village. You weren't just punishing them.

You were disciplining them to teach them to obey your laws."

"Yes. Some will learn their lesson. Some will foolishly reject it. But now, who will teach them my laws so they can obey them?"

Gabe's smile faded, and he bit his lip. "I guess that would be me." They sat in silence a minute. The King knew Gabe's mind was wrestling. "But I don't know what to say. I tried telling Mrs. Bollix about you, and she told me to leave her alone. My mother won't listen to me. How can I convince anyone you are even alive so that I can get them to listen about your law?"

"Have I ever made the way for you before?" Gabe laughed. "Lots of times. Okay. I'll try."

"Don't be afraid. I will make a way." The King's gentle eyes caught Gabe's and held them. "I always make a way."

Gabe smiled weakly and nodded. "I better get started before I lose my courage." That is what he said, but he wasn't feeling particularly courageous.

As Gabe stood to leave the throne room, the King gave him a reminder. "Don't forget that you aren't alone in this. You'll see me again."

"I know I'm not alone. I won't forget."

Gabe ran down the mountain, but his heart was pounding because of the task the King had given him. He decided that trying again at Mrs. Bollix's house was the best way to conquer his fear. The sun hadn't long been up when he knocked on the door and was invited in by Sally.

He stood waiting for Mrs. Bollix to join them and to give him permission to speak. "Mrs. Bollix, I apologized to you years ago when your husband died. I told you I was sorry because the King had told me the storm was coming, and I didn't warn you. What I said is true. The former King is alive, and I meet with him every day up on King's Hill, and he told me the storm was coming and that it would be bad. He told me to get in our kitchen and stay there when the winds picked up. I didn't tell anyone but my family. They were all safe and our inn was undamaged. The King kept us safe."

Mrs. Bollix sat quietly and fixed her gaze on the boy. She'd known him his whole life, and here he stood before her, a young man, full of a confidence she'd never seen in him before this moment. "I almost believe you," she said softly, but then her voice emptied of life. "But none of it matters now, does it? I don't hold his death against you."

At first Gabe agreed with her. It didn't matter now. *It was too late. But then a light dawned on Gabe's face.* "It does matter. You matter. You can choose to believe. I can teach you the King's law. It's not too late for you to listen to the King."

His earnestness took her aback. There were times she'd thought he couldn't put together more than two words. Now here he was, addressing her passionately. There was something else. She felt his compassion toward her, as if he truly cared.

"Okay," she said. "You can teach me about the King's law. I will listen to you. Come whenever you please."

"Thank you, Mrs. Bollix. Why don't you and your children join us at the inn this evening. Every night I teach my father and Angela about the King. Come. We can share a meal, and I will teach about the King's law."

"We will. Thank you."

The old Gabe was back. He gave a nod and wordlessly made his exit. He exhaled when he got outside, then made a beeline for another farmhouse. He remembered the people there had shooed him away when he had come to offer help during the plague.

He took a deep breath and knocked on the heavy wooden door. An elderly gentleman welcomed him in without asking his business. He offered Gabe a glass of water and motioned to his wife to bring one. Gabe began his speech, apologizing for not having told them sooner about the King being alive. At the mention of the King, the man laughed out loud.

"Alive? Did you miss his funeral? I thought the whole village was there. Do you think I'm a fool? Why would I believe a child telling a fairy tale? If that's all you've come for, you can go ahead and leave."

Gabe thanked them for the water and left without argument.

Gabe was relieved when he recognized Emily at the next farmhouse he entered. She and her husband remembered Gabe's kindness when their son, John, had been sick and were happy to welcome him in.

"Can I get you a glass of water?" Gabe declined, remembering the half-drunk glass he left at the last house.

"I have something I wanted to apologize for." Gabe looked with kindness at their confused faces. "I have known for more than three years that the King is alive. I have been meeting with the King on his hill and learning about his law. I have been teaching my sister and father about the King all these years, but I haven't told you about him before. I'm sorry that I have waited so long, but I would like to invite you now to come to our home this evening to share a meal and to learn about the King and his law."

Gabe said it all in one breath and now practically gasped for air. For a moment, his audience sat stunned. Emily looked to her husband, who looked to Gabe. "We would be happy to come and learn more. We know that you are a good boy and wouldn't be playing a trick on us. If your father is listening to what you have to say, we are willing to as well."

"Thank you," Gabe said in relief. He shook their hands and went out the door. While there were a few homes that rejected him, there were many who wanted to believe Gabe because of his kindness and bravery during the plague.

Gabe eventually made it through the farmhouses along the stretch from the inn to the Square and turned back home. He had thought that the next day he would continue farther, that word of the King had only made it to the farmers, but as the farmers made it to the markets that day, news of the King being alive traveled with them.

Standing by the village well, Vulpine's senses were on high alert as he detected a change of tone in the harmony of the village. He was certain he discerned discord among the villagers. Phineas had made an announcement and not everyone was parroting his words. When they did, it was a beautiful melody to Vulpine. Now a sour note was written into the strain. Insistent on rooting it out, he directed his spies to report on all village activity and discourse. By moonrise, he had his finger on the key. It was the King.

That evening two meetings were held. While the Brothers and Sons met at one of the member's homes, the farmers, some with wives, some with children, ventured over to the inn. Some felt a little foolish, some bubbled with anticipation, but all brought a gift of food to share with the others who had come to hear about the King.

Gabe, along with Angela and their father, welcomed the guests. Mother and Tabitha kept to the family quarters upstairs, but the rest shared a meal and listened to Gabe tell about his years at the King's feet. When he finished, they all stood under the golden glow of the lanterns overhead and sang the King's song.

The other meeting that night had a very different tone. "How could this have happened?" Vulpine fumed before his fellow secret society members. "Why is there talk of the King being alive? Who has the answers? How did this ugly rumor of the King's death being falsified get circulated?" A few snickered at the question, but Vulpine silenced them with one shot from his eyes. "These rumors must be squelched at once! For the peace and unity of the village!"

Lesson 161

1. Read chapter 10 of the *The King Will Make a Way*.
2. Why did Vulpine send troops up King's Hill? (Answers)
3. How did Vulpine become king? (Answers)
4. What is brewing among some of those at the meetings at the inn? (Answers)

"For the peace and unity of the village!" Vulpine was now ardently addressing the Assembly.

"For the peace and unity of the village!" The members of the Assembly rallied around their leader. Phineas led the villagers in the same battle cry. "For the peace and unity of the village!"

Ironically, to accomplish this peace, Vulpine turned to General Writ. He issued orders that the General lead his troops up King's Hill. If someone was sitting on the throne, then he was an imposter and must be killed. "We cannot let an imposter disrupt the peace and unity of the village!"

Very early the next morning, a trumpeter rallied the troops to the square. There were several notable absentees, but roll was not called. The troops marched behind their subordinate leader toward the hill. Percy Katrid kept in line as he marched, wanting to see what Vulpine was up to.

At the base of the mountain, General Writ divided his troops into three squads. Two were to march up the right and left flanks; the third was to come from the front. They would converge at the summit when the signal was given. They were ordered to destroy nothing except any man found sitting on the throne. He was to be killed without hesitation.

Gabe, who had stopped on his way up the hill to wait and watch what was happening, shivered when he heard a rallying cry ring out from the troops. The village men were fearless, even though—or maybe because—they had never actually fought in battle before. They had trained but few weapons had been created for them. So while some were armed with swords and bows and arrows, even more were armed with pitchforks and knives. A team of ten had the unenviable task of transporting a cannon up the face of the hill.

The animals remained hidden as the squads progressed slowly up the unfamiliar terrain. At the edge of the pine forest, the troops awaited the signal to charge. First, the cannon, only to be used if they were ambushed at the peak, had to be in place. The men had rammed the charge down the cannon's barrel, rolled in the cannonball and placed the fuse. One man stood poised with a flint in his hand.

General Writ raised his saber. The signal. The charge. Men from all sides marched double time up the final ascent, brandishing their weapons and releasing guttural cries. Some relished the thought of piercing through the imposter and becoming a hero, perhaps a legend in the village. The prospect spurred them on.

Now the cave was in view. The cries grew louder, the men's animal instincts possessing them, enabling them to kill or be killed. The three squads converged at the summit, and in one great, climactic moment, everything fizzled. The throne was empty. The trees and streams and flowers and rocks were silent.

General Writ ordered a thorough search of the cave, but it was small and solid and no hiding places were found. Before all the adrenaline disappeared, Vulpine himself appeared. He had followed the troops at a safe distance but had been prepared for such an outcome.

"Men! Do not be disappointed! You are the great ones of this village!" Vulpine's grandiose words struck a chord with his audience. He had their attention and held it as he made his way toward the cave.

"This village has suffered greatly recently from the terrible sickness, and it is now suffering again from rumors that the old King is living and ruling from this empty spot. You bravely put yourselves in harm's way to defend the honor of the village. You stood for the truth and the truth prevailed today!" The men cheered.

"We can't allow the suffering to continue. The village needs a leader, a real leader who is strong enough to make firm decisions and to guide our village into the future. Not a distant king who never makes himself seen or heard." He paused and placed his hand on his heart.

"The village has suffered, as we all know. And the weak ones of the village have turned to these lies about the King as a way to comfort themselves. So I propose that in order to accommodate the weaker members of our village, we should give them a king. A true leader who will speak for all members of the village, one who understands the weak, but who is man enough to lead the strong." The members of the Brothers and Sons were listening intently for their cue. It had all been decided beforehand. "And who do you think is the only one able to fill this role with wisdom and dignity?"

It was time. "King Vulpine! King Vulpine!" The chant began among a dozen scattered men but was soon picked up by others. "King Vulpine! King Vulpine!"

Vulpine thrilled to hear his name exalted. He put on regal airs and glided toward the throne. Two men came after him, carrying a king's robe and a bronze scepter. They raised the blood-red robe, and Vulpine slipped his arms inside. He took up the scepter and thrust it skyward.

Gabe had remained at the hill's base anxiously waiting, plucking up shoots before they could bloom in all their golden glory. Watching for a sign of what was happening past the shield of the forest, he heard the men's voices steadily rising and falling like the call of a kingbird, but he couldn't fathom the meaning of the din. Percy Katrid understood all too well.

"King Vulpine! King Vulpine!" The men urged him on with their repetitious shout. He lifted his other hand, motioning for silence, and the men quieted. "Let the will of the people be accomplished!" He sat on the throne. Vulpine luxuriated in his rich surroundings. Percy took one look at Vulpine sitting there and spat on the ground.

The men of the village whooped and cheered. Then a new chant emerged from within their midst. "Long live King Vulpine!"

Phineas Tract knew all was going as planned. Now he was to head up the next phase. Standing on the far side of the mass of men, he called out, "Men, let us go into the village and announce the tremendously good news that King Vulpine has begun his reign!"

Vulpine remained behind, tended by servants. Phineas shepherded his herd back to the village where the chant was taken up again. "Long live King Vulpine!" They moved slowly through the streets. Curious women and children emerged from their homes, trying to understand what their senses were taking in. Once in the square, Phineas proclaimed the day a holiday and welcomed everyone to come in the evening for feasting and dancing.

The men scattered to spread the news and to relate all that had taken place that morning on the hill. Gabe's father, who had remained at home, was visited by Percy, their friendship deepened by their agreement over Vulpine.

Gabe returned home and paced around behind the inn, kicking at pebbles and deep in thought. He couldn't make any sense out of what was happening. He reviewed the facts. *They hadn't found the King. Where was he? Vulpine now is king. Says who? Everyone. Not me. Vulpine wants the King dead. But he can't find him. I don't know where he is either. Today was the first day in three and a half years I didn't pay a visit to the King.*

At the realization, he slumped into the dirt. He felt like that ten-year-old boy again, being bellowed at by Vulpine and wishing he would just go away. He picked up a stick and started doodling in the dirt. His heart flooded his eyes, and a tear rolled down his cheek. He let the tear tickle his chin. *What now? Where are you, King? How can I talk to you?* A thought came to him. If he couldn't physically sit at the King's feet and hear his words spoken to him, he could read his words in the Book of Law.

His countenance brightened, and he felt that again the King had somehow been responsible for lifting his heavy burden. He flew up the stairs to the family's quarters and found Angela had beaten him to it. Sitting with their great-grandfather's papers on her lap, she grinned at him and, as if reading his thoughts, handed him some sheets. "Do you know he's gone?" Gabe asked as he squatted next to her.

She shook her braids back and forth. "He's not. He's right here with us. His words are in his law and in our hearts. We'll sing his song and share his words. He promised to come back to the village one day. You'll see him again, and I'll see him too." Gabe remembered the last thing the King had said to him and clung to the words of encouragement— he wasn't alone and he would see the King again.

"We need to keep meeting with the others," Gabe said, having caught Angela's infectious enthusiasm. "We can't let this stop us. We know the truth. The truth hasn't changed.

We need to keep telling others. They need to know that Vulpine is the imposter and the real King lives and reigns over our village."

Gabe sprang to his feet. "I'm going to tell everyone that we are still meeting tonight at the inn. We won't let anyone forget about the King."

Gabe wasn't the only busy one that afternoon. It seemed that half of the village women had fluttered about most of the day preparing for the party and were finally satisfied with their work as the sun began to set. Lanterns encircled the festivities, each lit as it hung in front of one of the shops lining the Square.

The women prattled on and on about their new king while a group of men gloated over their numerous kills. They had been sent to King's Hill that morning to hunt for the feast and had found an abundance of game. The children, dressed in their best, held hands and skipped and twirled to the music of their lighthearted laughter.

Phineas, standing on the steps of the Hall attracted everyone's attention. "In honor of our king, King Vulpine, let the festivities begin!" Cheers went up. Music played. The strings twanged. The brass trumpeted. The winds whistled. The percussion boomed. The people stamped and clapped and forgot all about their troubles.

They feasted on roasted bear, deer, pheasant and quail. They gorged on apricots, cantaloupe, plums, mushrooms, potatoes, squash, nuts and dates. They drank their fill until only good memories of the village and Vulpine swam in their heads.

After several hours of revelry, a hush came over the celebration. Vulpine had come down to them. An excited whisper passed like a wave to and fro, undulating through the gathering. Vulpine climbed the steps of the Hall, his robe carried by two men who carefully draped it over the steps for an impressive effect. Vulpine still carried the scepter and looked every part a king.

He raised his arms and addressed his subjects. "My good people, we have this day begun on a new course that will lead us into a prosperous tomorrow. I humbly accept your decision to make me your king and ruler supreme over the village. I will rule with gentleness over all who seek the peace and unity of our village and with an iron fist over all who seek its destruction."

The villagers cheered. "My first royal edict will be to open up King's Hill. Too long has it remained shrouded. I will not be a king like the other before me, completely removed from the life of the village. I will be among you and together we will make our village great!" More cheers and clapping and stomping and banging.

Phineas took the stage. "We have a special treat for you. The children's choir from our school will sing for us the village song, improved for the occasion." It was the same song that had replaced the King's after his funeral, but one line had been changed. "Our village" had been changed to "King Vulpine" so that the children pledged before their parents, "King Vulpine we will serve."

The tune was started again and the congregation sang the familiar melody, stirring up patriotism and pride in their hearts. With one voice they sang, "King Vulpine we will serve."

That evening at the inn, away from the festivities, there was a meal and singing and reading of the law. Percy Katrid was there for the first time and recounted the morning's events for the group. Gabe sensed there was something strange in the atmosphere, almost palpable, but only almost; he couldn't put his finger on it. Gabe's father, however, knew what it was—rebellion.

Lesson 162

1. Read chapter 11 of the *The King Will Make a Way.*
2. What does the King's law say about vengeance and justice? (Answers)
3. Why is Assemblyman Stone upset with Vulpine? (Answers)

From among the newly trained village men, Vulpine hired guards to serve him; most were stationed on King's Hill just past the edge of the forest. The trees traced their way across the hill, separating king from commoner. Vulpine had parceled out land along the forest green demarcation for Phineas Tract, General Writ and Assemblyman Tate, all of whom had devoted themselves to his service and had proven themselves useful to him. Assemblyman Stone was resentful to not be included in this elite treatment. His beady eyes leered at Vulpine through the smoke emitting from his pipe as he thought how he would make a much better ruler for the village.

But most of the villagers were thrilled with their new king. They were now free to use the forest and field for picnics and berry picking. Since Vulpine's coronation, hunting was allowed on the hill as well, and men were fashioning bows and arrows to catch their prey. Families began growing fat from their kill.

Vulpine continued to win the favor of the villagers. He took a small table made of gold from the throne room and had it melted down and made into little cubes of gold, which were given out to each family in the village. There was only one other thing Vulpine changed in the throne room. He had the wooden cabinet moved to the Assembly Hall. The single plate was carefully moved with it.

The cabinet became a tourist attraction among the villagers themselves. They loved to file past and find their homes on the intricately carved walls. They also loved Vulpine, praising his generosity and leadership—truly worshipping him.

No one was surprised when during the summer Vulpine decided the village song, in which villagers sang their pledge to serve Vulpine, would be sung daily in the square at midday. By fall, he had decided that attendance at the singing ceremony would be required on Sundays. Phineas announced the new law on a Saturday.

"King Vulpine has issued a new decree. From this day forward, each Sunday at midday, every villager, unless ill, must attend the singing ceremony in the square. Together we will proclaim our loyalty to King Vulpine. King Vulpine, in his wisdom, has decreed this to ensure the peace and unity of our village." Gabe never followed Phineas down to the square. He heard about the new law that night at the meeting.

"What are we going to do?" Mrs. Bollix asked the group. "We'll have to sing. It's the law." A short, wide man shared his opinion.

"I will not pledge to serve Vulpine." Percy Katrid was on his feet. "I refuse to call him king!"

"Can't we just go and not sing?" A timid woman offered her suggestion.

"That wouldn't feel right." Gabe's father stood by Percy. "Do you want to look like you're supporting Vulpine? It's time to take a stand."

"I don't—" Gabe saw his father's paternal glare meaning "this is not the time for you to be heard" and bit his lip.

Several men agreed and walked over to stand by Percy and Father.

Percy walked over to one of the tables and leaned his calloused hands on the oak slab. "This is only the beginning. Little by little he has changed our lives. He doesn't want just change though. He wants control. He's hungry for power. He wasn't satisfied with being head of the Assembly. He wanted all the power to himself. He made himself king. He has made it so he will never have to face an election. And he will get away with whatever he wishes, unless someone stops him. There is no longer any law in the village to use against him. Since he's put himself above the law, the only way to stop him is by force."

Many mumbled their agreement. Gabe retreated to the kitchen. Mother was rubbing salt between her fingers, raining it down on the simmering soup. "What's the matter? Not getting bored with King talk are you?" Gabe really wanted to talk to someone, but his mother wouldn't understand. He wandered out back. *At least Betty is a good listener.*

He stroked Betty's tan fur. "Everything was so perfect, Betty. Now I don't know. I wish I could go ask the King what was happening, what was right. They don't even want to hear me speak at the meeting." Betty mooed sympathetically. "They are listening to Percy Katrid, and he doesn't know anything about the King. He just doesn't like Vulpine. Vulpine is more important to him than the King. He doesn't care about the King. He's just using our meetings to gather support because he knows we don't like what Vulpine is doing." *Whining isn't helping. What am I supposed to do?*

The law. Gabe began reasoning to himself. *If the King were to rule, then we would be following his law. If they really want Vulpine out and the King in, then they should obey the King's law.* Gabe wandered up to the family quarters and found the stack of papers marked with his great-grandfather's ink scrawl. *Now where in these pages does it talk about all this?*

Gabe knew the King didn't want them to fight. All these years had passed, and the King had never encouraged a revolt against the village leaders. He just knew it wasn't the King's way to encourage his people to rebel against their leaders. But he couldn't prove it without finding it in the law. He knew the King's ways because he had sat at the King's feet and had learned straight from the King's mouth, but no one was listening to a kid right now. I'm just a kid. He tried to forget about that last thought, though he wasn't so good at forgetting. He'd been trying to forget for years about the time he fell into the well in the square because he had been showing off, trying to walk the cross bar where the bucket is tied.

Focus. King! His heart cried in desperation. *Where do I find your words about all this? They are going to go to war for your sake and you don't want them to.* He flipped through the pages of the law barely glancing down, despairing at the task. It was like searching for a star in the sky without knowing your constellations. You need the constellations to guide you, and Gabe needed the

King. He tossed the papers onto the floor, and they glided to a standstill. Gabe held his head in his hands and closed his eyes.

He saw the King. He was on his throne, smiling. Gabe felt a little light-headed in his presence but was still in control of himself. He could hear part of what the King was saying. "The law is just and justice will prevail. Vengeance is mine. I am the only one able to rule with justice. No one else can see with the clarity that I am able to see from my throne above the whole village. I know the moves and motives of everyone in the village. Justice will be done, but justice cannot be delivered except by a pure hand." Gabe's eyes remained shut fast, but he could no longer see the King. He remembered that day. The King had taught him about justice and revenge. *Now to find those words...*

Gabe snatched up the top sheet and with the same momentum, propelled himself up onto his feet. He started doing a jig, hopping, leaping and kicking around the upper room. He had found it. Had it been right there on top all this time? Gabe didn't stop to ponder. He did a few more leaps and laughed, wondering what they were hearing down below.

He made it down the stairs in two bounds. From the kitchen, he barreled through the door so hard it bashed against the wall. He didn't slow until he had jumped with two feet and landed on a bench.

He didn't need to quiet everyone to get their attention. His grand entrance had left them speechless. He held up the aged paper and began to read:

Gabe snatched up the top sheet and with the same momentum, propelled himself up onto his feet. He started doing a jig, hopping, leaping and kicking around the upper room. He had found it. *Had it been right there on top all this time?* Gabe didn't stop to ponder. He did a few more leaps and laughed, wondering what they were hearing down below.

He made it down the stairs in two bounds. From the kitchen, he barreled through the door so hard it bashed against the wall. He didn't slow until he had jumped with two feet and landed on a bench.

He didn't need to quiet everyone to get their attention. His grand entrance had left them speechless. He held up the aged paper and began to read:

"Vengeance belongs to the King. Do not take revenge, but trust the King to bring justice. Do not pay back evil with evil, but pay back evil with good. If someone slaps you on one cheek, turn and give him your other cheek. Love your neighbor and treat him as you want to be treated. Above all, love the one and only King. Serve him and obey his laws. This is your first and most important duty."

"This is the King's law." Gabe had stopped reading and was speaking unrehearsed words from his heart. "These are his own words that he gave us to live by. Percy Katrid would have you believe that we are to fight Vulpine to win back the throne for the King, but he doesn't know the King. I know him and now you know what he says about this. If you believe the King exists, then you better obey his law. If you don't believe, then go with Percy to your destruction."

As soon as he had finished speaking, reality smacked him in the face. He was standing taller than everyone else and telling adults what to do. He deflated like a balloon and flopped limply onto the bench, wanting only to slither under the table and hide.

Most were too flabbergasted to speak, but Percy was angry enough to let off steam, a teapot at full boil.

"Kid. You have no idea what you are talking about. We aren't playing here. We're talking people's lives. Vulpine isn't going to stop his rule by our being nice to him. We need to take action. Every minute delayed is another minute Vulpine's vice-like grip on the village tightens. I'm leaving this meeting. I will only be where the real men are. Anyone who wants to fight for freedom can follow me." To add emphasis, he trod heavily across the floor and exited the inn without looking back.

Several men left without further deliberation. Those with wives at their sides dragged them out the door too. Marcus Winsley stood up slowly, hat in hand. "I just want to do what's best for the village. This is my home." He looked down at his grown son sitting next to him. "My children's home. I can't let it all be taken away." He apologized and left after the others. His son followed.

Father turned his attention to Gabe. "You know I believe in the King, but Vulpine is restricting us so we can't even follow all of the King's laws if we wanted to. If Vulpine were gone, we could follow the King's ways. It's just never going to happen while Vulpine is ruling. Don't you think the King wants to sit on his throne again? He would want us to get Vulpine out of there. We need to do something. I just don't see any other way." Gabe's father walked out the door of his own inn.

It was Gabe's turn to be stunned. He felt like Betty had kicked and knocked the air out of him. He couldn't think of anything to say. Then he heard Angela's voice, strong and steady like the tolling of the village bell so that everyone could hear its message.

"Vengeance belongs to the King. Do not…." Angela had picked up the yellowed, tattered paper and was reading as Gabe had done. When she came to the end, the lilting words of the King's song followed. Those remaining, men and women alike, some younger than Gabe, some shriveled with age, all stood and joined in the refrain. They sang their devotion to the King, the one true King. They sang the song that had been silenced on the hill.

Lesson 163

1. Read chapter 12 of the *The King Will Make a Way.*
2. Who is part in the rebellion against Vulpine? (Answers)
3. What is their plan? (Answers)
4. Gabe says he serves the King. He says he doesn't serve who and what? (Answers)

Percy led the way around the back of his home, the only light a single candle in a window. He pushed aside a couple of bales of hay which concealed the cellar entrance, and a well-fed rat scurried out of the way. For a moment, Father questioned his wisdom in following Percy into the dark with the small mob of angry men. Tobacco smoke startled his senses and unhinged his thoughts. He followed Percy down the steps into the cellar and left his doubts out in the cold, dark night where they could vanish with the warm morning light.

The smoke was curling from the lips of four men relaxing in arm chairs. A few dozen men filled the hideout. No one was talking. They were watching and waiting. The other dozen men with Percy felt like animals being shown to buyers at the market. All eyes were on them. They tried not to show fear—they were pretty sure the others would be able to smell it.

Percy broke the silence. "We need all the good men we can get. Tomorrow is the day. We'll see what Vulpine and each of us are made of. I'll let Assemblyman Stone bring everyone up to date with the details."

"Thank you." Stone put down his pipe and spoke from his seat. "I will say outright that you are the wisest men in our fine village. You have seen beyond the masks and lies and have discovered the truth for what it really is. I commend you all. The imposter Vulpine surely is cunning, but his arrogance has led him to believe he can control us with bribes and fancy words. He thinks too highly of his own power.

"I offer to you that this is his blind spot. With a precise blow, we can bring him down. He has already stripped the Assembly of its power. The four of us upright Assemblymen have not bowed to Vulpine. The majority have, however. They are greedy for money and power and despise virtue." Stone rose and began methodically pacing the length of the room. Every eye trailed him. His words were working their charm, building confidence in each of them that they were on the side of right. Doubts drifted away and disappeared with the tobacco smoke. Stone had attracted them to the lure and now was ready to hook them.

"You are the saviors of the village. You are standing for freedom instead of becoming servants to that imposter. You are the ones able to right this tremendous wrong committed against you and your families. Our village needs you to rescue it. Your children need you. Even those foolish enough to follow Vulpine need you. Look around. There are many able-bodied men here. We are not at a disadvantage.

"We know Vulpine's weakness, do we not? He doesn't think it is possible that he could lose control of such a large number of his subjects." He spat the word. "He won't see it coming. We will be victorious! Let me explain the plan." He took his seat, reclining again and grinning as if he were at a party and not a war counsel.

"Our spies tell us that in the morning Vulpine will condescend to be among the common folk," Stone mocked. "He wants to see for himself the results of his edict that everyone be at the village singing ceremony. Vulpine has kept silent as to what he intends to do to violators. That is one of the few unknowns we face. But I don't see it as a complication, as we don't intend to let him do a thing. Let me get back to the plan.

"While confident of our sources, we don't want to risk being caught unprepared, so we will cover King's Hill as well. Percy here will lead a dozen men up the hill early in the morning. They will go under the pretense of hunting. By late morning, they will be in position. Percy will lead the charge. He will give them more details when they are in the forest tomorrow morning. Percy, have you chosen which men you want to take with you?"

"I'll take the ones I brought with me tonight. I trust them with my life." The men who stood behind Percy were sure he had spoken the truth and their chests swelled.

"Very well. The remainder of you will be under the orders of Perkins and Howe. Perkins will hide a half dozen of his men behind the Assembly Hall. Another dozen will be inside, oohing and aahing over the architecture and that cabinet of theirs with the carving of the village." Stone was enthralled with his own cleverness.

"That leaves Howe. He and his men will be with those singing in the square. When Vulpine is announced, they will rush the Assembly Hall where Vulpine will be on the porch in front of his adoring crowd. Vulpine will be surrounded. Percy and Howe, divvy up your men."

There was a short burst of commotion as the men divided the troops between them. Stone was back on his feet and pacing again. As the men's energy focused again on him, he stopped behind his high-backed chair. Leaning into it, he gripped its faded brown leather.

"Men, your leaders have already discussed this next point, but I would like to know what you think. We are in this all together, are we not?" The rhetorical question only brought forth a few grunts. The grin was back on Stone's face. "What do you think? Should we make Vulpine surrender as our prisoner, or does the dastardly devil deserve to die?" Each word was spoken with more force than the one before. The crescendo climaxed with a war whoop from the men. "Kill him!" "Let him die!" Gabe's father was surprised by the sudden transformation of the men. They had become ravenous sharks, attacking when they smell blood. At the mention of Vulpine's name, the scent wafted through the air.

Vulpine had been watching the movements in the village. He considered the villagers pieces on a giant chess board.

The pawns he didn't have any concern for, since their movements were easily manipulated. For now he would leave the bishops be and watch how the game progressed. He knew of their meetings at the inn and their disloyalty, but they were a bunch of weaklings: women, children and old men. Only a few straggly others joined them. There were the rooks, his guards; the queen, his devoted servants whom he could bid come at a moment's notice; and he, of course, was the king. That left the knights, those horses that fancied themselves special—the only pieces on a chess board allowed to jump over another. Vulpine was sure if they tried to maneuver over him, he would knock them down.

Saturday night Vulpine gathered to his throne his inner circle: Phineas Tract, General Writ and Assemblyman Tate, all members of the Brothers and Sons. "Word has spread that I will be at the singing ceremony tomorrow in the square. From our information, it seems our rogues will try and attack me during the ceremony, using the Assembly Hall as the center of their attack. I will speak to each of you privately about your role. Phineas and Tate will be at the ceremony with several of the guards. Writ will be right here. Do not say a word to anyone until necessary. Just have all your men present and alert. I have tested you each and found you trustworthy, but even now I will not speak freely. Do not trust anyone until this rebellion has been thoroughly stamped out. But men, this is an exciting day dawning. We knew this had to come. It's part of the birth pains of any new government. The leaders of the rebellion speak of freedom, but they are hypocrites and really just seek after power for themselves."

Each man had a whispered session with Vulpine. Not one mentioned a thing to another as they stood in the blackness of the night.

Lesson 164

1. Read chapter 13 of the *The King Will Make a Way.*
2. What does it tell us to know that the guards are standing by lanterns lit by order of Vulpine? (Answers)

A hawk swept over the village. The sun hadn't peeked over the horizon yet, but light was beginning to fill the expanse of the sky. Farmers were tending to their animals. Babies cried for milk. Children rolled over and snuggled into their blankets. A long, thin black dog sniffed his way through the streets, searching for a discarded treat. A calico cat walked a fence rail. It was Sunday.

Gabe and Angela had slipped from bed when it was still dark. They sat with a candle beside them, casting both light and shadows on the words of the King's law. Reading those words was all they could think of to help them prepare. They felt as if they were headed into a dark tunnel with no light yet showing at the far end. They didn't know what the day would bring. They didn't know Percy's plans. They didn't know what Vulpine would do. They didn't know what would happen to people who didn't show up to sing in the square. People like them.

A jarring sound clashed with the early morning tranquility. Whack. Thwack. Tap. Tap. Tap. Whack. Thwack. A hammer pounded a code that echoed off King's Hill, delivering the message to the inn. What did it mean? Angela and Gabe wanted to know and raced each other down to the Square. Watching from afar, they crouched in the shadows of the Assembly Hall.

They couldn't make out what they were seeing, but it certainly was altering the appearance of the Square. Two men knelt on a wooden platform. What they were pounding on was lying flat. Shortly the workers stopped and together raised the first form.

One man leaned on the frame while the other started hammering again at its base. The wooden form had an upright post, shorter than the man holding it, and a cross bar making it look like a squat capital letter T. The beam across the top had three holes cut in it, one large in the middle, two smaller ones at either side.

Feeling that this was important, they patiently waited for the workmen to finish. The seconds felt like minutes and the minutes like hours, but they watched as the workmen secured another wooden frame to the platform. And another. And another. And another.

Gabe and Angela weren't sure what they were looking at but knew it was unlike anything they had seen before. An ominous feeling tied Gabe's stomach in knots. "Let's get out of here." Angela didn't need more. They wouldn't have run faster if a black bear had been chasing them. They tumbled into the inn and into their father.

"Where have you two been?"

"Down to the square. There are men constructing something. I don't know what it is." Gabe proceeded to describe it.

"They are a punishment for criminals," Father explained. "The neck fits in the larger hole and the wrists in the smaller holes. That top bar opens. The criminal is put in place and then the top is locked down. He has to stand out there all day in front of everyone. You're sure they built one of those down there?"

"They built five." Gabe delivered the bad news to his father.

Father looked down the road. "I'm going hunting this morning with Percy and some others. Tell Mother not to expect me home until evening." Father was distracted and left without saying goodbye.

After watching Father leave, Angela turned to Gabe. "Ten hours of hunting? What's going on?"

"They're using it as an excuse." Gabe fixed his gaze on King's Hill. "They will all be gathered with their weapons in hand. Maybe they are planning to attack Vulpine today. Maybe they just want to be prepared in case Vulpine does something drastic. Father hasn't said anything. I don't know Percy's plan, but we know he wants to fight." Gabe looked at Angela. He had to look up a little as she had sprouted before he had. "There's nothing we can do. Let's just act like it's any other day."

Angela opened her mouth to speak, but she closed it again seeing Gabe turn his back to her and head calmly into the kitchen. They set about doing their chores.

Brad Winsley finished up his own chores in the barn and struck out with his father. He had made them each a set of bow and arrows. Having bonded over target practice, Marcus was proud to have his son in step with him. They smiled at each other knowingly as Marcus patted the dagger in its sheath under his vest. Gabe's father strode up alongside them, but they didn't greet each other. Their pinpoint focus was at the top of the hill.

The dozen men arrived in installments—a few here, a few there—each disappearing into the pines and then reconnecting at their designated meeting point. Gabe's father reported what he had learned from his children. Then Percy laid out the plan.

"We'll spend some time this morning hunting in two groups. We'll keep close and maintain contact. We'll work our way up the hill throughout the morning. We will be all together at the upper edge of the forest on the left flank before midday. When we hear the bell stop ringing, we'll attack the guards. With Vulpine at the ceremony and expecting there might be trouble, there shouldn't be more than a few guards. We'll outnumber them and take them easily." Percy was feeling cocky.

“Then we can take turns sitting on the throne.” He laughed out loud and put the men at ease, all but Gabe’s father. He couldn’t stop thinking about seeing his son standing in front of everyone the night before, reading from the King’s law. For some reason, he couldn’t remember the words.

Those same words permeated Gabe’s mind. He replayed the night over and over, setting his jaw to hide the heartache each time he thought of his father leaving the meeting. *What is he doing now?*

Mother noticed Father’s absence right away. Gabe gave Father’s message with such sadness she couldn’t help but feel nervous. She hummed to herself as she peeled apples to try and not think about it. She would just be glad that her children were there with her.

Angela was putting Tabitha’s hair in braids, singing silly songs to escape her worries. When their mother called, they came promptly and sat at the table for breakfast. No one noticed if it was good or not. Mother jabbered on about the Griver’s chickens running loose, about the size of the pumpkins at the market and how she had heard the Henkin’s boy had almost set fire to his family’s barn. If you had asked them afterwards, not even Mother could have told you what she had mentioned.

When the children pushed back their bench to rise from the table, she grabbed Gabe’s arm. “Listen, I know we think differently on some things these days, but I am your mother, and I want what’s best for you. I don’t know what’s going on, but I can feel in my bones it’s no good. Your father has himself mixed up in a fine mess, I’m afraid. I’m so glad you two are not out with him. But later today, I will be in the square with Tabitha, obeying our king. I hope to see you there. Vulpine is our king,” she repeated for emphasis.

“We won’t be there, Mother,” Gabe answered sullenly.

“Then don’t go for King Vulpine. Go for the sake of the village,” Mother begged.

“We don’t serve the village either. We serve the King. We can’t go to the square today. I know you don’t understand. Punish us if you must, but we can’t go.”

“I wash my hands of it. I won’t feel guilty for whatever becomes of it. This is your decision. You will take the consequences.” Mother stomped out of the kitchen.

“What are we going to do?” Angela was the one searching for answers this time.

“I don’t want to be around here. Let’s go to King’s Hill. It’s the most peaceful place I know.”

“Gabe, what about Father and the hunters?” Angela shook her head in disbelief at his suggestion.

“We’ll stay near the bottom of the hill. I don’t want to be here.” His sad eyes stared at the door where their mother had just left the room.

“All right, let me say goodbye to Tabitha, and I’ll be ready.”

In the forest, Gabe and Angela made a nest of pine needles for a place to wait out the morning. Their father, Percy Katrid, and almost a dozen other rebels were gathering at their meeting point and inching their way to the uppermost edge of the forest, where General Writ and his men guarded the throne room.

Nearly twenty rebels were in the square, hidden among the waiting crowd, while the rest were either behind or inside the Assembly Hall. Phineas was on the steps of the Hall, speaking with the villagers. Vulpine was just inside the Hall doors, waiting to be announced. His guards were stationed at intervals around the square, each standing in front of a shop with a lantern hanging out front—the lanterns had been lit by order of Vulpine.

The midday sun continued on its arc, rising to the highest point in the sky.

Lesson 165

1. Read chapter 14 of the *The King Will Make a Way.*
2. What was Vulpine's plan? (Answers)
3. What happened to the rebels? (Answers)

Phineas motioned to the boy who rang the bell to stop pulling the rope and smiled broadly at his audience, enjoying the clear, still day. Tabitha whined, asking when the music would start. She was shushed. The restless rebels shifted their feet and itched at their pockets. The sun reached its full potential.

The doors of the Hall were opened with flair as Phineas made his introduction, "Our great leader, his royal majesty, King Vulpine!"

****

Gabe's father stormed out of the forest following Percy.

They had spied just two guards in front of the throne room and were full of confidence. The two Winsley men ran across to their position and fired arrows at the guards. One guard was struck but not killed. As the arrow hit its target, the hill shook with a deafening boom.

"What was that?" Angela's voice quivered.

"I don't know, but I'm going to see. What if Father's in trouble?"

Angela caught his sleeve. "Gabe, no. If you go up there, they will think you are part of the rebellion. We can't let that happen." Gabe shook himself loose, but stayed.

****

The rebels rushed forward as one toward Vulpine. Their formation stretched clear across the front of the Assembly Hall. They leapt up the stairs of the Hall and muscled everyone standing there into the building. Phineas had jumped to safety, but Vulpine was trapped in the middle of the mob.

The crowd panicked. Shrieks and cries came from the women and children, angry shouts from the men. Gabe's mother dragged Tabitha into the glass blower's shop to hide from the chaos. She didn't notice the lantern was gone from out front.

****

Gabe's father was knocked backwards, hitting his head hard. His comrade had fallen into him, crushed under a cannonball. From inside the throne room, armed men emerged, a swarm of angry bees ready to sting. The Winsleys ran into the cover of the forest and didn't stop running, abandoning their weapons along the way. Percy swatted at the first bee which stung him, slicing at his arm, but these bees didn't die after they stung—they fought on. Percy was absorbed with the fight, his sword clanging against another's. The others were valiant at his side, all equally engrossed. They were outnumbered though, and each fell as a second or third guard surrounded him. Noticing Gabe's father on the ground, one of Vulpine's guards pierced his side with a sword.

Soon nothing moved other than Vulpine's guards. Several were being bandaged, but all had survived. General Writ congratulated his men as he surveyed the still landscape. "Toss the bodies over there. Leave them for the animals, a thank you for keeping our secret." General Writ thought he was witty and chuckled. The bodies were heaped by the edge of the forest. "A good day's work, men. A good rain should take care of the rest. You have my permission to take leave for the remainder of the day."

****

"Fire!" One of the rebels was the first to sound the alarm. Vulpine's guards had taken the lanterns, and some tossed them in through the windows of the Hall while others torched the porch. The fire raged on all sides, climbing the four walls of the Assembly Hall. The wood crackled. The men inside shouted. In the glass shop, Mother crumbled to the floor and rocked Tabitha against her chest.

The rebels from behind the Hall formed a bucket brigade. They were promptly arrested by Vulpine's guards. Other villagers took their place, passing a bucket back and forth, hand to hand, from the well to the fire. Still more brought containers, sending water onto the thirsty flames, which licked up the water as soon as it was poured out. The still air aided the firefighters; the fire never spread beyond its target—a bull's-eye.

Inside the Assembly Hall, the wooden cabinet with its intricately carved map of the village ignited. The flames snaked their way through the carving of the village, consuming it as it went: the Assembly Hall, the school house, the shops, barns, homes, farmland, the inn. The cabinet collapsed in ashes before the fire destroyed the image of King's Hill. Outside, the pillars adorning the front entrance snapped and crashed onto their foundation. There were no more cries from within. Outside, women wept and screamed and their frightened children imitated them. The firefighters carried on their work, passing buckets, vases and jugs—hand to hand, hand to hand.

****

Gabe and Angela ducked into their pine tree fort when they heard footsteps. Gabe spotted Brad and Marcus Winsley darting across their line of sight. "Did they go with Father this morning?" Angela whispered into Gabe's ear. He nodded and whispered back, "I think so." Angela hated not knowing what was happening. They strained to hear what they could, but they weren't getting many clues.

It didn't seem long before they heard more footsteps coming down the mountain. These footsteps were very different though, unhurried and accompanied by talking, even laughing. Members of

Vulpine's guard breezed past. Angela was happy she was closeted away behind their barricade of needles.

Gabe lay down flat on his back and stared up into the tangle of branches. "Gabe? Gabe?" He wasn't answering. He was wondering if he could see where the tip of the tree speared the sky. He wondered if a low-lying cloud could feel the pierce of the pine needles. He wondered what it felt like to be pierced through with a dagger, a sword. He wondered how his father had felt before he died. "Gabe? Gabe?"

"Don't you understand? No one else is coming down the mountain. Father is dead."

"Don't say that, Gabe." Angela's head started to swirl. "Maybe he escaped. Maybe he's hiding on the hill somewhere." Angela was desperately searching for an alternative explanation.

"Those guards weren't looking for people hiding in the woods, Angela."

Angela's world went tumbling, spinning. She was weak and dizzy. She grabbed hold of the dirt with both hands to try and hold on. She couldn't see straight. She felt like she couldn't breathe.

"Angela? Angela?" She had fainted, and Gabe was gently touching her cheek. "Angela? Angela?" Her eyelids fluttered. They cracked open and pinched shut. She took a deep breath. Her eyes opened and stared up at the wooden ladder. She wondered what she could see if she climbed limb by limb up the rungs to its top. She wondered if she would be able to see Father from up there. She wondered if she would see him lying on the ground, dead.

Gabe lay back down in their pine needle nest, and together they wondered.

Lesson 166

1. Read chapter 15 of the *The King Will Make a Way.*
2. Who taunts Gabe to give up? (Answers)
3. How does the King make a way for Father to get home? (Answers)
4. Phineas is whistling a happy tune. What do you think that means? Does ending the chapter that way make you curious as to what will happen next and make you want to read more?

Gabe was dozing and Angela was singing softly to herself when a sparrow alighted on Gabe's hand. Gabe twitched and sat up with a start. The bird didn't budge. Angela propped herself up on her elbows. "I thought you might sleep all—" She caught sight of the bird on Gabe's hand, and whispered, "How long has that been there?"

"It just landed, but it doesn't seem to want to go anywhere."

Gabe wasn't quite right about that. The bird pecked gently at Gabe's wrist.

"What do I do, Angela?"

"Gabe, remember your first trip up King's Hill?"

"Yes, so? Help Angela, it's pecking me!"

"Gabe; the toad, the deer! This is not a normal bird. It should be scared of you instead of you being scared of it. Do you think the King sent him?"

"I do. You're right." Gabe spoke quietly, as if afraid his voice would startle the bird and scare it away. "Angela, maybe this means Father is okay." The sparrow stopped pecking as if it knew its message had been understood. Immediately, it flew up to a branch and then out of the pine tree fort. "I guess we'd better follow him," Gabe said as he scrambled to his feet and ducked out of the hiding place.

The sparrow flitted from limb to limb, tree to tree. Gabe and Angela floated along after it. Their heartache had been lifted from them. That's how Gabe knew for sure the King was there, somewhere. Are we about to see the King? They both tingled with excitement at the thought. They wore bright smiles and almost laughed as they climbed. They refreshed themselves slurping cool, clean water from a stream. They nearly skipped along after the sparrow, their hearts suddenly so light. Angela looked at Gabe with sparkling, dancing eyes. Then she looked around to find the sparrow and screamed in horror.

Shaking, stammering, she dropped to her knees and covered her face with her hands. Gabe froze in dismay. An icy cold shot down his spine. *Whatever made her scream is behind me right now.* He wanted to bolt, hide, anything but turn and see what had brought his sister to hysteria. He had that ten-year-old feeling again. *Be a man, Gabe.* The self-pep talk was short and to the point. He was the man here now, the only one his sister could count on.

Muscle by muscle, he slowly turned. First, his knees swiveled. Then his hips. Next his torso. Shoulders. *Be a man, Gabe.* As his neck inched his head around the bend, his eyes squinted closed. *Be a man, Gabe.* He lifted his lashes to peek, pulling in his shoulders, flinching at the air.

He saw. Everything drooped. His eyes relaxed and opened. His jaw hung loose. His arms weighed down his shoulders. He, too, sank to his knees. It was the pile of discarded bodies, the rebels crushed under Vulpine's iron fist.

The sparrow had landed on the mound. Gabe didn't understand all that he was feeling as he looked at the pile. The tumult of emotion inside of him brewed and boiled over, spewing out at the innocent sparrow. "Why did you bring us here?" He screamed it as loud as he could, his face crimson. "I don't want to be here. I don't want to see this! Get away from us! Go!"

Despair circled Gabe like a vulture, taunting, laughing. "He's dead. He's dead. They're all dead. Lifeless bodies left for the birds. You might as well join them. Vulpine will be after you next." Gabe pounded the ground, sure he was going mad. The sparrow landed in front of him then lifted off again and back to the stack of bodies.

"I said go!" Gabe grabbed up a stone and heaved it at the bird. The sparrow escaped, and the stone landed with a moan.

A moan? "Angela, someone's still alive!"

She picked up her head. "What?"

"Didn't you hear that? Someone moaned. Someone's alive."

"Alive?" Angela was shaking her head, her body still trembling too much to move. "Gabe, I can't. I can't go over there. Don't make me go over there." The thought of those bodies sent a new ripple of tremors through her.

"Okay. Okay. It's okay. You don't have to do anything. I'll do it. It's okay." The sight of his sister so frail unnerved him.

Be a man, Gabe. He drew in a quick breath and held it as he launched out toward the pile. He was there in four long strides. Standing there close to it, he didn't see a pile—he saw men. Familiar faces with blank stares. He vomited. Another moan emitted from one of the men.

"Father?" The word slipped out. *Could it be him?* As he made his way around them, his eyes scanned the men frantically until they rested on his father's face. Gabe moved over to him and knelt gently by his head. "I'm here, Father. It's okay." His father let out a gasp of air that carried Gabe's name.

Gabe exhaled, and with the release his tears flowed. The dam had broken and everything he had felt and experienced that day came flooding out. He cried for his father. He cried for the rebellion. He cried over thinking his father was dead. He cried knowing he still might die. He cried for his mother and Tabitha in the Square. He cried for the terror Angela went through. He cried for the King.

Finally, Gabe's river of tears ran dry. It had washed away all his strength. He was drained, empty. "Father, I don't know what to do. I don't know how I could possibly help you." The sparrow returned and landed on his father's hand. It flitted up and then returned to rest on his father's hand. Again and again.

"You want to lead my father somewhere?" Gabe was too worn to concern himself over talking to an animal. "He can't even move!" Despair started cackling in his ear.

Angela thought of the King and the tremors stilled. "The King." Angela's voice broke Despair's spell.

Gabe shivered and shook off his enemy. "What? The King?"

"Gabe, the King is here. I don't know where, but he is here. There's no doubt he sent that bird to lead us to Father." Her voice broke off at his name. She hadn't gotten up the nerve to go look at him, but she called to him now. "Father, I'm here with Gabe. You're going to be fine. We're going to take care of you. I love you!" She grew quiet and reflective.

"Angela, the King? I don't know what you're thinking yet."

"Sorry. The sparrow led us to Father. We know the King must have sent him. That bird isn't that smart or that caring on his own. So, somehow the King knows what's going on. He sees us somehow. If that sparrow wants to lead Father somewhere, then it's the King wanting to lead him somewhere."

"Angela, I believe the King sent the sparrow. I truly, truly do." He came next to her and sat down beside her. Holding her arm, he leaned into her ear. "Father can't even speak. He has no strength, barely any life in him. He can't move or even be moved."

"Gabe, listen. Think. If the King wants us to move Father, then he will make a way. He has to. He always has made a way."

The memories flashed before his eyes. The thousand times he slipped past the guard. The nightmare before the hailstorm. The inn and his family kept from harm. The words and boldness to speak out. The guilt removed and burdens lifted.

"He always makes a way. You're right. There's a way here. He's made a way somehow."

"Gabe!" A weak voice called to him. He jumped to his feet and ran to his father's side. "I can do it. Help me up." Gabe and his father both winced as Gabe lifted Father to help him sit, then stand.

Angela came along Father's right side. Gabe held him up on his left. One step. Two steps. Three steps. Four steps. They had hobbled about a foot's length. Their father was breathing like he had just finished a marathon. Gabe looked at Angela and shook his head.

Angela's face lit up. With her chin, she pointed to beyond Gabe. "The King!" He swung around, longing to see the King again! But it wasn't the King. A small but sturdy horse was coming their way. The golden mare walked slowly with her head held high as if in a royal parade. Her hair was a white diamond between her eyes, adding to her majestic airs.

Gabe swallowed down his longing for the King and explained to his father that the horse had come to carry him down the mountain. Before they could worry about how he was to mount her, she lay down. They helped their father onto her back and laid him down against her mane. She lifted him effortlessly, and they began their descent. Before they reached the road home, while still under the cover of the pines, they heard someone walking past. Gabe peeked through the branches and saw Phineas Tract heading up the hill—whistling a happy tune.

Lesson 167

1. Read chapter 16 of the *The King Will Make a Way.*
2. What does Gabe say is their goal? (Answers)
3. What concept is so hard for one woman at the meeting to accept? (Answers)
4. Author's Note: Gabe has another dream. His last one came true and this one will as well.

Mother stumbled back a bit when she first saw Father— the sight was awful but the smell was worse. Spending part of the day among corpses brought home an unwelcome perfume. Mother regained her composure and managed to strip and bathe her loved one, getting a glimpse of where the sword had pierced his side. The children helped her get him settled comfortably in bed. He smiled faintly and slept.

Back in the kitchen, Mother dished up stew for all of them. Tabitha was in bed already, exhausted by the trauma of the day. Mother listened to the children's story, and then she shared her own. Gabe remembered seeing smoke, but he had been too consumed with himself to stop and consider what it had meant.

"I want to go see what's happening in the Square." Gabe was resolute. "If the fire is still going, maybe I can help. I need to see if everyone's been killed but Father. And Vulpine, did he die in the fire?"

Mother shook her head. "I don't see how anyone who had been inside could have survived."

"Mother, do you want me to stay with you?" Angela asked. Relief swept across her mother's face. "All right, I'll stay and help you."

"You don't need to help. Just stay here with me. My heart can't take any more separation today. Gabe, you stay away from any trouble. It'll be dark in an hour. Please try and be home."

"Yes, Mother."

Gabe was in the square in minutes. The fire was down to embers. The Assembly Hall had been reduced to ashes. The smell of fire usually brought cozy images of warm milk and porridge, but this smell was choking, nauseating, flesh and bone cooked into the ashy soup stirring before him as embers popped. The King's pearl plate sat in the ashes, the only thing that had escaped the fire other than the thick black smoke which billowed up into the sky.

Finally taking a good look around the square, he spotted the wooden frames. He had forgotten about them, a year's worth of events had taken place since the day had begun. He shuffled across to the platform at the other end with only the empty market stalls behind it and saw that the wooden frames had been filled just as Father had described. Heads and hands hung out of the three holes in each frame. One other man was bound hand and foot and tied to one of the posts. Six men had been arrested.

Gabe searched the grounds, littered during the earlier bedlam. He found a bowl of sorts and filled it with water from the well to give each man a drink, returning to the well when the bowl was emptied. None of the men spoke except for murmured thanks. As he tipped the bowl to the last man's lips, a rock stung him in the back.

"Ow!" He spun around. A white haired woman scowled at him.

"Leave them to die!" she hissed. "One of them your old man or are you one of them? Maybe you deserve to die too!"

She grabbed up the closest thing to her and hurled it at him. He ducked. It had been a vase used earlier by the bucket brigade and then abandoned. Now it was shards. Another casualty.

"I don't know them!" He spoke forcefully to the old woman and surprised himself. "I'm not a rebel either. I serve the King, the one true King. But there has been enough death today. I don't want to see another man die." He was intensely earnest. The woman spat at him then backed away.

Gabe sat on the edge of the platform. *What now?*

"Who are you?"

Gabe turned around but couldn't tell which of the men had asked. All of their heads hung weighted with defeat.

"No one. I just wanted to help you."

"Why? Who are you?" The middle-aged man heaved his head up to see the boy. After a glimpse it flopped back down like week-old parsley, his long, unkempt hair covering his face.

"I'm a servant of the King."

"If you serve Vulpine, why are you helping us?" There wasn't any anger in his voice; no fight was left in him. He just thought it dubious that a servant of the king would help them.

"No, I serve the one true King. Vulpine may sit on the throne up on the hill, but he is not the King. He does not really rule us. I know the true King, and I will serve him until I die. You weren't serving him by fighting today. You were serving yourselves and maybe Percy Katrid and the others, but not the King. I brought you water because I serve the King."

"My name is Caleb. It's nice to meet you, servant of the King. Thanks for the water."

"If you are still here tomorrow night, I will try and come back to give you another drink." Gabe slipped off the platform and headed home.

When Gabe entered the inn, he was surprised to see people gathered—more than the night before. Everyone was looking to him.

He spoke fervently about the King, his law, his love, his return one day. He urged them to submit to the village leaders except when it would require them to break the King's law. He reminded them that the two most important laws were to love and serve the King and to love and serve each other.

"There must never again be fighting. It will not accomplish our goal." His mind flashed wildly. *Our goal? What is our goal?* "Our goal is to see the King not only sitting on the throne but honored by everyone in the village. The King has been away from the village for decades, but he has never tried to force his way in. He wants the villagers to seek him, to come to him, to learn from him. We need to show people the King. We need to get them to believe he is real and worthy of our honor and obedience. We can show them by our love for each other and by our love for our enemies."

"Love for our enemies! My husband was burned alive today by Vulpine's men. My only comfort is that devil burned with him!" Fire was in her eyes and hate was in her voice. Her hands were trembling. "Why should I love those men? Why would I serve a King who loves those hateful men?"

"We don't have to love them like we love our brothers. But we have to treat them like we would want to be treated. It means if one of them is dying of thirst, we don't drag him out into the hot sun; we give him a drink of water. It means we welcome them into our meeting if they begin to follow the King. Please, no more hate. No more fighting. Today's tragedy should be enough for anyone to learn that lesson."

Gabe looked at Angela. She read from the King's law and led everyone in singing the King's song. They sang it over and over. The words washed away their burdens and fears. Tears cascaded from the woman's eyes, putting out the fire they had contained just minutes before.

Everyone slept deeply that night, exhaustion a friend of sleep. Gabe dreamed the King had returned. All the villagers knelt before him as he stood on a platform in the Square. Gabe was standing next to him, wearing brilliant white. Then the people started shouting, "The King is alive! The King is alive!" He smiled and stirred.

"Gabe, what is it? Gabe, are you awake?" Angela leaned over Gabe trying to get him up. "Gabe, what are they saying? What's going on?"

Gabe returned to consciousness, still remembering his dream. Or was he still dreaming? It was only the cusp of dawn, but the village bell was tolling. A crier was galloping on horseback through the streets calling out. Turning around past the inn, the rider's words rang out clearly as he rode back. "The king is alive! The king is alive! Everyone to the Square!"

Gabe and Angela stared dumbly at each other until Mother shooed them out of bed. "Go find out what's going on! I'll stay home with Father. And look, Tabitha is sleeping right through it as usual. I couldn't wake that child if I dropped her on her head."

Angela and Gabe pulled on clothes. Gabe hopped out the door as his right leg hadn't yet found the end of its tunnel.

They were out of the inn before Gabe had even spoken a word. All along the road, doors were opening as bewildered people stepped out of their homes. Gabe told Angela about his dream.

"Do you think it could really be him?" Angela asked, afraid to get her hopes up.

"I…I don't know. My dream about the storm happened, right?" *Please let it be you, King.* "Let's hurry." They were off again, just like the day before.

On the far side of the Square with the sun rising before them, the men, limp on their wooden hangers, cast long shadows. Inside the bell tower, a young boy tugged a tattered rope to rock the bell, and with each rock back, the bell tugged at the boy.

As the villagers arrived in the Square, they gathered in front of the platform. Everyone was trying to decipher the message of the crier. They were bursting with curiosity. Bewilderment gave way to excitement. Gabe's heart ached with the anticipation.

General Writ and numerous guards stood off to the side, and as Phineas stepped up onto the platform, the bell quieted. The crowd was as silent and still as those mornings when ice has glassed over the world.

He simply said, "May I present to you, your king!" Angela squeezed Gabe's hand. *Could it be?*

Lesson 168

1. Read chapter 17 of the *The King Will Make a Way.*
2. Who had a "miraculous reappearance"? How is he still alive? (Answers)
3. What does Gabe realize when Caleb asks how he can start reading the King's law? (Answers)
4. What did those at the meetings start calling themselves? (Answers)
5. The chapter ends with Vulpine pulling on his "iron glove." He had told the villagers he would rule with an "iron fist" over those who were working against the peace and unity of the village. What do you think might happen next?

"King Vulpine!" At Vulpine's name, the crowd didn't cheer or applaud. If everyone had been still and silent before, they were now frozen. No one dared do anything that might break the spell of those words. Then in a dramatic, magical moment, Vulpine emerged from among the guards. He leapt onto the platform. Hundreds of icebergs thawed.

One woman screamed. Another fainted. One man just started laughing hysterically. The baffled villagers started asking each other questions all at once. Phineas decided to help the dumbfounded commoners by shouting, "Long live King Vulpine!" The guards and the members of the Brothers and Sons joined in. "Long live King Vulpine!" Scattered groups took up the chant. "Long live King Vulpine!" The words picked up strength in numbers and in volume. And for the second time in twenty-four hours, Gabe vomited.

"Let's go home," Angela said as she took Gabe's arm and led him through the crowd. They walked past the ash heap, out of the square and headed home. *How could he have escaped?* Without discussion, they slipped into the inn and back into bed.

Scarcely an hour passed before their mother shook them awake. "You have guests" was all she would say. She pulled open the curtain and unlatched the window only to shut it again, muttering something about a draft.

Downstairs in the dining hall, people had been arriving, but they were more family than guests. "Welcome everyone! No, no, it's fine to come now." Angela was a gracious host. "We don't always need to wait for nightfall. Please, come, sit down." People from their nightly meetings had come straight from the Square. Too much had happened to digest alone.

Gabe and Angela learned what had happened after they left the unveiling of Vulpine that morning. Winnie Goss shared the story with them.

"You were there at first, so you know what it looked like with everyone there crazy over Vulpine just showing up after we all thought he was dead." She struggled with a pin in her pepper black hair, which had noticeably begun turning salty. "He gets everyone yelling, 'Long live King Vulpine!' except those of us who were happy when we thought he was dead. Well, I did see some folks shouting along with them that I've also seen right here in this inn." Her plump fingers fiddled with the collar on her pale blue frock.

"Well, when all the commotion settles down, Vulpine doesn't even explain what happened—how he's alive—just starts talking about how he had fulfilled his promise to defend the peace and unity of the village. He told everyone it wouldn't happen again because the rebels were either killed or taught the 'invaluable lesson'"— she did her best impersonation of Vulpine —"that he knew everything that was going on and would always be one step ahead of anything the rebels tried. Then he had everyone sing that song. And you know who was singing? Those Winsley boys, father and son, just singing away. I left though, and I don't care who saw me. It wasn't law we sing today."

"I can tell you what happened after that. Do you recognize me?" He was addressing Gabe. Gabe squinted, trying to put the memory in focus.

"Caleb! You're free! Is that what happened next?"

Caleb smiled and rubbed his wrists. "I'm free. Vulpine had us freed. He told everyone it was to show his desire to keep the village united. He said he was sure we were convinced now by his 'miraculous reappearance,'"— it was Caleb's turn to try to imitate the baritone —"that he was the only king or something. All right, maybe I wasn't paying close attention. But I know that I'm free."

Gabe had one more question for Caleb. "How did you find me here?"

"I asked around about a boy who would offer a drink to a stranger." Caleb laughed. "It was pretty easy to find you."

Gabe only shrugged in response.

After the meal, Gabe took again to the bench and told everyone about his years at the King's feet. With tears in his eyes and a catch in his throat, he told them of the King's love and pleaded with them to follow the King's law. Angela read to everyone from the Book of Law and led the singing of the King's song.

As the others left, Caleb sidestepped over to Gabe. "I listened to you today, and I believe you. I believe you about the King. And I was wondering, how I can get to know him like you do."

"You can learn his words in the Book of Law. They will teach you who the King is. And by coming and being here with me and the others, you can feel what it's like to sit with the King and be loved. Most of the people here have dedicated themselves to following the King."

"I would really like to follow the King. How can I start reading the law book?"

Gabe felt foolish. *Why didn't I realize before this moment that I have the only copy of the law? We need to get it to everyone*. He gave a few pages to Caleb to start copying, and he and Angela worked on copying pages into the night.

At the next meeting, everyone was given a page, golden with age, to take home and copy as many times as they could. Every day they traded pages and went home and made more copies. In a month, they each had their own copy of the King's law and copies to share with others.

Now Gabe wasn't the only one teaching others the King's law. Everyone became a servant of the King, taking the King's law to their families and neighbors, and more and more people joined their meetings. Mrs. Bollix started teaching the King's law to her brother-in-law. She visited his family often to tell them what she was learning. He listened out of curiosity at first but eventually became interested in reading the King's law for himself. Mrs. Bollix was ready with a copy. Soon he was attending meetings at the inn.

Gabe and Angela started visiting Caleb and his wife and children daily. As a family, they studied the King's law eagerly. His five children, ranging from little to big, all learned the King's laws. Soon Caleb started meetings in his home for his relatives and close neighbors.

Sundays came and went and the servants of the King, as those at the meetings started calling themselves, stayed home from the singing ceremony, keeping quiet and hidden around midday. No one seemed to notice or mind—or, so they thought.

Vulpine had been watching those bishops to see what their next move would be. He knew they had mostly kept to themselves, but as the snow and ice enveloped the village, he noticed things heating up. The servants had begun teaching their neighbors about the King. Thirty servants became one hundred.

The quiet, straggly bishops were strengthening and getting louder. Vulpine wasn't blind or deaf to it. He knew how to take care of them. He would just need to pull on his iron glove.

Lesson 169

1. Read chapter 18 of the *The King Will Make a Way.*
2. How did Gabe escape arrest? (Answers)
3. What is the prison like? (Answers)
4. What metaphor is used to describe the pillory stocks scene? (Answwres)
5. The villagers beat the servants to death in this chapter. Why do you think they did it? When answering, consider that no one had beaten them up the day before.
6. Throughout history populations have been guilty of many awful crimes against targeted minorities. From reading different historical accounts, I've come to the conclusion that they did those things because they were given permission to. If society says it's okay–condones or even encourages it, then people will do it. The lynching of African Americans in America's south continued because no one stopped it. They even had picnics to watch them. Would people still do it today if the same permissive atmosphere existed?

Another Sunday morning dawned. Caleb, having wanted to be alone, was on King's Hill reading the King's Book of Law. Angela and Gabe were sitting by a candle, wrapped in blankets, doing the same. They were preparing again. For what they didn't know, except that there had been rumors that Vulpine would make arrests.

Mornings started later in the winter, and by the time Betty had been cared for, the water fetched, the wash hung, the wood chopped and breakfast eaten, it was nearly noon. The children went upstairs to the family quarters. Father still spent his days in bed, but he could sit propped up for a short time. Angela brought him food while Gabe read to him from the King's law. Father had learned while lying almost dead on the hill that he should always listen to Gabe when he spoke the King's words.

The bell in the Square rang its chorus, its chime slipping easily over the icy fields through the bare branches of the trees and into the inn. Gabe and Angela tried not to be nervous, but they both stiffened at the sound. When the bell sang its last note, to those inside the inn, outside seemed lifeless. From their vantage point, the village seemed vacant, like the inn in the dead of winter.

"It feels like the day of the hailstorm," Angela said, standing at the window. "We kept watching and waiting, and then it sprung at us all of a sudden. Everything is so quiet and calm out there. I'm anxious though. I keep expecting something to happen." And then it did.

Coming at a quick pace down the snowy path from King's Hill came six of Vulpine's guards. Behind them was a horse-drawn cart with a cage built on top of it. Angela described it to her father. Gabe didn't wait to hear the description and darted to the window.

Closer and closer they trotted until they turned toward the inn. "They're coming here." Gabe catapulted himself out of the room.

Their pounding shook the door as the guards demanded it be opened. Gabe was there to obey the order.

"Sirs, welcome." He tried to act casual.

"We are under orders to arrest everyone not attending the singing ceremony today. You'll have to come with us. Is there anyone else at home?"

"Yes, my sister and I are here caring for our father. He's upstairs in his bed. Would you like to see them?"

"Take us."

Gabe led four of the guards up the stairs to the family quarters. Angela had heard them and sat by Father's bedside, wiping his face. He did his best to look miserable.

"They're just kids and the sick one. The law says you can stay home if you aren't well. Forget them."

Never before had Gabe been so thankful for his slight build. He was trying hard not to breathe, willing himself to be invisible. *Yes, just leave us here.*

"Come on." The guards found their own way out. Gabe didn't let out his breath until he heard the cart wheels in the snow. Angela was already at the window and flung it open.

"Gabe, quick! Look in the cage!"

Gabe hustled to the window. "Caleb!" Without thinking, he called out his name. Caleb heard, looked up at the window and smiled.

In dismay, Angela slumped to the floor. "What's happening out there?"

Gabe shut the window and without turning his gaze from the foggy pane, he started singing. Angela and Father added their soprano and bass, creating a memorable harmony with Gabe's tenor. He finally turned and looked at the others. "A beacon leading us out of our darkest night," he sang, repeating the line again. "When the King wrote the song, he was talking about this. Right now. Except we're not coming out of the darkest night, we're about to go into it. We can't forget the King. He's the one who will lead us out. We need to go tell Caleb." Then he added, "And any others."

There were others. The guards had swept through the whole village, house to house, arresting those who had defied Vulpine's mandate. The guards were shocked as they made their arrests. No one fought their captivity; some had even turned themselves in. Apart from the servants of the King, no one had defied Vulpine since the fatal attempt at rebellion. Even Assemblyman Stone was heard wishing Vulpine a long and illustrious reign.

The arrested servants were thrown into the village prison, one almost entirely dark and bare room. They were given bread and water and a bucket for a chamber pot that they were all expected to share. Men and women together were crammed into the stone room with nothing to sit or to lie on except the cold dirt floor. When the door was closed, there was no source of light except for the sliver at the bottom of the door.

Five men were chosen from their number to set an example for the others. They were locked into the wooden frames in the Square. The orders: the locks were not to be opened until the men were dead. That evening, the five men sang the King's song while the sun set behind them.

Gabe heard the news and after dark, took food and water to the captives in the square. Caleb was not one of them this time. With whispered encouragement, he helped them take bites of bread and cheese and sips of water. Before the sun came up again, Gabe had turned fifteen.

The next three days were unusually warm and pleasant. The snow and ice melted, and everyone who was able was outdoors. Angela even moved Father's bed next to the window. For the next two nights, Gabe tiptoed to the platform with a basket of food. The men were hungry, not only for food but for the King's words. Gabe fed them both. Each night, he slipped away promising to do whatever he could to come back again.

The third day, Vulpine conferred with his inner circle. "Someone's been feeding them. They should be wilted by now. They look happy!" The word "happy" had never before been spoken with such venom. He struck the golden arm of his throne, making his hand throb and him all the more livid. "Call the villagers to the Square. Let's be done with them."

The bell summoned the villagers, who hurried to see what was happening. Vulpine was on the platform, smiling, but his eyes were full of malice. He opened his arms wide to address the villagers.

"My loyal subjects, I come to you asking for your help. Together we will bring about our vision of peace and unity in our beloved village. But we must act together, united. Here behind me on this platform are five hideous creatures. They are disloyal, disobedient, a threat to the crown and to the village. To show your loyalty to the village, I ask you each to take a part in the destruction of these loathsome characters. Do what you will to them until they are all dead. That is your duty to the crown and to the village."

Vulpine stepped down quickly from the platform and concealed himself among his guards and officials. Phineas and Assemblyman Tate stood among them. At first, no one moved, unsure of what had just been asked of them. Then suddenly, a roar erupted from within the assembled crowd. A man rushed the platform and with a bound was on top of it. In an instant, he started boxing the face of one of the servants of the King, who was utterly helpless to defend himself.

The sight egged on others. More climbed onto the platform for their turn. They punched, stabbed, kicked, spat, yanked, stomped, elbowed. No bell brought a break in this boxing match without rounds. The men were beaten unceasingly for an hour. By the time the knockout was declared, the five servants were dead.

Lesson 170

1. Read chapter 19 of the *The King Will Make a Way.*
2. Who has newly joined the meetings at the inn and has started helping Gabe? (Answers)
3. How did the King make a way for the people in jail? (Answers)
4. Who is asked to leave the meetings? Why? (Answers)
5. What do you think would give the prisoners joy? (Answers)

Winnie was asked to leave the meeting that evening because she wouldn't stop gabbing about the deaths of the servants that afternoon and everyone she had seen at the square and what they had done. Gabe escorted her to the door and told her she could rejoin the meetings when she learned to hold her tongue. When he shut the inn door behind her, he shuddered at what he had just done. *How did I get the courage to do that?*

The meeting was small that evening. Gabe guessed more than half of their number had been imprisoned, although he wasn't really sure what that number was—he had never counted. Gabe wondered about the men and women missing. *Had they been arrested or did they just switch loyalties, like Marcus and Brad Winsley?*

He had run into Marcus in the square one day. Marcus had taken his hat in his hand and had averted his eyes. He had repeated the same thing he had said at the meeting: he was just doing what was best for his village and his family. After apologizing, he had walked away without ever having looked Gabe in the eyes. Gabe had decided not to go after him.

He wandered around the inn's dining hall, greeting people. He heard one man recount how he had escaped arrest on Sunday. Hearing the happy ending, Gabe repeated to himself, "The King made a way." At one table, he stopped to introduce himself to a young man, a few years his elder.

"Hello." Gabe reached out a hand. The young man took it and returned the greeting.

"My name's Gabe."

"I'm John, and I know who you are." John smiled and pointed at Emily and her husband, sitting across from him at the table. "Those are my parents. You came and helped them out when I was so sick with that virus that went around the village. Now it's just the three of us at home; my brother died then. My parents have been coming around here ever since then I guess, but this is my first time joining them."

"I remember coming to your farmhouse. I was glad to help out." Gabe spied Angela drifting by, watching. He pulled her over and introduced his sister.

John said hello, but Angela just smiled back shyly. Gabe had guessed John was about eighteen, but there was something else he could tell just by looking—he was handsome. Gabe could see that in Angela's eyes.

After a time, the meeting fell into its familiar routine: Gabe's impassioned plea and Angela's melodic voice. Even when she read from the King's law, you could hear music in her voice.

Before everyone had emptied the inn, Gabe took John aside. Gabe wondered if in a few years, he would be able to look him straight in the eye, but presently he got an eyeful of Adam's apple. He tilted his head and asked John why he had come to the meeting.

"When Vulpine asked us to kill those men in the square, I knew I couldn't have anything to do with the man. It made me sick. Listening to you talk about the King…it was just the opposite. I know he's someone I can honor."

Gabe was ready with another question. "Tomorrow I'm going to try and visit our friends who were arrested for not attending the singing ceremony. Would you like to come with me?" John shook on it and a new partnership was formed.

Bread and cheese filled two long baskets along with apples Mother had stored in the cellar to preserve during the winter. Angela had tucked a copy of the King's law into the bottom of one of the baskets and covered it with a plain white cloth edged with roses. She thought of the nights she had spent with red thread wrapped around her pointer finger doing the fine work, and she was happy that her labors could serve such a purpose. She admired her cornucopias but knew they would only feed each prisoner a small amount.

"Come home" was all she said as Gabe took up the basket handles.

"The King will make a way." He matched her reticence and was gone.

John was already waiting for him in front of the inn. "Let me help you with that." He took one of the baskets. With the wind chilling their cheeks, they walked the full length of the village: they left King's Hill behind them, passed John's family farm, peered in the shops in the square, skated over a bit of the lake and, for the first time in their lives, walked into the jail.

The guard had opened the door for them without hassle. Inside, another leaned his wooden chair against the wall, warming his hands on a cup of coffee. "What business do you have here?"

"We've brought some food for your prisoners," John answered.

"And for me I hope." The guard's voice was calm and casual, as if they were old friends.

John looked to Gabe.

"Sir, I see you have a warm cup of coffee there and probably had a warm breakfast this morning too. Have your prisoners even had a cold meal today?"

"What do I care about the prisoners?" The guard turned gruff. "Let me see what you have there." The front legs of his chair struck the hard floor. He took his time getting up and walking over to them, boring a hole through Gabe with his stare. He poked through the baskets and said in disgust, "Bird food. But the wife might like this here." He tugged hard and quick on the cloth and yanked it out from under the food spilling a dozen bread rolls onto the floor. "Clean up this mess," he ordered and then laughed.

John and Gabe dropped to the ground and quickly put the rolls back in the basket, thankful the heavy cheese and apples remained in the bottom covering their secret contents. They looked at each other, unsure of what to do next, when the guard helped them out unexpectedly.

"Go and feed the birds. It'll save me the trouble later." He was back in his chair, leaning against the wall and watching the steam rise from his cup.

The boys followed the other guard. The cell door had no window, just another small door through which food could be passed. When the guard was about to open the smaller door, Gabe interrupted.

"We can't really pass a whole basket through that little opening. Couldn't we just take it in to them? I'm sure they haven't been causing you trouble, and if we cause trouble, you could always lock us in there too."

John's eyes widened in disbelief at what Gabe had just said.

The guard just shrugged and opened the larger door. He shut and locked the door behind them. John wondered if he would ever see that door opened again.

"It's me, Gabe."

"Gabe, it's me, Caleb."

"Hi. Hi everyone," Gabe greeted the inmates anonymously in the pitch black room. "I don't even know where you are. I can't see a thing." Gabe elbowed John and covered his nose with his shirt. The prisoners obviously weren't allowed out of the room for any reason.

"My name's John. I've come with Gabe. I'm new to the meetings. We've brought some food." John felt awkward talking to unseen strangers.

Voices came from every angle, greeting, thanking, asking for food.

"I don't know how to get the food passed out. How many are you?" Gabe asked the blackness.

"Forty-two." Caleb seemed to be the leader of the group. "Your eyes will adjust in a bit. There is a tiny bit of light coming from under the door. Not enough, but at least you can tell if someone's right in front of you."

"There's only a small amount for everyone: half a bread roll, a bit of cheese and half an apple. Sorry." Gabe hoped no one would be disappointed.

"Don't be sorry. Sounds like a feast to us," Caleb assured him.

The prisoners organized themselves and came one at a time to get their portion. John handed out the food, and Gabe gave out encouragement.

While they ate, Gabe reminded them of the words of the King's song about his love leading them out of their darkest night. "It will be literally true for you all when you get out of here." Everyone quieted at the comment. "You will get out of here. He will lead you out." He started to sing, and everyone joined in.

"I guess it's time to see if the guard intends to open the door and let us out. I brought a copy of the King's law, but I don't see how you could ever read it in here." Gabe held the precious papers in his hands.

"Leave it with us anyway," Caleb decided. "The King may make a way, right?"

"The King will make a way." The words passed over everyone's lips. Gabe placed the papers into Caleb's hands.

John rapped on the door with his knuckles. All was quiet for a while. "Do you think anyone's going to let us out?" John's voice was unsteady.

"The King always makes a way, John. He always makes a way." Gabe's sure voice gave John confidence, at first.

John took his fist to the door this time. No one spoke. Everyone was waiting to see what would happen.

John bit his lip and tried again—this time knocking continuously. They heard the clang of keys against the metal door. Light flooded in. John thanked the guard. Gabe took a good look at all the faces and saw joy. "We'll try and come tomorrow," he said on his way out of the cell.

"Thank you, sir. We will see you again." Gabe spoke to the guard who was still sitting in his tipped-back chair leaning against the wall. John was pretty sure he was asleep. Outside John confessed his anxiety. "I thought I was trapped in that reeking black hole forever. How were you so calm? You didn't know we were going to be let out."

Gabe smiled. "I guess I should tell you my story. It started with a toad." Gabe shared with John about all the times he had seen the King make a way. "It's just that…it's just that I know the King. I know him." Gabe shrugged, not knowing how to explain. "When you know him, you just know that he has to make a way. It doesn't mean never being locked in a dark room. But for those people in there, he's made a way for them to be okay. I'm…I don't know how to tell you any better than that." Gabe felt inadequate, but John had understood.

"We'll go back tomorrow, right?" John was ready for more.

Gabe hadn't even finished his story when the King had done it again. Before the guard had closed the door, he had asked the prisoners about the song he had heard them singing. "I haven't heard that in years. It kind of brings back memories. If I left the delivery door open, do you think you could sing it again, so I can hear it better?"

"Of course," Caleb said with a smile. Boom. The guard closed the heavy metal door. Clank. He turned the lock. Creak. The little delivery door was opened. Light, enough light to read by, seeped into the cell.

Lesson 171

1. Read chapter 20 of the *The King Will Make a Way.*
2. What does Vulpine want everyone to do? (Answers)
3. Who refuses to give people the tattoo? (Answers)

Gabe and John took Angela with them when they went back to the prison the next day, Friday. The guard let the light shine in through the hatch, and Angela sang for him. They all enjoyed eggs, hard-boiled by John's mother. Several people recited parts of the King's law that had changed their lives in some way.

One woman recited from memory, "Do not let your heart be troubled, and do not be afraid." She told how these words ended her suffering from panic. She explained how she had developed a fear of being inside after the hailstorm had sent the ceiling crashing down around her. She would jump at every noise and constantly look up at the ceiling, nervous it was going to collapse on her again.

"But when I learned those words," she said, continuing her story, "it was as if all I had to do was to say yes to those words, and the fear disappeared. All I had to do was to decide that I would obey those words of the King, and somehow he did the rest. The fear and anxiety were gone."

Gabe, John and Angela left the prison with full hearts. Before they could go back on Saturday, Caleb bounded into the inn, his shaggy hair bouncing along with him. "You're home!" Angela cried out. Gabe came, shook his hand and asked what had happened.

"I don't know. The guard just opened the door and said, 'Go.' We were too excited to ask him why. We just ran. And I didn't stop running until I got here."

"Now what?" Angela wondered out loud. "What's going to happen tomorrow?"

"I don't know." Caleb didn't have the answer. They would know soon enough.

That evening they decided to meet in the middle of the day on Sunday. They didn't like the worrisome feeling of not knowing what was happening to the others. The next day, most were present for the meeting.

They were singing the King's song when the same six guards burst into the inn. They didn't bother with knocking this time. The servants didn't try to run or hide. The head guard looked around and ordered the others each to take one prisoner. Six servants were hauled off in the cage. Caleb escaped arrest this time—John had not.

Monday was a blustery day, and Phineas held his cloak close while addressing the crowd. He announced the reconstruction of the Assembly Hall. He also announced that from that day forward, it was illegal to sing the King's song. The door guard at the prison hadn't heard though—he had been on duty—and John got to serenade him with the others that evening. John also got to enjoy a bowl of warm stew which Angela had made herself. She and Gabe hauled it all the way to the prison on a borrowed cart.

Returning home they were laughing as they walked up to the inn and wondered if it was wrong to have such a good time visiting the prison. Their laughter abruptly stopped when they reached the door and saw a notice had been nailed to it. The inn had been closed to the public, their meetings and their business shut down by order of Vulpine. Again they were unsure of the future, tomorrow even. It was getting to be a familiar feeling.

Mother was furious over Vulpine's edict. "What have I done? What have I done? You are the ones having the meetings. I held my peace about it. Now look what you've all done."

Gabe and Angela stood mutely before their scolding mother. Father still kept to the family quarters upstairs and could not come to their defense. Without interrupting, they let her speak her mind.

"What are we going to eat? I ask you. What are we going to do? Spring is around the corner and the inn would finally be getting in some guests and now….What are we going to do?" She put her hand over her mouth and began to cry, her tears watering the seeds of bitterness.

Gabe had a suggestion. "You could take Father's woodwork to the market to sell. It's just like the King had it planned all along. Father's been making them for years now, and you've always complained they are just sitting around. Why don't you try and sell them?"

Mother wouldn't acknowledge that the King had made a way for their family to have another business. She just shrugged her shoulders and said, "Maybe." Gabe smiled at Angela but didn't say another word.

That night, as people showed up for the daily meeting, they were turned away. Many gathered in various homes. Some just returned to their own homes, unsure. Although Gabe and Angela couldn't tell people what would happen to them, there were two things they absolutely knew for sure: the King was alive and he always made a way.

It was on those two points that Gabe spoke at John's house that night. Then John's father spoke with every bit the passion of Gabe.

Gabe and Angela were back to the prison on Tuesday. While everyone ate, Angela told John about Mother's tirade. He tried to comfort her. "She still loves you. She just doesn't understand. She couldn't possibly understand. The King will make a way for your family to survive. You believe that, right?" Angela nodded and smiled, and to John her smile lit the dark room. When he was released from prison on Saturday, John's first stop was the inn.

Gabe was glad to have his partner back because Angela could no longer go on prison visits. Mother had her working around the inn while she was in the market selling Father's wood carvings. Father continued to spend part of his days whittling but also took some time each day to work on copying the King's law to give out to others. Gabe and Angela didn't have time for that any longer.

The winter daylight was short, but the work days were long for Gabe and John. Tirelessly they spent their days giving out copies of the King's law, teaching other servants and visiting the prison. Each Saturday the jail was emptied, and each Sunday it was filled again. Those arrested were glad there was always a group of them. The body heat of the others was the only thing keeping them from freezing in the bitterly cold cell.

Climbing up King's Hill in the icy cold, the members of the Brothers and Sons grumbled at Vulpine for deciding to meet at Assemblyman Tate's residence just beyond the forest. At the meeting, Vulpine's mood matched the weather. His words were darts with no target to aim at other than those present. Some felt the need to duck.

"I've become king, and here I am still with those who refuse to submit to me." Vulpine spat his words, practically foaming at the mouth. "There is still talk of the previous king living. There is talk of following his law. What are you doing about it?"

Everyone stirred, but no one answered. It was common knowledge that remaining silent was the best response when Vulpine's anger seethed. "I want everyone serving me. We need to end this rebellion permanently." Vulpine paced. Everyone waited for the plan. Vulpine always had a plan.

He stopped his movement and looked piercingly into each pair of eyes. "We need to know who is with us. We need some sort of sign, a mark that would show someone has devoted himself to my service. What can we use?"

Assemblyman Tate suggested a pin that looked like the village banner. Vulpine shook his head. "They could take it off at will and be loyal or disloyal depending on who was present. I want the villagers to be loyal. I want them to be mine." The village doctor cringed at the word "mine."

"What are you thinking then?" Tate posed the question.

"A tattoo: distinct, obvious at a casual glance, permanent." The word permanent landed heavily in the middle of the room.

Vulpine turned again to the doctor. "Are you able to help with this?"

The doctor shook his head. "I've never tried it." He paused and then added, "Isn't there another way, a way other than scarring people?"

Vulpine ignored the doctor's question and repeated his instead. "Are you able to help with this?" Vulpine wasn't asking politely. The words squeezed out through clenched teeth.

"I've never done it." The doctor shook his head. "I don't think I can do it."

Vulpine's left eye twitched at the thought of someone saying no to him. For an achingly long moment, he just glared at the doctor. Everyone was tense. Would Vulpine accept no for an answer?

Vulpine broke off his stare and addressed the whole group again. "Who can help us?"

Tate's adult son spoke up. "I know someone who can make tattoos, a cousin of mine. I'm sure that if he were paid for the job, he would be happy for the work." Tate nodded in approval at his son's suggestion.

"Fine. Make arrangements with Phineas for the payment. The design will be a simple letter V tattooed onto the back of the right hand. I expect you all to be first in line." When he spoke, he looked only at the doctor. The doctor kept his head down.

"Phineas will make the announcement this week and will encourage people to take the mark to show their loyalty. Please show favor to those who take the mark. Give them the best service when in your shops. Show them respect. Do the opposite to those who refuse the mark. Leave them standing outside in the cold. Deny them whatever you like. Help people choose their loyalty swiftly. I'm counting on you all."

Vulpine's feet pounded out of the room, and everyone breathed a sigh of relief. The doctor didn't lift his head. He kept looking at that heavy weight which Vulpine had dropped in the middle of the room—permanent.

Lesson 172

1. Read chapter 21 of the *The King Will Make a Way.*
2. What does the good doctor tell Phineas? (Answers)
3. The doctor tells Gabe his name. What is it? (Answers)

Assemblyman Tate and his son were the first to receive their tattoos. Phineas introduced the idea of the mark to the villagers with a great deal of patriotic talk. He urged them to show everyone that they were loyal to the village and to Vulpine by taking the mark. He pointed out that it was free for everyone so the whole village could be united by this simple act. "For peace and unity" was again the explained inspiration behind the mark. No one could argue that peace and unity were not desirable things.

Most of the Brothers and Sons took the mark right away, though a few hesitated. Tate offered some bribes to get other more visible members of the village to take the mark. Tate also took his nephew out to the market stalls and encouraged each seller to take the mark right then in order to prove their loyalty to the others. Gabe's mother was in one of the stalls selling Father's woodcarvings. She looked around at the others and followed them in taking the mark on her right hand.

All of the sellers had taken the mark until they reached the farmers selling their produce. Many of them turned it down. Mother knew why. She shook her head, tsk-tsking them for being so foolish as to listen to her young son instead of listening to the king. She admired the dark V on her hand and was confident she was the wise one.

She showed it off at home. Gabe looked at it with sad eyes but without comment. His mind started thinking through the implications of a mark of loyalty, but he decided he couldn't know what was to come of it. Instead, he refocused his thoughts on serving the King.

Serving the king was exactly what Vulpine determined everyone should do. While having rewarded Tate's efforts to get the villagers marked for their allegiance, he was agitated that the doctor had yet to take the mark himself. He couldn't sleep for want of knowing if his loyalties had changed. One sleepless night, he decided the doctor must be forced to take the mark or take his punishment for abandoning his oath to serve him until death. If the doctor no longer served him, death must swiftly follow.

Vulpine knew his personal appearance in the square would cause quite a stir, so he sent Phineas to complete the assignment—the doctor must be forced to choose. Phineas strolled into the doctor's store front along the edge of the square. "I've come to see the good doctor," he called out in a friendly tone.

The doctor pulled back the curtain to see who had entered and then closed it again to finish tending to his patient. He wasn't in a hurry. He had expected Vulpine to make a move. He knew he couldn't refuse the mark for long without being noticed by Vulpine's eagle eyes, or at least his spies.

He locked the door after his patient left and invited Phineas behind the curtain for a private discussion. The doctor was the first to speak. "I know why you've come, but I'm not taking the mark. I'm not going to be permanently branded for Vulpine. He's only a man." He sighed.

"He's more than just a man now. He's the king, and he can do whatever he likes. And it's your job to do whatever he likes." Hearing Phineas talk in that sharp manner reminded the doctor why he had never liked Phineas, but he remained quiet and let Phineas deliver his message. "You made an oath in order to join the Brothers and Sons, and you have enjoyed the privileges of membership. You pledged to give your life to serve Vulpine, King Vulpine. You have only two options here. Fulfill your pledge or lose your life."

Phineas thought the choice obvious, but the doctor didn't respond. He pulled back the curtain and walked over to the front window. Looking out over the square, he reassured himself he was making the right decision. He turned and looked Phineas in the eye. "I can't serve him any longer. I am a doctor, but in serving Vulpine I have used these hands to kill rather than to heal. That's not what I agreed to. I agreed to use my skills to serve Vulpine and, by extension, the village. You know we all thought things would be better if we controlled the village. But now things are worse, and we don't control anything. Vulpine just wants to control us. I'm taking myself out of his hands."

"That's not so easy," Phineas retorted.

The doctor looked out the window and watched the villagers passing by. They were ignorant of the decision he had just made. He wondered how many of them had thought through the consequences of taking Vulpine's permanent mark. He smiled faintly at the innocent children chasing each other, bobbing in and out of the crowds.

Suddenly, a man started kicking the door. He was carrying a small boy in his arms. Blood rushed from an open wound in the boy's head. Phineas was the first to the door and used the key to open it. He talked to the man then slammed the door shut and locked it again.

"What are you doing?" The doctor asked Phineas as he approached the door to open it. Phineas blocked his path and held fast to the key.

"What? That man? He isn't marked. He's not loyal to the king and so does not deserve to see the doctor." Phineas' cold-blooded comment sounded every bit as if Vulpine had said it himself.

"I can't do this. I won't serve Vulpine any longer."

Phineas saw that the doctor had made up his mind and shrugged his shoulders.

"What is to happen to me? What has Vulpine said?"

Phineas whistled in response. "I'm not sure he's decided. Neither of us expected you'd actually refuse the mark."

The doctor looked closely at Phineas. "Where is your tattoo?" The doctor's eyes grew cold.

"No one questions my loyalty to the king." Phineas returned the hard look.

"Do you have any loyalty to yourself?" Phineas made no response except to turn the key in the lock and let himself out.

The doctor looked out the open door and noticed Gabe and John walking through the square, carrying baskets of food on their way to the prison. Seeing Gabe with the food basket sent a picture flashing into the doctor's mind of the kind boy who had brought soup during his lowest moment. As if by impulse, he dashed over to them. The sight of the gray-haired man chasing the boys across the square gave many a reason to chuckle, but when he stopped running and the amusement faded, they turned their attention back onto themselves without wondering further what had been the reason for his rush.

Gabe was surprised by the doctor's approach, but he greeted him respectfully. Then, right there by the well in the center of the square, the doctor shared his heart with the boys. "Gabe, right?" Gabe only nodded. "I didn't remember right away when you brought me that soup, but it came to me later who you were. You're not marked, are you?" Gabe shook his head.

"Good. Good. You are a smart boy. I haven't been marked either. I…I don't want to serve Vulpine anymore. I followed him too far, until it cost others their lives. Now, in recompense, I am going to give up my life."

Gabe and John had no idea what the doctor was saying to them, and they especially didn't know why the doctor was saying it to them. They weren't sure the doctor knew why either. They just listened in silence until they saw the desperation in his eyes. Gabe looked deep into the man through those portholes and saw the frantic searching of his heart. Gabe remembered the desperation he had felt before he had met the King.

Gabe reached out and took hold of the doctor's arm and said, "The King says whoever seeks him finds him."

The doctor blinked questioningly and studied the boy's face. The peace he saw there was what he longed for, what he had lacked since signing over his life to Vulpine for a few perks and a feeling of power. "The King? You know the King is alive?" The doctor smiled. "Of course you do. You are the boy from the inn, and the inn had those meetings about the King until Vulpine shut them down."

Gabe was startled that the doctor knew so much.

"You are right," the doctor continued. "The King is alive. I know he is. I know the King's death was faked. I know…I know too many things. Do you still have meetings somewhere?"

Gabe looked at John, who offered an invitation to come to his house for the meeting that night. The doctor looked relieved. They offered to take him to John's house with them after they returned from the prison. The doctor took them up on the offer but made a further request.

"I don't want to wait here." The doctor glanced around nervously. "Could I walk with you? I could wait for you out by the lake."

"Of course you can join us, Doctor. You can stay with us the rest of the afternoon and evening." Gabe's friendly reply comforted the doctor.

As they were walking, the doctor asked one last favor. "Please, just call me Robert. I'm not the village doctor anymore."

Lesson 173

1. Read chapter 22 of the *The King Will Make a Way.*
2. What proved to Robert that everything Gabe had told him was true? (Answers)
3. Why were they able to forgive Robert? (Answers)

Robert was obviously nervous, watching over his shoulder and hunching into his cloak. Gabe tried to point out the sun reflecting off the water which shone in the waning afternoon sun, but Robert didn't seem to hear or notice. Gabe whispered to John, asking him to take the food in alone. John nodded and left Gabe and Robert by the lake.

The day was sunny and without wind, though winter's chill still found its way under their skin as they sat watching the light on the still lake. It was too cold for the children to play by its shores now, and the men, young and old, were alone.

Gabe knew the King could relieve Robert of whatever heavy burden he was obviously carrying, so Gabe broke the silence with talk of the King. He talked on his favorite subject, the King's love. Gabe was watching the lake slowly change from silver to gold as he told about the King's ability to take away burdens and didn't even glance toward Robert until he heard him softly say no.

He was shaking his head. "No, you're wrong. There is no love for me. I worked for Hate and Selfishness himself. There is no love for me. I deserve to die, and I will die. No, I don't deserve love."

Gabe wished he knew what Robert was talking about. He was sure that the King could remove any burden, so he told Robert again of the King's great love.

Robert listened intently and wanted to believe him. "Tell me. Tell me everything from the beginning. Tell me everything about the King. I don't have much time. This is my last chance to know."

John walked up to the two and felt like he was interrupting something, even though the two sat for the moment in silence. Looking up at John, Gabe took a deep breath and said, "We should get going before the sun is down." He rose to his feet and helped Robert up. "It all started with a toad."

John laughed to himself, remembering Gabe giving him the same talk in the same place. Robert kept his head down as they walked and instead of acting distracted and agitated, he kept his attention on Gabe's words.

Gabe continued talking with Robert when they reached John's house. The time slipped by and soon Angela had joined them for the evening meeting. John took a seat next to her at the table. Other servants arrived, and Gabe introduced Robert to everyone, though he couldn't bring himself to use his name. He was warmly welcomed by all the servants until Caleb entered and froze at the table's edge.

Gabe stood uneasily when he noticed Caleb's grim expression. "Caleb, why are you here? Is everything okay?"

Gabe was wondering why Caleb had left the meeting in his home to come and stare at Robert.

Caleb broke his stare and answered Gabe. "Okay? Thanks to the King everything is okay. But thanks to him," Caleb said and pointed at Robert, who had no idea who this man was, "my youngest son could have died today. Why are you here? Do you even know who I am?" Caleb wasn't yelling, but the usual lightness in his voice had faded to black.

Robert's confusion lifted, and he asked, "Are you the man Phineas refused entrance?" The servants looked at each other with raised eyebrows, asking each other if they knew what had happened. They shrugged their shoulders and shook their heads and waited to see how the drama would unfold.

"That was me. Weren't you there?"

"I was there. I'm sorry he locked you out. I wanted to help. I…I'm sorry. I was too consumed in my troubles to fight Phineas for your sake. Your son's okay?"

Caleb released his frustration and let the King remove its weight. He hung his head.

"I'm sorry too. I am glad to see you here. Are you really here to seek the King?"

Robert's heart leapt with joy. "I am. And I can't believe you are welcoming me here. Then it's really true. Everything Gabe told me about the King is true if you can stand there and forgive me just like that. The boy. Your boy. Tell me what happened."

The servants' hearts rejoiced as they watched Robert welcomed into their number and as they heard Caleb's remarkable tale.

"He's our youngest. He was playing in the barn and fell and cut his head open on a plowshare. He screamed, and I came running to find him bleeding badly from the head. I could see the deep opening in his forehead. I scooped him up and started running. My wife is in prison this week along with my eldest son, but I called out to my other children that I was going to the doctor and would be back. I didn't stop to tell them. I just hollered over my shoulder as I was running past the house.

"My boy stopped screaming, but he looked so scared that it scared me. I got to the doctor's, and it was locked. I just started crazy-like kicking at the door. It opens and who comes out but Phineas. I was startled by that and stepped back instead of trying to just push my way in the open door. He asked me if I was loyal to Vulpine and asked to see my mark. When I had to tell him I didn't have a mark, he said nothing, just slipped back in the door and locked it.

"I was stunned. I was really stunned. I didn't know what to do. My arms were so heavy from carrying my boy, but he looked asleep at that point. So I just headed home, the whole time saying, 'The King will make a way,' over and over to myself. Halfway back, I noticed his head wasn't bleeding anymore. When I got home, he still looked asleep. I got a wet rag and wiped away the blood on his forehead. It startled him awake, but I was even more surprised because the wound was gone. There wasn't any cut. There wasn't anything on his forehead."

Everyone was in awe.

"I don't know how, but I know the King did it. He made the way for my son to heal when the doctor didn't." Caleb looked at Robert when he spoke but showed no signs of being upset. "And why did he turn me away for not having Vulpine's mark? Is that a new law?"

Robert was the best qualified to answer. "It's not law yet, but it will be. Right now, certain people have been told to discriminate against those without the mark in order to encourage more people to take it."

"Why do they want people to have the mark? Why is it important?" Caleb asked Robert, who everyone had now realized had a lot more knowledge about what Vulpine was doing than the rest of them.

Robert sighed. "Eventually, everyone will be marked, either by showing their allegiance by wearing the 'V' tattoo, or by showing their disloyalty by not. Then Vulpine can move to rid the village of all traitors."

John saw Angela's face crease with concern. He reached over and laid his hand on top of hers to reassure her. She held her breath until he took his hand away. She let her eyes wander to look at him. His gentle, kind eyes smoothed the lines on her face, but she quickly put her focus back on Robert. John was still looking at Angela when Robert added, "And I will be the first to go."

John turned sharply at the comment to look at Robert. "Why?"

Robert looked weary, his eyes still showing the burden he was carrying. "Let's eat. Maybe later I can answer your question."

Everyone agreed, and Caleb finally returned to his home where other servants were gathered for a meeting.

Robert didn't have much appetite and several around the table noticed he had barely touched his food. No one pushed him to have more. They could all see he was troubled.

After the meal, Gabe spoke, as always, about the King's love for the villagers and shared about the King's law of forgiveness. "No matter how many times your friend has to come to you to say he's sorry, you are to forgive him. Think of all the King has forgiven us. We deserve to die according to his law because we all spent years not obeying any of it, but he pardoned each of us when we began following him. He is so merciful and understanding of our failings. As long as we are still seeking him and desiring to live by his law, he will help us to know his law and will help us follow it. If he can do all that for us, we can forgive each other for any wrong."

Robert's heart burned within him at Gabe's words. He had believed him about the King's love, and now forgiveness? Yes, he decided he could believe the King would forgive him, especially as he was prepared to give his life instead of following Vulpine. But he wondered if these people could forgive him? It would be the ultimate test of the truth of their words.

When Gabe finished, he looked at Robert and raised his eyebrows. Robert nodded and stood before the group. "Can you forgive? That's the question I want to ask you. I was asked why I believed I was going to be the first from among you to be killed for not taking the mark. Phineas was in my office today giving me an ultimatum, take the mark or die. He could do that because I am part of a group of villagers who had pledged themselves to serve Vulpine. We have met for years to scheme to place him on the throne. And at his bidding, I have participated in much evil." The shock of the confession sent whispers around the room.

"I couldn't bear his ways any longer and refused the mark. I know Vulpine will see to it that I don't live out the week, if not the day. I know the man well."

Gabe looked around the room trying to catch everyone's eyes and finally spoke for the group. "We forgive you for your part in helping Vulpine. We are so happy you have realized your error and have come to learn about the King. He teaches us to love our enemies, so we welcome you here, though we don't consider you an enemy now."

Gabe had hoped to see light come into the haunted eyes, but they remained darkened. Robert shook his head. "You don't understand what I've done. You don't know or you wouldn't be so quick to forgive, and you could never forget."

Gabe looked at the other servants, all equally unaware of what the doctor was hiding. He sat down and waited for Robert to speak.

"The virus." Robert spoke the words looking straight at Gabe. Again, confused looks shot around the room. The servants shook their heads, not understanding. "The virus that killed close to two hundred people last winter. I created it."

The servants still weren't understanding and looked intently at Robert to uncover his meaning. He continued to speak, now with his head down, surprising everyone by his display of weakness.

"Vulpine wanted to create fear in the village so that the villagers would want a leader, a king that they could look to for protection. He asked me if I could create a virus that would spread through the village and kill many in order to create the fear he needed to become king. I had pledged to serve him and unthinkingly unleashed the destroyer on all of you last winter."

In the silence that followed, realization began to dawn among the servants. It was hard for any of them to fathom his story to be true, yet there was no reason to doubt him. Gabe quickly looked around the room. Was anyone angry? Was anyone ready to strike out at Robert?

John's father was the first to speak. "This is my home you've been welcomed into." His voice was calm, betraying no emotion. "Last winter, I lost a son to that virus. He died in this very home. But I still welcome you."

Tears sprang into Robert's eyes as he looked up, disbelieving the grace just offered him.

John saw the good doctor's brokenness and wanted to help in mending it. "I lost a brother to the virus, and I welcome you here with us."

John's mother, Emily, spoke quietly. "I lost a son, and I welcome you."

An elderly man spoke. "I lost my wife, and I welcome you."

A young lady spoke. "I lost a friend, and I welcome you."

Each servant took a turn, helping to restore the fragile figure before them. When everyone had spoken, Gabe took the last turn. "You've been forgiven, Robert." Gabe had called him by name. Robert looked Gabe in the eyes, and Gabe saw that light had replaced the darkness and peace had replaced the burden. He had found what he had been searching for.

Lesson 174

1. Read chapter 23 of the *The King Will Make a Way.*
2. What does Robert find so funny? (Answers)
3. Why could Robert say he was free when he was held bound by a guard? (Answers)

Gabe and Robert sat alone in the long empty dining hall at the inn. Only one candle burned but gave them enough light to talk together late into the night. Robert mostly kept quiet. He wanted only to listen to the boy with the wisdom and understanding of the King and the humility to know he had no wisdom and understanding of his own.

Gabe obliged and continued sharing about the King. "I don't know if you'll believe me, but you weren't in control of that virus." Robert looked puzzled. "You weren't, and Vulpine wasn't either. The plague was a punishment for the village sent by the King."

Robert's surprised and confused look made Gabe grin. "I don't know how to explain it to you other than the fact that the King is always in control. He somehow always knows what's happening and is in control of the village and what happens to it. It's mind-boggling. I know I don't understand it except to know that it's true. He's proven it true to me thousands of times.

"You thought you were planning in secret and using it all to your own ends, but the King knew about it all and was using it all to his ends. No matter what it looked like."

Robert suddenly burst out laughing. He had to hold his belly he laughed so hard. Tears filled his eyes and he gasped for air. Gabe couldn't help but laugh too at the sight of the sad, worn doctor rolling with laughter. Robert took deep breaths to calm himself, still letting bursts of laughter escape at times.

"Tell me what's so funny. I was laughing at you. You looked pretty hilarious, laughing like a little kid being tickled. What were you laughing at?"

"Vulpine." Robert said with a chuckle.

"I've never found him funny," Gabe said, shaking his head.

"Vulpine thinks he's so smart. He thinks he's five steps ahead of everyone else. And all this time, he's just a part of the King's bigger plan." This time Gabe laughed with Robert, instead of at him.

"It's late, Robert. Stay the night at the inn. We'll see what tomorrow brings. The King always makes a way."

"Thanks for the offer. I would like to stay here with you. And don't worry about me. I know Vulpine won't rest until he's got me, but I'm not scared. Even when he gets his hands on me, I'll know I'm free."

Gabe looked into Robert's eyes; they were bright and clear.

The morning passed peacefully at the inn. Robert looked relaxed. He was sitting in the dining hall with his feet propped up, reading the King's law when the copper bell tolled. He dropped the papers onto the table. Gabe came running into the room.

"Do you know what it's about?" Gabe asked Robert directly.

Robert nodded, stood and used his hands to iron out the wrinkles in his clothes. He calmly put on his cloak and hat and opened the door before he replied. "They're calling me to the Square. I won't keep them waiting." With a nod, he exited the inn.

Gabe ran to fetch Angela. John was waiting for them by the time they left the inn.

“Do you know what’s going on?” John looked at Angela, but Gabe answered.

“Robert seemed pretty sure it’s about him.”

“He still thinks they’re going to kill him?” Angela’s stomach knotted at the question.

“He hasn’t really said much of anything,” Gabe explained. “But, he’s really changed from yesterday. He was so distraught. Since last night he’s really been at peace, even laughed a long time last night.”

“Laughed? At what?” Angela wanted to know the joke. “Vulpine.” Gabe started chuckling again, thinking about it. “I’ll explain later.”

The three teens walked in silence even though the hum of curious villagers surrounded them on all sides. By the time they reached the Square, Robert had already been arrested. He was standing on the Assembly Hall porch with a guard on one side of him and Phineas, greeting the villagers, on the other.

Gabe elbowed his way through the crowd until he was right in front of Robert. Their eyes met, and Robert smiled sincerely. Gabe wouldn’t allow himself to be distracted. He wanted to keep his eyes always on Robert so if he needed encouragement, he could find it in Gabe’s countenance.

Fellow servants of the King arrived and huddled together in front of the good doctor. Many of them clasped hands, hoping for the best but dreading the worst. The bell finished its welcome, and Phineas spoke.

“Thank you for coming. I know it’s a cold day, but we waited for the sun to be its warmest before calling you out.” Robert rolled his eyes at Phineas’ description of himself as considerate of others. “We were sure that you would want to see justice carried out. King Vulpine, with his vast insight, has uncovered a terrible crime. Never has a crime such as this been committed in our village. It is hard to even speak of. A year ago, a terrible plague descended on our village. Likely more than two hundred people were killed: your fathers, mothers, husbands, wives, your sons and daughters, killed by the devastating virus. It took King Vulpine to lift us up out of our despair.”

Robert looked at Gabe. Gabe was relieved that though his face was solemn, his eyes were clear. Phineas gestured toward Robert, who stood straight but not proud. “This man was the cause of that plague. I know it is hard to understand, but it has been proven true. He deliberately made the men training for King Vulpine’s guard sick with that virus. It’s his fault entirely that your loved ones are dead.”

“Give him to us,” an angry voice in the crowd shouted up to Phineas. “We’ll see that justice is served.” The villagers around the man started shouting their agreement and moved toward the platform. Shoving and shouting, their anger festered and the crowd throbbed with violence.

“Justice will be done!” Phineas didn’t think more than a few heard him. Phineas gave the guard his orders to take Robert through the square to the platform at the far end and to lock him into one of the wooden frames. The guard hesitated on the first step of the Assembly Hall, seeing the seething crowd. Phineas assured him that they would be more than pleased to let him pass to get his prisoner to his punishment. With a tug at Robert's arm, they started across the Square. They never even made it to the well.

At first, the servants of the King were there to encourage Robert with a word, a pat on the back. Robert had to shout to make himself heard, even to those next to him. "Don't worry about me. I know I'm free!" Gabe felt relief at his words. As Robert stepped out of their reach, Gabe quickly motioned to the other servants to move up and onto the Assembly Hall porch. They all sensed the danger and followed him up the steps.

The crowd pulsated with their hate. The guard shouted at them to give way and resorted to pushing aside those blocking his path. Then someone pushed back. The guard knocked into Robert, causing him to lose his balance. The crowd plunged forward, trying to get at the prisoner, but not even the guard could see him now.

Butting and ramming, the villagers were goats fighting over the single grain dropped in the farm yard. Shouts, grunts and cries emitted from those in the middle of the mass being squeezed in from all sides.

The guard pushed his way out and ran along the edge of the square back to Phineas. "He's gone. My guess is he's trampled under that mob out there." Phineas didn't respond to the report, never even acknowledging the guard. He just looked straight ahead with a satisfied smirk on his face.

"Please Gabe, let's go," Angela begged her brother. He put his arm around her, and they jumped down from the side of the porch, away from the angry mob. The other servants followed. Gabe turned to Caleb and asked him to stay so they would know what had happened. Caleb nodded and remained.

It was a long time before Phineas sensed the crowd had expended its venom and called out for the villagers to quiet, waving his short arms above his head.

"Please, everyone, step back. Please move toward the edges of the square. Let us see what has become of our guilty prisoner." He asked repeatedly until eventually the center of the square lay bare, save for the trampled body of Robert.

Lesson 175

1. Read chapter 24 of the *The King Will Make a Way.*
2. What was Father's conviction and how was it tested? (Answers)
3. What is Father's current fate? (Answers)
4. What is Angela pondering? (Answers)

Spring thawed the patches of snow remaining around the village but not the hate that had begun to permeate the hearts of everyone who bore Vulpine's "V"—hate directed at everyone who didn't.

Marked villagers began refusing to sell anything to the servants, the bare backs of their hands showing their disloyalty to Vulpine. Many of the servants were farmers and were thankful they still could provide food for their families and the other servants, but they were no longer allowed to sell their produce in the market.

The servants who had once bought and sold now gave and received. They borrowed from each other freely and offered to each other everything they could spare and some things they couldn't.

When there was a need that couldn't be met among them, there were still plenty of Vulpine loyalists who were willing to make an unfair trade for the item, and one of the servants would find something of value to sacrifice in order to help out their family, as that's what the servants considered each other.

Too many, like Gabe, had flesh and blood family members that mocked or scolded them for their disloyalty to Vulpine. Others, like Caleb, had the joy of living in a home where everyone served the King together.

Although the servants were quick to help and were learning to put each other first, they were still sure the King was helping in many ways as well. One older man with wispy white hair whose cheeks folded over themselves when he smiled loved to tell the others of the time the King had brought his wife dinner. He had been in prison and his wife had been left home alone. One day, she had run out of food but decided to sit down at the table at mealtime just the same. When she went to sit down, she heard a knock at the door. She opened it to find a roast chicken, as plump and savory as she had ever tasted, just sitting there on a platter in front of the door with not a soul in sight. Whenever he told the story, he ended it with a belly laugh and a slap on the thigh.

Some abandoned the meetings for fear of reprisal—they were being bullied, or worse, bloodied. Those servants who remained, grew daily in their understanding of the King's watchful eye and ever caring heart towards them. They also grew in their understanding of the King's law and followed it more closely than ever, always encouraging each other with their stories of failure and restoration as the King had made a way for them.

Gabe's father was always ready to share his story of how he had tried to fight back for the King and had almost lost his life. He never hesitated to share the lesson he learned and to embolden others not to take revenge.

Father had his new conviction tested one day walking home at sunset when it still was cold enough to see your breath. A few teenage boys were skulking behind a stone wall, lying in wait for one of the servants to pass. Father was the unfortunate one to walk past first. A rock pelted him behind his left ear and laughter erupted from behind the stones. Father paused momentarily, putting his hand on the wound. There was blood on his hand when he pulled it away. He kept walking without trying to see who had done it. The boys wanted to get a reaction out of him and weren't going to stop until they had had their thrill. More stones pegged their target, but Father just walked steadily on, not allowing the urge to retaliate to come over him. He had learned his lesson well.

Slowly, it seemed everyone was turning against the servants. The door guard at the jail, when faced with losing his job, took Vulpine's mark. He told Gabe that he was no longer allowed to visit the prisoners, which included Father that week. He also told Gabe and John that the prisoners would not be released until they received Vulpine's mark. Gabe told the other servants the news during the meetings that evening. He played the messenger going from house to house, bringing one more piece of bad news to the weary servants.

John's house was his last destination. He came upon Mrs. Bollix's brother-in-law on his way to the meeting. They walked together until Gabe noticed a "V" blazoned on the back of his right hand. Gabe froze like a deer listening for danger in the woods.

"You have Vulpine's mark," he blurted out, not taking his eyes off the tattoo.

"I had to take it. How was I supposed to carry on with my business if no one would buy from me or sell to me?" the man answered in a defensive tone.

Gabe peeled his eyes off his hand and was speechless at first. He shook his head and said, "The King would have made a way. You can't join us tonight at the meeting."

The man was offended. "This mark doesn't mean I don't serve the King."

Gabe spoke with a firm voice and sorrowful eyes. "Yes, it does. It means you serve Vulpine. You have chosen to serve the wrong king. Only servants of the true King can come to the meetings and gather around the table."

"Who are you to say?" The angry response came, but he didn't try and follow Gabe. He turned around in a huff and walked away.

Gabe let out a deep breath and slipped quietly in the door when he arrived at John's house. He sat down with the others and listened in as they talked about the new developments at the jail. Gabe was thankful John had already delivered the news. He knew the changes at the prison would be a devastating blow to the morale of the servants, and he would much rather bring encouragement.

"How many of you had only the visits and the reading of the King's law to look forward to each day in prison?" asked a teenage boy. "Now they're gone. What will keep them from going crazy in that black pit?"

"They have each other," Emily responded. "They'll encourage each other. Do we know who's in there this week?"

"My wife is in there," said a young man at the table. "When she was arrested, I wasn't even that upset. It wasn't the first time, and we had always been able to count on Saturday releases, even if Sunday they just arrested more. Now, I don't know if I'll ever see my wife again."

Gabe was empathetic. "My father is in prison now too." Then Gabe added his familiar encouragement, "The King will make a way." John's father spoke to the group at his home that night. He read a portion of the King's law: "The King is a refuge and a shield to those who trust him. He will save them from harm, and they will not fear the terrors of night, the arrow by day, nor pestilence or plague. He will send his punishment on the village, but he will protect those who love him."

John's father laid down his copy of the law and looked at each face before him.

"Do you love the King? He tells us that we love him by obeying the commands he gave us. If you are obeying the commands you know, then you can know you are protected. Do you trust the

King? Then you won't let fear into your hearts. It doesn't matter what happens. Vulpine could order us all arrested, or killed. Vulpine could order another sickness from the new doctor. It doesn't matter. Above it all, the King is in control and can save us from harm as the law says.

"I remember John telling me how Gabe first tried to explain these things to him. They had just been to visit the prison. It had been John's first experience of the dark and the smell and the feeling of finality when the door locked shut. Afterwards, Gabe taught John about how the King makes a way for his servants. He said that didn't mean never being arrested. He pointed out how he had seen joy on the faces of the prisoners. The King had made a way for them to be okay. We may want to see it as harm to be arrested, or whatever else we'll have to face, but knowing that the King gives us peace and joy takes the sting out of whatever they can try to do to us.

"Remember that the true harm is what those with Vulpine's mark face every day. Don't you see it? How their hearts are turning to stone? It's like their hearts and minds have been poisoned. That's true harm, and I am thankful I have been saved from it."

Angela smiled at his calm reassurance. John's heart grew full to see her at peace like that. The spring months had gone by in a blur of early mornings and late nights for Angela. As Tabitha grew more proficient at the work around the inn, Angela was able to spend more time helping Gabe and the other servants. She worked from dawn to dusk and in the evenings joined the other servants to gain strength for the next day.

The only break in the routine came at the beginning of summer on a warm June day when Sally Bollix married. Angela, at fifteen, was just a year younger than Sally. Angela didn't join in the festive spirit of the celebration. Feeling pensive, she kept to herself. Standing alone and watching the ceremony with its music and dancing, flowers and laughter, she thought of John. She had heard his mother make a comment or two about Angela turning sixteen in the coming winter. She was thinking Angela and John would marry. Angela watched Sally's groom take her away and pondered what she would have to give up if she had a groom come and take her away.

The days flashed by seemingly without beginning or end. No more arrests were made. Vulpine just left the pressure on those remaining in the prison to take the mark or rot in the dank jail. The rest of the servants had the heavy burden of living in a place where each day, someone new turned against them.

Over the winter, Gabe and Angela celebrated their sixteenth birthdays together. In the spring, John spent a week helping Mother with repairs around the inn since Father was still in prison indefinitely. Mother told Angela that John was "a fine man." Angela couldn't keep her face from flushing at the mention of his name. Yet from time to time, Angela would look at him and ponder the same question, *What would I have to give up if I let him take me away?*

Lesson 176

1. Read chapter 25 of the *The King Will Make a Way.*
2. Who returned to the meetings? (Answers)
3. What did Angela help John realize? (Answers)

Gabe lay on the floor exhausted. It was too hot to move anyway. Angela was prone on her bed, blubbering, her pillow soggy with tears.

"I didn't think it would be so hard to say no, Gabe. I was so sure. But the look on his face…I don't think he'll ever want to see me again." She wiped her scarlet nose.

"John will understand." Gabe tried in vain to console her. "Just give him time. He just hadn't realized your commitment to the King. He's committed too. He'll understand."

That morning John had told Angela that he loved her and asked her to marry him. Now he was pacing along a row of corn behind their family's home, wondering where he had missed the mark. So many nights he had sat awake in the dark prison, thinking about that moment and Angela's joyful response. He had had lots of time to think about it; he had been in prison often. It seemed only Angela and Gabe managed to avoid it. But he had been lying to himself. All of his daydreams were just that – dreams. He ripped off part of a stalk.

Gabe felt helpless. Whenever someone was in trouble, he would say, "The King will make a way." He believed it fully, and he used the line often. Now it didn't seem like those words could mend these two broken hearts, two hearts he dearly loved.

Angela sniffled. "Gabe, could you talk to him? Check on him for me. See if he's okay. Explain to him again for me."

Gabe didn't answer right away. He was thinking he'd rather visit Vulpine than go on this mission. *I'd rather jump in the lake in winter. I'd rather live out on the roof for a week. I'd rather eat a slug.* Gabe let out a little laugh before he caught himself and pretended his throat needed clearing. "I'll go tonight when it's cooler outside," Gabe answered. *And when John is cooler.*

That evening Angela went to the meeting at Caleb's house. Gabe went alone to John's. He purposely showed up late so he wouldn't have to talk to John, not yet at least. John's father spoke to the group. He lived the King's words, and they flowed out of him with little effort.

When he finished his message, Winnie stood up. In his preoccupation with John and Angela, Gabe hadn't noticed her. She looked each person in the eye. "I need to say I'm sorry to everyone. I used to come and talk foolishly with you all. I talked too much and told too much and cared too much about what everyone was doing. Basically, I was a gossip. I haven't been to meetings for a long while, but I have been reading the King's law. He has hard words for people like me. Well, hopefully, people like I was. I think I have learned my lesson." With a smile, she added, "And I'd like to thank Gabe for kicking me out of your meetings and sending me home until I learned it."

The group seemed as if they were waiting for Gabe to make a response. He was bowled over by her openness and her courage to keep seeking the King on her own, and he stood up and told her so. "And welcome home. You're part of our family again."

Everyone was on their feet. The women hugged her and kissed her cheeks. It was a thrill for everyone to see this happy ending after having seen others leave the meetings never to return.

After the meeting, Gabe lingered as the others left. John knew he was there to talk to him and eventually made it easy. "Do you want to come see the corn?"

Gabe saw through the offer and acted eager to see the crop's progress. The two walked out past the barn and hopped over the fence rail into the field with only the sound of the crickets accompanying them. John halted on the other side of the fence and leaned against it. He reached down, plucked a tall piece of grass and started ripping it into little pieces.

"It's been a bad day," John started. Gabe had been hoping John would do all the talking. "I've been driving myself crazy thinking about the past year, more than a year, every moment I've ever spent with her. I know it was all the King's work she was doing. I know she wasn't doing it to be with me but maybe some of the time, I was doing it to be with her." He stopped fidgeting and looked at Gabe. "That's what I've realized today, going over everything over and over in my head. I realized that I wasn't only serving the King. I was also serving myself by wanting to be with your sister." He rubbed his forehead.

Gabe realized John wasn't going to say anything else, and he was going to have to think of something to say. He scanned the night sky and took in the stars. Something came to him. "Well, I guess the question is now, do you want to serve the King even if it means never being with Angela?" Gabe bit his lip.

John didn't turn to look at Gabe; he set his gaze over the horizon and spoke into the hazy night sky. "King, I've never met you, but I know you are out there. Gabe says that somehow you know everything, so know this: I choose to serve you until I die, whether tomorrow or a hundred years from now. I love Angela and will always love her as another one of your servants, but I give her up to serve you. In fact, I want to be like her and give up my own life to serve you all the way."

He understands. The King did make a way.

"I want to go tell Angela I understand her decision. Let's go to the inn."

The night was warm but a relief from the baking sun. Angela was looking out the window when she saw them in the distance. She pulled on a shawl to cover her bare arms and leaned out the window, resting her elbows on the window sill. Her eyes met John's as he approached, and she knew from their warmth everything was okay. "I'll be right down," she called to him and withdrew from the window. She walked down the stairs one at a time, taking a breath with each step. She wanted to look calm when she walked out the door. She had been anything but calm all day.

John thought the first frost would nip before Angela managed to get outside. He hung his head and decided she must have changed her mind and didn't want to see him.

"Gabe, I'm going to—"

"Hi, John." Angela cut off his exit.

"Angela." At first, that was all he could say. Looking at her with the full moon reflected in her eyes, he almost forgot, just for a moment, his confession to the King.

Gabe came to the rescue. "John really understands, Angela. He wants to tell you."

John snapped to from Angela's mesmerizing eyes. "Yes, I do. I understand why you said no. And I've told the King." He stopped and smiled. Angela smiled back but raised her eyebrows. This time he avoided being drawn in by her shining eyes. "I did. I told the King that I wanted to be like you and commit myself completely to his service."

Angela held onto Gabe's arm, trying to draw on his strength by osmosis. It would take strength not to think about her past with John or the 'what ifs' of the future. "That's really wonderful, John." She looked at Gabe while she spoke.

She could feel the calm slipping away.

She looked up at John and smiled. His heart skipped a beat when he saw her tear-filled eyes. Now it was his turn to feel weak.

Angela pressed the corners of her eyes with her finger to stop the tears from spilling. She looked away and said, "Mrs. Bollix brought over some food for us to deliver to Widow Jenkins tomorrow. I think I'll go get it packed up so it's ready." She braved one more glance at John and whispered, "Goodnight, John."

Angela hurried inside and John swallowed hard, unable to speak. He slowly walked home and made one last trip to the corn field. He sighed heavily and spoke to the corn. "If this was supposed to be one of the best days of my life, what's tomorrow going to be like?"

Lesson 177

1. Read chapter 26 of the *The King Will Make a Way.*
2. What happened to Father? (Answers)
3. What does Phineas request of the villagers? (Answers)
4. What was set up in the Square? (Answers)

"We're not deterring them. Their numbers remain steady. Maybe we've encouraged some to defect, but it's not enough!" Vulpine railed at Phineas and Writ, who stood at attention before the throne. "Have you seen these?" He grabbed a page of the King's law and crumpled it in his hand. His eyes were fixed on the paper and flared red hot. He contorted his face like the thing was putrid and dropped it like it was diseased.

"We've tried to control them through their money." He spoke calmly now, his eyes fixed. "We've tried imprisonment, even death. Those bishops," he snarled, "are loyal to the wrong king, and I won't stand for it."

He blinked and the life came back to his eyes. He scanned the men before him and steadied his focus on General Writ. "Send your men in as spies. You saved some loyal guards to remain without the mark, right?" The General gave a crisp nod.

"Have them find the meetings under the pretense of wanting to be a follower of that ancient man. They are to watch the meetings carefully and arrest the leaders. They are to be taken to the Square.

We'll have ourselves a bonfire." Vulpine turned his attention to Phineas and nodded, setting him to action as if he had wound up his mechanical doll.

The servants were in action too. In the morning, John made his way to the inn to meet Gabe and Angela. Together they traversed the length of the village to Widow Jenkins' house. Angela worked on cleaning the house while John made some repairs. Gabe sat by her side and read to her from the King's law.

"Thank you," she said to the three before they left. "I know my old body won't last much longer, but I am thankful I lived long enough to hear those words and experience your kindness. Thank you." Angela gave her a warm embrace before they left. She felt satisfied and wished the good feeling would remain.

Before heading home, they stopped by the lake to cool off. Splashing the water and laughing, the teens felt as free as children again. It was in this brightened moment that John had the impulse to try again to visit the prisoners. The jail was in sight but a distance away. Gabe and Angela agreed, with a flicker of hope that they might get the chance to see Father after a year and a half.

They chased each other along the bank of the lake and stumbled into each other as they reached the prison door. The guard who had at one time wanted to hear the King's song was standing in front of the door.

Angela decided to ask the question. "Sir, do you think you could allow us, just this once, to visit with the prisoners?"

The guard looked forward and unblinkingly responded, "There are no prisoners."

"My father's in there," Angela countered.

"There are no prisoners," the unflinching guard repeated. Gabe tried. "Our father was arrested two winters ago. We know he hasn't been released. There were at least a dozen others with him." The guard didn't answer.

Angela started to softly sing the King's song. Quickly the guard turned to her. "Be silent. Your father and fourteen other prisoners were executed for refusing Vulpine's mark. Their heads were chopped off and their bodies buried in a heap behind the prison. Now go from here quickly and don't return."

But they didn't move at all. Their feet had turned leaden and their minds lost their direction. Angela suddenly felt like maybe she was dreaming, but a sharp "Go" from the guard made her bolt like a frightened kitten, just wanting to run to the nearest place to hide. She found it at the well and sat propped up against it, with her arms wrapped tightly around her knees. She buried her tear-streaked face in her arms.

The boys chased after her and slid down the well wall along with her, and sat on the dirt, dry and dusty from the scorching summer sun. No one spoke, but their thoughts were racing, tripping over each other, piling up like in a race when the lead runner goes down. The doubts, the fears, the unknowns, the realities came at them with a feverish pace. They were helpless, unable to just dig in their heels and make it all stop before it ended in tragedy.

As if to confirm every dark suspicion of what was to come, across the square, they spotted a large metal cage, three times the size Caleb's had been. Two horses pulled the unsteady cart while four of Vulpine's guards walked alongside, balancing the cage. When they reached the platform, the guards took axes to it and to the wooden frames as well, reducing it all to kindling. With great strain, the guards placed the bottomless cage over the pile of wood, its metal bars striping the sky beyond them. Satisfied with their job, the guards left, leading the horses and cart behind them.

John, Gabe and Angela stared at the oversized cage, its bars a web built to hold its prey. They moved toward it haltingly, like in a nightmare when you want to run but somehow you can only move slowly.

"How many people do you think they expect to round up in there?" Angela wished she hadn't spoken.

"Let's not talk about it," Gabe replied with sadness in his voice. "Let's be about the King's business." His eyes grew steady and his posture more confident.

Not a minute had passed when the bell resounded. "Now what's going on?" Angela's stomach was starting to feel like Gabe's at Vulpine's unveiling.

They found a shady place to sit and waited for the rest of the villagers to gather. The sun was high, promising another sweltering day. The three teens sat together in silence. Gabe once opened his mouth but shut it again without uttering a sound. John dozed off, physically and emotionally exhausted. Phineas' raised voice woke him.

"My friends," Phineas opened his arms to the awaiting crowd, "we have called you out this morning for an important reason. We need your help again. Traitors to the crown have been on the prowl. There are rumors of another attempt on Vulpine's life." Some in the audience gasped. John quickly turned to Gabe and mouthed, "Have you heard anything?" Gabe shook his head and formed a rounded "No" with his lips.

"I know it is the utmost concern of all our good and upright citizens to maintain the peace and unity of our village. These rascals want to steal these treasures from us. We won't let them, will we?" Deep huts and huzzahs bellowed out from the pits of the men's bellies.

"Once again we ask your help. Anyone refusing to attend the singing ceremony is a rebel! Tell us where the rebels meet. Also, his royal majesty King Vulpine has forbidden the production and distribution of literature. These thieving scoundrels have been spreading lies about our wise and noble king with their papers. Please gather any of these papers you find and throw them in there." He pointed directly to the cage in the Square. "Tonight we'll have a bonfire to celebrate our victory over these inferior weaklings who dare to consider standing up to our powerful king."

The majority cheered as victors. The remainder, though scattered, spoke with one small voice in that moment. "The King will make a way."

John, Angela and Gabe set off at a hectic pace. They stopped to talk with all of the servants, encouraging them to remember the King. They went from house to house, talked across fence rails, walked arm in arm. Everyone they could get a hold of they did, and their message was always the same—the King will make a way. At the same time, other villagers were giving names and locations to Vulpine's guards, reporting on family members and neighbors. Mother was among them.

At the evening meeting, Gabe finally shared the news of the prisoners' execution. The servants rallied around the newly widowed and fatherless. There were tears and laughter. There was a new man in attendance that was discomforted by the sight of their love and joy in the midst of pain and loss.

He listened as different servants shared lessons they had learned from the lives of those who had remained loyal to the King to their death. Gabe was proud that his father's testimony of learning not to pay back evil with evil had had such an impact on others.

After the meeting, Gabe shook hands with the new man in attendance and welcomed him. He just shook Gabe's hand, gave a nod and left. Gabe asked John if he knew who he was and where he had come from. John didn't have a clue.

The man, Todd, shuffled down the dirt path. He had followed orders and found the meeting, but it wasn't anything like he expected. There was no plotting to overturn Vulpine. It sounded like they wouldn't swat a fly if it landed on their noses. He couldn't figure out who the leader had been. They all had spoken in turn.

On the road ahead, he saw his colleagues escorting bound prisoners down the road. No one was fighting. He broke into a jog and caught up with a guard leading John's father from Caleb's home.

"Need any help?" Todd was eager to look like he was accomplishing something.

"Help? Does it look like it? Where's your man?"

"I couldn't make out a leader."

The other guard laughed. "Did you forget our orders? Make an arrest. They want bodies. Don't show yourself to the General without one."

Like a cat pouncing, reality hit. He remembered the "do or die" way the order had been given. He had been sent to arrest the leader and had left without making an arrest. He became resolute that he couldn't lose his job, or his head, no matter how nice these people were. Running back to the house, he saw Gabe and Angela walking home but decided he'd have to get someone who lived at the meeting house in order to be confident that he had someone worthwhile.

Breaking into a sprint, he tore up the path and with full force banged in through the front door, not stopping until he had shoved John to the ground. With a heavy boot pinning John to the floor, he bound John's hands behind his back.

He hoisted John to his feet. "Are you taking me to the prison?" John asked stoically.

"No," Todd said coolly. "I'm taking you to the Square." He broke out in a nervous laugh, knowing John didn't comprehend what was about to happen. As he led his captive out the door, he told him, "You're going to the bonfire."

Lesson 178

1. Read chapter 27 of the *The King Will Make a Way*.
2. What did Vulpine do to try and stop the "bishops?" (Answers)
3. What was one woman's reaction to the bonfire? (Answers)
4. Author's Note: Each time I mention this woman, I mention her holding onto her son to help the reader know who she is.

"Father!" John shouted across the confusion. John was in the square with Todd firmly holding his left arm. His father's eyes searched until they found their target—his son. His heart stopped. He gasped and gave himself a shake to pull himself together. The guard thought he was trying to escape and struck his stomach. His breath left him. Again he gasped and this time, in stillness, garnered the fortitude to face his son.

Todd stopped in front of the cage, and John stood next to his father. "This thing is what I told you about earlier." John had to use his chin to point to the menacing cage that loomed behind them. "Do you know what's going on?" John watched one of the guards throw copies of the King's law into the cage.

His father hadn't answered and John kept talking. "So, that's what this bonfire is about? They're burning all our copies of the King's law. Don't they know we'll just make more? Why the big show?"

Todd moved to face John. "Listen, the bonfire is for you. They don't need bars to hold the papers, do they?"

John's face scrunched in a quizzical expression. He turned to his father who was looking straight at him with a deadly serious expression. Realization dawned. For the longest moment, they just stared at each other. They weren't blank stares, though. They were expressing to each other a lifetime's worth of 'I love you' and 'I'm proud of you.'

"Like father, like son, right?" John tried to laugh off the knowledge of his fate.

Gabe and Angela came running across the square. Another one of the servants had rushed to the inn to tell them what was happening. They headed straight for John.

Catching her breath, Angela started bombarding John with questions. "How did you end up here? What's going on? What are they going to do to you?"

"I was arrested after you left. Go home now, Angela. I'll be okay. The King will make a way."

Gabe learned from John's father what was going on at the bonfire that night, and he told Angela. Shocked, she looked up at John and saw in his eyes that he knew the truth too. "John—"

"Angela, no. It's okay. I told the King yesterday I was going to serve him until I died. I'm going to keep my promise. I'm at his service, and tomorrow you'll serve him just as today." John's voice was solid, and his eyes showed more concern for Angela than for himself.

Angela tried to speak as she held back her tears. John didn't need to hear it; he could see it in her eyes. She finally managed to whisper, "I love you." John took a step toward her but was jerked back by Todd.

Gabe put his arm around Angela and started to lead her away from the scene. With a final glance back at John, Angela was escorted part way across the square. Gabe found a friend to walk with her back to the inn and returned to the cage. He wanted to be there to ensure there would be an honest account of what took place. He spoke to each of the seven men, bound and lined up in front of the dark enclosure, praising them for their bravery, assuring them that their sacrifice was worth the cost and encouraging them to remember the King in their last moments.

One of guards shooed him away like a pesky puppy sniffing at his heels. Gabe retreated into the shadows of the shops. He wanted to run away and hide but determined to stand his ground.

Music began playing. *How can you celebrate such an event?* Gabe felt queasy. Phineas took his place beside the cage, and shouted out to the gathering, "Bring all the illegal papers you found to help us light the bonfire!"

A line formed, an ever-shifting centipede, a hundred legs taking little steps forward, bringing copies of the King's law. Everyone took part, children asking their parents if they could be the ones to throw the papers onto the pile. Phineas congratulated them on their successful efforts to end the illegal distribution.

The seven men started quoting the King's law out loud. Neither the guards, nor those tossing in the papers, recognized their words. With each phrase, peace filled their hearts and minds and strengthened their resolve to face the hour with dignity.

Then one woman heard their words and pointing accusingly, shouted to Phineas, "Those are the filthy words! They are saying what's on these papers!" Phineas turned to General Writ who issued the orders for the cage to be opened and the prisoners thrown in. Phineas couldn't risk word getting back to Vulpine that he had allowed the King's law to be taught at the bonfire!

Two guards leaned over and lifted the front wall of the cage. The hinges screamed with the movement. No one fought their escort as the guards shoved them into their final prison. With a screech, the door was released. It crashed closed, and the heavy bang reverberated back and forth across the square before being swallowed up by the night.

"Light the fire!" Writ's order sent shivers down Gabe's spine. He looked at his feet. A torch was thrown into the cage which easily sent the papers into a blaze. Some in the crowd were yelling, urging the flames on, when a soulful note sounded. Gabe knew instantly what was happening. John had begun to sing the King's song. At first, the others suffering the heat didn't join in the song, such was the power of those first notes.

Then John looked to his father; he joined in and the others followed. The seven men with deep, full voices sang of their love for the King and the King's love for them. A woman watching the inferno rage slipped the papers she held into her blouse, grateful Phineas had stopped her before she had abetted this crime. She felt the power of the words and wanted to know them for herself. She excused herself and hurried home, dragging her four-year-old by the wrist.

The men crumbled to the floor of the cage, hidden in the golden glow of the flames; their song was finished.

Gabe took a detour on his way back to the inn. Thinking of John, he jumped the fence lining his family's corn field. It was incomprehensible to think only yesterday he had stood here speaking with John. Following John's example, uninhibited, he spoke to the King.

"Where were you tonight? Where are you ever? Where have you gone?" All the long days, the beatings, the deaths, the imprisonments, the closures, the secrecy, the bonfire; any of it and all of it finally overwhelmed him in that moment of questioning. He roared into the night sky and tears raced each other from both corners of his eyes. They slipped and sledded down his cheeks, streaking his face and dripping steadily off his chin. He ignored it all; his focus was on the King.

"You promised to come back to us down here one day. I know you are coming. Why not now? Why not tonight? What are you doing? Why are you letting all this happen? I want to talk with you! I love your words, your law, but I love you too, and I want to see you again! I want to be at your feet!"

His gut was twisted in knots. He flopped down in the grass and rolled onto his back, spent. He gazed into the starry night sky and started to doze off. He startled himself awake with a jerk of his limbs. Calmed, he struck up his conversation again.

"I'm sorry, King. I know I will see you again. You made the way for me to see you in the first place. You will make a way again. And you made a way tonight for those men. They weren't afraid. Somehow you kept them at peace. They didn't cry out in pain. They sang your song. You made a way. You always make a way."

Lesson 179

1. Read chapter 28 and 29 of the *The King Will Make a Way.*
2. Why is Vulpine excited that Gabe is the leader of the servants of the King? (Answers)
3. What does the marked woman who now believes in the King do? (Answers)
4. This was something else I wanted to put in the book. In that same book series I mentioned before, there was a man who receives the mark being forced into it by his parents. Instead of turning himself in, he is encouraged to keep the mark and use it to his (their) advantage. I think that is a seriously dangerous example. The Bible says that those who take the mark will go to hell. Well, it says, "...the smoke of their torment rises for ever and ever." The Bible also says that if your right hand causes you to sin, you should cut it off. I'm NOT encouraging anyone to maim themselves, I just wanted to provide a more biblical response to the situation. And, I didn't have her cut it off. She just turned herself in.
5. The climactic scene has been set. What's going to happen to Gabe? Is Vulpine finally going to be rid of his enemies and rule without disturbance? Will the King come back?

The homes where the seven men had been arrested were boarded up in the morning. The inn bustled again as Caleb's family and John's mother, Emily, moved in. Caleb's sons helped Emily with her farm and both families helped supply the inn. Having guests at the inn should have brought the color back to Mother's cheeks, but bitterness had left her pale and drawn. Her love had grown cold; now scorn marked her face.

Tabitha was growing into her mother's image daily. Now a young lady of eleven, she was a constant helper to Mother in Angela and Gabe's absences. She mirrored her mother in more than looks. She parroted her thoughts on the King.

More copies of the King's law were made and given to those who had lost theirs in the raid. There wasn't much reaching out to tell others about the King's law any more. The village seemed entirely segregated—them versus us. No one knew where it would all lead.

Over the winter, Gabe and Angela didn't celebrate when their seventeenth birthdays passed on a drab, gray day. Another sweep of arrests were made, and the servants tried not to think the worst. The only light in the dreary winter months was the servants' sweet time of fellowship which seemed to stretch longer each day.

Daily they felt the weight of their persecution. Spring came but didn't lighten the load. It wasn't until the oppressive heat of summer pressed in on them that much of the other oppression suddenly lifted.

"The King will make a way," parodied Vulpine from his throne. "The King is dead!" he bawled, heaving himself forward as if to throw his words over the trees and into the valley below. Leaning back and looking disgusted he added, "Didn't anyone tell you?"

General Writ had just given his status report and looked agitated by Vulpine's state. Vulpine gripped the arms of the throne. "I'm waging a war against an enemy who doesn't fight back, and I can't even win. How is that possible?" He growled the question.

Writ knew better than to answer. He remained at attention and let Vulpine go on his verbal rampage. "We need to find the one." Vulpine held up one long finger. "We need to find the one who had the first copy of that outdated law book. Learn where it all began, and then take out the backbone of the operation. Stop the arrests. Let up for a while so they'll feel more open. Then find him."

Writ understood the last command was not optional. It would be his life or that backbone. He had to find it and break it. He started by calling off all sweeps of homes by the guards. The guards were told to keep away from any meetings and to stop any harassment of the servants that they witnessed. They even released the prisoners from the jail. The extremely thin but joyfully alive prisoners returned to their families.

Relief swept through the meetings. The worst was over. The King had kept his word and brought them out of their darkest night. They no longer had that anxious feeling that they were about to get some horrendous news. Everything seemed better—the air fresher, the sky bluer, their steps bouncier.

Maybe it was this free feeling that kept Emily from seeing anything wrong with listening to Mother speak of Gabe's visits to the King in the market place. Squeezing vegetables, stroking fabric, bartering prices, they weaved their way through the stalls. Mother was talking about her children and how much things had changed once Gabe had started climbing King's Hill daily.

They came to the well and rested their bodies and their bags against it. "He said he was visiting with the King." She looked at Emily a bit sarcastically. "You know which King I'm talking about. He would wake up while it was dark, even in summer when the sun's up earlier than the roosters, and would be gone a few hours every day.

"He rarely said anything at all for a long time. I guess none of us listened to him, except Angela. She has always loved that boy. But now all these people listen to him. Even if I think he teaches some fool ideas, I'm still kind of proud of him."

She chuckled, thinking of Gabe as a young boy. "When he was a wee thing, he wouldn't even say hello to people. He was six before he would reply to a friendly greeting. It's the truth. Now look at him, talking at your meetings." Her eyes and her voice dropped. "But what good is his having confidence if it just gets people killed." Emily had no reply.

They hadn't noticed that the woman drawing water from the well continued to do so until their conversation had ended and then had left without taking any water with her. Hoisting their bags to begin the walk home, they were completely unaware of the part they had just played in Vulpine's plan.

"A boy?" Vulpine repeated incredulously.

"Yes, Your Majesty, a boy." General Writ was pleased to serve Vulpine the information he had desired. "And not just any boy. Do you remember Gabe from when we had our meetings at the inn?" Vulpine searched his memory and found a mop-haired boy, who had never spoken a word or looked a soul in the eye for all the time they had used the inn for their meetings.

"Gabe?" The surprise still hadn't left Vulpine's voice.

"Yes, sir. He was only ten when he started visiting the King, and he hasn't seen nor heard from him since he disappeared, and you took the throne."

Vulpine sat higher than the morning sun, which was making its daily morning climb as Gabe had done for three and a half years. At ease, Vulpine lounged in the throne and ruminated on the information. Moments passed before a wry smile cracked his face.

Abruptly, he jumped to his feet, as excited as a school boy just promised his own horse. "This will all be finished soon, General, my brilliant General, who brought me this delectable delicacy today." Vulpine was intoxicated with the assured final victory over this defiant enemy.

"Let's bide our time, a few weeks—just before the harvest. Until then, watch the boy. Learn his daily routine. Know where he goes. We need to be able to find him when the time comes. Don't let him escape. Set your guards around the perimeter of the village watching for an escape attempt.

"I will question the boy myself at a trial. When he fails before the entire village, the whole of it will crumble with him. He'll be hung for treason." Cackling, Vulpine slid back into his seat. He finished his chortling with a happy sigh.

Chapter 29

With the exception of Mother and Tabitha not joining in their meetings, everything seemed just about perfect. So it came like a bolt of lightning on a clear summer night when the door guard from the prison brought news to the inn early one morning.

"You're to be arrested." The guard made no other introduction and looked directly at Gabe as he spoke.

"What?" Gabe didn't comprehend what had just happened.

"I can't stay. I wanted to warn you. I remembered your kindness and well…" He stopped and looked over his shoulder nervously. "I have to go, but just know they're preparing a special cell for you. They're going to arrest you after dark, tonight. I need to go." In a flash, the lightning faded, but the dark storm clouds remained.

Gabe's family surrounded him and sat him down with them at a table. Caleb's family and Emily huddled around. All at once, everyone started talking.

"We can sneak you out of the village this afternoon."

"We can hide you in the cellar."

"If we can get you over to our place, no one is checking the boarded up homes anymore."

Gabe started shaking his head, slightly at first and then more vigorously until he vocalized its message. "No!" Everyone backed off at his firmness. "Let me stand, please." Gabe's mother moved and let her son out from the bench. She sat and looked up at her son.

"For seven years, I've been escaping." He spoke to the floor as he paced back and forth. "I didn't run away. The King just…" He stopped pacing and smiled at his audience. "The King just made a way. So, if he's not making a way for me to avoid arrest this time, he must be making some other kind of way. Look, we've all known this was probably going to happen someday. They must have finally realized who I was. I'm sure most of the time they didn't pay attention to me because I was a child." Gabe stood as tall and straight as a soldier at attention. "Now I'm as tall as Father ever was and can't hide anymore. I won't hide."

He leaned on the table. "I'm not saying I'm looking forward to whatever is going to happen tonight, but I'm not scared either, and I don't want you to be. And I'm thinking, if I'm going to be arrested anyway, I might as well do something worthwhile to get arrested for. I don't want to be arrested just sitting at home."

Gabe pushed himself back from the table. "I'm going to go speak about the King in the Square. Maybe I can convince some new people about the King before they finish my special cell."

No one argued with him. They knew he wouldn't back down from his plan. Mother set her jaw, slid out from the table, tugged at her apron and said evenly, "Before you go, you'll need a big meal." Emily followed her into the kitchen.

Caleb helped Gabe gather up all the copies of the King's law, leaving just the one original copy in the inn. He planned on giving out all he could. Caleb rejoined the family and Gabe sat alone with the King's words. He had turned to them time and time again in order to prepare for whatever lay ahead. Knowing at least a sliver of what was to come, he consumed those words again to gain the strength and wisdom he would need.

Angela was sent to fetch Gabe to eat. She peeked in the door to the family's quarters to find her brother in a familiar posture, bent over those tattered papers. She thought it amazing they hadn't disintegrated with use. She dreaded pulling him away from this comfortable scene. She had lost John and Father; her stomach was churning just thinking about not wanting to think about what might happen to Gabe.

"Gabe," she called to distract herself, "Mother has your food ready. She's expecting you to come now. She and Emily made so much you might not be able to stand afterwards."

Angela laughed but thought maybe Mother was thinking the same thing and making a desperate shot at keeping him home. Gabe didn't mind the reasons behind it; he just enjoyed the food. Whole eggs, rolls laced with cinnamon, cheese and meat slices, apples with sugar. He feasted like it was his last meal, thinking maybe it was.

When the last crumb was eaten and every last finger licked, there was nothing left to do but say goodbye. Gabe wanted to march straight out the door, but he dutifully hugged and shook hands with everyone at the inn—Caleb's family first, then his own. Mother's tears were a mixture of sadness and anger. Tabitha hugged him quickly, and while Angela's arms were wrapped around him, she whispered to him one more time, "The King will make a way."

He strode out of the inn without looking back. He made straight for the Square without knowing exactly what he was going to do when he got there.

He stepped into the openness of the square. It was abuzz with activity. He started strolling along the shops and saw a weaver busy at his trade, sitting at his loom, weaving threads into cloth with a steady clapping of wood and the smooth slide of the shuttle back and forth.

Gabe walked past the glassblower, who had garnered an audience. He was blowing the glass up like a balloon. When his onlookers were sufficiently awed, he pricked the balloon. Pop! The light reflected off a hundred flecks of glass being carried by the wind like the seeds of a dandelion. Gabe reached out a finger to catch one as it fluttered by.

The light breeze gently encouraged Gabe forward. He left the shelter of the shops at the edge of the square and crossed towards the well in the center. Gabe let a laugh escape as he remembered calling it the Square's belly button when he was little. He looked around quickly to see if anyone had been watching.

The ground was wet around the well, a sure sign of fall. He debated climbing onto the wall of the well to speak, but remembering his mishap and the dark chill of the well water, he chose to remain on the ground.

He took a deep breath and plunged in. "There is only one King who rules our village," he shouted over the clamor in the Square. "Vulpine is the imposter. He has lied to you, to me, to the whole village. The one true King is alive! I have seen him and met with him. I will tell you about him."

At first, people scurried away from him, embarrassed to be standing by the shouting young man. Others further back stopped to listen. Their ears were ringing with the foreign words of love and a living King. Some laughed, thinking him crazy, while others were drawn in by his passion—either way they gathered to listen.

He told them of his days at the feet of the King. He told them that the King would return to rule and that they would be sorry if they weren't found on the side of the King. He told them of the King's laws and quoted them by heart. The words of the King were burned on his mind and filled his heart until they poured out from him wherever he was.

He didn't need to think about what he was saying. The words flowed past his lips as easily as a river passes over a pebble and they flowed with as much power as a river cascading over a waterfall. Tears filled the eyes of a woman standing several feet from Gabe; she was holding the hand of her five-year-old son. She recognized the words from the papers she had tucked away the night of the bonfire. She called out, interrupting him, "Have you really seen him?"

Gabe dammed the current. He stepped forward to speak directly to the woman. "I've seen him. For three-and-a-half years, I met with him daily. I sat at his feet and learned from him and was loved by him." She searched his eyes and found a treasure of love and truth.

"I believe you."

A man standing next to her, having heard and seen the encounter, asked loud enough for everyone to hear, "If we believe this is all true, what can we do?"

Gabe reflected as he walked back to his post by the well. "If you believe, then there is only one thing you must do. You must give yourself entirely to serving the King and obeying his laws. The King must be your first and only and everything. You must be prepared to give up your home, your family, your belongings, your last breath in order to serve him alone."

The man was shaken by the answer, but the woman walked up to him and stood in the mud by the well. "I'm willing." She slipped her son's hand into her sister's. Several stepped back and faded away. One reported to a guard what was being said at the well.

The guard hurried to break up those congregating by the water. He knew he could lose his head if he allowed this kind of chatter under his guard. When he saw the copies of the King's law, he grew frantic. He knew he couldn't let those get out of the Square. He ordered everyone to throw their copies into the well then asked who had broken the law by distributing them. Gabe turned himself in.

The woman chased after Gabe and the guard. The head prison guard recognized Gabe and told his captor of the big fish he had just reeled in. Then he asked about the woman.

She spoke for herself. "I deserve to be arrested. I am no longer loyal to Vulpine."

The guards all looked at each other. Spotting her marked right hand, the head guard said, "I can help you with that," and walked out of the prison.

The others waited in wondering silence. Gabe grimaced when he saw the guard return with a hatchet. "Put your hand on the table." The woman hesitated for just a moment then placed her hand on the table and pinched her eyes shut. The hatchet came down heavy and wedged into the wooden table. The woman pulled her arm away without her right hand.

"Thank you," she said calmly but stared at her arm, unmoving. Gabe started to pull off his shirt, and the guard released him so he could wrap it around the woman's wound. She smiled at him and walked out of the prison. Free.

Lesson 180

1. Finish the *The King Will Make a Way.*
2. Why is Vulpine wrong to equate schooling with wisdom? (Answers)
3. How does Gabe prove he has seen the King? (Answers)
4. Who is walking down the road by the inn? (Answers)
5. Author's Note: When I wrote in the plate with Gabe's name on it in the beginning, I had no idea that it would be so important later on. That was just a gift the Lord gave me.

When Gabe was alone with his captors, they stripped him and shut him into the cell, which was more like an indentation in the wall. There was no window or even a little delivery door. Apparently, no one expected to be feeding him.

There was no room to sit, so Gabe would be forced to stand all day and all night. He leaned has bare back against the wall, closed his eyes and sang. When he finished, he started again. Then he worked on reciting the King's law word for word, starting with page one. He had read it so many times he could just about do it. The song and the words had the same effect. He was experiencing his darkest night, but he was at peace. Despair no longer hunted him, stealthily encircling him, waiting for a weak moment in which to pounce. Despair had no home there with him. In its place there was hope.

Mother, on the other hand, had no hope or peace. When she felt she couldn't stand the torment of not knowing any longer, she sent Angela to the Square to see what was happening. Angela sped out the door as fast as a falcon swoops towards its prey.

Stopping to catch her breath in the southeast corner of the square, she noticed a gathering at the well and went over to investigate. It wasn't hard to discover what had happened. Everyone was talking about Gabe and the King.

Gabe's river of words had spilled its banks. More and more people had gathered around the well. The guard returned from the prison and threatened them with arrest if they didn't disperse. They slowly edged away. But the guard had just created tributaries, each person a rivulet meandering through the Square leaving sedimentary news that the King might be alive.

Angela didn't speak to anyone. She felt detached from the scene, floating from pair to pair, listening in on the chatter. Angela's feet touched the ground right in front of the Assembly Hall where her eyes transfixed on General Writ. He was standing on the porch of the Hall listening to the reports of two guards. One told of arresting Gabe, the other of talk that the King was alive.

Writ was noticeably flustered by the intelligence he had received. "Bring me a horse!" he barked at no one in particular, but a horse was promptly provided. Angela stood in the settling dust watching the galloping horse trace its way to King's Hill and wondered what response the news would bring.

"He's altered the plan!" Vulpine was irked by the revelation. "The arrest was to be made in secret tonight. He was to be kept in his cell without food or drink or sleep for two days before we announced his arrest and trial to the public. I want him weakened for that trial!" Vulpine realized what he had just admitted in front of the General and quickly recanted.

"Never mind. All the better. Let's be done with him and the whole thing. We need to stop the spread of those vicious rumors he started. Send Phineas to announce his arrest and to warn people of his harmful, scandalous talk. He's to announce that the trial will be in the morning." General Writ gave a curt nod and set off.

Vulpine spoke to himself. "He's already weak. He's a boy. He never even went to school. I am a learned man. He can't cope with my wisdom. He will fall before me, and I will prove to everyone Lord Vulpine is the king!"

Hooves frantically drumming the road was not an everyday sound in the village. Caleb opened the door to see who was racing past the inn, not once, but twice that afternoon. Smiling, he noted to those gathered that Gabe had Writ dashing madly about, trying to fix whatever damage had been done by his speaking in the Square.

The dust was flying again, and Angela backed out of the way of the speeding equestrian. She lurked in the shadows of the Assembly Hall on a reconnaissance mission to discover her brother's fate. She scouted General Writ recovering his composure after his frenetic race to the Square. He disappeared into the Assembly Hall and reappeared with Phineas, who gestured to the villagers in the Square.

"I'm calling on every man and woman to be in attendance for a trial in the Square tomorrow morning. Our protectors have succeeded in capturing a dangerous criminal who has been spreading vicious rumors. King Vulpine himself will question the liar and expose his lies. Our village will not tolerate anyone sowing seeds of disunity. Do not believe his lies or spread them further. King Vulpine will lead us all to the truth!"

Angela hurried home with the report. The inn, though full of familiar sights and smells, felt odd and empty without Gabe. The families quickly gathered around Angela, and she shared all the details she knew.

Caleb took off to spread word of the trial. Other servants began filtering into the inn, feeling the need to be together at the loss of Gabe, who up until that day had seemed untouchable. For the first time in more than three years, they sang the King's song all together in the inn.

Hours went by and the candles were lit, no one wanting to leave the inn or the feeling of strength that comes with numbers. Mother, however, went up to the family quarters with Tabitha, as usual, while the meeting was still going on.

Angela went to sleep reluctantly that night, not wanting the comfort of fellowship to end and to have to face the long, dark, unknown of the night alone. She dreamed she and Gabe were down in the Square, watching them build those wooden frames. Whack. Thwack. Tap. Tap. Tap. She stirred from her sleep. Her eyes shot open wide. Whack. Thwack. Tap. Tap. Tap. The hammering echoed through the village, sending another code. But what was its message?

She raced alone to the Square. She didn't need an explanation of what she was seeing this time. There was a new wooden platform next to the Assembly Hall with a tall neck. From its bowed head swung a hangman's noose. The gallows. She swallowed hard. She made a hasty retreat like a roach when a candle is suddenly lit. She felt exposed and wanted to hide. She wanted to bury herself in her bed under pillows and covers as she did as a child to feel safe from a thunderstorm. But she knew this was a storm she'd have to face.

Chapter 31

The servants were sober in the morning as they made the journey together from the inn to the Square. The bell rang out its welcome, inviting everyone to the event. The whole village was turning out—mothers with still swaddled babies, old men barely moving with canes, the merchants, the farmers. Everyone with eyes and ears wanted to be in the square to see and hear Vulpine and his foe.

The bell's ring slowed, sounding more and more distant as Gabe was brought nearer and nearer to the Assembly Hall. Vulpine had ordered him dressed in a plain night shirt that hung to his calves. His feet were bare, and his wrists bound behind him. One of Vulpine's personal guards led him on a leash, like an untamed animal needing to be reined in.

Gabe walked without struggling. His head was up and his eyes were steady. A full day without any nourishment or sleep had accomplished an unexpected result in Gabe; he was steeled to prove the truth about the King.

Gabe's leash was tied to a pillar on the Assembly Hall porch. His fellow servants amassed just in front of him and could see the calmness in his eyes. Angela and Gabe locked their eyes on each other and neither blinked as Vulpine was announced. Angela moved her lips to form the familiar phrase, "The King will make a way." Gabe knew it was true—he just didn't know if that meant release or peace at his execution.

Two guards opened the door to the Assembly Hall. With all royal pomp and pride, Vulpine stepped forward onto the porch. With a scepter in his raised right hand, he greeted his subjects.

"Thank you for your presence at this trial. We need your help in order to end, once and for all, the lies being spread by this weasely scoundrel. You, my beloved subjects, will act as jury. You will do your duty to denounce his lies and to order his treachery ended by means of the gallows!"

Cheers erupted from around the Square. Silence was present as well in the circle of servants before Gabe and in a one-handed woman clinging to her five-year-old son.

Vulpine spun on his heels to face Gabe, his robe twisting behind him. "Do you plead guilty to the charge brought against you yesterday at the time of your arrest; namely, the unlawful distribution of literature in the village?"

"I do," Gabe answered evenly.

"Please repeat your answer again. Are you guilty or not guilty?" Vulpine was exceedingly pleased with himself and his immediate victory in the trial.

"Guilty." Gabe spoke in the same even manner.

"Let everyone in the jury know that the defendant, Gabriel, has pleaded guilty." Vulpine walked to the edge of the porch and egged on the crowd. "Am I not being proved correct that this is a scoundrel that should be done away with?" Vulpine relished the yells and cheers of the villagers.

"Now let's turn to a more serious matter. You have been spreading vicious lies around the village. The most serious lie is that the previous King is still alive. Have you spoken this lie to anyone in the village?"

Gabe caught Vulpine's crafty words. "I have not lied," Gabe called out, his voice stronger, "but I have told many people that the true King is still alive." A muffled cheer came from the small circle in the crowd in front of him. The servants may have been outnumbered, but to Gabe, that dot was like the North Star in a sky cluttered with constellations—all that was needed to lead him home.

Vulpine didn't back down. "So you admit you've spoken this outrageous falsehood numerous times. A lie, I may point out, which amounts to treason."

Gabe didn't respond but kept his eyes on the North Star to steer him straight.

"This trial will then quickly come to a close, for from what you have openly admitted your only recourse is to prove this King is alive. I leave it in your hands. Can you prove it?" Vulpine was gleeful.

Gabe pierced the expectant silence. "I have seen the King!" The fullness of his lungs and diaphragm supported the words and carried them to the edges of the crowd. The words were met by gasps and guffaws. Vulpine quickly intervened.

"Another lie! You can't keep wielding your slippery tongue without evidence. If you say the King is alive because you have seen him, then again I say to you, where is the proof? Show us the evidence that you have seen him." Vulpine's eyes narrowed into slits, arrow slits made for one purpose only, to destroy the enemy.

The North Star seemed to dim. In all the years they had listened to Gabe speak of the King, he had never offered evidence that the King was alive. They each had felt it for themselves, but how could it be proven?

Gabe searched the sky again for the words as he had done his last night with John. Instead of finding a solution, he spotted a star. A new star seemingly had appeared in the sky, bright enough to be seen by day. Gabe squinted and tilted his head back trying to get a better look.

Villagers started to follow his stare. They began pointing and whispering. The blood was rising in Vulpine's face at having lost the momentum and focus of the trial. He brought everyone back to attention, shouting, "The defendant must provide evidence of having seen the King or be hung!"

The solution came. Gabe addressed his jury. "After it was announced that the King had died, a beautifully carved cabinet was brought to be kept in the Assembly Hall. Where did that cabinet come from?"

"The King's throne room." Everyone knew the answer. A chorus of voices responded, a cacophony of sound.

"It came from the throne room of the previous King, who is still the true King of the village."

Vulpine burst again in his rage, "Where is your proof?"

Gabe remained as steady as a cat on its feet and continued his conversation with the jury. "And what was the one thing that was kept in that cabinet?"

"A plate," the crowd answered eagerly, enjoying the game they were playing.

"Not any plate but a plate made out of solid pearl and trimmed in gold, the plate of a King."

Vulpine had regained control of himself and now just rolled his eyes at Gabe's antics. "Having had a cabinet and a plate does not prove the man alive nor that you have seen him." A few chortled along with Vulpine.

Gabe ignored the interruption. Angela was beside herself. She was the only one in a thousand who knew what Gabe was doing. Her stomach flip flopped. She didn't think she could bear the suspense of waiting to see the outcome. It was a horse race and her stallion had just come from behind and was pulling into the lead. Don't trip now!

"The first time I visited the King on the hill, he showed me that plate and told me it was my invitation to sup with him whenever I wanted. I request that the plate be removed from its shelf where it's been since the fire and shown to the jury as evidence."

Knowing the whole village had shuffled past that plate time and time again to inspect it, Vulpine waved his fingers at a guard to bring it out. Waiting for the guard, Gabe again spied the golden star in the sky which seemed to have grown larger. He gaped at it along with half of the villagers.

Bellowing again, Vulpine restored everyone's attention to the proceedings. He didn't like Gabe speaking so much and wanted to draw this to an end as soon as possible.

The guard had brought out the plate. Gabe looked at the plate expectantly, but with his hands tied behind his back, he couldn't touch it. His name had been there seven years ago. It had to still be there, right? He wondered if the fire could have seared off the writing. His hesitancy made Angela's heart skip a beat. Taking a deep breath, she called out, "The King has made a way." She quickly shrank into the crowd as guards advanced toward her, but the damage had been done. Gabe had regained his footing.

"I ask that a member of the jury be permitted to join us on the porch to examine the evidence." Gabe was again as confident as a lion ruling his pride.

Vulpine was leery. "As villagers, the guards are part of your jury. I permit this guard here holding the plate to observe it for the jury at large."

Todd, the guard, nodded at Gabe. He remembered the last time he had seen him, just before pushing John into the bonfire cage. He gave Gabe a questioning look.

Gabe eyed the seemingly approaching star and somehow drew on its energy. He lifted his voice and called out, "Please clearly tell your fellow jury members what is the only word written on the back of my invitation to visit the King."

Vulpine shuddered and went pale. Todd carefully turned the costly plate over to reveal its underside. There was only one word there. "Gabriel!" Todd shouted it loud and clear.

The crowd erupted at Gabe's name and so did Vulpine. He grabbed the plate and smashed it to the ground, sending fragments in every direction. He grabbed Todd fiercely by the throat as if by shouting alone he wouldn't get his orders across. "Hang him!"

Todd was shaken, but fear of Vulpine's wrath spurred him to move quickly. He untied Gabe and dragged him stumbling to the gallows. He slipped the noose around his neck while the crowd screamed and roared.

Vulpine stormed across the porch to knock Gabe off and cause him to swing to his death. As his heavy boots thundered their way to Gabe, an even louder sound split the scene.

An earthquake violently shook the Square. The terrified villagers were knocked to the ground and tossed about. The Assembly Hall split from its foundation and, toppling backwards, was shredded by the trees behind it. The whole square reeled. Crashes came from around the square as shops creaked and cracked and threw their stock. The long neck of the gallows snapped in two. Gabe slipped himself free from its grasp and stood steady on its platform. Vulpine was flung off the Assembly Hall porch, which splintered. The other servants of the King were still right in front of the remains of the Hall when the earth ripped in two and a sinkhole opened on the far side of the Square, swallowing hundreds of villagers, who disappeared under the earth before most had any idea what was happening.

When the tremors lessened and the stunned villagers regained their bearings, they began to stand to survey the damage. What they saw knocked them right back to the ground. The star had disappeared from the sky, and not only was Gabe dressed in brilliant white, but beside Gabe on the platform stood the King.

Chapter 32

"The king is dead!" Phineas had scrambled over to Vulpine, lying prone on the ground. Seeing his chest still, he had made his final announcement to the village. He eyed the King and slunk away. Heading toward the hill, Phineas froze in front of the inn when he saw a few dozen people all dressed in white approaching him. When he recognized Robert, the good doctor, among them, his heart stopped and he collapsed in the road. They walked past his body on their way toward the Square, while the birds rejoiced above them.

In the Square, the villagers were on their knees before the King, more majestic in appearance and presence than they could have imagined possible. Vulpine, in comparison, had been a slug.

The servants, all now clothed in white, bowed in awe. Without a word from the King, the other villagers remained bowed to the ground and began weeping in guilt and fear. At the same time, a nightingale began to sing. A skylark alighted on the broken neck of the gallows and warbled. A dove perched on the platform and cooed. More birds began circling in the blue sky, adding their voices.

Angela was the first to pick it out. She recognized the birds' song—it was the song of the King. She stood, a lone tree on the savannah, and sang with the birds. The servants began to cry tears of their own. Years of terror had broken them, and the beauty of Angela's voice and the lyrics of love washed their wounds. By the song's end, they had been made whole.

Angela began the song again, and this time all of the servants stood and sang the King's song. With one voice they praised the King, *His love a banner waving over all of us, a beacon leading us out of our darkest night.*

The King had made a way.

Answers

Lesson 91

2. Katy wasn't sure whether Birch's loyalty was to the British or Americans, although she lived in his house for many years. She did mention that he had expressed the feeling that it was unnatural for a far away country like England to rule a country like America.

Vocabulary 1A, 2C, 3D, 4C, 5A, 6A, 7C, 8B, 9B

Lesson 92

2. When Frances, attempting to help her brother, mentioned that he had contact with Birch, who was regarded as a Royal spy. Why did Colonel Singleton feel a special ugency to help save Captain Wharton? Because Singleton's wounded son had been cared for in the house of Captain Wharton's father, and Frances Wharton had been the last one with his daughter Isabella when she died.

Lesson 93

2. At first they were hopeful that General George Washington would be merciful and pardon him; but then word arrived that Washington had approved Wharton's execution. Then, as they were in mourning and preparing for the impending execution, they recalled the offer of Harper (the guest at the Wharton house from the first chapters) to help Capt. Wharton should he find himself in this very situation. When they mentioned Harper's name to Dunwoodie, he was surprised and seemed certain that Harper would be able to intercede with Washington and save Capt. Wharton. When Dunwoodie went off to find Harper, however, he was not able to locate him immediately. He returned with this disappointing news, leaving the family again in a state of uncertainty.

Lesson 96

2. The British (and Americans) assume Birch is a British spy. But Harper is on the side of the rebels. If Capt. Wharton saw them together and reported it to his superiors, Birch would be killed by the British as a spy.

Lesson 97

2. It was the only way she could delay him to give her brother the necessary time to escape; and also she truly loved Dunwoodie, and was worried that if he went quickly and captured her brother again, the execution of her brother would forever separate her from Dunwoodie by making it impossible for her to want to marry him.

Lesson 98

2. He was led by Birch to a British frigate, which he persuaded to allow him aboard to safety.

Lesson 99

2. Dunwoodie was allowed to spend weeks recovering with Frances as his nurse; then he was allowed to go live at his plantation with her in order to regain his health, and they spent a happy winter together.

Lesson 100

2. He is revealed to be a spy for George Washington himself, although he has been thought to be a loyalist spy by both the British and the Americans.

Lesson 101

2. This chapter jumps to 1814, when the Americans are again fighting the British, and Harvey Birch is in his 70s. He meets two young soldiers, one of whom turns out to be the son of Dunwoodie and Frances. He hears the young man and his companion talking of various people Harvey knew. Harvey then accompanies them to their camp, and after the ensuing battle he is discovered dead in the middle of the battlefield. The paper written for him by G. Washington years ago is found by the young soldier, revealing Harvey's identity as a servant to and martyr for his country.

Lesson 109

2. Jim understands about the mutiny and that the pirates are killing those not joining the mutiny. He thinks he could be next.

Lesson 110

2. the doctor

Lesson 111

Analogies: 1. hexagon, 2. green, 3. question, 4. mechanic, 5. woman

Lesson 112

2. Jim
3. "Again, this chapter shows the theme of Stevenson's use of moral ambiguity. In the book, although there are 'good' and 'bad' sides it is not if as if you are choosing between the sides based on their morality - both are after the same prize, using the same methods of deceit, etc. in order to obtain it. Choosing a moral side in Treasure Island is more like choosing between two baseball teams based on their morality: it is pointless."
   from http://www.gradesaver.com/treasure-island/study-guide/section3/
6. Todd seems to be embarrassed because he dropped something on the floor. Mary was sick. Thomas is a slob.

Lesson 113

Analogies: 1. minute, 2. inch, 3. up, 4. screw, 5. small

Lesson 114

2. The pirates were getting drunk which is a sin. Also, any sin the devil can use to cause more trouble unless there is repentance.
3. It's only sort of buy one get one free; only a cheaper one is free and only through a certain date. The best? That's subjective. It's not real information. It doesn't tell us anything. He'll fight for me? He doesn't know me. He can't be on everyone's side.

Lesson 116

2. The parrot calls it out. No.
6. mice, team, thoughts, cool, vegetable

Lesson 117

2. "First, he made a 'hash of the cruise.' Second, he let their enemies out of the stockade. Next, he refused to allow the pirates to attack the enemies when they left and finally, he is protecting Jim Hawkins." from http://www.gradesaver.com/treasure-island/study-guide/section5/

Lesson 118

2. He yells at Jim. It shows that the treasure is more important to him than Jim.

Lesson 119

2. doctor, Gunn, Gray
4. In the first and last chapter it is shown to be told in retrospective. It's all over and done and he's remembering it. There is no current peril in the situation, just the memory of it.

Lesson 120

Answers will vary

1. narrators: Jim, the doctor; settings: inn, the Hispanolia, Treasure Island; Billy Bones, Long John Silver; pieces of eight; British flag and Jolly Roger

Lesson 121

2. a kind of good luck charm

Lesson 122

5. God destroyed it by fire and sulfur.
6. He is a knight serving with the Crusaders on some sort of errand, riding alone in the desert.
7. He meets a Muslim warrior, a Saracen. At first, they fight each other, but later they decide to ride together.

Lesson 123

3. Water freezes in the winter and the horses can walk across a frozen lake or river.
6. The Christian feels that alcohol is a gift from God and a husband should be devoted to one lady, like one precious gem. The Muslim thinks alcohol is a poisonous drink and that a man should be surrounded by many devoted ladies, a central jewel set in a circle of smaller gems.
7. I think they like each other as two warriors can respect one another, but I don't think they understand each other's culture and they do not respect one another's faith.

Lesson 125

3. He hates Islam and views the Saracen as an enemy of the cross.
4. Ephesians 6:12 says that our battle is not against people but against Satan and his demons.
6. I feel that even the "violent" acts are described lightly and that he doesn't take his characters too seriously.

Lesson 126

3. To a small room with an altar and a veil. Next, the hermit leads him upstairs to a large "holy" space with another altar and perhaps a piece of the cross of Jesus.
4. First he sees nothing because he is in darkness, but then a group of maidens come into the room. He thinks he sees that one of them is his adored lady love because he recognizes her hand and she gives him a rose.
5. He is "over the moon," because he thinks that this lady, who is far above him in social rank, has noticed him and perhaps even returned his affection.
6. The high-born lady that Sir Kenneth loves.

Lesson 127

2. Two strange dwarfs
3. They appear out of an opening in the floor.

Lesson 128

3. Strong, brave, impetuous, proud
4. He is very ill and he doesn't trust the other leaders of the Crusaders. He thinks they want to look out only for themselves and he thinks they want to give up and he can't do anything about it.
5. I think he really cares about King Richard and Richard respects him and de Vaux is not afraid of much.

Lesson 129

3. De Vaux does not trust Scotsmen; he thinks they are inferior to Englishmen and they have attacked some of his lands in the past.
4. He has brought a physician, though Muslim, who says he can cure King Richard of his illness.
5. I might think that the Muslim would try to poison the King.

Lesson 130

3. Saladin, the leader of the Muslim armies
4. He plans to challenge Saladin to single combat and win.
5. De Vaux goes to visit the tent of Sir Kenneth to see how much success the physician has had in curing Sir Kenneth's sick servant.
6. He is accompanied by a bishop. I don't like the bishop. He is a coward for one thing and will not come near the sick man. Besides, he is a little mysterious.

Lesson 131

3. The Council of the Princes of the Holy Crusade. He was to find out if the Muslims would accept a permanent peace. King Richard is furious. He can only accept total victory.
4. Next King Richard is visited by the Marquis of Montserrat and the Grand Master of the Knights Templar. They have come to try to dissuade Richard from trusting the Muslim physician. I don't trust them because the author has let me know that many people are suspicious of their motives.
5. Yes, I think it will work because it seems like Sir Kenneth and King Richard are main characters in the book and the success of this cure is important to both of them. Besides, I want it to work.

Lesson 132

3. They hate King Richard. The success of the Crusades? They think they will be better off if the Crusades fail and they can make their own deals with Saladin.
4. The Marquis would like to be Prince of Jerusalem and the Grand Marshall would like to keep the power of the Knights Templar even if it means serving Saladin. The Grand Marshall, at least, is willing to kill King Richard. The Marquis is more inclined to try to break up the political alliances and destroy the Crusading army by many desertions.
5. Yes, these men seem very evil.

Lesson 133

2. Richard is fierce and strong, very skilled in battle; I think his lifestyle is a little rough. The Archduke prefers to eat well, to be entertained, to drink a lot of wine. He likes a rich lifestyle even on the battlefield.
3. He makes some remarks that make the Archduke feel jealous of King Richard. Then the Archduke decides to place his banner beside the English banner in the center of the camp.

4. He gets up from his sickbed, leaves his tent, pulls down the Austrian banner and tramples on it.
5. He reminds everyone of their mission.
6. Who is prudent and calm? King Phillip of France. Who is impetuous and violent? King Richard

Lesson 134

3. He is thinking about his "love," Lady Edith, who attends the Queen. He knows that she is still too far above him in social status, but he is grateful that the King has given him this trust. He thinks that at least it gives him some importance.
4. The strange dwarf, Nectabanus, appears and he has a ring that Sir Kenneth recognizes. Nectabanus says that Sir Kenneth is summoned by his lady.
5. I think he should stay at his guard duty. I think this invitation is some sort of test of his faithfulness to his duty. Besides, the author introduced this chapter with the quote, "'Tis woman that seduces all mankind." I think that Sir Kenneth is going to be in BIG TROUBLE, but I could be wrong.

Lesson 135

3. He is behind a partition in the Queen's tent.
4. They had used Edith's ring to convince him to leave his post. They seemed to want to embarrass Edith, who I guess always thought she was good and right.
5. He likes to be near Edith, and then it is very dark when he leaves the Queen's tent and he has to move cautiously so as not to be seen.

Lesson 136

3. Hakim, the Muslim physician who is attending King Richard, appears. He offers to tend the wounds of the dog and perhaps heal him.
4. Hakim tells Sir Kenneth to get out of town and go to the Saracens. He thinks that Saladin will like him and eventually give him some rewards.
5. He learns that there is a plan to seal a peace between the King Richard and Saladin through the marriage of Saladin to Dame Edith, Richard's cousin (and Sir Kenneth's adored one.)
6. It looks like he is going to tell King Richard about the marriage proposal. I wonder who took the banner. I wonder if the dog will later be able to identify his assailant.

Lesson 137

2. He is angry because Sir Kenneth allowed the banner of England to be taken without even a struggle, and he is angry because the knight spoke to him about Edith's possible marriage. Richard knows that Kenneth adores Edith, and he feels that he has no right to even think about her because her rank is so above his. What happens to Edith, thinks Richard, is no concern of Sir Kenneth's.
3. I think Sir Kenneth is too ashamed that he was so easily tricked.
4. I am thinking he will not be executed because I think he is the hero of the story and it's only the middle of the book. Maybe the Queen will explain the trick to King Richard, but even if she does, I don't know if that would be enough to make the king change his mind.

Lesson 138

2. She is 21. Her picture should show a young woman with wavy, blond hair.
3. Green
4. She thinks that her husband likes to have conversation with Lady Edith because he thinks that she is more intelligent than his wife.
5. I think she may not be successful because I am not sure that King Richard would allow a woman to change his mind when he feels that the honor of England is at stake.

Lesson 139

2. I think I might add stubborn. He certainly continues to be strong, brave, impetuous, and proud. Those traits were on my list.
3. The confessional is where a person tells (confesses) his sins to a priest, who assures the person of God's forgiveness. (A priest can't forgive sins, but the Bible says that if we confess our sins God is faithful and just to forgive us our sins and cleanse us of unrighteousness.) The priest is sworn to secrecy. He is never to tell what someone has confessed to him. I wonder what Sir Kenneth's secret is.
4. She seems very calm about the fact that Sir Kenneth will soon die.
5. Misanthropy means hatred, dislike, or distrust of humankind. I guess if a person is going to be chopping off other peoples' heads it might be helpful to him if he didn't like people.

Lesson 140

2. We learn that the medicine that cured King Richard is a "talisman," which has certain rules for its use. One rule is that the one who seeks to use the talisman must cure at least 12 people every month or something terrible will happen to the physician and to the last person he has cured.
3. Hakim tells King Richard that he needs one more "cure" before the month ends. He wants that "cure" to be the life of Sir Kenneth.
4. The hermit of Engaddi. He tells Richard that he dare not destroy the unity of the Crusaders and that Richard's life is in danger, but he may be spared for a time.

Lesson 141

3. The Archbishop of Tyre comes to invite the King to a general meeting of the council of Crusaders and to urge him to consider a possible marriage between the Soldan, leader of the Muslims, and his cousin Edith Plantagenat.
4. Being too bossy and proud and treating everyone else like slaves.
5. He agrees that his character might be too proud, but he says his heart is in the right place, to regain Jerusalem, and somehow he persuades the others to follow him into battle even when they really want to go home.
6. He repeats the Lord's prayer to himself.
7. They already know of an assassin who will kill him.
8. Once a wise man has made a decision he doesn't hesitate, doesn't rethink it over, second guess. He doesn't retract, doesn't take back what he had said he had purposed to do. He resolves; he's completely determined that this is the course and he will complete it. He executes; he does it; he accomplishes what he determined to do.

Lesson 142

3. Because he let the Scottish knight go free, not at her suggestion but at the suggestion of the Muslim physician, Hakim.
4. Because King Richard had sent him many gifts, including the dwarfs.
5. It is disrespectful because Muslims are not supposed to drink alcohol. However, the marabout seems very willing and soon falls into a drunken stupor just outside King Richard's tent.
6. For some reason, I am feeling suspicious because he is so close to the King's tent and the Marquis and the Templar talked about an assassin.

Lesson 143

3. He sees the marabout reflected in the shield he is polishing.
4. They fear the poison and they do not think a black slave is worth the risk to their lives.
5. A message to the Lady Edith Plantagenet
6. He cannot speak, he writes English very well, and he seems to understand the spirit of chivalry.

Lesson 144

2. Sir Kenneth's horse nearly stumbles because of his rider's inattention.
3. They listen to some stories from their musician.
4. They see a party of Crusaders riding swiftly in their direction. Hakim is concerned because they are Knights Templar whom he does not trust. He says "their peace is war, and their faith is falsehood."
5. They easily outrun the Crusaders, leaving Sir Kenneth breathless.
6. At the oasis, the Diamond of the Desert, where Sir Kenneth met the Saracen warrior, Emir Sheerhohf, or Ilderim.

Lesson 145

2. He is sleeping in a luxurious tent, and Hakim the physician turns out to be the same person, Ilderim, that he had met days ago in the desert.
3. He wanted to see the women that Sir Kenneth had told him about. Sir Kenneth thinks that is insulting.
4. He offers to let him return disguised to the Crusaders' camp and take his dog who he thinks will be able to identify the thief who took the banner of England and wounded the faithful dog. And he wants him to carry a message from Saladin to Lady Edith.

Lesson 146

3. I must admit that I was still "in the dark," so to speak, and had to read on before I figured out that mystery.
4. The Nubian is Sir Kenneth. I think I figured it out when I read, "Richard said to the slave with some scorn, 'Thy success in this enterprise, my sable friend, even though thou hast brought thy hound's sagacity to back thine own, will not, I fear, place thee high in the rank of wizards, or much augment thy merits towards our person.'"
5. He is too powerful (the battle would be unfair); he owes them money; he is too valuable to his own country.
6. Somewhere of Saladin's choosing and under his protection.

Lesson 147

2. I do think that King Richard is acting a little more wisely and giving more thought to his actions and reactions. For example, he did let the Council persuade him not to fight the Marquis himself.
3. One is from Saladin to Edith Plantagenet requesting that she marry him. The other is from King Richard to Saladin asking him to provide a neutral place for the joust and inviting him to observe it if he wishes.
4. She recognizes him.
5. He will not speak to her; he preserves his "identity" as a slave and his allegiance to King Richard, who had forbidden him to speak to Edith.

Lesson 148

2. "The Bloody Vest" - love between a Princess and a lowly knight
3. It is a story similar to Edith Plantagenet and Sir Kenneth's.
4. She says "No." She could not marry a heathen prince.
5. "that thy marriage shall reconcile me with a powerful enemy, and that thy husband shall be Christian, leaving thus the fairest ground to hope that the conversion of the Soldan and the bringing in of the sons of Ishmael to the pale of the Church, will be the consequence of thy wedding with Saladin."

Lesson 149

3. At the same oasis, the Diamond of the Desert, which the author has used twice before.
4. I guess they respected each other's strength and leadership.
5. King Richard has a mighty sword that can slice a bar of iron; Saladin has a sharp, thin scimitar that can slice through a cushion or a scarf.
6. That Sir Kenneth and the black Ethiopian are the same person, and that Hakim, the physician, is really Saladin, the Muslim leader, which means he is also Ilderim, the Saracen friend of Sir Kenneth in the first chapter.
7. She will do nothing; she will not marry either an infidel or a lowly adventurer.
8. They have gone or are planning to go back to their own countries.

Lesson 150

2. They might be killed, and they must not die without having confessed their sins to God.
3. He fears that Conrade will be confessing their plots against King Richard and naming the Grand Master as a participant in those plots. Later, the Grand Master kills Conrade so that he cannot confess, and Saladin, in turn, kills the Grand Master – before he has drunk his wine or the law of hospitality would have prevented any punishment for him.
4. Sir Kenneth wins. He is revealed to be David the Earl of Huntingdon, Prince Royal of Scotland. When the King of Scotland had refused to send troops to the Crusades, the son had decided to come on his own and keep his identity a secret.
5. The hermit had thought that the prophecy was about the conversion of Saladin to Christianity, but it was about Edith's marrying someone who was already a Christian and thus uniting the enemies England and Scotland. The hermit is humbled by his mistake, but in that humbling he is somehow set free to accept forgiveness for his sin.
6. King Richard envies Sir Kenneth because he actually got to participate in single combat with Saladin in the desert when he was pretending to be Ilderim. King Richard wants Saladin to

agree to fight him man to man for Jerusalem, but Saladin refuses because Jerusalem is already his and his people need him to be their leader.
7. He gives them the talisman.
8. It seems to me that he says we can deeply disagree with our "enemies," but still respect them deeply as human beings and honorable persons. What do you think?

Lesson 152
2. He's shy and has a hard time speaking up.
3. Gabe isn't thinking highly of himself here.
4. right-hand man, mouthpiece

Lesson 153
2. a copy of the Book of Law
3. The Law says that the King will come back to the village, but he hadn't.
5. to be king

Lesson 154
2. "a haughty look comes before the fall"
3. a pearl plate with his name, Gabriel, etched in gold on the back

Lesson 155
2. law
3. The village took away his invitation.
4. joy, love, knowledge and wisdom

Lesson 156
2. dream
3. the hail storm
4. the antichrist

Lesson 157
2. She told him to leave her alone.
3. Percy found other men who were against Vulpine ruling.
4. He didn't want anyone to see it/read it.

Lesson 158
2. The doctor dipped an arrow in a decomposing body and had it shot into one of the soldiers.
3. She's more quiet, submissive.
4. He is called to obey the King's law and help others when no one else will.

Lesson 159
2. the King
3. the golden rule, though he doesn't call it that
4. She's being molded into the image of Christ; she became more gentle, less know-it-all.

Lesson 160
2. He used it as discipline to show them things aren't right, and then he sent Gabe to teach them the King's law.
3. Vulpine
4. teaching others about the King/Jesus, "teaching them to obey all that I have commanded..." Matthew 28:20, being held accountable for obeying His commands to live as His light before others

Lesson 161
2. to counter talk of the King being alive
3. talked his way into it, and mob mentality
4. rebellion

Lesson 162
2. We aren't to take revenge, but to trust it to God; justice can only be carried out by a pure hand.
3. He's not part of the inner circle.

Lesson 163
2. Percy, Assemblyman Stone, Father…and more
3. Their plan is to form a line across the Square and barge into the Hall taking Vulpine with them. There are also rebels in and behind the Hall as well as on King's Hill.
4. Vulpine, the village

Lesson 164
2. He's got a plan involving the lanterns.

Lesson 165
2. light the Hall on fire
3. killed or arrested

Lesson 166
2. despair
3. a horse

Lesson 167
2. to see the King honored by everyone
3. love your enemies

Lesson 168
2. Vulpine, we don't know
3. They need copies of the King's law.
4. servants of the King

Lesson 169
2. They decided he was just a kid.
3. one bare room, dark, dirt floor, chamber pot
4. boxing match

Lesson 170
2. John
3. The jailer opened the delivery door, so he could hear them singing better, and they got enough light to read the King's law.
4. Winnie Goss, a gossip
5. knowing they stood up for the King and didn't submit to fear

Lesson 171
2. get a V tattooed on their right hand
3. the doctor

Lesson 172
2. He won't take the mark.
3. Robert

Lesson 173

2. He was forgiven.
3. because the King had forgiven them

Lesson 174

2. Vulpine thinks he's in control but really the King is, and just as Vulpine thought he was using everyone to his purposes, the King is using Vulpine for His purposes. If the King and Vulpine are doing the same thing (or trying to), what makes them different? One is evil; one is good.
3. He had been a prisoner to Vulpine and to sin and now was free of them.

Lesson 175

2. not take revenge, he ignored boys pelting him with stones
3. in jail unless takes the mark
4. what she would have to give up if she married John

Lesson 176

2. Winnie Goss
3. In turning down his marriage proposal, she helped him realize that in part he was serving himself and not just the King, and he commits himself to serving the King wholly.

Lesson 177

2. head chopped off
3. tell where the servants meet and bring in copies of the King's law to be burned
4. large cage

Lesson 178

2. arrested leaders and burned them alive
3. She held onto the papers she had.

Lesson 179

2. He's young and unschooled, and Vulpine remembers him as being quiet and lacking confidence.
3. turns herself in

Lesson 180

2. Gabe had been gaining wisdom from the King for years.
3. His name is on the plate.
4. the resurrected saints

ABOUT

Easy Peasy All-in-One Homeschool

Easy Peasy All-in-One Homeschool is a free, complete online homeschool curriculum. There are 180 days of ready-to-go assignments for every level and every subject. It's created for your children to work as independently as you want them to. Preschool through high school is available as well as courses ranging from English, math, science and history to art, music, computer, thinking, physical education and health. A daily Bible lesson is offered as well. The mission of Easy Peasy is to enable those to homeschool who otherwise thought they couldn't.

Made in the USA
Coppell, TX
05 August 2020